Edited and designed by

Time Out Guides Limited
Universal House
251 Tottenham Court Road
London W1P 0AB
Tel + 44 (0)171 813 3000
Fax + 44 (0)171 813 6001
Email guides@timeout.com
www.timeout.com

Editorial

Editorial Director Peter Fiennes
Editor Anne Hanley
Deputy Editor Nick Rider
Proofreader Alison Bravington
Indexer Richard Wright

Design

Art Director John Oakey
Art Editor Mandy Martin
Senior Designer Scott Moore
Designers Benjamin de Lotz, Lucy Grant,
Thomas Ludewig, Paul Mansfield
Picture Editor Kerri Miles
Picture Researchers Kit Burnet, Olivia Duncan-Jones
Scanning & Imaging Chris Quinn

Advertising

Group Advertisement Director Lesley Gill
Sales Director Mark Phillips
International Sales Manager Mary L Rega
Advertisement Sales Representative Margherita Tedone
Advertising Assistant Ingrid Sigerson

Administration

Publisher Tony Elliott
Managing Director Mike Hardwick
Financial Director Kevin Ellis
Marketing Director Gillian Auld
General Manager Nichola Coulthard
Production Manager Mark Lamond
Accountant Bridget Carter

Features in this guide were written and researched by:

Introduction Anne Hanley. **Rome by Season** Anne Hanley. **History** Ferdie McDonald. **Rome Today** Anne Hanley.
Architecture Paul Duncan, Ros Belford. **Sightseeing** Anne Hanley, William Ward, Ros Belford, *The Ghetto* Lee
Marshall, *The Vatican City* Anne Hanley, Philippa Hitchen, William Ward. **Accommodation** Michelle Hough.
Restaurants Lee Marshall. **Snacks** Anne Hanley **Wine bars & *birrerie*** Lee Marshall. **Cafés & Bars** Anne Hanley,
Sarah Delaney, *Handling the Roman bar* Lee Marshall. **Ice cream** Anne Hanley. **Shopping & Services** Anne
Hanley, Peter Douglas, Charles Lambert.**Children** Anne Hanley, Sarah Delaney. **Contemporary Art** Charles
Lambert. **Film** Lee Marshall. **Gay & Lesbian** Peter Douglas, Charles Lambert. **Media** Anne Hanley, Andrew
Gumbel. **Sport & Fitness** Chris Endean. **Theatre & Dance** Linda Bordoni. **Music: Classical & Opera** Robert
Adams. **Music: Rock, Roots & Jazz** Paul Toohill, Mike Cooper. **Nightlife** Paul Toohill, Kier Fraser. **Trips Out of
Town** Lee Marshall, Sam Cole, Charles Lambert. **Directory** Michelle Hough, Yamin Tun, Jane Shaw, Peter
Douglas, *Using the Lingo* Anne Hanley.

The Editor would like to thank the following:

Marina Moscetti and Davide Cecilia of DM Studio for antiques advice, the indefatigable Fulvia Angelini, Martha
Boyden and Anne Donnelly. Special thanks to Lee and Clara Marshall.

Maps by LS International Cartography. Via Sanremo 17, 20133 Milan.

Photography by Adam Eastland except: page 5 Associated Press; pages 20, 72 and 241 AKG London; pages 127,
134, 139 and 238 Francesca Yorke; page 185 Catherine Randall; page 199 (top) The Callender Co 1987; page
199 (bottom) Artificial Eye; page 209 (top) and 210 Empics Ltd; 211 Sam Cole; page 217 CM Falsini; page 220
Stefano Ghidini - SoleLuna/Mercury; page 234 The Bridgeman Art Library; page 237 and 247 Anne Hanley; pages
87, 89, 91, 93, 239 and 243 Il Dagherrotipo; page 245 Courtesy of The Italian State Tourist Board, London.
Black and white printing by Adam Eastland.

Contents

About the Guide

This fourth edition of the *Time Out Rome Guide* has been reassessed, revised and rewritten by a team of writers who live and work in Rome. It is one of an expanding series of city guides that includes London, Berlin, New York, Barcelona, Budapest, Las Vegas, Sydney, Florence & Tuscany, Venice and many more cities around the world. The *Time Out Rome Guide* gives you a complete picture of the Eternal City, from its ancient relics and artistic glories to *gelaterie*, star restaurants, hip bars and tiny corner shops. Many guides linger on Rome's astonishing millennial past; the *Time Out Rome Guide* takes in the city's contradictory, very living present.

Checked & correct

As far as possible, all the information in this guide was checked and correct at time of writing. However, Roman owners, managers and café-keepers are often very erratic and imprecise in their answers to questions about opening times, the dates of exhibitions, prices and even their address and telephone number. In mid-summer, especially, opening times can vary unpredictably. If possible, it's a good idea to phone before visiting anywhere out of your way. We have also tried where possible to include information on access for the disabled, but, again, wherever you can it's useful to phone to check that your needs can be met.

Prices

The prices listed throughout this guide should be taken primarily as guidelines. Fluctuating exchange rates and inflation can cause prices, in shops and restaurants especially, to change rapidly. However, if prices or services ever vary wildly from those we have quoted, ask if there's a good reason. If not, go elsewhere and then please let us know. We try to give the best and most up-to-date advice, so we always want to hear if you've been overcharged or badly treated.

Credit Cards

Throughout the guide, the following abbreviations have been used for credit cards: **AmEx** American Express; **DC** Diners' Club; **EC** Eurocheque; **JCB** Japanese Credit Bank card; **MC** Mastercard; **V** Visa.

Bold

Where we mention people, places or events that are listed elsewhere in the guide, or in detail later in a chapter, they are usually **highlighted in bold** – this means that you'll be able to find them in the index.

Telephone numbers

Since the end of 1998 area codes must be dialled with all Italian phone numbers, even for local calls. In Rome, therefore, all ordinary numbers must be preceded by the code **06**, whether you're calling from the next street or the other end of the country. This does not apply to freephone (800) lines and some other numbers. *See also page 267.*

Right to reply

It should be stressed that in all cases the information we give is impartial. No organisation or enterprise has been included in this guide because its owner or manager has advertised in our publications. We hope you enjoy the *Time Out Rome Guide*, but if you disagree with any of our reviews, let us know. Your comments on places you have visited are always welcome and will be taken into account when compiling future editions of the guide. For this purpose, you will find a reader's reply card at the back of the book.

> There is an online version of this guide, as well as weekly events listings for several international cities, at
> http://www.timeout.com

Introduction

There's a panel attached to the wire fence that for some years has surrounded a messy, stalled dig at the foot of the Portico d'Ottavia, in Rome's Jewish Ghetto. The panel explains what you're looking at in the weed-filled, masonry-strewn jumble: its ancient lay-out, its historical significance.

Scrawled across the panel, in thick blue marker, is a less wordy but more eloquent explanation of the significance of the Portico and its immobile dig for the inhabitants of the Ghetto today: *'ridateci er portico,'* it says. Give us back our portico. It's a cry from the heart.

For Romans in their history-gorged city, an excavation has, ironically, something anachronistic about it. If it's confined to an obviously 'historical' area – the Imperial Fora, say, or the Colle Oppio – then that's fine: let the archaeologists get on with their scrabbling about in the mud. But when it interferes with everyday life, that's quite another matter.

More than any other city in the world, Rome has taken its history on board as an integral part of everyday life. Other cities chaff uneasily against their World War II bomb craters or their towering '60s monstrosities; Rome lives exuberantly alongside its crumbling outcrops of ancient aqueducts and its impossibly complicated topography, dictated by an astounding mish-mash of Roman, medieval and Renaissance town planning.

Other cities mothball their meagre archaeological remains, putting them carefully behind glass in such a way that the descendants of the people who produced them could not feel more removed. Romans, on the other hand, could not feel closer (albeit in antagonistic fashion) to the forebears who built their ancient city walls, which cause massive traffic tailbacks out of the city each weekday evening. They follow instinctively in ancient footsteps when they meander through street entertainers along the traffic-free Via dei Fori Imperiali on Sunday mornings, or take their summer evening strolls through the Roman Forum (which now, thanks to local pressure, is open to all for free, after years of ticket-paying isolation.).

For the visitor to Rome, it's easy to mistake this Roman insouciance towards history for callousness or even ignorance. It isn't (or at least, it usually isn't).

The Portico d'Ottavia is a case in point. The frustrated scribbler was not, no doubt, worried about the damage being done by the non-advancing excavation to Rome's international reputation for keeping up its archaeological sites. Nor was he (or she) concerned about the possible effects of traffic pollution or acid rain on the masonry, which had been so

safely buried under earth and cobblestones for centuries. No, uppermost in his mind when he took out his indelible pen was the fact that, when not hemmed in by wire barricades, the portico was a handy wall for Ghetto kids to kick footballs at, a back-drop against which elderly Ghetto-dwellers propped their fraying folding beach chairs for an afternoon argument or pea-shelling session, and a friendly, familiar sentinel keeping watch over the not-quite legal carpark at its foot. All key functions that, for years now, have been rendered impossible by the dig.

And all (apart from the car parking) functions that he might have felt equally concerned about being denied access to had he lived 2,000 years ago, rather than on the verge of the third millennium. But suggest that the portico be dismantled and moved behind glass, that the Ghetto be given a real car park, or a football pitch, or a shady garden for its elderly and all hell would break loose. In their own, abrupt way, Romans love their monuments. The portico is a centuries-old witness to the life of the Ghetto: it gives a sense of identity-through-continuum that's unique to Rome. Rome's remains are, in fact, as much part of the present – and treated as such – as they are of the past.

So cast aside your museum-fuelled preconceptions and enter into the spirit of past-in-present, avoiding any temptation to look down on Rome's seemingly cavalier treatment of its heritage. Feel what it is to be part of this heritage. History will never have seemed so alive. *Anne Hanley*

In Context

DIESEL
FOR SUCCESSFUL LIVING

STOP CRIME NOW!

In order to stop young people from turning into criminals we must have one policeman per every five youngsters. People who are willing to turn on a fire hydrant today, will most probably be pyromaniacs and flashers tomorrow. Thank you for agreeing with us.

IF WE PUT ALL YOUNG PEOPLE IN JAIL TODAY, WE WILL HAVE NO CRIMINALS TOMORROW!

Number 97

WHERE
In a series of Diesel "How to..." guides to SUCCESSFUL LIVING.

INFO
Call Diesel Italia
0424-4855   www.diesel.com

Rome by Season

**Papal processions, street festivals and the city's own birthday,
number 2,750-plus – Rome's events calendar is utterly unique.**

Bad bunions, bishop: Easter foot-washing.

Ancient Rome had over 150 public holidays a year, which perhaps contributed significantly to its demise. Today there are only ten – well within the EU average. Romans are fond of their breaks, often extending them by taking a day or two off between the end of an official holiday and the preceding or following weekend, a practice known as *il ponte* (the bridge). At the faintest hint of sun, citizens will brave hours of fumes waiting at an *autostrada* toll-booth for a glimpse of sea or mountain – plus an ample feast in a rustic spot to help forget all the stresses of city life.

Different districts of Rome celebrate their own patron saints with anything from a bit of limp bunting on a church to days of parading and feasting. For really special events, makeshift stages are erected in squares, and occupied far into the night by lusty crooners of Roman love songs. **Public holidays** are marked below with an asterisk.

Spring

Festa di Santa Francesca Romana (Patron Saint of Motorists)

Church of Santa Francesca Romana. Metro Colosseo/bus to Via dei Fori Imperiali. **Map 8/2C**
Monastery of the Oblate Sisters, Via del Teatro di Marcello. Bus to Via del Teatro di Marcello.
Date 9 March. **Map 6/1A**
Santa Francesca Romana (1384-1440) had the gift of dislocation – being in several places at the same time – which endeared her to Italy's pioneer motorists, who adopted her as their patron saint in the 1900s. Motor vehicles of all descriptions are blessed at her church, near the **Roman Forum**, while the magnificently frescoed Tor de' Specchi convent of the Oblate order, which she founded, is opened up to the public for the day.

Festa di San Giuseppe

Around Trionfale. Metro Ottaviano/bus to Piazza Risorgimento. **Date** 19 Mar. **Map 2/2C**
Although no longer an official public holiday, the feast of Saint Joseph, legal father of Jesus, remains popular, especially in the Trionfale district. Only carpenters and woodworkers still get the day off. In the run-up to the feast, the city's cafés and *pasticcerie* are piled high with deep-fried batter-balls called *bigné di San Giuseppe*.

Roma City Marathon

Via dei Fori Imperiali. Bus to Piazza Venezia.
Information 06 3018 3022/06 3018 3302/06 3018 3016. **Date** 3rd Sun in March. **Map 8/1-2C**
Rome's annual run may not be at the level of London or New York, but it has a growing reputation and now attracts big-name runners. A city-to-sea half-marathon is held three weeks before the big event.

Festa di Primavera – Mostra delle Azalee

Piazza di Spagna. Metro Spagna/bus to Via del Tritone or Piazza San Silvestro/.
Dates end Mar-early Apr. **Map 5/1C**
Spring arrives early in Rome, bringing masses of flowers. When the azaleas come out, some 3,000 vases of them are arranged on the Spanish Steps, displacing the resident army of tourists.

Settimana Santa & Pasqua

Vatican Bus Piazza Risorgimento or Piazza della Città Leonina. **Map 3/1C**; **Colosseum/Palatine** *Metro Colosseo/bus to Piazza del Colosseo.* **Map 8/2B-C**; **Information** 06 6982. **Dates** Mar, Apr.

Pyrotechnics and pageantry for Rome's birthday celebrations, the **Natale di Roma**.

On the Saturday before Palm Sunday the city is flooded with tour groups from all over the world, here to attend the open-air mass in Saint Peter's Square. During the *Settimana Santa* (Holy Week) that follows, Rome offers Christendom's nearest equivalent to the collective fervour of Mecca, with non-stop services, rituals and chants in the city's 610 places of Catholic worship. Specific information on events and times is best obtained from street posters. Events culminate in the Pope's stations of the cross and Mass at the Colosseum late on the evening of Good Friday; in Holy Year, naturally, crowds are expected to surpass all records.

On *Pasquetta* (Easter Monday) the city empties again, as Romans then traditionally have their first picnic *fuori le porte* (outside the city gates), of *porchetta* (Roman roast pork) and *torta pasqualina* (cheese bread, with salami and hard-boiled eggs).

Natale di Roma

Campidoglio *Bus to Piazza Venezia.* **Map 6/1A;**
Giardino degli Aranci/Viale Aventino
Metro Circo Massimo. **Map 9/1C;**
Information 06 488 991. **Date** 21 Apr.
It may seem odd for a city to have a birthday, but not to Romans, whose city was 'born' in 753 BC (*see chapter* **History**). The spectacular main celebrations take place at the Campidoglio. The City Hall and the other palazzi on the Capitol are illuminated, and enormous quantities of fireworks are set off.

Settimana dei Beni Culturali

Various locations. **Information** 06 589 9359.
Dates Variable, usually April.
All public museums and monuments are open to the public without charge for a week. As well as saving money, you can visit many museums and sites that are usually closed. Check dates on the ministry web-site: *www.beniculturali.it*

Festa della Liberazione*

Piazza Venezia *Bus to Piazza Venezia.* **Map 6/1A;**
Mausoleo delle Fosse Ardeatine *Via Ardeatine, 174.* **Information** 06 514 6742. **Date** 25 Apr.
The liberation of Italy in World War II is celebrated in relatively subdued fashion. The main ceremony is at the Ardeatine Caves, where the Nazis murdered

335 Romans in 1944. The President also lays a wreath at the Tomb of the Unknown Soldier on the **Vittoriale** monument in Piazza Venezia.

Concorso Ippico Internazionale di Piazza di Siena

Villa Borghese. Metro Spagna or Flaminio/bus or tram to Piazzale Flaminio or Via Vittorio Veneto/train to Piazzale Flaminio. **Information** 06 327 9939. **Dates** end Apr-beginning May. **Map 4/2C**
The international show-jumping event at Piazza di Siena in Villa Borghese is one of few truly jet-set occasions Rome still has to offer, as smart and self-consciously *all'inglese* as can be imagined.

Primo Maggio*

Piazza San Giovanni. Metro San Giovanni/bus or tram to San Giovanni or Piazzale Appio. **Information** 06 847 6514. **Date** 1 May. **Map 8/2A**
The main event of May Day in Rome is a big free rock concert by the basilica of San Giovanni, sponsored by the main trades unions. Top Italian acts from mid-afternoon into the night.

Campionato Internazionale di Tennis (Italian Open)

Foro Italico, Viale dei Gladiatori. Bus to Lungotevere Maresciallo Cadorna. **Information** 06 323 3807.
Dates 1-15 May.
Italy's annual tennis championships are one of the first big events in the European tennis season.*See also chapter* **Sport & Fitness.**

Mostra dell'Antiquariato

Via de' Coronari. Bus to Corso Rinascimento, Corso Vittorio Emanuele or Lungotevere Tor di Nona. **Information** 06 488 991. **Dates** mid-end May; mid-end Oct. **Map 3/1B**
Via de' Coronari is the hub of Rome's antiques trade. During its 20-day antiques fairs, shops stay open late, allowing you to browse to your heart's content.

Fiera Internazionale di Roma (Rome International Trade Fair)

Ente Autonomo Fiera di Roma, Via Cristoforo Colombo, 281. (06 513 8141/fax 06 5138 1415).
Bus to Piazza Navigatori.
Dates 26 May-early June. **Admission** L4,000-6,000.

Rome is not a major industrial city like Milan or Turin. However, of the 20 or so fairs at the Fiera di Roma site each year, this is the most important, a chance to see what Italians call *il Made in Italy*.

Fiera d'Arte di Via Margutta

Via Margutta. Metro Spagna/bus to Piazza del Popolo or Piazzale Flaminio. **Information** 06 812 3340. **Dates** end of May; end of Oct. **Map 2/2A**
If Via Veneto was where the *Dolce Vita* set hung out at night, Via Margutta was where they did their daubing. Few active painters still live here, but the street is still chock-full of art galleries. High points of their year are the two art fairs, each of four days; paintings range from so-so to downright terrible.

Summer

Festa delle Forze Armate (Armed Forces Day)

Via dei Fori Imperiali. Bus to Via dei Fori Imperiali or Piazza Venezia. **Information** 06 488 991.
Date 2 June. **Map Map 8/1-2C**
Today's military parades down Via dei Fori Imperiali are muted compared with the extravagant shows put on by Mussolini. Proceedings are limited to a fly-past and a wreath-laying ceremony on the Tomb of the Unknown Soldier in Piazza Venezia.

Estate Romana

Various locations. **Information** 06 488 991.
Dates June-Aug.
After some time in the doldrums, the *Estate Romana* (Roman Summer) festival has again become a major date in the calendar, bringing an embarrassing choice of culture to a city that for much of summer is too empty to absorb the wealth of events available. *Piazze*, *palazzi*, parks and courtyards come alive to the sound of local jazz and pop bands, and films are shown on makeshift screens late into the night.

Festa di San Giovanni

San Giovanni in Laterano. Metro San Giovanni/bus or tram to Piazza San Giovanni or Piazzale Appio.
Information 06 6982. **Date** 23 June. **Map 8/2A**
This saint's day has has lost its resonance except in San Giovanni district, where singing, dancing and games go on all night. It's *de rigueur* to eat *lumache in umido* (stewed snails) and *porchetta* (roast pork). The religious highlight is a candlelit procession, usually led by the Pope, to San Giovanni in Laterano.

Tevere Expo

Tiber Embankment. Bus to Lungotevere Castello or Lungotevere Tor di Nona. **Information** 06 686 9068.
Dates 23 June-31 July. **Map 3/1B**
A handicrafts fair along the banks of the Tiber, between Ponte Sant'Angelo and Ponte Cavour. It's open during the day, but most spectacular at night. There are also entertainers, sports, bars and bands.

San Pietro e San Paolo*

San Paolo fuori le Mura. Metro San Paolo/bus to Piazzale San Paolo or Via Ostiense.
Information 06 541 0341. **Date** 29 June.

The two founders of Catholicism share the honours as twin patron saints of Rome, and each are duly honoured in their respective basilicas, Saint Peter's and San Paolo fuori le Mura. Outside San Paolo there is also an all-night street fair along the Via Ostiense.

Teatro dell'Opera Summer Season

Information *06 481 7003/fax 06 488 1253).*
Dates July-mid-Aug. **Map 5/2B**
This open-air opera and ballet season tends to be shunted around, as venue after venue runs into bureaucratic hitches. Programmes are generally dominated by classical favourites.

RomaEuropa Festival

Information 06 474 2286. **Dates** July-Oct.
This ambitious pan-European arts festival presents the best of the participating countries' avant-garde cultural offerings, although the event's worthy tone limits its potential as a showcase for new talent. *See also chapter* **Music: Classical & Opera**.

Palio Madama Margherita

Castelmadama. By car: A24 to Castelmadama/ train to Avezzano from Termini/bus COTRAL from Metro Rebibbia. **Information** 0774 44078/0774 448 210. **Dates** 10, 11 July.
While not quite as spectacular as its more famous Siena counterpart, this horse race and parade in sixteenth-century costumes around a small town near Tivoli (*see chapter* **Trips Out of Town**) saves you a much longer journey. It is held in honour of the town's sixteenth-century ruler, Margaret of Parma, also remembered in Rome's Palazzo Madama.

Roma Alta Moda

Piazza di Spagna. Metro Spagna/ bus to Piazza San Silvestro. **Information** 06 482 8933. **Dates** mid-July. **Map 5/1C**
Rome's fashion community has long been overshadowed by trendier Milan, but strikes back with *Alta Moda*. The Piazza di Spagna and major hotels host sneak-preview shows of the coming year's collections, by Roman designers and other top labels.

Festa di Noantri

Viale Trastevere. Bus or tram to Viale Trastevere.
Information 06 488 991. **Dates** mid-July. **Map 6/2B**
Roughly translatable as 'a knees-up for us plebs', and theoretically in honour of the Madonna del Carmine, with whose procession the events begin, *La Festa di Noantri* is one of the last surviving glimmers of Trastevere's old working-class culture. For two weeks the busiest part of Viale Trastevere and some streets around it are blocked to traffic and filled with stalls, open into the small hours. Spectacular fireworks round off the closing night.

Festa delle Catene

Chiesa di San Pietro in Vincoli, Piazza di San Pietro in Vincoli. Metro Cavour/bus to Via Cavour.
Information 06 6982. **Date** 1 Aug. **Map 8/1B**
Chains alleged to be those in which Saint Peter was dragged to his execution are solemnly displayed in a special Mass at **San Pietro in Vincoli** (*see p80*).

Festa della Madonna della Neve

Basilica di Santa Maria Maggiore. Bus to Piazza dell'Esquilino. **Information** 06 483 195.
Date 5 Aug. **Map 5/2A**

For Romans sweating through a sticky August, snow is an enticing thought. Perhaps that's why the legend of the snowfall over the Esquiline Hill on 5 August 352 still has such resonance (*see p80*). To commemorate it, a deluge of rose petals flutters down on Mass-goers in Santa Maria Maggiore.

Ferragosto – Feast of the Assumption*

Date 15 Aug.

The Feast of the Assumption is the high point of summer; even those who remain in Rome for August go away for this long weekend, and practically everything is closed. The very few restaurants that do stay open serve the traditional Ferragosto dish of *pollo con i peperoni*: chicken with peppers.

Autumn

Ognissanti*/Giornata dei Defunti

Cimitero Il Verano, Piazzale del Verano. Bus or tram to Piazzale Verano. **Information** 06 491 511/06 6982.
Dates 1, 2 Nov.

Otherwise known as *Tutti Santi*, All Saints' Day is followed by *La Commemorazioni dei Defunti* (or *Tutti i Morti*), when the Pope celebrates Mass at the vast cemetery of Il Verano. Flower-sellers make a killing as Romans en masse visit family graves.

Winter

Immacolata Concezione*

Piazza di Spagna *Metro Spagna/bus to Piazza San Silvestro or Via del Tritone.* **Map 5/1C; Santa Maria Maggiore** *Bus to Piazza dell'Esquilino.* **Map 5/2A. Information** 06 6982. **Date** 8 Dec.

The statue of the Madonna in Piazza di Spagna is the day's focal point, when, with the Pope looking on, the fire brigade runs a ladder up Mary's column, and a lucky fireman gets to place a wreath over her outstretched arm (in times past, popes themselves did the climbing). At the base of the column locals and dignitaries deposit immense quantities of flowers. Later in the day, the Pope goes on to Santa Maria Maggiore to say Mass.

Natale* and Santa Stefano*

Dates 25, 26 Dec.

Oddly enough, the world centre of Catholicism is no great shakes at Christmas. The traditional trappings of northern Yuletide consumerism, with *Babbo Natale* (Father Christmas) much in evidence, have asserted themselves strongly in recent years, however, with extra-long opening hours, Sunday shopping and classy street decorations in the fashion streets. A walk among the throng on Via del Corso the weekend before Christmas could put you off present-buying for life. All this is a recent import: until a few years ago it was Epiphany that really counted. For a taste of a more traditional Roman

Christmas, get tickets to the papal midnight Mass in **Saint Peter's** (from the *Prefettura*, 06 6988 3017; make you request months ahead), or visit the cribs: you'll find one in most churches: there's a good one half-way up the **Spanish Steps**; but Saint Peter's Square boasts the biggest crib of all, plus an immense Christmas tree.

San Silvestro/Capodanno*

Dates 31 Dec, 1 Jan.

New Year's Eve is a night to stay inside, and not only because most restaurants are shut: the firework mayhem that builds to a crescendo in the minutes around midnight is unforgettable from a hotel window, but reminiscent of a war zone if you're caught up in it at street level. Best experienced in down-home areas like Testaccio or San Lorenzo, but there are hazards here too: some older residents still honour the tradition of chucking unwanted consumer durables off their balconies. Alternatively, make your way to the free concert, disco and fireworks in Piazza del Popolo

Epifania – La Befana*

Piazza Navona. Bus to Corso Rinascimento.
Date 6 Jan. **Map 3/2A-B**

Reflecting Romans' pagan spirit, the Feast of the Epiphany is better known by the name of a very un-Christian character, *La Befana*, the old witch. As the legend goes, this Mother Christmas only brought presents to good children; bad ones found their shoes filled with bits of coal. Today, all Roman *bambini* get their presents anyway, and coal comes in the form of a sickly black sweet. From mid-December to 6 January Piazza Navona fills with market stalls, selling sweets and cheap tat. The climax comes late on 5 January, when *La Befana* herself touches down in the piazza.

Sant'Eusebio

Via Napoleone III. Metro Vittorio/bus to Piazza Vittorio Emanuele. **Date** 17 Jan. **Map 8/1A**

Animal lovers keen to ensure their pets a place in heaven have them blessed at the little church of Sant'Eusebio, in a ceremony that used to go on for days and was loved by Grand Tourists, crowds of whom caused traffic jams as they cooed over this rare example of Italian devotion to animal welfare.

Carnevale

Date the week before Lent (usually late Feb-Mar).

In the Middle Ages, this riotous pagan farewell to winter before the rigours of Lent was celebrated in lurid abandon outside the city walls on Monte Testaccio. Anxious to keep a check on their libidinous subjects, the Renaissance popes brought the ceremony back within the walls to the Via Lata, renaming it Via del Corso in honour of the Carnival processions and races held along it. Nowadays, an array of diminutive princesses, Zorros and characters from Disney's latest release swarm about the city with their proud parents by day, while older kids shower the streets (and your best coat) with shaving foam and confetti by night.

History

Emperors, popes, barons, megalomaniac schemes and revolts from below: everything changes and nothing changes in the Eternal City.

Romulus & Remus

Out of their legends Roman historians created a self-glorifying chronicle, complete with exact dates, for the foundation of the city and its earliest rulers. According to them, Rome was founded by Romulus, on 21 April 753 BC, a date still celebrated as the city's official 'birthday' (*see page 6*).

The twins Romulus and Remus were the result of a rape by the god of war, Mars, of a local princess called Rhea Silvia. Cast adrift as babies on the Tiber and washed up in the marshy area below the Palatine Hill, they were suckled by a she-wolf until found by a shepherd. In time, Romulus rose to be leader of his tribe, quarrelled with and killed his brother, founded the city and, deciding his community was short on females, abducted all the women of the neighbouring Sabine tribe.

The true origins of Rome are lost, but traces of ninth-century BC huts have been excavated on the Palatine – proof that there was a primitive village there at least. The first historically documented king of Rome was an Etruscan, Tarquinius Priscus, who reigned from 616 BC. It was probably Etruscans who drained the marshy area between the seven hills to create the **Forum**, hub of the city's political, economic and religious life.

According to Roman historians, in 509 BC the son of King Tarquinius Superbus raped Lucretia, the wife of a Roman, Collatinus. The next day, before killing herself, she told her husband and his friend Brutus what had happened, and in revenge they led a rebellion against the Tarquins. The Etruscan dynasty was expelled and the Roman Republic was founded, with Brutus and Collatinus as the first *Consuls* or chief magistrates.

This is doubtless a romanticised account of what happened, but in time Etruscan influence over the region did wane and authority passed to Rome's magistrates. Chief among them were the two annually elected Consuls, guided by a council of elders called the *Senate*. The number of people who could participate in the political life of the Republic was limited to a few ancient families or clans who formed the Patrician class. Only they could vote, be appointed to the Senate or hold the more important public and religious offices.

The lower classes, or Plebeians, struggled for a greater say in their own affairs. In 494 BC, the office of *Tribune of the Plebs* was created to represent their interests, and by 367 BC a Plebeian could hold the office of Consul. The class system, however, was maintained – rich or successful Plebeians were simply designated Patricians.

All the Romans of the Republic were united by a belief in their right to conquer other tribes. Their superb military organisation, and an agile policy of divide-and-rule in making alliances, allowed them to pick off the neighbouring peoples of central and southern Italy, and bring the other Latin communities – including the Etruscans – under Roman control. To ensure the spread of Roman power, new cities were established in conquered territories, and an extensive infrastructure was created to support the many conquests. The first great Roman road, the **Via Appia**, was begun in 312 BC, and shortly afterwards work started on the Acqua Appia, the first great aqueduct to bring fresh water to the city. The port of Ostia, founded at the mouth of the Tiber in 380 BC, expanded rapidly, as streams of barges plied the river, bringing corn, wine, oil and building materials to Rome.

Rome's expansion brought her into conflict with two equally powerful peoples, the Carthaginians of North Africa and Spain, and the Greeks, who had colonised southern Italy and Sicily. The latter were expelled from mainland Italy in 272 BC, but the Punic Wars against the Carthaginians lasted almost 120 years, and Rome was more than once in danger of annihilation. In 219 BC Hannibal made his historic crossing of the Alps, gaining control of much of Italy, but was too cautious to press home his advantage with an assault on Rome. Carthage was finally destroyed in 146 BC, leaving Rome in control of the western Mediterranean.

In the early days of the Republic most Romans, rich or poor, had been farmers, tending to their own land or livestock in the surrounding countryside. Wars like those against Carthage, however, required huge standing armies. At the same time, much of the land in Italy had been laid waste, either by Hannibal or the Roman armies. Wealthy Romans bought huge estates at knockdown prices, while landless peasants flocked to the capital. By the end of the second century BC, the Romans were a race of soldiers, engineers, administrators and merchants, supported by tribute in the form of money and goods from defeated enemies and the slave labour of prisoners taken in battle. Keeping the mass of the Roman poor contented required the

Key Events

Romulus & Remus

* = *Traditional dates*
753 BC Romulus kills Remus and founds Rome.
750 BC Rape of the Sabine Women.
616 BC Tarquin elected king. Forum is drained.
509 BC Tarquins are ousted after rape of Lucretia.
507-6 BC Roman Republic founded. The Latins and Etruscans declare war.
499 BC Thanks to Castor and Pollux, Romans beat Latins at Battle of Lake Regillus.
494 BC Plebeians revolt. Tribunate founded.
450 BC Roman Law codified into Twelve Tables.
434 BC War against the Etruscans.
390 BC Gauls sack Rome.
264-146 BC Punic Wars against Carthage. In 212 Rome conquers Sicily; in 146 Carthage is destroyed.
200-168 BC Rome conquers Greece. Greek gods introduced to Rome.
186 BC 1,000 men and women executed for immoral acts during the Bacchanalia.
100 BC Birth of Julius Caesar.
92-89 BC Social Wars against former Italian allies.
60-50 BC First triumvirate: Caesar, Pompey, Crassus.
55 BC Caesar invades Britain.
51-50 BC Caesar conquers Gaul and crosses Rubicon.
48 BC Caesar defeats Pompey and meets Cleopatra.
45 BC Caesar declared *imperator* (emperor).
44 BC Caesar assassinated by Brutus and Cassius.
43-32 BC Second triumvirate: Octavian, Mark Antony and Lepidus.

Pax Romana

31 BC Battle of Actium. Antony and Cleopatra defeated and Octavian (Augustus) becomes sole ruler.
14 AD Death of Augustus. Tiberius becomes emperor.
37 Caligula accedes.
41 Caligula assassinated. Claudius accedes.
64 Nero clears city slums by setting fire to Rome.
67 Saints Peter and Paul are martyred.
80 Colosseum begun.
106 Trajan conquers Dacia.
125 Pantheon rebuilt to designs by Hadrian.
164-180 Great Plague throughout the Empire.
270 Military disasters: Dacia lost to the Goths.
284-305 Diocletian splits Empire into East and West.

A New Religion

313 Constantine proclaims Edict of Milan, allowing toleration of Christianity.
382 Severe persecution of pagans.
410 Alaric the Goth sacks Rome.
475-6 Byzantium becomes seat of empire. Goths rule Rome.
567 Lombards overrun much of Italy.

778 Charlemagne defeats last Lombard King.
800 Pope crowns Charlemagne Holy Roman Emperor.
1084 Holy Roman Emperor Henry IV sacks Rome. Robert Guiscard and the Normans sack Rome again.
1097 First Crusade begins.
1300 First Holy Year. Thousands of pilgrims flock to Rome – the tourist industry has begun.
1309 Pope Clement V moves the papacy to Avignon.
1347 Cola di Rienzo sets up Roman republic.
1417 End of Great Schism in the papacy.

The Renaissance

1494 Charles VIII of France invades Italy.
1508 Michelangelo begins the Sistine ceiling.
1527 Sack of Rome by Imperial army.
1556 Roman Jews confined to the Ghetto.
1563 Council of Trent launches Counter-Reformation.
1585 Sixtus V begins to change the layout of Rome.
1626 The new Saint Peter's is consecrated.
1689 Death of Queen Christina of Sweden.
1721 Bonnie Prince Charlie born in Rome.
1773 Jesuits expelled from Rome.
1798 French exile Pope and declare Rome a republic.
1806 End of Holy Roman Empire.
1808 Rome made 'free city' in Napoleon's Empire.
1821 Death of Keats in Rome.
1848 Revolutionaries declare Roman Republic; put down by French troops, who occupy the city until 1870.

A Capital Again

1870 Italian army enters Rome which becomes capital of united Italy.
1922 Mussolini marches on Rome.
1929 Lateran Treaty creates the Vatican State.
1944 Rome liberated. Vittorio Emanuele III abdicates.
1946 A national referendum makes Italy a republic.
1957 Common Market Treaty signed in Rome.
1959 Fellini's *La Dolce Vita* released.
1960 Olympic Games held in Rome.
1962 Second Vatican Council: major Church reforms.
1981 John Paul II shot in Saint Peter's Square.
1993 *Tangentopoli* corruption investigations begin: political parties crumble; **summer** Mafia bombs kill 11 in Rome, Florence, Milan; **December** Francesco Rutelli becomes Rome's first Green mayor.
1994 Right-wing coalition of media tycoon Silvio Berlusconi wins election; government falls apart after seven months.
1995 Seven-times premier Giulio Andreotti on trial for collusion with the Mafia.
1996 Romano Prodi's left-wing coalition wins election.
1997 Rutelli wins second term as Rome's mayor.
Oct 1998 Massimo D'Alema becomes first ever ex-Communist prime minister.

exaction of still more tribute money from the conquered territories. A parasitic relationship was thus established, in which all classes in Rome lived off the rest of the Empire.

The political situation in the first century BC became more and more anarchic. Vast armies were required to fight distant wars on the boundaries of the Empire, and soldiers came to owe greater loyalty to their general, who rewarded them with the fruits of conquest, than to the government back in Rome. The result was a succession of civil wars between rival generals.

Caesar and Pompey, the two greatest generals of the first century BC, tried to bury their differences in a three-man Triumvirate with Crassus, but in 49 BC Caesar, then Governor of Gaul, defied the Senate by bringing his army into Italy ('crossing the Rubicon', the muddy stream that marked the border). All opposition was swept aside, and for the last six years of his life Caesar ruled Rome

Theatre of bad dreams: the Colosseum

Improving the emperor's image after the public relations havoc wreaked by arson-prone Nero was a priority for his successor Vespasian (AD 69-79), who lost no time in placating the plebs by restoring to the populace some of the land usurped by Nero for his private pleasure gardens. To make sure they knew he was on their side, he also put up a temple to Roman blood-sports as well.

Properly called the **Flavian amphitheatre** (but later known as the *Colosseum* not because it was big, but because of a gold-plated colossal statue, now lost, which stood alongside), the arena was a third of a mile in circumference, could seat 50,000 people and could be filled or emptied in ten minutes through a network of *vomitoria* – exits – which remains the basic model for stadium design today.

Nowhere in the world was there a larger or more glorious setting for the mass slaughter and gore so loved by the brutal Romans. If highly-trained (and so costly) professional gladiators were often spared at the end of their bloody bouts, not so the slaves, criminals, war prisoners, deserters and assorted unfortunates roped in to do battle against them. Fights were to the death: any combatant who disappointed the crowd by not showing enough grit was put to death anyway, and corpses were prodded with red-hot pokers to make sure no one tried to elude fate by playing dead.

It was not only human life which was sacrificed to Roman blood-lust: wildlife, too, was legitimate fodder, and the more exotic the animal, the better the show. Animals fought animals; people fought animals. In the ten-day carnage held to inaugurate the amphitheatre in AD 80, 5,000 beasts (plus an unrecorded number of humans) perished. By the time wild animal shows were finally banned in AD 523, the elephant and tiger were all but extinct in north Africa and Arabia.

Entrance to the Colosseum was free for all, although a membership card was necessary, and a rigid seating plan kept the sexes and social classes in their rightful places. The emperor and senators occupied marble seats in the front rows; on benches higher up came priests and magistrates, then foreign diplomats. Women were confined to the upper reaches – all, that is, except the Vestal Virgins, the chaste females who lived in pampered seclusion in the **Temple of Vesta** in the Forum to guard over the sacred flame, the continuity of which was believed to be essential for the survival of Rome itself. Less addicted to blood-letting than their fellow Romans, these hapless females, Suetonius reports, were often carried out from their privileged seats near the emperor fainting in shock. *See also chapter* **Centro Storico**.

as a dictator. The Republican spirit was not quite dead, though, and in 44 BC he was assassinated. Ironically, his death did not lead to the restoration of the Republic but to a power struggle between Mark Antony and Caesar's nephew, Octavian, which escalated into a full-blown civil war.

PAX ROMANA

Octavian eventually defeated Mark Antony and Cleopatra at the Battle of Actium, in 31 BC. The Empire now stretched from Gaul and Spain in the west to Egypt and Asia Minor in the east, and to hold it together a single central power was needed. Octavian naturally felt the person to embody such authority was himself, and took the name Augustus, implying that he enjoyed the favour of the gods.The transformation from Republic to Empire was not declared immediately, but he quickly acquired permanent power over the Roman state.

To give greater authority to his assumption of absolute power, Augustus encouraged the cult of his uncle Julius Caesar as a god, building a temple to him in the Forum. The **Ara Pacis**, decorated with a frieze showing Augustus and his family, was a reminder that it was he who had brought peace to the Roman world. Later in his reign statues of Augustus sprang up all over the Empire, and he was more than happy to be worshipped as a god himself.

Augustus lived on the **Palatine** hill in a relatively modest house, but later emperors indulged their apparently limitless wealth and power to the full, building a series of extravagant palaces. The last member of Augustus' family to inherit the Empire was the megalomaniac Nero, who built himself the biggest palace Rome had ever seen, the *Domus Aurea* or 'golden house' (*see page 80*). Extending from the Palatine across the valley now occupied by the Colosseum – land cleared of dwellings in a massive fire in AD 64, while Nero, reportedly, was plucking his lyre – it boasted outer walls clad in gold and mother-of-pearl, ceilings of ivory, and a park full of exotic beasts.

When Nero died in 68, with no heir, the Empire was up for grabs, and generals converged from across the Empire to claim the throne. The eventual winner of this struggle was a bluff soldier called Vespasian, founder of the Flavian dynasty.

ROME AT THE TOP

Over the next hundred years Rome enjoyed an era of unparalleled stability. The Empire reached its greatest extent during the reign of Trajan (98-117). Thereafter it was a matter of protecting the existing boundaries, and making sure civil war did not threaten the Empire from within.

Peace throughout the Mediterranean encouraged trade and brought even greater prosperity to Rome. At the same time, however, the power and influence of the capital and its inhabitants declined. Many talented imperial officials, generals and even emperors were Greeks, north Africans or Spaniards. Trajan and Hadrian, for example, were both born in Spain.

To keep an increasingly disparate mass of people content, emperors relied on the policy neatly summed up in the poet Juvenal's phrase 'bread and circuses'. From the first century AD a regular hand-out of grain was given to the poor, ostensibly to maintain a supply of fit young men for the army, but also to ensure that unrest in the city was kept to a minimum. Such a degree of generosity to the poor of Rome necessitated still further exploitation of the outlying provinces of the Empire. Even in years of famine, Spain and Egypt were required to send grain to Rome.

The other means used to keep over a million fairly idle souls quiet and loyal to their emperor was the staging of lavish public entertainments. The most famous venue for such spectacles was the **Colosseum**, built by the emperors Vespasian and Domitian and completed in AD 96. The appetite of the Roman crowd for blood was almost unappeasable, and sometimes hundreds of people and animals were massacred for entertainment's sake in a single day.

Imperial Rome was the most populous metropolis the world had ever seen. In Augustus' day its population was about one million. By the reign of Trajan a century later it had risen to 1,500,000. No other city even approached this size until the nineteenth century. It was superbly equipped in its public areas, with eight bridges across the Tiber, magnificent major buildings and 18 large squares.

The golden age of Rome ended with the death of Marcus Aurelius in AD 180. Defending the eastern provinces and fortifying the borders along the Danube and the Rhine placed a huge strain on the imperial purse and the manpower of the legions. Moreover, the exploitative relationship between the Roman state and its distant provinces meant that the latter were unable to defend themselves.

The threat from barbarian invaders and civil wars became so serious that in the third century the Emperor Aurelius was obliged to fortify Rome itself with massive defences. The **Aurelian Wall**, later reinforced by medieval popes, still surrounds much of the city. It is a splendid – but misleading – monument to the engineering skills of the ancient Romans. In its heyday, the city needed no defences. Its protection lay in the vastness of its Empire and the guaranteed security of the *pax romana*.

A new religion

The end of the third century AD was a turning point in the history of Rome. Radical decisions taken by two powerful emperors, Diocletian (284-305) and Constantine (306-37), ensured that the

city's days as head of a great empire were number-
ed. Diocletian established new capital cities at
Mediolanum (Milan) and Nicomedia (in present-
day Turkey) and divided the Empire into four
sectors, sharing power with a second 'Augustus',
Maximian, and two 'Caesars', Constantius and
Galerius. The priorities of the over-extended
Empire were now to defend the Rhine and Danube
borders against invading Germanic tribes, and the
eastern provinces from the Persians. Rome was
abandoned to look after itself.

The reign of Diocletian is also remembered as
one of the periods of most intense persecution of
Christians in the Empire. Christian communities
had been established in Rome very soon after the
death of Christ, centred in clandestine meeting-
houses called *tituli*. Christianity, though, was just
one of many mystical cults that had spread from
the Middle East through the Roman Empire. Its
followers were probably fewer than the devotees
of Mithraism, a Persian religion open only to men
(*see p95*). Christianity, with its promise of personal salvation in the afterlife, had great appeal
among the oppressed – slaves, freedmen, women.
However, within two decades of the persecutions
of Diocletian, Emperor Constantine would first
tolerate and then recognise Christianity as the
official religion of the Roman Empire.

BORN AGAIN

When Constantius, Constantine's father and commander of the western provinces, died at York in
306, his army acclaimed young Constantine as
'Augustus' in his place. The early part of his reign
was taken up with campaigns against rival
emperors, the most powerful being Maxentius,
who commanded Italy and North Africa.

The decisive battle was fought just to the north
of Rome at the Milvian Bridge (Ponte Milvio) in
312. Before the battle a flaming cross is said to
have appeared in the sky, with the words 'by this
sign shall you conquer' written on it in Greek. As
the legend goes, Constantine's cavalry then swept
Maxentius' superior forces into the Tiber. The
following year, in the Edict of Milan, Constantine
decreed that Christianity be tolerated throughout
the Empire. Later in his reign, when he had gained
control of the eastern Empire and started to build
his new capital city at Byzantium (Constantinople),
it became the religion of the state.

Christianity was much stronger in the east than
in the west, and its effect on Roman life was at first
limited, the new faith simply co-existing with the
other religions. Constantine's reign saw the building of three great basilicas, but these were situated
on the outskirts of the city. Saint Peter's and Saint
Paul's without the Walls (**San Paolo fuori le
Mura**) were built over existing shrines, while the
Bishop of Rome was given land by the Laterani
family to build a basilica beside the Aurelian Wall
– **San Giovanni in Laterano**. To give Rome
credibility as a centre of its new religion, fragments
alleged to be of the 'True Cross' were brought from
the Holy Land by Constantine's mother Saint
Helena (*see page 15*). Meanwhile, life in fourth-century Rome went on much as before. The departure

Early Christians break into song and dance to celebrate end of the persecutions.

The Palatine: *home to ancient Rome's movers and shakers.*

of part of the imperial court to the east was a heavy blow to a city accustomed to considering itself *caput mundi*, the capital of the world, but the old pagan holidays were still observed, games were staged, and bread was doled out to the poor.

The Roman world, however, was beginning to fall apart. Constantine learned nothing from the conflicts created by Diocletian's division of power, and on his death left the Empire to be split between his three sons. From this point on, the Western Empire and the Byzantine Empire were two separate entities, united for the last time under Theodosius in the late fourth century. Byzantium would stand for another thousand years, while Rome's glorious palaces, temples, aqueducts, statues and fountains would be destroyed by successive waves of Germanic invaders.

The first great shock came in 410, when Alaric's Visigoths marched into Italy and sacked Rome. Even more significant was the conquest of north Africa by the Vandals in 435, cutting Rome off from its main source of grain. In 455 the Vandals too sacked Rome, removing everything of value they could carry. After this, the Western Empire survived in name alone. The great aqueducts supplying water to Rome ceased to function, while much of the Italian countryside was laid waste. The emperors in Rome had become the puppets of the assorted Germanic invaders who controlled the Italian peninsula.

The last emperor, Romulus, was given the diminutive nickname Augustulus, since he was such a feeble shadow of the Empire's founder. In 476 he was deposed by the German chieftain Odoacer, who gave himself the title King of Italy. He was in turn deposed by Theodoric the Ostrogoth, who invaded Italy with the support of Byzantium and established an urbane court in Ravenna that ruled stably for the next 30 years.

In the sixth century much of Italy was reconquered by the Eastern Empire. Then, in around 567, yet another Germanic tribe swept in. The Lombards overran much of the centre of the peninsula, but when they threatened to besiege Rome they met their match in Pope Gregory the Great (590-604), who bought them off with tribute. Gregory was a tireless organiser, overseeing the running of the estates that had been acquired by the church throughout western Europe, encouraging the establishment of new monasteries and convents, and sending missionaries as far afield as pagan Britain.

He also did a great deal to build up the prestige of the papacy. Rome had been merely one of the centres of the early Church, the others – Byzantium, Jerusalem, Antioch and Alexandria – all being in the east. Disputes were sometimes referred to the Bishop of Rome, but many Christians, particularly in the eastern Churches, did not acknowledge him to have any overall primacy. The collapse of all secular government in the west, however, and above all in Italy, meant that the papacy emerged almost by default as the sole centre of authority, a political leader as well as head of the Roman Church.

Rome in the badlands

The Dark Ages must have been particularly galling for the inhabitants of Rome, living among the magnificent ruins of a vanished golden age. There was no fresh water, as the aqueducts cut during the invasions of the fifth century had never been repaired. People took most of their water from the Tiber, and disease was rife. Formerly built-up areas reverted to grazing land, or were planted as vegetable gardens by monks, who owned much of the land. Fear of invasion meant that the country-

Saint Helena goes collecting

In 327, at the age of 72, Constantine's redoubtable mother Helena set out for Palestine, becoming the forerunner in two fashions that were to leave an indelible mark on the Middle Ages: pilgrimages – and later Crusades – to the sites associated with Christ's life, and relic-lust.

Not that relics were not already popular: the mortal remains of local holy men and women were jealously guarded by the persecuted early Christians, as miracle-working fetishes. Helena's finds took this grisly pastime onto another plane, though, for the emperor's Ma claimed to have brought home part of the True Cross, the one that Jesus died on. Relic one-upmanship was born.

A fervid convert to Christianity, Helena had no doubts that the bits of wood she found in Jerusalem beneath a temple to Aphrodite were the Real Thing: a handy dying woman was laid down on them, and miraculously cured. The ease with which she had made her lucky find convinced streams of pilgrims, and subsequently Crusaders, to follow in her footsteps. All believed that the flotsam sold them at high prices by wily Palestinians must surely be the remains of Christ and his revered mother. Nowadays, it is estimated that the pieces of 'true' cross in existence would suffice to build something the size of an aircraft carrier.

Helena took part of her finds back to Rome, where she had her palace converted into the church of **Santa Croce in Gerusalemme**, where her sacred souvenirs can still be seen. The bulk of her discovery became a crucial political statement when, in her son's spanking new capital of the Eastern Empire, Constantinople, a lump of cross was hoisted atop the milestone from which distances throughout the known world would be measured. There could be no clearer sign of the supremacy of Byzantium.

Rome, on the other hand, boasted a slough of apostle parts. **Saint Peter's** was built over the body of the saint, and the chains in which he was brought to Rome can be seen in **San Pietro in Vincoli**. Saint Paul's remains may or may not be in **San Paolo fuori le Mura** (Saracens made off with his sarcophagus in the ninth century, but a stone flag over what you will be assured is his tomb has holes allowing visitors to poke cloth through, thus impregnating it with the sacred aura of his dust and ashes). The finger that dubious Saint Thomas stuck in Christ's wound can be seen in Santa Croce in Gerusalemme. Alas, however, the Rome area's most bizarre relic – Christ's foreskin – was stolen some years ago from the church in Calcata, north of the city, never to be recovered.

---

side around the city was practically deserted. After reaching over a million at the height of the Empire, Rome's population could be counted in no more than hundreds by the sixth century.

As the city shrank, the ancient ruins became convenient quarries for builders. Marble and other limestone was burned to make cement, most of which was used to repair the city's fortifications. Rome saw more wars, invasions, sieges and disturbances in the Middle Ages than it had ever witnessed under the Republic and Empire.

For several centuries the city still owed nominal allegiance to the emperor in Byzantium and his representative in Italy, the *exarch*, whose court was at Ravenna. However, the *exarch's* troops were normally too busy defending their own cities in north-east Italy to be of much help to Rome. The city did have a military commander, a *dux*, and a *comune* (city council) that met, as the *Comune di Roma* still does today, on the Capitoline Hill, but the papacy also had its parallel courts and administration. In the end the power of the Church prevailed. In time, this would lead to a permanent rift with Byzantium and the eastern Orthodox Churches.

A NEW EMPIRE

During the Dark Ages the Roman nobles who controlled the papacy and the city set out to re-establish something akin to the old Empire. When the Lombards seized Ravenna in 751 and threatened to do the same to Rome, Pope Stephen II enlisted Pepin, King of the Franks, as defender of the Church. The papacy's alliance with the Franks grew with the victories of Pepin's son, Charlemagne, over the Lombards, and was sealed on Christmas Day 800, when the Pope caught Charlemagne unawares in Saint Peter's and crowned him Holy Roman Emperor.

Rome appeared to have recovered much of its long-lost power and prestige. It had an Emperor to protect it, blessed by the Pope, who in return was rewarded by the gift of large areas of land in central Italy. As things turned out, this arrangement caused nothing but trouble for the next 500 years, as popes, emperors and other monarchs vied to determine whose power was greatest. Roman nobles took sides in these disputes, seizing every occasion to promote members of their own families to the papacy and frequently reducing the city to a state of anarchy. At regular intervals one faction or another would idealistically declare Rome to be a Republic once more, to no real effect.

The prestige of the papacy reached a low ebb in the tenth century, when the Frankish Empire collapsed and the papal crown was passed around between a series of dissipated Roman nobles. One of these, John XII (955-64), was obliged to call on the Saxon King Otto for assistance and crowned him Holy Roman Emperor, but then immediately thought better of it. He began to plot against Otto, who rushed to Rome and commanded the clergy and people never again to elect a Pope without the consent of himself or his successors.

Papal independence was reasserted in the second half of the eleventh century by Pope Gregory VII (1073-85), who also established many of the distinctive institutions of the Catholic Church. It was Gregory who first made celibacy obligatory for priests, and he set up the College of Cardinals, giving them sole authority to elect all future popes. He also insisted that no bishop or abbot could be invested by a lay ruler such as a king or emperor, which led to a cataclysmic struggle for power with the Emperor Henry IV.

In 1084 Henry entered Rome, bringing with him a new candidate to replace Gregory VII, who had taken refuge in the **Castel Sant'Angelo**. At this point a Norman army arrived to rescue the Pope, but unfortunately they also took the opportunity to sack the city (*see page 16*). Gregory left Rome a broken man, and died the following year.

Despite never-ending conflict between rival factions, usually headed by the powerful Colonna and Orsini families, the twelfth and thirteenth centuries were a time of great architectural innovation in Rome. The creative spirit of the Middle Ages is preserved in beautiful cloisters like those of **San Giovanni** and **San Lorenzo fuori le Mura**, and in Romanesque churches with graceful brick bell-towers and floors of fine mosaic.

Rome's prestige, however, suffered a severe blow in 1309, when the French overruled the College of Cardinals and imposed their own candidate as pope, who promptly decamped to Avignon. A pope returned to Rome in 1378, but the situation became farcical, with three separate popes competing for the papal throne. Stability was only restored in 1417, when Oddo Colonna was elected as a single Pope Martin V at the Council of Constance, marking the end of the Great Schism. He returned to Rome in 1420, to find the city and the surrounding Papal States in a ruinous condition.

Renaissance Rome

With the reign of Pope Martin V (1417-31) some semblance of dignity was restored to the office of Christ's Vicar on Earth. It was at this time that the perennial uncertainty as to who ruled the city was solved: henceforth, the city councillors would be nominees of the pope. At the same time, the popes

1084 and all that

Decades before William the Conqueror set out for Hastings, a rowdy bunch of his footloose Norman cousins had made their way into southern Italy. Fighting as mercenaries for local barons, the Normans wisely took land in payment. By 1059, when Pope Nicholas II invested Robert Guiscard 'the crafty' – the brilliant military strategist who had emerged as the Normans' leader – with the non-existent titles of Duke of Puglia, Calabria and Sicily, the Gallic newcomers were major landowners, and a fighting force to be reckoned with.

Pope Nicholas and his successor Gregory VII needed Robert Guiscard. With the backing of Norman muscle they dared to challenge the authority of the invasive Holy Roman Emperors. When would-be emperor Henry IV marched on Rome in 1083, demanding to be crowned, Gregory called for Robert (who was busy across the Adriatic, attempting to conquer Byzantium). Guiscard came directly to the pope's aid… but

not before the Romans-of-little-faith had already capitulated to Henry's army.

The massive Guiscard, whose 'eyes shot out sparks of fire' was not one to tone his wrath down: 'Robert's bellow, so they say, put tens of thousands to flight', recorded the Byzantine chronicler Anna Comnena. Reaching Rome in May 1084, he found not a city to be delivered, but a city gone over to the enemy; so he let his lads loose in a three-day orgy of looting. So brutal was their pillaging that even the supine Romans revolted. The peeved Normans set fire to the little that was still standing. From the Palatine to San Giovanni in Laterano, nothing remained but the blackened hulks of once-great palazzi and the smoking ruins of churches.

The horrified Romans were ready to prostrate themselves and beg for mercy. Robert, however, had already lost interest in his Roman conquest, and was heading back towards defeat and his final come-uppance in Byzantium.

Fragments of early Christianity.

chose to make the Vatican their principal residence, as it offered greater security than their traditional seat in the Lateran Palace.

Successive popes took advantage of this new sense of authority, and Rome became an international city once more. Meanwhile, the renewed prestige of the papacy enabled it to draw funds from all over Catholic Europe in the form of tithes and taxes. The papacy also developed the money-spinning idea of the Holy Year, first instituted in 1300 and repeated in 1423, 1450 and 1475 (*see page 106*). Such measures enabled the Church to finance the lavish artistic patronage of Renaissance Rome.

Nicholas V (1447-55) is remembered as the pope who brought the spirit of the Renaissance to Rome. A lover of philosophy, science and the arts, he founded the **Vatican Library** and had many ancient Greek texts translated into Latin. He also made plans for the rebuilding of **Saint Peter's**, the structure of which was found to be perilously unstable. The Venetian Pope Paul II (1464-71) built the city's first great Renaissance palazzo, the massive **Palazzo Venezia**, and his successor, Sixtus IV, invited leading artists from Tuscany and Umbria – Botticelli, Perugino, Ghirlandaio and Pinturicchio – to fresco the walls of his new **Sistine Chapel** in the Vatican.

Since the papacy had become such a fat prize, the great families of Italy redoubled their efforts to secure it, and always had younger sons groomed and ready as potential popes. The French and Spanish kings, too, usually had their own candidates. Consequently, Renaissance popes are not associated with any great spirituality. Sixtus IV and his successors Innocent VIII and Alexander VI (the infamous Rodrigo Borgia) devoted far more of their energies to politics and war than spiritual matters, and papal armies were continually in the field, carving out an ever-increasing area of central Italy for themselves.

ROMAN AMBITIONS

The epitome of the worldly Renaissance pope, Julius II (1503-13), made the idea of a strong papal state a reality, at the same time reviving the dream of restoring Rome to its former greatness as spiritual capital of the world. He began the magnificent collection of classical sculpture that is the nucleus of today's **Vatican Museums**, and invited the greatest architects, sculptors and painters of the day to Rome. Chief among them were Bramante, Michelangelo and Raphael. Julius' rule was not as enlightened as he liked to think, but he did issue a bull forbidding simony (the buying or selling of church offices) in the election of a pope. In his own financial dealings, he depended on the advice and loans of the fabulously wealthy Sienese banker Agostino Chigi, whose beautiful villa beside the Tiber, now known as the **Villa Farnesina**, still gives a vivid impression of the luxurious way of life of the papal court.

Julius' successors were less successful. Some were simply *bons viveurs*, like Giovanni de' Medici who, on being made Pope Leo X in 1513, said to his brother, 'God has given us the papacy. Let us enjoy it.' Enjoy it he did. A great patron of the arts, his other passions were hunting, music, theatre and throwing spectacular dinner parties. He plunged the papacy into debt, spending huge sums on French hounds, Icelandic falcons, and banquets of nightingale pies, peacock's tongues and lampreys cooked in Cretan wine.

Future popes had to face two great threats to the *status quo* of Catholic Europe: the protests of Martin Luther against the Catholic Church – and Roman extravagance in particular – and the growing rivalry between Francis I of France and Charles V, Holy Roman Emperor and King of Spain, who were establishing themselves as the dominant powers in Europe.

The year 1523 saw the death of Pope Adrian VI, a Flemish protégé of Charles V and the last non-Italian pope until 1978. He was succeeded by Clement VII, formerly Giulio de' Medici, who rather unwisely backed France against the all-powerful Emperor. Charles captured the Duchy of Milan in 1525, and threatened to take over the whole of Italy in retaliation for the Pope's disloyalty. In 1527 a large, ill-disciplined Imperial army, many of whom were Germans with Lutheran condemnations of Rome ringing in their ears, sacked the city. The looters were chiefly interested in gold and ready money, but they also destroyed churches and thousands of houses, burnt or stole countless precious relics and works of art, looted tombs, and killed indiscriminately. The dead lay unburied in the streets for months.

Pope Clement held out for seven months in Castel Sant'Angelo, but eventually slunk away in disguise. He returned the following year, and shortly afterwards crowned Charles as Holy Roman Emperor in Bologna. In return, Charles grudgingly confirmed Clement VII's sovereignty over the Papal States.

COUNTER-REFORMATION

The Sack of Rome put an end to the Renaissance popes' dream of making Rome a great political power. The primary concerns now were to rebuild the city and push forward the Counter-Reformation, the Catholic Church's response to Protestantism.

The first great Counter-Reformation pope was Alessandro Farnese, Paul III (1534-49), who had led a riotous youth and produced four illegitimate children. He realised that if Catholicism was to hold its own against austere Protestantism, lavish ecclesiastical lifestyles had to be restrained. Paul summoned the Council of Trent to redefine Catholicism, and encouraged new religious groups such as the Jesuits – founded by the Spaniard Ignatius of Loyola and approved in 1540 – over older, discredited orders. From their mother church in Rome, the Gesù, the Jesuits led the fight against heresy and set out to convert the world.

Pope Paul IV (1555-9), the next major reformer, was a firm believer in the Inquisition, the burning of heretics and homosexuals, and the strictest censorship. He expelled all Jews from the Papal States, except those in Rome itself, whom he confined to the Ghetto in 1556 (see chapter Centro Storico).

By the end of the sixteenth century, the authority of the papacy was on the wane outside Rome, and the papal treasury was increasingly dependent on loans. Nevertheless, in the following century different popes continued to spend money as if the Vatican's wealth was inexhaustible, commissioning architects of the stature of Bernini and Borromini to design churches, palazzi, and fountains that would transform the face of the Eternal City (see chapter Architecture). The inevitable result, however, was to draw off wealth from other parts of society, and the economy of the Papal States became chronically depressed.

If two centuries of papal opulence had turned monumental Rome into a spectacular sight, squalor and poverty were still the norm for most of its people: the streets of Trastevere and the Monti district (earlier the Suburra or great slum quarter of ancient Rome) were filthy and danger-

ous, and the Jewish population lived in even more insanitary conditions in the Ghetto. Even having glorious open spaces such as the Piazza Navona, with its fountains playing, at the end of your dirty, unpaved, sewage-strewn alley cannot have been all that uplifting.

At least the city was now a more peaceful place to live. The rich no longer shut themselves up in fortress-like palazzi, but built delightful villas in landscaped parks, such as Villa Borghese and Villa Pamphili. Rome had many attractions, in spite of the waning prestige of the popes. A Europe-wide resurgence of interest in the classical past was also underway, and shortly the city would discover the joys – and earning powers – of tourism. Rome was about to be invaded again.

GRAND TOURISTS

By the eighteenth century a visit to Rome as part of a 'Grand Tour' was near-obligatory for any European gentleman who aspired to be cultured (see page 58), and Romans responded eagerly to this new influx. Rome itself, however, produced little great art or architecture at this time, due in part to the poor state of papal finances. The two great Roman sights that date from this period, the Spanish Steps and the Fontana di Trevi, are really a late flowering of earlier Roman baroque. The few big building projects undertaken were for the benefit of tourists, notably Giuseppe Valadier's splendid park on the Pincio and the neo-classical facelift he gave to Piazza del Popolo.

Although on the surface Rome was a cultured city, there were many customs that reeked of medieval superstition. Foreign writers like Smollett, Gibbon and Goethe, forgetting the full brutality of ancient Rome, all remarked on the contrast between the sophistication of that vanished civilisation and the barbarism lurking beneath the surface of papal Rome. Some executions were still carried out by means of the martello, in which the condemned man was beaten about the temples with a hammer before having his throat cut and his stomach ripped open. This humane method remained in use until the 1820s.

Executions were traditionally staged in Piazza del Popolo, and often timed to coincide with the Carnival, a period of frantic merrymaking before Lent. For a few days Via del Corso resembled a masked ball, as bands played and people showered each other with confetti, flour, water and more dangerous missiles. The centrepiece was the race of riderless horses along the Corso. They had heavy balls filled with spikes dangling at their sides, and boiling pitch pumped into their recta to spur them on as they ran.

Rome was a city of spectacle for much of the rest of the year, too. In summer, Piazza Navona was flooded by blocking the outlets of the fountains, and the nobility drove around the piazza in their

From Grand Tourism to mass tourism... the **Spanish Steps** *remain a mecca.*

carriages while street urchins frolicked in the water, begging for coins. The only time the city fell quiet was in late summer, when everyone who could left for their villas in the Alban Hills, to escape the stifling heat and the threat of malaria.

Romantic rebellions

In 1798 everything changed. French troops under Napoleon occupied the city, and Rome became a Republic once more. Pope Pius VI, a feeble old man, was exiled from the city and died in France.

Like most attempts to restore the Roman Republic, this one was short-lived. The next pope, Pius VII, elected in Venice, signed a Concordat with Napoleon in 1801, which allowed him to return to Rome. The papacy was expelled a second time when French troops returned in 1808. Napoleon promised the city a modernising, reforming administration, but Romans were not keen to be conscripted into his armies. When the Pope finally reclaimed Rome after the fall of Napoleon in 1814, its noble families and many of the people welcomed his return.

Goethe takes a break from Roman barbarism in the Roman countryside (see page 18).

The patchwork of duchies, principalities and kingdoms that had existed in Italy before Napoleon's invasions was restored after 1815. The Papal States were also handed back to Pius VII. Nevertheless, the brief taste of liberty under the French helped inspire a movement for unification, modernisation and independence from the domination of foreign rulers, such as Austria in the north and the Bourbon Kingdom of the Two Sicilies in the south.

Italy's *Risorgimento* was a movement for the unification of the country, but in itself it was very diverse. Its supporters ranged from liberals who believed in unification for economic reasons, to conservatives who looked to the papacy itself to unify Italy. Initially, the most prominent were the idealistic republicans of the *Giovane Italia* (Young Italy) movement headed by Giuseppe Mazzini. They were flanked on the left by more extreme groups and secret societies such as the *Carbonari*.

Two reactionary popes, Leo XII (1823-9) and Gregory XVI (1831-46), used a network of police spies and censorship to put down opposition of any kind. Most of the unrest in the Papal States, though, was in the north; in Rome life went on much as before. Travellers continued to visit, and Shelley, Dickens and Lord Macaulay all passed through, only to be horrified at the repressive regime of the papacy.

The election of a new pope in 1846 aroused great optimism. Pius IX had a liberal reputation, and immediately announced an amnesty for over 400

What the Savoias did...

To today's visitor, the massive, pompous constructions beloved of post-Unification architects seem an integral part of the Roman scenery. Not so when they were first erected, as Augustus Hare wrote in *the* guide book for late-nineteenth-century visitors, *Walks in Rome* (1883):

'Twelve years of rule by the Savoias (the House of Savoy, the Piedmontese royal family who became Kings of Italy) have done more for the destruction of Rome, with its beauty and interest, than all the invasions of the Goths and Vandals', Hare opined. 'The whole aspect of the city is changed, and the picturesqueness of old days must now be sought in such obscure corners as have escaped the hand of the spoiler.'

The Rome inherited by the new king and his planners in 1870 was a magnificent jumble of the political prisoners. However, the spate of revolutions that spread through Europe in 1848 radically altered his attitude. In November that year his chief minister was assassinated, and Pius fled in panic to Naples. In his absence a popular assembly declared Rome a Republic. Seizing the chance to make his dream reality, Mazzini rushed to the city, where he was chosen as one of a triumvirate of rulers. Meanwhile, another idealist arrived in Rome at the head of 500 armed followers – Giuseppe Garibaldi, a former sailor who had gained his military experience fighting in a variety of wars of liberation in South America.

Ironically, it was Republican France, with Napoleon I's nephew Louis Napoleon as president, which decided it was her duty to restore the pope to Rome. Louis Napoleon's motivation was simple, and not especially religious: he wished to counter the power of Austria within Italy. A French force marched on Rome, but was repelled by the *Garibaldini* (followers of Garibaldi) – a ragbag mixture of former papal troops, young volunteers and enthusiastic citizens. The French attacked again with greater numbers, mounting their assault from the gardens of Villa Pamphili. For the whole of June 1849 the defenders fought valiantly from their positions on the Gianicolo, but the end of the Republic was inevitable.

For the next 20 years, while the rest of Italy was being united under King Vittorio Emanuele of Piedmont, a garrison of French troops protected Pope Pius from invasion. Garibaldi protested vainly to the politicians of the new state – it was, he said, a question of *Roma o morte* ('Rome or death') – but the Kingdom of Italy, established in 1860, was not prepared to take on Napoleon III's France. Meanwhile, the policies of the former liberal Pius IX were increasingly reactionary. In 1869 he convened the first Vatican Council in order to set down the Catholic Church's response to the upheavals of the industrial age. It did so with intransigence, making the doctrine of papal infallibility an official dogma of the Church for the first time.

Tomb of Umberto I, a short-lived Savoy.

Rome, Italy

Even though it was still under papal rule, Rome had been chosen as the capital of the newly unified kingdom. In 1870, with the defeat of Napoleon III in the Franco-Prussian war, the French withdrew from Rome, and Italian troops occupied the city. Pius IX withdrew into the Vatican, refusing to hand over the keys of the **Quirinale**, the future residence of the Italian royal family. Troops arriving in the city had to break in.

There followed the most rapid period of change Rome had experienced since the fall of the Empire. The new capital needed government buildings and housing for the civil servants who worked in them. Church properties were confiscated, and for a time government officials worked in converted monas-

medieval, the Renaissance, and the baroque, interspersed with nature-engulfed remains of the ancient world. To architects used to the French-style order of Turin, this was anarchy at its worst, and certainly not fitting for the showpiece capital of a newly-united nation. Moreover, the hordes of northern pen-pushers who flooded in to man the new country's ponderous bureaucracy had to be provided with offices and accommodation. The consequences, Hare believed, were devastating.

'Precious street memorials of medieval history have been swept away; ancient convents have been levelled with the ground or turned into

barracks; the glorious cloisters of Michelangelo have been walled up; the pagan ruins have been denuded of all that gave them picturesqueness or beauty.'

Many stones that were left unturned by the Savoys were later heaved well out of the way by Mussolini, whose obsession with the glories of the Empire led him not to conserve its remains, but to stamp his mark upon them with a characteristically heavy hand. The great sweep of **Via dei Fori Imperiali** was knocked through a forest of *fora* to link – geographically and symbolically – *Il Duce*'s HQ at Palazzo Venezia with the Colosseum.

*Traffic mills around the **Vittoriale**, monstrous tribute to united Italy's diminutive first king.*

teries and convents. Two aristocratic *palazzi* were adapted to house the Italian parliament: **Palazzo di Montecitorio** became the Chamber of Deputies, and **Palazzo Madama** the Senate.

The city's great building boom lasted for over 30 years (*see pages 20-21*). Entirely new avenues appeared: Via Nazionale and Via Cavour linked the old city with the new Stazione Termini in the east, and Corso Vittorio Emanuele was driven through the historic centre. The new ministries were often massive piles quite out of keeping with their surroundings, and still more extravagant was the monstrous **Vittoriale**, the marble monument to Vittorio Emanuele erected in Piazza Venezia.

Rome was little affected by World War I, but following the war social unrest broke out, with the fear of socialism encouraging the rise of Fascism. Benito Mussolini was a radical journalist who, having become alienated from the far left, shifted to the extreme right. Like so many before him, he turned to ancient Rome to find an emblem to embody his idea of a totalitarian state: *fasces* were the bundles of rods tied round an axe carried by the Roman *Lictors* (marshals) as they walked in front of the city's Consuls. In 1922 Mussolini sent his blackshirt squads on their 'March on Rome', demanding, and winning, full power in the government. He had been prepared to back out at the first sign of real resistance by the constitutional parties, and himself made the 'March' by train.

Mussolini's ambition was to transform the country into a dynamic, aggressive society. Among other things, he wanted to put Italians in uniform and stop them eating pasta, which he thought made them lazy and un-warlike. His ideas for changing the face of Rome were equally far-fetched. He planned to rebuild Rome in gleaming marble, with *fora*, obelisks, and heroic statues proclaiming the *Duce* (Leader) as a modern Augustus

at the head of a new Roman Empire. The most prominent surviving monuments to his megalomania are the suburb of **EUR** (*see page 100*), planned to house an international exhibition of Fascism, and the **Foro Italico** sports complex.

When put to the test in World War II, Fascist Italy rapidly foundered. Mussolini was ousted from power in 1943, and the citizens of Rome had no difficulty in changing their allegiance from the Axis to the Allies. During the period of German occupation that followed, Italian partisans showed themselves capable of acts of courage that had never been displayed in the cause of Fascism. Rome was declared an open city – the *Roma Città Aperta* of Rossellini's great film – meaning that the Germans agreed not to defend it, pitching their defence south of the city around Frascati. While other Italian cities and towns were pounded by shells and bombs, Rome suffered only one serious bombing raid during the whole war.

After the war Italy voted to become a Republic, and Rome quickly adapted to the new political structures. *Partitocrazia* – government by a group of political parties sharing power and dividing up lucrative government jobs and contracts between them – suited the Roman approach to life well. The political unrest of the 1970s affected Rome less than it did Milan or Turin, and the Romans simply swam with the political tide, voting in their first Communist mayor in 1976.

The city has benefited greatly from Italy's post-war economic boom. It has spread radially along its major arterial roads. The problem of the city authorities since the war has been how to preserve the old city and yet encourage development. Rome's main industry is still being itself, whether as capital of Italy or historical relic, and the city continues to thrive, trading as it has done for the last 1,500 years on its unforgettable past.

Rome Today

The Millennium is nigh, but Rome is still not sure what it will make of it.

Today's Rome has many faces. The face that the city centre presents to the visitor is charming, lively, absorbing; it manages to be imposing while also remaining full of character and characters. So much so, in fact, that it's almost a caricature of everything that strangers to Rome want and expect to find: packs of nuns peering greedily into the windows of designer boutiques; Fiat 500s hurtling the wrong way down one-way streets; politicians looking shady; priests looking shadier; suave men hassli ng lone females; over-dressed females snapping dangerous looks at predatory males. All against a background of such indescribable beauty and imbued with such a sense of historical significance that the inconveniences, the patchy service and the threat to life and limb from passing traffic can (almost) be overlooked.

To the Roman, however, that same centre has a very different look. From earliest times, the relationship between the city and its inhabitants has never been an easy one.

When the Western world was ruled from here, only a tiny minority actually did the ruling and reaped the benefits of domination directly; the rest were spoon-fed bread and circuses to keep them docile and pliable, a historical precedent that may explain why the Romans on today's streets sit back and do little to improve their own backyard. Instead, they wait for the powers that be to do it for them, grumbling when they don't, but grumbling equally loudly if any work to improve the city causes them the least personal discomfort. Then they'll slip, in self-satisfied fashion, into possession of the end result, as if it were nothing more than they deserved.

Through the Middle Ages, Rome slid further and further into decline, a decline made all the more poignant by its crumbling architectural reminders of the power it once was. Renaissance Romans wreaked their schizoid revenge by using those ruins as building materials. Even into the twentieth century the havoc was further compounded as, during the economic boom of the '60s and '70s, Rome's citizens surrounded their ancient relics with apartment blocks of astounding ugliness. Its wealth of art, too, was treated in cavalier fashion, hidden away in museums with erratic opening times or completely under wraps in eternal restoration projects.

Rome's everyday life is steeped in history.

Yet modern Romans are neither ignorant about nor insensitive towards their cultural heritage. Rather, this devil-may-care attitude towards ruins, art and the beauties that surround them is due to being so totally steeped in their history that it is an integral part of modern life: part of its beauty, and part of its frustrations. If opening a unique monument to the public means working overtime, lock the doors; if it's in a field where you want to build a new block of flats, build around it; if there's no way round it, knock a hole through it… there's plenty more of the old stuff elsewhere, anyhow. Old buildings are not pickled in nostalgia; they are part of the surroundings and accepted as such. Kids kick footballs around the pillars of the Pantheon, girls totter across centuries-old cobblestones in chunky platforms, and drivers barrel down medieval alleys, squeezing their cars into parking places too small for an ancient handcart.

ALL CHANGE OR SMALL CHANGE?

When Rome became capital of Italy in 1870 it, and the papacy it housed, were a political irrelevance residing in a provincial backwater. Today, despite more than a century of tawdry growth, and the changes for the better of the last few years, the city is still struggling to find a role it can be proud of.

Since 1993 a wind of change has been blowing through the city hall on the Capitoline Hill. Over two terms in control of the mayor's office, a team led by one of the country's most prominent Greens, Francesco Rutelli, has brought about palpable changes. Church façades blackened over centuries are suddenly clean. The opera house, once run with legendary extravagance but little talent, is under new management. Museums galore have been opened and re-opened. Parking regulations have been revolutionised, new tramlines have been laid and an overhaul of the lumbering bus system has begun.

But Rome remains far away from Italy's economic powerhouse in Milan and Turin and the economically miraculous North-east. The capital was traditionally lumbered with the massive machinery of state industry and banking which, until recently, provided jobs for the highly unqualified boys, and lost money hand over fist. More recently, new, young, go-getting managers have presided over the dismantling of great parts of this state conglomerate and its sale to the private sector, following which operations have tended to shift to more productive areas of the country.

Naturally, Rome is still home to central government: definitely a dubious honour given the universal mistrust with which politics and politicians are regarded in Italy, despite the collapse in the early '90s of the corrupt old guard. The new political generation may be more honest than its predecessor, but it has some way to go before convincing voters it is any better at getting things done. This nationwide scepticism spills over by extension onto the capital as a whole, and there is still a tendency elsewhere in the country to regard all Romans as pen-pushing time-servers and parasites of an ineffective state.

Romans, equally naturally, reject this, and do so by doing what they do best: simply being Roman. They may be brusque and stroppy, but

Rome by numbers

Population (1997)	2,653,000	Murders (1998)	31
Rubbish produced yearly		Attempted murders (1998)	84
per resident (1996)	497kg	Rapes (1998)	115
Rubbish recycled yearly		Drug traffickers and dealers	
per resident (1996)	8.5kg	arrested (1998)	3,032
Parks and gardens		Total beds for hire in hotels, hostels,	
per resident (1996)	11.8 sq m	religious institutes in Rome (1998)	95,000
Cars per 100 residents (1996)	65.8	Beds in hotels (1998)	70,300
Traffic police (1998)	5,800	Beds in four and five	
Fines issued by traffic police		star hotels (1998)	35,000
(Jan-June 1998)	800,000	Beds in one and two star	
Parking fines issued by		hotels (1998)	11,700
licensed wardens (1998)	351,000	Total pilgrims expected	
Cars towed away (Jan-June 1998)	35,000	during 2000 Holy Year	29.4 million
Buses (1998)	2,485	Non-Italian pilgrims expected	
Trams (1998)	125	during 2000 Holy Year	9.9 million
Km covered by buses (1998)	116.6 million	Rubbish generated by	
Bus passengers (1998)	750 million	29.4 million pilgrims	90,650 tonnes
Tram passengers (1998)	65 million	Pilgrims expected at	
Ticket inspectors on buses		Holy Year services on:	
and trams (1998)	352	Ash Wednesday, 8 March	500,000
People fined for travelling without		Workers' Jubilee, 1 May	1.3 million
tickets on buses and trams (1998)	44,237	Youth rally, 19-20 August	2-3 million
Non-Italian female tourists who think			
Romans sexiest men in Italy	34%	**Sources** Eredi Pisanò; Comune di Roma; Istat;	
Roman surfaces		Corpo della Polizia Municipale;	
covered by graffiti	15,000 sq m	Holy See Jubilee Committee; Polizia di Stato;	
Thefts (1998)	151,591	Arma dei Carabinieri; ATAC; Agenzia Romana	
		per la Preparazione del Giubileo.	

The Millennium plan

For Rome's Green-led city council, the Holy Year celebrations planned for Millennium year (*see also page 106*) – or at least the vast amounts of public funding that have accompanied them – have truly come as manna from heaven. For over 30 years there had been virtual stasis as far as improving Rome's traffic system and other infrastructure went (apart from a small hiatus for the World Cup in 1990, when projects blossomed everywhere, only to collapse as pockets were lined and chronic foot-dragging set in). Then suddenly, with the promise – or threat – of unprecedented numbers descending on the city, things had to improve, or implode.

It was not until 1997, however, that the L2.8 trillion (£1 billion/$1.6 billion) earmarked for preparing the province of Rome for the new millennium started trickling in. And, in one horrendous mess, thousands of building sites mushroomed simultaneously. Projects ranged from scraping the dirt of centuries off Renaissance facades, to tunnelling beneath Castel Sant'Angelo to ease traffic flow along the riverside, and extending the metro.

For Romans, whose lives degenerated into an infuriating obstacle race around scaffolding and holes in traffic-choked roads, it became increasingly difficult to see the glimmer of a functioning modern city at the end of the tunnel of frustration. As this guide went to press, a dispiritingly small proportion of the work had been completed. Still, Romans are past masters at last-minute spurts, and there was every reason to believe that many of the projects promised for the Holy Year would be finished by 31 December 1999 or, failing that, during the festivities.

There can be no doubt that, when the scaffolding finally comes down and the holes are paved over, the Rome offered to the tourist will be more beautiful than ever. Museums have been renovated, collections re-hung, reorganised and re-lit. There's hardly a blackened building left in the city centre. Parks are looking spruce and manicured. And the Eternal City's eternal traffic snarl? Well… some small steps forward have been taken.

For Romans themselves the benefits are not so overwhelming. Much of the revamping has taken place in the centre, leaving residents in the dismal (and not so dismal) suburbs feeling bitter and left out. Many feel the daily torture they have had to bear in the run-up to 2000 has outweighed any advantage the overhaul might bring. Then again, Romans are moaners by nature, and far from rejoicing if things do go well, they will simply take changes for the better for granted, as their God-given right. They will use the improvements to the full, too, frequenting their own museums, parks and gardens with as much relish as any out-of-towner.

Millennial programmes

The cultural programme drawn up for the 2000 Holy Year is exhaustive and exhausting, with exhibitions throughout the year. Among the most important are:

Medieval Holy Years Palazzo Venezia, Oct 1999-Feb 2000
Francesco Borromini Palazzo delle Esposizioni, Dec 1999-Feb 2000
Roy Lichtenstein Santa Maria della Pace, Dec 1999-Apr 2000
Tapestry designs by Rubens and Pietro da Cortona Palazzo Barberini, Jan-Mar 2000
Paintings on musical themes by late Renaissance masters Palazzo Barberini and Auditorium-Città della Musica, Mar-May 2000
Classical myth in depictions of Rome from 1780-1900 Palazzo Venezia, Oct 2000
Raphael's works for the Borghese family Galleria Borghese, Oct 2000-Feb 2001
The Barberini family in the seventeenth century Palazzo Barberini, from Nov 2000
For up-to-date information on all 2000 events, visit official tourist information booths (*see chapter* **Directory**), or check the websites below:
www.romagiubileo.it The city hall-sponsored Agenzia Romana per la Preparazione del Giubileo
www.jubil2000.org The Vatican's own Council for the Great Jubilee
www.comune.roma.it Rome city council
www.beniculturali.it Cultural Heritage ministry
www.enit.it The Italian national tourist board.

they manage to be so with sunny, Mediterranean gusto. It's hard not to fall in love with the exuberant play they act out daily against their glorious city backdrop. Behind the play-acting is a wheeler-dealing determination which used to be employed (as the rest of the country suspected) in getting as much as possible for as little as possible out of the state and its trappings. Those opportunities are fast drying up, but Roman ingenuity remains. Who knows – in the new Millennium it might just be put to better use, making Rome into a truly vital capital again. Until then, the city's infuriating, enigmatic and restless soul remains very much alive.

Architecture

Ruins, Renaissance, and Renzo Piano: Rome's architecture keeps pace with the times.

The ancient city

'The beauty of Rome lies in what is in ruins,' wrote a visitor to the city in 1444, and the relics of the Republican and Imperial eras strewn around the **Forum**, **Palatine** and **Imperial Fora** prove him right. But wonderfully evocative as they are, decaying ruins can be fiendishly tricky to interpret; consequently, it's very fortunate there are still some superbly preserved structures such as the **Colosseum**, **Pantheon**, **Trajan's Markets** and **Trajan's Column**, to give an idea of just how splendid the ancient city really was.

Major buildings expressed all the glamour and sophistication of ancient Rome. In imitation of ancient Greece, important façades followed the system of orders, each of different proportions, based on the width of the columns. The main Greek orders were *Doric*, plain and sturdy; *Ionic*, more slender and ornate; and *Corinthian*, the most delicate and ornate of all. The Colosseum is a good example of how they were used: hefty and rooted Doric at the bottom to support the construction; lighter, more elegant Ionic in the middle to provide a suitable visual link between the tiers; and the delicate, decorative Corinthian top layer. Further embellishment was often provided by statues, reliefs and, in some cases, painted façades.

Whole genres of building were based on Greek models. Temples were usually colonnaded, and either rectangular, like the temples of Saturn or Portunus, or circular like the temples of **Vesta** and **Hercules Victor**. Other common building forms were Greek-style theatres and their Roman relative the amphitheatre, an elliptical arena designed for blood sports. The Romans did also develop some forms of building themselves: the first known basilicas – rectangular meeting-houses flanked by columns – are in Rome, as are the first baths with heated running water.

The commonest stone found around Rome was soft, volcanic tufa. This was not an ideal building material, and as early as the third century BC a form of concrete had been developed, made of pozzolana (a volcanic ash), lime and tufa rubble. As this was not aesthetically pleasing, later buildings were faced with thin veneers of coloured marble or travertine (a calcareous limestone). Without concrete, constructing the Pantheon would have been impossible. The huge hemispherical dome is the largest cast-concrete construction made before the twentieth century. Other feats of cast-concrete engineering include the **Baths of Diocletian** and **Baths of Caracalla**. If you look at the ruined domes of the latter, you can see the layers of brick, concrete and marble, and get an idea of how the building was put together. Brick, the other fundamental Roman building material, was used to face buildings, to lend internal support to concrete walls, and as a material in its own right. The most impressive example is **Trajan's Markets**.

Early Christian Rome

There are traces of the early Christians everywhere in Rome – and not confined to the dank **Catacombs** and grisly reliquaries of martyrs. Scores of early churches survive, even though in many cases the original building is hidden beneath later accretions and decoration. The tell-tale signs are there if you know what to look for.

Early Christian basilical churches are the ghosts of ancient Roman basilicas. Churches founded in the fourth and fifth centuries such as **San Paolo fuori le Mura**, **San Giovanni in Laterano**, **Santi Quattro Coronati**, **Santa Maria in Trastevere**, **San Pietro in Vincoli** and **Santa Sabina** are the most tangible connection we have with the interiors of ancient civic Rome: go into any of them and imagine them shorn of their later decoration. The construction is generally simple and stately. Most are rectangular, with a flat roof and a colonnade separating a tall nave from lower aisles. Natural light enters the nave from high windows, while the aisles are lit from the ground-floor windows. Behind the altar, opposite the entrance, is an apse topped by a conch.

Santa Sabina on the Aventine has survived virtually unchanged, and still evokes the taste for classical forms that lasted long after the demise of pagan Rome. Built between 422 and 432, and stripped of later accretions in 1936, it even retains its original selenite windows.

The fortunes of the Catholic church are well reflected in architecture. When it was poor, as in the fifth century, buildings were plain and functional; when it was rich, in periods such as the eighth and twelfth centuries, churches were adorned with brilliant mosaics. The most magnificent to have survived are in **Santa Maria Maggiore**, **Santa**

The **Pantheon**: *a splendidly-preserved monument to the glories of concrete.*

Prassede and **Santa Maria in Trastevere**. Many churches were decorated with Cosmati-work: exquisitely carved pulpits, walled choirs, candlesticks decorated with glass and gilding, and inlaid marble floors (*see page 83*). Very occasionally circular churches were built, perhaps inspired by Roman tombs like Hadrian's mausoleum (now **Castel Sant'Angelo**) and the **Mausoleum of Augustus**. The dazzling mosaic-caked **Santa Costanza** was probably built in the fourth century as a mausoleum for the daughters of Emperor Constantine, while its contemporary, **Santo Stefano Rotondo**, was a seat of the cult of protomartyr Saint Stephen. Its shape may be due to its occupying the site of an earlier circular building that was perhaps part of the Roman market, the *macellum magnum*. Equally, it may have been inspired by the church of the Holy Sepulchre in Jerusalem.

As for civic architecture, this was a period in which the main families of Rome were in an almost constant battle for power. Consequently most felt it necessary to live in fortresses with lookout towers. The Torre delle Milizie, behind Trajan's Markets, and Torre degli Anguillara in Trastevere are good examples.

The Renaissance

In the late fourteenth century, while a huge revolution in art, architecture and thought was underway in Tuscany, Rome was still a crumbling, dirty, medieval city. Only in the following century, when the great revival in art, literature and humanistic thought trickled down to Rome, was the Tuscan influence felt.

In 1445 the Florentine architect Filarete created Rome's first significant Renaissance work: the magnificent central bronze doors of **Saint Peter's**. However, it was not until the reign of Pope Nicholas V (1447-55) that the Renaissance really began to flourish. Nicholas was a highly educated man, who knew the architectural theorist Leon Battista Alberti and other key protagonists of the early Renaissance. He decided that the Church had to be reconciled with secular culture, and that Rome should become worthy of its glorious past; much of the city as he found it was in a state of collapse, its streets filled with cattle, sheep and goats. His motivation, however, was more evangelistic than humanistic. If Rome was to take on fully its role as focus of Christianity, it had to look the part. Nicholas believed faith would be strengthened if people were surrounded by 'majestic buildings, lasting memorials, witnesses to their faith planted on earth as if by the hand of God'. After consultations with Alberti, Nicholas began to rebuild Saint Peter's itself, which at the time was in imminent danger of collapse. Meanwhile, those with lucrative church connections built fabulous palaces: in 1508 papal banker Agostino Chigi commissioned a lavish villa, now the **Villa Farnesina**, and in 1515 work started on **Palazzo Farnese** for Cardinal Alessandro Farnese.

The Roman Renaissance gathered momentum under Pope Pius II (1458-64), a cultured Tuscan, steeped in classical literature and an acclaimed orator and poet, who forbade the destruction of ancient buildings. Under Sixtus IV (1471-84), roads were paved and widened, churches such as **Santa Maria della Pace** and **Santa Maria del Popolo** were rebuilt, the **Ponte Sisto** was begun and the **Sistine Chapel** was built and decorated by some of the foremost artists of the time, among them Ghirlandaio, Pinturicchio and Signorelli.

Architect Donato Bramante came to Rome from Milan in 1499, and in 1502 built the **Tempietto** to mark the spot traditionally thought to be that of Saint Peter's execution. A domed cylinder

Architectural terms

Amphitheatre – open-air elliptical theatre.
Apse – large recess at the high-altar end of a church.
Baldacchino – canopy supported by columns above an altar.
Basilica – ancient Roman rectangular public building; Christian rectangular church with apse and aisles, but no transepts.
Campanile – bell tower.
Caryatid – supporting pillar carved in the shape of a woman.
Confessio – crypt beneath a raised altar.
Cupola – a dome-shaped roof or ceiling.
Cryptoporticus – underground corridor.
Entablature – section above a column or row of columns including the frieze and cornice.
Greek cross – (church in the shape of a) cross with arms of equal length.
Latin cross – (church in the shape of a) cross with one arm longer than the other.

Loggia – gallery, open on one side.
Mithraeum – temple to god Mithras.
Narthex – enclosed porch in front of church.
Nave – main body of a church; the longest section of a Latin cross church.
Palazzo – important and/or large building (not necessarily a palace).
Pendentives – four concave triangular sections on top of piers supporting a dome.
Peristyle – temple or court surrounded by columns.
Piazza – town or city square.
Rococo – highly decorative style, popular in the eighteenth century.
Transept – shorter, 'side' arms of a Latin-cross church (see above).
Triclinium – dining room.
Triumphal arch – arch in front of apse, usually over the high altar.
Trompe l'œil – deceptive stylistic effect (often to make a surface appear three-dimensional).

surrounded by a Tuscan Doric colonnade, it came closer than any other building to the spirit of antiquity. Miniature in scale but exquisitely proportioned, with perfectly detailed capitals, entablatures and dome, it is a masterly evocation of the majesty of ancient Rome – precisely what the Renaissance sought to emulate.

Rome's Renaissance reached its peak with Julius II (1503-13), who made Bramante his chief architect, and commissioned Michelangelo to sculpt his tomb and fresco the ceiling of the Sistine Chapel, and Raphael to decorate the *stanze* in the Vatican Palace. Not satisfied with the restoration of Saint Peter's initiated by his predecessors, Julius decided to scrap the old building and start again. The job was given to Bramante, and in 1506 the foundation stone for a new **Saint Peter's** was laid.

Work began on Bramante's Greek-cross design, but was halted after his death in 1514. In 1547 Michelangelo took over, keeping to the centralised design but increasing the scale tremendously. After his death in 1564 it was left to Giacomo del Duca to erect the dome, in the papacy of Sixtus V (1585-90), an obsessive planner responsible for the layout of much of modern Rome. However, the Greek design was wrecked by Paul V (1605-21), who commissioned Carlo Maderno to lengthen the nave in line with the new ideals of the Counter-Reformation.

The Baroque

The second half of the sixteenth century in Rome was dominated by the austere reforms of the Council of Trent (1545-63), designed to counter the ideas of Luther's Reformation, and by the estab-

lishment of heavy-handed new orders such as the Jesuits and Oratarians. Consequently, the earliest churches of the period, such as the **Chiesa Nuova**, were plain and provided with long naves, suitable for processions. The **Gesù**, with its wide nave and barrel-vaulted ceiling, was deemed ideal for the preaching purposes of the Jesuits, as no architectural obstacles came between the preacher and his congregation.

As the Counter-Reformation gathered pace, great cycles of decoration preaching the mysteries of the faith (such as the *Cappella Sistina* of **Santa Maria Maggiore**) or inspiring the onlooker to identify with the sufferings of martyrs (as in the bloodthirsty frescoes of **Santo Stefano Rotondo**) began to appear. On their heels came an increasingly exuberant and theatrical style of art and architecture, the baroque.

It is to a great extent the endlessly inventive confections of the baroque that make Rome what it is today, creating a magnificent backdrop for everyday life. The style is found not only in churches, but in villas, fountains, squares and palaces, and their painted, sculpted and gilded adornments.

Architects like Giacomo della Porta (1532/3-1602), who worked on **Sant'Andrea della Valle**, and Domenico Fontana (1543-1607), who worked at **Santa Maria Maggiore** and **San Carlo alle Quattro Fontane**, set the scene in which the real shapers of the baroque grew up. These were the architects Gian Lorenzo Bernini (1598-1680), poet, playwright, sculptor and painter; Francesco Borromini (1598-1667; *see pages 64-5*), an eccentric genius with a passion for archaeology; and Pietro

San Carlo alle Quattro Fontane.

da Cortona (1598-1669), master of architecture, painting and theology. All three worked on the **Palazzo Barberini**.

Bernini virtually made the baroque his own, with his imaginative use of coloured marble, bronze and stucco, his combination of sensuality and mysticism and the inspired sense of movement and immediacy he gave to his sculpture. For over 20 years he was artistic dictator of Rome, and was jealously guarded by his Barberini patrons. He carried out much of the decoration of the interior of Saint Peter's for the Barberini Pope Urban VIII (there are bees, the Barberini family emblem, all over the *baldacchino*) and dominated all the arts to the extent of causing the relative neglect of Borromini, Rome's other great genius of the era.

Bernini said that quarrelsome, neurotic Borromini 'had been sent to destroy architecture'. For centuries Borromini was vilified as a wild revolutionary. Today he is recognised as one of the great masters of the period, perhaps greatest of all in the inventive use of ground plan and the creation of spatial effects. The most startling examples of his work are **San Carlo alle Quattro Fontane** and **Sant'Ivo alla Sapienza**, both of which broke all established rules. Perhaps because of his temperament (he eventually committed suicide), he never attained anything like the acclaim awarded to Bernini, but his patrons allowed him a freedom to develop his ideas that he might not have enjoyed had he worked for popes such as Urban VIII or Alexander VII.

Like Bernini, Pietro da Cortona created some of his greatest works for the Barberini popes. He was principally a painter, and his most significant con-

tribution to architecture was his three-dimensional treatment of the wall. At **Santa Maria della Pace** he combined opposing convex forms that, curving sharply at the ends, are almost flat in the middle. The result is almost theatrical. Squeezed into a tiny piazza, the church resembles a stage set.

The hallmarks of the buildings by Bernini, Borromini and da Cortona are the preference for curves, complex forms, massive scale, dramatic effects of light and shadow, and movement and counter-movement – spirals, ovals, and curves moving in opposite directions. Interiors were adorned with an undiluted richness, produced with coloured marbles and gilded stucco. In statues and paintings, saints and martyrs were depicted in hideous misery or orgasmic ecstasy. Architecture, painting and sculpture were sometimes combined, most successfully in the Cornaro chapel in **Santa Maria della Vittoria** and the *baldacchino* in **Saint Peter's**, by Bernini.

None of this would have been possible without the patronage of the popes, their families and the various religious orders. Popes commissioned the decoration of Saint Peter's (Urban VIII, 1623-44); the colonnade in front of it (Alexander VII, 1655-67); the layout of **Piazza Navona** and the redecoration of **San Giovanni in Laterano** (Innocent X, 1644-55). Their cardinal-nephews inspired a great many lesser building schemes: the redecoration or restoration of existing churches, and private villas, gardens, palaces and picture galleries.

The religious orders were no less profligate. The great churches of the time were the initial testing ground – none more than the **Gesù**, which, although begun in the 1560s, was not completed until the baroque period. It was originally intended to have bare interior walls, and only in the 1640s did it begin to acquire the alarming profusion of decoration, illusion and ornament we see today. Other churches decorated by the orders in high-baroque style include **Sant'Ignazio**, **Sant'Andrea della Valle** and the **Chiesa Nuova**.

Marking time

In the eighteenth century the baroque gained something of a rococo gloss, with Francesco de Sanctis' **Spanish Steps**, Filippo Raguzzini's pretty **Ospedale di San Gallicano** in Trastevere, Nicola Salvi's **Fontana di Trevi** and Fernando Fuga's hallucinatory **Palazzo della Consulta** on Piazza del Quirinale. Rome saw little significant building during the nineteenth century until 1870, when the city became capital of a united Italy, triggering a whole new phase of urban development in the city (*see chapter* **History**). Examples include the neo-classical **Piazza Vittorio Emanuele**, the flamboyant **Palazzo delle Esposizioni** and the imperious, jingoistic **Vittoriale** monument in Piazza Venezia.

Not computer mice but concert halls: Renzo Piano's state-of-the-art **Auditorium**.

Twentieth-century Rome

The architectural triumphs of twentieth-century Rome are largely confined to the Fascist era. **Stazione Termini** is a strident and impressive example. It was begun just before World War II, and its wide, overhanging entrance portal, repeated arches and huge foyer are still stunning half a century after their completion. Other Fascist buildings are dotted around the periphery of the city. North of the Tiber is the **Foro Italico**, a magnificent sports complex – although it's doubtful whether its builders intended the huge statues of naked male athletes to be quite as homo-erotic as they are. The best buildings from the period are at **EUR** south of the city, a surreal, clinical example of 1930s town planning, where structures such as the **Palazzo della Civiltà del Lavoro** and **Museo della Civiltà Romana** look as though they were designed to feature in de Chirico cityscapes (*see chapter* **Other parts of town**). The **Palazzo dello Sport**, built by Pier Luigi Nervi and Marcello Piacentini for the 1960 Olympics, has a reinforced concrete dome that, with a diameter of 100 metres, took from the Pantheon the record for being the world's largest free-standing concrete dome.

Today there are still few modern buildings in central Rome, although there would have been scores if Mussolini had got his way. Addressing the city council, he said that 'In five years, Rome must appear wonderful to the whole world: immense, orderly and powerful, as she was in the days of the first empire of Augustus. The approaches to the Theatre of Marcellus, the Campidoglio and the Pantheon must be cleared of everything that has grown up round them during the centuries of decadence. Within five years the hill of the Pantheon must be visible through an avenue leading from Piazza Colonna.' Fortunately the war first distracted his attention and then removed him from power before he could wreak too much havoc.

You need only look at the **Via dei Fori Imperiali** that links the Colosseum with Piazza Venezia to see the result of Mussolini's unenlightened attempts to 'improve' the city. The grand avenue bludgeoned its way across the ruins of the ancient *fora*, covering and in some cases obliterating them. Work is currently under way to remove part of this road and turn the area between the Colosseum and the Piazza Venezia into a huge archaeological park.

From the 1950s to the 1970s, Rome, in common with other European cities, received its share of functional office blocks; high-rise apartments to house the children of the economic boom, covered what until then had been unspoilt countryside. In recent years, building projects have been considerably more positive. The visionary **mosque** by postmodernist Paolo Portoghesi was opened in the early 1990s near the Catacombs of Priscilla. As this guide went to press, work was surging ahead on an ambitious **auditorium**, designed by Renzo Piano and due for completion by the millennium (*see chapter* **Music: Classical & Opera**).

Sightseeing

Introduction

The Eternal City's attractions are endless; it pays to concentrate your gaze, and take your time.

Over 2,000 years of history – many of them at the centre of the Western stage – has left Rome with more magnificent piazzas, palaces, churches and ancient monuments than any other European city. Yet, far from being a sterile open-air museum, this is one of Europe's most vivacious capitals, and its accumulated glories form the backdrop for the chaotic exuberance of everyday Roman life.

For an essential first impression, forget the tourist trail and seat yourself at a table outside any central café. Take time just to breathe in car fumes, mixed with a hint of anarchy, as Rome rushes compulsively by. This done, you can proceed to outdoor sights, and there are enough of these to keep you busy for weeks. When you've absorbed a place by day, go back at night. Many sites are floodlit (don't miss the **Roman Forum** and the **Palatine**), and even those that are not look spectacular in a blend of moonlight and the soft glow of street lamps. After that, it's time to begin the museums, galleries, *palazzi* and churches, which are – and contain – Rome's seemingly inexhaustible artistic treasures.

In the following chapters, when a building or site is highlighted in **bold** this indicates that it has a detailed listing elsewhere in the Guide.

Ancient sites

The ancient sites of Rome have been treated in a rather cavalier fashion. Some have later buildings on top of or inside them, and most have been used at some time or other as a handy source of building materials. Some are still present, hidden under tangles of weeds and shrubs, while others are discernible only in the outlines they have handed down to modern streets and buildings. Still others, thankfully, are well preserved, well restored and on view.

The most concentrated and fully excavated cluster of ancient remains lies in the area bound by the Capitoline, Palatine, Esquiline and Quirinal hills, roughly south and east of the post-medieval centre of Rome. This was the official heart of the ancient city, where the fates of nations were decided, military triumphs celebrated, and citizens entertained by the death of gladiators and mass slaughter of wild animals. Here you'll find the world's first shopping mall, **Trajan's Markets**. Here too was the most desirable residential area in Rome, the **Palatine**, where – if ancient historians are to be believed – the sexual excesses of

emperors, empresses, politicians and poets were matched only by the passion with which they plotted against and poisoned one another.

Churches

Central Rome contains over 400 churches – excessive, perhaps, even for the headquarters of the Catholic Church and one of the birthplaces of western Christianity. Across the centuries popes, princes and aristocrats commissioned artists and architects to build, rebuild, adorn, fresco and paint their city's places of worship. Motives were not wholly pious. For many, it was a cynical means of assuring a place in Heaven, securing temporal power, increasing their prestige, or a combination of the three.

Whatever the reasons, the results of all this munificence form some of Rome's most spectacular sights. In addition, a flurry of restoration work in the run-up to the 2000 Holy Year has still further enhanced their extraordinary grandeur.

Churches are places of worship: visitors are expected to respect certain dress codes.

Lunedì chiuso

Sightseeing on a Monday can be a frustrating experience in Rome, as many museums and sites give themselves a day off to get over their strenuous weekends. Limit Monday roving to churches, and you will find few bolted doors. Otherwise, head for the following, which will be open:

The Colosseum (*see pxx*)
Mamertine Prison (*see pxx*)
The Roman Forum (*see pxx*)
Museo di Arte Ebraico (*see pxx*)
The Palatine (*see pxx*)
The Pantheon (*see p57*)
Galleria Doria Pamphili (*see p60*)
Keats-Shelley Memorial House (*see p60*)
Galleria Borghese (*see pp66-7*)
Palazzo delle Esposizioni (*see p69*)
Villa Farnesina (*see p72*)
Castel Sant'Angelo (*see pxx*)
Museo Nazionale
delle Arti e Tradizioni Popolari (*see pxx*)

Getting through locked gates

A surprising number of archaeological and other sites in Rome can only be visited with prior permission, obtained from the infamous *Ripartizione X* of Rome's city heritage office. The immense frustration of arriving at that ancient monument you've always wanted to see, only to find it firmly locked and open only by written application, can be avoided with a little forethought.

Once you have ascertained that permission is necessary (see individual listings in this Guide) phone 06 6710 3819, where you will find someone who will speak to you in passable English. Establish which sites you wish to visit on what days (individuals can usually be accommodated within hours or days of calling; groups should organise visits a week or so in advance). Then send a fax confirming your appointments (list sites and dates to make sure there are no mixups) to 06 689 2115. The fax should read:

All'attenzione della Ripartizione X

Il sottoscritto (*La sottoscritta* if you're a woman) [your name], *che sarà in visita a Roma dal* [starting date of holiday] *al* [finishing date of holiday] *chiede l'autorizzazione a visitare* [list of requested sites]. *Potrà essere contattato* (*contattata* if you're a woman) *a Roma al seguente indirizzo:* [name and phone number where you can be reached in Rome].

In fede, [signature].

Carry a shawl or long-sleeved shirt to hide bare shoulders, and do not wear very short (much above the knee) shorts or skirts. Consider taking binoculars and a torch to see into distant, badly-lit corners, and have a supply of coins (L100, L200, L500) for the meters that light up the most interesting nooks. Although you may be admitted to churches during services, you will be expected not to take photographs, talk loudly or wander around.

Museums & galleries

Until not many years ago, visitors to the artistic treasures of Rome were likely to be greeted by scaffolding and closed doors, as they ran a dispiriting gamut of eccentric opening hours, wildcat strikes and apparently endless restoration programmes. Recently, however, things have taken a definite turn for the better, and the approach of the 2000 Holy Year has provided a much-needed incentive to bring museums and galleries up to scratch.

The most significant ancient collections are in the **Vatican Museums**, the **Capitoline Museums**, the various sections of the **Museo Nazionale Romano** and the **Museo Nazionale di Villa Giulia**. Renaissance and baroque paintings are best seen in **Palazzo Barberini**, **Galleria Borghese** and **Galleria Doria Pamphili**.

Opening hours

Opening times given in the following chapters are for the winter timetable (roughly October-May). Summer hours can vary significantly, especially at major museums and archaeological sites, and are rarely the same from year to year; between May and October, check for current time-tables at tourist information kiosks (*see chapter* **Directory**).

Ancient sites, museums & galleries

Ticket offices normally stop issuing tickets ½-1 hour before closing times. On public holidays (*see pp5-8*) most museums keep Sunday hours. Times given in these chapters were correct at time of writing, but are liable to sudden variations, depending on the season, or official decisions. In summer, especially, hours may lengthen: in recent years many of Rome's attractions have stayed open until 10pm in mid-summer.

Churches

Times given can only be rough guidelines: most open and close an hour later in summer (May-Oct). In many, whether doors are open depends on the whims (and hunger pangs) of conscientious objectors assigned to lend a hand to the diocese of Rome.

Admission charges

Entrance to all publicly-owned museums and sites is free to EU citizens under 18 and over 60. Under-25s in full-time education may also be eligible for discounts. Make sure you carry appropriate ID.

A joint ticket for the **Museo Nazionale Romano** (**Palazzo Altemps**, **Palazzo Massimo alle Terme**, probably the **Terme di Diocleziano** when it reopens), the **Colosseum** and **Palatine** is available. It costs L20,000 and is valid for three days.

One week each year is designated *Settimana dei beni culturali* (cultural heritage week), when all publicly-owned museums and sites are open long hours and free of charge (*see chapter* **Rome by Season**).

Disabled travellers

Progress has been made, but many of Rome's museums and sites are far from wheelchair-friendly, and very few churches are equipped for people with mobility problems. For more on facilities for the disabled in the city, *see chapter* **Directory**.

Centro Storico

Sweeping baroque squares and medieval alleyways, churches and cycle repairers, hole-in-the-wall workshops and fashionable bars: there's nothing museum-like about Rome's historic core.

The tightly-knit web of narrow streets and *piazze* on the right bank of the river Tiber forms the core of Rome's *centro storico* (historic centre). By day it teems with small shops, markets, craft workshops and restaurants; by night it buzzes with clubs, bars and more restaurants.

There are sharp social and economic contrasts here. In ancient cobbled streets off Via dei Banchi Vecchi and Via del Governo Vecchio, dingy motor-cycle repair shops spill out onto pavements shared with chic lunchtime cafés, and exclusive boutiques stand cheek-by-jowl with grubby-looking junk shops. The inhabitants are also a mixed bunch: ever-higher local taxes have not yet succeeded in pushing all the centre's poor out to dismal suburbs, and down-at-heel pensioners still shuffle among

the fur-coated occupants of smart apartments that have been carved out of patrician *palazzi*.

In ancient times, much of the area on either side of the present-day Corso Vittorio Emanuele was relatively thinly populated, and a large section of it to the north was kept empty as the *Campus Martius*, the training ground reserved for games and exercises to keep Romans ready for war. The main centre of population in ancient Rome was to the south-east, around the Forum. The area now referred to as the *centro storico* was built up from the Dark Ages onwards under papal rule.

The inhabitants of the *centro* have been making a living out of tourists for centuries. Via de' Coronari is now home to some of the old centre's showiest antiques shops, but it started out in the

Piazza Navona: *take the weight off your feet and watch Rome rush by. See page 39.*

fifteenth century as the Via Recta, or straight street, designed to ferry pilgrims to the Vatican quickly with their money-bags intact. However, within a few years rosary-makers (*coronari*), ancestors of modern souvenir-sellers, had taken over the street and were making a killing out of the passing trade.

By the time of the high Renaissance there were over two dozen banks, hundreds of hotels and numerous courtesans in the area, servicing the financial deals and physical needs of visiting ecclesiastics, pilgrims and merchants. Survivors of the era include the sixteenth-century Banco di Santo Spirito, originally the papal mint; and a fifteenth-century inn, the Osteria dell'Orso (due to re-open in 2000 as a very up-market eatery) on Via dell'Orso, a street that during the Renaissance was inhabited mainly by upmarket courtesans.

In the 1880s Corso Vittorio Emanuele was driven through the district, carving what is now a heavily-trafficked and grimy fast-track to **Saint Peter's** past historic churches and *palazzi*. It is plied by the infamous 64 bus, main means of transport between central Rome and the Vatican, and much loved by petty thieves and frotteurs, attracted by the wallets, handbags and scantily-clad backsides of unwary tourists.

Museum checklist

The great art collections
Galleria dell'Accademia di San Luca (*see p60*)
Galleria Borghese (*see p67*)
Galleria Colonna (*see p60*)
Galleria d'Arte Moderna e Contemporanea Ex-Birreria Peroni (*see p97*)
Galleria Doria Pamphili (*see p60*)
Galleria Nazionale di Arte Antica, Palazzo Corsini (*see p75*)
Galleria Nazionale di Arte Moderna e Contemporanea (*see p67*)
Galleria Spada (*see p47*)
Museo di Palazzo Venezia (*see p51*)
Palazzo Barberini (*see p68*)

The relics of Ancient Rome
Antiquarium Comunale (*see p93*)
Museo Barracco di Scultura Antica (*see p47*)
Musei Capitolini (*see p36*)
Museo della Civiltà Romana (*see p101*)
Museo delle Mura (*see p93*)
Museo Nazionale Romano:
Palazzo Altemps (*see p47*);
Palazzo Massimo alle Terme (*see p82*);
Terme di Diocleziano (*see p82*)
Museo Nazionale di Villa Giulia (*see p67*)
Museo di Via Ostiense (*see p93*)

The history of other eras
Castel Sant'Angelo (*see p96*)
Museo dell'Alto Medioevo (*see p101*)
Museo di Arte Ebraica (*see p51*)
Museo del Folklore (*see p75*)
Museo Napoleonico (*see p47*)
Museo Nazionale d'Arte Orientale (*see p82*)
Museo Nazionale delle Arti e Tradizioni Popolari (*see p101*)
Museo Preistorico ed Etnografico L. Pigorini (*see p102*)
Museo Storico della Liberazione di Roma (*see p83*)

Literature, music
Keats-Shelley Memorial House (*see p60*)
Museo Nazionale degli Strumenti Musicali (*see p83*)

Exhibition spaces
Palazzo delle Esposizioni (*see p69*)
Palazzo Ruspoli (*see p61*)

Museums beyond classification
Museo delle Anime dei Defunti (*see p96*)
Museo Naz. delle Paste Alimentari (*see p69*)
Museo Storico Nazionale dell'Arte Sanitaria (*see p96*)

The Capitoline Museums

As this guide went to press, the Capitoline Museums were closed for major restoration, and due to re-open by the beginning of 2000. Until then, many of their great works of classical statuary can be seen at the **Palazzo Altemps** *(see page 47), and at the* **Centrale Montemartini** *(Via Ostiense, 106, 06 574 8030; open 10am-6pm Tue-Fri; 10am-7pm Sat, Sun), where they are displayed in a beautifully renovated former power station. Some of the statues may remain in the Centrale even after the main museums re-open. The layout of the Capitoline museums may also be changed after the revamp.*

Standing on opposite sides of Michelangelo's **Piazza del Campidoglio** and housed in the twin palaces of **Palazzo Nuovo** and **Palazzo dei Conservatori**, the Capitoline Museums are the oldest public museums in the world. The collection they house was initiated in 1471, when Pope Sixtus IV presented the Roman people with a group of classical sculptures. Until the creation of the **Vatican Museums**, Sixtus' successors continued to enrich the collection with examples of ancient art, most of which was sculpture, and, at a later date, some important Renaissance and post-Renaissance paintings. The entire collection was finally open to the public in 1734, by Pope Clement XII.

The **Palazzo Nuovo** (on your left as you come up Michelangelo's sloping ramp) houses one of Europe's most significant collections of ancient sculpture. The Hall of Philosophers is lined with Roman copies of busts of Greek politicians and philosophers. There are two rooms of Roman busts, providing a good indication of contemporary fashions and hairstyles; the most spectacular are those of women in the Emperor's room. They date from the Flavian period (first century AD), and show that pasta-spiral hair-dos were most definitely the new look for the new millennium. Not all the subjects are patrician: in the main gallery a drunken old woman clutches an urn of wine, while the Dove Room contains statues of children, including one of a little girl protecting a bird from a snake. The dove mosaic came from Hadrian's villa at Tivoli.

As was the fashion at the time there are several Roman copies of Greek works, including the *Capitoline Venus*. This was based on Praxiteles' *Venus of Cnodis*, considered so erotic by the fourth-century BC citizens of Kos that one desperate citizen was caught in flagrante with it. The most remarkable work in the collection, however, is the extraordinarily moving *Dying Gaul*, probably based on a third-century BC Greek original. On the ground floor

NEIGHBOURHOOD CHARACTER

Despite its wealth of historical treasures, the *centro storico* is in no sense a museum city preserved for tourists and academics. Corso Vittorio is a thundering office-lined thoroughfare; Via de' Coronari carries on its brisk antiques trade, barely deigning to notice passing tourists; and the myriad shops on Via del Governo Vecchio pitch their wares to residents as much as visitors. Even picturesque Via Giulia, with its abundance of art galleries and high, ivy-dripping walls, is predominantly a haphazard ante-chamber and moped-park for the high school at its far end.

The *centro*'s squares, too, may have venerable histories and architecture but also share the area's endearingly self-deprecating character, forming magnificent sets for the happenings of everyday life. For pedestrian activity, pride of place has to go to the great theatre of Baroque Rome, **Piazza Navona**. For all its gracious sweep, Bernini fountains and pavement cafés, its denizens range from soothsayers, caricature artists, buskers and suburban smoothies to tourists, nuns, businessmen, ladies of leisure and anyone who simply wants a gossip or an ice cream.

Just off Piazza Navona, in little Piazza Pasquino, stands the patron of the city's scandalmongers, a severely truncated classical statue lodged against one wall. Placed here in 1501, it is known as Pasquino, supposedly after a tailor who had his shop in the piazza and did work for the Vatican. The loose-tongued Pasquino become famous for regaling his mates with insider gossip. He left some of his best stories and lampoons pinned to the statue, and when other people joined in it became the Renaissance equivalent of a satirical magazine. Scurrilous and libellous verses, called *pasquinate* and usually targeted at the aristocratic and ecclesiastical establishment, were attached to the statue anonymously to be read by all. In papal Rome, this was just about the only channel of free speech. In time, Pasquino gained correspondents, as the lampoons he carried were 'answered' by others, and he engaged in dialogues with other 'talking statues' such as Madame Lucrezia (in Piazza Venezia), Luigi Abate (next to **Sant'Andrea della Valle**) and Marforio (in the Palazzo Nuovo courtyard of the **Capitoline Museums**). The occasional piece of barbed prose is still to be found tacked there today.

stands the gilded equestrian bronze of Emperor Marcus Aurelius (*see page 37*).

Across the square you enter the **Palazzo dei Conservatori**. The courtyard contains what is left of a colossal statue of Constantine (the rest was made of wood) that originally stood in the Basilica of Maxentius in the **Forum** (*see page 41*). Among the highlights of the exhibits in this part of the museum is the much-reproduced *She-Wolf*. This one is a fifth-century BC Etruscan bronze; the suckling twins were added during the Renaissance by, according to tradition, Antonio del Pollaiolo. The first-century BC bronze of a boy removing a thorn from his foot, known as the *Spinario*, is probably an original Greek work.

The **Pinacoteca Capitolina** in the same building contains a number of significant works. The most striking is Caravaggio's sensual 1596 *Saint John the Baptist*, but don't let it overshadow paintings by artists such as Rubens, Titian, Veronese, Domenichino, Dossi and Van Dyck.

Musei Capitolini

Piazza del Campidoglio, 1 (06 6710 2071).
Bus to Piazza Venezia. **Open** 9am-7pm Tue-Sun.
Admission L10,000. **Map 6/1A**

The streets in the area between Corso Vittorio and Via Arenula converge on the **Campo de' Fiori**. All have medieval names referring to the trades once practised in them (*see page 171*). Even after 500 years Via de' Giubbonari (jacket-makers) has kept the faith, with central Rome's highest concentration of clothes shops. Via de' Cappellari (hat-makers), on the other hand, has shifted emphasis but not character: its medieval buildings open up as workshops on the ground floors, and carpenters and furniture restorers work in the street. Despite the prices, the quality of the goods and services on offer is low: the smarter shops on Via Giulia and Via Monserrato offer better quality.

Between the Campo de' Fiori and Via Giulia is solemn, operatic **Piazza Farnese**, with its twin fountains. Overlooking them is **Palazzo Farnese**, designed by Michelangelo and now home to the French Embassy.

At night the whole area on either side of Corso Vittorio is chaotic, with obsessive to-ing and fro-ing between *pizzerie, trattorie, gelaterie* and bars. The most popular area for nightlife stretches from Piazza Navona towards the river, and is known as *il triangolo della Pace* after the eternally fashion-

able **Bar della Pace** on Via della Pace (*see pages 158, 229*). Smartly dressed Romans gather to drink, meet or pose in and around the bars along these narrow cobbled streets. Others get bottles of beer from cheap bars and hang out on the fringes.

The most historically significant part of the *centro*, the heart and hub of ancient Rome, lies beyond the Capitoline to the south-east. It was here that Rome had its birthplace, in the **Roman Forum** and the **Palatine**, and it's here that you will find the monument that for centuries has been the city's best-recognised landmark:the **Colosseum**.

Piazze & fountains

Campo de' Fiori

Bus to Corso Vittorio Emanuele/tram to Via Arenula. **Map 3/2B**

Home to Rome's most picturesque – but also most costly – food market in the mornings, Campo de' Fiori is an amiable piazza surrounded by houses with chafed walls, warped shutters and pigeons nesting on their sills. The Campo has been a focus of Roman life since the fifteenth century. Lucrezia Borgia was born nearby, her brother was murdered down the road, and Caravaggio played a game of tennis on the piazza, after which he murdered his opponent for having the temerity to beat him. The cowled statue in the centre is of Giordano Bruno, burned at the stake on this spot (*dove il rogo arse* – where the pyre burned, as the inscription says) in 1600 for reaching the conclusion that philosophy and magic were superior to religion.

The market begins around 6am and packs up in the early afternoon, when people flow into the Campo's restaurants for lunch. Afternoons are quiet and slow, with things beginning to pick up around 6pm, when the ever-popular **Vineria** wine bar (*see pp156, 229*) opens up. By 10pm the restaurants are full again, and by midnight the Vineria crowd has expanded to fill the whole square.

The Capitoline (*Piazza del Campidoglio*)

Bus to Piazza Venezia. **Map 6/1A**

Michelangelo designed this elegant piazza for Pope Paul III in the 1530s. It took about 100 years to complete, but, although some of his ideas were modified along the way, it is still much as he envisaged it. It stands on top of the Capitoline, politically the most important of ancient Rome's seven hills and site of the three major temples – to Jupiter, symbolic father of the city; Minerva, goddess of wisdom; and Juno Moneta, a vigilant goddess who was expected to sound the alarm in times of danger. The temple of Juno, the site of which is now occupied by the church of Santa Maria in Aracoeli, housed the sacred Capitoline geese, in commemoration of the gaggle that supposedly raised the alarm when the Gauls attacked Rome in 390 BC. The best approach to the Campidoglio is via the great ramp of steps called the *cordonata*, also by Michelangelo, sweeping up from Via del Teatro di Marcello. At the top they are

The palace of the Massimo

On one day each year a closed-up palazzo on the bustling Corso Vittorio Emanuele suddenly springs into life. The **Palazzo Massimo alle Colonne** looks almost derelict on the outside, its curving portico blackened by exhaust fumes, and offering just enough shelter for a couple of sleeping vagrants. But on the morning of March 16 (9am-noon) its gates are thrown open, and anyone who turns up is welcome to wander in.

The Massimo family is one of the oldest in Rome: its name is recorded as early as the beginning of the eleventh century, before even the equally heavyweight Colonna and Orsini clans. In 1797, Camillo Massimo was asked by Napoleon if it was true that his family was descended from the legendary Roman general Fabius Maximus, the opponent of Hannibal. The witty *marchese* replied that, 'I could not prove it – the story has only been told in our family for twelve hundred years'.

The facade of the palazzo follows the curve of Domitian's amphitheatre: it was designed by Baldassare Peruzzi in 1532 in a mannered classical style that has few parallels in Rome. A stuccoed passageway, presided over by a liveried family servant, gives access into an internal courtyard lined with classical statuary – a nod to the family's ancient lineage. On the first floor

is a frescoed loggia with its original painted wooden ceiling; above this a series of low rooms adorned with paintings celebrating military feats leads up to the family chapel, *la cappella di San Filippo Neri*.

It was in this very room (made into a chapel much later) on 16 March, 1583, that San Filippo Neri, that most Counter-Reformation of saints (*see p44*, **Chiesa Nuova/Santa Maria in Vallicella**), performed one of his most celebrated miracles. Called to administer the last rites to the young Paolo Massimo, the saint found the boy already dead; nothing daunted, he brought him back to life, chatted for a while, and then – when Paolo declared he was finally ready to die – commended him to God. With its heavy silk wall coverings, reliquary cases and Gothic paintings, this is one of the best examples of a private family chapel in Rome – albeit that it has the status of a church, due to the importance of the miracle. On the anniversary, after a private Mass, a procession of family, servants and altar boys escorts the presiding cardinal or archbishop to a room – off-limits to visiting plebs – where the remnants of Rome's nobility meet for a buffet lunch. To see the spectacle in all its Felliniesque glory, turn up around 11.30, just as Mass is ending. *See also page 40.*

flanked by two giant Roman statues of mythical twins Castor and Pollux, placed here in 1583. The palace facing you at the top of the steps is the Palazzo Senatorio, Rome's city hall, completed by Giacomo della Porta and Girolamo Rainaldi to a design by Michelangelo. To the left is the **Palazzo Nuovo** and to the right the **Palazzo dei Conservatori**, together forming the **Capitoline Museums** (*see p36*). For four centuries the central pedestal of the square supported a magnificent second-century equestrian statue of Emperor Marcus Aurelius, placed here by Michelangelo. The statue you see today is a faithful computer-generated copy; the original, after years of restoration, is now behind glass in the Palazzo Nuovo.

Fontana delle Tartarughe

Piazza Mattei. Bus or tram to Largo Argentina. **Map 6/1A**

One of Rome's most beautiful fountains lies in the maze of streets of the old **Ghetto**. Four elegant boys cavort around its base, gently hoisting tortoises up to the waters above them. According to legend, Giacomo della Porta and Taddeo Landini built the fountain in the 1580s in a single night for the Duke of Mattei (whose family palazzo, packed with loot-

ed antiquities and now home to an American study centre, is also in the square). The Duke, the story goes, had lost all his money and so his fiancée, and wanted to prove to her father that he could still achieve great things. The tortoises, possibly by Bernini, were added in the next century.

Largo Argentina

Bus or tram to Largo Argentina. **Map 3/2A**

Officially Largo di Torre Argentina (nothing to do with the Latin American country; the name refers to a tower (*torre*) in a nearby street, plus the fact that the local diocese was called *Argentoratum*, a word derived from *argento* – silver), this huge open space is a busy bus and tram junction. Between waiting for one piece of public transport or another, cast an eye into the hole in the middle of the square: there lies Rome's largest expanse of fully-excavated Republican-era remains. A narrow warren of streets that stood here was bulldozed in 1885, and then further obliterated in 1926-9, to reveal what is known as the **Sacred Area** (*Area Sacra Argentina*; access with prior permission only, *see p33*). Visible are columns, altars and foundations from one round and three rectangular temples dating from the mid-third-century BC to c100 BC. The frescoes on the taller brickwork are from the twelfth century church of San Nicola de' Cesarini, which was built into one of the temples here.

Piazza Farnese
Bus to Corso Vittorio Emanuele. **Map 6/1B**
Serene, elegant and dominated by the refined façade of Michelangelo's **Palazzo Farnese**, this piazza is a world away from the bustle of adjacent Campo de' Fiori. It's uncluttered save for its two fountains, created in the seventeenth century out of granite tubs from the **Baths of Caracalla** and topped with lilies – the Farnese family emblem. The area is most evocative at night, when the palace is lit up and chandeliers inside are switched on to reveal ceilings with sumptuous frescoes.

Piazza Navona
Bus to Corso Vittorio Emanuele or Corso Rinascimento. **Map 3/2A-B**
This tremendous theatrical oval, dominated by the gleaming marble composition of Bernini's **Fontana dei Quattro Fiumi**, is the hub of the *centro storico*. The piazza owes its shape to an ancient stadium, built in AD 86 by the Emperor Domitian, which was the scene of at least one martyrdom (Saint Agatha was thrown to her death here for refusing to marry), as well as sporting events. Just north of the piazza you can still see some remains of the original arena, sunk below the level of Corso Rinascimento (which can be entered with permission, *see p33*). The piazza acquired its current form in the mid-seventeenth century. Its western side is dominated by Borromini's façade for the church of **Sant'Agnese in Agone** and the adjacent Palazzo Pamphili, built for Pope Innocent X in 1644-50. The 'Fountain of the Four Rivers' at the centre of the piazza, finished in 1651, is one of the most extravagant masterpieces designed – though only partly sculpted – by Bernini. Its main figures represent the rivers Ganges, Nile, Danube and Plate, surrounded by geographically appropriate flora and fauna. The figure of the Nile is veiled, as its source was unknown, although for centuries the story went that Bernini designed it that way so the river god appeared to be recoiling in horror from the façade of Sant'Agnese, designed by his great rival Borromini (on the rivalry, *see p64*). In fact, the church was built after the fountain was finished. The obelisk in its centre came from the Circus of Maxentius on the **Via Appia Antica** (*see p102*).

The less spectacular **Fontana del Moro** is at the southern end of the piazza. The central figure (called the Moor, although he looks more like a portly sea god wrestling with a dolphin) was the only part designed by Bernini himself.

Piazza Venezia
Bus to Piazza Venezia. **Map 6/1A**
Piazza Venezia is dominated by the glacial **Vittoriale**, a piece of nationalistic kitsch that out-does anything dreamed up by the ancients. This vast pile, entirely out of proportion with anything around it, was constructed between 1885 and 1911

to honour the first king of united Italy, Vittorio Emanuele of Savoy. Centred on an equestrian statue of the king, who sports a moustache three metres long, it is also the home of the eternal flame, Italy's memorial to the unknown soldier. As for the piazza, six main roads converge here, making it a dizzying roundabout. The west side is formed by the **Palazzo Venezia**, now an art museum that also hosts temporary shows of varying standards (*see p51*). The palace, one of the first Renaissance buildings in Rome, was built in the late fifteenth century for the Venetian Pope Paul II. Centuries later Mussolini established his headquarters here, delivering regular orations to the crowds (brought together to order) from the balcony overlooking the piazza, where pedestrians were prevented from standing still by security-obsessed guards.

Palazzi

Palazzo della Cancelleria
Piazza della Cancelleria. Bus to Corso Vittorio Emanuele. **Closed to the public. Map 6/1B**
One of the most refined examples of Renaissance architecture in Rome, the Palazzo della Cancelleria was built, possibly by Bramante, between 1483 and 1513 for Raffaele Riario. He was the great-nephew of Pope Sixtus IV, who made him a cardinal at the age of 17, though Raffaele didn't allow his ecclesiastical duties to cramp his style. He is said to have raised a third of the cost of this palace with the winnings of a single night's gambling. He also got involved in anti-Medici plotting, and in retaliation the palace was confiscated for the Church when Giovanni de' Medici became Pope Leo X in 1513. It later became the Papal Chancellery, and is still Vatican property. The fourth-century church of San Lorenzo in Damaso was incorporated into one side of the building.

Palazzo Cenci
Vicolo dei Cenci. Bus to Lungotevere dei Cenci/tram to Via Arenula. **Closed to the public. Map 6/1A**
Hidden in the middle of the Ghetto, this unassuming palazzo was home to the Cenci family, which gained notoriety in 1598 when Beatrice Cenci, her mother and two brothers were arrested for hiring thugs to murder her father. Popular opinion came to her defence when it was revealed that the father had forced Beatrice to commit incest; nevertheless, the Pope condemned her to death and she was beheaded outside **Castel Sant'Angelo** in 1599. Shelley used the story in his play *The Cenci*, banned in Britain until 1886 because of its subject matter.

Palazzo Farnese
Piazza Farnese (06 687 4834). Bus to Corso Vittorio Emanuele. **Closed to the public. Map 6/1B**
This palazzo has housed the French Embassy since the 1870s and is not generally open to the public, but guided tours can sometimes be arranged by appointment (preference is given to art historians). Often considered the finest Renaissance palace in

Rome, the huge building was begun for Cardinal Alessandro Farnese (later Pope Paul III) in 1514 by Antonio da Sangallo the Younger. He died before it was completed, and in 1546 Michelangelo took over. He was responsible for most of the upper storeys and the grand cornice along the roof. After his death the building was completed by Giacomo della Porta. Inside it has superb frescoes by Annibale Carracci.

Palazzo Madama

Corso Rinascimento (06 670 61). Bus to Corso Rinascimento. **Open** first Sat of every month; free guided tours in Italian 10am-6pm. **Map 3/2A**
Home to the Italian Senate since 1871, this palazzo was built by the Medici family in the sixteenth century as their Rome residence. Its rather twee façade, with a frieze of cherubs and bunches of fruit, was added 100 years later. The *Madama* of its name was Margaret of Parma (1522-86), the illegitimate daughter of Emperor Charles V, who lived here in the 1560s before moving to the Netherlands, where she instigated some of the bloodiest excesses of the religious wars.

Palazzo Massimo alle Colonne

Corso Vittorio Emanuele, 141 (06 6880 1545). Bus to Corso Vittorio Emanuele.
Open March 16 only. **Map 3/2B**
The Massimo are one of the oldest aristocratic families in the city, claiming to trace their descent from ancient Rome. When their palace was built in the 1530s by Baldassare Peruzzi, its unique design – curved walls with a portico built into the bend – aroused suitable admiration. The interior is only open to the public on one day each year, 16 March (*see p38*), in commemoration of the day in 1583 when a young Massimo was allegedly raised from the dead by Saint Filippo Neri. At the rear of the palace is the Piazza de' Massimi, dominated by an ancient column originally from Domitian's theatre, which stood where **Piazza Navona** is today.

Ancient Rome

Arch of Constantine (*Arco di Constantino*)

Piazza del Colosseo. Metro Colosseo/bus to Piazza del Colosseo. **Map 8/2B**
Constantine's triumphal arch was one of the last great Roman monuments, erected in AD 315, shortly before he abandoned the city for Byzantium. Although it appears magnificent enough at first glance, a close look reveals its splendours to be shallow - most of the carvings and statues were simply scavenged from other monuments around the city.

Circus Maximus (*Circo Massimo*)

Via del Circo Massimo. Metro Circo Massimo/ bus or tram to Viale Aventino. **Map 9/1C**
Ancient Rome's major chariot-racing venue is now ringed by several lanes of traffic, but with a bit of imagination it's still possible to visualise the flat base of the long, grassy basin as the racetrack, and

the sloping sides as the stadium stands. At the southern end there are remains of the original seating, although the tower there is medieval. This was the oldest and largest of Rome's ancient arenas, and chariot races were held here from at least the fourth century BC onwards. It was rebuilt by Julius Caesar, and by the days of the Empire could hold as many as 300,000 people. The circus was also used for mock sea battles (with the arena flooded with millions of gallons of water), the ever-popular fights with wild animals, and the occasional large-scale execution.

Colosseum (Colosseo)

Piazza del Colosseo. (06 700 4261). Metro Colosseo/bus to Piazza del Colosseo. **Open** 9am-6pm Mon-Sat; 9am-4pm Sun. **Admission** L10,000; included in joint ticket with Palatine and Museo Nazionale Romano (*see p33*). **Map 8/2B**
Built in AD 72 by Vespasian on the newly-drained site of an artificial lake in the grounds of Nero's *Domus Aurea*, or Golden House, the *Anfiteatro Flavio*, to give this monument its proper name, hosted gory battles between gladiators, slaves, prisoners and wild animals of all descriptions (*see p80*).
If you climb to the top of the Colosseum and look down into the centre of the stadium, you can see a maze of passages, originally underground, through which animals were funnelled on their way into the arena. You can also appreciate the massive scale of the building, which held capacity crowds of 50,000. When gladiatorial blood sports went out of fashion in the sixth century, the Colosseum became one big quarry, where Romans turned to for stone and marble to build and decorate their *palazzi*. This pillaging was not halted until the mid-eighteenth century, when Pope Benedict XIV had stations of the cross built inside it, and consecrated it as a church. For another 100 years it was left to its own devices, becoming home to hundreds of species of flowers and plants. After unification in 1870 that flora was yanked up, in what English writer Augustus Hare described as 'aimless excavations'. 'In dragging out the roots of its shrubs,' he moaned in his *Walks in Rome* (1883), 'more of the building was destroyed than would have fallen naturally in five centuries'.

Mamertine Prison (*Carcere Mamertino*)

Clivio Argentario, 1 (06 679 2902). Bus to Via dei Fori Imperiali or Piazza Venezia. **Open** 9am-noon, 2.30-6pm, daily. **Admission** donation expected. **Map 8/1C**
Anyone thought to pose a threat to the security of the ancient Roman state was thrown into this dank, dark and oppressive little underground dungeon, squashed between the Roman Forum and Via dei Fori Imperiali at the bottom of the steps up to the Capitoline. In those days, the only way down to the lower level (built in the fourth century BC) was through a hole in the floor. The numberless prisoners who starved to death here were tossed into the **Cloaca Maxima**, the city's main sewer. The most famous of the prison's residents, legend has it, were Saints Peter and Paul. (*continued on p43*)

The Roman Forum

Numbers refer to the map on page 42.

In the earliest days of the Republic the *Foro Romano*, or Roman Forum, was much like any Italian piazza today: an open space where people would shop, gossip, catch up on the latest news and perhaps visit a temple. In the second century BC, when Rome had become the capital of an empire that included Greece, Sicily and Carthage, it was decided the city needed a more dignified centre. The food stalls were moved out, and permanent law courts and offices were built. In time this centre was also deemed too small, and emperors began to build the new **Imperial Fora** (*see page 78*). Nevertheless, the Roman Forum remained the symbolic heart of the Empire, and emperors continued to renovate and embellish it until the fourth century AD.

What we can see of the area today consists of little more than the layouts of floors and a few columns, but with a bit of imagination a tour around the Forum can still give an accurate impression of what ancient Rome looked like. Before entering, look down over the Forum from behind the **Capitoline** for a view of its overall layout. Its central thoroughfare, the **Via Sacra (1)**, runs almost directly through the middle. Going into the Forum from the Via dei Fori Imperiali entrance, to the left is the **Basilica Emilia (2)**. This was a large hall, originally built for business and moneylending in 179 BC, though what remains is mainly from later periods. The brown rusty marks dotted around the basilica at the end towards the Capitoline are bronze coins that fused into the floor during a fire in AD 410. The tall brick building at the coin end is a 1930s reconstruction of the **Curia (3)** or senate house.

Standing out to the left of the Curia is the best-preserved monument in this part of the Forum, the massive **Arch of Septimius Severus (4)**, built in AD 203 to celebrate a victory over the Parthians. Near here was the Golden Milestone (*Millarium Aureum*), from which all distances to and from Rome were measured.

Beyond the Arch of Septimius are the remains of Caesar's **rostrum (5)**, a platform from which speeches and demonstrations of power were made, and from where Mark Antony supposedly asked the Roman populace to lend him its ears. Further back, the eight massive columns that formed part of the **Temple of Saturn (6)**, built in the fifth century BC, stand out. The state treasury was housed underneath it. Also clearly visible from here is the solitary **Column of Phocas (7)**, erected in AD 608 by Pope Boniface IV to thank the Byzantine Emperor for giving him the Pantheon as a church. Visible on the other side of the Via Sacra are the foundations of the **Basilica Giulia (8)**, built by Julius Caesar in 55 BC and once a major – and by all accounts very noisy – law court. Ancient board games are carved into the steps.

Further into the Forum are three elegant columns that formed part of the **Temple of Castor and Pollux (9)**, the saviours of Rome. According to legend, these twin giants and their horses appeared to the Romans during a battle in 499 BC, and helped the Republic to victory.

Beyond the Temple are the remains of the round **Temple of Vesta (10)** and, within its garden (the *Atrium Vestae*), the rectangular **House of the Vestal Virgins (11)**. On the Via dei Fori Imperiali side of the Via Sacra are the columns, atop a flight of steep steps, of the **Temple of Antonius and Faustina (12)**, built to honour a second-century emperor and his wife and, since the eleventh century, part of the church of **San Lorenzo in Miranda**. The oldest graves ever unearthed in Rome were found here; the bodies are now housed in the Palatine Museum. The circular building further up the slope is the **Temple of Romulus (13)**, dating from the fourth century AD. It has nothing to do with the co-founder of Rome: this Romulus was a son of the Emperor Maxentius, who died in 309. The bronze door of his temple is still locked with the original ancient key.

Looming above these temples are giant vaults that were part of the **Basilica of Maxentius (14)**, also known as the Basilica of Constantine, begun in AD 306 and studied by Michelangelo and Bramante when they were designing Saint Peter's. By the southern exit, which leads down to the Colosseum, stands the **Arch of Titus (15)**, built in AD 81 to celebrate the sacking of Jerusalem; the event is depicted in the elaborate relic panels (note the sacred seven-branched candelabra). A path to the right of this arch leads to the Palatine; another beyond lead to the Colosseum.

The Roman Forum *entrance from Largo Romolo e Remo, Via dei Fori Imperiali; Piazza del Colosseo; Via Foro Romano (06 699 0110). Metro Colosseo/bus to Via dei Fori Imperiali or Via Luigi Petroselli.* **Open** 9am-4pm Mon-Sat; 9am-1pm Sun. **Admission** free. **Map 8/2B-C**

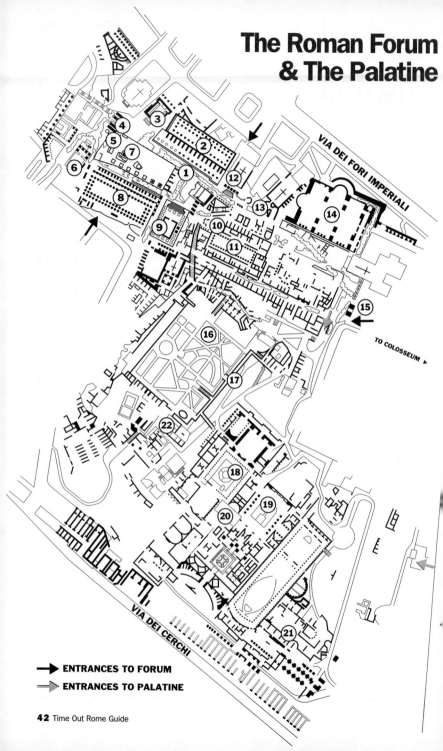

The Roman Forum & The Palatine

VIA DEI FORI IMPERIALI

TO COLOSSEUM ►

VIA DEI CERCHI

→ ENTRANCES TO FORUM

⇒ ENTRANCES TO PALATINE

The Palatine

Numbers refer to the map on page 42.

The Beverly Hills of ancient Rome, the Palatine Hill (*Palatino*) was where the movers and shakers of both Republic and Empire built their palaces. The choice of location was understandable: the Palatine overlooks the Roman Forum, yet is a comfortable distance from the disturbances and riff-raff down in the valley.

Entering the Palatine from the Forum, you pass the **Hortus Farnese (16)** on the right. Originally the *Domus Tiberiana*, these gardens full of orange trees and burbling fountains were laid out in the sixteenth century, making them one of the oldest botanical gardens in Europe. The gardens were created for a member of a papal family, Cardinal Alessandro Farnese, who used them for lavish garden parties. The pavilion at the top of the hill is seventeenth-century, with a good view over the Forum. Underneath the gardens, behind the pavilion, is the **Cryptoporticus (17)**, a long semi-subterranean tunnel built by Nero for hot-weather promenades or as a secret route between the Palatine buildings and his palace the *Domus Aurea* (**Nero's Golden House**, *see page 80*), across the valley on the Oppian hill. Lit only by slits in the walls, the Cryptoporticus is welcomingly cool in summer, and at one end there are remnants of a stucco ceiling-frieze and floor mosaics.

South of the gardens are the remains of the imperial palaces built by Domitian at the end of the first century AD, which became the principal residence of the emperors for the next three centuries. The nearest section, the **Domus Flavia (18)**, contained the public rooms. According to the biographer Suetonius, Domitian was so terrified of assassination that he had the walls faced with shiny black selenite

so he could see anybody creeping up behind him. Sadly for him this did not prevent his eventual murder. You can see the foundations of a strange room, with what looks like a maze in the middle, which was the courtyard; next to this was the dining room, where parts of the marble floor have survived, although it's usually covered for protection. The brick oval in the middle was probably a fountain.

Next door is the emperor's private residence, the **Domus Augustana (19)**. The oval building close to it may have been a garden, or a miniature stadium for Domitian's private entertainment. Sandwiched between the Domus Flavia and Domus Augustana is a tall grey building that houses the **Palatine Museum** (*Museo Palatino*, **20**). Downstairs are human remains and artefacts from the earliest hut communities of Rome, founded in the Forum and Palatine areas from the ninth century BC: room II has a model of an eighth-century village. Emerging from the floor are foundations of Domitian's dwelling. Upstairs are busts, Gods and some fascinating eave-edgings from the first to the fourth centuries AD. To the south of the Domus Augustana lie the remains of the comparatively small palace and baths of **Septimius Severus (21)**, some of the best-preserved buildings in the area.

Back towards the Farnese gardens is the **Domus Livia (22)**, named after Augustus' wife. The wall paintings here date from the late Republic, and include *trompe l'œil* marble panels and scenes from mythology.

The Palatine: *entrance from the Roman Forum; Via di San Gregorio (06 699 0110). Metro Colosseo/bus to Via dei Fori Imperiali.* **Open** 9am-6pm Mon-Sat, 9am-1pm Sun. **Admission** L12,000; included in joint ticket with Colosseum and Museo Nazionale Romano (*see p33*). **Map 8/2C**

(*continued from p40*) Peter head-butted the wall in the ground-level room, leaving his features impressed on the rock (or so the plaque says). He also caused a miraculous well to bubble up downstairs in order to baptise his prison guards, whom he converted by his shining example.

Ponte Rotto & the Cloaca Maxima

Views from Ponte Palatino, Isola Tiberina and Lungotevere Pierleoni. Bus to Piazza Sonnino, Piazza di Monte Savello, Lungotevere Pierleoni, Lungotevere Ripa. **Map 6/2A**

The 'broken bridge' was the first stone bridge in Rome (142 BC). Parts of it fell down at least twice, before the bridge's final collapse in 1598. Near its

west side there is a tunnel in the embankment, the gaping mouth of the **Cloaca Maxima**, the city's 'great sewer', first built under the Tarquins (Rome's Etruscan kings) in the sixth century BC to drain the area round the Forum, and given its final form in the first century BC.

Portico of Octavia (*Portico d'Ottavia*)

Via del Portico d'Ottavia. Bus to Piazza di Monte Savello or Via del Teatro di Marcello. **Map 6/2A**

These remains have been nonchalantly built around and into over the centuries, and are now held together by rusting braces to form the porch of the church of Sant'Angelo in Pescheria. They originally formed the entrance to a massive colonnaded square containing shops, libraries and temples. Emperor Augustus rebuilt the portico in the first century BC and dedicated it to his sister Octavia; the isolated columns outside belong to a later (AD 213) restoration by Septimius Severus. For centuries the portico also formed part of Rome's main fish market, hence the name of the church. At the time of writing, a dig in progress around the base of the portico has allowed fascinating glimpses of ancient urban infrastructure, but has also severely marred the attractiveness of this most Roman of quarters.

Theatre of Marcellus (*Teatro di Marcello*)

Via del Teatro di Marcello. Bus to Via del Teatro di Marcello. **Open** with prior permission only (*see p33* **Getting through locked gates**). **Map 6/2A**
If you haven't had time to seek formal permission to enter, don't give up: the theatre is visible from the street outside. This is one of the strangest and most impressive sights in Rome – a Renaissance palace grafted onto an ancient, time-worn circular theatre. Julius Caesar began building a massive theatre here to rival the one erected by Pompey in the Campus Martius, but it was finished in 11 BC by Augustus, who named it after his favourite nephew (*see p57* **Mausoleum of Augustus**). At one time the theatre was connected to the adjacent **Portico of Octavia**, and originally had three tiers in different styles (Ionic, Doric and Corinthian), but the top one has collapsed. After the theatre was abandoned in the fourth century AD it had various uses, including that of fortress, before Baldassare Peruzzi built a palace for the Savelli family on top of the crumbling remains in the sixteenth century. This palace has now been converted into luxurious and hugely expensive apartments. To the north of the theatre are three columns that were part of the Temple of Apollo, built in 433 BC.

Temples of Hercules Victor and Portunus (*Tempio di Vesta e Tempio di Fortuna Virilis*)

Piazza della Bocca della Verità.
Bus to Piazza Bocca della Verità. **Map 6/2A**
Like the **Pantheon**, both these diminutive Republican-era temples owe their exceptional state of preservation to their conversion into churches during the Middle Ages. The round one, which looks like an English folly, was built in the first century BC and dedicated to Hercules. Early archaeologists were confused by its round shape, which is similar to the Temple of Vesta in the **Roman Forum**, and mistakenly dubbed it the Temple of Vesta. Romans still tend to refer to it by this name. The second temple, square but similarly perfect in form, is a century older and was dedicated to Portunus, god of harbours, since this was the port area of ancient Rome. This was also misattributed as being dedicated to 'manly fortune'. Both temples were deconsecrated and made ancient monuments in the 1920s on orders from Mussolini.

Churches

Chiesa Nuova/Santa Maria in Vallicella

Piazza della Chiesa Nuova (06 687 5289).
Bus to Corso Vittorio Emanuele.
Open 8am-noon, 4.30-7pm, daily. **Map 3/2B**
Filippo Neri (1515-1595) was a Florentine businessman who gave up his career to live and work among the poor in Rome. He was a personable character, who danced on altars and played practical jokes on priests, and became one of the most popular figures in the city, his fame helped along by a miracle or two (*see p38*). He founded the Oratorian Order to continue his work. Work began on the Chiesa Nuova, the order's headquarters, in 1575, with funds raised by his followers. Neri wanted a large and simple building, but after his death the whitewashed walls were covered with exuberant frescoes and multi-coloured marbles. Pietro da Cortona painted Neri's *Vision of the Virgin* (1664-5) in the vault, the *Trinity in Glory* (1647) in the cupola and the *Assumption of the Virgin* (1650) in the apse; Rubens contributed three paintings, the *Virgin and Child* (1607) over the altar, and *Saints Gregory* and *Domitilla*, right and left respectively of the main altar (1607-8). The result is one of the most satisfying church interiors in Rome. The body of Neri, canonised in 1622, lies in a chapel ornately decorated with marble to the left of the main altar; his rooms are open to the public on May 26, his feast day. Singing was an important part of Oratorian worship, and oratory as a musical form developed out of the order's services. Next to the church, Borromini designed the fine Oratorio dei Filippini, which is still used for concerts.

Il Gesù

Piazza del Gesù (06 697 001). Bus or tram to Largo Argentina or Piazza Venezia. **Open** *church* 6am-12.30pm, 4-7.15pm, daily; *Loyola's rooms* 4-6pm Mon-Sat; 10am-noon Sun. **Map 6/1A**
The huge Gesù is the principal church of the Jesuits, the order founded by Basque soldier Ignatius Loyola in the 1530s. Realising the power of appealing directly to the emotions, he devised a series of 'spiritual exercises' aimed at training devotees to experience the agony and ecstasy of the saints. The Gesù itself was designed to involve the congregation as closely as possible in the proceedings, with a nave unobstructed by aisles so the view of the main altar was unobstructed. Work began in 1568, and the façade by Giacomo della Porta was added in 1575. His design was repeated *ad nauseam* on Jesuit churches across Italy (and the world) for decades afterwards. A large, bright fresco by Il Baciccia (1676-79) – one of Rome's great baroque masterpieces – decorates the gilded ceiling of the nave, which seems to dissolve on either side as stucco figures, by Antonio Raggi, and other painted images are sucked up into the dazzling light of the heavens. The figures falling back to earth are presumably Protestants. On the left is another spectacular baroque achievement, the chapel of Sant'Ignazio by Andrea Pozzo (1696-1700),

Bernini et al *revamped classical statuary now in the* **Palazzo Altemps**. *See page 47.*

adorned with gold, silver and coloured marble. The statue of Saint Ignatius is by Antonio Canova. Towering above the altar is what was long believed to be the biggest lump of lapis lazuli in the world. In fact, it's covered concrete. Outside the church, at Piazza del Gesù, 45, you can visit the rooms of Saint Ignatius, which contain a wonderful painted corridor with *trompe l'œil* special effects by Pozzo, and mementoes of the saint including his death mask.

Sant'Agnese in Agone

Piazza Navona (06 679 4435). Bus to Corso Vittorio Emanuele or Corso Rinascimento. **Open** 4.30-7pm Tue-Sat; 10am-1pm Sun. **Map 3/2B**

The virgin martyr Saint Agnes was stripped in public when she refused to abjure Christ, who kindly caused a miraculous growth of hair to cover her embarrassment; the flames of her execution pyre then failed to consume her, so her pagan persecutors lopped her head off, supposedly on the exact spot where the church of Sant'Agnese, the grandest building on **Piazza Navona**, now stands. Sant'Agnese was begun by Carlo and Girolamo Rainaldi for Pope Innocent X in 1652. It was intended to be their masterpiece, but they quarrelled with the pope, and Borromini was appointed in their place. He revised the design considerably, and added the concave façade that is one of his greatest achievements. The *trompe l'œil* interior is typically Borromini, with pillars distributed irregularly to create the illusion that the apses are the same size.

Sant'Agostino

Piazza di Sant'Agostino (06 6880 1962). Bus to Corso Rinascimento.

Open 8am-noon, 4-8pm, daily. **Map 3/1A**

This fifteenth-century church stands on the site of a ninth-century one, and has one of the earliest Renaissance facades in Rome, fashioned out of travertine filched from the Colosseum. The third column on the left bears a fresco of *Isaiah* by Raphael (when its commissioner complained that the artist had charged him too much for the work, Michelangelo is said to have snapped 'the knee alone is worth that'), near which there is a beautiful scupture of Mary, her mother Anne and Jesus by Andrea Sansovino. In the first chapel on the left is Caravaggio's depiction of the grubbiest, most threadbare pilgrims ever to present themselves at the feet of the startlingly beautiful *Madonna of the Pilgrims*. So dirty were they, in fact, that the church that originally commissioned the picture refused point blank to have it. The main altar was designed by Bernini, who personally sculpted the two highest angels.

Sant'Andrea della Valle

Piazza Sant'Andrea della Valle (06 686 1339). Bus to Corso Vittorio Emanuele. **Open** 8am-1pm, 4-7.30pm, daily. **Map 3/2A**

Sant'Andrea was originally designed by Giacomo della Porta for the Theatine order in 1524, but the church's façade and dizzyingly frescoed dome both date from about a century later, when the Church was in a far more flamboyant frame of mind. The dome, by Carlo Maderno, is the second largest in Rome after **Saint Peter's**. Giovanni Lanfranco nearly died while painting the dome fresco – supposedly because his rival Domenichino had sabotaged the scaffolding on which he was working. Puccini set the opening act of *Tosca* in the first chapel on the left inside the church.

Santi Cosma e Damiano

Via dei Fori Imperiali, 1 (06 699 1540).
Metro Colosseo/bus to Via dei Fori Imperiali.
Open 8am-1pm, 3-7pm, daily. **Map 8/2C**
This small church on the fringe of the **Forum** incorporates the pagan Temple of Romulus. It has a wonderful sixth-century mosaic in the apse, representing the Second Coming, with the figure of Christ appearing huge against a blue setting as he descends a staircase of clouds. This massive style was the last phase in the development of late Roman mosaic, just before the Byzantine conquest brought the self-consciously classical mosaics of **Santa Pudenziana**.

Sant'Ivo alla Sapienza

Corso Rinascimento, 40 (06 686 4987). Bus to Corso Rinascimento. **Open** 9am-noon Sun. **Map 3/2A**
Perhaps Borromini's most imaginative geometrical design, with a concave façade countered by the convex bulk of the dome, which terminates in a bizarre corkscrew spire. The interior is based on a six-pointed star, but the opposition of convex and concave surfaces continues in the floor plan, on the walls and up into the dome, in a dizzying whirl that can bring on an attack of vertigo.

San Luigi dei Francesi

Piazza San Luigi dei Francesi, 5 (06 688 271) Bus to Corso Rinascimento. **Open** 8.30am-12.30pm, 3.30-7pm, Mon-Wed, Fri-Sun; 8am-12.30pm Thur. **Map 3/2A**
Completed in 1589, San Luigi is the church of Rome's French community. That the interior is lavish to the point of gaudiness goes unnoticed by the majority of visitors, who are here for one thing: Caravaggio's spectacular scenes from the life of *Saint Matthew* in the fifth chapel on the left. Painted in 1600-02, they depict Christ singling out Matthew (left), Matthew being dragged to his execution (right) and an angel briefing the evangelist about what he should write in his gospel (over the altar). Don't let Caravaggio's brooding brilliance and dramatic effects of light and shade blind you to the lovely frescoes of scenes from the life of *Saint Cecilia* by Domenichino (1615-7), in the second chapel on the right.

Santa Maria in Campitelli

Piazza di Campitelli, 9 (06 6880 3978).
Bus to Via del Teatro di Marcello.
Open 7am-noon, 4-7pm, daily. **Map 6/1A**
This church was commissioned in 1656 to house the medieval icon the *Madonna del Portico*, to which the population had prayed (successfully) for a prompt release from a bout of the plague. Carlo Rainaldi completed his masterpiece in 1667: a solemn, austere exercise in mass and light. The floor plan is complex: Greek cross, plus (hidden) dome, plus apse, with a series of side chapels. Inside are some fine baroque paintings, and a spectacularly over-the-top gilt altar tabernacle by Giovanni Antonio de Rossi.

Santa Maria in Cosmedin

Piazza della Bocca della Verità, 18 (06 678 1419).Bus to Piazza della Bocca della Verità.
Open 9am-6pm daily. **Map 6/2A**

Santa Maria in Cosmedin was first built in the sixth century, next to the **Temple of Hercules Victor**. It was enlarged in the ninth century, and given a beautiful campanile in the twelfth. Between the eleventh and thirteenth centuries much of the decoration was replaced with Cosmati work (*see p83*): the spiralling floor, the throne, the choir, the thirteenth-century *baldacchino*, over the ultimate example of recycling, a Roman bath tub used as an altar. If you want to prove a point, stick your hand into the *Bocca della Verità* (the 'Mouth of Truth') a worn stone face under the portico that was probably an ancient drain cover, and is said to bite the hands of liars. According to legend it was much used by husbands to test the faithfulness of their wives. The scene in *Roman Holiday* where Gregory Peck ad-libs getting his hand bitten, eliciting a (reportedly) unscripted shriek of genuine alarm from Audrey Hepburn, is one of the most delightful moments in cinema (*see pp198-9*). In the sacristy is a fragment of an eighth-century mosaic of the *Holy Family*, brought here from the original **Saint Peter's**.

Opening times of this church depend on the whims of whoever's on guard at any given time, and you may find it closed between 1.30 and 2.30pm on weekdays. On Sunday mornings at 10.30 a Byzantine rite mass is sung in the church

Santa Maria della Pace

Vicolo del Arco della Pace, 5 (06 686 1156).
Bus to Corso Rinascimento. **Open** 10am-noon, 4-6pm, Tue-Sat; 9-11am Sun. **Map 3/2B**
As the front door is usually locked, you're likely to enter this church via a simple, beautifully harmonious cloister by Bramante, his first work after arriving in Rome in the early 1500s. The church itself was built in 1482 for Pope Sixtus IV, while the Baroque façade was added by Pietro da Cortona in 1656. The church's most famous artwork is Raphael's *Sybils*, painted in 1514 for Agostino Chigi, the playboy banker and first owner of the **Villa Farnesina**, which is just inside the door.

San Nicola in Carcere

Via del Teatro di Marcello, 46 (06 6830 7198).
Bus to Via del Teatro di Marcello.
Open *Sept-July* 7.30am-noon, 4-7pm, Mon-Sat; 10am-1pm Sun. **Map 6/2A**
This church was built in the eleventh century, within the ruins of three Republican-era temples. These were dedicated to the two-faced god, Janus, to the goddess Juno, and to Spes (Hope). They overlooked the city's fruit and vegetable market, the *Forum Holitarium*, the columns of which can still be seen embedded in the wall.

Museums & galleries

Galleria Spada

Vicolo del Polverone, 15B (06 686 1158).
Bus to Largo Argentina/tram to Via Arenula.
Open 9am-7pm Tue-Sat; 9am-1pm Sun.
Admission L8,000. **Map 6/1B**

Bernini's Four Rivers fountain dominates the theatrical oval of **Piazza Navona**. *See page 39.*

One of Rome's prettiest palaces, built for Cardinal Girolamo Capo di Ferro in 1540, Palazzo Spada was acquired by Cardinal Bernardino Spada in 1632. Its most famous feature is Borromini's ingenious *trompe l'œil* colonnade in the garden, which is 9m long but appears much longer. Today, the palace houses high court offices as well as the art collection of Cardinal Spada, displayed in its original setting. Spada's portrait by his protegé Guido Reni is on show in Room 1. More portraits follow in Room 2, including Titian's wonderful, unfinished *Musician*. Don't miss the wacky-hatted *Cleopatra* by Lavinia Fontana in the same room. Room 3 contains massive, gloomy paintings such as Guercino's *Death of Dido* and Jan Breughel the Elder's very un-Roman *Landscape with Windmill*, plus a couple of Dutch seventeenth century globes. Room 4 has two powerful works by Artemisia Gentileschi, *Saint Cecilia playing a Lute* and *Madonna and Child*, and *Martyrdom of a Saint* by Domenichino. Copious notes in many languages are provided for each room.

Museo Barracco di Scultura Antica
Piazza dei Baullari, 1 or Corso Vittorio Emanuele, 168 (06 6880 6848). Bus to Corso Vittorio Emanuele. **Open** 9am-7pm Tue-Sat; 9am-1pm Sun. **Admission** L3,750. **Map 3/2B**
This small collection of mainly pre-Roman art was amassed by Senator Giovanni Barracco in the first half of the twentieth century. His interests covered the gamut of ancient art, and there are extraordinary Assyrian reliefs, Attic vases, sphinxes and bas-reliefs and Babylonian stone lions, as well as Roman and Etruscan exhibits and superb Greek sculptures. Don't miss the copy of the *Wounded Bitch* by Lysippus, on the second floor. Notes in Italian only.

Museo Napoleonico
Via Zanardelli, 1 or Piazza Ponte Umberto, 1 (06 6880 6286). Bus to Corso Rinascimento. **Open** 9am-7pm Tue-Sat; 9am-1pm Sun. **Admission** L3,750. **Map 3/1B**
Although Napoleon spent only a short time in Rome, other members of his family, including his mother Letizia and sister Pauline, settled here. This collection of art and memorabilia relating (sometimes tenuously) to the family was left to the city in 1927 by Napoleon's last descendants, the Counts Primoli. The museum has been restored and redecorated in keeping with an aristocratic palazzo of the early nineteenth century. You will find portraits of family members, including one by David of Napoleon's sister Carlotta, alongside uniforms, clothes and some of Canova's studies for the infamous sculpture of Pauline (now on show at the **Galleria Borghese**), including a cast of her right breast. *Wheelchair access.*

Museo Nazionale Romano – Palazzo Altemps
Piazza Sant'Apollinare, 46 (06 683 3566). Bus to Corso Rinascimento. **Open** 9am-6.45pm Tue-Sat; 9am-1.45pm Sun. **Admission** L10,000; included in joint ticket with Colosseum and rest of MNR (*see p33*). **Map 3/1B**
The fifteenth/sixteenth century Palazzo Altemps, just north of **Piazza Navona**, has been beautifully restored to house part of the state-owned stock of Roman treasures (the rest is spread between **Palazzo Massimo alle Terme** and the **Terme di Diocleziano**, *see p82*). Here, in perfectly-lit salons, loggias and courtyards, you can admire gems of classical statuary originally in the private Boncompagni-Ludovisi, Altemps and Mattei collections.

"And then there were tourists that thought they could leave without..."

...International Phone Cards.

What they probably don't know is that Telecom Italia's Phone Cards are more valuable than ever with

CALLING COSTS NOW REDUCED BY AS MUCH AS 50%. Not only, you always know how much you are paying for each minute of conversation, even from your hotel room. They are HANDY to use for placing international calls from private and pubblic phones, which eliminates the need for coins or local phone cards. International Phone Cards: two solutions, many destinations.

EUROPE AND NORTH AMERICA

REST OF THE WORLD

Two solutions, many destinations.

The Ghetto

Rome's Jews occupy a unique place in the history of the Diaspora. They have maintained an uninterrupted presence in the city for over 2,000 years, making this Europe's longest-surviving Jewish community, and one that enjoyed a surprising degree of security, even at times (such as in the years following the Black Death) when waves of anti-semitism were sweeping the rest of Europe. Some Italian Jews even applied a rather fanciful Hebrew etymology to *Italia*, deriving from it *I Tal Ya* – island of the dew of God.

It may seem odd that the city that was the great centre of power for the Christian Church represented such a safe haven, but security came at a price. The popes took on the double role of protectors (curbing popular violence against Jews) and oppressors, bringing Jews under their direct jurisdiction and making sure they paid for the privilege. The first documented tax on Roman Jews dates back to 1310, and set the pattern for the tradition of blackmail that characterised the Church's relations with the Jewish community until the nineteenth century. Payment exempted Jews from the humiliating Carnival games, where they were liable to be packed into barrels and rolled from the top of **Monte Testaccio**.

The historic memory of this exploitation was revived in September 1943, when the German occupiers demanded 50kg of gold from the Jewish community, to be produced in 36 hours. After an appeal to which both Jews and non-Jews responded, the target was reached, but this time accepting blackmail did not bring security. On 16 October over a thousand Jews, mostly women and children, were rounded up and deported in cattle trucks to Auschwitz. A quarter of Rome's Jews died in the camps, a proportion that would have been higher had it not been for the help given by wide sections of Roman society, including the Catholic priesthood (but not, many believe, the Vatican).

Rome's Jews had originally settled in Trastevere, but by the thirteenth century they had started to cross the river into the area that would become the Jewish Ghetto: three cramped hectares in one corner of the *centro storico*, immediately north of the Tiber island. Its chief landmark today is the imposing synagogue, begun in 1874. It incorporates the **Museo di Arte Ebraica**, a small museum of Roman Jewish life and ritual.

The *Ghetto* (the word is Venetian in origin) was definitively walled off in 1556 after the bull *Cum nimis absurdam*, issued by the anti-semitic Pope Paul IV, ordered a physical separation between Jewish and Christian parts of cities.

'Wasn't that..? but... Damn, and I thought it was Tuesday.' See page 41.

Many Jews actually welcomed the protection walls and curfews afforded, despite the fact that they were also obliged periodically to attend Mass in churches, to be lectured on their sinfulness. However, overcrowding, the loss of property rights and trade restrictions imposed on the community all took their toll, and the Ghetto experienced a long decline from the sixteenth to the eighteenth centuries.

By Italian unification in 1870, conditions for the more than 5,000 people who lived there were desperately squalid. The new government ordered that the walls be destroyed, and large sections of the district rebuilt.

The **Via Portico d'Ottavia**, an anarchic hotchpotch of ancient, medieval and Renaissance architecture, used to mark the Ghetto's boundary.

Nowadays, this is still the centre of Jewish life, even though many of the old people you'll see sitting around chatting during the evening have come in from the suburbs. It's also a good place to sample the unique hybrid that is Roman Jewish food. Restaurants like **Sora Margherita** (*see page 147*) specialise in such delicacies as artichokes fried Jewish-style, while at one end of the street, in a tiny unmarked corner shop (the **Forno del Ghetto**, *see page 163*), an all-female bakery turns out a *torta di ricotta e visciole* – ricotta and damson tart – that has achieved legendary status among Roman gourmets.

Museo di Arte Ebraica

Lungotevere dei Cenci (06 684 0061).
Bus to Via Arenula or Piazza di Monte Savello.
Open 9am-4.30pm Mon-Thur; 9.30am-1.30pm Fri; 9am-noon Sun. Closed Jewish holidays.
Admission L10,000. **Map 6/2A**
As well as luxurious crowns, Torah mantles and silverware, the museum presents vivid reminders of the persecution suffered by Rome's Jewish community at various times during its long history. Copies of sixteenth-century papal edicts banning Jews from an ever-growing list of activities are a disturbing foretaste of the horrors forced on them by the Nazis, which in turn are commemorated by stark photographs and heart-rending relics from the concentration camps. Admission includes a visit to the synagogue, built in the 1870s.

The Ludovisis were great ones for having contemporary artists re-do bits of statues that had dropped off over the ages, or simply didn't appeal to the tastes of the day, as copious notes(in English) by each work explain. In Room 9, for example, is a stately *Athena with Serpent*, revamped in the seventeenth century by Alessandro Algardi, who also had a hand in 'improving' the *Hermes Loghios* in Room 19 upstairs. In Room 20, the former dining room with its pretty fifteenth century frescoes on foody themes, is an *Ares* touched up by Bernini. Room 21 has the museum's greatest treasure – or greatest hoax, if you subscribe to the theory of the late, great art historian and polemicist Federico Zeri – the 'Ludovisi throne'. On what may or may not be a fifth century BC work from Magna Grecia (Zeri insisted it was a clumsy nineteenth-century copy of an original now in Boston). Aphrodite is being delicately and modestly lifted out of the sea spray from which she was born; on one side of her is a serious lady burning incense, and on the other is a naked one playing the flute.

In Room 26 there is a Roman copy of a Greek *Gaul's Suicide*, which was ordered to be made, recent research has suggested, by Julius Caesar; also here is the Ludovisi sarcophagus, with some action-packed high-relief depictions of Roman soldiers thoroughly trouncing barbarians. Room 34 has a graceful *Bathing Aphrodite*, an Imperial Roman copy of a Greek bronze originally dating from the third century BC.
Wheelchair access.

Museo di Palazzo Venezia

Via del Plebiscito, 118 (06 679 8865).
Bus to Piazza Venezia. **Open** 9am-2pm Tue-Sun.
Admission L8,000. **Map 6/1A**
A hotch-potch of everything from medieval decorative art to Bernini's terracotta models for major statues. In Room 1 are Venetian odds and ends, including a double portrait by Giorgione; room 4 has a glorious zodiac motif on the ceiling. Amid the seventeenth- and eighteenth-century offerings in room six is a touching group portrait of Duke Orsino's children, and a very sad *Saint Peter* by Guercino. Room 8 has pastel portraits of eighteenth-century aristos. In the long corridor are collections of Italian ceramics, and porcelain, including some Meissen. In Rooms 18-26 are Bernini's terracotta musings for the **Fontana del Tritone**, and one for the angels on Ponte Sant'Angelo (built to link **Castel Sant'Angelo** with the *centro storico*). The huge *Sala del Mappamondo*, so called because of an early map of the world kept there in the sixteenth century, was Mussolini's office.
Wheelchair access with assistance.

BALL○ON
SETA
COTONE
CASHMERE

ROMA   MILANO   LONDRA   MADRID

ROMA: Piazza di Spagna, 35 - Via Cola di Rienzo, 303/309 - L.go di Villa Paganini, 24 - P.zza Apollodoro, 24/28 - P.zza di Santa Anastasia,

The *Tridente*

Fashionable Rome and a tourists' home-from-home: the Spanish Steps, the Trevi fountain, classic cafés, the Via Condotti shopping run...

Fontana di Trevi. *See page 55.*

Via del Corso shoots down from **Piazza del Popolo** to **Piazza Venezia**, jammed with traffic and hemmed in by clothes shops, shoe shops and banks. It forms the central prong of three streets (the others are Via del Babuino and Via di Ripetta) known, for reasons that are obvious from any map, as *Il Tridente*, the 'trident' of Rome. At weekends busloads of teenagers from the suburbs swarm to this grid of narrow streets to strut among cheap clothing outlets, while during the week well-heeled Romans browse in Armani, Gucci and Bulgari and crowds of Japanese visitors queue patiently to enter the Prada fashion pagoda.

Via del Corso is the last urban stretch of the ancient Via Flaminia, which linked Rome with the north Adriatic coast. Over the past 2,000 years it has been successively a processional route for Roman legions, a country lane, a track for Carnival races and, from the late nineteenth century, a showcase principal street for the capital.

The street's liveliest period began in the mid-fifteenth century, when Pope Paul II began to fret over the debauched goings-on at the pre-Lenten Carnival celebrations in **Testaccio**. He decided to transfer the races and processions to somewhere more central, where he and his troops could keep an eye on things. The obvious spot was the Via Flaminia – then known simply as Via Lata, or wide street – at the end of which he built his new **Palazzo Venezia**. He had the street paved (using funds raised by a tax on prostitutes) and renamed *Il Corso* (the Avenue). For over four centuries Romans flocked there at Carnival time to be entertained by such edifying spectacles as races between press-ganged Jews, hunchbacks, prostitutes, and horses with hot pitch up their recta to make them run faster.

These grotesqueries only stopped after Italian unification in the 1870s, when the new national government set up shop half-way along Via del Corso. The cheap shops and eateries that lined the street were shut down, to be replaced by pompous neo-classical offices for banks and insurance companies. This set the tone for what remains the country's political heart: the Lower House (*Camera dei Deputati*) is in **Palazzo Montecitorio**, in the piazza of the same name, and Palazzo Chigi, the prime minister's office, is in Piazza Colonna.

Legends of Machiavellian wheeler-dealing cling to every restaurant and bar around the parliament building. Older MPs can be distinguished by their shapeless green Tyrolean swing coats, which inexplicably never went out of fashion in Roman political circles. Younger ones tend to look like somebody's secretary. More impressive are the ministers' chauffeurs in their sharp suits, mirror shades and identical haircuts, lined up outside Palazzo Chigi during cabinet meetings.

GREAT *PIAZZE*

At the northern end of Via del Corso is the symmetrically elegant **Piazza del Popolo**, once the papacy's favourite place for executions; now, gloriously restored and virtually traffic free, it's a popular meeting point. And though Federico Fellini no longer graces the **Canova** bar, his spirit hovers above it and its equally famous rival across the way, **Rosati** (*see chapter* **Cafés & Bars**).

Palazzo Chigi. See page 53.

To the west of the Corso is the charmingly Rococo **Piazza Sant'Ignazio** with its severe Jesuit church, while in the Piazza di Pietra the columns of the **Temple of Hadrian** can be seen embedded in the walls of Rome's singularly inactive stock exchange. Further over still lies Piazza della Rotonda, home to the **Pantheon** and adorned with a central fountain the steps of which provide an ever-popular hang-out for hippies, punks and other counter-cultural varieties. All seem oblivious to the well-heeled tourists paying over the odds for coffee at tables in the square, and to the terrible smell that pervades when the wind blows the wrong way over the square's branch of McDonald's. Piazza San Silvestro, to the east, has been reduced to a noisy bus terminus. It's a short walk from here to the **Fontana di Trevi**.

The most famous piazza in the area, the **Piazza di Spagna**, was at the centre of what eighteenth-century Romans called *er ghetto de l'inglesi* (the English ghetto), despite having its fair share of Grand Tourists from all over Europe (to Romans, all foreigners were English, and all equally fleece-able). The whole area was given over to sheep and ruins until Pope Sixtus V (1585-90) subjected it to a touch of his favourite hobby, town planning. Nowadays, the piazza has lost little of its charm, despite the fact that since its metro stop opened in the 1980s it has become a favourite hang-out for suburban youths, who fill the square and the Spanish Steps above it, importuning foreign females. A vast McDonald's, the opening of which was fiercely contested by local designers headed by Valentino, feeds the flirting and flitting hordes.

The grid of streets below the Piazza di Spagna is home to the latest creations of the best-known Italian designers, with Via Condotti still un-challenged as the city's chic-est shopping thoroughfare. The Spagna district also has relics of the Rome of the original Grand Tourists such as Keats, Shelley, Byron, Goethe and the Brownings. You can still have coffee at **Caffè Greco**, whose clients have included Casanova and mad King Ludwig of Bavaria, or a cuppa at **Babington's Tea Rooms**, set up by two Victorian spinsters, or

visit the house where Keats died of consumption and a broken heart (*see page 61*). For a price, you can sleep in the **Hotel d'Inghilterra**, where the rooms still resemble those of a London gentlemen's club (*see chapter* **Accommodation**).

Leading out of Piazza di Spagna to the north-west is Via del Babuino, once home to artists and composers such as Poussin and Wagner and now lined with serious antique and opulent interior design shops. The street is named after a statue that was considered so ugly it was named 'the baboon'. It's close to the incongruously neo-gothic All Saint's Church, designed by the English architect GE Street and looking for all the world like a stray from an English village – an impression confirmed by the tea and biscuits served in the garden at the back on sunny Sundays.

Tucked in beside Via del Babuino is Via Margutta, synonymous with the bohemian art boom of the 1950s and 1960s and with Rome's great mythologist Federico Fellini, who lived here until his death in 1993.

Halfway down the third arm of the *Tridente*, Via di Ripetta, is the emphatic Piazza Augusto Imperatore, built by Mussolini around the rather neglected family funeral-mound of the Emperor Augustus, with the intention of having himself buried there with the Caesars. Above is the magnificent **Ara Pacis**, erected by Augustus to celebrate peace in the Mediterranean after his conquest of Gaul and Spain. South of the square are two fine churches, San Girolamo degli Illirici, serving Rome's Croatian community, and San Rocco, built for local innkeepers and Tiber boatmen by Alexander VI (1492-1503), and, heading back towards the *centro storico*, the giant, curving walls of the Palazzo Borghese, acquired in 1506 by Camillo Borghese, the future pope Paul V, and later the home of Napoleon's sister Pauline.

Piazze & fountains

Fontana di Trevi

Piazza di Trevi. Metro Spagna/bus to Piazza San Silvestro or Via del Tritone. **Map 5/2C**
Known the world over as the fountain where Anita Ekberg cooled off in *La Dolce Vita*, and into which you should throw a coin if you want to be drawn back to Rome. Although tucked away in a tiny piazza, it's almost impossible to miss, as the alleys approaching it are glutted with souvenir shops and takeaway pizzerias, and full of the sound of water. Permanently surrounded by crowds, the fountain's creamy travertine gleams beneath powerful torrents of water and constant camera flashes. The attention is justified: it's a magnificent rococo extravaganza of rearing sea horses, conch-blowing tritons, craggy rocks and flimsy trees, cavorting below the wall of the Palazzo Poli. In a relief high on the palace wall is the virgin of legend showing three thirsty Roman

soldiers to a handy spring (hence the *Acqua Vergine*, the name of the source that still feeds the fountain). According to one version of the story, the unfortunate maid was called *Trivia*; the fountain's name is more likely to come from its position at the meeting of three roads, *tre vie*. Designed by Nicolò Salvi for Pope Clement XII, the fountain was finished in 1762, although the aqueduct bringing the Acqua Vergine has been here since Roman times. Would-be Ekbergs should think twice before plunging in: not only are they likely to be arrested, but the water contains unpalatable quantities of bleach.

Piazza della Minerva & Bernini's Elephant ('*Il Pulcino della Minerva*')

Bus or tram to Largo Argentina. **Map 3/2A**
The otherwise unremarkable square-cum-car-park of Piazza della Minerva is home to *Il Pulcino della Minerva*, aka Bernini's elephant. This cuddly marble animal, with wrinkled bottom and benign expression, has stood here since 1667. It was designed by Bernini as a tribute to Pope Alexander VII; elephants were both a symbol of wisdom and a model of sexual abstinence. They were believed to be monogamous and to mate only once every five years, which, the Church felt, was the way things should be. The sixth-century BC Egyptian obelisk perched on its back was taken from an ancient temple to the goddess Isis.

Piazza del Popolo

Metro Flaminio/bus or train to Piazzale Flaminio. **Map 2/2A**
For centuries Piazza del Popolo was the first glimpse most travellers got of Rome, for it lies at the end of the ancient Via Flaminia and directly inside the city's northern gate, the Porta del Popolo. If Grand Tourists were unlucky enough to arrive during Carnival time, they were likely to witness condemned criminals being tortured here for the edification/entertainment of the populace. The piazza was given its present oval form by Rome's leading neo-classical architect Giuseppe Valadier in the early nineteenth century; the obelisk in the centre was brought from Egypt by Augustus and stood in the Circus Maximus until 1589, when it was moved to its present site by Pope Sixtus V. It appears to stand at the apex of a perfect triangle formed by Via di Ripetta, Via del Corso and Via del Babuino, although this is an illusion. The churches on either side of Via del Corso – Santa Maria dei Miracoli and Santa Maria di Monte Santo – appear to be twins, but are actually different sizes. Carlo Rainaldi, who designed them in the 1660s, made them and the angles of the adjacent streets appear symmetrical by giving one an oval dome, and the other a round one. The immense gate was given a facelift by Bernini in 1655 to welcome Sweden's Queen Christina, who had shocked her subjects by abdicating her throne to become a Catholic (*see p72*). The plaque wishing *felice fausto ingressui* (a happy and blessed arrival) was addressed to the Church's illustrious new signing. The piazza's greatest

No more executions: **Piazza del Popolo**.

monument, though, is the church of **Santa Maria del Popolo**. In the piazza itself are the eternally fashionable meeting points, the **Rosati** and **Canova** cafés (*see chapter* **Cafés & Bars**).

Piazza di Spagna

Metro Spagna/bus to Piazza San Silvestro. **Map 5/1C**
Piazza di Spagna has been a compulsory stop for visitors to Rome ever since the eighteenth century, when a host of poets and musicians stayed nearby (*see p58*). The square takes its name from the Spanish Embassy to the Vatican, which has been here for several centuries, but is better known for the **Spanish Steps**, the elegant 1720s staircase that cascades down from the church of Trinità dei Monti. At Christmas a crib is erected half-way up; in spring and summer, the steps are adorned with huge tubs of azaleas for the fashion shows held here (*see pp5, 7*). At the foot of the stairs is a delightful boat-shaped fountain, designed in 1627 by either Gianlorenzo Bernini or perhaps his less famous father Pietro, and which is ingeniously sunk below ground level to compensate for the low pressure of the delicious *Acqua Vergine* that feeds it.

Palazzi

Palazzo di Montecitorio
Piazza di Montecitorio (06 67 601). Bus to Via del Corso or Piazza San Silvestro. **Open** first Sun of every month; free guided tours (in Italian) 10am-5.30pm; on weekdays, guided group visits by appointment only. Closed Aug. **Map 3/1 A**
Since 1871 this has been the Lower House of Italy's parliament, which is why police and barricades sometimes prevent you from getting anywhere near its elegantly curving façade. The building was designed by Bernini in 1650 for Pope Innocent X, and although much of it has been greatly altered since, the clock tower, columns and window sills of rough-hewn stone are his originals.

Ancient Rome

Ara Pacis Augustae
Via di Ripetta (06 3600 3471). Bus to Piazza Augusto Imperatore. **Open** *Oct-Mar* 9am-6pm Tue-Sat, 9am-1pm Sun; *Mar-Oct* 9am-7pm Tue-Sat, 9am-1pm Sun. **Admission** L3,750. **Map 3/1 A**
Inside a glass pavilion above the Tiber is a reconstruction of the Ara Pacis, or altar of peace, one of the most artistically distinguished monuments of ancient Rome. It was inaugurated in 9 BC to celebrate the wealth and security that Augustus' victories in Spain and Gaul had brought to the Empire. Originally located near Piazza San Lorenzo in Lucina, the altar was rebuilt on this site earlier this century, from ancient fragments amassed through a fiendishly difficult excavation over many years and a trawl through various Italian and French museums. The altar itself sits in an enclosure carved inside and out with delicately realistic reliefs. The lower band of the frieze is decorated with a relief of swirling acanthus leaves and swans with outstretched wings; the upper band shows a procession, thought to depict the ceremonies surrounding the dedication of the altar. With the help of a booklet on sale at the entrance, you can put names to the faces of Augustus and his family. At the time of writing the Ara Pacis had disappeared under scaffolding, but is due to re-emerge some time in the third millenium with an enlarged pavillion and exhibition space for showing the Ara-related artefacts that have languished in storage for decades. *Wheelchair access.*

Column of Marcus Aurelius (*Colonna di Marco Aurelio*)
Piazza Colonna. Bus to Via del Corso. **Map 3/1 A**
This 30-metre-high column was built between AD 180 and 196 to commemorate the victories of that most intellectual of Roman emperors, Marcus Aurelius. Author of the famous *Meditations*, he died while campaigning in 180. The reliefs on the column, modelled on the earlier ones on Trajan's Column in the **Imperial Fora**, are vivid illustrations of Roman army life. A statue of Marcus Aurelius on top of the column was replaced by one of Saint Paul in 1589.

Mausoleum of Augustus (*Mausoleo di Augusto*)
Piazza Augusto Imperatore or Via di Ripetta. Bus to Piazza Augusto Imperatore. **Open** with prior permission only (*see p33* **Getting through locked gates**). **Map 3/1 A**
It's hard to believe this forlorn-looking brick cylinder was once one of the most important monuments of ancient Rome. It was originally covered with marble pillars and statues, all of which have long since been looted. Two obelisks that stood either side of the main entrance are now in the **Piazza del Quirinale** and Piazza dell'Esquilino. It was built in honour of Augustus, who had brought peace to the city and its Empire, and begun in 28 BC. The first person buried here was Augustus' nephew, favourite son-in-law and probable successor Marcellus, also commemorated in the **Theatre of Marcellus**, who died young in 23 BC. Augustus himself was laid to rest in the central chamber on his death in AD 14, and many more early Caesars went on to join him. In the Middle Ages the mausoleum was used as a fortress, and later hosted concerts, but Mussolini had it restored, perhaps because he thought it a fitting place for his own illustrious corpse. He also planted the cedars and built the Fascist-classical-style square that now surrounds the tomb.

Pantheon
Piazza della Rotonda (06 6830 0230). Bus to Largo Argentina or Via del Corso/tram to Largo Argentina. **Open** 9am-6.30pm Mon-Sat; 9am-1pm Sun. **Admission** free. **Map 3/2A**
The Pantheon is the best preserved of the remains of ancient Rome. It was built by Hadrian in AD 119-128 as a temple to the 12 most important classical deities, although the inscription on the pediment records an earlier Pantheon built 100 years earlier by Augustus' General Marcus Agrippa – which confused historians for centuries. Its fine state of preservation is due to the building's conversion to a Christian church in 608, when it was presented to the Pope by the Byzantine Emperor Phocas. The Pantheon has nevertheless suffered over the years – notably when bronze cladding was stripped from the roof in 667, and when Pope Urban VIII allowed Bernini to remove the remaining bronze from the beams in the portico to melt it down for his *baldacchino* in **Saint Peter's** in the 1620s. The simplicity of the building's exterior, though, remains largely unchanged, and it retains its original Roman bronze doors.

Inside, the key to the Pantheon's extraordinary harmony is its dimensions. The radius of the dome is exactly equal to its height, so it could potentially accommodate a perfect sphere. At the centre of the dome is a circular hole 9m in diameter, the *oculus*, which is the only source of light and a symbolic link between the temple and the heavens. The building is still officially a church, but it's easy to overlook this, in spite of all the paraphernalia added over the years and the tombs of eminent Italians, including the Renaissance artist Raphael and the first king of united Italy, Vittorio Emanuele II. Until the eighteenth century the portico was used as a market: supports for the stalls were inserted into the notches that can be seen in the stonework of the columns. *Wheelchair access.*

Temple of Hadrian (*Tempio di Adriano*)
Piazza di Pietra. Bus to Via del Corso. **Map 3/2A**
Along the south side of a building in the otherwise unremarkable Piazza di Pietra are eleven 15m-high Corinthian columns, now embedded in the grimy wall of Rome's highly inactive stock exchange (*Borsa*). These originally formed part of a temple built to honour Emperor Hadrian by his adopted son, Antoninus Pius, in AD 145.

Churches

Sant'Ignazio di Loyola
Piazza Sant'Ignazio (06 679 4406).
Bus to Via del Corso. **Open** 7.30am-12.15pm, 4-7.30pm, daily. **Map 3/2A**
Sant'Ignazio was built to commemorate the canonisation of Saint Ignatius, founder of the Jesuit order, in 1626. *Trompe l'œil* columns soar above the nave,

and architraves by Andrea Pozzo open to a cloudy heaven into which figures are ascending. Trickery was also involved in creating the dome: The Dominican monks next door claimed that a real dome would rob them of light, so, rather than tussle with seventeenth-century planners, Pozzo simply painted a dome on the inside of the roof. The result is pretty convincing if you stand on the disc embedded in the floor of the nave. Walk away, however, and the illusion collapses.

San Lorenzo in Lucina
Piazza San Lorenzo in Lucina, 16a (06 687 1494).
Bus to Via del Corso or Piazza Augusto Imperatore.
Open *church* 9am-7pm daily; *Roman remains* 4.30pm, last Sat of each month; other Sats by appointment for groups of 15 or more. **Admission** *Roman remains* L3,000. **Map 3/1A**
This twelfth-century church was built on the site of an early Christian place of worship, which in turn is believed to stand on the site of an ancient well sacred to Juno. A guided tour of the lower levels takes place on the last Saturday of the month. The church's exterior incorporates Roman columns, while the seventeenth-century interior contains a wealth of

Literary footsteps

So thick on the ground were Grand Tourists in the streets around Piazza di Spagna in the eighteenth century that it became known as the 'English Ghetto'. In among the aristocracy – on mind-expanding trips or fleeing debt, duels or dowager mothers – and their downtrodden tutors, there were also artists and writers a-plenty.

By 1821, when Keats breathed his last in No. 26 Piazza di Spagna, Rome was an obligatory stop-over for any pen-wielder worth his – or more rarely, her – salt. Edward Gibbon had been here researching his *Decline and Fall* in 1765, and James Boswell had done some close examination of the Roman breed of foreigner in the same year. On the cusp of the new century, Wordsworth blazed a trail for what was to become a steady flow of Romantics. Coleridge nipped down in 1805, convinced that a close-quarters brush with the ancients would help him kick his opium addiction; it didn't. Byron passed through in 1817, and Shelley and his wife Mary pitched up in the spring of 1819, only to see their son William expire. Keats – undeterred by such proof of Rome's lack of therapeutic qualities – followed a year later, hoping the city's air would help his lung infection; it didn't. Like the Shelleys, father and son, he is nowadays to be found in the **Protestant Cemetery** in Testaccio (*see page 95*).

Such melancholy connections, plus the awe struck into visitors by Rome's ponderous ruins and history, may have contributed to the heavy output – stylistically, emotionally and on the kitchen scales – of many later visitors.

Charles Dickens discoursed at length on uncouth Romans after witnessing the *Carnevale* shenanigans in 1845; Nathanial Hawthorne drew his inspiration for *The Marble Faun* from visits between 1857 and 1859; George Eliot's Roman experiences in 1860 coloured Dorothea's dire honeymoon in *Middlemarch*; and Henry James, here from 1873-5, had his *Daisy Miller* expire after an evening breathing in the foul air of the **Colosseum**.

Rome lost none of its inspirational allure in the twentieth century. EM Forster came to call in 1902, DH Lawrence dropped in to pour cold water over the ancient Romans in 1919 after falling head over heels in love with the raunchier Etruscans, and the Catholic GK Chesterton made pilgrimages to the Eternal City at various times between 1920 and 1934. Eccentric Ezra Pound came to Rome to visit Mussolini in 1933, no doubt to express his admiration: subsequently, his pro-Fascist broadcasts on Italian radio during World War II would earn him 12 years in an American asylum for the criminally insane after the war.

Casanova sipped caffè between conquests in the **Caffè Greco**. See page 59.

treasures including Bernini portrait busts in the Fonseca Chapel, a kitsch seventeenth-century *Crucifixion* by Guido Reni, and a monument to French artist Nicholas Poussin, who died in Rome in 1665. In the first chapel on the right is an ancient grill, reputed to be the one on which the martyr Saint Lawrence was roasted to death (*see p100*).

Santa Maria del Popolo

Piazza del Popolo, 12 (06 361 0836).
Metro Flaminio/bus to Piazzale Flaminio.
Open 7am-noon, 4-7pm, Mon-Sat; 8am-1.30pm, 4.30-7.30pm, Sun. **Map 2/2A**

According to legend, Santa Maria del Popolo occupies the site of a garden in which Nero's nurse and mistress secretly buried the hated emperor's corpse. A thousand years later the site was still believed to be haunted by demons, and in 1099 Pope Paschal II built a chapel there to dispel them. Nearly four centuries later, beginning in 1472, Pope Sixtus IV rebuilt the chapel as a church, financing it by taxing foreign churches and selling ecclesiastical jobs.

In the apse are Rome's first stained-glass windows, created by French artist Guillaume de Marcillat in 1509. The apse itself was designed by Bramante, the Chigi Chapel by Raphael, and the choir ceiling and two of the chapels in the right aisle (first and third) were frescoed by Pinturicchio, the Borgias' favourite artist. In Pinturicchio's exquisite works, the Virgin and a host of saints keep company with some very pre-Christian sibylls. Most intriguing is the Chigi Chapel, designed by Raphael for Agostino Chigi. The mosaics in the dome depict God creating the sun and the seven planets, and

Agostino's personal horoscope: with binoculars, you can just about make out a crab, a bull, a lion and a pair of scales. The chapel was completed by Bernini, who, on the orders of Agostino's descendant Pope Alexander VII added the two theatrical statues of Daniel and Habakkuk. The church's most-gawped-at possessions, however, are the two masterpieces by Caravaggio in the Cerasi Chapel, to the left of the main altar. On a vast scale, and suffused with lashings of the master's own particular light, they show the stories of Saint Peter and Saint Paul. Note, also, the bizarre memorial of seventeenth century notable GB Gisleni, left of the main door: grisly skeletons, chrysalids and butterflies remind us of our brief passage through life and exit the other end.

Santa Maria sopra Minerva

Piazza della Minerva, 42 or Via Beato Angelico, 35 (06 679 3926). Bus or tram to Largo Argentina.
Open 7am-7pm daily. **Map 3/2A**

Santa Maria is Rome's only Gothic church, built on the site of an ancient temple of Minerva. The best of its art works are Renaissance: on the right of the transept is the superb Carafa chapel, with late fifteenth-century frescoes by Filippino Lippi (1457-1504), commissioned by Cardinal Oliviero Carafa in honour of Saint Thomas Aquinas. Carafa took Renaissance self-assurance to extremes: the altar painting shows him being presented to the Virgin, right at the moment when Gabriel informs her she's going to give birth to Christ. The tomb of the Carafa Pope Paul IV (1555-59) is also in the chapel. He was one of the prime movers of the Counter-Reformation, chiefly remembered for persecuting the Jews and ordering Daniele da Volterra to paint loincloths on the nudes of Michelangelo's *Last Judgment.* A bronze loincloth was also ordered to cover Christ's genitals on a work by Michelangelo here in Santa Maria. The statue was finished by Pietro Urbano (1514-21) and depicts a heroic Christ holding up a flimsy cross. An early Renaissance work is the *Madonna and Child,* believed by some to be by Fra Angelico, in the chapel to the left of the altar, close to the artistic monk's own tomb. The father of modern astronomy Galileo Galilei, who dared suggest in the early sixteenth century that the earth revolved around the sun and not vice versa, was tried for heresy in the adjoining monastery.

Santa Maria in Via

Via Santa Maria in Via (06 679 6760). Metro Barberini/bus to Piazza San Silvestro or Via del Tritone. **Open** 7am-3.30pm daily. **Map 5/2C**
An ornate baroque façade, completed in 1681 by Carlo Rainaldi, a pupil of Bernini, hides a little chapel containing a well where, in 1256, a stone bearing an image of the Virgin's face floated to the surface, or so the story goes. Shots of the water, which supposedly has the power to cure the sick, are handed out in little plastic cups from the altar rail in exchange for a donation in a box.

Museums & galleries

Galleria dell'Accademia di San Luca

Piazza dell'Accademia, 77 (06 679 8850). Metro Barberini/bus to Piazza San Silvestro. **Open** 10am-12.30pm Mon, Wed, Fri and last Sun of each month. Closed July and Aug. **Admission** free. **Map 5/2C**
This august institution was founded in 1577 to train artists in the grand Renaissance style. The highlight of the collection is a fragment of a Raphael fresco, but there are also works by Titian, Rubens, Reni and Van Dyck, and fascinating self-portraits by the few women members of the Academy, such as Lavinia Fontana (1552-1614) and Angelica Kauffman (1741-1807). Note the curious elliptical staircase near the entrance, a typically original addition by Borromini. *Wheelchair access with assistance.*

Galleria Colonna

Via della Pilotta, 17 (06 679 4362). Bus to Piazza Venezia. **Open** 9am-1pm Sat. **Admission** L10,000. **Map 5/2C**
It's well worth making the effort one Saturday morning to see this lavish six-roomed gallery (completed in 1703), in the still family-owned Palazzo Colonna. The Great Hall has a dramatic frescoed ceiling depicting the *Apotheosis of Marcantonio Colonna;* next to it is the Hall of the Desks, so named because of two lavish writing desks, one decorated with *pietra dura* and bronze statuettes, the other covered in carved ivory. The ceiling is a fantasy of evil cherubs, endangered maidens and threatening Turks, by Sebastiano Ricci. Other highlights include the wonderfully sensuous *Venus and Cupid* by Bronzino, the nightmarish *Temptation of Saint*

Anthony by a follower of Hieronymus Bosch, and Annibale Carracci's appropriately earthy *The Bean-Eater,* a familiar, much-reproduced face. Groups of ten or more can arrange guided tours of the gallery (L30,000 per person), the private apartments (L25,000) or both (L45,000) during the week. *Wheelchair access with assistance: call ahead.*

Galleria Doria Pamphili

Piazza del Collegio Romano, 2 (06 679 7323). Bus to Piazza Venezia. **Open** 10am-5pm Mon-Wed, Fri-Sun. **Admission** *museum* L13,000; *private apartments* L5,000. **Map 3/2A**
One of Rome's finest private art collections, housed in the rambling palace of the Doria Pamphili family, a pillar of Rome's aristocracy now headed by two half-British siblings. For many years the collection was crammed onto the walls of four corridors. It has now spilled into the fifteenth-century wing of the palace, although the best is definitely still in the gallery proper. Among those on show are a portrait by Raphael of two gentlemen(1500s room), Correggio's unfinished *Allegory of Virtue* (Wing 3), four Titians, including *Religion Succoured by Spain* (Aldobrandini room) and a self-possessed *Salome* holding the head of John the Baptist (1500s room). Caravaggio is represented by a Penitent *Magdalen* and the early *Rest during the Flight into Egypt* (both in the 1600s room). Of the paintings by Guercino, the martyred *Saint Agnes* (Wing 3) as she fails to catch light at the stake stands out. There are many works by Guido Reni, darling of the Victorians but rarely to end-of-millennium tastes. The suite of rooms that leads off the far end of Wing 2 houses Italian and some Flemish works, arranged chronologically by century; Wing 4 contains a number of works by Dutch and Flemish artists, including Brueghel. The collection's greatest jewel is arguably the extraordinary portrait by Velázquez of the Pamphili pope *Innocent X,* displayed in a separate room off Wing 1, alongside a Bernini bust of the same pontiff. Landscapes by the Carracci, Claude Lorrain and others are found in Wing 1. In the series of rooms en route to the gallery proper, a spectacular eighteenth-century ballroom leads into the Yellow Room, with its Gobelin tapestries, and a series of elegant rooms beyond. The chapel, by Carlo Fontana (1689), though repeatedly altered, has its original *trompe l'œil* painted ceiling.
For an extra L5,000 there are guided tours of the private apartments, in Italian (with a brief summary in English). Tours begin about every 30 minutes, from 10.30am-12.25pm. There are important pictures here too, such as a delicate *Annunciation* by Filippo Lippi, and Sebastiano del Piombo's portrait of the Genoese admiral and patriarch Andrea Doria as Neptune.

Keats-Shelley Memorial House

Piazza di Spagna, 26 (06 678 4235). Metro Spagna/bus to Piazza San Silvestro. **Open** 9am-1pm, 3-6pm, Mon-Fri; 11am-2pm, 3-6pm, Sat. **Admission** L5,000. **Map 5/1C**
The house at the bottom of the Spanish Steps where the 25-year-old John Keats died of tuberculosis in

Cheap clobber for kids from the 'burbs along Via del Corso.

1821 is crammed with mementoes of Keats, Shelley and Byron: a lock of Keats' hair and his death mask, a minuscule urn holding tiny pieces of Shelley's charred skeleton, copies of documents and letters, and a massive library make this a Romantic enthusiast's paradise. Devotees should also make the pilgrimage to the **Protestant Cemetery** in Testaccio, where both Keats and Shelley are buried.

Palazzo Ruspoli

Via del Corso, 418 (06 6830 7344). Bus to Piazza San Silvestro. **Open** exhibition times vary. **Admission** depends on exhibition. **Map 3/1 A**
The palace of one of Rome's old noble families is now used for touring exhibitions of art, photography, archaeology and history. It stays open late at least one or two nights a week. The basement rooms often host photo exhibitions, and admission is sometimes free.
Wheelchair access.

Parks & gardens

Pincio

Piazza del Pincio. Metro Flaminio/bus or train to Piazzale Flaminio. **Map 2/2A**
Overlooking **Piazza del Popolo** is one of the oldest gardens in Rome. The Pinci family began the first gardens here in the fourth century, although the present layout was designed by Valadier in 1814. The garden is best known for its view of the Vatican at sunset, with the dome of **Saint Peter's** silhouetted in gold. There are also beautiful views of the **Gianicolo** and the **Fontana Paola**. Don't miss the squat dome of the **Pantheon**, and the statue on top of the **Column of Marcus Aurelius** in Piazza Colonna. The paved area behind the viewpoint is popular with cyclists (bikes can be hired nearby) and skaters. To the south-east is the Casino Valadier, with an exorbitantly expensive restaurant and tearoom, but a stupendous view

Via Veneto
& the Quirinale

The Vita may no longer be Dolce, but there's a unique concentration of art for all tastes around the lush Villa Borghese.

Rome's most famous modern street – officially Via Vittorio Veneto – cuts through what was once the heart of the palace and gardens of the Villa Ludovisi, laid out in 1662. It was one of the largest of the princely villas that dotted Rome until the post-1870 Piedmontese influx, when most were sold off by their aristocratic owners to the new breed of building speculators. Fortunately for Rome, the **Villa Borghese**, just to the north, was taken over by the state and made into a public park (*see page 66-7*).

Prince Boncompagni Ludovisi (whose two surnames have been given to major roads) sold off his glorious estate in 1885, and with the proceeds built a massive palazzo in part of the grounds. Crippled by running costs and the tax bill on the sale of the land, he sold it to Margherita, widow of King Umberto I. The renamed Villa Margherita, half-way down Via Veneto, is now the US Embassy.

The area was swiftly built up, immediately acquiring the reputation for luxury that it retained right up until the late 1960s. The area on the hill, known as the *quartiere Ludovisi*, largely consists of late nineteenth-century palazzi and villas; the lower part, extending as far as Via XX Settembre and Piazza Barberini, was mostly rebuilt in the Fascist era, when Via Barberini and Via Bissolati were relentlessly bulldozed through the urban fabric. These two streets are now the heart of Rome's airline and travel business, while the *quartiere Ludovisi* is synonymous with the upper end of the finance and service industries.

Via Veneto itself is lined with major hotels and the headquarters of publishers, banks and insurance companies. With its impersonal expense-account restaurants and unenticing glass-fronted cafés, the broad sweep of Via Veneto could be a

'You will be what we are now.' Grim lessons at the **Immacolata Concezione**. *See page 65.*

*Divine love gets earthy in **Santa Maria della Vittoria**. See page 69.*

B & B: brilliant and baroque

If the Gothic passed Rome by and the Renaissance was slow to take off, the baroque exploded like one of the firework displays that the Eternal City still loves, thanks above all to the extraordinary works of two sworn enemies, two men who were diametrically opposed in character, background, and approach.

After an initial period of collaboration that produced such masterpieces as the *baldacchino* in **Saint Peter's** and the **Palazzo Barberini**, bitter rivalry erupted between the witty, charming **Gianlorenzo Bernini (1598-1680)**, always at ease with his rich, aristocratic patrons, and the irascible **Francesco Borromini (1599-1667)**, who inevitably alienated his.

Bernini was confident, brilliant, a master of all the arts, and enjoyed the patronage of eight successive popes. His saints were sensual, and his church designs showy, delighting in intellectual and visual tricks. A devout Catholic, Bernini was convinced that all art had to be didactic and propagandistic, and he adhered unerringly to the prevailing opinion that, since man was created in God's image and therefore perfect, the fundamental tenets underlying art always had to be anthropomorphic.

Borromini was altogether a nervier, spikier character, who, bitter to the end, took his own life in a fit of what commentators would later describe as schizophrenia. A stonemason who worked his way up from the bottom, he had little time for the intellectual concepts of the age, preferring to place his professional trust in sound, concrete geometry. His work is characterised by its sculptural quality and a complex and innovative use of geometric forms: in ground-breaking constructions such as **Sant'Agnese in Agone** (*right, behind Bernini's* **Fontana dei Quattro Fiumi**), **San Carlo alle Quattro Fontane** and **Sant'Ivo alla Sapienza**, he pushed contemporary architectural tenets to the limits and beyond, bringing opprobrium upon his head, but radically redefining ideas about what was structurally possible.

---

street in any northern-European business district. The worldwide reputation it acquired in the 1950s was largely due to the enormous American presence at **Cinecittà** (*see chapter* **Film**). Fellini's 1959 film *La Dolce Vita*, starring the late and much lamented Marcello Mastroianni, consecrated the scene and originated the term *paparazzo* – the surname of a character in the film, modelled on the legendary photographer Tazio Secchiaroli.

Nowadays, there is little *vita* on Via Veneto, apart from droves of middle-aged visitors. The local tourist industry tries desperately to resurrect the corpse for them. What they get are bimbos on the doorsteps of wildly expensive night-clubs, enticing them in for atrocious floorshows, terrible food and sleazy company.

At the foot of Via Veneto is Piazza Barberini, overlooked by the huge **Palazzo Barberini**, with Bernini's **Fontana del Tritone** as its centrepiece. In ancient times, this site was occupied by the Flora Circus, where erotic dances would mark the coming of spring. From Piazza Barberini, Via delle Quattro Fontane shoots to the top of the Quirinal hill, where it bisects the equally straight Via del Quirinale. From the crossroads here there are extraordinary views of the obelisks at Trinità dei Monti and **Santa Maria Maggiore** . The finest point of the Quirinal is the polygonal **Piazza del Quirinale** at the far end of the street, from where the view over the city is just as spectacular, above all at sunset.

Piazze & fountains

Fontana dell'Acqua Felice

Piazza San Bernardo. Metro Repubblica/bus to Piazza della Repubblica. **Map 5/1B**
The Acqua Felice, designed by Domenico Fontana in the form of a triumphal arch, was completed in 1589. It was one of many urban improvements that were commissioned in Rome by Pope Sixtus V, and provided this district with clean water from an ancient aqueduct (*see chapter* **History**). The statue of Moses in the central niche of the fountain, by Leonardo Sormani, has been roundly condemned as an atrocity against taste ever since it was unveiled in 1586.

Fontana del Tritone & Fontana delle Api

Piazza Barberini. Metro Barberini/bus to Piazza Barberini. **Map 5/1B**
Like many Bernini figures this cheerful Triton, now stranded at a hellish major traffic junction, has a well-developed abdomen. Completed in 1642, he sits, his two fish-tail legs tucked beneath him, on a shell supported by four dolphins, and blows water through a conch in his mouth. The bees on the coat of arms on the fountain were a symbol of the Barberini clan, the family of Bernini's great patron, Pope Urban VIII. Similar Barberini bees naturally also feature prominently on another Bernini fountain, the **Fontana delle Api** (Fountain of the Bees), which stands just across the piazza at the foot of the Via Veneto. This time they are trying to crawl out of the water.

Piazza del Quirinale

Bus to Via Nazionale. **Map 5/2C**

One of the centres of official Rome, this expanse is dominated by the huge, orange **Palazzo del Quirinale**. At the centre of the piazza is an obelisk originally from the **Mausoleum of Augustus**. The square is dominated by disproportionately large Roman statues of the heavenly twins Castor and Pollux, each 5.5m tall, atop a fountain that was moved here in the 1800s after – legend has it – centuries of use as a cattle trough in the Roman Forum.

Quattro Fontane

Bus to Piazza Barberini or Via Nazionale. **Map 5/2B**

At the fume-filled crossroads between Via delle Quattro Fontane and Via XX Settembre, these four charming baroque fountains date from 1593 and represent four gods. The river god accompanied by the she-wolf is obviously the Tiber, although it is unclear whether the other male figure is meant to represent the Nile or the Aniene. The females are probably Juno (with duck) and Diana.

Palazzi

Palazzo del Quirinale

Piazza del Quirinale (06 46 991). Bus to Via Nazionale. **Open** 8.30am-12.30pm, second and fourth Sun of each month. **Admission** L10,000. **Map 5/2C**

The Quirinale was begun in 1574 only as a papal summer residence, but soon became more popular with pontiffs as a permanent base than the low-lying Vatican palace. So that they should not have to return to the other place for conclaves, the *Cappella Paolina*, a replica of the **Sistine Chapel** (in size and shape, not decoration), was built in the following century, and accommodation for the cardinals was provided in the *Manica Lunga*, the immensely long façade running the length of Via del Quirinale. Popes Pius VI and VII were forcibly removed from the palace and deported by Napoleon, in 1799 and 1809 respectively; republican rebels forced Pius IX to sneak ignominiously out the back door in 1848. After his return to Rome, the disgruntled Pius refused to hand over the keys of the Quirinale to Italy's new king in 1870, and soldiers had to break into the palace before Vittorio Emanuele could take up residence there (*see chapter* **History**). Since the end of the monarchy in 1946 it has been home to the president of Italy. The graceful door in the main façade is by Bernini. The lofty public rooms and beautiful gardens open to the public twice a month. *Wheelchair access.*

Churches

L'Immacolata Concezione

Via Vittorio Veneto, 27 (06 487 1185). Metro Barberini/bus to Piazza Barberini. **Open** *church* 6.45am-noon, 4.30-7pm, daily; *crypt* 9.30am-noon,3-6pm, Fri-Wed. **Admission** *crypt* donation expected. **Map 5/1B**

Commonly known as *I Cappuccini* (the Capuchins) after the long-bearded, brown-clad Franciscan sub-

Round and round the (Borghese) garden

In 1580 the wealthy and noble Borghese family bought a vineyard in a semi-rural area north of Rome. Two decades later, the plot caught the fancy of pleasure-loving Cardinal Scipione Borghese, the favourite nephew of Pope Paul V, who was seeking a location for a *giardino delle delizie*, a garden of earthly delights. In 1608 he began buying up land all around it, and hired architects Flaminio Ponzio and Jan van Santen (Italianised to Giovanni Vasanzio) to produce a worthy backdrop for his sybaritic leisure activities and matchless collection of art. Work on the magnificent gardens, the **Villa Borghese**, went on until Scipione's death in 1633.

The result was a baroque fun-park, complete with trick fountains that sprayed unwitting passers-by, automata and erotic paintings, aviaries, menageries of wild beasts, and an *al fresco* dining room (still visible, to the right as you look at the façade of the **Galleria Borghese**), where the cardinal entertained his guests with due magnificence on warm summer evenings. At the centre of the park, flanked by formal gardens with exotic plants and fruit trees, rose the *Casino* (now the Galleria Borghese), an elaborate construction intended not as a residence but as a permanent home for Scipione's mushrooming collection of canvas and marble.

Successive generations of Borgheses altered Scipione's park according to changing fashions, and added to (or, tragically, partly sold off) his superlative art collection. When Rome became capital of Italy, the clan looked set to sell off the 80-hectare estate to property speculators. In a rare example of civic far-sightedness the state stepped in in 1901, wresting possession of the Villa from the family in a bitter court battle.

Today the Borgheses' park is used for jogging, dog-walking, picnics and cruising. Wandering around it is a great way to recuperate from an overdose of sightseeing and carbon monoxide, although culture vultures can continue to sweat it out in three of Rome's greatest art depositories, the Galleria itself, the Etruscan museum in **Villa Giulia** and the **Galleria Nazionale d'Arte Moderna**. The park also houses the **Dei Piccoli** children's cinema (*see chapter* **Film**) and Rome's **Zoo**. Other sights worth looking out for include the Piazza di Siena, an elegantly-shaped arena used for opera and show-jumping, imitation ancient temples, and a lake with rowing boats (for hire from 9.30am to sunset, daily). There is also a good view of the *Moro Torto* section of the **Aurelian Wall** from the bridge between the Pincio and Villa Borghese. Once a favourite suicide spot, this is now strung with nets to make sure no depressed Romans plunge onto the constant stream of traffic below.

Galleria Borghese

Piazzale Scipione Borghese, 5 (information and bookings 06 32 810, 9am-7pm Mon-Fri; 9am-1pm Sat). Bus to Via Veneto, Via Pinciana or Corso D'Italia. **Open** 9am-7pm Tue-Sun. **Admission** L12,000; booking advisable at all times, and essential in high season, when you should call at least two weeks prior to visiting. **Map 4/2B**

Il Casino was designed in 1613 by Jan van Santen to house Cardinal Scipione Borghese's art collection. One of Bernini's greatest patrons and a collector of classical sculpture, the cardinal was also a man with as good an eye for a bargain as for a masterpiece, and picked up many works – even the odd Caravaggio – at bargain prices after they were rejected by the disappointed or shocked patrons who had commissioned them. After a 15-year closure, when it was shrouded in scaffolding, the Gallery re-opened in 1998 with decorations and art works fully restored. The imposing entrance salon has fourth-century AD floor mosaics showing gladiators fighting wild animals, and ancient Roman statuary; next to it in Room 1 is one of the Gallery's sculptural highlights, Canova's 1804 figure of Pauline, sister of Napoleon and wife of Prince Camillo Borghese. She is portrayed as a topless Venus; Camillo thought the work so provocative he forbade even the artist to see it after completion (asked by a shocked friend how she could bear to pose naked, Pauline is said to have snapped: 'the studio was heated').

Rooms 2-4 contain some spectacular sculptures by Bernini, made early in his career but already showing his genius: notice how Pluto's hand presses into Proserpine's marble thigh in *The Rape of Proserpine*. Room 3 houses perhaps his most famous work, *Apollo and Daphne*, showing the nymph fleeing the sun god, her desperate attempt at flight hampered as she turns, fingertips first, into a laurel tree.

Room 5 contains important pieces of classical sculpture, many of them Roman copies of Greek originals. Among the most renowned are a Roman copy of a Greek dancing faun, and a copy of a sleeping hermaphrodite, displayed with his/her back to the onlooker so that the breasts and genitals are invisible. Bernini's *Enea e Anchise* dominates Room 6, while Room 7 contains more classical statues. In room 8 are six works by Caravaggio, including *David Holding Aloft the Head of Goliath*, his luscious *Boy with a Basket of Fruit* and an uncanny *Madonna of the Serpent*. His *Sick Bacchus* is believed to be a self-portrait.

The first-floor picture gallery is packed with one masterpiece after another. Look out in particular for: Raphael's *Deposition* and Pinturicchio's *Crucifixion with Saints Jerome and Christopher* (Room 9); Correggio's *Danae*, commissioned as sixteenth-century soft porn for Charles V of Spain, and Lucas Cranach's *Venus and Cupid with Honeycomb* (10); a dark, brooding *Pietà* by Raphael's follower Sodoma (12); two self- portraits and two sculpted busts of Cardinal Scipione Borghese by Bernini (14); Ruben's spectacular *Pietà* and *Susanna and the Elders* (18); Titian's *Venus Blindfolding Cupid* and the recently-restored *Sacred and Profane Love* are the centrepieces of Room 20, which also contains works by Veronese, Giorgione and Carpaccio, and a stunning *Portrait of a Man* by Antonello da Messina. *Wheelchair access.*

Galleria Nazionale d'Arte Moderna e Contemporanea

Viale delle Belle Arti, 131 (06 322 981).
Bus/tram to Viale delle Belle Arti.
Open 9am-7pm Tue-Sun. **Admission** *permanent collection* L6,000; *permanent collection plus special exhibitions* L12,000. **Map 4/1C**

Italy's national collection of modern art, housed in a massive neo-classical palace from 1912, with a recently-opened modern wing, covers the nineteenth and twentieth centuries. Italian art of this period is relatively unknown outside Italy. Most of what's on display here will make you understand why, but a few works (and the cool, quiet elegance of the gallery itself) make it worth crossing Villa Borghese to take a look. The nineteenth-century collection contains works by the *macchiaioli*, who used dots of colour to create their paintings. The twentieth-century component is stronger, with many works by De Chirico, Carrà, Sironi, Morandi, Marini and others, as well as representatives of contemporary movements such as *Arte povera* and the *Transavanguardia*. There's an interesting assortment of works by international artists, among them Klimt, Kandinsky, Cézanne and Henry Moore. The museum has a well-stocked shop and excellent café-restaurant, the **Caffè delle Arti** (*see chapter* **Restaurants**). *Wheelchair access from Via Gramsci, 71.*

Museo Nazionale di Villa Giulia

Piazzale di Villa Giulia, 9 (06 322 6571). Bus/tram to Viale delle Belle Arti. **Open** 9am-7pm Tue-Sat; 9am-2pm Sun. **Admission** L8,000. **Map 2/1A**

Villa Giulia was built for pleasure-loving Pope Julius III in the mid-sixteenth century and was, like the Borghese Casino across the park, intended for entertainment rather than living in. Extensive gardens and pavilions were laid out by Vignola and Vasari, while Ammannati and Michelangelo both had a hand in the creation of the fountains. The villa was transformed into a museum in 1889, and houses an exhaustive collection of Etruscan art and artefacts.

Most of the exhibits here came from tombs: very few Etruscan buildings have survived (*see chapter* **Trips out of Town**). A fifth-century BC terracotta relief from a temple pediment from the port of Pyrgi depicts life-size episodes from the Theban cycle, indicating the Greek presence in Etruscan art. The Faliscan crater, an urn from the fourth century BC, depicts Dawn rising in her chariot, and the Chigi vase features hunting tales from the sixth century BC. Even the jewellery is covered with carved animals, as are the hundreds of miniature vases, pieces of furniture and models of buildings made to accompany the dead to their eternal life. Red, black and white pottery in the villa shows scenes of dancing, hunting and more intimate pleasures. The sixth-century BC terracotta *Sarcofago degli Sposi*, presumably made as a tomb for a husband and wife, is adorned with a sculpture of the happy couple reclining on its lid.

In the garden is a reconstruction of an Etruscan temple. Look out too for the frescoes in the colonnaded loggia, and the sunken *nymphaeum* (water garden) in the courtyard, decorated with mosaics, fountains and statues. The Santa Cecilia academy presents breathtaking concerts here each summer (*see chapter* **Music: Classical & Opera**). *Wheelchair access with assistance.*

Bioparco & Museo di Zoologia

Bioparco *Via del Giardino Zoologico, 1 (06 360 8211);* **museo** *Via Aldovrandi, 18 (06 321 6586). Bus to Via Pinciana or Via Mercadante/tram to Via Aldovrandi.* **Open** *Bioparco* 9.30am-6pm daily; *museo* 9am-5pm Tue-Sun.
Admission *Bioparco* L10,000; L7,000 6-12s. *Museo* L5,000; free under-18s. **Map 4/1B**

Rome's ropey old zoo, with morose animals in cramped cages, has been relabelled the *Bioparco* and is gradually being given an eco-friendly once-over. It has all the regular furry and feathered friends, a snazzy reptile house, and free organised games and face-painting for kids daily in school holidays, at weekends at other times.

On the north-east side of the zoo is the **Museo di Zoologia**, the zoological museum, with a vast and glorious collection of dusty and moth-eaten stuffed animals in its old wing, and a state-of-the-art permanent exhibit on *Animals and their Habitats* in a spanking new wing. Access is possible from Via Aldovrandi or the zoo. *Wheelchair access to Bioparco only.*

The Barberini Gallery

Maderno, Bernini and Borromini all contributed to the design of the **Palazzo Barberini**, built for the Barberini Pope Urban VIII between 1627 and 1633. Borromini's handiwork can be seen in the characteristic oval secondary staircase on the right, while Bernini was responsible for the rectangular main staircase to the left. The most famous feature of the interior is the *Gran Salone*, dramatically frescoed by Pietro da Cortona in 1633-39 with depictions of *The Triumph of Divine Providence*.

The art collection tends to be re-arranged from time to time, and will undergo further changes in 2000 when Armed Forces officers are evicted from their club on the ground floor and the gallery expands. Highlights of the collection include: Filippo Lippi's *Madonna* (with possibly the ugliest Christ-child ever painted); an enigmatic portrait of a courtesan, *La Fornarina*, traditionally (although probably wrongly) believed to represent Raphael's mistress (*see page 72*, **Casa della Fornarina**); a portrait of *Erasmus* by Flemish artist Quentin Metsys; a *Nativity* and *Baptism of Christ* by El Greco; Tintoretto's dramatic *Christ and the Woman taken in Adultery*; Titian's *Venus and Adonis*; two Caravaggios, one of Judith rather gingerly cutting off Holofernes' head; a Holbein portrait, *Henry VIII Dressed for his Wedding to Anne of Cleves* (although it has been suggested this may be a copy); Bronzino's forceful portrait of *Stefano Colonna*; Guido Reni's *Penitant Magdalene* and portrait of incest-victim *Beatrice Cenci* (*see chapter* **Centro Storico: Palazzo Cenci**); a Bernini bust and painted portrait of Pope Urban VIII, who commissioned the palace; works by Raphael's best-known follower, Sodoma (the nickname, apparently, was accurate), including a *Rape of the Sabine Women* with predictably compliant subjects and *The Mystic Marriage of Saint Catherine*; a self-portrait by Artemisia Gentileschi; and Venetian scenes by Canaletto and Guardi.

Visitors also have access to a suite of small private rooms, exquisitely painted and furnished for Princess Cornelia Costanza Barberini in the eighteenth century (note the charming natives in the room decorated with depictions of the discovery of America). Cornelia was the last of the Barberinis, and the name died out when she was married off to one of the Colonna family at the age of 12. These rooms also house some Barberini family clothes and furniture.

Palazzo Barberini

Via delle Quattro Fontane, 13 (06 481 4591/bookings 06 32 810). Metro Barberini/bus to Piazza Barberini. **Open** *9am-7pm Tue-Sat, 9am-1pm Sun.* **Admission** *gallery* L10,000; *private apartments* L2,000. **Map 5/1B** *Wheelchair access with assistance.*

order to which it belongs, this baroque church at the foot of Via Veneto has a *Saint Michael* (1635) by Reni (first chapel on the right) that was a major hit with English Grand Tourists, and a fine rendition of *Saint Paul's sight being restored* (1631) by Pietro da Cortona (first chapel on the left). Its real attraction, though, lies below in the crypt, where the dry bones of generations of monks have been removed from the order's short supply of soil from Jerusalem and attractively arranged in swirls, sunbursts and curlicues all over the walls, as a reminder (as a notice states) that 'you will be what we now are'.

Sant'Andrea al Quirinale

Via del Quirinale, 29 (06 474 4801).
Bus to Via Nazionale. **Open** 8am-noon, 4-8pm, Mon, Wed-Sun. **Map 5/2C**
This oval church, decorated in pink marble, is a typically theatrical Bernini production, finished in 1670 and cleverly designed to create a sense of grandeur in a small space. Inside, every surface is lavishly decorated, but pride of place must go to a plaster Saint Andrew floating through a broken pediment on his way to Heaven.

San Carlo alle Quattro Fontane

Via del Quirinale, 23 (06 488 3261). Bus to Via Nazionale. **Open** 9.30am-12.30pm, 4-6pm, Mon-Fri, Sun; 9.30am-12.30pm Sat. **Map 5/2B**
This was Borromini's first solo commission (1634-41), and is an ingenious building for a cramped site. The most remarkable feature is the oval dome. The geometrical coffers in its decoration decrease in size towards the lantern to give the illusion of additional height, and the illumination, through hidden windows, makes the dome appear to be floating in mid-air. At the time of writing the church was closed for extensive restoration, but the charming if somewhat austere courtyard in the adjoining monastery has remained open.

Santa Maria della Vittoria

Via XX Settembre, 17 (06 482 6190). Metro Repubblica/bus to Largo Santa Susanna or Via XX Settembre. **Open** *Sept-July* 7.30-11.30am, 4.30-7pm, daily; *Aug* 7-10.30am, 5-7pm daily. **Map 5/1B**
This modest-looking baroque church, its interior cosily candle-lit and lovingly adorned with marble and gilt, holds one of Bernini's most famous works. *The Ecstasy of Saint Teresa,* in the Cornaro chapel (the fourth on the left), shows the Spanish mystic floating on a cloud in a supposedly spiritual trance after a teasing, androgynous angel has pierced her with a burning arrow. The result is more than a little ambiguous (writing of the angel incident in her *Life,* Teresa recalled 'so intense was the pain I uttered several moans; so great was the sweetness caused by the pain that I never wanted to lose it.') As a former president of France commented after seeing Bernini's work, 'if that is divine love, I know all about it'. When the chapel is seen as a whole, with the heavens painted in the dome, the light filters through a hidden window, reflecting gilded rays and bathing Teresa in a heavenly glow. She is sur-

rounded by a row of witnesses – members of the Cornaro family sitting in a balcony and earnestly discussing the spectacle.

Santi Vincenzo ed Anastasio

Vicolo dei Modelli, 73 (06 678 3098).
Bus to Piazza San Silvestro or Via del Tritone. **Open** 7am-noon, 3-7pm, daily. **Map 5/2C**
Your chance to stand in the presence of the livers, spleens and pancreases of every pope from Sixtus V (1585-90) to Leo XIII (1878-1903). After each pope's death his innards were bottled, labelled and deposited here – but you cannot see them, yet. After many years under wraps, they are *in restauro,* and may be unveiled during Y2K.

Museums & galleries

Galleria Comunale d'Arte Moderna e Contemporanea

Via F. Crispi, 24 (06 474 2848).
Metro Barberini/bus to Via del Tritone. **Open** 9am-7pm Tue-Sat; 9am-2pm Sun. **Admission** L10,000. **Map 5/1C**
This city-run gallery concentrates on smaller shows, with the emphasis on one-person exhibitions and retrospectives. The permanent collection contains works by such figures as Rodin, De Pisis, Morandi, Guttuso, Afro and Capogrossi.
Wheelchair access in Via Zucchelli, 7; ring bell in Via Crispi first.

Museo Nazionale delle Paste Alimentari

Piazza Scanderbeg, 117 (06 699 1119).
Bus to Via del Tritone. **Open** 9.30am-5.30pm daily. **Admission** L12,000. **Map 5/2C**
This grandly-named tribute to pasta is one of the best-organised museums in Rome. Visitors are issued with a portable CD player, with commentary in six languages, to talk them through the collection of pasta-making equipment, labels, art inspired by Italy's national dish and prints and photos of famous – and not so famous – people enjoying pasta. You hear more than strictly necessary on the techniques of pasta making, and some of the displays (particularly a set of eighteenth-century prints that seem to appear in every room) are a bit repetitive, but for anyone with a passing interest in the national dish the museum is worth a visit.
Wheelchair access with assistance.

Palazzo delle Esposizioni

Via Nazionale, 194 (06 488 5465). Bus to Via Nazionale. **Open** 10am-9pm Mon, Wed-Sun. **Admission** L12,000. **Map 5/2B**
Dating from the late nineteenth century, the Palazzo was one of Rome's first purpose-built exhibition halls. After years of neglect and restoration it reopened in 1990 to become Rome's most prominent cultural centre, holding exhibitions, film screenings, conferences and many other events. Incorporated into the complex are a bookshop, design shop, bar and rooftop restaurant.
Wheelchair access from Via Milano, 9A.

Trastevere

Cloisters and art cinemas, restaurants and craft workshops: the Tiber's west bank is one of Rome's most characterful quarters.

There has been a small colony on the west bank of the Tiber (across the Tiber – *trans Tiberim* – hence Trastevere) since the foundation of Rome, reached by a ford where the Ponte Palatino now crosses from Piazza Bocca della Verità. During the Empire, Trastevere was sufficiently important to be included within the **Aurelian Wall**, the main gates of which still exist (now Porta Portese and Porta San Pancrazio). The area consisted mainly of vegetable gardens, orchards and hunting forests owned by noble families, most famously the Caesars (Cleopatra is thought to have stayed here).

After the fall of the Empire Trastevere was gradually colonised by Syrian and Jewish trading communities, and the remains of an early synagogue can still be seen in Vicolo dell'Atleta. In the early Middle Ages the Jews moved out and across the Tiber to the **Ghetto**, and in time Trastevere became established as the main working-class district of the papal capital.

In the two centuries prior to Italian unification, and for a while after, there was a strong tradition of violent rivalry between the *bulli trasteverini*

(Trastevere toughs) and the *monticiani* (the boys from **Monti**). The gangs, their leaders, and their stone-throwing battles, knife-fights and frequent fatalities became enshrined in popular lore, a prototype *West Side Story* duly written down by dialect poet Giuseppe Gioacchino Belli (1791-1863) and illustrated by Hogarth-meets-Goya cartoonist Bartolomeo Pinelli (1781-1835). The 200-odd sonnets by the former (whose top-hatted statue now graces Piazza Belli, the taxi-rank at the beginning of Viale Trastevere) are still a useful way to make sense of the character and philosophy of the modern-day Roman. Despite the fact that Trastevere strove hard to prove itself a separate city, the good-humoured cynicism, proud independence and fun-loving vulgarity that set it apart have now come to be regarded as quintessentially Roman traits.

Today, Trastevere contends with **Testaccio** across the river for the title of *er core de Roma* – the heart of Rome. Trastevere still puts up a good fight. Although many of its apartments have fallen into the hands of assorted foreigners, the locals have not allowed this to throw them off their stride:

Only Trastevere kids disturb the silence of the **Orto Botanico.** *See page 75.*

old ladies sit outside their kitchen doors commenting on passers-by as they shell the peas; neighbours shout to one another across the street from high windows; and carpenters whittle and floury bakers bake in shops and workshops sandwiched between wine bars and restaurants.

THE LAYOUT

Trastevere is divided into two sharply different sectors by the traffic-snarled avenue of the same name. South of the *viale* is a quiet, evocative enclave where you will find the highest concentration of genuine locals. The warren of lanes around the church of **Santa Cecilia** is a good place to wander aimlessly, watching local craftsmen at work. This area faces the ***Isola Tiberina***, or Tiber Island. Connected to the mainland by two bridges, both of ancient origin, the island is peopled during the day by pyjama-clad patients from its venerable Fatebenefratelli (Do-Good Brothers) hospital. To the north of the *viale* lies the true tourist mecca: all streets seem to lead to the stunning **Piazza di Santa Maria in Trastevere**. This still manages to preserve an aura of ancient calm, despite the impromptu football matches played against the walls of its church and the fiendish mandolin-strummers who serenade the diners at its two over-priced restaurants.

In some streets in this area, notably Vicolo del Cinque and Via della Scala, it seems that every ground-floor space is a restaurant, a 'piano bar', or a herbal bookshop with tea-room attached. When the bustle gets too much, escape with a stroll along Via della Lungara. Widened and paved by Pope Julius II to mirror his Via Giulia on the other bank of the Tiber, it contains some of Rome's finest *palazzi*, including the Raphael-frescoed **Villa Farnesina**, and the **Palazzo Corsini**, backing onto the beautiful **Orto Botanico** botanical garden. Not to mention the notorious Regina Coeli, a medieval prison still in use.

Above the prison, the hillside park of the **Gianicolo** offers a chance for prisoners' spouses to shout messages down to their locked-up loved-ones during exercise hour. Reached by the tortuous Via Garibaldi, which passes by the baroque **Fontana Paola**, the Gianicolo provides Rome's most spectacular view. The spreading pine tree and statue-dotted gardens are dominated by an enormous equestrian statue of Giuseppe Garibaldi, close to which a cannon is fired every day at noon.

Santa Cecilia's hidden garden. See page 73.

from the original **Saint Peter's** basilica. The fountain was designed in 1612 by Flaminio Ponzio and Giovanni Fontana for Pope Paul V, from whom it takes its name. It was built to celebrate the reopening of an ancient aqueduct, built by Emperor Trajan (AD 98-117) to bring water from Lake Bracciano.

Piazza di Santa Maria in Trastevere

Bus/tram to Piazza Sonnino. **Map 6/2B**
This is the heart and soul of Trastevere, a traffic-free cobbled square. Overlooking the fountain, designed by Carlo Fontana in 1692, are the fantastic thirteenth-century mosaics on the façade of **Santa Maria in Trastevere**, one of the oldest churches in Rome. Legend has it that a miraculous well of oil sprang from this spot when Christ was born, and flowed to the Tiber all day. A small street leading out of the piazza, Via della Fonte dell'Olio (Oil Well Street), commemorates the miracle.

Palazzi

Casa della Fornarina

Via di Santa Dorotea, 20. Bus to Lungotevere Sanzio or Piazza Sonnino. **Map 6/2B**
This unassuming house, with a pretty window high on the façade and a granite column embedded in its wall, is believed to have been that of Margherita, *La Fornarina* (the Baker's Girl), Raphael's model and lover for many years. Universally considered a fallen

Piazze & fountains

Fontana Paola

Via Giuseppe Garibaldi. Bus to Gianicolo or Via G. Carini. **Map 6/2C**
This huge fountain on the Gianicolo hill was intended, like the **Fontana dell'Acqua Felice**, to resemble a triumphal arch. The columns used came

woman for her very publicly untoward conduct with the artist, poor Margherita was then rejected by Raphael on his death-bed, as he sought to atone for his life of sin and debauchery. According to local lore, she took refuge in the convent of Sant'Apollonia in the Piazza Santa Margherita, just around the corner from her home.

Villa Farnesina

Via della Lungara, 230 (06 6880 1767). Bus to Lungotevere Farnesina or Piazza Sonnino. **Open** 9am-1pm Mon-Sat. **Admission** L8,000. **Map 6/1B**
This pretty villa was built in 1508-11 by Baldassare Peruzzi, as a pleasure palace and holiday home for the rich papal banker and party-giver Agostino Chigi. The powerful Farnese family bought and renamed it in 1577, when the Chigis went bankrupt. Chigi was one of Raphael's principal patrons, and in its day the villa was stuffed with great works of art, although many were later sold to pay off debts. The stunning frescoes in the ground floor Loggia of Psyche were designed by Raphael but executed by his friends and followers, including Giulio Romano; according to local lore the master himself was too busy dallying with *La Fornarina* (*see above*) to contribute any more than was strictly necessary. The *Grace* with her back turned, to the right of the door,

Queen Christina: did she want to be alone?

Pope Alexander VII was overjoyed when Europe's best-known Protestant monarch, Queen Christina of Sweden, abdicated her throne to embrace Catholicism in 1655. But he – and his three successors – came to regret the massive welcome put on for her arrival, when Bernini redesigned the **Piazza del Popolo** in her honour (*see page 55*).

The witty, learned Christina (1626-89) had become queen-elect on the death of her father in 1631, when she was just five. His last wish – that she be educated as a boy – was carried out to the letter. By the age of 14, this child prodigy was having her say in council meetings. In 1644 she was crowned, and promptly banished her advisors and took power into her own hands. Her court was packed with scholars and writers; Descartes spent the last years of his life with her. Then, in 1654, pleading illness, she shocked her country by abdicating in favour of her cousin. It was not, though, illness that drove her to abandon her throne, but terror of marriage and a religious crisis.

Christina's existential hiccough did nothing to undermine her self-confidence, as the pope found to his dismay. Not long after her triumphal entry into Rome she publicly condemned the church's empty public acts of piety; and, not sated by building up a huge collection of books and Venetian art in her Trastevere palazzo, she took to politicking. Clearly at a loose end with no country to run, she made a pact with the French (unbeknown to the pope) to oust the Spanish from Naples and place her on the Neapolitan throne. The French got cold feet about their queen-designate and pulled out in 1657, when she had her equerry executed for no apparent reason while on a visit to Paris. Later, in 1667, she attempted to snatch the Polish throne from her second cousin. The current pope, Clement IX, must have heaved a sigh of relief, followed by a shudder of horror when she gave up her plan because she had realised it would take her too far from her much-loved home in the Eternal City.

To keep herself busy in Rome she also entered fully into the Machiavellian manoeuvring in the Vatican. In doing so she took as her lover the brilliant and influential Cardinal Decio Azzolino. Their letters show real affection, but this was of little comfort to the pope: on the streets of Rome, denigrators jeered at a Church that imported foreign converts only to have them seduce its priests.

*Wise and foolish virgins get together at **Santa Maria in Trastevere**. See page 71.*

is attributed to him. Around the corner, in the Loggia of Galatea, Raphael took brush in hand to create the victorious goddess in her sea-shell chariot. Up the white-panelled stairs is the *Salone delle Prospettive*, painted by Peruzzi with views of sixteenth-century Rome. Next to it is Agostino Chigi's bedroom, with a fresco of the *Marriage of Alexander the Great and Roxanne* by Sodoma. Like most of his paintings, this is a rather sordid number showing the couple being relieved of their clothes by vicious little cherubs.

Churches

Santa Cecilia in Trastevere

Piazza Santa Cecilia (06 589 9289).
Bus or tram to Viale Trastevere. **Open** *church, crypt and excavations* 8am-6pm Mon, Tue, Thur, Fri, Sun; 8am-2pm, 4-6pm Wed, Sat. *Cavallini frescoes* 10-11.30am Tue, Thur; occasional Suns.
Admission *excavations & crypt* L4,000; *Cavallini frescoes* donation expected. **Map 6/2A**
This pretty church stands on the site of a fifth-century building that was built in turn over a Roman house, the bath and store rooms of which can still be visited beneath the church. According to legend it was the home of Valerio, a Roman patrician who was so impressed (or perhaps frustrated) by his Christian wife Cecilia's maintaining her vow of chastity that he too converted. Valerio was martyred for his pains, and Cecilia was arrested while trying to bury his body. Her martyrdom was something of a botched job – after a failed attempt to suffocate her in the hot steam baths of her house, her persecutors tried to behead her with three strokes of an axe (the

maximum permitted). She took several days to die, which, the legend goes on, she spent singing. Hence she became the patron saint of music. Her tomb was opened in 1599, revealing her still-undecayed body. It rapidly disintegrated, but not before a sketch had been made, on which Stefano Maderna based the astonishingly delicate sculpture that lies below the high altar. Her sarcophagus can be seen in the crypt.

Make sure your visit to this church coincides with the very short periods when you can see a small remaining fragment of what must have been one of the world's greatest frescoes. Pietro Cavallini's late thirteenth-century *Last Judgment* is high up in the gallery, and miraculously survived later rebuildings. While still working within a Byzantine framework, Cavallini floods the seated apostles with a totally new kind of light (note the depth of the faces) – the same light that was to reappear in Giotto's work, and which has led a growing number of scholars to believe that Cavallini, not Giotto, was responsible for the Saint Francis fresco cycle in Assisi.

San Francesco a Ripa

Piazza San Francesco d'Assisi, 88 (06 581 9020).
Bus or tram to Viale Trastevere.
Open 7am-noon, 4-7pm, daily. **Map 7/1B**
In a quiet corner of Trastevere, this seventeenth-century church stands on the site of the hospice where Saint Francis of Assisi stayed when he visited Rome in 1219. The original church was built by Rodolfo Anguillara, one of Francis' richer followers, in the thirteenth century. It was entirely rebuilt in the 1680s, and today its unremarkable baroque interior rings to the guitar-strumming of a thriving

parish church. It's most visited for Bernini's sculpture of the *Beata Ludovica Albertoni* (1674), showing the aristocratic Franciscan nun dying in one of those agonised, sexually ambiguous baroque ecstasies (*see p69*, **Santa Maria della Vittoria**). A near-contemporary portrait of St Francis hangs in the cell said to have been occupied by the monk himself; if the sacristan is feeling so inclined, he'll take you in and show you the rock that Francis used as a pillow. The *Ripa* of the church's name refers to its position a stone's throw from what was Rome's main riverside port area, the *Ripa Grande*.

Santa Maria in Trastevere

Piazza Santa Maria in Trastevere (06 581 4302).
Bus or tram to Viale Trastevere.
Open 7am-1.30pm, 3.30-7pm, daily. **Map 6/2B**
The first church on this site was begun in 337 by Pope Julius I, one of the first in Rome to be dedicated to the Virgin. The present building was erected for Pope Innocent II in the twelfth-century, and has wonderful mosaics. Those on the façade – from the twelfth and thirteenth centuries – show Mary breast-feeding Christ, and ten women with crowns and lanterns on a gold background. Their significance is uncertain, as they have been altered over the years, but they may represent the parable of the wise and foolish virgins. Inside, the apse has a twelfth-century mosaic of Jesus and his mother; the figure holding the church on the far left is Pope Innocent. Lower down, between the windows, there are beautiful thirteenth-century mosaics showing scenes from the life of the Virgin by Pietro Cavallini (*see* **Santa Cecilia**), whose relaxed, realistic figures represent the re-emergence of a Roman style after long years of hegemony of Byzantine models. The *Madonna and Child* with rainbow overhead is also by Cavallini. Through the wooden door on the left, just before entering the transept, there are two tiny, exquisite fragments of first century AD mosaics from **Palestrina** (*see chapter* **Trips out of Town**), and in the chapel immediately to the left of the high altar is a very rare sixth century painting on wood of the Madonna.

Tempietto di Bramante
& San Pietro in Montorio

Piazza San Pietro in Montorio, 2 (06 581 3940).
Bus to Porta San Pancrazio or Viale Glorioso.
Open 8am-noon, 4-6pm, daily. **Map 6/2C**
High up on the **Gianicolo**, on the spot where Saint Peter was once believed to have been crucified, San Pietro in Montorio commands the finest view of any church in Rome. It also has one of Rome's greatest architectural gems in its courtyard: the **Tempietto**, designed by Bramante in 1508. This much-copied round construction was the first modern building to follow exactly the proportions of the classical orders (in this case, Doric, *see chapter* **Architecture**).

Hidden cloisters & secret gardens

Trastevere's lesser-known areas conceal cloisters and gardens that rank among Rome's loveliest. Beginning in the noisy market square of **Piazza San Cosimato**, enter the gateway of the **Nuova Regina Margherita** hospital at number 76, and follow the signs to the *Endoscopia Digestiva* department. In this unlikely setting you will find a Romanesque cloister from the eleventh century, its arches supported by a double row of delicate columns, around a central lawn packed with dressing-gowned patients and their visitors. The wall to your left has early Christian reliefs set into it; a set of steps (helpfully signposted *Day Hospital Gastroenterologia*) leads to a fifteenth-century cloister with octagonal columns.

Cross the traffic-clogged **Viale Trastevere** on the other side of the hospital, then take **Via San Francesco a Ripa** to the square at its end, and turn right into **Via Anicia**. Beyond the sixteenth-century church of **Santa Maria dell'Orto**, there is a wooden door that opens (only *Apr-Oct* 3-6pm, Tue and Thur; *Nov-Mar*, 2-4pm Tue and Thur; ring the bell marked *Sposito* to get in) into a glorious flower-filled cloister with a well at its centre, part of a fifteenth-century hospice for Genoese sailors. Concealed among the octagonal columns supporting the double loggia is a plaque commemorating Rome's first ever palm tree, planted here in 1588.

At the northern end of Via Anicia take a right into **Via dei Genovesi**, and then first right again into **Via di Santa Cecilia**. Behind a high wall on your right lies the beautiful garden of the church of **Santa Cecilia**, its climbing roses and jasmine perfuming the air. From outside the church, cross **Piazza dei Mercanti** and turn left into **Vicolo Santa Maria in Cappella**. In the courtyard at number six is the tiny chapel after which the street is named; its diminutive bell tower is believed to be the oldest in Rome. Ring the doorbell at the door to your right; a friendly nun will allow you a look at the garden inside, created in the seventeenth century for a sister-in-law of Pope Innocent X. This little oasis has tidy garden beds surrounded by citrus trees and cascading plumbago. Pensioners from the old people's home that now occupies it knit and picnic among the verdure.

Bernini got his hands on it in 1628, adding the staircase that leads down to the crypt. The church itself, founded in the ninth century and rebuilt in the late fifteenth, contains a chapel by Bernini (second on the left) and one by Vasari (fifth on the right). Paintings include Sebastiano del Piombo's *Flagellation*, and a *Crucifixion of Saint Peter* by Guido Reni.

Museums & galleries

Galleria Nazionale d'Arte Antica (Palazzo Corsini)

Via della Lungara, 10 (06 6880 2323).
Bus to Lungotevere della Farnesina or Piazza Sonnino. **Open** 9am-7pm Tue-Fri; 9am-1.30pm Sat, Sun. **Admission** L8,000. **Map 6/1C**

This palace, designed in stages by Ferdinando Fuga between 1738 and 1758, incorporated the Palazzo Riario of 1510, once the Roman residence of the seventeenth-century's highest-profile convert to Catholicism, Queen Christina of Sweden (*see p72*). A plaque marks the room in which she died in 1689. Today the palace houses part of the national art collection, the bulk of which is in the **Palazzo Barberini** (*see p68*). The galleries are beautifully painted with frescoes and *trompe l'œils* and mostly house paintings from the sixteenth and seventeenth centuries. There are the usual scores of Holy Families, and Madonnas and Children (the most memorable a *Madonna* by Van Dyck). Other works include a sensual pair of Annunciations by Guercino; two Saint Sebastians, one by Rubens, the other by Annibale Carracci; Caravaggio's unadorned *Narcissus*; and a triptych by Fra Angelico. The works by Guido Reni also stand out, notably the melancholy *Salome*. The original palace grounds behind the building are now Rome's botanical garden, the **Orto Botanico**.

Museo del Folklore e dei Poeti Romaneschi

Piazza Sant'Egidio, 1b (06 581 6563). Tram to Viale Trastevere. **Open** 9am-7pm Tue-Sat; 9am-1pm Sun. **Admission** L3,750. **Map 6/2B**

Rome's folklore museum is housed in a seventeenth-century convent formerly occupied by Carmelite nuns. It contains an entertaining collection of period paintings and prints, along with a series of waxwork tableaux relating to the life, work, pastimes and superstitions of the man in the street in eighteenth- and nineteenth-century Italy. Don't miss the riotous nativity scene set in the busy back streets of Naples. Closed for restoration for some time, it was due to reopen in October 1999 with new spaces for one-off exhibits on salt-of-the-earth themes.

Parks & gardens

Gianicolo

Bus to Gianicolo. **Map 6/2C**
The hill of the Janiculum, as it was known in ancient times, offers the best view over the city and, on a clear day, to the mountains beyond. In 1849 it was

Patriots galore on the **Gianicolo***.*

the scene of one of the fiercest battles in the struggle for Italian unity, when Giuseppe Garibaldi and his makeshift army defended the Roman Republic against French troops sent to restore papal rule (*see chapter* **History**). There is an equestrian statue of him in the middle of the square, while the busts that line the road are those of the thousand martyrs of Italy's *Risorgimento*. If you carry on past the equestrian statue of Garibaldi's equally heroic wife Anita, you will reach a curious lighthouse, the patriotic gift of Italian emigrants in Argentina. The view from this part of the hill takes in the ochre shades of medieval and baroque Rome. At the Vatican end of the walk, opposite the Bambino Gesù children's hospital, you overlook **Saint Peter's** and the **Castel Sant'Angelo**.

Orto Botanico

Via Corsini (06 4991 7106). Bus to Lungotevere Farnesina or Piazza Sonnino. **Open** 9am-5.30pm Mon-Sat. **Admission** L4,000. **Map 6/2C**

Established in 1883, when part of the grounds of the **Palazzo Corsini** was donated to Rome University, the Orto Botanico contains some 7,000 species in wondrous green exuberance, barely held in check: here there is none of the sterile order that can render botanical gardens in northern climes so cold. Plants tumble over steps and into fountains and fishponds, creating verdant hidden corners disturbed only by frolicking children, parked here by Trastevere mums.

Monti & Esquilino

Amid pompous palazzi and fume-filled streets, Monti and Esquilino contain some of Rome's most impressive ancient relics and grandest papal basilicas.

Stretching from the **Imperial Fora** to **Stazione Termini** and Rome's main university campus, these two *rioni* (districts) are criss-crossed by some of the city's busiest and least interesting streets dominated by more than their fair share of dismal bureaucratic *palazzi*. This said, there are several unmissable sights, such as **Trajan's Markets** and the **Museo Nazionale Romano**, not to mention a great market and the nearest thing Rome has to a multi-cultural zone.

A single *rione* until 1874, Monti and Esquilino were once ancient Rome's most exclusive suburbs, their green heights dotted with patrician villas and temples. Paradoxically, they overlooked one of the city's worst slums: the grimy, thronging *Suburra* area, in the marshy swamp between the Quirinal, Viminal and Esquiline hills.

Barbarian invasions forced Rome's élite down from their hilltop residences to the relative safety of what is now the *centro storico*, close to the Tiber. The hill areas went into decline and, despite being well within the **Aurelian Wall**, remained almost uninhabited until the Middle Ages, when Monti became the battleground of bullish families such as the Conti, Frangipani, Annibali, Caetani and Capocci, who are remembered in the names of local streets. Each clan constructed its own fortress, with its own *torre* (tower). At the end of the thirteenth century, when anarchy reached its peak, Rome bristled with 200 towers; of the dozen that remain over half are in this area, including the Torre delle Milizie behind **Trajan's Markets**.

In the sixteenth century Sixtus V, the great town planner of Counter-Reformation Rome, definitively reincorporated the area into the city. He ordered the building of the great Via Felice, which stretches (nowadays changing names several times along its length) from the top of the **Spanish Steps** in the north to **Santa Croce in Gerusalemme** in the south, a dead-straight 3.5km sweep. Until the building of Via Nazionale and Via Cavour 300 years later, the whole *rione* developed around this axis. However, as late as the 1850s 70 per cent of Monti and Esquilino was still farmland or classical ruins.

Italian unification brought dramatic changes to the area. As well as being split into two separate *rioni*, Monti and Esquilino became a hub of the newly-formed state. Architect Quintino Sella

Cavorting in **Piazza della Repubblica**.

designed a ministerial and administrative district focusing on the semi-circular, arcaded **Piazza della Repubblica**, from which Via Nazionale descends to the old centre. The arrival of the railway at Termini in the 1860s had already attracted a rush of frenzied speculators, who snapped up most of the surrounding land. A decade later, with Rome the capital of unified Italy, they made an even bigger killing. The ancient ruins dotting the area were swept away, and a whole new city-within-a-city was built in the grid mode favoured by the ruling Turinese, covering nearly 300 hectares.

Aesthetically, the fruits of the Unification building boom have little to offer. Dotted among them, however, are such gems as the **Baths of Diocletian**, **Trajan's Markets**, and a clutch of stunning early churches (**San Pietro in Vincoli**, **Santa Prassede** and **San Martino ai Monti**). Moreover, the ancient *Suburra* slum still has a real life of its own. Here you find Via dei Serpenti, the villagey high street that connects Via Nazionale and its carbon-copy high-street fashion emporia with dreary Via Cavour; Piazza degli Zingari, the pretty site of a medieval gypsy encampment; and Via dei Capocci, long a centre of prostitution.

The area between Termini and **Piazza Vittorio Emanuele** is as close as Rome gets to an ethnic zone. Shops selling food and goods from around the world are frequented mostly by natives of the countries in question, which can be a refreshing change from the overwhelmingly Roman atmosphere of the rest of Piazza Vittorio market. After dark, this area gets seriously sleazy, and its very advisable to take care.

If you've had your fill of the picturesque and need a shot of the Kafkaesque, take a look at such monolithic examples of Italian public architecture as the Interior Ministry in Piazza del Viminale, the Bank of Italy headquarters at Palazzo Koch on Via Nazionale, the **Teatro dell'Opera** in Via Firenze, and the Sisde secret police headquarters on Via Lanza. Or wander down undulating Via Panisperna, past the lab where in 1934 Enrico Fermi and Ettore Majorana first split the atom.

Other highlights include the massive basilica of **San Giovanni in Laterano**, immediately recognizable by the host of gigantic statue-saints partying atop its façade, and the remains of Nero's *Domus Aurea* (*see page 80*) in the Colle Oppio park, which is frequented at night by Rome's far-right youth and a sprinkling of its more foolhardy gays. In their rush to cover the two *rioni* with lucrative bricks and mortar, Unification planners gave little thought to greenery. Besides the Colle Oppio, the only green lung is the endearing hanging garden of **Villa Aldobrandini**.

Piazze & fountains

Piazza dei Cinquecento & Stazione Termini

Metro Termini/bus to Piazza del Cinquecento.
Map 5/2A

Piazza dei Cinquecento had a major facelift in the 1990s, and now provides a fitting setting for Stazione Termini, one of the most remarkable modern buildings in Italy. Architect Angiolo Mazzoni produced a triumph of undulating horizontal geometry, complete with tubular towers of metaphysical grace straight out of a De Chirico painting. Building began in 1938 but was interrupted by the war, and the station was not inaugurated until 1950.

Piazza della Repubblica

Metro Repubblica/bus to Piazza della Repubblica.
Map 5/2B

Better known to Romans as Piazza Esedra, this heavily-trafficked roundabout is the traditional starting point for major demonstrations, and a favourite hang-out for the motley overflow from **Stazione Termini**. The Fontana delle Naiadi at its centre was due for unveiling in 1901, but the nudity of the art-nouveau nymphs cavorting seductively with sea monsters around it so shocked authorities that it was boarded up again for years. Locals fed up with the eyesore tore the planks down, in an undignified inauguration. Sculptor Mario Rutelli is said to have returned to Rome once a year for the rest of his life just to take his buxom models out to dinner.

Piazza Vittorio Emanuele

Metro Vittorio/bus to Piazza Vittorio Emanuele.
Map 8/1A

The neighbourhood around this large square – always abbreviated to Piazza Vittorio – was designed to be one of Rome's smartest when it was built at the turn of the twentieth century. You'd never know it now. A steady decline into characterless slum-hood was halted in the 1980s by the arrival of a multi-ethnic community, which has injected some life and colour into the run-down streets around the square. The piazza continues to host central Rome's biggest and most cosmopolitan morning food market (*see chapter* **Shopping**), despite plans (proposed for decades) to remove it to a more salubrious location nearby. Behind the market stalls, the revamped gardens at the heart of Piazza Vittorio offer a cool place to rest in the shade of palm trees. As you do so, have a go at breaking the still-encoded recipe for changing base metal into gold on the *Porta Magica*; this curious door, with hermetic inscriptions dating from 1688, is all that remains of the Villa Palombara, an estate that once occupied this site.

Ancient Rome

Baths of Diocletian (*Terme di Diocleziano*)

Via Enrico de Nicola, 79; Via Romita, 8 (06 488 0530). Metro Repubblica/bus to Piazza della Repubblica. **Map 5/1A**

Diocletian's baths, built from AD 298-306, were the largest in Rome, covering over a hectare and able to accommodate 3,000 people at a time. For an idea of the immense size of the structure, tour the remaining fragments: the *tepidarium* and part of the central hall are in the church of Santa Maria degli Angeli (Piazza della Repubblica); a circular hall can be seen in the church of San Bernardo alle Terme (Piazza San Bernardo); and the *aula ottagona* (Octagonal Hall), which used to house Rome's planetarium, is in Via Romita (open 9am-2pm Tue-Sat; 9am-1pm Sun; admission free). A convent complex was built around the largest surviving chunk of the baths by

Michelangelo in the 1560s. For years this housed Italy's state collection of Roman artefacts, the **Museo Nazionale Romano**. This has now been comprehensively reorganised, and the bulk of the collection relocated to **Palazzo Altemps** (*see chapter Centro Storico*) and **Palazzo Massimo alle Terme**. The baths building will reopen in 1999-2000 (*see p83*).

Imperial Fora (*Fori Imperiali*)

Via dei Fori Imperiali. Metro Colosseo/bus to Colosseum. **Open** with prior permission only (*see p33* **Getting through locked gates**). **Map 8/1C**

This area, across Via dei Fori Imperiali from the main **Forum** (*see chapter Centro Storico*) and all clearly visible from the main road, consists of five separate *fora*, each built by a different emperor. As the existing *fora* became too small to cope with the legal, social and commercial life of the city, the emperors combined philanthropy with propaganda, and created new ones of their own. All but one was built to celebrate a military triumph. Mussolini thought fit to slice through the remains to build the multi-laned Via dei Fori Imperiali (he was, after all, planning to create a bigger, better empire of his own). Archaeologists are now hard at work to redress the balance, digging up every square inch that doesn't have traffic thundering over it, but a drastic plan for doing away altogether with the Via dei Fori Imperiali is unlikely to take shape in the foreseeable future.

The earliest of the Imperial Fora was begun by Julius Caesar in 51 BC, after he had conquered Gaul. Augustus built his in 31 BC after he had avenged Caesar's death. In the 'Temple of Peace' in the Forum of Vespasian, of AD 71, the treasures looted from the Temple of Jerusalem were displayed. This event was also commemorated in the reliefs on the **Arch of Titus** in the **Roman Forum**. A Temple to Minerva was the main feature of the Forum of Nerva, dated AD 98. Part of its original frieze survives. Most ambitious of all the *fora* was the Forum of Trajan, built in AD 113 after the emperor had annexed Dacia – roughly present-day Romania. The story of his campaign against the Dacians is told in the beautifully carved reliefs spiralling up **Trajan's Column**, which stands on the western fringe of Piazza Venezia. The column is 38m high, and has over 100 scenes carved up its sides. They were originally painted, and would have been easily visible from galleries on the nearby buildings. They are difficult to see today, but there are replicas in the **Museo della Civiltà Romana** in **EUR** (*see chapter Oher parts of town*), which help appreciate the extraordinary detail. The statue of Saint Peter atop the column was added by Pope Sixtus V in 1587 to replace the original one of Trajan. East of the column are **Trajan's Markets**.

Trajan's Markets (*Mercati Traiani*)

Via IV Novembre, 94 (06 679 0048).
Bus to Via Nazionale. **Open** 9am-6.30pm Tue-Sun.
Admission L3,750. **Map 8/1C**
This indoor market was built on the orders of Trajan in the first decade of the second century AD. Designed by Apollodorus of Damascus (later executed by Hadrian on suspicion of treachery), it is an ancient Roman equivalent of a shopping mall. The most distinctive feature is a multi-storey brick crescent or *hemicycle*, which gives access into Trajan's Forum in the **Imperial Fora**. At the back of the crescent is a large hall, which may have been used for the distribution of the corn dole (*see chapter* **History**). In total there were five levels to the building, containing about 150 small shops. They were probably organised into areas – the ground floor for wine and oil, first floor for fruit and flowers, and so on. The shops are all empty now, but are mostly intact, and you can still see some of the ridges into which shutters were dropped at closing time.

Attached to the market are several medieval buildings, including the Torre delle Milizie (militia tower), part of a fortress built for Pope Gregory IX in the thirteenth century. For years it was erroneously believed to be the place from where Nero watched Rome burn, after he had supposedly set fire to it.

Churches

Santa Croce in Gerusalemme

Piazza di Santa Croce in Gerusalemme, 12 (06 701 4769). Bus or tram to Piazza di Porta Maggiore. **Open** 8am-7pm daily.
Founded in 320 by Helena, the redoubtable mother of Emperor Constantine (*see chapter* **History**), this church just east of **San Giovanni in Laterano** (**Map 8/2A**), began as a hall in her home, the Sessorian palace. It was rebuilt and extended in the twelfth century, and again in 1743-4. The outline of the original building can be seen from the grounds of the **Museo Nazionale degli Strumenti Musicali**. It was built to house the fragments of Christ's cross brought back from the Holy Land by Saint Helena, which are now housed behind glass in a Fascist-era chapel, with lashings of grey marble, off the left side of the nave. As well as three pieces of the cross and a nail, there are two thorns from Christ's crown, a section of the good thief's cross and the finger of Saint Thomas – allegedly the very one the doubting saint stuck into Christ's wound. Bagfuls of soil from Calvary lie under the tiles in the charming lower chapel beneath the altar; the chapel's mosaics were laid in the fifth century, but redesigned around 1484 by Melozzo di Forlì. A plaque on the wall states that women are only allowed into the chapel on one day a year, a rule that is now overlooked.

San Giovanni in Laterano

Piazza di San Giovanni in Laterano, 4 (06 6988 6433). Metro San Giovanni/bus or tram to Piazza San Giovanni. **Open** *church* 7am-5.45pm, *baptistry* 9am-1pm, 4-6pm, *cloister & museum* 9am-6pm, daily.
Admission *cloister & museum* L4,000. **Map 8/2A**
San Giovanni was built in around 313, on a site given to Pope Melchiades for the purpose by the Emperor Constantine himself. It is Rome's official cathedral. Little remains of the original basilica, which has been sacked, destroyed by fire and earthquake and

heavily restored and rebuilt over the centuries. San Giovanni long suffered from being in an under-populated area of the city, near-impossible to defend.

The façade, surmounted by 15 huge statues, dates from the final rebuilding and was designed by Alessandro Gallei in 1735. The interior was last transformed in 1646 by Borromini, who encased the original columns in pillars and stucco. The enormous bronze doors in the main entrance came originally from the Senate House in the **Roman Forum**. A thirteenth-century mosaic in the apse survived the modernisation, as did a fragment of fresco attributed to Giotto (behind the first column on the right); it shows Pope Boniface VIII announcing the first Holy Year in 1300 (*see chapter* **History**). Another survivor is the Gothic *baldacchino* over the main altar; the two busts behind the grille were once believed to hold the heads of Saints Peter and Paul. Off the left aisle is the thirteenth-century cloister: the twisted columns, studded with mosaics, were made by the Vassalletto family. Remains from the original basilica also appear around the walls. The central well is ninth-century. A small museum off the cloister contains vestments, and manuscripts of music by Palestrina.

The north façade was added in 1586 by Domenico Fontana. On its right is the octagonal baptistry, founded by Constantine and rebuilt in 432 and 1637. Now restored after a bomb exploded nearby in 1993,

it holds fine fifth- and seventh-century mosaics. On the eastern side of Piazza San Giovanni are the remaining sections of the former papal residence, the Lateran Palace, the recently-restored (but, sadly, inaccessible to the public) *Sancta Sanctorum*, formerly the pope's private chapel, and the *Scala Santa*, or Holy Staircase. These 28 steps were once the ceremonial staircase of the old palace, but are traditionally believed to be those Christ climbed on his way to trial at Pontius Pilate's house in Jerusalem. They were supposedly brought to Rome by Constantine's mother, Saint Helena. Devout pilgrims ascend on their knees, particularly on Good Friday. In 1510 Martin Luther gave this a go, but half-way up the steps decided that relics were a theological irrelevance, and walked back down again.

Santa Maria Maggiore

Piazza Santa Maria Maggiore (06 483 195).
Bus to Piazza Esquilino or Piazza Santa Maria
Maggiore. **Open** *church* 7am-7pm , *loggia* 9.30am-5pm, daily. **Admission** *loggia* L5,000. **Map 8/1B**
Behind this blowsy baroque façade is one of the most striking basilica-form churches in Rome. Local tradition says a church was built on this spot c366; documents place it almost 100 years later. The fifth-century church was first extended in the thirteenth century, and again prior to the 1750 Holy Year, when Ferdinando Fuga overhauled the interior and attached the façade that we see today.

Inside, a flat-roofed nave shoots between two aisles to a triumphal arch and apse. Above the columns of the nave, heavily-restored fifth-century mosaics show scenes from the Old Testament. Thirteenth-century mosaics in the apse by Jacopo Torriti show Mary, dressed as a Byzantine Empress, being crowned Queen of Heaven by Christ. The Virgin theme continues in fifth-century mosaics on the triumphal arch. The ceiling in the main nave is said to have been made from the first shipment of gold extracted from the Americas by Ferdinand and Isabella of Spain, and was presented to the church by the Borgia Pope, Alexander VI. The Borgias' bull heraldic device is very much in evidence. In the sixteenth and seventeenth centuries, two incredibly flamboyant chapels were added. The first was the *Cappella Sistina* (last chapel on right of nave), designed by Domenico Fontana for Sixtus V (1585-90), and decorated with multi-coloured marble, gilt and precious stones. Sixtus had ancient buildings ransacked for materials, and employed virtually every sculptor working in the city. Directly opposite is the *Cappella Paolina*, an even gaudier Greek-cross chapel, designed by Flaminio Ponzio in 1611 for Paul V to house the ninth- (possibly twelfth) century icon of the Madonna on the altar.

To the right of the main altar a plaque marks the burial place of Rome's great baroque genius Gianlorenzo Bernini, and his father Pietro. In the loggia high up on the front of the church (tours leave the baptistry about every ten minutes; notes are provided in English) are thirteenth-century mosaics that

Trajan's Column in the **Imperial Fora** *(left).*

decorated the façade of the old basilica, showing the legend of the foundation of Santa Maria Maggiore. The lower row shows Mary appearing to Giovanni the Patrician who, with Pope Liberius, then sketches the plan for the basilica. The legend goes that the Virgin told Giovanni to build a church on the spot where snow would fall the next morning. The snow fell on 5 August, 352, a miracle that is commemorated every year, when thousands of flower petals are released from the roof of the church, in the **Festa della Madonna delle Neve** (*see p8*). The Capella Paolina also contains a relief (1612) by Stefano Maderno showing Liberius tracing the plan of the basilica in the snow.

San Pietro in Vincoli

Piazza di San Pietro in Vincoli, 4a (06 488 2865). Metro Cavour/bus to Via Cavour. **Open** 7am-12.30pm, 3.30-6pm, daily. **Map 8/1B**

Built in the fifth century over an earlier church and third-century BC ruins, Saint Peter in Chains was touched up in the eighth, eleventh and fifteenth centuries, and baroque-ified in the eighteenth. Dominating the church is the monument to Pope Julius II and Michelangelo's imposing *Moses* (1515). Julius wanted a final resting place five times this size, with forty statues, in the larger and more prestigious **Saint Peter's** across the Tiber, but he died too soon to check that Michelangelo put in the required work (the artist was otherwise engaged in the Sistine Chapel at the time). His successors were less ambitious. As a result, the mighty Moses (his horns prompted by a bad translation of the Old Testament, where the old Hebrew word for 'radiant' was mistaken for 'horned') is wildly out of proportion with everything else, and infinitely better than the offerings of Michelangelo's students who threw

Nero's golden home

The Emperor Nero, Suetonius tells us, was born as rosy-fingered dawn stretched her digits earth-wards; she poked the new-born babe before she touched the earth, he says. Ancient history does not record whether this early brush with sun-stroke helped to unbalance the adult. It did, however, give Nero a lasting taste for dazzling things.

In the summer of AD 64, a fire devasted a large part of central Rome. The ashes of patrician palaces were mingled with those of slums. Nero sat the conflagation out calmly, strumming on his lute. Afterwards, anything in the area east of the Forum left unsinged (plus a great deal untouched by the fire, but which stood in the way of his masterplan) was knocked down, to make way for a home fit for the sun-god he liked to think he was.

Work began on the ***Domus Aurea***, the 'Golden House', just after the great fire had died down. A three-storey structure, its main, south-facing façade was entirely clad in gold; inside, every inch not faced with mother-of-pearl or inlaid with gems was frescoed by Nero's pet aesthete Fabullus. Fountains squirted rich perfumes, and baths could be filled with sea or mineral waters. In one room, wrote Suetonius, an immense ceiling painted with the sun and stars and signs of the zodiac revolved constantly, keeping perfect time with the heavens.

The house stood in 80 hectares of parkland, stretching from the Palatine to the Celio and Esquiline hills; almost a quarter of the ancient city. Lakes were dug, forests planted, and a gilded bronze statue of Nero 35m high erected:

seven rays of sun shot out of the colossus' crown, and the face was turned up to Nero's heavenly counterpart. 'Now,' said the emperor when his house was complete, 'I can begin to live like a human being.'

Nero's subjects were not so sure he qualified. The moment he was in his grave in AD 68 work began to eradicate every vestige of the hated tyrant. Vespasian drained the lake to build his amphitheatre (the tight-fisted emperor kept Nero's colossus, simply putting a new head on it, and so the stadium became known as the **Colosseum**). Enraged locals dug up the park, and Trajan used the brickwork as a handy foundation for his baths. So thorough was the cover-up job that for decades after the house's frescoes were first rediscovered, in 1480, no one realised it was Nero's *Domus Aurea* that they had stumbled across. The frescoed 'grottoes' became an obligatory stopover for Renaissance artists, inspiring – among many other things – Raphael's weird and wonderful frescoes in the **Vatican** (and incidentally giving us the word 'grotesque').

After years of restoration, some 30 rooms of the *Domus Aurea* re-opened in June 1999. Visits should be booked in advance, especially in high season. Over 100 rooms remain off-limits, and a further 200-odd still wait to be excavated.

Domus Aurea

Viale della Domus Aurea (reservations & information 06 3974 9907/credit card bookings 06 481 5576). Metro Colosseo/bus to Piazza del Colosseo or Via Labicana. **Open** 9am-5pm daily. **Admission** L10,000. **Map 8/2B**

Soaring gilt-trip in the snow-inspired **Santa Maria Maggiore** *(see page 79).*

together the rest. The master's hand can be seen in the statues of *Leah* and *Rachel* either side of the patriarch. He clearly had nothing to do with the statue of poor Julius himself, by Maso del Bosco. Julius was never placed in his tomb, ending up in an unmarked grave across in the Vatican.

If tourists flock here for Michelangelo, believers come for the chains. Eudoxia, wife of Emperor Valentinian III (445-55), was given a set of chains said to have been used to shackle Saint Peter in Jerusalem; when she gave them to Pope Sixtus III, the story goes, he placed them next to others used on the saint in the **Mamertine Prison** and they became miraculously entangled. They are now conserved in a reliquary on the main altar. There are several relics of Saint Peter in Rome – footprints in the church of Santa Francesca Romana, a head print where he butted the wall in the **Mamertine Prison**, his head in **San Giovanni in Laterano** – but the chains are the most venerated of all. They are paraded around Rome every 1 August.

Santa Prassede

Via Santa Prassede, 9a (06 488 2456).
Bus to Piazza Santa Maria Maggiore.
Open 7am-noon, 4-6.30pm, daily. **Map 8/1B**
This church is a scaled-down copy of the old **Saint Peter's**, a ninth-century attempt to recreate an early Christian basilica. Unfortunately, as the uneven brickwork shows, the Romans had lost the knack. The home-grown mosaic artists were no better, so Pope Paschal I decided to import mosaicists from Byzantium to decorate the church. The results are exotic and rich, and what they lack in subtle

modelling they make up for in glorious colours, flowing drapery and fluid movement. In the apse, Christ riding on a cloud is being introduced to the martyr Saint Praxedes by Saint Paul on the right, while Saint Peter is doing the honours on the left for her sister Pudenziana. Pope Paschal is there too, holding a model of the church and sporting a square halo because he was alive when the mosaic was made. Beneath, twelve lambs represent the apostles. The triumphal arch shows the heavenly Jerusalem, with palm-frond-toting martyrs heading for glory.

Off the right side of the nave is the chapel of Saint Zeno, with some of Rome's most spectacular mosaics. Entered beneath a carved architrave pilfered from an ancient site, the chapel is a dazzling swirl of Byzantine blue and gold, punctuated with saints, animals and depictions of Christ and his mother. Wall and ceiling mosaics are ninth-century; the jolly Mary clutching a dwarf-like Jesus and flanked by sister-saints Praxedes and Pudenziana in the niche above the altar is thirteenth century. In a room to the right is a portion of column, said to be part of *the* one that Jesus was tied to for scourging.

Santa Pudenziana

Via Urbana, 160 (06 481 4622).
Metro Cavour/bus to Piazza Esquilino.
Open 8am-noon, 3-6pm, daily. **Map 5/2B**
The mosaic in the apse of Santa Pudenziana dates from the fourth century (although it was hacked about in a brutal restoration in the sixteenth), and so pre-dates the arrival in Rome of the stiff Byzantine style. It is a remarkable example of the continuity between pagan and Christian art, depict-

Hairstyles at **Palazzo Massimo alle Terme**.

ing Christ and the apostles as wealthy Romans framed by very Roman architectural details and wearing togas, against an ancient Roman city-scape and a glorious Turner-esque sunset. Were it not for Christ's halo and symbols of the four evangelists in the sky, it could be taken for a portrait of senators.

Santi Silvestro e Martino ai Monti

Viale del Monte Oppio, 28 (06 486 3126). Bus to Piazza Santa Maria Maggiore or Via Merulana. **Open** *church* 9am-noon, 4.30-6pm, daily; *excavations* 9am-noon, 4.30-6 pm, Mon-Fri. **Admission** *excavations* donation expected. **Map 8/1B**
The main reason to visit here is to see the third-century *titulus* or early Christian meeting-house that is underneath the ninth-century church. It's a spooky and rarely visited place, littered with bits of sculpture, decaying mosaics and frescoes. It does not have the usual jungle of newer foundations sunk through Roman brickwork, and so it's not difficult to picture this as an ancient dwelling and/or place of worship. The church above the *titulus* is chiefly remarkable for two frescoes: one showing San Giovanni in Laterano as it was before Borromini's changes (by Dughet, to the left of the entrance), and the other portraying the original **Saint Peter's** (by Gagliardi, left of the altar).

Museums & galleries

Museo Nazionale d'Arte Orientale

Via Merulana, 248 (06 487 4415). Bus to Via Merulana. **Open** 9am-2pm Mon, Wed, Fri, Sat; 9am-7pm Tue, Thur; 9am-1pm Sun. Closed first & third Mon of each month. **Admission** L8,000. **Map 8/2A**
For a break from unrelenting Roman artefacts try this impressive collection of oriental art, in a gloomy palazzo near Santa Maria Maggiore. It's arranged geographically and roughly chronologically. First are ancient artefacts from the Near East – pottery, gold, votive offerings – some from the third millennium BC. Then come eleventh- to eighteenth-century painted fans from Tibet, sacred sculptures and some Chinese pottery from the fifteenth century; Perhaps most unusual are artefacts from the Swat culture, from Italian-funded excavations in Pakistan. *Wheelchair access.*

Museo Nazionale Romano – Palazzo Massimo alle Terme

Largo di Villa Peretti, 1 (06 481 5576/06 4890 3501). Metro Repubblica/bus to Termini, Piazza della Repubblica. **Open** 9am-7pm Tue-Sat; 9am-2pm Sun. **Admission** L12,000; included in joint ticket with Colosseum, Palatine, rest of MNR *(see p33).* **Map 5/2A**
The Italian state's spectacular collection of ancient art, has undergone a radical reorganisation in the run-up to 2000. It is now divided between the **Baths of Diocletian, Palazzo Altemps** in the *Centro storico* and Palazzo Massimo alle Terme.

In the basement of Palazzo Massimo is an extensive collection of coins from earliest times, Roman luxuries, descriptions of trade routes, and audio-visual aids (all of which make this floor especially appealing to kids). On the ground and first floors are busts of emperors, their families and lesser mortals, in chronological order (allowing you to track changing fashions in Roman hairstyles). The ground floor covers the period up to AD 69. In Room 5 is a magnificent statue of Augustus as *Pontifex Maximus*; Room 8 has a very graceful Muse. The first floor begins from the age of Vespasian (AD 69-79), the first of the Flavians: his pugilistic portrait bust can be seen in Room 1. Room 5 contains statues of Apollo and a young girl holding a tray, both from Nero's villa south of Rome in Anzio, and a gracefully crouching *Aphrodite* from Hadrian's Villa at **Tivoli** *(see chapter* **Trips out of Town**). Room 6 has a marble Roman copy of a Greek discus thrower, cast in bronze in the fifth century BC. In Room 7 is a peacefully sleeping hermaphrodite, a second-century AD copy of a Greek original.

The real treat of the Palazzo Massimo, though, lies on the second floor, where rare wall paintings from different villas have been reassembled (you will be assigned a time for a guided visit when you buy your ticket). The spectacular fresco from the *triclinium* (dining room) of the villa of Augustus' wife Livia in Prima Porta, just north of Rome, has a fruit-filled garden bustling with animal life, and perspective rarely seen again until the Renaissance. A *triclinium* from the original Villa Farnesina (Room 3) has delicate white sketches on a black background, surmounted by scenes of courts handing down sentences that have had experts baffled for centuries. Also in Room 3 is a lively naval battle, from a frescoed corridor in the same villa. The three *cubicoli* (bedrooms) in Room 5 have decorative stuccoed ceilings. Room 10 contains Botero-like larger-than-life (megalographic) paintings, and Room 11 dazzlingly bright marble *intarsio* works. On the ground floor is an excellent gift and bookshop, with many titles in English and a fine range for children. *Wheelchair access.*

Museo Nazionale Romano – Terme di Diocleziano

Via Enrico de Nicola, 79 (06 4880 530). Metro Termini/bus to Termini station. **Open** check locally before visiting; will probably be included in joint MNR ticket *(see p33).* **Map 5/1A**

For years the fourth-century **Baths of Diocletian** (*see p77*) was the main home of the Museo Nazionale Romano, but, despite their size, the baths proved inadequate, and much of the collection was usually in cold storage. It is now divided between **Palazzo Massimo alle Terme** and **Palazzo Altemps**. When the baths building re-opens in 2000, it will contain the stone inscriptions, as well as being presented as an archaeological site in its own right.

Museo Nazionale degli Strumenti Musicali

Piazza Santa Croce in Gerusalemme, 9a (06 701 4796). Metro San Giovanni/bus to Piazza Santa Croce in Gerusalemme. **Open** 9am-7pm Tue, Thur; 9am-2pm Wed, Fri, Sat; 9am-1pm Sun. **Admission** L4,000.

In the early twentieth century opera singer Evan Gorga collected over 800 rare and beautiful musical instruments. The collection gives a comprehensive overview of the history of European music since ancient times. Look out for the exquisite, triple-stringed Barberini harp, a seventeenth-century harpsichord, and elegantly curving lutes and viols.

Museo Storico della Liberazione di Roma

Via Tasso, 145 (06 700 3866). Metro San Giovanni/bus to Piazza San Giovanni in Laterano. **Open** 4-7pm Tue, Thur, Fri; 9.30am-12.30pm Sat, Sun. **Admission** free. **Map 8/2A**

Prisoners of the Nazis were brought to this grim building for interrogation during the occupation of Rome in 1943-4. This haunting museum is a tribute to them: resistance fighters; passive victims taken in reprisal; and members of the Nazis' proscribed groups such as Jews, homosexuals, gypsys and Communists. The walls are covered with pictures and biographies of those who passed through on their way to die, and several cells have been preserved, complete with prisoners' farewell messages to their families. It's a moving and a chilling place, not forgotten in a hurry. *Wheelchair access.*

Parks & gardens

Villa Aldobrandini

Via Mazzarino, 11. Bus to Via Nazionale. **Open** 7am-dusk daily. **Map 8/1C**

The villa here was built in the sixteenth century for the Dukes of Urbino, and later bought by the Aldobrandini Pope Clement VIII. It's now state property and closed to the public, but the gardens remain open. Reached through a gate off Via Mazzarino, they are formal, with neat gravel paths and well-tended lawns. During renovations, the gardens were raised some 30m above street level, behind the high wall which dominates the southern end of Via Nazionale. A picturesque place where weary tourists can sit and enjoy splendid views over the city.

Multi-coloured ages

Ravenna's mosaicists made their city the centre of Italian art in the so-called Dark and Middle Ages, but Rome did not lag far behind, as the mosaics scattered around the city show. From the classical fourth-century examples in **Santa Maria in Domnica** and **Santa Pudenziana** and the fifth-century ones in **Santa Maria Maggiore**, the shift towards naturalism can be traced through **Santi Cosma e Damiano** and **San Lorenzo fuori le Mura** (sixth century), **Sant'Agnese fuori le Mura** (seventh), **Santa Maria in Cosmedin** (a beautiful eighth-century fragment of a *Madonna, Saint Joseph and Child* from the first **Saint Peter's**), **Santa Prassede** (*photo*) and, again, **Santa Maria in Domnica** (ninth century).

Mosaic techniques were revolutionised in the twelfth century by the Cosmati family. They put the many assorted bits and pieces from ancient buildings to excellent us, sawing up columns into round disks to create inlaid marble floors, thrones, tombs and fonts. Called *Cosmatesque*, this work can be seen at its breath-taking best in **Santa Maria in Cosmedin**.

That Rome's capacity for creating great art was not lost in the city's Dark Age is clear from the few but stunning surviving works of Pietro Cavallini (c1250-1330), creator of mosaics in **Santa Maria in Trastevere** and frescoes in **Santa Cecilia**. His pupil Filippo Rusuti did his master proud in fine work to be seen in the loggia of the basilica of **Santa Maria Maggiore**.

Aventino, Celio & Testaccio

South-central Rome is a place of contrasts: ancient oddities and the funkiest after-dark zone in town; exclusive, leafy residential zones, and a hub of working-class city life.

The exclusive and green Aventine hill boasts Rome's highest property prices, and hosts a sovereign passport-issuing territory in the headquarters of the Knights of Malta, in the square of the same name (**Piazza dei Cavalieri di Malta**). Two delightful parks offer spectacular views, particularly at sundown, and the churches are an added bonus: the glorious fifth-century **Santa Sabina**, and Santa Prisca, which stands on top of Rome's best-restored Mithraic shrine.

There are still elderly people on the Aventine and its sister hill San Saba, just across the busy Viale Aventino, who remember farmers herding sheep and goats into the area's *piazze* of an evening before taking them to market the next morning. And, until the debris left by an influx of Latin American transvestite prostitutes made it a health hazard, old ladies could until very recently be seen picking *rughetta* (rocket) for salads amid the grass at the foot of the **Aurelian Wall**.

The south side of old Rome contains some of the most fascinating, spectacular and unusual remains of the ancient city, in the **Baths of Caracalla**, **Monte Testaccio** and the many ruins along the **Via Appia Antica** (*see p102*). For a taste of what large swathes of Rome must have been like as the Barbarians swept in and sent the locals fleeing to what is now the *Centro storico*, head for the wilder areas of the Celio. Approached by the steep winding street opposite the sprawling white marble cuboids of the UN's Food and Agricultural Agency, first built to house Mussolini's Colonies Ministry, the Celio is lush and unkempt, containing a massive ramshackle structure in which nuns of Mother Teresa of Calcutta's order grow broad beans, and the immense false-fronted church of **San Gregorio Magno**, with its picturesquely overgrown vegetable garden. It was from here that Saint Augustine was dispatched to convert the pagans of far-off Britain in the sixth century.

An arcaded street leads past the church of **Santi Giovanni e Paolo**, built over a street of Roman houses, to the **Villa Celimontana** park. The grid of narrow streets on the hill's lower slopes contain three ancient churches: **San Clemente**, **Santi Quattro Coronati** and **Santo Stefano Rotondo**.

Further south, though still within the ancient Wall, is the wedge-shaped **Testaccio** district. This is one of the few areas of central Rome where a sense of community is strongly felt, and where the line between courtyard and street is blurred enough to allow old ladies to pop into the local *alimentari* in their dressing-gown and slippers. Elsa Morante chose this as the setting for her sprawling Marxist novel *La Storia* (*History*). The best place to begin is in Piazza Testaccio, home to one of Rome's best-stocked and liveliest food markets. Once a desperately poor area, Testaccio has reaped the benefits of post-war prosperity without losing either its character or its original residents, who remain resolutely salt-of-the-earth, despite encroaching health-food shops and other trappings of gentrification. Many of the apartment blocks are still publicly owned, and let at controlled rents. At the beginning of the twentieth century a quarter of all families here slept in their kitchens, and tenants were forced to brave the suspended walkways (*ballatoi*) connecting the apartments on each floor. For a glimpse of these *ballatoi* venture into the recently-restored courtyard of the block at Piazza Testaccio, 20.

You'll meet few non-residents in Testaccio by day, the only tourist destinations being the **Protestant Cemetery**, the **Pyramid of Caius Cestius** and the more obscure **Monte Testaccio** and **Emporium**. By night, however, the area is inundated with outsiders who flock to the cheap pizzerias and myriad clubs burrowed into the flanks of Monte Testaccio (*see chapter* **Nightlife**).

Piazze

Piazza dei Cavalieri di Malta
Metro Circo Massimo/bus to Via di Santa Sabina.
Map 7/1 A
Designed by the great fantasist Piranesi in the eighteenth century, this diminutive square with its mysterious reliefs and orderly cypress trees looks

like the set for some surrealist drama. It takes its name from the Knights of Malta, whose priory is at number 3. If you look through the little hole in the priory doorway, you'll see one of Piranesi's most spectacular illusions: at the end of a neat avenue of trees sits the dome of **Saint Peter's**, apparently only a few metres away. This is probably the only keyhole in the world through which you can see three sovereign territories: Italy, the Vatican, and the aristocratic, theocratic Knights of Malta themselves, a sovereign order that enjoys extra-territorial rights, has its own head of state, and issues its own number plates (starting SMOM) and passports.

Palazzi

Il Mattatoio

Piazza Giustiniani. Bus to Via Marmorata or Lungotevere Testaccio. **Map 7/2B**

With its Doric arches and bizarre statuary, the *Mattatoio*, the municipal slaughterhouse, was considered Europe's most advanced abbatoir when it opened in 1891. It coped with an eightfold increase in the city's population, and provided Testaccio's residents with work (not to mention noise and smells) until it was finally pensioned off in 1975. For decades constant bickering between politicians, architects and planners over what to do with the structure caused complete stasis: now, finally, the whole area, including the Campo Boario cattleyards next door, seems destined to become an up-market shopping complex, complete with gallery and performance spaces. Some small corner will also be reserved – or so the city council says – for the **Villaggio Globale** *centro sociale* (*see chapter* **Music: Rock, Roots & Jazz**), which for a while looked as if it might be made homeless.

Ancient Rome

Baths of Caracalla (*Terme di Caracalla*)

Viale delle Terme di Caracalla, 52 (06 575 8626). Metro Circo Massimo/bus to Viale Aventino or Viale delle Terme di Caracalla.
Open *Oct-Apr* 9am-1pm Mon, Sun; 9am-4.30pm Tue-Sat. *May-Sept* 9am-1pm Mon, Sun; 9am-6pm Tue-Sat. **Admission** L8,000. **Map 9/2B**

These high-vaulted ruins, surrounded by trees and grass, are pleasantly peaceful today, but were anything but tranquil in their heyday, when up to 1,600 Romans could sweat it out at any one time in their baths and gyms. You can get some idea of the original splendour of the baths from the fragments of mosaic and statuary littering the ground, although the more impressive finds are to be seen in the **Vatican**'s **Pio Cristiano** museum. The baths were built at the beginning of the third century AD, the fifth to be built in Rome, and the largest up to that time (although the later Baths of Diocletian were even bigger). They remained in use until well into the sixth century. The two large rooms down the sides were gymnasia. After exercising, Romans

cleansed themselves in saunas and a series of baths. The baths were usually open from midday until sunset, and were opulent social centres where people came to relax after work. The complex also contained a library (still identifiable on one side of the baths), a garden, shops and stalls.

Emporium (*Porto Fluviale*)

Lungotevere Testaccio. Bus or tram to Piazza dell'Emporio. **Open** for guided tours, see below. **Admission** varies according to tour. **Map 7/1A**

From the second century BC, the bank just south of the modern Ponte Sublicio (built in 1919) was Rome's *Emporium*, the ancient wharf area, from which steps led up to the *Porticus Emilia*, a huge covered warehouse 60m wide and almost half a kilometre long. Behind the Porticus were the *horrea*, or grain warehouses, built under Tiberius (AD 14-37) to help control the imperial grain monopoly; the occasional outcrop of bricks from these buildings can still be seen among Testaccio's apartment blocks. Stop-go excavations of the **Emporio-Porto Fluviale** (emporium-river port) have been ongoing for years, but have recently been completed. Guided tours are organised frequently (but irregularly) by local archaeological groups; consult the local listings magazines such as *Roma C'è* and *Time Out Roma* (*see chapter* **Media**) for contact addresses and information and details of current tours.

Monte Testaccio

Via Zabaglia, 24. Metro Piramide/bus to Via Marmorata or Via Zabaglia/tram to Piazza San Paolo. **Open** with prior permission only (*see p33* **Getting through locked gates**). **Map 7/2A**

Known locally as the *Monte dei cocci* – the hill of shards – Monte Testaccio is just that: although it's covered by soil and scrubby plants, underneath the 'hill' is nothing but a pile of broken *amphorae*, ancient earthenware jars, flung here between AD 140 and 255 after being unloaded at the **Porto Fluviale**. Most came from the Roman province of Betica (Andalusia), and contained olive oil. In the Middle Ages, Monte Testaccio and the area below it were famous as the site of the Carnival celebrations, in which the horse races and religious pageants of the nobility vied with the less refined sports of the people. Pigs, bulls and wild boar would be packed into carts at the top of the hill and sent careering down; any survivors of the impact were finished off at the bottom with spears. Jews, too, were subjected to indignities of all kinds, although they were spared the coup de grace. Today some of Rome's most buzzing clubs and restaurants, such as **Akab** and **Alibi**, have been built into the base of the hill (*see chapter* **Nightlife**), and some afford glimpses of the *amphora* mound beyond.

Pyramid of Gaius Cestius (*Piramide di Caio Cestio*)

Piazza di Porta San Paolo. Metro Piramide/bus or tram to Piazza di Porta San Paolo. **Open** with prior permission only (*see p33* **Getting through locked gates**). **Map 7/2A**

Standing out from the brick **Aurelian Wall** is a miniature Egyptian pyramid. It was built by an obscure first-century BC magistrate and tribune who was so impressed by the tombs of the pharaohs that he decided he wanted one of his own. He did not build it with as much technical care as the Egyptians had used (it's made of brick and only clad in marble) but nevertheless it has survived remarkably well since Cestius was buried here in 12 BC.

Churches

San Clemente

Via San Giovanni in Laterano (06 7045 1018). Metro Colosseo/bus to Colosseo or Via Labicana. **Open** 9am-12.30pm, 3-6pm Mon-Sat; 10am-noon, 3-6pm Sun. **Admission** *excavations* L4,000. **Map 8/2B**

San Clemente is one of the most intriguing of all Rome's buildings: three layers of history one on top of the other, and a narrow first-century alley you can still walk down, thanks to excavations begun in 1857 by the Irish Dominicans who have been in charge of the church since the seventeenth century. The existing basilica is a smaller twelfth-century copy of its fourth-century predecessor, which in turn was built over an early Christian *titulus*, or meeting place. The original church was burnt down when the Normans sacked Rome in 1084 (*see p16*), but the *schola cantorum*, a walled marble choir, survived and was moved upstairs to the new church, where it still stands. The most striking feature, however, is a vivid twelfth century mosaic in the apse, showing the vine of life spiralling around delightful pastoral scenes. Peasants tending flocks and crops are interspersed with saints and prophets, and the whole mosaic centres on the crucified Christ. The chapel of Saint Catherine of Alexandria (to the left, facing the altar) has frescoes by Masolino (possibly helped by Masaccio) showing scenes from the life of the saint, who was tortured to death strapped to a wheel, and so, much later, gave her name to the firework.

Steps lead down from the sacristy to the fourth-century basilica, the layout of which is much obscured by walls built to support the church above. Rapidly fading frescoes illustrate episodes from Saint Clement's miracle-packed life. According to legend, Clement, the fourth pope, was exiled to the Crimea by Trajan, but continued his proselytising undaunted and was hurled into the sea, tied to an anchor, for his pains. When the sea receded a year later, a tomb containing the saint's body miraculously appeared; from then on, the sea would recede again once a year, and another miracle would occur.

At the end of the underground basilica, past the strange modern Slavic memorial to Saint Cyril – inventor of Cyrillic script, great figure of the Orthodox churches, and responsible for bringing Clement's body back to Rome – a stairway leads down to the remains of a second-century apartment block or *insula*, where the cult of the god Mithras was celebrated. Mithraism, Christianity's main rival in the late Empire, was a complex mystical religion of Persian origin (*see p95*). Three rooms have been excavated: the anteroom, with benches and a stucco ceiling; the sanctuary, with an altar depicting Mithras killing a bull; and a school room. On the other side of the lane, meanwhile, are the ground-floor rooms of a Roman house that was used by early Christians as a meeting place.

Santi Giovanni e Paolo

Piazza Santi Giovanni e Paolo, 13 (06 700 5745). Bus or tram to Via di San Gregorio. **Open** 8.30am-noon, 3.30-6.30pm, daily. **Admission** *excavations* donation expected. **Map 8/2B**

Goths and Normans did their worst to the original church built here in the fourth century, but remains of it can be seen embedded in the twelfth-century façade of the current construction, in a square that has scarcely changed since medieval times. The interior, however, suffered heavy-handed decorating in the eighteenth century and now looks like a luxury banqueting hall, with creamy stucco work and extravagant chandeliers. Excavations beneath the church have revealed Roman houses of the first and second centuries that were evidently used as places of Christian worship (*tituli*), and a cellar used for secret Christian burials. The site has been identified as the home of Pammachius, a senator who gave all his money to the poor and embraced Christianity, converting his house into the original church; his story was recorded for posterity by his friend Saint Jerome. Wall frescoes have been restored for the reopening of the *titulus* in 2000. Ask the sacristan for permission to view the (separate) remains of the Temple of Claudius, which once dominated the Celian hill, and is now hidden under the church, monastery and bell tower. Down the left of the church runs the Clivio Scauro, a lane which bears the same name as it did in Roman times, but has long been crossed by fifth-to-fourteenth century buttresses shoring up the church.

San Gregorio Magno

Piazza di San Gregorio, 1 (06 700 8227). Bus or tram to Via di San Gregorio. **Open** 8.30am-12.30pm, 1.45-6.30pm, daily. **Map 9/1C**

Now essentially a baroque building, finished by Giovanni Battista Soria in 1633, this church is most famous as the starting point for Saint Augustine's sixth-century mission to convert England to Christianity. It was originally the family home of one of the most remarkable popes, Gregory the Great, who had it converted into a monastery in 575. In the chapel to the right of the altar is a marble chair dating from the first century BC, reputed to have been used by Gregory as his papal throne. Also here is the tomb of Tudor diplomat Sir Edward Carne, who came to Rome several times to persuade the pope to annul the marriage of Henry VIII and Catherine of Aragon, so he could marry Anne Boleyn.

Santa Maria in Domnica

Piazza della Navicella, 10 (06 700 1519). Bus to Via della Navicella. **Open** *usually* 9am-6pm daily. **Map 9/1B**

San Clemente: *Rome's historical triple-decker.*

Santa Maria dates from the ninth century, but its sixteenth-century portico and ceiling were added by Pope Leo X. In the apse, behind the modern altar, there is one of the most charming mosaics in Rome. It was commissioned in the ninth century by Pope Paschal I, and shows the Virgin and Child surrounded by a crowd of saints. The pope kneels at their feet, with a square halo to indicate that he was still living at the time. Above their heads, the apostles are apparently skipping through a flower-filled meadow, with Christ in the centre. Opening hours depend on the priest roping in someone to watch over the church: when he finds no one, you'll find it closed from noon to 3.30pm.

Santi Quattro Coronati

Via dei Santi Quattro Coronati, 20 (06 7047 5427). Bus or tram to Via Labicana. **Open** *church 9.30am-noon, 3.30-6pm, Mon-Sat; 10.45am-noon, 4-6pm Sun; cloister & oratory 9.30-11.45am, 4.30-6pm, Mon-Sat; 9am-10.45am, 4-6pm Sun.* **Admission** donation expected at cloister and oratory. **Map 8/2B**

This basilica dates from the fourth century but, like **San Clemente** and **Santi Giovanni e Paolo**, was burnt down by the Normans in 1084 (*see p16*). It was rebuilt as a fortified monastery, with the church itself reduced to half its original size; the outsize apse, visible as you look uphill along Via dei Santi Quattro, hails from the original church. The early basilica form is still discernible, and the columns that once ran along the aisles are embedded in the walls of the innermost courtyard. The church has a fine *cosmatesque* floor (*see p83*). There is also a beautiful cloister, from about 1220, with a twelfth-century fountain playing amid its flowerbeds.

In the oratory next to the church (ring the bell and ask the nuns for the key) is a fresco cycle depicting the *Donation of Constantine*, the legend that for centuries was put forward by the papacy as a primary source of its authority, according to which an early pope, Sylvester, cured the Emperor of leprosy (or another similarly unpleasant disease), after which he was so grateful that in return he granted

The original American steakhouse.

Delightful small chain of American steakhouses, ideally
in Wild West Stations, serving legendary portions of best
T⊕Bone steak and offering authentic American cooking
grills and burgers. The dining room atmosphere is perfect for a bu
ness lunch, as well as the cocktail bar is an excellent spot wher
stay till 3.00am.

Daily noon⊕03.00 ⊕ Air conditioning system
All major credit cards accepted

T⊕Bone Station 1: Via F. Crispi 25 metro stop Barberini or Spagna tel 06 67 8
Parking Ludovisi complimentary
T⊕Bone Station 2: Via Flaminia 525/527 corner Corso di Francia tel 06.33 33

The Baths of Caracalla: *where ancients went for a wash and brush up (see page 85).*

the Bishops of Rome spiritual and worldly authority over the whole empire. The frescoes, painted in the thirteenth century as a defence of the popes' temporal powers, show a pox-ridden Constantine being healed by Sylvester, and then crowning him with a tiara and giving him a cap to symbolise the pope's spiritual and earthly authority. Just to make sure there are no lingering doubts about Sylvester's capacity for heroics, he resuscitates a bull killed as a sacrifice, and frees the Romans from a dragon. The monastery is still home to an enclosed order of nuns, who ask visitors to be as silent as possible.

Santa Sabina
Piazza Pietro d'Illiria, 1 (06 574 3573).
Bus to Piazzale Ugo La Malfa. **Open** 6.30am-
12.45pm, 3.30-7pm, daily. **Map 7/1A**
This magnificent basilica is another that was built, in the fifth century, over an early Christian *titulus*. Added to and decorated over the centuries, it was shorn of later accretions in a merciless restoration in the 1930s: what you see today is arguably the closest thing to an unadulterated ancient church that Rome has to offer. Santa Sabina has a high nave with towering, elegant Corinthian columns, supporting an arcade decorated with original marble inlay work.

The floor is fifth century, as are the wooden doors carved with scenes from the New Testament, including one of the earliest renderings of the crucifixion. The selenite windows date from the ninth century, as does the choir. The very few later additions remaining in the church include the sixteenth-century fresco in the apse (said to be opied from the original mosaic) and the roundels flanking it, by Taddeo Zuccari. A sloping corridor near the main door leads to a peaceful thirteenth-century cloister.

Santo Stefano Rotondo
Via di Santo Stefano Rotondo, 7 (06 7049 3717)
Bus to Via della Navicella or Piazza di Porta
Metronia. **Open** 2-4pm Mon; 9am-1pm, 2-4pm,
Tue-Sat. **Map 9/1B**
One of very few round churches in Rome, Santo Stefano dates from the fifth century. The many mystics whose imaginations have been captivated by the place over the centuries believed it to have been modelled on the Holy Sepulchre in Jerusalem; in its measurements, they argued, lies the secret of the Holy Number of God. The church originally had three concentric naves separated by antique columns; the simplicity of the place was disturbed when arches were built to shore it up in the twelfth

American Bar - Piano Bar

An exclusive meeting place for a cockta
to listen some good music after dinner.
From 11.00 a.m. to 02.00 p.m.

Ristorante - Piano Bar

An elegant restaurant with Italian
and international cuisine and Grande
Parte with selection of wines.
Sale Privèe for reservation dinner.
From 12.30 a.m. to 15.00 p.m. and
from 19.30 p.m. to 01.00 p.m.

Bistrot

Straight on Via Veneto with a
wonderful view of Porta Pinciana.

Closed on Sunday
All credit cards accepted
For information and reservation: Harry's Bar Roma
Via Vittorio Veneto, 150
00187 Roma Tel. 06/484643 fax. 06/4883

The Walls of Rome

Rome's **Aurelian Wall** (*Mura Aureliane*) was built around AD 270 by Emperor Aurelian, at a time when Rome's power was waning, and formidable defences were required. It originally had 16 gates around its 20km length, was four metres thick, and stood seven metres high. Its top level was later raised to over ten metres. This massive contruction still forms a near-complete circle around central Rome: the best-preserved parts of the ancient construction today are the *Muro Torto* (crooked wall) section between the Pincio and Villa Borghese; the *Porta Ostiense* (*above*), renamed Porta San Paolo in honour of Saint Paul, who walked through it on the way to his execution; and the area around the Porta San Giovanni. Of the remaining gates, the Porta San Sebastiano, originally Aurelian's *Porta Appia* at the head of the Via Appia Antica, is the most impressive, and now houses the **Museo delle Mura**, dedicated to the history of the walls.

Of the earlier **Servian** walls, believed to have been built in the reign of Servius Tullius (579-534 BC), little remains. The pile of bricks to the right as you exit from **Termini** railway station is a rare fragment of the original 11km belt. The **Leonine** walls, which surround the Vatican, are altogether more satisfying. Built between 847 and 852 by Pope Leo IV, they were extended by Nicholas III in the thirteenth century. Caught up in the battle between Hapsburgs and Angevins for control of Sicily, Nicholas wisely had a covered walkway built along the stretch of the wall that joined the Vatican palace to the fortified, impregnable **Castel Sant'Angelo** (*see p96*). In the event he himself never needed to high-tail it to the papal bolt-hole, but Pope Clement VII must have blessed his predecessor's foresight in 1527 when he made use of this *corridoio* to survive the Sack of Rome by Charles V's troops (*see chapter* **History**).

There's something *comfortable* in old Rome

Is there a design hotel right in the heart of Trastevere
with 170 suites that have been renovated
to provide guests with all the latest conveniences?
With a restaurant that uses produce
from the proprietor's own farm, is open for lunch,
and accomodates after-theater diners?
Where you can organize an art exhibition
or a meeting for 180 people, providing hospitality,
efficiency and a large garage?

Yes, indeed. There's really something new in Rome.

RIPA
ALL SUITES
HOTEL

via degli orti di trastevere 1, 00153 Rome
telephone 06 58611 fax 06 5814550 e mail: ripa@uni.net
http//www.travel.it/roma/ripa/ripa.html
Worldwide Hospitality Golden Tulip Hotels
Planet Hotels & Resorts

Reservation office 06 5861857

century, and the outer ring was walled in in 1450. The haunting peace diminished in the sixteenth century when the outer interior wall was frescoed with graphic scenes of ghastly martyrdoms. A *mithraeum* beneath the church can be visited by seeking permission at the phone number above.

Museums & galleries

Antiquarium Comunale
Viale del Parco del Celio, 22 (06 700 1569).
Bus or tram to Colosseum or Via di San Gregorio.
Open 9am-7pm Tue-Sat; 9am-1pm Sun.
Admission L3,750. **Map 8/2B**
There's something charmingly provincial about this quiet museum in a villa on the Celio hill. Like any local museum, it houses the ancient finds of the area; this being Rome, however, the collection is rather better than you would find in most places elsewhere. Many of the exhibits were unearthed when the city was expanding at the end of the nineteenth century. Big collections took the pick of the finds, but this little museum hung on to a wonderful range of domestic artefacts, tools and kitchen equipment, many of which look surprisingly similar to their modern equivalents. Perhaps most touching is a jointed doll, a sort of ancient (small busted) Barbie, found in the tomb of a young girl who died shortly before she was due to be married; it's exquisitely carved, even detailing the complicated hairstyle fashionable in the second century AD.

Museo delle Mura (Museum of the Walls)
Via di Porta San Sebastiano, 18 (06 7047 5284).
Bus to Piazza Numa Pompilio, then a long walk, or to Via delle Mura Latine. **Open** 9am-7pm Tue-Sun.
Admission L3,750. **Map 9/2A**
Housed in the Porta San Sebastiano, which was built by the Emperor Aurelian (AD 270-75) as the exit-gate from the city onto the Appian Way, the little Museum of the Walls has a smallish collection of artefacts associated with Roman walls and roads, and – best of all – allows its visitors access to the walkway atop a substantial stretch of the **Aurelian Wall** itself (*see p91*).

Museo di Via Ostiense
Via R. Persichetti, 3 (06 574 3193). Metro Piramide/bus or tram to Piazza San Paolo. **Open** 9am-1pm, 2.30-4.30pm, Tue, Thur; 9am-1pm Wed, Fri, Sat. **Admission** L4,000. **Map 7/2A**
This small museum is dauntingly placed in the middle of a frantic traffic roundabout, and just opposite the station for **Ostia Antica**. A visit can be handily combined with one to the excavations of the ancient port city (*see chapter* **Trips out of Town**). The ancient gatehouse, the Porta di San Paolo, contains artefacts and prints describing the story of the historic Via Ostiense – the Ostian Way – built in the third century BC to join Rome to its port and the vital salt-pans at the mouth of the Tiber. The museum has two large-scale models, of old Ostia and the port of Trajan.

*The **Antiquarium Comunale**: a taste of ancient domestic life.*

Parks & gardens

Parco Savello

Via di Santa Sabina, Aventino. Bus to Piazzale Ugo La Malfa or Via di Santa Sabina.
Open dawn to dusk daily. **Map 7/1A**
Inside the walls of the Savello family's twelfth-century castle is a pretty garden, full of orange trees and massive terracotta pots of dark green plants. Close by on Via di Valle Murcia are the city rose gardens, which are especially sweet-smelling – but also very crowded – in late spring and early summer.

Protestant Cemetery (Cimitero Accattolico)

Via Caio Cestio, 6 (06 574 1900).
Metro Piramide/bus to Via Marmorata/tram to Porta San Paolo. **Open** *Oct-Mar* 9am-5pm, *Apr-Sept* 9am-6pm, Tue-Sun. **Admission** free (donation expected). **Map 7/2A**
'It might make one in love with death to know that one should be buried in so sweet a place.' So Shelley described the final resting place of his friend Keats in the preface to his poem *Adonais*, little knowing that he too would be taking up permanent residence there, after a fatal boating accident just a year later.

Miraculously, given that only a wall divides it from the chaos of Piazza di Porta San Paolo, it remains a haven of peace. The inhabitants of the cemetery – the official title of which is the *cimitero accattolico*, the non-Catholic cemetery – are not limited to Protestants: there are Russian Orthodox, Chinese, Buddhist and even atheist tombs as well. To get in, ring the bell. A detailed map is available at the entrance, and will help you discover the graves of other distinguished residents such as Goethe's son Julius, Joseph Severn, faithful companion to Keats, and Antonio Gramsci, founder of the Italian Communist Party.

Villa Celimontana

Via della Navicella (no phone). Bus or tram to Via di San Gregorio, bus to Via della Navicella.
Open dawn to dusk daily. **Map 9/1B**
A pretty, leafy, walled garden, its swings and climbing frames swarming with local kids and its lawns packed with bits of ancient marble from the collection of the Mattei family, which owned the property from 1553 until 1928 when it became a public park. The best bits of the Mattei collection can now be admired in the **Palazzo Altemps** (*see chapter* **Centro Storico**).

Blood & sperm: the trail of Mithras

The ancient Persian cult of Mithras, mentions of which have been found in cuneiform texts from as early as the fifteenth century BC, enjoyed a sudden revival in second and third-century Rome. Why this rather bloody sun-deity, god of contracts and loyalty, should have become so popular at that time is unclear; the fact, however, that the bulk of his followers were military men (women were excluded from Mithraism) suggests that emperors and generals encouraged the cult to ensure that loyalty was a virtue aspired to by even the most battle-weary troops.

The Mithraic myth is a creation story: the sun-god Apollo ordered Mithras to sacrifice a bull, a task he carried out unwillingly as his averted face in pictures of this act shows. But, as the bull died, the animal became the moon, while Mithras' mantle became the starry sky. The bull's blood became the first corn and grapes, and its semen, collected in a handy bowl, was the seed from which everything else was made. Awoken by the celestial light ignited by the sacrifice, evil appeared in the shape of a scorpion and a snake, drinking blood and semen and beginning the eternal battle between good and evil. Having loyally done his bit, Mithras was taken up to a banquet in the sun by Apollo.

That the Mithraic cult included animal sacrifices is certain. It is also believed to have included some form of initiation rite, but there is no agreement over what this consisted of. Ritual chastisement seems to have been popular. Ceremonies were held in narrow caves holding no more than 100 adepts, each belonging to one of seven grades that could be achieved by followers of the cult.

Mithraeums can be visited in the digs beneath the churches of **San Clemente**, **Santo Stefano Rotondo** and Santa Prisca on the Aventine (in Via di Santa Prisca **Map 7/1A**; open to visitors by appointment only, *see page 33*). Another, with a large relief of Mithras killing the bull, is in Via dei Greci, near the **Circus Maximus**; again, this can only be seen by appointment. The ancient Roman port at **Ostia Antica** (*see chapter* **Trips out of Town**) boasts seven Mithraic sites.

The cult of Mithras was still going strong at the outset of the fourth century, battling for supremacy against another foreign import: the newly-established cult of Christianity. Unfortunately for the sun-god, it was a blazing cross rather than a blazing bull that led Constantine to victory at the Battle of Ponte Milvio in 312 (*see p13*). The emperor threw all his weight behind Jesus. By the time Mithraism was banned in 395, it was the religion of a small, reactionary, pagan minority.

Other parts of town

Beyond its historic core, Rome has sprawling suburbs, ancient Christian shrines and catacombs, and yet more museums in a Fascist-inspired model city.

Prati

On the west bank of the Tiber and bordering on the **Vatican**, this residential area was largely built in the nineteenth century, on the flat meadowland (*prati*) behind **Castel Sant'Angelo**. Closer to the castle and Piazza San Pietro it fades into the narrower, characterful streets of the old Borgo, the district that grew up in the Middle Ages around **Saint Peter's**. A wander for lunch or retail therapy down Prati's main shopping street, Via Cola di Rienzo, is a good antidote to a surfeit of culture. Otherwise, the area's main features are the **Trionfale** flower market, on the west side of Prati (*see chapter* **Shopping**), the endless military barracks lining Viale delle Milizie, some quiet, tree-lined streets close to the river, and the headquarters of RAI, the Italian state broadcaster.

Castel Sant'Angelo

Lungotevere Castello, 50 (06 681 9111). Bus to Lungotevere del Vaticano or Piazza Cavour. Open 9am-8pm Tue-Sun. **Admission** L8,000. **Map 3/1B**
Begun by the Emperor Hadrian in AD 135 as his own mausoleum, Castel Sant'Angelo has since functioned as a fortress, prison and papal residence. The passageway connecting it to the Vatican is still visible, a reminder of the days when petrified popes, threatened by invading forces, scampered from **Saint Peter's** to the relative safety of the castle. Although it now plays host to temporary art shows (displays of stolen paintings and artefacts recovered by the police are regular choices), the real pleasure of a visit to Castel Sant'Angelo lies in wandering from Hadrian's original ramp-like entrance to the upper terraces, with their superb views of the city and beyond. In between, there is much to see: the lavish Renaissance salons, decorated with spectacular frescoes and *trompe l'œils*; the chapel in the *Cortile d'Onore*, designed by Michelangelo for Leo X; and, half-way up an easily-missed staircase, Clement VII's surprisingly tiny personal bathroom, painted by Giulio Romano. Puccini had Tosca hurl herself from the top of Castel Sant'Angelo in the final tragic, stirring act of the opera of the same name.

Note, also, that in recent summers it has remained open until 11pm on Saturdays. *Limited wheelchair access.*

Museo delle Anime dei Defunti

Lungotevere Prati, 12 (06 6880 6517). Bus to Piazza Cavour. **Open** 7-11.30am, 4.30-7pm, Mon-Sat; 7am-noon Sun. **Admission** free. **Map 3/1B**
This macabre collection, attached to the church of the Sacro Cuore del Suffragio, contains the hand- and finger-prints left on the prayer books and clothes of the living by dead loved ones, reminding their survivors to say Mass to release their souls from Purgatory into Heaven. Begun just over a century ago, the collection is intended to convince the sceptical of life after death. A startling exhibit is the incandescent handprint supposedly left by Sister Clara Scholers on the habit of fellow-nun Margarita Hahrendorf in Westphalia in 1696. Another dead soul apparently left hand-scorched bank notes outside a church where he wanted his Mass to be said.

Museo Storico Nazionale dell'Arte Sanitaria

Lungotevere in Sassia, 3 (06 6835 2353). Bus to Borgo Santo Spirito or Lungotevere in Sassia. **Open** 10am-noon Mon, Wed, Fri. **Admission** L3,000. **Map 3/1C**
This gruesome collection of medical artefacts, from ancient times to the nineteenth century, is housed in a few rooms on one side of the hospital of Santo Spirito. As well as the usual collection of skeletons, organs, anatomical charts and surgical instruments, there is a collection of wax votive offerings, left at churches and shrines to encourage God to cure parts of the body conventional medicine could not reach. There are also reconstructions of a seventeenth-century pharmacy and an alchemist's laboratory.

Northern suburbs

Flaminia

The dead-straight Via Flaminia shoots north from **Piazza del Popolo**, crossing the river at the ancient Ponte Milvio, where the Emperor Constantine is supposed to have had his battle-winning vision of Christ (*see chapter* **History**). On

View from the pope-bunker: scared pontiffs scampered to **Castel Sant'Angelo**.

the way, the road passes through affluent residential areas that contain a host of sports facilities: the **Stadio Flaminio** and **Acqua Acetosa** running tracks in the east, and the **Foro Italico** and **Stadio Olimpico** football stadium across the river to the west (*see chapter* **Sport & Fitness**).

Monteverde

Climbing the steep hill behind Trastevere is Monteverde Vecchio, a leafy, well-heeled suburb that is home to the vast, green, tree-filled expanses of the **Villa Pamphili** park, and to the smaller but equally lovely **Villa Sciarra** gardens (*see chapter* **Children**). Further west is Monteverde Nuovo, a charmless, more downmarket and predominantly post-war addition.

Nomentana

Via Nomentana is the main road leading out of Rome to the east, crossed at right-angles by the once-majestic Via Regina Elena. It's flanked on either side by another fairly middle-class residential area. To the south-east, the area around the Via Tiburtina is rather more low-rent.

Sant'Agnese fuori le Mura & Santa Costanza

Via Nomentana, 349 (06 861 0840). Bus to Via Nomentana. **Open** 9am-noon Mon; 9am-noon, 4-6pm, Tue-Sat; 4-6pm Sun. **Admission** *catacombs* L8,000.
The circular fourth-century mausoleum of Santa Costanza, 2km beyond the beginning of the Via Nomentana at Porta Pia (**Map 4/2A**), was built for

Constantine's daughters, Constance (a saint only by popular tradition, never having been canonised) and Helen, and is decorated with the world's earliest surviving Christian mosaics. They do not look very Christian – simple pastoral scenes with a spiralling vine encircling figures joyfully collecting and treading grapes – but historians insist the wine being made represents Christ's blood. In the adjoining church of Sant'Agnese, also dating from Constantine's time, there is a seventh-century apse mosaic showing a diminutive figure of Saint Agnes standing on the flames of her martyrdom, flanked by two popes. Like the mosaics of **San Lorenzo fuori le Mura**, there is little of the classical tradition here. Saint Agnes was almost certainly buried in the catacombs below this church, after her martyrdom in what is now **Piazza Navona**. The catacombs are among the least-visited and most atmospheric in Rome.

Galleria Comunale d'Arte Moderna e Contemporanea (ex-Birreria Peroni)

Via Reggio Emilia, 84 (06 884 4930/ galleria.moderna@comune.roma.it). Bus to Piazza Fiume or Via Nizza. **Open** 10am-6.30pm Tue-Sun. **Admission** L8,000. **Map 4/2A**
As well as being a fascinating example of industrial archaeology and the recycling of disused spaces, this refurbished former brewery is a valuable addition to the capital's public galleries and a strong indication of Rome city council's interest in new art. It will provide a permanent home for the Rome council's own collection of some 4,000 works of modern and contemporary art, predominantly Italian, with artists such as Marini, Guttuso and Morandi well

*Fascist-era **Garbatella**: short on fresh paint, long on community camaraderie.*

represented. The ex-brewery will also host temporary and touring contemporary art shows. *Wheelchair access.*

Parioli

North of the Villa Borghese, this is one of the dearest but also one of the dullest residential areas of the city, built between the late nineteenth century and the 1930s on the hilltop estates of some of baroque Rome's finest private villas. When Romans refer to *pariolini*, they have in mind the sort of brash rich kids who feel naked without a designer jacket, jeans pressed by the family's *filipina* maid, a cellphone and a four-wheel drive.

Southern suburbs
Ostiense/Garbatella

These districts south of **Testaccio** are similarly interesting areas of late nineteenth-early twentieth century workers' housing: many of their apartment blocks are architecturally outstanding. Despite some urban blight, they have a strong community feel.

San Paolo fuori le Mura

Via Ostiense, 186 (06 541 0341). Metro San Paolo/bus to Piazzale San Paolo. **Open** *basilica* 8am-6pm; *cloister* 9.30am-1pm, 3-6pm, daily.
Constantine founded San Paolo to commemorate the martyrdom of Saint Paul at nearby Tre Fontane – named after fountains that sprang up as his severed head bounced three times. The church, 3km beyond

the Porta San Paolo (**Map 7/2A**) along the Via Ostiense, has been destroyed, rebuilt and restored several times, and the present building is only 150 years old, although a few details and a wonderful cloister survive from its ancient beginnings. The greatest damage to the basilica occurred in a fire in 1823, but subsequent restorers have also contributed to the destruction of the older building. Features that have survived include eleventh-century doors, decorated with biblical scenes; the elegant thirteenth-century *ciborio* (painted canopy) above the altar, by Arnolfo di Cambio; and a strange twelfth-century Easter candlestick, featuring human-, lion-, and goat-headed beasts spewing the vine of life from their mouths.

The cloister is a good example of *Cosmatesque* work (*see p83*), its twisted columns inlaid with mosaic, and supporting an elaborate arcade of sculpted reliefs. In the sacristy are the remnants of a series of papal portraits that once lined the nave. The modern church has carried on this tradition, replacing the originals with mosaic portraits of all the popes from Peter to the present incumbent. There are only eight spaces left; once they are filled, apparently, the world will end.

San Giovanni

A nineteenth-century area, built outside the wall beyond the ancient basilica of Rome's official cathedral, **San Giovanni in Laterano**. It's now a busy shopping district, surrounded by swathes of monotonous apartment blocks.

San Lorenzo

Badly built, densely populated and still showing wounds from World War II, San Lorenzo is scarred like an alley cat. It's also one of Rome's liveliest neighbourhoods, full of restaurants, artists, graffiti and cultural diversity, plus the spill-over from the nearby campus of Rome's La Sapienza university. The area has a history of rebellion. It was 'designed' in the 1880s as a working class ghetto, with few public services or amenities, and soon developed into Rome's most radical area, where anarchist workers bravely battled the rising tide of Fascism. The street battles of the 1920s between *squadracce fasciste* and the *sanlorenzini* form part of Italian left-wing legend.

San Lorenzo fuori le Mura

Piazzale del Verano, 3 (06 491 511).
Bus or tram to Piazzale del Verano.
Open 7am-noon, 3.30-7.30pm daily.
This basilica on the ancient Via Tiburtina, 1km to the west of Termini station (**Map 5/2A**), was donated by Constantine to house the roasted remains of **Saint Lawrence** (*see p100*). Rebuilt in the sixth century by Pope Pelagius II, it was later united with a neighbouring church, using the Pelagius church as the chancel. Successive restorations were undone in the 1860s, when some unfortunate frescoes were added. A couple of wayward bombs plunged through the roof in 1943, making San Lorenzo the only Roman church to suffer war damage, but it was painstakingly reconstructed by 1949. On the right

The Catacombs

Most of the 300km of catacombs running through the soft volcanic rock beneath suburban Rome date from the fourth century BC to the first century AD. In ancient Rome burial within the city walls was forbidden, while flashy overground tombs like those along the Via Appia Antica were costly for all but the élite. Hence, the mortal remains of Rome's humbler occupants ended up underground.

Many of the tombs are pagan, among them the **Columbarium** (literally, dovecote) **of Pomponius Hylas**, in the Parco degli Scipione; a few are Jewish. The most famous, however, are those of the Christians, for whom the catacombs offered one special advantage: in the underground chambers, ceremonies could be carried out, and the dead buried, far from the prying and vindictive eyes of their pagan persecutors.

The standard form of burial was in a niche carved in the rock. The body, wrapped in linen and often embalmed, was laid in the niche, which was then sealed with tiles or slabs of marble. The grander, arched niches tend to be the graves of martyrs or other important members of the flock, while some wealthy families had their own crypts where they could all be buried together. Frescoes on the walls often illustrate the indomitability of faith. Popular symbols include representations of Christ as a fish or a shepherd, while a lamb or a sheep represents humanity.

When Christianity became Rome's official religion and came up to the surface, the catacombs took on a special significance; here were the bones of the heroes of the early church, including Saints Sebastian, Agnes and Cecilia. It is possible that the **Catacombs of Saint Sebastian** may also have been used to house the relics of Saint Peter and Saint Paul during the third century, when worship at their shrines was still strictly forbidden. Like so many of Rome's ancient monuments, the catacombs were forgotten for long periods, then rediscovered. In the ninth century huge quantities of bones were dug up and reburied in **Saint Peter's** and elsewhere; it was not until the sixteenth century, however, that their full extent became apparent. Of the many catacombs beneath suburban Rome, the most frequently visited are those of **San Callisto**, **San Sebastiano** and **Domitilla** along the **Via Appia Antica**. More atmospheric, however, are the **Catacombs of Priscilla** outside the Villa Ada park near Parioli, and those beneath the church of **Sant'Agnese fuori le Mura** (*see p97*).

The Catacombs of Rome

Catacombs of Domitilla *Via delle Sette Chiesa, 282 (06 511 0342). Bus to Via delle Sette Chiese.* **Open** 8.30am-noon, 2.30-5.30pm , Mon, Wed- Sun. **Admission** L8,000.
Catacombs of Priscilla *Via Salaria, 430 (06 8620 6272). Bus to Via Salaria.* **Open** 8.30am-noon, 2.30-5pm, Tue-Sun. **Admission** L8,000.
Catacombs of San Callisto *Via Appia Antica, 110 (06 5130 1580). Metro Colli Albani then bus to Via Appia Antica.* **Open** 9.30am-noon, 2.30-5.30pm, Thur-Tue. **Admission** L8,000.
Catacombs of San Sebastiano *Via Appia Antica, 136 (06 788 7035). Metro Colli Albani then bus to Via Appia Antica.* **Open** 9am-noon, 2.30-5pm, Mon-Sat. **Admission** L8,000.
Columbarium of Pomponius Hylas *Via di Porta Latina, 10. Metro Circo Massimo.* **Open** with prior permission only (*see p33* **Getting through locked gates**). **Map 9/2A**

San Lorenzo alla griglia

Saint Lawrence was a kindly Spaniard who came to Rome in the early third century, and won the hearts of the city's poor by feeding them, tending to their material wants and generally directing the Christian community's funds to those in need. His familiarity with ecclesiastical economics won him a brief stay of execution when the Emperor Valerian had him arrested on 6 August, 258. Valerian wanted to know where the dosh was stashed, but when Lawrence pointed to a bunch of poor and sick Christians, saying 'here are the treasures of the Church', the emperor's patience ran out. Lawrence was thrown into a dark hole of a prison, where he remained just long enough to convert and baptise some fellow prisoners before meeting a fiery end, roasted on a gridiron.

In his *Walks in Rome* (1883), Augustus Hare suggests the following itinerary: 'Those who wish to fix the scenes and events of Roman history securely in their minds will do best perhaps to take them in groups. Suppose, for instance, that any travellers wish to study the history of Saint Lawrence, let them first visit the beautiful little **Chapel (of Pope Nicholas V)** in the Vatican (*see chapter* **The Vatican City**), where the whole story of his life is portrayed in the lovely frescoes of Fra Angelico. Let them stand on the greensward by the Navicella (on the **Celio**, *see p84*), where he distributed the treasures of the Church in front of the house of Saint Ciriaca. Let them walk through the *cryptoporticus* of the **Palatine** (*see chapter* **Centro Storico**) up which he was dragged to his trial. Let them visit **San Lorenzo in Fonte** (Via Urbana 50 [06 482 5361], open 7-11.30am, 4.30-7pm, daily. **Map 8/1B**. Ask in the sacristy for keys to the prison), where he was imprisoned, and baptised his fellow-prisoners in the fountain that gives the church its name. Let them go hence to **San Lorenzo in Panisperna** (Via Panisperna, 90, open 4-7pm Sat; 10am-1pm, 4-7pm, Sun. **Map 8/1B**), built upon the scene of his terrific martyrdom, which is there portrayed in a fresco. Let them see his traditional chains and the supposed gridiron of his suffering at **San Lorenzo in Lucina** (*see p58*). And, lastly, at the great basilica of **San Lorenzo fuori le Mura** (*see p99*), let them admire the mighty church, which for 1,200 years has marked the site of that little chapel which Constantine built near the lowly catacomb grave in which the martyr was laid'.

---

side of the thirteenth-century portico are frescoes from the same period, showing scenes from the life of Saint Lawrence.

Inside the triumphal arch are sixth-century mosaics reflecting Byzantine influence. The figures are flat, stiff and outlined in black, floating motionless against a gold ground. There is little modelling or play of light and shade, and the colouring is not as subtle as in the earlier mosaics. This is partly due to the Greek-inspired use of marble, instead of the glass *tesserae* normally favoured by the Romans.

EUR

Italian Fascism managed to be simultaneously monstrous and absurd, but its delusions of grandeur helped produce some of the most interesting European architecture and town planning of this century. In the early 1930s, Giuseppe Bottai, Mussolini's governor of Rome and the leading arbiter of Fascist taste, had the bright idea of expanding landbound Rome well along the Via Ostiense (**Map 7/2A**) towards the sea, some 20km away. He combined this with the notion of a Universal Exhibition, pencilled in for 1942 and intended to combine permanent cultural exhibition spaces with a monument to Fascism.

Popular Fascist architect Marcello Piacentini was charged with co-ordinating the vastly ambitious project, but in the event few of the original designs were ever built. The planning committee became so bogged down in argument that little had been achieved when the outbreak of World War II forced work to be suspended. After the war, work was resumed, but with a different spirit. Renamed EUR – *Esposizione universale romana* – the project went ahead disassociated from its Fascist ambitions. Some of Italy's best architects – Giovanni Muzio, Mario de Renzi, Ludovico Quaroni and partners Luigi Figini and Gino Pollini – left their mark on it; many consider the results an archetype of bombastic modernism, but EUR is certainly memorable. Fascist-inspired buildings such as Guerrini's **Palazzo della Civiltà del Lavoro**, popularly known as *il colosseo quadrato* – the square Colosseum – and Arnaldo Foschini's toy-town church of Santi Pietro e Paolo can be seen alongside post-war *palazzi* like Adalberto Libera's highly original Palazzo dei Congressi and Studio BBPR's superbly functional Post Office.

The 1960 Olympic Games offered another stimulus for filling out the area. The masterpiece is Nervi and Piacentini's flying saucer-like **Palazzo dello Sport**, hovering over EUR's artificial lake and now often used – despite its abysmal acoustics – for big rock concerts and political conventions. The area contains several other attractions, such as the **LUNEUR Park** funfair, the **Piscina delle Rose** swimming pool (*see chapters* **Children** *and* **Sport & Fitness**) and, most interesting for the visitor, a clutch of museums.

Most Romans never visit EUR except on business or to go to a concert. At night, however, and especially in summer, it becomes the playground of fun-loving, suntanned, wealthy brats. Rome's desire to be a little bit of California finds its most eloquent expression in EUR's relatively unsnarled, tree-lined boulevards, and there's a definite whiff of rich-kid, good-time culture in the air.

Museo dell'Alto Medioevo

Viale Lincoln, 3 (06 5422 8199).
Bus to Piazza Guglielmo Marconi. **Open** 9am-2pm Tue-Sat; 9am-1pm Sun. **Admission** L4,000.
This museum concentrates on the decorative arts of the period between the fall of the Roman Empire and the Renaissance. Exhibits of intricately carved gold- and silver-decorated swords, buckles and horse tackle have survived, along with more mundane objects: painted ceramic bead jewellery, and the metal frames of what may be Europe's earliest folding chairs. Church masonry carved with Celtic designs and fragments of rich embroidery from medieval priests' robes are also worth checking out.
Wheelchair access with assistance.

Museo della Civiltà Romana

Piazza Giovanni Agnelli, 10 (06 592 6041).
Metro EUR Palasport/bus to Piazza Guglielmo Marconi. **Open** 9am-7pm Tue-Sat; 9am-1pm Sun.
Admission L5,000.

The exhibits here date from 1937, when Mussolini mounted a massive celebration to mark the bi-millennium of Augustus becoming the first emperor. Any parallels between Augustus' reign and his own were, of course, coincidental. The building – vast blank walls and massive straight columns – is Fascist-classical at its most grandiloquent.

Models detail the construction of ancient Rome's main buildings, and there is a fascinating cutaway model of the Colosseum's maze of tunnels and lifts. There are also full-scale casts of the reliefs on the Column of Trajan in the **Imperial Fora** which enable you to examine their intricate details. The centrepiece is a giant model of Rome in the fourth century AD, showing the famous buildings in their original state. All in all, this outwardly daunting museum manages to put Rome's scattered fragments and artefacts into context very helpfully.
Wheelchair access.

Museo Nazionale delle Arti e Tradizioni Popolari

Piazza Guglielmo Marconi, 8 (06 592 6148).
Metro EUR Palasport/bus to Piazza Guglielmo Marconi. **Open** 9am-2pm Mon-Sat; 9am-1pm Sun. Closed second and fourth Sun of each month.
Admission L4,000.
An enormous collection dedicated to Italian folk art and rural tradition. There are elaborately decorated carts and horse tack, and a bizarre collection of votive offerings left to local saints (depictions of horrible diseases, or wax models of affected bits of anatomy). Malevolent-looking puppets fill one room; another has costumes and carnival artefacts, plus an exquisite collection of traditional jewellery, with photos showing how it was worn.
Wheelchair access.

Blueprint for the new Wembley? Scaled-down history in the **Museo della Civiltà Romana***.*

**Museo Preistorico
ed Etnografico L. Pigorini**
Piazza Guglielmo Marconi, 14 (06 549 521).
Metro Palasport/bus to Piazza Guglielmo Marconi.
Open 9am-2pm Tue-Sat; 9am-1pm Sun.
Admission L8,000.
This museum displays prehistoric Italian artefacts together with ethnological material from a range of world cultures. The lobby contains a reconstruction of the Guattari cave, with a genuine Neanderthal skull. On the first floor is the ethnological collection, with an all-too-predictable range of spears, pottery, jewellery, head dresses, masks, a few textiles and a couple of shrunken heads. The second floor has archaeological finds brought together from digs all over Italy, including mammoth tusks and teeth, and some human bones.
Wheelchair access.

Along the Appian way

Begun in the late fourth century BC by the statesman, lawmaker and sometime official censor Appius Claudius Caecus, the **Via Appia Antica** is one of the oldest Roman roads. It eventually reached as far as Brindisi on the Adriatic coast, making it the Romans' main route to their eastern provinces. In addition, because of a fifth-century BC law banning burials within the city, the road became lined with the tombs and mausoleums of Rome's important families.It is now a favoured retreat for lovers, ensconced in parked cars with steamed-up windows, and popular with men visiting the handful of elderly prostitutes who sit by their braziers at the Raccordo Anulare end.

However, it is the tombs of the ancient families and three sets of **Catacombs** (*see p99*) that attract the bulk of the road's visitors. Near the Porta di San Sebastiano (**Map 9/2A**), built by Aurelian when he walled the city in the fourth century AD, is the austere church of **Domine Quo Vadis?** Its main claim to fame lies just inside the door – the imprints of two long flat feet that are supposed to have been left by Christ when he appeared to Saint Peter, who was running away from Rome and crucifixion. Christ told him he himself was going back to Rome to be crucified again, and Peter was thus shamed into returning himself. The painting to the left side the altar depicts his martyrdom.

A memorial to a more recent act of barbarity stands beyond the **Catacombs of Domitilla**. This is the Fosse Ardeatine, formerly a quarry, where 335 Italians were shot by the Nazis in 1944 as a reprisal for a Resistance attack. They now lie here in an underground mausoleum; a memorial ceremony is held every year on 25 April (*see page 6*). Beyond the **Catacomb of San Sebastiano** are three of the road's most famous ancient sites. At the junction with Vicolo della Basilica are the overgrown remains of the fourth-century Tomb of Romulus, the same beloved son of the Emperor Maxentius who is commemorated in the Temple of Romulus in the

Roman Forum. The red brick walls behind it are the ruins of the Circus of Maxentius, also built by Romulus' father, for chariot racing.

On top of a hill to the south is a squat brick cylinder that is the Tomb of Cecilia Metella, from the first century BC. Cecilia had only married into the wealthy Metella family, who nevertheless gave her this unusually lavish tomb. During the fourteenth century the Caetani family, relatives of Pope Boniface VIII, turned the tomb into a fortress, adding the crenellations around its top, and proceeded to extract tolls from passers-by.

After the tomb comes a long stretch of road that in parts still retains the original flagstones used by the Romans. The tombs that line it are picturesquely overgrown and have been attracting artists for centuries. Much further on, about half-way between the crossings with Via Erode Attico and Via Del Casal Rotondo, is the site of the second century AD Villa of the Quintilli. Beyond this point the road is quieter and the landscape wilder, with fragments of aqueduct standing in the fields. Any turning to the left will take you eventually to Via Appia Nuova, the main modern route back to the centre of Rome.

Parco dell'Appia Antica
Information *Via Appia Antica, 42 (8000 2 8000) Bus 218 to Via Appia Antica.*
Open 9am-5.30pm daily.
The information office of the Parco dell'Appia Antica (in the stretch between Porta di San Sebastiano and Domine Quo Vadis?) has maps and information on the ancient road. It also organises tours and special events for children. Also pleasant, and easy, are walks or bike rides along the old road (*see chapter* **Directory: cycle hire**) on Sunday, when the whole length of the road from Porta San Sebastiano is closed to traffic.
Getting There Bus 218 from San Giovanni in Laterano stops by Domine Quo Vadis? before turning west onto Via Ardeatina. You can also approach the Via Appia from the far, south-eastern, end: take the Metro to Colli Albani, then the 660 bus, which stops near the Tomb of Cecilia Metella.

The Vatican City

Spectacular at any time, the papal headquarters is geared up for a millennial mega-event.

The Vatican State was given its current status in 1929 under a treaty with Mussolini known as *La Conciliazione*, or Lateran Pact. This was the papacy's consolation prize for having lost its temporal, political, power over Rome and its region in 1870, when Italy united and became a secular country. As such prizes go, it wasn't bad. Italy gave the Vatican 750 million lire and the income from a billion lire in state bonds, exempted it from taxes and duty on imported goods, and agreed to adopt canon law in marriage and make Catholic teaching compulsory in all schools.

Falling church attendance and the steady decline of Vatican influence over Italian politics have since encouraged the Italian state to backpedal. Divorce, contraception and abortion are legal, religious education is optional, and the Vatican is taxed on profits from the stock market, although its own employees are still not taxed on their earnings and it remains a duty-free zone.

The Vatican City occupies a hilly area west of the Tiber. Until Caligula, and then Nero, decided to build a circus there in the middle of the first century AD, the area was mainly used for the execution of religious troublemakers like the early Christians – the most famous being Saint Peter. Several decades on, in AD 90, the first monument was built over what was believed to be the site of Peter's martyrdom, and in the periods when the new faith was tolerated this became a popular spot for pilgrims. In the mid-fourth century, Constantine built a basilica over Peter's tomb, nevertheless he chose **San Giovanni in Laterano** as headquarters for the new official religion. Christians, however, preferred Peter's tomb, and dozens of buildings appeared in what became known as the *Borgo* (village).

After a series of invasions by Saracens and Lombards in the eighth and ninth centuries, Pope Leo IV encircled the area with a 12-metre-high defensive wall (*see page 91*) incorporating Hadrian's tomb, fortified as the **Castel Sant'Angelo**. In the Middle Ages, during the incessant battles for power between popes, the aristocracy and the Holy Roman Emperors (*see chapter* **History**), popes often fled down the covered passageway connecting the Vatican to the castle.

After the sack of Rome by Charles V's troops in 1527, the *Città Leonina* lost its strategic importance for ever. The papacy moved across the Tiber,

first to the Lateran Palace, then to the **Palazzo del Quirinale**, where it stayed until ousted by the Piedmontese royals in 1870, when Pius IX scuttled back behind the safety of the Vatican walls. On the creation of the independent Vatican City, the *Borgo* remained part of Italy and the city of Rome.

VISITING THE VATICAN

Note that dress codes are strictly enforced, in Saint Peter's and throughout the Vatican, including the museums, gardens and the Sistine Chapel. Ensure that you have something to cover exposed shoulders and/or legs above the knee; if you do not, you will almost certainly be turned away.

Saint Peter's Basilica

After 120 years as the world's most elegant building site, the current Saint Peter's was consecrated on 18 November 1626 by Urban VIII – exactly 1,300 years after the consecration of the first basilica on the site. The earlier building was erected on the orders of the first Christian emperor, Constantine the Great. Records show that it was a five-aisled classical basilica, fronted by a large courtyard and four porticoes. It was steadily enlarged and enriched, becoming the finest church in Christendom. By the mid-fifteenth century, however, its south wall was on the point of collapse. Pope Nicholas V commissioned new designs and had 2,500 wagonloads of masonry from the **Colosseum** carted across the Tiber, but never got further than repair work. No-one wanted to demolish the most sacred church in Christendom. It took the arrogance of Pope Julius II and his pet architect Bramante to get things moving. In 1506, 2,500 workers tore down the 1,000-year-old basilica, and Julius laid the foundation stone for its replacement.

Following Bramante's death in 1514, Raphael took over the work, and scrapped his predecessor's plan for a basilica with a Greek cross plan (*see page 28*), opting for an elongated Latin cross. In 1547, Michelangelo took command and reverted to a Greek design. He died in 1564 aged 87, but not before coming up with the design for a massive dome and supporting drum. This was completed in 1590, the largest brick dome ever constructed.

In 1607 Carlo Maderno won the consent of Pope Paul V to demolish the remaining fragments of the

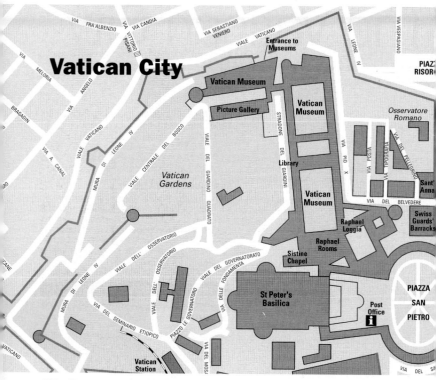

old basilica and put up a new façade, crowned by enormous statues of Christ and the Apostles. After Maderno's death Bernini took over, and despite nearly destroying both the façade and his reputation by erecting towers on either end (one of which fell down), he became the hero of the hour with his sumptuous *baldacchino* and famous piazza. This latter was built between 1656 and 1667, its colonnaded arms reaching out towards the Catholic world in a symbolic embrace. The main oval measures 340m by 240m, and is punctuated by the central Egyptian obelisk (dragged from Nero's Circus in 1586) and two symmetrical fountains, by Maderno and Bernini. The 284-columned, 88-pillared colonnade is topped by 140 statues of saints. In the portico (1612), opposite the main portal, is a mosaic by Giotto (c1298), a survivor from the original basilica. There are five doors leading into the basilica: the central ones come from the earlier church, while the others are all twentieth century. The last door on the right is only opened in Holy Years (*see page 106*) by the pope himself.

Inside, the basilica's size is emphasised on the marble floor, where a boastful series of brass line inscriptions measure the lengths of other church-es around the world which haven't made the grade. But it is Bernini's huge curlicued *baldacchino* (1633), hovering over the high altar, that is the real focal point. This was cast from brass purloined from the **Pantheon** (prompting local wits to joke *quod non fecerunt barbari, fecerunt Barberini* – what the Barbarians didn't do, the Barberini did, referring to Bernini's patron Pope Urban VII, of the Barberini clan), and is bathed in light flooding in from windows in the dome above. The canopy stands over Saint Peter's tomb; two flights of stairs lead beneath the altar to the Confessio, where a niche contains a ninth-century mosaic of Christ, the only thing from old Saint Peter's that stayed in the same place when the new church was built.

Catholic pilgrims head straight for the last pilaster on the right before the main altar, to kiss the big toe of Arnolfo da Cambio's brass statue of Saint Peter (c.1296); the toe has been worn down by centuries of pious lips. Tourists, on the other hand, make a bee-line for the first chapel on the right, where bullet-proof glass now protects Michelangelo's *Pietà* (1499) from unwanted attentions. This is the only work that Michelangelo ever bothered to sign, on the band across the Virgin's chest. Proceeding around the basilica in an anti-clockwise direction, notice the monument to Queen Christina of Sweden (*see page 72*) to the left of the *Pietà* chapel. The third chapel has a tabernacle and two angels by Bernini, plus the only remaining painting – a *Trinity* by Pietro da Cortona – in Saint Peter's (others have been replaced by mosaic copies). In the first chapel beyond the right transept is a tear-jerker of a neo-classical tomb (of Pope Clement XIII) by Antonio Canova (1792).

Bernini's *Throne of Saint Peter* (1665), flanked by papal tombs, stands at the far end of the nave beyond the high altar, under an almost psychedelic stained-glass window. Encased within Bernini's creation there is a wood-and-ivory chair, probably dating from the ninth century but for many years believed to have belonged to Saint Peter himself. Immediately to the right of the throne is Bernini's 1644 monument to his patron Urban VIII, who commissioned the bronze portrait, between statues of charity and justice, before his death. On the insides of the pillars supporting the main dome there are much-venerated relics including a chip off the true cross and the cloth that Veronica used to mop Christ's sweaty brow on the way to Calvary, only to find he'd left a face-print to remember him by.

Near the portico end of the left aisle is a group of monuments to the Old Pretender James Edward Stewart, his wife Maria Clementina Sobieski and their sons Charles Edward (Bonnie Prince Charlie) and Henry Benedict. They are buried in the grottoes below.

The **Vatican Grottoes** – the Renaissance crypts beneath the basilica, with more papal tombs – are open to visitors. The **Necropolis**, where Saint Peter is believed to be buried, is beneath these Grottoes and can be visited with permission. In the treasury off the left nave of the basilica there is a small historical museum, containing some stunning liturgical relics. The **dome** (reached via a cramped lift and hundreds of stairs) offers fabulous views of the **Vatican Gardens**, which can be toured.

Saint Peter's (*San Pietro*)

Metro Ottaviano/bus to Piazza del Risorgimento or Piazza della Città Leonina. **Map 3/1C**
Basilica *Oct-Mar* 7am-6pm, *Apr-Sept* 7am-7pm, daily. **Admission** free.
Free guided tours of the basilica in English set off from the information office at 2.15pm Mon-Sat; 3pm Mon, Wed-Fri; 2.30pm Sun.
Dome *Oct-Mar* 8am-4.45pm, *Apr-Sept* 8am-5.45pm, daily. **Admission** L7,000; *with lift* L8,000.
Grottoes *Oct-Mar* 7am-5pm, *Apr-Sept* 7am-6pm, daily. **Admission** free.
Necropolis apply at the *Uffizio degli Scavi (06 6988 5318/fax 07 6988 5518/uff.scavi@fabricsp.va).*
Open 9am-5pm Mon-Sat. English-language tours must be booked at least 25 days ahead of your visit. **Admission** L15,000.

Mega-Pope presides over mega-Holy Year.

Treasury Museum *Oct-Mar* 9am-5.15pm, *Apr-Sept* 9am-6.15pm, daily. **Admission** L8,000.
Vatican Gardens phone the Vatican Tourist Office (06 6988 4466) to book a tour, at least three or four days in advance. **Admission** L20,000.

The Vatican State

Apart from the massive sprawl of the basilica, the papal apartments and the magnificent structure that houses the Vatican museums, the 44 hectares encompassed by the Vatican walls include smaller churches, foreign seminaries and minor papal residences. On a more mundane level, there are also post offices, a railway station, a heliport, a pharmacy, a supermarket and a petrol station.

Leading up to the Vatican is Via della Conciliazione, an austere foil to Bernini's elaborate curves. For centuries, popes had planned to clear the labyrinthine Borgo streets and create a monumental approach to Saint Peter's Square; it was Mussolini who finally did it in the 1930s.

For **papal audiences**, apply to the *Prefettura della Casa Pontificia* (06 6988 3273/fax 06 6988 5863; open 9am-1pm Mon-Sat). Tickets are free, and entrance is through the bronze door at the basilica end of Bernini's colonnade. For a private audience, your local bishop has to make a written request, which can take between three months and a year to be granted.

Mother of all Holy Years

The first ever Holy Year – or, to give it its proper name, Jubilee Year – was celebrated in 1300, when Pope Boniface VIII (1294-1303) noticed Church coffers were depleted. Pilgrims converging from all over Christendom, he thought, ready to splash cash in return the remission of the odd sin, might help rectify the situation. He was right. Boniface envisaged the Jubilee junket as a once-a-century event, but by 1342 Pope Clement VI had fully grasped its economic implications and reduced the gap to 50 years. Which was not enough for Paul II, who in 1470 declared that a Jubilee was needed every 25 years.

If Clement could justify speeding things up from scripture (Leviticus 25;8 states that every 50th year was a sabbatical year for the people of Israel, when fields lay fallow and slaves were freed), Paul's reduction was harder to explain; harder still the practise, introduced in 1560, of calling 'special' Holy Years whenever a pope's fancy took him (any connection to economic difficulties being purely coincidental). However, the year 2000 does have all the requisites of holy year-ness, and the *Great Jubilee* promises to be the Holy Year to beat all Holy Years, with 25 million pilgrims expected to swell Rome's usual tourist army over the twelve-months-and-a-bit during which celebrations last.

Motives for making the trip to Rome have changed since Holy Years started. Then (as now), every Jubilee pilgrim earned a plenary indulgence (any outstanding penance on earth or in purgatory needed to earn a place in heaven was erased, leaving you with a clean slate). Today, however (unlike then), indulgences are highly unfashionable - too medieval for the modern Church - and it is the sheer kudos of being able to say 'I was there' and of receiving a blessing from an old man in white that keeps the faithful faithful.

The 2000 Jubilee party, as tradition dictates, begins on 24 December 1999, when the pope takes his hammer and knocks down the bricks and mortar that have blocked the Holy Door (*see page 104*) in **Saint Peter's** since the special Jubilee in 1983 (the blow will be symbolic, and the door will have been rigged with handle and hinges). More holy doors are opened in the basilicas of **San Giovanni in Laterano** (25 Dec), **Santa Maria Maggiore** (25 Dec) and **San Paolo fuori le Mura** (18 Jan).

Then begins a series of rallies, designed to make sure no one feels left out. If you're not planning to participate, avoid the pilgrim onslaught by visiting Rome on a date when no festivities are scheduled. Where no venue is given, it had not been definitively decided at time of writing. Check the official Jubilee website (*www.jubil2000.org*) for updated information on all aspects of Holy Year.

Holy Year Calendar

Christmas Urbi et Orbi blessing Dec 25 1999. *Venue* Saint Peter's
Prayer vigil for the new millennium 31 Dec 1999. *Venue* Saint Peter's
Children's Jubilee 2 Jan 2000. *Venue* Saint Peter's
Mass children's baptism 9 Jan. *Venue* Saint Peter's
Priests' Jubilee 2 Feb. *Venue* Saint Peter's
Jubilee of the sick 11 Feb. *Venue* Saint Peter's
Artists' Jubilee 18 Feb. *Venue* Santa Maria Maggiore
Ash Wednesday Procession 8 Mar. *Venue* Santa Sabina
Craftsmen's Jubilee 20 Mar.
Women's Jubilee 25 Mar. *Venue* Santa Maria Maggiore. With a video link-up to Marian shrines around the world.
Jubilee of migrants and refugees 10 Apr.
Good Friday Way of the Cross 21 Apr. *Venue* Colosseum
Easter Sunday Urbi et Orbi blessing 23 Apr. *Venue* Saint Peter's
Workers' Jubilee 1 May.
Clergy's Jubilee/Pope's 80th birthday 18 May. *Venue* Saint Peter's
Scientists' Jubilee 25 May.
Rome Diocese Jubilee 28 May.
Journalists' Jubilee 4 June.
Prisoners' Jubilee 9 July.
Jubilee for Youth 19-20 Aug.
University teachers' Jubilee 10 Sept. *Venue* Saint Peter's
Jubilee of the elderly 17 Sept.
Day of Jewish-Christian dialogue 3 Oct.
Bishops' Jubilee 8 Oct. *Venue* Saint Peter's
Families' Jubilee 15 Oct. *Venue* Saint Peter's
Jubilee for Sports people 29 Oct. *Venue* Stadio Olimpico
Jubilee of those involved in public life 5 Nov.
Agricultural Jubilee 12 Nov.
Police and military Jubilee 19 Nov.
World of entertainment Jubilee 17 Dec.
New Year's prayer vigil 31 Dec. *Venue* Saint Peter's
Holy Year Doors closed in **San Giovanni in Laterano, Santa Maria Maggiore, San Paolo fuori le Mura** 5 Jan 2001.
Holy Year Door closed in **Saint Peter's** 6 Jan 2001.

Bigger than thou: **Saint Peter's** *basilica displays no humility about its size (see page 104).*

The Vatican Museums

It's a brisk ten-minute walk from Saint Peter's to the entrance of the Vatican Museums. Begun in 1506 by Pope Julius II, this immense collection represents the accumulated fancies and obsessions of a long line of strong, often contradictory personalities. The popes' unique position allowed them to obtain treasures on favourable terms from other collectors, and artists often had little choice as to whether they accepted papal commissions.

The collections are so vast that it's impossible to take in more than a small portion on one visit. The museum authorities have laid out four colour-coded routes, ranging from a race to the Sistine Chapel to a conscientious five-hour plod around the lot. The following are selected highlights.

There are four special itineraries for wheelchair users, with disabled toilets en route; a brochure is available at the ticket office. Wheelchairs can be hired at the museums by calling (06 6988 3860) prior to visiting. Note that opening times are liable to change at short notice, and will almost certainly be lengthened in Holy Year; ring 06 6988 3333 to check.

The Vatican Museums
Metro Ottaviano/bus to Piazza del Risorgimento.
Open *Mar 1-Oct 29, Dec 20-30* 8.45am-3.45pm Mon-Fri; *rest of year* 8.45am-12.45pm Mon-Fri; *all year* 8.45am-12.45pm Sat; *last Sun of each month* 8.45am-12.45pm. **Admission** L18,000; students L12,000; last Sun of month free.

Egyptian Museum
Founded by Gregory XVI in 1839, in rooms partly decorated in Egyptian style, this is a representative

---

The Jubilee trail

As an integral part of Jubilee devotions, pilgrims must do the rounds of the four big basilicas – **Saint Peter's**, **San Giovanni in Laterano**, **Santa Maria Maggiore** and **San Paolo fuori le mura** – in the 24 hours between vespers one evening and the next. To clock up even more heavenly brownie points, sprightlier pilgrims can add to the list the basilicas of **San Lorenzo fuori le Mura**, **Santa Croce in Gerusalemme** and San Sebastiano, a church built in the fourth century and rebuilt in the seventeenth, containing an arrow supposedly shot into Saint Sebastian and the column he was tied to while the arrows were flying… and totally overlooked by most visitors as they make for the **catacombs of San Sebastiano** (*see page 99*), on top of which the basilica stands.

---

selection of ancient Egyptian art from 3,000-600 BC. It includes statues of a baboon god, painted mummy cases and a white marble statue of Antinous, Emperor Hadrian's lover, who drowned in Egypt and was declared divine by the emperor. A couple of real mummies will help make this the most exciting bit of the whole Vatican if you have grisly-minded kids in tow.

Chiaramonte Gallery
Founded by Pius VII in the early nineteenth century and laid out by the sculptor Canova, this is an eclectic collection of Roman statues, reliefs and busts. Don't miss the replica of a Greek statue by Polyeuctos of stuttering orator Demosthenes, and a much-reproduced copy of a *Resting Satyr* by the Greek sculptor Praxiteles.

Pio-Clementino Museum
In the late eighteenth century Pope Clement XIV and his successor Pius VI began the world's largest collection of classical statues, which now fills 16 rooms on two floors. Essential viewing are the first-century BC headless *Belvedere Torso* by Apollonius of Athens; the *Apollo Sauroctonos*, a Roman copy of the bronze *Lizard Killer* by Praxiteles; and, in the octagonal Belvedere Courtyard, the exquisite *Belvedere Apollo* and *Laocoön*, who is being throttled by sea serpents as punishment by the goddess Athena for warning the Trojans that the wooden horse was full of wily Greeks.

Etruscan Museum
Founded in 1837 by Gregory XVI, and enlarged in this century, this collection contains Greek and Roman art as well as masterpieces from Etruria, including the spectacular contents of the Regolini-Galassi Tomb from c650 BC, the Greek-inspired fourth-century BC *Mars*, and the fifth-century BC young man and small slave.

Galleria dei Candelabri & Galleria degli Arazzi
Roman marble statues, in a long gallery studded with candelabra. In the next gallery are ten huge tapestries woven by Flemish master Pieter van Aelst from the cartoons by Raphael that are now in London's Victoria and Albert Museum.

Galleria delle Carte Geografiche
Pope Gregory XIII (he of the Gregorian calendar, which we use today) had a craze for astronomy, and was responsible for this 120-metre-long gallery, with its Tower of the Winds observation point at the north end. Ignazio Danti of Perugia drew the maps that cover its walls, showing each Italian region, city and island, with extraordinary precision for the time (1580-3).

The Raphael Rooms, Raphael's Loggia and the Chapel of Nicholas V
One of the masterpieces of the collection, these rooms were part of Nicholas V's palace, originally decorated by Piero della Francesca. Julius II then let

*A God's-eye view of the Pope's back yard from **Saint Peter's** dome (see page 105).*

Perugino, Lorenzo Lotto and others loose on them, until he discovered Raphael, whereupon he gave the young artist carte blanche to re-design four rooms of the Papal Suite.

The order of the visit changes from time to time, but it makes sense, if possible, to see the rooms in the order in which they were painted. The Study (*Stanza della Segnatura*) was Raphael's first bash (1508-11), and features philosophical and spiritual themes – the triumph of Truth, Good and Beauty. Best known is the star-packed *School of Athens* fresco, with contemporary artists as classical figures: Plato is Leonardo; the thinker on the steps – Heraclitus – is Michelangelo; Euclid is Bramante – note the letters RUSM, Raphael's signature, on his gold collar – and Raphael himself stands to the left of a capped man, believed to be his pupil Sodoma). Raphael next turned his hand to the Waiting Room (*Stanza di Eliodoro*, 1512-14), frescoed with political themes such as *The Expulsion of Heliodorus*, a re-reading of a biblical episode designed to highlight Pope Julius II's supreme political savvy.

The Dining Room (*Stanza dell'Incendio*, 1514-17) is devoted to the feats of Popes Leo III and IV, among them *The Fire in the Borgo*, which Leo IV halted with the sign of the cross. The Reception Room (*Sala di Constantino*, 1523-5) was completed by Giulio Romano after Raphael's death in 1520, but was based on Raphael's sketches of the Church's triumph over paganism.

The long *La loggia di Raffaello*, with a beautiful view over Rome, was started by Bramante in 1513 and finished by Raphael and his assistants. It features 52 small paintings on biblical themes, and leads into the *Sala dei Chiaroscuri* (Raphael's frescoes here were obliterated by Gregory XIII, but the magnificent ceiling remains). The adjacent *Cappella di Niccolò V*, has outstanding frescoes of scenes from the lives of Saints Lawrence (*see page 100*) and Stephen by Fra Angelico (1448-50).

Borgia Rooms

A six-room suite adapted for the Borgia Pope Alexander VI (1492-1503) and decorated by Pinturicchio and his school with a series of frescoes on biblical and classical themes. In 1973, some 50 rooms of the Borgia Apartments were renovated to house the *Collezione d'Arte Religiosa Moderna*, featuring modern religious works.

The Sistine Chapel (*Cappella Sistina*)

The world's most famous frescoes cover the ceiling and one wall of a chapel built by Sixtus IV in 1473-84. For centuries it has been used for popes' private prayers and papal elections (conclaves). In the 1980s and '90s the 10,000 square feet of *Creation*, on the ceiling, and the *Last Judgment* on the wall behind the altar were subjected to the most controversial restoration job of all time, funded by the Japanese television company NHK in exchange for a period of exclusive broadcasting rights.

In 1508 Michelangelo was commissioned to paint a some kind of undemanding decoration on the ceiling of the Sistine Chapel. Julius II may have been egged on to give the job to a sculptor with no experience in fresco by Bramante, who was jealous of the pope's admiration for Michelangelo and desperately wanted to see him fail. Michelangelo responded by offering to do far more than mere decoration, and embarked upon his massive venture alone. He spent the next four years on top of scaffolding on his back, with paint and plaster dripping into his eyes, and his pay arriving so infrequently that he complained to his brother in 1511 'I could well say that I go naked and barefoot'.

The work, completed in 1512 (so Michelangelo was working a short corridor away from Raphael while he frescoed the *stanze*), was done in the heady days of the high Renaissance when optimistic artists were nobly bent on the pursuit of beauty. Beginning at the *Last Judgment* end, scenes depict the

Separation of Light from Darkness, the *Creation of Sun, Moon and Planets*, the *Separation of Land and Sea* and the *Creation of Fishes and Birds*, *Creation of Adam*, *Creation of Eve*, *Temptation and Expulsion from Paradise*, *Sacrifice of Noah* (which should come after the Flood, but was put here for space reasons), the *Flood*, and the *Drunkenness of Noah*. Michelangelo painted these scenes backwards, beginning with Noah's drunkenness. They are framed by monumental figures of Old Testament prophets and classical sibyls.

Twenty-two years after completing this masterpiece, the aged and embittered artist rolled up his sleeves again and started work on the *Last Judgment* to fill the altar wall. In the interim, Rome had been sacked (1527) – an episode seen by many, including Michelangelo, as the wrath of God descending on the corrupt city – and the atmosphere was altogether more pessimistic. It took him seven years to complete the work, in 1541. It is altogether more doom-laden, as befits the subject. Hidden among the larger-than-life figures that stare, leer and cry out from their brilliant blue background, Michelangelo painted his own, frowning, miserable face on the wrinkled human skin held by Saint Bartholomew (*see page 110*), below and to the right of the powerful figure of Christ the Judge. Pius IV objected to so much nudity and wanted to destroy the fresco; thankfully he was persuaded to settle for loincloths, most of which were removed in the restoration.

Dwarfed by Michelangelo's work, the sorely-neglected paintings on the side walls of the chapel are a *Who's Who* of Renaissance greats, painted before Michelangelo began. On the left-hand wall as you look at the *Last Judgment*, going anti-clockwise around the chapel, are: *Journey of Moses* by Perugino; *Events from the life of Moses* by Botticelli; *Crossing the Red Sea* by Cosimo Rosselli; *Moses receives the tablets of the law* by Cosimo Rosselli; *Testament of Moses* by Luca Signorelli; *Dispute over Moses' Body* by Matteo da Lecce; *Resurrection* by Arrigo Paludano; *Last Supper* by Cosimo Rosselli; *Handing over the Keys* by Perugino; *Sermon on the Mount* by Cosimo Rosselli; *Calling of the Apostles* by Ghirlandaio; *Temptations of Christ* by Botticelli; and *Baptism of Christ* by Perugino. The papal portraits are by the same masters.

Pinacoteca

Founded by Pius VI in the late eighteenth century, the *Pinacoteca* (Picture Gallery) includes many of the pictures the Vatican hierarchy managed to recover from Napoleon after their forced sojourn in France. The collection ranges from early paintings of the Byzantine School and Italian primitives to eighteenth century Dutch and French masters, and includes Giotto's *Stefaneschi Triptych*, a *Pietà* by Lucas Cranach the Elder, several *Madonnas* by Fra Filippo Lippi, Fra Angelico, Raphael and Titian, Raphael's very last work *The Transfiguration*, Caravaggio's *Entombment* and a monochrome *Saint Jerome* by Leonardo.

Spot that Saint

Saints are Rome's stock-in-trade, and symbols of the best-remembered martyrs and figures of the Church are found all over the city. Below are a few references to recognise:

Agatha breasts on a plate (a spurned Roman senator and suitor had hers cut off)
Agnes Lady Godiva look-alike (stripped naked in Piazza Navona, she was covered up by her conveniently-growing hair)
Anthony of Padua carries a child (he was spotted by a follower carrying the baby Jesus about)
Bartholomew complete human skin (he was flayed alive)
Catherine of Alexandria a cartwheel (tortured strapped to a wheel, she gave her name to the firework)
Francis of Assisi brown robes, tonsure, and stygmata (sure proof that he had God on his side)
Jerome red robes, with a lion lurking nearby (he took a thorn out of its paw)
John the Baptist long spindly cross, bear-skin attire (from living rough out in the desert)
Lawrence a grill iron (he was roasted to death)
Lucy eyes on a tray (hers were put out)
Martyrs (in general) carry palm fronds
Paul big sword (he was a soldier, after all)
Peter big key (to Pearly Gates)
Sebastian shot full of arrows (just one of the hiccoughs he suffered on the way to martyrdom)
Stephen big rock in his skull (he was stoned to death)
Virgins (in general) carry lilies, symbol of purity

Museum of Pagan Antiquities

This collection of Roman and neo-Attic sculpture has been housed since 1970 in the *Museo Paolino*. Highlights include the beautifully draped statue of Sophocles from Terracina, a *trompe l'œil* mosaic of an unswept floor and the wonderfully elaborate Altar of Vicomagistri.

Pio Cristiano Museum

The upper floor of the *Museo Paolino* is devoted to a collection of early Christian antiquities, mostly sarcophagi carved with reliefs of biblical scenes.

The Vatican Library

Founded by Pope Nicholas V in 1450, this is one of the world's most extraordinary libraries, with 100,000 medieval manuscripts and books and over a million other volumes. It is open to students and specialists on application to the *Prefettura* (06 6988 3273). *See also chapter* **Directory**.

Staying in Rome

Accommodation

Imperial opulence, pads in palazzi and budget bunks: Rome has beds for every class of pilgrim.

Predominantly privately run, Rome's hotels retain their original charm.

Rome is not a cheap place to stay, and price does not always reflect quality. One compensation for the expense, though, is that the city has also resisted the encroachment of impersonal chains. Most hotels are still privately run, and most of those that are not retain their original charm.

Italian hotels are classified on a star system, from one to five. One star usually indicates *pensioni*, which are cheap but have very few facilities, and you may have to share a bathroom. The more stars, the more facilities a hotel will have; a higher rating, however, does not guarantee friendliness, cleanliness or decent service. Pricewise, a double room in a one-star can set you back L70,000-L200,000; two-star, L90,000-L280,000; three-star, L150,000-L400,000; four-star roughly L200,000 to L790,000. Five-star prices start at about L280,000, and don't stop until most people would need a second mortgage just for one night.

Hotels listed here offer value for money. In the luxury category the emphasis is on opulence. Those in mid- to upper-price ranges are smaller, many in old *palazzi* with pretty, if often small, bedrooms. *Pensioni* are fairly basic,but those listed here are clean, friendly and usually family run.

Few Roman hotels have even heard of non-smoking areas, and not many have access for the disabled. Staff are generally very willing to help guests with mobility problems, but most places have so many stairs there's not much they can do (*see chapter* **Directory: Disabled travellers**).

Booking a room

Most hotels fall roughly into certain areas: **Campo de' Fiori**, strong on low- to medium-priced hotels with lots of character; **Piazza di Spagna**, with elegant, traditional, well-refurbished hotels in the upper price ranges; **Termini**, with countless cheap *pensioni* and a few mid-price hotels (but single and female travellers should remember that the station area can be unpleasant after dark); and **Piazza Navona**, with rooms in mid- to-upper-brackets. Some hotels are a bit further afield, in **Trastevere**, near the **Vatican** or on the **Aventine**.

Always reserve a room well in advance, especially at peak times. If you're coming for (or at the same time as) any major events on the 2000 Holy Year calendar (*see page 106*), book weeks or months ahead. The high season begins at Easter and continues until June, resumes in September and October, and then has another burst over Christmas and New Year. July and August, though busy, are not generally difficult times to find accommodation.

Many hotels will ask you to fax confirmation of a booking, with a credit card number as deposit. Smaller hotels may ask you to send a eurocheque or money order to secure rooms in high season.

If you arrive with nowhere to stay, the **APT** tourist office provides hotel lists, and **Enjoy Rome** will also book one for you (*see chapter* **Directory: Tourist information**). The **Hotel Reservations** agency (06 699 1000; open 7am-10pm daily), with desks at Termini and Fiumicino, has details on availability in 200 hotels at all prices. Staff speak English. It's best not to accept help from the touts that hang around Termini – you're likely to end up paying more than you should for a grotty hotel.

Prices quoted are for peak rates in 1999, and are subject to change: in popular areas (notably Campo de' Fiori) they are likely to go on rising, especially for Holy Year. Some hotels have low weekend rates, and it's always worth asking about discounts for longer stays or groups. Unless stated, prices are for rooms with bathrooms, and include breakfast.

If you're visiting with **children**, most hotels will be happy to squeeze a cot or camp bed into a room, but will probably charge 30 to 50 per cent extra for the privilege. Self-catering accommodation (*see page 129*) can be a cheaper alternative.

De luxe

Aldovrandi Palace

Via Ulisse Aldovrandi, 15 (06 322 3993/fax 06 322 1435/hotel@aldovrandi.com). Bus to Via Bruno Buozzi/tram to Via Aldovrandi. **Rates** *single* L580,000; *double* L680,000; *suite* L950,000.
Credit AmEx, DC, EC, JCB, MC, V. **Map 4/1C**
A haven of luxurious tranquillity on a busy road at the edge of the Villa Borghese, and one of few central (ish) hotels with a garden and swimming pool. Public areas are magnificent, and it has two fine restaurants, one overlooking the garden.
Hotel services *Air-conditioning. Bar. Car park. Currency exchange. Fax. Garden. Garage. Gym. Laundry. Lifts. Multi-lingual staff. Non-smoking rooms. Restaurant. Safe. Swimming pool (outdoor).*
Room services *Hair dryer. Mini-bar. Radio. Room service. Safe. Telephone. TV (satellite).*
Website: www.aldovrandi.com

Ambasciatori Palace

Via Vittorio Veneto, 62 (06 47 493/fax 06 474 3601/ambasciatorirome@diginet.it). Metro Barberini/bus to Via Veneto. **Rates** (breakfast L27,000 extra) *single* L350,000-L450,000; *double* L450,000-L650,000; *suite* L850,000.
Credit AmEx, DC, EC, JCB, MC, V. **Map 5/1B**
A *fin de siècle* hotel with elegant lounge and bar. Upstairs there are 110 large, comfortable rooms, several with two bathrooms and small balconies. Guests are mainly business people; staff are very friendly.
Hotel services *Air-conditioning. Babysitting. Bar. Car park (nearby). Conference facilities. Currency Exchange. Fax. Laundry. Lifts. Multi-lingual staff. Non-smoking rooms. Restaurant. Safe. Sauna.*

Room services *Air-conditioning. Hair dryer. Mini-bar. Radio. Room service (24-hour). Safe. Telephone. TV (satellite).*
Website:www.hotelambasciatori.com

Atlante Star

Via Vitelleschi, 34 (06 687 3233/fax 06 687 2300/ atlante.star@atlantehotels.com). Metro Ottaviano/bus to Piazza del Risorgimento or Piazza Cavour. **Rates** *single* L390,000; *double* L530,000; *suite* from L850,000.
Credit AmEx, DC, EC, JCB, MC, V. **Map 3/1C**
A comfortable 70-room hotel well placed for the Vatican and not far from the *centro storico*. Ultra-modern bedrooms are in dark colours, which can be soothing or claustrophobic, depending on size – some rooms are small. Its roof garden-restaurant has wonderful views of Saint Peter's. Free airport pick-up is provided; outward journeys cost L60,000.
Hotel services *Air-conditioning. Babysitting. Bar. Car park. Car rental. Garden. Conference facilities. Currency exchange. Disabled: adapted rooms (2), wheelchair access. Fax. Laundry. Lifts. Multi-lingual staff. Non-smoking rooms. Restaurant. Safe. Solarium. Tours arranged.*
Room services *Hair-dryer. Jacuzzi in suites. Mini-bar. Radio. Room service (24-hour). Telephone. TV.*
Website:www.atlantehotels.com

Crowne Plaza Minerva

Piazza della Minerva, 69 (06 6994 1888/fax 06 67 94 165/minerva@pronet.it). Bus or tram to Largo Argentina. **Rates** (breakfast L30,000-L45,000 extra) *single* L555,000; *double* L700,000-L770,000; *suite* L1,300,000. **Credit** AmEx, DC, EC, JCB, MC, V. **Map 3/2A**
The Holiday Inn empire took over this seventeenth-century *albergo* within spitting distance of the Pantheon in the 1980s, and brought in Paolo Portoghesi to give a postmodern redesign to its public rooms, with truckloads of marble, stained glass and neo-classical motifs. The hotel has now left the chain, and been revamped yet again: the very friendly and helpful 'have a nice day staff' have remained.
Hotel services *Air-conditioning. Babysitting. Bars. Car Rental. Conference facilities. Currency exchange. Disabled: adapted room (1), wheelchair access. Fax. Fitness room. Laundry. Lifts. Multi-lingual staff. Non-smoking rooms. Ticket desk.*
Room services *Fax point. Hair dryer. Mini-bar. Radio. Room service. Safe. Telephone. TV (satellite).*
Website: www.crowneplaza.com

Eden

Via Ludovisi, 49 (06 47 8121/freephone within Italy only 800 820 088/fax 06 482 1584/ reservations@hotel-eden.it).
Metro Spagna/bus to Via Veneto. **Rates** (breakfast L36,000-L53,000 extra) *single* L693,000-L737,000; *double* L990,000-L1,155,000; *suites* L2,530,000-L3,850,000; *Imperial Suite* on request.
Credit AmEx, DC, EC, JCB, MC, V. **Map 5/1C**
Just off Via Veneto, the Eden has opulent reception rooms, tastefully decorated bedrooms and a roof terrace with top-rank restaurant and truly spectacular views. It's a celeb favourite, but the atmosphere is more relaxed than in other hotels in this bracket.

In the afternoon you can sip tea listening to a harpist, and at weekends take brunch on the terrace to jazz. The Imperial suite is Europe's most expensive. **Hotel services** *Banqueting/conference facilities. Bars. Car rental. Currency exchange. Fax. Garage nearby. Gym. Laundry. Non-smoking rooms. Reservations for airlines, theatres. Restaurant. Safe. Tours.* **Room services** *Fax. Hair dryer. Internet access. Mini-bar. PC point. Radio. Safe. Telephone. TV (satellite).*
Website:www.hotel-eden.it

Excelsior

Via Vittorio Veneto, 125 (06 47 081/fax 06 472 6205). Metro Barberini/bus to Via Vittorio Veneto. **Rates** (breakfast L35,000-L55,000 extra) *single* L506,000-L550,00; *double* L814,000-L924,000; *suite* L1,430,000-L7,370,000. *Ambassador Suite* on request. **Credit** AmEx, DC, EC, JCB, MC, V. **Map 5/1B**
The entrance and bar are decorated in luxurious blue and gold, with thick carpets, chandeliers, and antique clocks. Above, the 377 bedrooms are more Hollywood historic fantasy than genuine stately home; an ultra-luxurious suite is a recent addition. Staff and management are appropriately attentive. **Hotel services** *Air-conditioning. Babysitting. Bar. Beauty salon. Car park (nearby). Conference facilities. Currency exchange. Fax. Laundry. Lifts. Multi-lingual staff. Non-smoking rooms. Restaurant. Safe.* **Room services** *Fax point. Hair dryer. Mini-bar. Radio. Room service (24-hour). Telephone. TV (satellite). Video (on request).*
Website: www.sheraton.com
www.luxurycollection.com

Le Grand Hotel

Via Vittorio Emanuele Orlando, 3 (06 47 091). Metro Repubblica/bus to Piazza della Repubblica. **Rates** not available at time of writing.
As this guide went to press, Le Grand was undergoing a complete, very secretive overhaul, and due to re-open in November 1999. When unveiled, the 170 rooms will probably be of an opulence that will put even its sister hotel, the Excelsior, to shame.

Hassler Villa Medici

Piazza Trinità dei Monti, 6 (06 699 340/fax 06 678 9991/hasslerroma@mclink.it). Metro Spagna/ bus to Piazza Barberini. **Rates** (breakfast L38,000-L58,000 extra) *single* L540,000-L790,000; *double* L860,000-L1,080,000; *suite* on request.
Credit AmEx, DC, EC, JCB, MC, V. **Map 5/1C**
One of Rome's classic hotels, the Hassler is marvellously located by the top of the Spanish Steps, with tremendous views. Opened in 1885 and owned by the same Swiss family for decades, it has 100 bedrooms soothingly decorated in wood and marble, and a delightful rooftop terrace and restaurant. The Hassler prides itself on being a home away from home (if your home happens to be a castle), combining Roman hospitality with Swiss courtesy. **Hotel services** *Air-conditioning. Babysitting. Bars. Car park. Conference facilities Currency exchange. Fax. Interpreters. Laundry. Lifts. Multi-lingual staff. Restaurant. Safe. Secretarial services. Tours*

arranged. **Room services** *Fax point. Hair dryer. Mini-bar. PC point. Radio. Room service (24-hour). Safe. Telephone. TV (satellite & cable).*
Website:www.hotelhasslerroma.com

d'Inghilterra

Via Bocca di Leone, 14 (06 69 981/fax 06 6992 2243/reservation-hir@charminghotels.it). Metro Spagna/bus to Piazza San Silvestro. **Rates** (Breakfast L37,000 extra) *single* L449,000; *double* L668,000; *suite* L877,800-L1,229,800.
Credit AmEx, DC, EC, JCB, MC, V. **Map 3/1A**
Founded in the Victorian era, this celebrated hotel takes itself and its illustrious past so seriously that its much-vaunted atmosphere of dignity can lapse into plain rudeness. Still, the setting, in a quietish street near Piazza di Spagna, is splendid, and so is the plush, English colonial-style décor. Public rooms are opulent, while the 105 bedrooms are relentlessly tasteful. Some have balconies; many are cramped. **Hotel services** *Air-conditioning. Babysitting. Bars. Car park (nearby). Currency exchange. Fax. Laundry. Lift. Multi-lingual staff. Restaurants. Ticket desk.* **Room services** *Fax point. Hair dryer. Mini-bar. PC point. Room service. Safe. Telephone. TV (satellite).*
Website: www.charminghotels.it

Majestic

Via Vittorio Veneto, 50 (06 486 841/fax 06 488 0984). Metro Barberini/bus to Via Vittorio Veneto. **Rates** *single* L500,000-L580.000; *double* L690,000-L790,000; *suite* L900,000-L2,600,000.
Credit AmEx, DC, EC, JCB, MC, V. **Map 5/1B**
A peaceful but rather formal atmosphere. The downstairs lounge is richly furnished in eighteenth-century style, while the 95 bedrooms are more modern, with striped wallpaper and big, glitzy bathrooms, most of which include a jacuzzi. **Hotel Services** *Air-conditioning. Babysitting. Bar. Conference facilities. Car park. Currency exchange. Fax. Laundry. Lifts. Multi-lingual staff. Safe. Restaurant.* **Room services** *Fax point. Hair dryer. Jacuzzi. Mini-bar. Radio. Room service. Safe. Telephone. TV (satellite).*

Plaza

Via del Corso, 126 (06 6992 1111/fax 06 6994 1575/plaza@italyhotel.com). Bus to Piazzale Flaminio or Piazza San Silvestro. **Rates** (breakfast L42,000 extra) *single* L370,000; *double* L550,000; *suite* L900,000. **Credit** AmEx, DC, EC, MC, V. **Map 3/1A**
Just around the corner from Via Condotti and Piazza di Spagna, the Plaza retains a certain *fin de siècle* atmosphere, and the staircase leading up from the rococo-style lounge has probably been trodden by more famous feet than any other in Rome. It has 207 bedrooms; those on upper floors have little private terraces. The roof terrace is for the use of all guests. **Hotel services** *Air-conditioning. Babysitting. Bar. Car rental. Currency exchange. Disabled: adapted rooms (8), wheelchair access. Fax. Laundry. Lifts. Multi-lingual staff. Non-smoking rooms. Restaurant. Safe.* **Room services** *Hair dryer. Mini-bar. Radio. PC point. Room service. Safe. Telephone. TV (satellite).*
Website:www.venere.it/roma/plaza

The **Valadier**: *romantic hideaway with mirrored ceilings and padded walls.*

Valadier

Via della Fontanella, 15 (06 361 1998/ fax 06 320 1558/valadier@venere.it). Bus to Piazza del Popolo. **Rates** *single* L410,000; *double* L520,000; *suite* L600,000-L700,000.

Credit AmEx, DC, EC, JCB, MC, V. **Map 2/2A**

This quiet, exclusive hotel, close to the Ara Pacis, prides itself on being a romantic hideaway, and has an appropriately seductive atmosphere that has drawn such celebrities as David Bowie. The 49 bedrooms are slickly decorated, some with mirrored ceilings and padded walls. If you like that kind of thing.

Hotel services *Air-conditioning. Babysitting. Bar. Car park. Car Rental. Currency exchange. Lift. Multilingual staff. Roof garden. Restaurant. Safe.* **Room services** *Fax point, Hair dryer. Mini-bar. Phone. Radio. Room service. Safe. Telephone. TV (satellite). Website: www.italyhotel.com/roma/valadier*

Upper range

Carriage

Via delle Carrozze, 36 (06 699 0124/fax 06 678 8279). Metro Spagna/bus to Via del Corso. **Rates** *single* L300,000; *double* L400,000; *triple* L500,000; *suite* L600,000.

Credit AmEx, DC, EC, MC, V. **Map 3/1A**

A pretty, comfortable hotel in one of the quieter streets of the Piazza di Spagna shopping area. In the 27 rooms there are reproduction antiques and brass beds, and it has small suites for up to four people. As well as a breakfast room there's a small terrace, and some rooms have patios. Staff are very helpful.

Hotel services *Air-conditioning. Babysitting. Currency exchange. Fax. Laundry. Lifts. Multi-lingual staff. Tours.* **Room services** *Hair dryer. Mini-bar. Radio. Telephone. TV (satellite).*

Due Torri

Vicolo del Leonetto, 23/25 (06 6880 6956/fax 06 686 5442). Bus to Corso del Rinascimento. **Rates** *single* L180,000-L200,000; *double* L290,000-L320,000; *suite* L380,000.

Credit AmEx, DC, EC, MC, V. **Map 3/2A**

A peaceful hotel in a quiet alley near Piazza Navona. The 26 recently-redecorated bedrooms are pretty and cosy, while the lounges and breakfast room are comfortable and gracious. Ask the friendly staff about the building's history (it has been a residence of cardinals – at least one of whom became pope).

Hotel services *Air-conditioning. Babysitting. Bar. Car park (nearby). Currency exchange. Fax. Laundry. Lifts. Multi-lingual staff.* **Room services** *Hair dryer. Mini-bar. Radio. Room service. Safe (in reception). Telephone. TV (satellite).*

Fontana

Piazza di Trevi, 96 (06 678 6113/fax 06 679 0024). Bus to Via del Tritone. **Rates** *single* L290,000; *double* L350,000-L390,000; *suite* L470,000.

Credit AmEx, DC, EC, MC, V. **Map 5/2C**

The only hotel in Piazza di Trevi. A great place, unless you want peace and quiet – the Fontana is so close to the Trevi Fountain you could almost dive in from some of the rooms. The noise of rushing water and shrieking tourists is overwhelming, but the rooms, in odd shapes and sizes to fit into the rambling old building, are bright and spacious.

Hotel services *Babysitting. Bar. Currency exchange. Fax. Laundry. Lift. Multi-lingual staff. Reservation for airlines and theaters. Safe.* **Room services** *Air conditioning (L20,000 extra). Hair dryer (from reception). Room service. Telephone. TV.*

Forum

Via Tor de' Conti, 25-30 (06 679 2446/fax 06 678 6479/ Forum@venere.it). Metro Colosseo/bus to Via Cavour or Via dei Fori Imperiali. **Rates** *single* L250,000-L380,000; *double* L350,000-L550,000. **Credit** AmEx, DC, EC, MC, V. **Map 8/1C**

A very civilised, calm hotel in the remains of a Renaissance palace behind the Imperial Fora. The low-ceilinged downstairs lounge was refurbished recently and is particularly relaxing for a post-sightseeing drink, while the rooftop restaurant has wonderful views. The 80 bedrooms are very comfortable as well.

Hotel services *Air-conditioning. Babysitting. Bar. Car park. Car rental. Conference facilities. Currency exchange. Fax. Laundry. Lifts. Multi-lingual staff. Restaurant. Safe.* **Room services** *Hair dryer. Radio. Room service. Safe. Telephone. TV (satellite). Website:www.hotelforum.com*

Raphael

Largo Febo, 2 (06 68 28 31/fax 06 68 78 993/info@rafaelhotel.com). Bus to Corso Rinascimento. **Rates** *(breakfast L23,000-L33,000 extra) single* L335,000-L395,000; *double* L495,000-L590,000; *suite* L680,000-L785,000. **Credit** AmEx, DC, EC, MC, V. **Map 3/2A**

Its owner has filled this stately, ivy-draped building with antiques, and the 70 bedrooms are individually decorated with pictures and well-chosen furniture. Close to the Senate in Palazzo Madama, the Raphael has long been popular with politicians.

Hotel services *Air-conditioning. Babysitting. Bars. Conference facilities. Currency exchange. Fax. Laundry. Lifts. Multi-lingual staff. Non-smoking rooms. Restaurants. Safe.* **Room services** *Hair dryer. Mini-bar. Room service. Safe. Telephone. TV (satellite). Website: www.rafaelhotel.com*

La Residenza

Via Emilia, 22-24 (06 488 0789/fax 06 485 721/hotel.la.residenza@venere.it). Metro Barberini/bus to Via Veneto. **Rates** *single* L155,000; *double* L320,000; *junior suite* L375,000. **Credit** AmEx, MC, V. **Map 5/1B**

As its name suggests, this quiet 28-room hotel off the bustling Via Veneto prides itself on having the feel of a (rather grand) private home. Its colours are muted and soothing, and the comfortable, elegant furniture is there to be used; the overall tone is hushed and formal. Some of the well-equipped rooms have terraces, and there's also a roof garden for guests' use.

Hotel services *Air-conditioning. Bar. Car park (nearby). Fax. Laundry. Lifts. Multi-lingual staff. Massage. Safe. Sunbed. Ticket desk. Tours.* **Room services** *Hair dryer. Mini-bar. Radio. Room service. Telephone. TV (satellite). Website:www.italyhotels.it*

The cosy **Due Torri** *(see page 117).*

Scalinata di Spagna

Piazza Trinità dei Monti, 17 (06 69 40 848/fax 06 6994 0598). Metro Spagna or Barberini/bus to Piazza Barberini or Via del Tritone. **Rates** *single* L380,000; *double* L500,000; *triple* L550,000; *suite* L800,000. **Credit** AmEx, DC, EC, MC, V. **Map 5/1C**

A hotel with one of the most romantic settings in Rome, at the top of the Spanish Steps looking down over Keats' house to Piazza di Spagna. It's lovely inside, with rambling staircases; the 15 bedrooms are pleasantly old-fashioned, even if some are small. There's a wonderfully secluded roof garden.

Hotel services *Air-conditioning. Babysitting. Car park (nearby). Currency exchange. Disabled: semi-adapted room (1), wheelchair access. Fax. Laundry. Multi-lingual staff. Safe. Ticket desk.* **Room services** *Hair dryer. Mini bar. Room service (24-hour). Safe. Telephone. TV.*

Sole al Pantheon

Piazza della Rotonda, 63 (06 678 0441/fax 06 6994 0689/ hotsole@flashnet.it). Bus to Largo Argentina. **Rates** *single* L380,000; *double* L550,000; *suite* L750,000. **Credit** AmEx, DC, EC, MC, V. **Map 3/2A**

This attractive hotel traces its history back to 1467, and former guests range from the Renaissance poet Ariosto to Jean-Paul Sartre. It has been sensitively refurbished, with tiles and frescoes. Bedrooms are cool and fresh; some have painted ceilings. Ten of the 27 rooms have superb views of the Pantheon.

Hotel services *Air-conditioning. Bar. Fax. Laundry. Lifts. Multi-lingual staff.* Room services *Hair dryer. Jacuzzi in most rooms. Mini-bar. Radio. Room service (24- hour). Safe. Telephone. TV (satellite). Video.* Website: *www.italyhotel.com/roma/solealpantheon/*

Teatro di Pompeo

Largo del Pallaro, 8 (06 687 2566/fax 06 6880 5531). Bus to Corso Vittorio Emanuele. Rates *single L270,000; double L350,000.* Credit AmEx, DC, EC, MC, V. Map 3/2A.

A Campo de' Fiori hotel that's a bit smarter than its neighbours. It can claim, at least in part, to be the oldest hotel in Rome: you have breakfast in what was part of the first century BC Theatre of Pompey. The décor of the bar and 12 bedrooms is unfussy. Hotel services *Air-conditioning. Bar. Conference facilities. Fax. Laundry. Lift. Multi-lingual staff.* Room services *Hair dryer (on request). Mini-bar. Radio. Room service. Safe. Telephone. TV (satellite).*

Moderate

Campo de' Fiori

Via del Biscione, 6 (06 6880 6865/06 6830 9036/fax 06 6830 9036). Bus to Corso Vittorio Emanuele. Rates *single without bath L150,000; single L180,000; double without bath L180,000; double L230,000; suite L250,000.* Credit MC, V. Map 3/2B

Campo de' Fiori: *at the heart of the Centro.*

Housed in an ochre palazzo, this 27-room hotel has loads of character. A roof terrace gives great views of the *centro storico*, and the entrance is lined with mirrors and columns to give a *trompe l'œil* effect as you struggle in with your bags. Bedrooms are small but imaginatively decorated. A third have bathrooms; four more have box showers. Hotel services *Currency exchange. Fax. Multi-lingual staff. Reservations for airlines and theatres. Safe.* Room services *Radio. Telephone.*

Celio

Via SS Quattro, 35c (06 7049 5333/fax 06 709 6377). Metro Colosseo/bus to Via Labicana. Rates *single L250,000-L320,000; double L270,000-L390,000; suite L590,000.* Credit AmEx, DC, MC, V. Map 8/2B

This small hotel near the Colosseum is a gem of tasteful decoration and comfort. It has rooms beautifully frescoed with details inspired by Renaissance masters, and everything is designed to please the eye. Breakfast is served in rooms. Hotel services *Air-conditioning. Babysitting. Bar. Car park (nearby). Currency exchange. Disabled: adapted room (1), wheelchair access. Fax. Laundry. Multi-lingual staff. Non-smoking rooms. Safe.* Room services *Hair dryer. Mini-bar. PC point. Radio. Room service (24-hour). Telephone. TV (satellite). Video.*

Domus Aventina

Via di Santa Prisca, 11B (06 574 6135/fax 06 5730 0044). Metro Circo Massimo/bus to Viale Aventino. Rates *single L200,000; double L300,000.* Credit AmEx, DC, EC, MC, V. Map 9/1C

Domus Aventina is next to the church of Santa Prisca, and has lovely views from its roof terrace. Public rooms are frescoed with *trompe l'œil* views of Rome; its 25 spacious bedrooms (some with balconies) are in soothing colours, with reproduction antiques. The staff are friendly and attentive. Hotel services *Air-conditioning. Bar. Car parking (public car park). Fax. Laundry.* Room services *Hair dryer. Mini-bar. Radio. Room service (24 hour). Telephone. TV (satellite).*

Fontanella Borghese

Largo Fontanella Borghese, 84 (06 6880 9504/06 6880 9624/fax 06 686 295). Bus to Via del Corso or Piazza Augusto Imperatore. Rates *single L200,000; double L320,000.* Credit AmEx, DC, EC, MC, V. Map 3/1A

The Fontanella Borghese offers a mix of first-class service and family-run intimacy. Very near Via Condotti and Via del Corso, it's ideal for retail fiends who don't want to carry shopping bags too far. Hotel Services *Air-conditioning. Bar. Disabled: adapted rooms (2), wheelchair access. Fax. Lifts. Multi-lingual staff. Safe.* Room services *Fax point. Hair dryer. Mini bar. PC point. Room service. Safe. Telephone. TV (satellite).*

Hotel Locarno

Via della Penna, 22 (06 361 0841/fax 06 321 5249). Metro Flaminio/bus to Via di Ripetta. Rates *single L215,000; double L330,000-360,000; triple L420,000; suite L390,000.* Credit AmEx, DC, EC, MC, V. Map 2/2A

The Locarno, on a street between the Tiber and
Piazza del Popolo, was founded in the 1920s and
looks like a set for an Agatha Christie film. It
retains some original details: a Tiffany lamp, a
grandfather clock, a wrought-iron cage lift. The
lounge has a real fire in winter, and there's a lovely
patio with fountain. All of its 48 rooms and suites
have been refurbished recently. Regulars include
director Peter Greenaway, and Bernard Weber set
his 1976 film *Hotel Locarno* here. Some of the
extras are still on the staff.
Hotel services *Air-conditioning. Bar. Bicycles (free
for guests). Disabled: adapted room (1), wheelchair
access. Garage. Laundry. Lifts. Multi-lingual staff.
Safe.* **Room services** *Fax point. Hair dryer. Mini-
bar. Radio. Safe. Telephone. TV (satellite).*

Hotel Parlamento

*Via delle Convertite, 5 (tel & fax 06 6992 1000). Bus
to Piazza San Silvestro.* **Rates** *single* L170,000;
double L190,000; *triple* L235,000-L260,000; *quadruple*
L300,000. **Credit** AmEx, DC, EC, MC, V. **Map 3/1A**
The Parlamento's rooms, although not large, are
spotlessly clean and tastefully decorated. Some have
access to a pretty leafy terrace, and there's also a roof
garden for guests who want to relax before descending into the hustle and bustle of Via del Corso.
Hotel services *Air conditioning. Bar. Fax. Garage
(nearby). Lifts. Multi-lingual staff.* **Room services**
*Air conditioning (most rooms). Hair dryer. Radio.
Room service (breakfast only). Safe. Telephone. TV.*

Marcus

*Via del Clementino, 94 (06 68 30 03 20/06 687
3679/fax 06 6830 0312). Bus to Via del Corso or
Via Tomacelli.* **Rates** *single* L140,000-L160,000;
double L200,000; *triple* L260,000; *quad* L280,000.
Credit AmEx, MC, V. **Map 3/1A**
Tucked into a quiet street two minutes' walk from
the Spanish Steps, the Marcus is ideal for those who
want to be in the centre of Rome without paying any
top-of-the-range prices. Family-operated, it
combines efficient service with comfort; the décor is
relatively plain, but for its price and location it's
worth remembering.
Hotel services *Air conditioning. Bar. Currency
exchange. Fax. Lifts. Multi-lingual staff. Safe. Ticket
desk.* **Room services** *Hair dryer. Mini bar. Room
service. Safe. TV.*

Marghera

*Via Marghera, 29 (06 44 57 184/06 445 4237/fax
06 446 2539). Metro Termini/bus to Termini.*
Rates (breakfast L25,000 extra) *single* L190,000;
double L290,000. **Credit** MC, V. **Map 5/2A**
Opposite the main Italian tourist office and not far
from Termini station, this hotel has 20 spotlessly
clean rooms, with white bedspreads and huge
pillows. The atmosphere is calm and civilized; the
owner and many guests are musicians, and you may
hear gentle strumming from other rooms.
Hotel services *Air-conditioning. Babysitting. Bar.
Fax. Lifts. Multi-lingual staff.* **Room services** *Hair
dryer. Mini-bar. Radio. Room service (for breakfast).
Trouser press. Telephone. TV. Video.*

Margutta

*Via Laurina, 34 (06 322 3674/fax 06 320 0395).
Metro Spagna or Flaminio/bus to Piazzale Flaminio.*
Rates *single* L165,000; *double* L175,000.
Credit AmEx, DC, EC, MC, V. **Map 2/2A**
A very reasonable, quiet hotel in a pricey area.
Don't be put off by the utilitarian reception and
breakfast area: all 24 rooms are bright and sunny,
and some on the top floor open onto a balcony.
Three ground-floor rooms can be adapted for
wheelchair access.
Hotel services *Bar. Car park (on Piazza del
Popolo). Disabled: adapted rooms (3). Fax. Lifts.
Multi-lingual Staff. Tours.* **Room services**
Hairdryer. Phone.

Nerva

*Via Tor de' Conti, 3 (06 678 1835/fax 06 6992
2204). Bus to Piazza Venezia.* **Rates** *single* L250,000;
double L360,000; *suite* L450,000-L600,000.
No credit cards. Map 8/1C
The Nerva is excellently located for the Forum, the
Colosseum and other ancient sites. The rooms have
been beautifully refurbished without losing their
original features, and each one is different: some look
out onto Nerva's Forum, some onto pretty courtyards, and from others you can see the Palatine.
Excellent facilities for disabled travellers.
Hotel services *Air-conditioning. Bar. Currency
exchange. Disabled: adapted rooms (2), wheelchair
access. Laundry. Multi-lingual staff. Safe.* **Room
services** *Safe. Telephone. TV (satellite).*

Portoghesi

*Via dei Portoghesi, 1 (06 686 4231/fax 06 687
6976/ info@hotelportoghesiroma.com).
Bus to Corso del Rinascimento.* **Rates** *single*
L190,000-L210,000; *double* L250,000-L290,000; *suite*
L320,000-L480,000. **Credit** MC, V. **Map 3/1A**
A peaceful 28-room hotel in the *centro storico*, a
couple of minutes from Piazza Navona. All rooms
have antique furniture. There is a roof terrace.
Hotel services *Air-conditioning. Bar. Car park
(nearby). Currency exchange. Fax. Laundry. Lift.
Multi-lingual staff. Safe. Small animals accepted.
Ticket desk.* **Room services** *Hair dryer. Room
service. Telephone. TV (satellite).*
Website: www.hotelportoghesiroma.com

Residenza Zanardelli

*Via G. Zanardelli, 7 (06 6821 1392/fax 06 6880
3802). Bus to Via Zanardelli or Lungotevere Tor di
Nona.* **Rates** *single* L160,000; *double* L250,000; *suite*
L250,000. **Credit** AmEx, DC, EC, MC, V. **Map 3/1B**
A pleasant, family-run residencein the heart of the
centro storico, just around the corner from Piazza
Navona and 15 minutes from Saint Peter's. The
owner used to be an architect, and has decorated the
rooms in impeccable taste – including silk and gold
leaf Versace wallpaper.
Hotel Services *Air conditioning. Breakfast room.
Fax. Lifts. Multi-lingual staff. Non-smoking rooms.
Safe. Tours.* **Room services** *Air conditioning
(L20,000 extra). Hair dryer on request. Room
service. Telephone. TV (satellite).*

The bed & breakfast concept

There are essential differences between Italian and British ideas of Bed & Breakfast. For a start, Italians are not about to cook up any bacon-and-egg breakfasts; they will, however, do a mean coffee and *cornetti* – Roman croissants. Secondly, Rome's B&Bs are rooms in private houses or flats, most of which bear no resemblance to an English boarding house. And the bed & breakfast phenomenon has only been around since 1997. With the approach of Holy Year (*see pages 25, 106*) and its expected pilgrim avalanche, the city council has begun encouraging anyone with any spare room to turn it to advantage.

Rooms for rent are either double or single and, according to city by-laws, no household can rent out more than three rooms. Many rooms have private bathrooms, but in some cases you share with your hosts. All guests must be given a key so they can come and go as they please. Official instructions advise hosts to allow guests as much privacy as possible. Bear in mind, though, that while some may stop at a mild invitation to an after-dinner *grappa*, others will insist on taking you forcibly into the bosom of the family.

Bed & Breakfast Association of Rome

Piazza del Teatro di Pompeo, 2 (tel & fax 06 687 7348/Info@b-b.rm.it). Bus to Largo Argentina. **Open** 9am-6pm Mon-Fri.
Rates *single rooms* L75,000-L90,000; *doubles* L120,000-L160,000; *apartments* from L160,000 for two, from L220,000 for three, from L230,000 for four. **Credit** MC, V. **Map 3/2B**
Set up in 1997, and one of the most reputable b&b associations. Many of the apartments are in the centre and around the Vatican. All hosts and flats are carefully vetted, and guests are given a feedback form to air their views. Minimum stay is two days. The Association also rents private apartments.
Website:www.b-b.rm.it

Promoroma
– Rome Chamber of Commerce
Website: www.promoroma.com/b&b
The Chamber of Commerce website lists dozens of private homes offering bed & breakfast. Rather short-sightedly, it's only in Italian. From the home page, click on *Dove sono i B&B*, then zoom in on the area of Rome where you wish to stay. From there, you must note down phone numbers and contact hosts yourself. Prices range from around L50,000 to L100,000 per person per night; payment, unless you arrange otherwise with your host, is cash only.

Rinascimento
Via del Pellegrino, 122 (06 687 4814/fax 06 683 3518/ htlrinascimento@iol.it). Bus to Corso Vittorio Emanuele. **Rates** *single* L180,000; *double* L240,000-L280,000. **Credit** AmEx, EC, MC, V. **Map 3/2B**
In an appealing old palazzo in the heart of the Campo de' Fiori district, the Rinascimento has refurbished its 18 rooms, all of which are well-equipped for the price (although bathrooms are small). One room has a terrace, and there's a small bar/breakfast room.
Hotel Services *Air-conditioning. Currency exchange. Bar. Disabled: adapted room (1), wheelchair access. Fax. Laundry. Lift. Multi-lingual staff.* **Room services** *Mini-bar. Radio. Telephone. TV (satellite).*
Website:www.venere.it/roma/rinascimento/

La Rovere
Vicolo Sant'Onofrio, 5 (06 6880 6739/fax 06 6880 7062). Bus to Lungotevere Gianicolense.
Rates *single* L210,000; *double* L280,000; *triple* L320,000. **Credit** DC, MC, V. **Map 3/2C**
Tucked up a cutesy alley off Lungotevere Gianicolense, near the river below Saint Peter's and the Vatican, this former *pensione*, now upgraded to three-star hotel status, is well-placed for sightseeing, but there's a 15-minute hike to the nearest decent restaurant. Book early, especially for rooms with terraces.

Hotel services *Air-conditioning. Bar. Car park (nearby). Currency exchange. Fax. Laundry. Lifts. Multi-lingual staff. Non-smoking rooms. Safe.* **Room services** *Hair dryer. Room service. TV (satellite).*

Sant'Anna
Borgo Pio, 34 (06 6880 1602/fax 06 6830 8717/ santanna@travel.it). Metro Ottaviano/bus to Piazza della Città Leonina. **Rates** *single* L230,000; *double* L300,000; *triple* L330,000; *quad* L360,000.
Credit AmEx, DC, EC, MC, V. **Map 3/1C**
Throw open your shutters in the morning, look up the road and try to catch the Swiss Guards yawning as the sun rises over the Vatican. Just 200m from the Vatican walls, this is a quiet hotel with 20 rooms pleasantly decorated in pastels. Two rooms open onto a small courtyard garden.
Hotel services *Air conditioning. Babysitting. Currency exchange. Fax. Multi-lingual staff. Laundry. Lifts. Ticket desk. Tours.* **Room services** *Fax point. Hair dryer. Mini bar. PC point. Radio. Safe. Telephone. TV (satellite).*

Sant'Anselmo
Piazza Sant'Anselmo, 2 (06 578 3214/06 574 8119/fax 06 578 3604/). Metro Circo Massimo/bus to Viale Aventino. **Rates** *single* L120,000-L190,000; *double* L200,000-290,000; *triple* L280,000-340,000; *quad* L360,000. **Credit** AmEx, DC, EC, MC, V. **Map 7/1A**

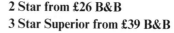

Hotel districts

Centro storico
Upper range *Due Torri, Raphael , Teatro di Pompeo;* **Moderate** *Campo de' Fiori, Portoghesi, Residenza Zanardelli, Rinascimento;* **Budget** *Casa Kolbe, Della Lunetta, Navona, Piccolo, Pomezia*

Tridente
De luxe *Crowne Plaza Minerva, Hassler Villa Medici, d'Inghilterra, Plaza, Valadier;* **Upper range** *Carriage, Fontana, Scalinata di Spagna, Sole al Pantheon;* **Moderate** *Hotel Locarno, Hotel Parlamento, Marcus, Margutta;* **Budget** *Abruzzi, Mimosa;* **Self-catering** *Residence Ripetta*

Via Veneto & Quirinale
De luxe *Aldovrandi Palace, Ambasciatori Palace, Eden, Excelsior, Majestic;* **Upper range** *La Residenza;* **Moderate** *Villa Borghese;* **Self-catering** *Aldovrandi Residence*

Trastevere
Moderate *La Rovere;* **Budget** *Trastevere Hotel*

Monti & Esquilino
De luxe *Grand Hotel;* **Upper range** *Forum;* **Moderate** *Marghera, Nerva, Villa delle Rose;* **Budget** *Fawlty Towers;* **Hostels** *Pensione Sandy, YWCA*

Aventino, Celio, Testaccio
Moderate *Aventino, Celio, Domus Aventina, Sant'Anselmo, Villa San Pio;* **Self-catering** *Villa Habsburg*

Prati & the Vatican
De luxe *Atlante Star;* **Moderate** *Sant'Anna, La Rovere;* **Hostels** *Pensione Ottaviano*

Northern suburbs
Hostels *Ostello della Gioventù Foro Italico (Youth Hostel)*

In the quiet, green residential area of the Aventine, this is an exceptionally pretty place housed in a villa with a garden. All the 45 bedrooms have antique furniture. The same owners have two more hotels nearby, the **Aventino** and **Villa San Pio**, both in similar tastefully-decorated Aventine country-house-style villas with delightful gardens, and at similar prices.
Hotel services *Air-conditioning. Babysitting. Bar. Car park .Currency exchange. Fax. Laundry. Lifts. Multi-lingual staff. Safe.* **Room services** *Mini bar. Room service. Telephone. TV (on request).*
Branches: Aventino Via San Domenico, 10 (06 574 5231/fax 06 578 3604). **Map 7/1A**
Villa San Pio Via Sant'Anselmo, 19 (06 574 5174/fax 578 3604). **Map 7/1A**
Website:www.aventinohotels.com

Villa Borghese
Via Pinciana, 31 (06 8530 0919/fax 06 841 4100/hotel.villaborghese@quipo.it). Bus to Via Pinciana or Via Po. **Rates** *single* L235,000; *double* L300,000; *triple* L360,000; *suite* L400,000.
Credit AmEx, MC, V. **Map 4/2B**
Once the family home of writer Alberto Moravia (who was born here), this cosy, friendly hotel overlooking Villa Borghese has a country house feel. Public rooms are intimate and beautifully decorated, with Persian rugs and chintzy furnishings; walls are decked with original prints, drawings and paintings. The 31 rooms vary in size and colour but are equally tasteful, and it has an ivy-draped patio.
Hotel services *Air-conditioning. Bar. Currency exchange. Fax. Laundry. Multi-lingual staff. Tours.* **Room services** *Hair dryer (on request). Mini-bar. Room service. Telephone. TV (satellite).*

Villa delle Rose
Via Vicenza, 5 (06 445 1788/fax 06 445 1639). Metro Termini/bus to Termini. **Rates** *single* L190,000; *double* L275,000; *suite* L275,000.
Credit AmEx, DC, EC, MC, V. **Map 5/1A**
A relaxed, family-run hotel, housed in a villa and with its own garden, a rarity so close to Termini. Some of the 35 bedrooms have air-conditioning. The décor is stark, but some rooms are split level, giving them a spacious feel and allowing for extra beds.
Hotel services *Bar. Car park. Fax. Laundry. Lifts. Multi-lingual staff. Non-smoking breakfast room. Safe.* **Room services** *Hair dryer (from reception). Room service. Telephone. TV.*

Budget

Abruzzi
Piazza della Rotonda, 69 (06 67 92 021). Bus or tram to Largo Argentina. **Rates** *single without bath* L72,000-L98,000; *double without bath* L110,000-L140,000. **No credit cards.** **Map 3/2A**
Facilities in this 25-room place are basic (there are only eight shared bathrooms), but rooms are a good size and several have a view of the Pantheon (and cost more). It's an interesting old building, but ask for a room at the back if you want quiet at night.
Hotel services *Multi-lingual staff. Safe.*

Casa Kolbe
Via San Teodoro, 44 (06 679 4974/fax 06 6994 1550). Bus to Piazza Bocca della Verità or Via dei Cerchi. **Rates** (breakfast L7000 extra) *single* L105,000; *double* L135,000; *suite* L170,000-L190,000
Credit AmEx, MC, V. **Map 8/2C**
You can practically touch the Palatine from Casa Kolbe's street-facing rooms. Spartan decor, spiky beds (definitely not for un-nun-like activities), and school-cooking smells remind you you're in a converted convent, but it's excellent value. All 69 rooms have bathrooms, and there's a big garden and restaurant. It's often part-occupied by big student and tour groups; the staff are very helpful.
Hotel services *Bar. Conference room. Laundry. Restaurant.* **Room services** *Telephone.*

Della Lunetta

Piazza del Paradiso, 68 (06 686 1080/06 687 7630/fax 06 689 2028). Bus to Corso Vittorio Emanuele. **Rates** *single without bath* L80,000; *single* L100,000; *double without bath* L120,000; *double* L160,000; *triple without bath* L165,000; *triple* L210,000. **Credit** EC, MC, V. **Map 3/2B**
A rambling, shabby old building in the *centro storico*. Nearly half the 35 rooms have bathrooms. There is a big lounge with TV downstairs, and several small sitting areas upstairs. No breakfast.
Hotel services *Fax. Multi-lingual staff. Safe.*
Room services *Telephone.*

Fawlty Towers

Via Magenta, 39 (06 445 0374/fulang@flashnet.it). Metro Termini/bus to Termini. **Rates** *single without bath* L60,000; *single* L75,000 *double without bath* L90,000; *double* L120,000; *dormitory* L30,000-L35,000 per person. **No credit cards. Map 5/1A**
Part *pensione*, part hostel. Guests can share a room with up to two others, or have their own. A homely atmosphere makes it easy to forget you're so near Termini; there's a bright sitting room and terrace, guides to browse through, and satellite TV. A good base for anyone travelling alone, with no curfew.
Hotel services *Fridge. Internet access. Microwave. Multi-lingual staff. Terrace. TV (satellite). Website: www.enjoyrome.it/ftytwhtl.htm*

Mimosa

Via di Santa Chiara, 61 (06 6880 1753/fax 06 683 3557). Bus to Largo Argentina. **Rates** *single without bath* L95,000; *double without bath* L130,000; *double* L150,000; *triple without bath* L190,000.
No credit cards. Map 3/2A

Navona: *Agrippa downstairs, Keats up top.*

In medieval times the Mimosa housed the Cavalieri della Croce, an order of Crusading soldiers; for anyone wanting to go AWOL there was a handy escape tunnel to the Tiber. Today, it may not have the most beautiful interior, but is comfortable, clean and family-run. Five of its 12 rooms have bathrooms; the others share five between them. The hotel is owned by Roman nobility, and its profits go to charity.
Hotel services *Bar. Fax. Non-smoking bedrooms. Multi-lingual staff.*
Room services *Telephone (2 rooms).*

Navona

Via dei Sediari, 8 (06 686 4203/fax 06 6880 3802). Bus to Corso Rinascimento. **Rates** *single without bath* L110,000; *single* L130,000; *double* L160,000; *suite* L200,000. **No credit cards. Map 3/2A**
There's a welcoming, communal atmosphere at this 30-room hotel, making it a good choice for lone travellers. Most rooms have showers. It's an attractive, romantic old building, close to Piazza Navona. The ground floor dates back to AD 1, and was the site of the baths of Agrippa; the top floor housed Keats and Shelley. Rooms are spacious and comfortable, and staff and owners are very helpful and friendly.
Hotel services *Air conditioning. Fax. Multi-lingual staff. Non-smoking rooms. Restaurant (groups only). Safe.* **Room services** *Air conditioning (L20,000 extra). Hair dryer (on request). Room service.*

Piccolo

Via dei Chiavari, 32 (06 6880 2560). Bus to Corso Vittorio Emanuele. **Rates** (breakfast L7,000 extra) *single without bath* L100,000; *single* L120,000; *double without bath* L120,000; *double* L150,000; *triple* L160,000. **Credit** AmEx, EC, MC, V. **Map 3/2A**
A family-run hotel near Campo de' Fiori. All 16 immaculately clean rooms have bidets; only three have full bathrooms, but five have showers. There's a TV in the breakfast room, and a 1am curfew.
Hotel services *Air conditioning. Bar. Multi-lingual staff. Safe.* **Room services** *Telephone.*

Pomezia

Via dei Chiavari, 12 (06 686 1371/fax 06 686 1371). Bus to Corso Vittorio Emanuele. **Rates** *single without bath* L120,000; *single* L150,000; *double without bath* L150,000; *double* L200,000. **Credit** AmEx, EC, MC, V. **Map 3/2A**
One of a number of good cheap hotels near Campo de' Fiori. This one has a small terrace, and 10 of its 24 rooms have en suite bathrooms; bedrooms are clean but small. Unusually for a hotel of this class, there is a small bar in the reception area.
Hotel services *Bar. Currency exchange. Laundry. Multi-lingual staff.* **Room services**. *Room service. Telephone.*

Trastevere Hotel

Via Luciano Manara, 24 (06 581 4713/fax 06 5881 0116). Bus to Piazza Sonnino/tram to Viale Trastevere. **Rates** *single* L100,000; *double* L130,000; *triple* L160,000; *quad* L180,000.
Credit AmEx, EC, MC, V. **Map 6/2B**

*More Hollywood than stately home, the **Excelsior** (see page 116) has Rome's plushest suite.*

A very friendly, cheap *pensione*, well placed for the clubs and bars of Trastevere (all guests have a night key) and within walking distance of the *centro storico*. All its bright, cheery rooms have showers. **Hotel services** *Bar. Fax. Lifts. Multi-lingual staff. Restaurant.*

Hostels

Women are better served than men, thanks to the **YWCA** and the **Protezione delle Giovane**, which has an office at Termini that will help out if you arrive without a bed booked.

Ostello della Gioventù Foro Italico

Via delle Olimpiadi, 61 (06 324 2571/06 323 6267fax 06 324 2613).
Bus to Lungotevere Maresciallo Cadorna.
Rates *bed & breakfast* L25,000 **No credit cards**.
There are 400 beds in dormitories at this neobrutalist building near the Stadio Olimpico, a fair distance – but well connected by public transport – from the centre. This is the IYHF's main Rome hostel (standard category), open to members only, although you can join here. There's a garden, restaurant and bar. It's well adapted for wheelchairs.

Pensione Ottaviano

Via Ottaviano, 6 (06 39 73 72 53/
gi.costantini@agora.stm.it). Metro Ottaviano/bus to Piazza Risorgimento. **Rates** L25,000 per dormitory bed; L70,000 double room. **No credit cards. Map 2/2C**
A short stroll from Saint Peter's, this hostel is fairly basic; however, one of the owners looks like George Clooney, which (for some) may compensate. Guests can use the *pensione*'s e-mail.
Website:www.pensioneottaviano.com

Pensione Sandy

Via Cavour, 136 (06 488 4585/
gi.costantini@agora.stm.it). Metro Cavour/
bus to Via Cavour. **Rates** L25,000 per bed.
No credit cards. Map 8/1B
A sister hotel to the **Ottaviano** and **Fawlty Towers**, offering rooms with up to six beds each.
Website:www.sandyhostel.com

Protezione della Giovane

Via Urbana, 158 (06 488 1489). Metro Cavour/
bus to Piazza Esquilino. **Rates** L24,000-L27,000 per person. **No credit cards. Map 8/1B**
This Catholic organisation 'for the protection of young women' offers cheap accommodation to women under 27. There is a 10pm curfew.

YWCA

Via Cesare Balbo, 4 (06 48 80 460/06 48 83 917/
fax 06 48 71 028). Metro Cavour/bus to Piazza dell'Esquilino. **Rates** *single without bath* L60,000; *single* L80,000; *double without bath* L100,000; *double* L120,000; *triple/quad* L40,000 per person; *meals* L20,000. **No credit cards. Map 5/2B**
Bedrooms for women with from one to three beds in each. A little too close to Termini station for comfort, but lone females may feel safer here than in mixed hostels or *pensioni*. Midnight curfew.

Self-catering

If you're staying in Rome for more than a couple of weeks, especially if there are more than two of you, it's worth considering renting a flat or staying in a residential hotel. They are cheaper than normal hotels, while offering similar services (maid service, and usually a restaurant or bar).

Best hotels for...

That Roman Holiday experience

Walk straight out of the **Hassler Villa Medici** (*see p116*) and go down the Spanish Steps. Buy an ice-cream. Pose for a moment, looking wonderful in Gucci, and try not to fall for the charms of Gregory Peck – or any other smoothie who's lurking about.

Joining the Dead Poets' Society

The **Navona** (*see p126*) may have housed the baths of Agrippa in AD 1, but for a bit of romanticism go up to the beautiful attic rooms and stay where Keats and Shelley laid their heads when first in Rome.

Miss Marples & Hercule Poirots

From its cage lift to Tiffany lamps, the **Locarno** (*see p120*) is straight from the world of Agatha Christie – with the added attraction of fold-away bidets.

Sleeping as soundly as cardinals

A central hotel cocooned in a quiet alley away from the madness of beeping horns, the **Due Torri** (*see p117*) was formerly the residence of a series of cardinals, one of whom became pope. Today its discreet elegance is favoured more by writers and artists.

Being 'On top of the world, Ma!'

At the roof-top restaurant at the **Eden** (*see p115*) the view is stupendous, and glorious food is served by waiters who cater to your every whim. It's a real paradise, without the disturbance of a naked couple rummaging in the foliage looking for fig leaves.

*Poirot meets Greenaway at the **Locarno**.*

Aldovrandi Residence

Via Ulisse Aldovrandi, 11 (06 322 1430/fax 06 322 2181). Bus or tram to Piazza Pitagora. **Rates** *flat for one* from L3,300,000 per month; *flat for two* from L4,730,000 per month. **Credit** AmEx. **Map 4/1C**
One of the best-equipped residential hotels in Rome, just north of Villa Borghese.
Hotel services *Air-conditioning. Bar. Car park (nearby). Garden. Lift. Multi-lingual staff. Restaurant.* **Apartment services** *Radio. Telephone. TV (satellite).*

IDEC

Via Poliziano, 27 (06 7045 4074/fax 06 7045 4455/df.idec@agora.it). **Rates** *weekly* L500,000-L1,400,000; *monthly* L1,600,000-L3,700,000.
This reliable agency rents out apartments – from studio flats to four- bed ones – all over central Rome. Prices, naturally, depend on size and location.
Website: www.idecroma.com

Residence Ripetta

Via di Ripetta, 231 (06 323 1144/fax 06 320 3959/Info@ripetta.it). Bus to Ponte Cavour. **Rates** *studio flats for 1-2 (weekly)* from L1,850,000; *flats for 1-2 (two weeks)* from L3,400,000; *flats for 1-2 (monthly)*

from L5,300,000; *flats for 3 (weekly)* from L2,550,000; *flats for 4 (two weeks)* from L4,350,000; *flats for 4 (monthly)* from L6,700,000, plus tax.
Credit AmEx, MC, V. **Map 2/2A**
In a good, central location close to both Via del Corso and the *centro storico*, the Ripetta consists of 69 self-catering flats. Kitchens are fully equipped, and the flats are cleaned daily. Some look over the Tiber.
Apartment services *Air-conditioning. Fax. Garage. Lift. Radio. Safe. Telephone. TV (satellite).*

Villa Habsburg

Piazza di Porta Metronia (reservations to 00 43 1 712 5091/fax 00 43 1 715 4291). Bus to Via Amba Aradam or Porta Metronia. **Rates** approx. L1,720,000-L2,600,000 per week. **Map 9/1B**
Vienna-based Odile Taliani (who is British, despite the name) rents out two (soon to be four) charming apartments, each sleeping 4-6 people, in an early twentieth-century villa in one of Rome's largest private gardens, nestling up to the Aurelian Wall and with a sweeping view across the Baths of Caracalla to Saint Peter's. Each flat has its own corner of garden with tables and chairs. There's a large swimming pool nearby.

Restaurants

The vine-covered pergola is still around... and what's served beneath it is getting better.

A pavement table beneath a vine-covered pergola. The animated buzz of people with something to talk about. Though so much has changed over the last few years, this image of the classic Roman *trattoria* retains its hold on the collective imagination. For the nostalgic, the good news is that such places can still be found. For those who value the gastronomic experience over the postcard setting, the other good news is that there are also restaurants in Rome that take their food and wine very seriously. For anyone who doesn't like Italian food, the bad news is that you're in the wrong city.

In the last few years there has been a slow revolution in the Roman restaurant scene. Many of the traditional white-linen restaurants with reputations formed in the *Dolce Vita* years – and whose success was consolidated by fat expense accounts in the '80s – have been weeded out, by recession and a greater demand for quality. Those that have kept going – **La Campana, Paris, Checchino dal 1887** – have done so for the simple reason that they look after their reputations, rather than living off them.

Into the void has stepped an army of new, younger establishments. Most are faithful to two constants: one, that a restaurant should at least appear to be family-run, and secondly that, however creatively interpreted, the cooking should be Italian. **Antico Arco, Tram Tram, Uno e Bino, Sangallo** – despite their differences – all fit this description. Rome is also beginning to get its first international-style 'concept' restaurants, the most talked about being **'Gusto**, opened only in 1998. However novel they are for Italians, many visitors from abroad are less than enthralled – after all, one great thing about eating out in Rome is precisely the lack of Conran-esque, design-led eating-places.

Italy in general and Rome in particular have never taken a *nouvelle* or post-modern approach to food. Cheap *trattorie* are always packed with locals, who eat out at least once a week, and tend to be discerning gourmands rather than finicky gourmets. You're just as likely to find a humble dish like *spaghetti cacio e pepe* (sheeps' cheese and black pepper) in a top-of-the-range restaurant as in a spit-and-sawdust neighbourhood *osteria*.

The regional nature of Italian society means that cuisine from other regions is seen almost as foreign, even if recipes or ingredients are very similar. *La cucina romana* sits heavily on the stomach, and is based on and around offal (*see* *page 152,* **The Offal Truth**. Luckily for vegetarians, though, Roman cuisine also boasts a large selections of vegetable dishes.

Equally, Rome is in no way an international restaurant city. Chinese restaurants abound, and Indian, Thai, Korean and Mexican food can be tracked down, but the standard is far lower than in London, Paris or New York. The one exception to the rule – a consequence of Italy's murky colonial history – is the range of good Eritrean, Somali and Ethiopian cuisine on offer (*see page 150*).

The Menu

Most meals consist of a *primo* – pasta course; *secondo* – meat or fish course; and *contorno* – vegetables or salad, served separately. An *antipasto* – hors d'oeuvre – is often an alternative to a *primo* but may merely precede it, while *dolci* – dessert – are often missed altogether. For a full menu vocabulary, *see pp146-7*.

You're under no pressure to order four courses. It's perfectly normal to order a first course followed by a simple salad or *contorno* (often the only option for vegetarians, *see p151*). Fixed-price meals are a rarity. Top-flight establishments occasionally offer a *menu degustazione* (taster menu), but anywhere offering a *menu turistico* should generally be avoided, especially if it is written in several languages.

Drinks

Most top-range restaurants have respectable wine lists, but *trattorie* and *osterie* tend to have a limited selection (*see page 148* **Select your wine**). House wine is usually uninspiring Castelli Romani white, or equally unimpressive Montepulciano d'Abruzzo red, but there are exceptions. There are several new-style eateries – **Uno e Bino, Antico Arco** – where wines are as important as food. Mineral water – *acqua minerale* – is *frizzante* or *gassata* (sparkling), or *naturale* (still), and usually in litre bottles. If you have a full meal, and they like you, you may be offered free *amaro* – bitter liqueur – with coffees.

Paying & tipping

In 1995 the city council forced restaurants to abolish the *pane e coperto* charge, which allowed them to add up to L4,000 a head for providing a tablecloth and bread. Be warned, though: some restaurants ignore the ban, and others get round it by crossing out *coperto* and leaving *pane*. Service is supposed to be included, but some places still add it on separately. Romans themselves tend not to tip much, especially in family-run places. However, if you are

Satisfaction at **Da Felice**: *not the food, but getting past the* riservato *signs. See page 145.*

Restaurant
Bar
Boutique

PLANET HOLLYWOOD

For reservations call
06 42 82 80 12

PLANET HOLLYWOOD
118, Via del Tritone – ROME
Metro stop: Piazza Barberini.
Rest. hours: Sun.-Thur. noon–12.30 am, Fri. & Sat. noon–1am.

Best restaurants for...

When you can't face another plate of pasta, try **Hasekura**. *See page 151.*

All-round dining pleasure at a good price
Antico Arco; Paris; Cantina Cantarini; Myosotis; Tram Tram; Uno e Bino

Eating outside
Checchino dal 1887; Paris; Albistrò; Caffè delle Arti; La Carbonara; Monserrato; San Teodoro; La Taverna degli Amici; Ar Galletto; Augusto; La Torricella; Trattoria-Pizzeria della Pace; Sahara

A romantic soirée
Agata e Romeo; Il Convivio; La Terrazza dell'Hotel Eden; Il Quadrifoglio; Sangallo; Taverna Angelica; Albistrò; Antico Bottaro; Il Dito e la Luna; San Teodoro

Seeing and being seen
politicians/journalists La Campana; Gino in Vicolo Rossini; **fashion/entertainment** Trattoria-Pizzeria della Pace; 'Gusto; Fiaschetteria Beltramme; Maccheroni; La Taverna degli Amici

Creative modern Italian cooking
Agata e Romeo; Il Convivio; La Terrazza dell'Hotel Eden; Antico Arco; Taverna Angelica; Ditirambo; Osteria dell'Ingegno; Uno e Bino; Tuttifrutti

Traditional Roman
See **The Offal Truth** *page 152.*

Italian regional cooking
Al Ceppo (Marches); Monte Caruso (Basilicata); Papà Baccus (Tuscany); Il Quadrifoglio, Nel Regno di Re Ferdinando II (Naples); Taverna Giulia (Genoa); Il Dito e la Luna (Sicily); Taverna Sottovento (Calabria)

Fish
Sangallo; San Teodoro; Cantina Cantarini

International
Hasekura

Wine
* indicates only a small mark-up on street prices
Agata e Romeo; Il Convivio; Checchino dal 1887; Al Bric; Al Ceppo; *Antico Arco; Paris; Sangallo; Sora Lella; *Albistrò; *Ditirambo; Il Dito e la Luna; *Myosotis; Tram Tram; *Uno e Bino

happy with a meal, leave 8-10%; equally, if service has been slack or rude, don't feel ashamed to leave nothing – or to check the bill in detail, as there is still the occasional restaurateur who becomes strangely innumerate when dealing with tourists.

Italy is still a cash society, so never assume you can use cards or travellers' cheques without asking first.

By law, when you pay a bill (*il conto*) you must be given a detailed receipt (*ricevuta fiscale*). In theory, if you leave a restaurant without it you can incur a fine, but this is chiefly aimed at tax-dodging restaurateurs.

General points
Taking **children** into restaurants – even the smartest – is never a problem in Rome. Enthusiastic

The Pizza menu

So orthodox is the range of toppings in Roman *pizzerie*, so eyebrow-raising any departure from the norm, that it's worth learning the main varieties by heart. You don't need to specify *una pizza con...* Just ask for *una Napoli, una funghi*, and so on. If you want it without tomato, ask for *una ... bianca*; for example, *una funghi bianca*.

It's customary in *pizzerie* to order gap-fillers while you're waiting for yours to be baked. A few of the most common extras are listed below.

Pizzas

calzone a doubled-over pizza, usually filled with cheese, tomato and ham; **capricciosa** ham, hard-boiled or fried egg, artichokes and olives; **funghi** mushrooms; **marinara** plain tomato, sometimes with anchovies; **margherita** tomato and mozzarella; **napoli** or **napoletana** tomato, anchovy and sometimes mozzarella; **quattro formaggi** four cheeses (in theory); **quattro stagioni** mozzarella, artichoke, egg, mushrooms.

Extras

bruschetta coarse toast with raw garlic rubbed into it and oil on top, and usually diced raw tomatoes; **crochette** potato croquettes, often with a cheesy centre; **crostini** slices of toast, usually with a grilled cheese and anchovy topping; **fagioli stufati** white cannellini beans in a sauce, often with raw onion; **filetto di baccalà** deep-fried salt cod in batter; **olive ascolane** deep-fried battered olives stuffed with sausage meat; **supplì** deep-fried rice balls held together by tomato sauce, with fresh mozzarella inside. Vegetarians beware: some contain mincemeat.

Thin and crispy vs deep and puffy: bite into the romana-napoletana *pizza war.*

waiters will oblige with a high chair (*un seggiolone*), and bring *mezze porzioni* – half portions – on request. **Women** dining alone, though, may attract unwelcome attention in cheaper restaurants, even from smirking waiters, and **single men** can have trouble getting a table in cheaper places at busy times. Eating out is a communal experience here.

Very few places impose a **dress code**, although shorts and T-shirts go down badly in formal, upmarket restaurants. Some restaurants now ban **mobile phones**, but **no-smoking areas** are a rarity.

Booking, once unusual, is becoming more of a habit, even in places that might appear to be spit-and-sawdust. Where 'Booking essential/advisable' is indicated below, it should be taken seriously, especially on Friday and Saturday evenings.

Restaurant categories

Restaurants listed here are arranged on the basis of price. In theory the words *ristorante*, *trattoria* and *osteria* (sometimes called *hostaria*) should indicate descending levels of quality, but they're often interchangeable and relate more to atmosphere than food quality. Average prices listed include a *primo*, a *secondo*, a *contorno* and a *dolce*, but not *antipasto*, wine or water. Note too that opening times can change according to time of year, and personal whim. Times given are those of the kitchen – in other words, when you can actually turn up and order – but many restaurants stay open for an hour or more after the cook goes home. *Pizzerie* generally open by 7pm, whereas few proper restaurants open before 8pm.

Splashing out: over L85,000

Agata e Romeo
Via Carlo Alberto, 45 (06 446 6115). Metro Vittorio Emanuele/bus to Santa Maria Maggiore. **Open** 1-2.30pm, 8-10.30pm, Mon-Sat. Closed two weeks Aug; two weeks Jan. **Average** L120,000. **Credit** AmEx, DC, EC, MC, V. **Map 8/1A**
The seedy area between Termini and Santa Maria Maggiore is not where you expect to find one of Rome's gourmet treats. Cooking – *nouvelle Romana* – is overseen by Agata Caraccio, while husband Romeo hovers in the dining room. Roman specialities like *pasta e broccoli in brodo d'arzilla* (pasta with broccoli and ray broth) mix with international dishes and in-house creations. Desserts are fabulous (try the dream-like *millefoglie*) – but at L20,000, they should be. For serious foodies, or serious romance. *Air-conditioning. Booking essential.*

Checchino dal 1887
Via di Monte Testaccio, 30 (06 574 6318). Bus to Via Marmorata or Via Galvani. **Open** 12.30-3pm, 8-11pm, Tue-Sat. Closed Aug, Christmas. **Average** L90,000. **Credit** AmEx, DC, EC, MC, V. **Map 7/2A**
Nestling among the trendy bars and clubs opposite Testaccio's former slaughter house (*see p85*) is Rome's leading temple of authentic *cucina romana*. Specialities include *insalata di zampetti* (hoof jelly salad), *animelle al vino bianco* (sweetbreads in white wine) and *coratel-*

la con i carciofi (veal heart with artichokes). Not content with offering the definitive versions of thos offally dishes that have kept Romans going for over 2,000 years, Checchino also has what is generally considered to be Rome's finest wine cellar, dug out of the ancient amphora tip which constitutes Monte Testaccio. There's also an outstanding selection of cheeses, with recommended wine combinations. *Air-conditioning. Booking advisable. Tables outdoors.*

Il Convivio
Vicolo dei Soldati, 31 (06 686 9432). Bus to Corso Rinascimento. **Open** 1-2.30pm, 8-10.30pm, Mon- Sat. Closed one week Aug. **Average** L120,000. **Credit** AmEx, DC, EC, MC, V. **Map 3/1B**
In this temple of foodie excellence the menu changes with the season and the moods of chef Angelo; maybe pasta strips with wild mushrooms in a quail and pesto sauce, or salt-cod in batter with gooseberry sauce. It ain't strictly Roman, but neither is it out-and-out culinary eclecticism. Add intimately tasteful surroundings, a fine wine list, impeccable service and outstanding desserts to make this one of the best places in Rome for a really special meal. *Air-conditioning. Booking essential.*

La Pergola dell'Hotel Hilton
Via Cadlolo, 101 (06 3509 2211). Bus to Piazza Medaglie d'Oro. **Open** 7.30-11.45pm Tue-Sat. Closed Jan. **Average** L150,000. **Credit** AmEx, DC, EC, MC, V. Who wants to eat in a hotel restaurant miles from the centre? The management of the Hilton-bunker on Monte Mario must have asked themselves this when they brought in young German chef Heinz Beck to revitalise their uninspiring rooftop restaurant. His cooking deserves the plaudits Italy's food critics have heaped on it, but some still find the luxury-hotel atmosphere stifling, despite the breathtaking views. The cuisine is international, with almost no pasta; Beck handles fresh fish, meat and vegetables with great finesse, and desserts are out of this world. Service, though, is pompous and oddly slow, and the 300 percent mark-up on wine is unforgivable. For dedicated foodies with understanding bank managers. *Air-conditioning. Tables outdoors. Booking essential.*

La Terrazza dell'Hotel Eden
Via Ludovisi, 49 (06 4781 2552). Bus to Via Veneto. **Open** 12.30-2.30pm daily. **Average** L150,000. **Credit** AmEx, DC, EC, MC, V. **Map 5/1C**
Cook Enrico Derflingher, formerly of Kensington Palace, has imposed his mod-Med approach at this roof-garden hotel restaurant with a truly spectacular view over the city. The service can be overbearing, and the dishes don't always match up to his ambitions, but he uses the freshest ingredients, and is always experimenting: on the right day this can be an unforgettable experience. To limit costs, go for a fixed-price menu: the L90,000 business lunch (Mon-Fri) is decent value and generally very good. In the evenings well-heeled health freaks can opt for a macrobiotic menu at L120,000, and there's even a special childrens' menu. *Air-conditioning. Booking essential.*

Antico Arco: *classic pasta and desserts in a class of their own. See page 138.*

Al Bric

Via del Pellegrino, 51 (06 687 9533). Bus to Corso Vittorio Emanuele. **Open** 7.30-11.30pm Tue-Sun. Closed two weeks Aug. **Average** L65,000. **Credit** AmEx, DC, EC, MC, V. **Map 3/2B**

The idea is sound, but Al Bric is still fine-tuning its formula of a restaurant where the wine is the thing. Its prime location, just west of Campo de' Fiori, and exposed-beam decor are all very nice, but the food – conservatively creative pasta, fish and meat, based on fresh or own-made ingredients – runs from quite good to unimpressive, which is a shame, especially in view of the bill. There's no wine list; clients choose their bottle after conferring with sommelier Roberto Marchetti (who speaks some English). Al Bric has the potential to move into a higher league. *Air conditioning. Booking essential.*

Al Ceppo

Via Panama, 2 (06 841 9696). Bus or tram to Piazza Ungheria. **Open** 12.45-3pm, 7.30-11pm, Tue-Sun. Closed three weeks Aug. **Average** L75,000. **Credit** AmEx, DC, MC, V.

This elegant restaurant run by the Milozzi sisters is the culinary hub of fur-coated, mobile-phoned Parioli. Cristina and Marisella's reworking of *cucina marchigiana* – with much use of mushrooms, fresh vegetables and seafood – is bold and original without being risky or overpriced. Try their delicious fettucine with broad beans, ham and pecorino. Seconds are dominated by fish and game: rabbit, cuttlefish, mixed grills. Desserts include great home-made ices, and there's a reasonably priced wine list. *Air-conditioning. Booking advisable.*

Antico Arco

Piazzale Aurelio, 7 (06 581 5274). Bus to Via Carini. **Open** 12.30-3pm, 8pm-midnight, Tue-Sun. **Average** L65,000. **Credit** AmEx, MC, V. **Map 6/2C**

Domenico, Maurizio and Patrizia have been working in this old house on the Gianicolo since 1996, and the promise they showed in their former home (Il Bacaro, now in sad decline) has turned into mature flair. First courses are Patrizia's forte: *risotto al castemagno* (risotto with Castelmagno cheese) is a classic, but *secondi* such as *branzino* (sea bass) with roast potato crisps are as impressive. The décor is effortlessly elegant, service ultra-affable, and afters deserve an entry to themselves. Add the trio's honest pricing policy – and the advantage of being able to turn up and eat after 11 – and you have one of the best-value gourmet experiences in Rome. Phone ahead to check they are open for lunch in summer. *Air-conditioning. Booking essential.*

La Campana

Vicolo della Campana 18 (06 6867 820). Bus to Lungotevere Marzio or Via Tomacelli. **Open** 12.30-3pm, 7.30-11.30pm, Tue-Sun. Closed Aug. **Average** L60,000. **Credit** AmEx, DC, EC, MC, V. **Map 3/1A**

Some things happily never change. La Campana, which claims to be the oldest *trattoria* in Rome, is one of them. Even its younger waiters seem stuck in a 1950s timewarp, and the clientele of journalists, politicos and Gucci wives appear equally unfazed by social and culinary revolutions. The kitchen does conservative but delicious renditions of Roman classics such as *ossobuco, spaghetti con le vongole*, even *vignarola* - a broad bean and ham soup hard to find these days. Wear pearls or a tweed jacket – or both. *Air conditioning.*

Monte Caruso

Via Farini, 12 (06 483 549). Metro Termini/bus to Santa Maria Maggiore. **Open** 8pm-midnight Mon; noon-3pm, 8pm-midnight, Tue-Sat. Closed Aug. **Average** L65,000. **Credit** AmEx, DC, EC, MC, V. **Map 5/2A**

Nothing is remarkable about the address or décor, but the food here is well worth a spin. Owner-waiter-sommelier Domenico Lucia and his chef-wife are almost alone in Rome in offering a highly personal version of *cucina lucana* – from Basilicata, in Italy's instep. There are plenty of *piccante* flavours in the pasta and vegetables, and unusual, herb-packed meat offerings and the quaintly-named *glu-glu* (chicken breast with orange). Its desserts are celebrated; house red is a tannic Aglianico della Vulture. *Air-conditioning.*

Papà Baccus

Via Toscana, 36 (06 4274 2808). Bus to Via Veneto. **Open** 12.30-3pm, 7.30-11.30pm, Mon-Fri; 7.30pm-midnight Sat. Closed one week Aug, one week Christmas. **Average** L70,000. **Credit** AmEx, DC, EC, MC, V. **Map 4/2B**

Cucina toscana at its best: all the raw materials – meats, oils, wine and cheeses – are imported from owner Italo Cipriani's native valley. Try the *crostini alla cacciagione* (toast with game) or the *filetto al Brunello* (fillet steak cooked in Brunello di Montalcino wine). It's also one of the few places in Rome to serve *ribollita*, delicious Tuscan soup made from beans, fresh vegetables and bread. Open until late. The wine list has honest mark-ups. *Air-conditioning. Booking advisable. Tables outdoors.*

Paris

Piazza San Calisto, 7a (06 581 5378). Bus to Viale Trastevere. **Open** noon-3pm, 8-11pm, Tue-Sat; noon-3pm Sun. Closed Aug. **Average** L65,000. **Credit** AmEx, DC, EC, MC. **Map 6/2B**

Despite its Trastevere location – a good hike from the Ghetto – simple, elegant Paris is the place to come to sample *cucina ebraica* at its finest, backed up by fine wines. The magnificent *fritto misto con baccalà* (fried vegetables with salt cod) is the star of the show, but simple dishes like the classic *pasta e ceci* (pasta and chickpea broth) and *minestra d'arzilla* (ray soup) make a fine supporting cast. *Air-conditioning. Booking essential. Tables outdoors.*

Il Quadrifoglio

Via del Boschetto, 19 (06 482 6096). Bus to Via Nazionale. **Open** 7.30-11pm Mon-Sat. Closed three weeks Aug. **Average** L70,000. Credit AmEx, MC, V. **Map 8/1C**

Restaurants by area

Shawerma: *Egypt comes to the Colosseum. See page 151.*

Centro storico

Splashing out *Il Convivio;* **Aiming high** *Al Bric; La Campana; Sangallo; Taverna Giulia;* **Affordable** *Albistrò; La Carbonara; Ditirambo; Monserrato; Myosotis; San Teodoro; La Taverna degli Amici;* **Bargain fare** *Ar Galletto; Da Sergio; Filletti di Baccalà; Sora Margherita;* **Pizzerie** *Acchiapafantasmi; Da Baffetto; Trattoria-Pizzeria della Pace;* **International** *L'Eau Vive; Thien Kim;* **Vegetarian** *L'Insalata Ricca*

Tridente

Affordable *Antico Bottaro; Edy; Fiaschetteria Beltramme; Maccheroni; Osteria dell'Ingegno;* **Bargain fare** *Gino in Vicolo Rosini;* **Pizzerie** *'Gusto; PizzaRé;* **Vegetarian** *Margutta Vegetariano; Supernatural*

Via Veneto & Quirinale/ Villa Borghese

Splashing out *La Terrazza dell'Hotel Eden;* **Aiming high** *Papà Baccus;* **Affordable** *Caffè delle Arti;* **Bargain fare** *Osteria del Rione;* **Affordable** *Cantina Cantarini*

Trastevere

Aiming high *Antico Arco; Paris;* **Bargain fare** *Augusto; Da Enzo;* **Pizzerie** *Dar Poeta; Panattoni – I Marmi; Da Vittorio;* **International** *ATM*

Monti & Esquilino

Splashing out *Agata e Romeo;* **Aiming high** *Monte Caruso; Il Quadrifoglio;* **Affordable** *Taverna Sottovento;* **Pizzerie** *Est! Est!! Est!!!; Pachi;* **International** *Africa; Sahara; Il Guru; Maharajah; Hasekura*

Aventine, Celio, Testaccio

Splashing out *Checchino dal 1887;* **Affordable** *Agustarello; Nel Regno del Re Ferdinando II;* **Bargain fare** *Al Callarello; Da Felice; Tuttifrutti; Pizzerie Remo;* **International** *Shawerma*

Prati/near the Vatican

Aiming high *Taverna Angelica;* **Bargain fare** *Osteria dell'Angelo*

Suburbs – north

Splashing out *La Pergola dell'Hotel Hilton;* **Aiming high** *Al Ceppo;* **Pizzerie** *Al Forno della Soffitta;* **International** *Thai Inn*

Suburbs – south & San Lorenzo

Affordable *Alfredo a Via Gabi; Il Dito e la Luna; Tram Tram; Uno e Bino;* **Bargain fare** *Betto e Mery;* **Vegetarian** *L'Arancia Blu*

Tasteful, relaxed surroundings and invisibly efficient service make this ideal for an intimate dinner. First courses such as the pasta-and-seafood *penne allo scarpariello* are in the best Neapolitan tradition – although there's a tendency to overcook the pasta. Cook Annamaria Coppola comes good with main courses, such as *totani ripieni* (stuffed baby octopus). As usual with southern Italian food, vegetarians find plenty to keep them going. The real treats, though, are its desserts – among Rome's best. Call ahead and they'll keep the kitchen open for you till midnight. *Air-conditioning.*

Sangallo

Vicolo della Vaccarella, 11A (06 686 5549). Bus to Corso Rinascimento. **Open** 8-11.30pm Mon-Sat. Closed two weeks Aug. **Average** L85,000. **Credit** Am Ex, MC, V. **Map 3/1A**

The walls are lime yellow, the artwork sub-Dali, the music easy-listening. What marks out player-manager Gianfranco Panattoni is his unbridled enthusiasm. This can be overwhelming – especially when you're railroaded into choosing the L85,000 seafood menu (the restaurant's *pièce de resistance*) rather than à la carte. See the meal as a battle of wills: smile defiantly at the po-faced waitress, send white wine back if it's warm (the bane of a recent visit) and object to kids being charged full whack. A place for focused foodies: fish and seafood – such as raw prawn *antipasto* – are impeccable, desserts sublime. *Air-conditioning. Booking advisable.*

Sora Lella

Via Ponte Quattro Capi, 16, Isola Tiberina (06 686 1601). Bus to Piazza Monte Savello. **Open** 1-2.30pm, 8-11pm, Mon-Sat. Closed Aug. **Average** L70,000. **Credit** AmEx, EC, MC, V. **Map 6/2A**

Sora Lella was the plump, homely sister of film star Aldo Fabbrizi. A Roman Hattie Jacques-cum-Queen Mother, she became a folk idol and TV star in her own right. Her son Aldo Trabalza set up this authentic Roman trat on Tiber island in her honour after she died in 1993. It avoids the obvious trap of folksy kitsch, and offers excellent Roman cooking, such as *pasta e patate* (pasta and potatoes) and *abbacchio brodettato* (lamb in broth). Great on cold winter days. *Air-conditioning. Booking advisable.*

Taverna Angelica

Piazza delle Vaschette, 14A (06 687 4514). Bus to Via della Conciliazione or Piazza Risorgimento. **Open** 7.30pm-midnight Mon; 12.30-2.30pm, 7.30pm-midnight, Tue-Sat. Closed three weeks Aug, Christmas. **Average** L70,000. **Credit** AmEx, EC, MC, V. **Map 3/1C**

Until this stylishly cool restaurant opened in 1994, Borgo – the warren of lanes in front of Saint Peter's – was a gourmet desert. The décor is minimalist-modern, the cuisine creative and fish-based. Dishes like nettle *tagliatelle* with curry sauce and *petto di pollo all'aceto e nero di seppia* (vinegared chicken breast with squid ink) establish the joint's *nouvelle* credentials. Service is attentive, and a well-selected wine list also includes *mescita* (by-the-glass) options. *Air-conditioning.*

Taverna Giulia

Vicolo dell'Oro, 23 (06 686 9768). Bus to Corso Vittorio Emanuele. **Open** 12.30-3.30pm, 7.30-11.30pm, Mon-Sat. Closed Aug. **Average** L65,000. **Credit** AmEx, DC, EC, MC, V. **Map 3/2C**

A pleasant, old-fashioned Genoese restaurant, in a charming fifteenth-century house, which now caters largely to a business or politico clientele. Ligurian specialities such as *trenette al pesto* or *stoccafisso alla genovese* (Genoese dried cod) are what they do best: other high points are the crème brûlée and a limited but well-balanced wine list. *Air-conditioning.*

Affordable: L40,000 – L60,000

Agustarello

Via Giovanni Branca, 100 (06 574 6585). Bus to Via Marmorata/Via Branca. **Open** 12.30-3pm, 7.30-11pm, Mon-Sat. Closed Aug. **Average** L40,000. **No credit cards. Map 7/2B**

The decor in this Testaccio *trattoria* couldn't be more basic, but what matters here is respect for Roman tradition in all its anatomical detail: *animelette e muscoletti con funghi* (cow's pancreas and thymus glands, assorted muscles, and mushrooms) is just one of the culinary delights that the sons of the late owner, Agustarello, cook to perfection. *Tables outdoors.*

Albistrò

Via dei Banchi Vecchi, 140A (06 686 5274). Bus to Corso Vittorio. **Open** 7.30-11pm Mon, Tue, Thur-Sat; 12.30-3pm, 7.30-11pm, Sun. Closed mid-July-mid-Aug. **Average** L45,000. **Credit** DC, EC, MC, V. **Map 3/2B**

The Swiss owner and his Italian wife have carved a bistrot ambience out of this narrow space in the *centro storico*, which spills out into a pretty courtyard. The cuisine is international and creative: try the nettle-stuffed ravioli or aubergine falafel if they have it – the menu is strictly seasonal. An intelligent wine list is offered at near-*enoteca* prices. *Tables outdoors.*

Alfredo a Via Gabi

Via Gabi, 38 (06 7720 6792). Metro Re di Roma/bus to Piazza Tuscolo. **Open** noon-3pm, 7.30-11pm, Mon, Wed-Sun. Closed Aug. **Average** L45,000. **No credit cards.**

A no-nonsense family trattoria near San Giovanni in Laterano (**Map 9/1A**). Alfredo mixes regional influences: there are hints of the Marches in *pasta e fagioli con frutti di mare* (pasta with beans and seafood) and a Roman Jewish component in the wonders they work with artichokes. Come on Saturday for hard-line *cucina romana*, innards and all. *Air-conditioning. Tables outdoors.*

Antico Bottaro

Passeggiata di Ripetta, 15 (06 323 6763/06 323 6812) Bus to Piazza Augusto Imperatore or Piazza del Popolo. **Open** 12.30-3pm, 8pm-1am, Tue-Sun. Closed three weeks Aug. **Average** L55,000. **Credit** AmEx, DC, EC, MC, V. **Map 2/2A**

Antico Bottaro: a Neapolitan slant.

There's a Neapolitan slant to this restaurant near Piazza del Popolo, a warren of elegant, pale yellow, vaulted rooms. The food is good (if not outstanding), with fish dominating. The risotto with asparagus and truffle is worth a try; vegetable dishes such as radicchio with gorgonzola are also given more space here than in many Roman eateries. Open late.
Booking advisable. Wheelchair access with assistance.

Caffè delle Arti
Via Gramsci, 73-5 (06 3265 1236).
Bus or tram to Via delle Belle Arti. **Open** 7.30am-6pm Mon; 7.30am-midnight Tue- Sun. **Average** L55,000. **Credit** AmEx, DC, EC, MC, V. **Map 4/1C**
The pleasant but uninspiring pan-Italian fare served (in generous portions) in this annex to the **Galleria Nazionale d'Arte Moderna** (*see page 67*) doesn't justify its prices, but the Villa Borghese location does. A huge terrace surrounded by the lush green of the park and sheltered by a billowing white awning is great for whiling away a summer lunch-hour. Alternatively, just sip a drink from the bar, or munch on a morning *cornetto*.
Tables outside. Wheelchair access.

Cantina Cantarini
Piazza Sallustio, 12 (06 485 528). Bus to Via XX Settembre. **Open** 12.30-3.30pm, 7.30-10.30pm, Mon-Sat. Closed Aug, Christmas. **Average** L40,000. **Credit** AmEx, DC, EC, MC, V. **Map 5/1A**
A high-quality *trattoria* in a smart neighbourhood, but with extraordinarily reasonable prices. The food

is *romana/marchigiana*; meat-based for the first part of the week, fishy from Thursday to Saturday. The atmosphere is as *allegro* as seating is tight, but the *coniglio al cacciatore* (stewed rabbit), *fritto misto di pesce* (fried mixed fish) and *spaghetti al nero di seppia* (squid ink) should quell concerns about comfort. *Booking advisable at weekends. Tables outdoors.*

La Carbonara
Campo de' Fiori, 23 (06 686 4783).
Bus to Corso Vittorio. **Open** 12.15-3pm, 7-11.30pm, Mon, Wed-Sun. Closed three weeks Aug. **Average** L50,000. **Credit** AmEx, MC, V. **Map 3/2B**
Looming at one end of Rome's most *folkloristico* square, those tables look like they have to be a tourist trap. In fact, this old trooper surprisingly honest *cucina romana*, with old favourites like *fritto di cervella e carciofi* (fried brains and artichokes). The wine list and desserts are uninspired, but it's the setting that counts. Keep an eye on your bag at outside tables: Vespa swoops have happened.

Ditirambo
Piazza della Cancelleria, 74 (06 687 1626).
Bus to Corso Vittorio. **Open** 1-3.30pm, 8-11.30pm, Tue- Sun. Closed Aug. **Average** L40,000.
Credit AmEx, DC, MC, V. **Map 6/1B**
This funky *trattoria* around the corner from Campo de' Fiori has tasty, good value food: it's regularly booked out in the evenings, despite the cramped conditions and occasionally hassled service. The cuisine is eclectic, mixing pasta such as *maltagliati con i fiori di zucca* (pasta with courgette flowers) with fish and vegetarian *secondi* and some great salads.
Air-conditioning. Tables outdoors. Booking advisable.

Il Dito e la Luna
Via dei Sabelli, 51 (06 494 0726). Bus to Via Tiburtina. **Open** 8pm-midnight Mon-Sat. Closed Aug, Christmas. **Average** L50,000. **No credit cards.**
A good place to bring that special person without anyone fainting over the bill. The softly-lit ambience of this Roman *bistrot* contrasts with its location in San Lorenzo. The menu changes according to the season – try the *caponata*, a Sicilian ratatouille, if they have it, and the *flan di cipolle di Tropea e fonduta di parmigiano* (onion flan with Parmesan sauce). The desserts are good, especially the *cannoli*. A modest wine list offers bottles at near-cost price. *Booking advisable.*

Edy
Vicolo del Babuino, 4 (06 3600 1738).
Metro Spagna/bus to Via del Babuino.
Open noon-3.30pm, 7pm-midnight, Mon-Sat. Closed one week Aug. **Average** L40,000.
Credit AmEx, DC, EC, MC, V. **Map 2/2A**
A vaguely arty *trattoria* with creative but genuine Roman cooking at reasonable prices: not bad in an area where the whiff of serious money is all-pervasive. The menu changes with the season, though the house speciality - *spaghetti al cartoccio con frutti di mare*, a spaghetti and seafood creation baked and served in its own silver-foil packet - is always on the menu.

Fiaschetteria Beltramme

*Via della Croce, 39 (no phone). Metro Spagna/bus to
Piazza Augusto Imperatore.* **Open** noon-3pm, 8-
11pm, Mon-Sat. Closed two weeks Aug. **Average**
L40,000. **No credit cards.** **Map 2/2A**
This historic *trattoria* in the Tritone shopping triangle is little more than a front-room with paintings
in dubious taste. But the 'no credit cards – no phone'
line and rustic atmosphere disguise its high-chic
appeal: Madonna once fled a gala dinner to eat here.
Specialities include *tonnarelli cacio e pepe* and *pollo
con i peperoni* (chicken with peppers).

Maccheroni

*Piazza delle Coppelle 44 (06 6830 7895).
Bus to Corso Rinascimento.* **Open** 1-3pm, 8pm-
midnight, Mon-Sat. **Average** L45,000. **Credit**
AmEx, DC, EC, MC, V. **Map 3/1A**
This young, funky eaterie opened only in 1998, but
is already an established favourite with locals, office
workers and thin girls who work in PR. Off a pretty
square, it has panelled walls, and long marble counters separating the eating area from the open-to-view
kitchens. The food? Italian home cooking of variable
quality, but mostly reliable.
Tables outdoors.

Monserrato

*Via Monserrato, 96 (06 687 3386). Bus to Corso
Vittorio Emanuele.* **Open** 12.30-3pm, 7.30pm-midnight,
Tue-Sun. Closed three weeks Aug. **Average** L55,000.
Credit AmEx, EC, MC, V. **Map 6/1B**
A reliable *trattoria* around the corner from Piazza
Farnese, with summer seating in the charming
square of Santa Caterina della Rota. It could get by
on setting alone, but the pan-Italian food is not at all
bad either. Fish is a strong point, especially grilled;
primi such as *bigoli* (fat spaghetti) with asparagus
and shrimps are generally spot on, and change
according to what's in the market.
Tables outdoors.

Myosotis

*Vicolo della Vaccarella 3/5 (06 686 5554). Bus to
Corso Rinascimento.* **Open** 12.30-3pm, 7.30-11pm,
Mon-Sat. Closed three weeks Aug. **Average** L55,000.
Credit AmEx, DC, EC, MC, V. **Map 3/1A**
There should be more restaurants like this in the *centro storico*: a friendly atmosphere, efficient service
and fine food , all at decent prices. In three light,
pastelly rooms, Myosotis (Latin for forget-me-not) is
the younger offshoot of a historic culinary mecca in
Rome's eastern outskirts. The house *antipasto* of
mozzarella, ricotta, focaccia and stuffed pimento sets
things off well; follow up with *stracci di basilico e
pachino* (pasta strips in basil, tomato and olive
sauce). Wines at near-*enoteca* prices.
Air-conditioning. Booking advisable.

Nel Regno di Re Ferdinando II

*Via di Monte Testaccio, 39 (06 578 3725).
Bus to Via Marmorata or Via Galvani.* **Open** 8-
11.45pm Mon; noon-2.30pm, 8-11.45pm, Tue-Sat.
Closed two weeks Aug. **Average** L50,000. **Credit**
AmEx, EC, MC, V. **Map 7/2B**

A good place to try Neapolitan specialities such as
sartù di riso (rice, mushroom, meat and cheese bake)
in pleasant surroundings without goggling at the
bill. This popular restaurant is built into the bowels
of Monte Testaccio, complete with picture-windows
onto broken pots (*see page 85*). Seafood is a speciality, and good pizza napoletana in the evening.
Air-conditioning. Booking advisable.

Osteria dell'Ingegno

*Piazza di Pietra, 45 (06 678 0662)
Bus to Via del Corso.* **Open** 12.50-3pm, 8pm-
midnight, Mon-Sat. Closed two weeks Aug. **Average**
L45,000. **Credit** AmEx, DC, EC, MC, V. **Map 3/2A**
The menu changes monthly in this friendly new
restaurant, with Chagall-inspired artworks on
salmon pink walls. The *gnocchi in salsa di tartufo*
(truffle sauce) is good, as are the *involtini di rombo
con finocchi e salmone* (turbot rolls stuffed with fennel and salmon); vegetarians have a wide choice.
Service is efficient even at peak times, and serious
drinkers will enjoy the reasonably-priced wine list.
Dessert fiends should not miss the crème brulée.
Air conditioning. Booking advisable. Tables outdoors.

San Teodoro

*Via dei Fienili, 49/51 (06 678 0933).
Bus to Via del Teatro di Marcello.* **Open** 1-3pm, 7.30-
11.30pm, Mon-Sat. **Average** L50,000.
Credit AmEx, DC, EC, MC, V. **Map 8/2C**
In summer this is one of the best places in Rome to
eat outside: on a raised terrace amid the medieval
houses of a small residential enclave in the shadow
of the Forum. Fish and seafood are the star turn;
among the *primi, tonnelli San Teodoro* (pasta with
courgettes, king prawns and tomatoes) stands out.
They also do great things with artichokes and mushrooms, in season. Another well-priced wine list.
Air-conditioning. Booking advisable for tables outdoors.

La Taverna degli Amici

*Piazza Margana, 36 (06 6992 0637). Bus to Piazza
Venezia.* **Open** 12.30-3.30pm, 7.30pm-midnight, Tue-
Sun. Closed two weeks Aug. **Average** L50,000.
Credit AmEx, DC, EC, MC, V. **Map 6/1A**
The setting is idyllic, on an ivy-draped square on the
Ghetto side of Piazza Venezia; the cooking doesn't
always match, but on a good day *bucatini all'ama-
triciana* and *tonnarelli cacio e pepe* are fine. Chicken
with peppers and fish and/or vegetarian options fol-
low. Service is friendly, the wine list short but ade-
quate; the outside tables are much sought-after.
Air-conditioning. Booking advisable. Tables outdoors.

Taverna Sottovento

*Via Ciancaleoni 31 (06 474 2265).
Bus to Santa Maria Maggiore/Via Milano.* **Open**
7.30-midnight Sun; noon-2.30pm, 7.30-midnight,
Mon-Sat. Closed one week Aug. **Average** L55,000.
Credit AmEx, DC, EC, MC, V. **Map 8/1B**
This Calabrian restaurant between Santa Maria
Maggiore and Via Nazionale has a wood-panelled
dining room done out in a nautical theme. The cui-
sine is full of southern flavour, based on specially-
delivered Calabrian products, some of which are

available for sale upstairs. Among the *primi* the *tagliolini* with courgette flowers and scampi stand out; main courses are fish-based, but vegetarians are well-served. For dessert, go for *tartufo* ice-cream.
Air conditoning.. Booking advisable.

Tram Tram
Via dei Reti, 44/46 (06 490 416).
Bus to Piazzale Verano/tram to Via dei Reti.
Open 12.30-3.30pm, 7.30-11.30pm, Tue-Sun. Closed Aug. **Average** L45,000. **Credit** MC, V.
Taking its name from its proximity to the tram tracks (something you're reminded of more than once during your meal), this good-value San Lorenzo *trattoria* attracts a young crowd. The menu is mainly southern Italian, and strong on fish and vegetables, as in *orecchiette vongole e broccoli*. There are also vegetarian main courses. Service is erratic but undeniably *simpatico*, and the wine list small but well-chosen, with reasonable mark-ups.
Air-conditioning. Tables outdoors. Booking advisable

Uno e Bino
Via degli Equi, 58 (06 446 0702) Bus to Piazzale Verano or Via Tiburtina/tram to Via dei Reti
Open 8-11.30pm Tue-Sun. Closed three weeks Aug. **Average** L50,000. **Credit** DC, MC, V.
This recently-founded *bistrot* in San Lorenzo is friendly in spite of its minimalist decor, and great value. Host Giampaolo Gravina can talk you through his excellent (and fairly-priced) wine-list in competent English. The food is creative Italian, with no regional bias; pasta courses such as *tortelli* stuffed with caprino cheese and cabbage in a spring onion sauce are convincing, and there's usually at least one vegetarian *secondo*.
Air-conditioning. Booking advisable. Disabled: wheelchair access, toilets.

Bargain fare: L20,000 – L40,000

Ar Galletto
Vicolo del Gallo, 1/ Piazza Farnese, 102 (06 686 1714). Bus to Corso Vittorio Emanuele/Lungotevere Tebaldi. **Open** noon-3pm, 7-11.15pm, Mon-Sat. Closed one week Aug. **Average** L35,000.
Credit AmEx, DC, EC, MC, V. **Map 6/1B**
You don't need to pay the inflated prices of overrated Camponeschi for a ringside view of Piazza Farnese. Ar Galletto, a far humbler *trattoria*, has tables on the square in summer. The food is standard Roman, but dishes like *penne all'arrabbiata* or *spaghetti alle vongole* are appetising and – for the location – well-priced. Service is brisk but friendly.
Tables outdoors.

Augusto
Piazza de' Renzi, 15 (06 580 3798). Bus to Lungotevere Sanzio/tram to Viale Trastevere. **Open** 12.30-3pm, 8-11pm, Mon-Fri, 12.30-3pm Sat. Closed mid-Aug-mid-Sept. **Average** L30,000. **No credit cards. Map 6/2B**
Don't miss this: one of the last really cheap *osterie* in Trastevere, serving classics of Roman cuisine such as *rigatoni all'amatriciana* and *pollo arrosto*

con patate at unbeatable prices. In a pretty piazza with tables outside in summer, it's frequented by older *trasteverini* and people with serious haircuts.
Tables outdoors.

Betto e Mery
Via dei Savorgnan, 99 (06 2430 5339). Bus to Via Casilina/Metro Arco di Travertino. **Open** 8-11pm Mon-Wed, Fri-Sun. Closed one week Aug, three weeks Jan. **Average** L35,000. **No credit cards**.
Way off the beaten tourist track, but very worth a detour. The fire burns merrily away, even in summer, in anticipation of the *grigliata mista* (mixed grill); alternatively, there are classic Roman offal dishes such as *pajata, coda alla vaccinara, animelle* – which can all be sampled if you order the *misto romano* taster. Of the *primi*, the own-made *gnocchi* and *gramiccia* (thin *tonnarelli*) are memorable.
Tables outdoors.

Da Enzo
Via dei Vascellari, 29 (06 581 8355).
Bus or tram to Viale Trastevere. **Open** 12.30-3pm, 8-11.15pm, Mon- Sat. Closed two weeks Aug. **Average** L30,000. **Credit** AmEx, MC, V. **Map 6/2A**
A rustic, unreformed Roman *trattoria* with perfectly acceptable renditions of traditional dishes like *penne all'arrabbiata, spaghetti alla carbonara* and *pajata* at affordable prices. It has six or seven tables inside and a few outside, on a lane in the quiet southern part of Trastevere. The young, friendly waiters work a democratic shift system: two serve while the other perches on his/her Vespa across the road for a smoke and a chat with passing mates.
Tables outdoors.

Da Felice
Via Mastrogiorgio, 29 (06 574 6800). Bus to Via Marmorata. **Open** 12.15-2.30pm, 8-10.30pm, Mon-Sat. **Average** L30,000. **No credit cards. Map 7/2A**
The thrill of this neighbourhood trat is not the food – good, traditional Roman cooking with lots of offal – but trying to get in. The inaptly-named Felice – not happy at all, but a morose septagenarian – covers every table in *riservato* signs well before he opens up for the day, just so that he can announce 'no room' in lugubrious fashion to anyone who comes in that he doesn't fancy (often, anyone that he hasn't known for 30 years). But the food is plentiful and cheap, and the satisfaction of being among the chosen few makes up for any lapses.

Da Sergio
Vicolo delle Grotte, 27 (06 686 4293).
Bus to Via Arenula. **Open** 12.30-3pm, 6.30-11.30pm, Mon- Sat. Closed two weeks Aug.
Average L35,000. **No credit cards. Map 6/1B**
It's cheap, it's friendly, it does good home cooking and it's always full of locals. Add a central location near Campo de' Fiori, honest-to-goodness *trattoria* ambience and the bonus of wood-oven pizzas in the evening and it's not hard to understand why there's often a queue going down the road and round the corner. Note too the early opening times.
Booking advisable at weekends.

Reading the menu

Pasti – meals

prima colazione breakfast; pranzo lunch;
cena supper; un spuntino a snack.

Materie prime – basic ingredients

aceto vinegar; latte milk; limone lemon;
olio d'oliva olive oil; pane bread;
pepe pepper; sale salt; zucchero sugar.

Modi di cottura – cooking techniques

al dente cooked, but still firm; al forno baked;
al sangue rare (for steaks); al vapore steamed; alla
griglia/grigliato grilled; bollito boiled; cotto
cooked; crudo raw; fritto fried; in bianco plain, just
with oil or butter (rice, pasta), or no tomato (pizza);
in brodo in clear meat broth; all'acqua pazza (of
fish) in thin broth; ripassato in padella (of
vegetables) fried with garlic and chilli after boiling or
steaming; in umido poached; stufato stewed.

Antipasti – hors d'oeuvre

alici marinati marinated anchovies; antipasto
di mare seafood hors d'oeuvre; antipasto misto
mixed hors d'oeuvre (usually marinated vegetables
and cold cuts); bresaola dry-cured beef;
bruschetta toast with garlic, oil and optional
tomatoes; fiori di zucca fried courgette flowers
stuffed with mozzarella and anchovy; olive
ascolane fried olives stuffed with mince meat;
prosciutto (cotto/crudo/con melone) cured
ham, raw (Parma) ham, ham with melon.

Pasta, sughi e condimenti – pasta, with sauces and toppings

spaghetti alle vongole spaghetti with clams;
ravioli, ricotta e spinacci ravioli stuffed with
cottage cheese and spinach, often served with *burro
e salvia* (butter and sage); agnolotti, tortellini
similar to ravioli but usually meat-filled; fettucine
long flat pasta strips; tonnarelli like large
spaghetti, square in cross-section; cannelloni long
pasta rolls, designed for filling; rigatoni short pasta
tubes; orecchiette ear-or hat-shaped pasta discs,
often served with a broccoli sauce; al pesto with a
sauce of pine nuts, pecorino and basil; al pomodoro
fresco with fresh, raw tomatoes; al ragù
'bolognese', with minced meat and tomatoes; al
sugo (di pomodoro) with puréed cooked tomatoes;
all'amatriciana with tomato, chilli, onion and

sausage; alla gricia the same without the tomato;
all'arrabbiata with tomato and chilli; alla
carbonara with bacon, egg, Parmesan; alla
puttanesca with olives, capers, garlic in hot oil;
cacio e pepe with sheep's cheese and black pepper.

Carne – meat

abbacchio, agnello lamb; capra, capretto goat,
kid; coniglio rabbit; maiale, maialino pork,
piglet; manzo beef; pancetta similar to bacon;
pollo chicken; prosciutto cotto, prosciutto
crudo 'cooked' ham, Parma ham; tacchino
turkey; vitello, vitella, vitellone veal.

Piatti a base di carne – meat dishes

bollito con salsa verde boiled meat with parsley
in vinegar sauce; carpaccio, bresaola very thinly
sliced types of cured beef; ossobuco beef shins with
marrow jelly inside; polpette, polpettine meatballs;
porchetta roast piglet; rognoni trifolati stir-fried
chopped kidneys, usually with mushrooms; salsicce
sausages; saltimbocca veal strips and ham;
spezzatino casseroled meat; spiedini kebabbed, on
the spit; straccetti strips of beef or veal, stir-fried.
See also page 152 The Offal Truth.

Formaggi – cheeses

cacio, caciotta young, coarse-tasting cheese;
gorgonzola strong blue cheese, in creamy (*dolce*) or
crumbly (*piccante*) varieties; parmigiano Parmesan;
pecorino hard, tangy Roman cheese used instead of
Parmesan; ricotta crumbly white cheese, often used
in desserts; stracchino creamy, soft white cheese.

Pesce – fish

Sarago, dentice, marmora, orata, fragolino,
which are all bream of various kinds;
alici, acciughe anchovies; baccalà salt cod;
branzino/spigola sea bass; cernia grouper;
merluzzo cod; pesce spada swordfish; razza,
arzilla sting-ray or thornback ray; rombo turbot;
salmone salmon; sarde, sardine sardines;
sogliola sole; tonno tuna; trota trout.

Frutti di mare – seafood

astice, aragosta lobster, spiny lobster; calamari,
calamaretti squid, baby squid; cozze mussels;
crostacei shellfish; gamberi, gamberetti
shrimps, prawns; granchio crab; mazzancolle

Filletti di Baccalà

Largo Librai 88 (06 686 4018).
Bus to Largo Argentina/ tram to Via Arenula.
Open 5.50-11.10pm Mon-Sat. Closed Aug. Average
L18,000. No credit cards. Map 6/1B

It's officially known as Dar Filettaro a Santa
Barbara, but habitués take their cue from the sign
over the door, which promises exactly what you get
– salt cod fillets in batter. Alongside the obligatory
filletti (L5,000) there are other goodies such as fried

courgettes. Service is brisk, the ambience spit and
sawdust, but it's in a pretty square, and dead cheap.
Opens early, if you like your fry-up before 6pm.
Tables outdoors

Gino in Vicolo Rosini

*Vicolo Rosini, 4, off Piazza del Parlamento (06 687
3434). Bus to Via del Corso.* Open 1-2.45pm, 8-
10.30pm, Mon-Sat. Closed Aug. Average L35,000.
No credit cards. Map 3/1A

king prawns; **moscardini** baby curled octopus; **ostriche** oysters; **polipo/polpo** octopus; **seppie, seppiette, seppioline** cuttlefish; **telline** wedge shells (small clams); **totani** baby flying squid; **vongole** clams.

Verdura/il contorno – vegetables/the side dish

aglio garlic; **asparagi** asparagus; **basilico** basil; **broccoli siciliani** broccoli; **broccolo** green cauliflower; **broccoletti** tiny broccoli sprigs, cooked with the leaves; **carciofi** artichokes; **carote** carrots; **cavolfiore** cauliflower; **cetriolo** cucumber; **cicoria** green leaf vegetable, resembling dandelion; **cipolle** onions; **fagioli** haricot or borlotti beans; **fagiolini** green beans; **fave** broad beans; **funghi** mushrooms; **funghi porcini** boletus mushrooms; **insalata** salad; **lattuga** lettuce; **melanzane** aubergines; **patate** potatoes **peperoncino** chilli; **peperoni** peppers; **piselli** peas; **pomodori** tomatoes; **porri** leeks; **prezzemolo** parsley; **puntarelle** bitter Roman salad usually dressed with an anchovy sauce; **radicchio** bitter purple lettuce; **rughetta, rucola** rocket salad; **sedano** celery; **spinacci** spinach; **verza** cabbage; **zucchine** courgettes.

Frutta – fruit

albicocche apricots; **ananas** pineapple; **arance** oranges; **cachi** persimmons; **ciliege** cherries; **coccomero** (also known as **anguria**) water melon; **fichi** figs; **fragole, fragoline** strawberries, wild strawberries; **frutti di bosco** woodland berries; **mele** apples; **nespole** loquats; **pere** pears; **pesche** peaches; **prugne, susine** plums; **uva** grapes.

Dolci/il dessert – desserts

gelato ice cream; **montebianco** cream, meringue and maron glacé purée; **pannacotta** 'cooked cream', a very thick, blancmange-like cream, often served with chocolate (cioccolata) or wild berry (frutti di bosco) sauce; **sorbetto** sorbet; **tiramisù** mascarpone and coffee sponge; **torta della nonna** flan of patisserie cream and pine nuts; **torta di mele** apple flan; **millefoglie** flaky pastry cake.

Situated right behind the Parliament, and nearly always filled to bursting with political journalists, *deputati* and their bagmen, this unreconstructed traditional trat is a monument unto itself. The cuisine is more varied than usual: the *coniglio al vino bianco* (rabbit in white wine) and *zucchine ripiene* (stuffed courgettes) are recommended, as is the home-made tiramisù. Come early, especially at lunchtime, or be prepared to wait around for one of the hotly-contested tables.

Osteria dell'Angelo

Via Giovanni Bettolo, 24 (06 372 9470).
Metro Ottaviano/bus to Via Ottaviano. **Open** 8pm-midnight Mon, Wed, Thur,-Sat; 1-2.30pm, 8pm-midnight, Tue, Fri. Closed three weeks Aug.
Average L35,000. **No credit cards. Map 2/2C**
You can't fault the food here: tasty traditional dishes to show that Roman cooking is not just offal. The *tonnarelli cacio e pepe* are among the best in Rome; *secondi* include meatballs flavoured with nutmeg, pine nuts and sultanas. In the evening, when booking is a must, there's a fixed-price menu of L35,000, including a glass of *romanella* (sweet wine) and *ciambelline* (aniseed biscuits). Photos of boxers and rugby players on the frescoed walls belong to host Angelo's sporting past. Non-Italian speakers may have a hard time. Bring your own boxing gloves.
Booking essential in the evenings. Tables outdoors.

Osteria del Rione

Via Basento, 20 (06 855 1057).
Bus or tram to Via Po or Viale Regina Margherita. **Open** noon- 2.30pm, 7.30-11pm Mon-Fri; 7.30-11pm Sat. Closed three weeks Aug; one week Dec.
Average L28,000. **No credit cards. Map 4/1A**
Had a hard morning in the quest for culture? This is the place for you: a cheap and cheerful *osteria* of one small room with seven tables, within striking distance of Villa Borghese. You'll find all the old Roman faves – *pasta e ceci, fiori di zucca* – plus some more creative dishes such as *penne con provola e crema di zucchine* (pasta with smoked cheese and courgette purée) and some *onesto* (just about drinkable) house wine, all for a risible outlay. For once, don't be put off by the *menu turistico* in six languages outside – the L28,000 fixed-price outlay is money well spent.
Booking advisable (evenings).

Sora Margherita

Piazza delle Cinque Scole, 30 (06 686 4002).
Bus to Via Arenula or Lungotevere de' Cenci. **Open** 12.10-3pm Mon-Fri. Closed Aug. **Average** L25,000. **No credit cards. Map 6/1A**
La padrona Margherita Tomassini and her husband have been running this wonderful *osteria* in the Ghetto for over 20 years, opening only for weekday lunches, and without even a sign over the door. Not light food, but no-one argues with Roman Jewish cooking at these prices. Classic pasta and meat dishes, including superlative *pasta e fagioli*, plus daily-changing fishy treats such as *baccalà al sugo* and *alicotti con l'indivia* (anchovies with endives).

Tuttifrutti

Via Luca della Robbia, 5 (06 575 7902).
Bus to Via Marmorata or Via Galvani. **Open** 8pm-midnight Tue-Sun. Closed Aug.
Average L35,000. **Credit** MC, V. **Map 7/2A**
The decor in this trat in a Testaccio side street may be unexpected, but the food served by the friendly, earnest young bunch who run it is very good indeed. Based on seasonal ingredients, the menu – pan-Italian with international touches – changes nightly, and the waiters insist on talking you through it.

Select your wine

In Paris, it's safe to assume the house wine will at least be drinkable. In Rome, it's safe to assume the opposite. In all but the highest-class restaurants house wine will be a cheap product from Calabria or **Frascati** – also known as **Castelli Romani**. No longer the nectar praised by Roman dialect poet Trilussa in the 1900s, most Frascati that goes into the carafe today is at best bland and at worst a cloudy yellow brew with a paint-stripper bouquet.

It's a good idea, therefore, to know your labels, and find an alternative. Most neighbourhood *trattorie* have only a limited choice of the most obvious, mass-produced wines, but some of these are not at all bad, and if you scan the list (or the shelves), there's usually at least one worth drinking. Most Roman waiters haven't a clue about how wine should be served, so it's wise to check the year and temperature, and ask for an ice bucket (*un secchiello di ghiaccio*) if the wine merits it. Most Italian whites should be drunk within a year of bottling.

Best of the big names

Chianti Avoid anything in a straw-covered flask. Reliable names include *Rocca delle Macie, San Felice, Agricoltori del Chianti Geografico, Frescobaldi* (*Chianti Nipozzano*), *Fattoria di Felsina, Isola e Olena, Vignamaggio, Macchiavelli* and *Melini*.
Corvo Bianco/Rosso Originating in the Duca di Salaparuta's huge Sicilian estates (now owned by Sicily's regional government), this is Italy's most mass-produced wine, with four million bot-

tles rattling off the line every year. It has improved steadily, and makes up in consistency what it lacks in character. If they have it, try *Colomba Platino* white.
Frascati Superiore A notch above standard house Frascati, but still bland unless you're lucky enough to find Fontana Candida's *Santa Teresa* cru. Drink, as a rule, as young as possible. Other good Frascatis: *Colle Picchioni, Villa Simone, Casale Marchese, Conte Zandotti, Cantine San Marco* and *Castel De Paolis*.
Montepulciano d'Abruzzo Most of the red house plonk in Roman trats is Montepulciano d'Abruzzo, and no great advertisement for its qualities. But if you can find it, Cantina Tollo's *Colle Secco* or, better still, *Colle Secco Rubino* should reconcile you to this warm, tannic wine, which goes well with red meat. The legendary Montepulciano d'Abruzzo produced in tiny quantities by *Edoardo Valentini* is in quite another league, and quite another price range.
Regaleali Bianco This Sicilian 'industrial' white is ever-reliable and great value. Drink young. *Villa Tasca* is a pricier (but good value) big brother.
Vini Bianchi Leggeri A new generation of slightly sparkling, fresh whites. The best known is *Galestro Capsula Viola*, produced by Tuscan giants Antinori. Another good bet is *Cala Viola*, made by Sardinian winery Sella & Mosca, and *Glicine*, by Corvo. Best drunk as young as absolutely possible.

The kitchen stays open late, when you may be caught up in poetry competitions or any of the other cultural experiences that Tuttifrutti regularly hosts. *Booking advisable.*

Pizzerie

Ten years ago, you could have any pizza you liked as long as it was Roman. The city's *pizzaioli* have always been proud of their thinner, flatter *pizza romana*, but recently the fickle public has defected to the puffier Neapolitan variety. Whichever you choose, avoid the reheated surface-of-Mars discs that congeal outside tourist bars. *Pizza rotonda* (round pizza, as against the square, tray-baked takeaway *pizza rustica, see page 153*) should be rolled and baked as you wait, preferably in a wood oven .

Average prices listed in this section are based on one pizza and one 'extra'. Note that *pizzerie* are usually open in the evenings only, but they generally allow you to sit down to eat early by Roman standards, from 7pm onwards. Very few *pizzerie* accept credit cards.

Achiappafantasmi
Via dei Cappellari, 66 (06 687 3462).
Bus to Corso Vittorio Emanuele. **Open** 7.30pm-1am daily. Closed Tue, Oct-Mar, & one week Aug.
Average L25,000. **Credit** DC, MC, V. **Map 6/1B**
The tongue-twisting name translates as 'Ghostbusters', a handle justified by the Calabrian owners' speciality: *pizza del campionato*, a vaguely spook-shaped tomato, mozzarella and aubergine creation with olives for eyes. Southern Italian treats like *pomodori secchi* and *bocconcini golosi* (mozzarella wrapped in bacon) are a change from the usual pizzeria extras. Service is erratic, like the décor. *Air-conditioning.*

Al Forno della Soffitta
Via dei Villini, 1E (06 440 4642).
Metro Policlinico/bus to Porta Pia. **Open** 7pm-1am Mon-Sat. Closed two weeks Aug. **Average** L30,000.
Credit AmEx, DC, EC, MC, V.
Not exactly central – outside Porta Pia on Via Nomentana (near **Map 4/2A**) – but the Neapolitan pizzas here are among the best in town. Watch the exhibitionist *pizzaioli* spin dough-circles in the air to

Restaurants

get the required shape, and tuck into the end result, served on wooden platters like giant table-tennis bats. Upstairs is a proper Neapolitan restaurant, whose extras and wines can be ordered downstairs as well. If you stray beyond pizza, the bill will leap. No bookings taken; the place fills up early.
Branch: Via Piave, 62 (06 4201 1164). **Map 5/1A**

Da Baffetto
Via del Governo Vecchio, 114 (06 686 1617).
Bus to Corso Vittorio. **Open** 6.30pm-1am daily.
Closed two weeks Aug. **Average** L20,000.
No credit cards. Map 3/2B
Perhaps Rome's best-known pizzeria, Da Baffetto is an institution on Via del Governo Vecchio in the *Centro*. It extends over two floors, and has lightning-quick, eat-up-won't-you-there's-a-queue-outside service. The pizza and other dishes are all first-rate, but come early (6.30-8pm) or late (you can order after midnight), or expect a very long wait.

Dar Poeta
Vicolo del Bologna, 45 (06 588 0516). Bus to Piazza Sonnino. **Open** 8-11.30pm Tue-Sun. **Average** L25,000. **Credit** AmEx, MC, V. **Map 6/2B**
These four pizza-making lads use the slow-rise method introduced in recent years by *nouvelle pizza* guru Angelo Iezzi. Dar Poeta's offerings have fluffy bases and creative toppings, including *taglialegna* (mixed vegetables, mushrooms, sausage and mozzarella) and *bodrilla* (apples and Gran Marnier). The varied *bruschette* are first-rate, and you can eat till late. No bookings are taken, so come early or wait.

Est! Est! Est!
Via Genova, 32 (06 488 1107). Metro Repubblica/bus to Via Nazionale. **Open** 7pm-midnight Tue-Sun. Closed three weeks Aug.
Average L22,000. **Credit** MC, V. **Map 5/2B**
One of the oldest, most old-fashioned *pizzerie* in Rome, usefully placed between the station and Piazza Venezia, Est! Est! Est! (after the wine of the same name) was renovated a few years back, but, with dark wood and the same starched, elderly waiters, it hasn't lost its conservative allure. The pizzas and *calzoni ripieni* (folded-over pizzas) are still good.
Air-conditioning.

'Gusto
Piazza Augusto Imperatore, 9 (06 322 6273).
Bus to Piazza Augusto Imperatore.
Open 1-3pm, 7.30pm-1am, Tue-Sun. **Average** L30,000 **Credit** AmEx, MC, V. **Map 3/1A**
A pizzeria-cum-restaurant-cum-winebar-cum-bookshop. The ground floor pizza and salad bar is packed with staff from surrounding offices at lunchtime, and just about everyone in the evening; wicker-and-beige décor may make you yearn for something more grittily Roman, but the fare is good-to-middling, the salads abundant and fresh. The upstairs restaurant blends stir-fry with Italian staples with varying degrees of success. There is also a good selection of wines by the glass.
Air-conditioning. Disabled: wheelchair access to ground floor only. Tables outside.

Pachi
Via Cavour 315 (06 6920 2164).
Bus to Via Cavour. **Open** noon-3.30pm, 7pm-midnight, Tue-Sun. Closed one week Aug. **Average** L22,000. **Credit** AmEx, DC, EC, MC, V. **Map 8/1B**
One of the most recent outposts of the Neapolitan invasion, Pachi is housed in a former garden centre at the Forum end of Via Cavour. The colour-scheme is dubious, and the huge space can feel very empty. But the pizzas are decent, toppings are generous, and there's a wider than usual range of side dishes. Note the lunchtime opening – unusual for a pizzeria.

Panattoni – I Marmi
Viale Trastevere, 53 (06 580 0919).
Bus/tram to Viale Trastevere. **Open** 6.30pm-2.20am, Mon, Tue, Wed-Sun. Closed two weeks Aug.
Average L18,000. **No credit cards. Map 6/2B**
Better known as *l'Obitorio* (the morgue) on account of its marble slab tables, but there's nothing deathly about Panattoni, one of the liveliest pizzerias in Trastevere, especially in summer when you can sit outside and watch the new super-trams glide past. Its pizzas, though, are not the best in Rome, and service is sharp to the point of being ruthless.
Tables outdoors.

PizzaRé
Via di Ripetta, 14 (32 11 468). Metro Flaminia/bus to Piazza del Popolo. **Open** 12.45-3.30pm, 7.30pm-12.30am, daily. Closed one week Aug. **Average** L20,000. **Credit** AmEx, DC, MC, V. **Map 2/2A**
Another leader of the Neapolitan invasion, just a few paces from Piazza del Popolo. This formulaic but still lively pizzeria offers 40 varieties of high-risers, various *antipasti* and a range of salads. You can even order a steak. Service is cheery and efficient, the surroundings pleasantly retro, and there are some acceptable bottles of wine on offer.
Air-conditioning.

Remo
Piazza Santa Maria Liberatrice, 44 (06 574 6270). Bus to Via Marmorata or Piazza Santa Maria Liberatrice. **Open** 6.30pm-12.30am Mon-Sat. Closed Aug.
Average L15,000. **No credit cards. Map 7/1A**
The best place in town for authentic *pizza romana*, Remo is a Testaccio institution, with a prime location on the district's main piazza. You can sit at wonky tables balanced on the pavement, or in the cavernous interior, overseen by Lazio team photos. The *bruschette al pomodoro* are the finest in Rome.
Tables outdoors.

Trattoria-Pizzeria della Pace
Via della Pace, 1 (06 686 4802). Bus to Corso Vittorio. **Open** *Oct-Apr* 1-3pm, 8pm-midnight, *May-Sept* 8pm-midnight only, Tue-Sun. **Average** L25,000. **Credit** MC, V. **Map 3/2B**
Owner Bartolo also runs the ever-trendy **Bar della Pace** next door (*see p158*), and the combination of a sharp PR instinct and strategic watch-and-be-watched pavement tables means that it's always packed. Most nights a few paparazzi or a camera crew will be hovering on the off-chance. The food

hardly matters: Neapolitan-style pizzas, decent, home-cookin' pasta, one or two more adventurous fishy and meaty mains, and a limited, reasonably priced wine list. It takes orders late (you can sit over your meal until around 2am) and doesn't accept bookings, so come late or early to be sure of a table.

Da Vittorio
Via di San Cosimato, 14A (06 580 0353). Bus to Viale Trastevere. **Open** 8pm-midnight Tue-Sun. **Average** L22,000. **No credit cards.** **Map 6/2B**
Vittorio was here way before Neapolitan pizzas became trendy, and no doubt will be when the fad has passed. He's as *napoletano* as they come, and so are his succulent pizzas. He has a couple of inventions of his own – like the self-celebratory *Vittorio* (mozzarella, Parmesan, fresh tomato and basil). The place is minute, but bursts with exuberance. *Tables outdoors.*

International

Such is the steamroller nationalism and regionalism of Roman diners that foreign cuisine has always been regarded with raised eyebrows. Younger Romans are more adventurous, and a number of usually middling-quality establishments have sprung up in recent years.

There have long been over 100 Chinese restaurants in the city, but it's a mystery how they survive, as the quality is generally low and the tables empty. Ethiopia and the Horn of Africa, too, are well-represented. Most of these restaurants are frequented by the community itself – few Italians have ever ventured into one. This is a pity, since this hot, spicy food is full of memorable dishes.

Overall, the range is still nothing like one finds in truly international cities. The main reason for eating in the restaurants listed below is that you simply can't face another pizza or pasta dish.

Ethiopian/Eritrean

Africa
Via Gaeta, 26 (06 494 1077). Metro Castro Pretorio or Termini/bus to Via Volturno orTermini.
Open 8am-11.30pm Tue-Sun. **Average** L30,000.
Credit AmEx, MC, V. **Map 5/1A**
Long-established Eritrean restaurant, offering specialities such as *sambussa*, a dish of cigar-shaped meat and spice rolls, and *taita* – a sour, spongy bread served with *zighini* (spicy meat), *spriss* (beef cubes with chilli, onion and spices) and other toppings; there's also a vegetarian version. Opens early in the morning for Eritrean breakfast of yoghurt and *ful.*

Sahara
Viale Ippocrate, 43 (06 4424 2583). Metro Bologna/bus to Viale Ippocrate. **Open** 12.30-2.30pm, 7.30-10.30pm, Mon, Tue, Thur-Sun. Closed one week Aug. **Average** L30,000. **Credit** AmEx, MC, V.
Try out Eritrean delicacies while sitting on a delightful and somehow un-Roman (if equally un-African)

patio north-east of Termini station. The dishes are mostly meat-based, and all very spicy. *Derho* (chicken with tomatoes) and *zilzil tibs*i (veal) are served on Eritrean bread. There's a vegetarian menu as well. *Tables outdoors.*

French

L'Eau Vive
Via Monterone, 85 (06 6880 1095). Bus to Largo Argentina. **Open** 12.30-3pm, 7.30-10.30pm, Mon- Sat. Closed three weeks Aug. **Average** L70,000. **Credit** AmEx, DC, EC, MC, V. **Map 6/1A**
Possibly the oddest culinary experience in Rome: if Fellini had ever directed a James Bond film, he would have set it here. Picture the scene: an obscure order of multi-ethnic Third World nuns runs a sophisticated French haute cuisine-inspired restaurant in a sixteenth-century palazzo, with Renaissance frescoes on the ceiling. At 9pm, the diners – many in the ill-fitting brown suits favoured by the international espionage circuit – are interrupted by the tinkle of a silver bell and invited to join in the Ave Maria. The only disappointment is the food: French à la school dinner. They also do a bargain-price tourist lunch. *Air-conditioning. Booking essential.*

Indian

Il Guru
Via Cimarra, 4/6 (06 474 4110). Bus to Via Nazionale or Via Cavour **Open** 7.30pm-midnight Tue-Sat. Closed two weeks Aug. **Average** L40,000. **Credit** AmEx, DC, EC, MC, V. **Map 8/1B**
If you're dying for an Indian, Il Guru is a reliable option. Like the **Maharajah**, it has a tandoori oven; the cuisine is standard pan-Indian, with a vegetarian menu, and the staff are friendly.

Maharajah
Via dei Serpenti, 124 (06 4747 144). Bus to Via Nazionale or Via Cavour. **Open** 12.30-2.30pm, 7-11.30pm, Mon-Sat; 7-11.30pm Sun. **Average** L45,000. **Credit** AmEx, DC, EC, MC, V. **Map 8/1B**
Very near the Guru, the Maharajah has the culinary edge, but is also more expensive. Classic Punjab food, with a tandoori oven and a vegetarian menu. *Air-conditioning.*

Japanese

ATM
Via della Penitenza, 7 (06 6830 7053). Bus to Lungotevere Farnesina. **Open** 7.30pm-12.30am Tue- Sun. Closed Aug. **Average** L45,000. **Credit** AmEx, MC, V. **Map 6/1C**
This new, fashionable sushi bar has the right post-Blade-Runner, post-Starck decor and lounge music, but is still trying to get its food entirely right. Sushi, sashimi and tempura are the main acts, none as faultless as the ambience leads you to expect, but it's a good place to go when other Trastevere kitchens have closed down. *Air conditioning.*

Hamasei
Via della Mercede 35/36 (06 679 2134).
Bus to Piazza San Silvestro. **Open** noon-2.30pm, 7-
10.30pm, Tue-Sun. **Average** L45,000.
Credit AmEx, DC, EC, MC, V. **Map 5/1C**
A branch of a famous Tokyo eaterie, this is Rome's
most traditional Japanese restaurant, oozing orien-
tal elegance and packed with a reassuringly large
slice of Rome's Japanese population. Try the serious
sushi, or Sashimi and Sukiyaki at candle-lit tables.
At lunch time, set menus start at L25,000.
Air-conditioning.

Hasekura
*Via dei Serpenti, 27 (06 483 648). Bus to Via
Nazionale or Via Cavour.* **Open** noon-2.30pm, 7-
10.30pm, Mon-Sat. Closed Aug. **Average** L55,000.
Credit AmEx, DC, EC, MC, V. **Map 8/1C**
The best value of Rome's five Japanese restaurants,
Hasekura is an intimate little place, with good sushi
and sashimi. You can opt for the generous fixed-
price lunch menus (tempura L25,000, sushi L45,000)
or go à la carte. Beautifully presented specialities
can be ordered if you phone ahead.
Air-conditioning.

Middle Eastern

Shawerma
*Via Ostilia, 24 (06 700 8101). Metro Colosseo/bus or
tram to Piazza del Colosseo.* **Open** noon- 3.30pm,
8pm-midnight, Tue-Sun. Closed ten days Aug.
Average L35,000. **Credit** AmEx, DC, V. **Map 8/2B**
You can sit downstairs on seats, or cross-legged on
cushions on a low balcony at this Egyptian eaterie
near the Colosseum. The cuisine is first-rate, with
great couscous and unusual milk-based desserts;
lubrication comes in the form of rose wine. By day
it's a café, with exotic beverages such as *hansun* and
erfa as well as mint tea and Egyptian coffee.
Air-conditioning. Tables outdoors.

Thai

Thai Inn
*Via F. Ozanam 94 (06 5820 3145). Bus or tram to
Piazza San Giovanni da Dio.* **Open** 11am-3pm, 8pm-
midnight, Tue-Sun. Closed one week Aug. **Average**
L40,000. **Credit** AmEx, DC, EC, MC, V.
The best of Rome's long-standing Thai restaurants,
with a pretty inner veranda. The cooking is standard Thai – crab soup, duck with fresh ginger – with
a Malay twist. It's out of the way, on the cusp
between Monteverde Vecchio and Nuovo.
Air-conditioning.

Vegetarian/salad bars

Italians have no great awareness of vegetarianism.
There are Italian vegetarians, but they tend to be
of the hard-line macrobiotic variety, and their
numbers fall every year, with the demise of the
comunes and cooperatives that fuelled them. That

Pick of the brunch

A recent arrival on the Roman eating scene, brunch
is spreading like wildfire. Five of the best…
Macrobiotic brunch: **Margutta
Vegetariano** (*p152*), 11am-3pm daily. A
healthy L16,000-L20,000, except on Sunday,
when live music pushes the price to L35,000.
Brunch with a dip: **Holiday Inn** (*see p210*).
Brunch-plus-pool formula at a cool L80,000 a head.
Brunch with a view: **La Terrazza
dell'Hotel Eden** (*p135*), noon-3pm Sat, Sun.
At L50,000, L60,000 and L70,000, you'll need a
head for heights.
Brunch over a book: **Bibli** (*see p170*),
noon-4pm Sun; tranquil brunch for bibliophiles
at L25,000.
Pub brunch: **Trinity College** (*see p156*):
the genuine Italo-Irish brunch article, all for
L20,000, 11am-4pm Sun.

said, it's a lot easier for vegetarians here than in
many European cities. The reason is simple: Italian
cuisine – especially the southern variety – includes
innumerable meat-free combinations of pasta,
cheese and vegetables.

As long as you avoid the seriously *cucina
romana* offal-with-everything places, you should
be able to assemble a perfectly satisfying meal by
choosing from among the *antipasti*, first courses,
salads or *contorni* and desserts. If in doubt, check
by asking *non c'è carne, vero?* (There's no meat, is
there?). Note too that many Italians don't consider
chicken (*pollo*) or fish (*pesce*) to be meat, so check.

Vegetarian-friendly first courses (*primi*)
orechiette ai broccoletti/cima di rape ear-
shaped pasta with broccoli sprigs/green turnip-tops;
pasta e ceci soup with pasta and chick-peas; **pasta
e fagioli** soup with pasta and borlotti beans; **pasta
alla puttanesca** or **alla checca** (literally 'à la
whore' or 'à la raging queen') based on olives, capers
and tomatoes, though anchovies (*alici*) are sometimes
slipped into the former; **penne all'arrabbiata**
pasta with tomato sauce and lots of chilli; **ravioli** OK
if filled with *ricotta e spinacci* (soft cheese and
spinach) and served *con burro e salvia* (with butter
and sage) or a simple *sugo di pomodoro* (tomato
sauce); **risotto ai quattro formaggi** risotto made
with four types of cheese; **spaghetti aglio, olio e
peperoncino** with garlic, olive oil; **spaghetti cacio
e pepe** with crumbled salty ewe-milk cheese and lots
of black pepper.

Main courses (*secondi*)
Second courses are more of a problem; often, you'll
have to make do with an unispiring *insalata mista*.

Among the standard options are:
carciofi alla giudia deep-fried artichokes; **fagioli all'uccelletto** haricot beans with tomato, garlic and olive oil (strictly speaking a *contorno*, but substantial enough to take the place of a main course);
melanzane alla parmigiana aubergine with Parmesan (this occasionally has meat in the topping); **scamorza** grilled cheese; specify without ham (*senza prosciutto*) or anchovies (*senza alici*).

Arancia Blu

Via dei Latini 65 (06 445 4105). Bus to Porta Tiburtina. **Open** noon-3pm, 8pm-midnight, daily. **Average** L40,000. **No credit cards.**
A friendly but upmarket vegetarian restaurant in San Lorenzo, which prides itself on its wine list. Very enjoyable pasta courses are mainly southern Italian in conception; the more macrobiotic *secondi* are a tad less convincing, but still satisfying. Since it is officially a private club, you need to fill in a nominal membership card to eat here. They also organise cooking and wine courses.
Air conditioning. Booking advisable.

L'Insalata Ricca

Largo dei Chiavari, 85 (06 6880 3656).
Bus to Corso Vittorio Emanuele. **Open** noon-4pm, 6pm-midnight, daily. **Average** L20,000. **Credit** AmEx, DC, EC, MC, V. **Map 3/2A-B**
The nearest Rome has to a fast-food salad bar. Not exclusively vegetarian, but a good cheap alternative to obligatory pasta and/or veggie ghettoes (although you can order pasta too). The main branch is geared to fast outdoor eating; the smaller one in Piazza di Pasquino is a shade more comfortable and intimate.
Tables outdoors.
Branch: Piazza di Pasquino, 72 (06 6830 7881).

Margutta Vegetariano – Ristorarte

Via Margutta 118 (06 3265 0577).
Metro Flaminia/Bus to Piazza del Popolo. **Open** 11am-midnight daily. **Average** L45,000. **Credit** DC, EC, MC, V. **Map 2/2A**
Rome's historic vegetarian diner has expanded into a surprisingly large plant-filled space on arty, exclusive Via Margutta. The décor pays homage to the area, with plenty of modern art; at weekends there is live piano. For lunch, a set-price all-you-can-eat option from brunch buffet (L20,000, with dessert) is an alternative to the more formal restaurant.The menu offers a wide choice: pasta, salads, soufflés, soya rolls and grilled vegetables.

Supernatural

Via del Leoncino, 38 (06 3265 0577).
Bus to Via Tomacelli or Via del Corso.
Open 12.30-3.30pm, 7.30-10.30pm, daily. **Average** L20,000. **Credit** MC, V. **Map 3/1A**
Rome's only vegetarian pizzeria. Service is rather uncertain and the tables outside are too flimsy for serious pizza-sawing, but it's cheap and fills a gap in the market: just about any vegetarian topping you like (even pesto). There's also a vegan menu, and even the own-made beer and cola are organic.
Tables outdoors.

The offal truth

The unspeakable parts of the beast have long been a major component in Roman culinary tradition. The so-called *quinto quarto* or 'fifth quarter', of tripe, intestines and the like, went by right to workers at the Testaccio slaughterhouse. It was here, in humble *trattorie* such as **Checchino dal 1887** (now one of the city's most highly-regarded restaurants) that inventive cooks learnt to put workers' offcuts to good use.

One Sora Ferminia came up with the recipe for *coda alla vaccinara* – literally, 'tail in the style of the slaughterhouse worker'. The popularity of this dish – in which an oxtail is braised in a celery broth – soon led to a run on tails. Other classic offal dishes are *rigatoni alla pajata* – pasta with a sauce of veal's intestines with the mother's milk still inside, cooked in lard, onion, celery and parsley; *fagioli con le cotiche* – beans with pork scratchings; *insalata di zampi* – hoof jelly salad; and *animelle* – the spongy white pancreas and thymus glands, generally fried. Tripe (*tripa*) is also big in Rome, and other bits of the animal you may see on menus include *cervello*, brain, *lingua*, tongue, *guanciale*, pig's cheek, cured in salt and pepper, and *nervetti*, strips of cartilage. *Buon appetito*!

For the full innards experience, take a deep breath and head for one of the following: **Checchino dal 1887** (*page 135*), **Sora Lella** (*page 141*), **Agustarello** (*page 141*), **Betto e Mery** (*page 145*).

Brains, glands, intestines... Mmmmm.

Snacks

Rome is learning to cater for grazing animals as the long Roman lunch becomes ancient history.

The Roman habit of tucking away two full, sit-down meals each day is fast disappearing, and as a result places designed for eating on the run are mushrooming. Roman snack culture, though, is a strange beast, lurking in un-obvious places. A bit of inside knowledge helps ferret it out.

Few new arrivals, for example, consider stepping into a humble *alimentari* (grocer) to have their picnic lunch prepared – and yet for fresh bread and high-quality fillings this is invariably the best option. In bars, you'll find the same white, triangular sandwiches everywhere, but some of these establishments are lunchtime Meccas, with full-scale *tavole calde* (buffets). What follows is a selective, centre-biased guide to how and where to snack in Rome. For further snacking options, *see also chapters* **Wine Bars** *and* **Cafés & Bars**.

Alimentari

From around noon until they close for lunch at 1.30, Roman *alimentari* play host to a (for some reason) mainly masculine tradition. The client enters and asks for *un panino con…* (a roll with…), waits while the man with the apron puts it all together, and wanders out again clutching the bundle and a can of something, usually beer. Favourite casing is the ubiquitous white Roman roll, *la rosetta*, or a slice of *pizza bianca* (plain oiled and salted pizza, eaten as is or filled); fillings are generally ham, salami or cheese (*alimentari* do not sell fruit and veg). Any Roman *alimentari* will do this for you; for upmarket delis serving gourmet versions (such as **Volpetti**), *see chapter* **Shopping**.

L'Antico Forno
Via delle Muratte, 8 (06 679 2866).
Bus to Via del Corso or Via del Tritone.
Open *Sept-May* 7am-9pm Mon-Wed, Fri-Sun; 7am-1pm Thur. *June-Aug* 7am-9pm daily. **Map** 5/2C
Right opposite the Trevi fountain, this bakery-general store does ready-made (but fresh) filled rolls, plus the usual *gastronomia* fare – rice and seafood salad and so on. Service is grumpy but efficient.

Fratelli Paladini
Via del Governo Vecchio, 29 (06 686 1237). Bus to Corso Vittorio Emanuele. **Open** 8am-8pm Mon-Wed, Fri-Sun; 8am-3pm Thur. Closed Aug. **Map** 3/2B
This ancient, family-run bread shop looks nothing special, but the crowd spilling outside at peak hours know different. The wood-fired *pizza bianca* is out-

standing, and is filled to order with hams, cheeses, fresh figs, dried tomatoes and other delights.

Bars

La Casa del Tramezzino
Viale Trastevere, 81 (06 581 2118). Bus or tram to Viale Trastevere. **Open** 7am-2am daily. **Map** 6/2B
In one of his struggles against foreign influences, Mussolini ordered that foreign words be replaced with newly-coined Italian ones. Sandwich became *tramezzino*. La Casa del Tramezzino has the widest choice of them in Rome. Apart from classics like mozzarella and tomato, try the fried aubergine, rocket and Gorgonzola, or cheese and caviar.

Galeani
Via Arenula, 50 (06 6880 6042). Bus to Lungotevere dei Cenci/tram to Via Arenula. **Open** 7am-10.30pm Mon-Sat. Closed two weeks Aug. **Map** 6/1A
A lively bar packed with customers from the Justice Ministry across the road. Filled *rosette* or slices of *pizza bianca* are made up on the spot. The edge-of-the-Ghetto location is reflected in kosher fillings like *bottarga* (mullet roe) and *pastrami* (salt beef).

Gran Caffè Strega
Piazza Viminale, 27-31 (06 485 670). Bus to Via Nazionale. **Open** 6am-midnight daily. **Map** 5/2B
Tucked under the imposing Interior Ministry, this is a good place for a fast inexpensive lunch. Highlights are pizza *a legna* (in a wood oven), a generous salad bar and cold buffet, and copious cakes and ice cream.

Il Seme e la Foglia
Via Galvani, 18 (06 574 3008).
Bus to Via Marmorata, Via Galvani.
Open 7.45am-1.30am Mon-Sat; 6pm-1.30am Sun.
Closed three weeks Aug. **Map** 7/2A
Once a po-faced macrobiotic affair, this has become a lively daytime snack bar and evening pre-club stop. At midday there's always a pasta dish, plus salads and exotic filled rolls.

Pizza a Taglio

Pizza a taglio or *pizza rustica* is classic Roman fast food – a slab of variously-topped pizza. Beware of outlets with a slow turnover, where the pizza is likely to have been out of the oven and congealing on the counter for hours. You won't have this problem in the places listed below.

Frontoni
*Viale Trastevere, 52 (06 581 2436). Bus or tram to
Viale Trastevere.* **Open** 11am-1am Mon-Thur; 11am-
2am Fri, Sat; 5pm-midnight Sun. **Map 6/2B**
Frontoni claims to have 60 different fillings for the
slabs of *pizza bianca* piled up behind its counter. Just
point to the ones you fancy.

Da Giovanni
*Piazza Campo de' Fiori, 39 (06 687 7992). Bus or
tram to Corso Vittorio Emanuele/tram to Via
Arenula.* **Open** *Sept-May* 8am-3pm, 4-9pm, *June-July*
8am-midnight, Mon-Sat. Closed Aug. **Map 3/2B**
Giovanni does the best takeaway sliced pizza in the
Campo de' Fiori area. Check out the *fiori di zucca* –
courgette flower pizza.

Pizzeria Leonina
*Via Leonina, 84 (06 482 7744). Metro Cavour/
bus to Via Cavour.* **Open** 7.30-10pm Mon-Fri.
Closed two weeks July; Aug. **Map 8/1B**
One of the best *pizzerie a taglio* in Rome. Avoid peak
times, as the queue is endless (take a number). Not
as cheap as one might hope, but with toppings like
spicy beans, tuna salad and even apple strudel, it's
still worth it.

Sisini
*Via San Francesco a Ripa, 137 (06 589 7110).
Bus to Viale Trastevere.* **Open** 9am-9pm Mon-Sat.
Closed three weeks Aug. **Map 6/2B**
Probably Trastevere's best *pizza a taglio* outfit. The
flavours on offer are fairly conservative, but there's
a wide range and they're all delicious.

Zi Fenizia
*Via Santa Maria del Pianto, 64 (06 689 6976). Bus
to Largo Argentina/tram to Via Arenula.* **Open** 9am-
9pm Sun-Fri. Closed Jewish holidays. **Map 6/1A**
Rome's only kosher pizza outlet. Auntie Fenizia does
over 40 flavours, including the speciality *con aliciotti
e indivia* (with anchovies and endives).

Rosticcerie & Tavole Calde

A *rosticceria* roasts things on spits – usually chick-
en. The concept tends to overlap with a *tavola
calda*, which offers hot (or reheated) pasta, meat
and vegetable dishes.

Er Buchetto
*Via del Viminale, 2f (06 488 3031).
Metro Repubblica or Termini/bus to Termini.*
Open 9am-9pm Mon-Fri; 9am-3pm Sat. Closed two
weeks Aug. **Map 5/2A**
A hole in the wall near the Opera specialising in one
of the great culinary triumphs of the Roman countryside: *porchetta* – strongly peppered cold roast
baby piglet – between slices of *casareccio* bread,
with a glass of Castelli white wine. Utterly delicious.

Volpetti Più
*Via Alessandro Volta, 8/10 (06 574 4306). Bus to
Via Marmorata.* **Open** 10am-3.30pm, 5-10.30pm,
Mon-Sat. Closed two weeks Aug. **Map 7/2A**

Close to the upmarket deli of the same name, this
snack bar does excellent high-rise *pizza a taglio* and
other hot and cold dishes. Unusually for a buffet, it
also has a range of good wines at *enoteca* prices.

Self-service/fast food

Brek
*Largo Argentina, 1 (06 6821 0353).
Bus or tram to Largo Argentina.* **Open** *bar* 7am-
1am; *restaurant* noon-3.30pm, 7-11.30pm.
Credit *restaurant* AmEx, DC, MC, V. **Map 3/2A**
A bar and slabs of pizza downstairs; a free-flow
restaurant with salad bar and meat grilled before
your eyes upstairs. All rather aggressively theatrical, in homage to the Teatro Argentina next door.

Indian Fast Food
*Via Mamiani, 11 (06 446 0792). Metro Vittorio/
bus or tram to Piazza Vittorio Emanuele.*
Open 9.30am-4pm, 5-10pm Mon-Sat. **Map 8/1A**
Rome's only Indian takeaway, just off Piazza
Vittorio. You can eat in too, accompanied by glor-
iously kitsch Indian music videos – and send a mon-
eygram while you consume your vegetable samosa.

Le Piramidi
*Vicolo del Gallo, 11 (06 687 9061). Bus to Corso
Vittorio Emanuele/tram to Via Arenula.* **Open**
10.30am-1am, Tue-Sun. Closed Aug. **Map 6/1B**
Around the corner from Campo de' Fiori, Le
Piramidi is the city-centre place to go if Italian food
is getting you down. Good, tasty Middle Eastern
snacks and sweets (plus perfectly acceptable pizza).

Paninoteca da Guido
*Borgo Pio, 13 (06 687 5491). Bus to Piazza della
Città Leonina or Piazza Risorgimento.* **Open** 8.30am-
4pm daily. Closed Aug. **Map 3/1C**
Lunchtime pasta, meat and vegetable dishes with a
real home cooking feel to them, served in a cup-
board-sized dive no distance from Saint Peter's. One
of few places in Rome where you can still eat a full
meal for L15,000, or they can just run you up a sandwich. Get there early, or be ready to be very patient,
if you want to grab the one outside table outside.

Ristorante Self-Service del
Palazzo delle Esposizioni
Via Milano, 9 (06 482 8001). Bus to Via Nazionale.
Open *Bar* 10am-9pm, Mon; *buffet* 12.30-3pm, Mon,
Wed-Sun. **Credit** AmEx, DC, MC, V. **Map 5/2B**
The ground-floor bar in this arts complex does standard bar food, with knockout Sicilian pastries (*see
chapter* **Cafés & Bars**). Go up in the glass lift to
find a reasonably priced buffet with a good salad
bar – a rarity in Rome.

Shawerma Express
*Via Calatafimi, 7 (06 481 8791). Bus to Termini or
Via Goito.* **Open** 11am-midnight daily. **Map 5/1A**
Good-value Arab and Middle Eastern specialities
such as felafel, *fuul* (spicy beans), couscous and
kebabs, served with pitta bread, to take away or to
eat in. There are tables outside in summer.

Wine Bars & *Birrerie*

Where to find the veritas in Roman vino.

Neighbourhood *enoteche* (wine shops) and *vini e oli* outlets have been around in Rome since time immemorial, complete with their huddle of old men drinking wine by the glass (*al bicchiere* or *alla mescita*). Recently a number of upmarket, international-style wine bars have also sprung up, offering snacks to go with their wines. Such is the Roman predilection for eating over drinking that some – **Il Brillo Parlante**, **Ferrara**, **Trimani Wine Bar**, **Il Simposio** – are best thought of as restaurants with great cellars.

Beer culture is far less developed, but the pub is an increasingly popular concept with young Italians – one reason for the fungal spread of 'authentic' Irish pubs in the city, with identical décor out of a kit supplied by Guinness. The pubs listed below are all a little more genuine and/or atmospheric. For just bottle-buying, *see page 183*.

Fratelli Tempera:*100 beery years (page 156).*

is equally popular, offering a great selection of salads, smoked fish, cheeses and a few pasta dishes.

Alla Corte del Vino
Via Monte della Farina, 43 (06 6830 7568).
Bus to Largo Argentina/tram to Via Arenula.
Open 6.30pm-1am Tue-Sun. Closed three weeks
Aug. **Credit** MC, V. **Map 6/1B**
A new wine bar between Campo de' Fiori and Via Arenula that's already on the serious wino's map of the *centro storico*. Run by three young, enthusiastic lads, it has a good range by the glass or bottle, plus cheeses, salami, salads and flans.

Cul de Sac
Piazza Pasquino, 73 (06 6880 1094).
Bus to Corso Vittorio Emanuele. **Open** 7pm-12.30am
Mon; 12.30-3.30pm, 7pm-12.30am Tue-Sun.
Credit AmEx, EC, MC, V. **Map 3/2B**
Rome's original wine bar, founded 1968. It's cramped inside and out, but anywhere that offers so many good bottles at such decent prices within sight of Piazza Navona (and with tables outside) has got to be worth a try. Food is standard fare, mainly cold: the Greek salad and lentil soup stand out.

The Drunken Ship
Campo dei Fiori, 20/21 (06 6830 0535).
Bus to Corso Vittorio Emanuele. **Open** 5pm-2am
daily. **Credit** AmEx, MC, V. **Map 3/2B**
Most popular meeting place on the Campo after the **Vineria**, the Ship has become a place to go if, like more and more trendy young Romans, you would not be seen dead drinking wine. Oddly, though, the

Centro storico

L'Angolo Divino
Via dei Balestrari, 12 (06 686 4413).
Bus to Largo Argentina. **Open** 10.30am-3pm Mon;
10.30am-3pm, 5.30-1am Tue-Sun. Closed two weeks
Aug. **Credit** EC, MC, V. **Map 3/2B**
This punningly-named bar on a quiet street near Campo de' Fiori has come up in the world since it opened as a humble *vini e oli* 50 years ago. The décor is simple: terracotta floor, beamed ceiling and government-surplus tables. Fifteen or so wines are available by the glass, many more by the bottle. There's an unusually good range of salads, an ample cheese-board and, in winter, at least one hot dish.

La Bottega del Vino da Anacleto Bleve
Via Santa Maria del Pianto, 9a-11 (06 686 5970).
Bus to Largo Argentina/tram to Via Arenula.
Open *enoteca* 4.30-8pm Mon; 9.30am-1pm, 4.30-8pm
Tue-Sat; *wine bar* 12.45-3pm Tue, Sat; 12.45-3pm, 8-10pm Wed-Fri. Closed three weeks Aug.
Credit AmEx, DC, EC, MC, V. **Map 6/1A**
Not a wine bar as much as a wine shop that turns into a very enjoyable restaurant five days a week (for dinner, only Wednesday, Thursday and Friday). The carefully selected range of bottles by top Italian producers means that it is well patronised by locals. The restaurant, with tables among shelves of bottles,

main act – beer – is limited to three varieties. Great location (with tables on the piazza) and slick design distinguish it from nearby rivals. Student discounts, and DJs in the evening; happy hour 5-8pm.

Il Goccetto
Via dei Banchi Vecchi, 14 (06 686 4268).
Bus to Corso Vittorio. **Open** 11am-2pm, 5.30-10.30pm, Mon-Sat. Closed three weeks Aug.
Credit AmEx, MC, V. **Map 3/2B**
One of the more serious *centro storico* wine bars, occupying part of a medieval bishop's house, with original painted ceilings and a cosy, private-club feel. Wine is the main point, with a satisfying range by-the-glass from L4,500, but there's a good choice of cheeses, salami and salads.

La Vineria
Campo de' Fiori, 15 (06 6880 3268). Bus to Corso Vittorio Emanuele. **Open** 9.30am-3pm, 5pm-1am, Mon-Sat. **Credit** AmEx, DC, EC, MC, V. **Map 3/2B**
Everyone calls in here sooner or later. Also known as Da Giorgio, this is an authentic local wine bar, with a great position on the Campo and decent wine by the glass from L2,000 – cheaper than most. It's evocatively portrayed in Michael Dibdin's novel *Vendetta*, as the favourite drinking haunt of his cop hero Aurelio Zen. By day and in the early evening it throngs with lived-in locals and historic expatriates; by night, it's a seriously hip hang-out for bright young things (and some slightly tarnished older ones) who crowd its pavement tables. Also a good place to pick up a bottle after hours.

Tridente

Antica Enoteca di Via della Croce
Via della Croce, 76b (06 679 0896). Metro Spagna/ bus to Piazza Augusto Imperatore or Piazza di Spagna. **Open** *enoteca* 11.15am-1am, *restaurant* 12.30-3pm, 7-10.30pm, daily.
Credit AmEx, DC, EC, MC, V. **Map 2/2A**

The best

...wine bars for wine:
Cavour 313
Cul De Sac
Il Goccetto

...wine bars for meeting people:
La Vineria

...wine bars for eating:
La Bottega del Vino da Anacleto Bleve
Trimani Wine Bar

...pubs:
The Fiddler's Elbow
The Druid's Den
Ombre Rosse

A good selection of wines by the glass for L4,000-10,000, plus a cold buffet at the counter and a full restaurant in the long back room. When this place first opened in 1842 it was a favourite haunt of painters living in nearby Via Margutta. A tasteful revamp has retained most of the original fittings, including the marble wine vats and venerable wooden cash desk. There are also fine wines to take away.

Birreria Fratelli Tempera
Via di San Marcello, 19 (06 679 5310).
Bus to Piazza Venezia. **Open** 12.30-2.45pm, 7.30-11.30pm, Mon-Fri; 7.30pm-midnight Sat. Closed two weeks Aug. **Credit** MC, V. **Map 5/2C**
Much better known by its traditional name, Birreria Peroni, after the Roman brewery, this is the perfect place for a lunchtime snack. Service is canteen-style, and the food – always with a couple of pasta options – is good and cheap. It still retains its original, beautiful art nouveau décor, featuring slogans like 'drink beer and you'll live 100 years'. Arrive early to avoid the lunchtime rush.

Il Brillo Parlante
Via della Fontanella, 12 (06 323 5017).
Bus to Via di Ripetta or Piazza Augusto Imperatore.
Open *bar* 11am-2am Mon-Sat; 7.30pm-1am Sun; *restaurant* 12.30-2.45pm, 7.30pm-1am, Mon-Sat; 7.30pm-1am Sun. Closed two weeks Aug.
Credit AmEx, DC, EC, MC, V. **Map 2/2A**
In the first-floor bar, you can drink wines by the glass and have the odd nibble sitting at the marble counter, or two tiny outside tables; downstairs, this wine bar around the corner from Piazza del Popolo opens out into a vaulted cellar, with heraldic frescoes. Unusually for a wine bar, it does pizzas – not exactly the best – as well as hot and cold dishes.

Nando Severini
Via Bocca di Leone, 44a (06 678 6031).
Metro Spagna/bus to Piazza San Silvestro.
Open 8.30am-1pm, 5-8pm, Mon-Sat. Closed two weeks Aug. **No credit cards. Map 3/1A**
Nando is a legend in the *Tridente*. This may be Rome's most cosmopolitan shopping area, but he was born here, and his family have owned a local *vini e oli* for over 40 years. The eclectic clientele comes to drink his superlative, own-label *prosecco*, and delicious *fragolino* – rosé made from *uva fragola*, strawberry grapes. Food consists of a few *tartine* with olive or mushroom paste. Perch on a crate next to Nando's dog and look at his collection of news cuttings and neo-cubist paintings; note the early evening closing. On a sign outside, Nando amends his official hours to 'closed Saturday if Lazio playing; open Sunday 2-9pm if Roma playing and it's sunny... maybe.' If you're left in any doubt as to his allegiances, the *enoteca* is plastered with Lazio's sky blue and white colours.

Trinity College
Via del Collegio Romano, 6 (06 678 6472).
Bus to Via del Corso. **Open** 11.30am-3am daily.
Credit AmEx, DC, EC, MC, V. **Map 3/2A**

City-centre pub much frequented by hip students of the Visconti *liceo* (high school), and thirstier employees of the cultural heritage ministry opposite.

Via Veneto & Quirinale

The Albert
Via del Traforo, 132 (06 481 8795).
Bus to Via del Tritone. **Open** 11am-3am Mon-Sat; 5pm-1am Sun. **No credit cards. Map 5/2C**
Until about 10pm, when the teen crowd moves in and the volume is turned up, the Albert is a peaceful oasis in the Trevi Fountain area. Friendly staff (the owner once had a pub in Scotland) serve basic pub grub through the day, with a generous 'happy hour' (L5,000 a pint, spirits half-price) all day until 9pm.

Trastevere

Enoteca Ferrara
Via del Moro, 1a (06 580 3769). Bus or tram to Viale Trastevere. **Open** 8.30pm-2am Mon, Wed-Sun. **Credit** AmEx, DC, EC, MC, V. **Map 6/2B**
In a surprisingly big space for Trastevere, the Paolillo sisters run a tasteful imbibery with a well-stocked cellar. The apartheid wine lists (one book for whites, one for reds) provide a happy evening's reading, and Mary in the kitchen puts together wonderful soups that, with the desserts, are highlights of a varied and interesting menu. In summer (when the *enoteca* closes on Sunday rather than Tuesday) you can wine and dine in a pretty, quiet garden at the back.

Ombre Rosse
Piazza Sant'Egidio, 12 (06 588 4155). Bus to Viale Trastevere or Piazza Sonnino. **Open** 7am-2am Mon-Sat; 5pm-2am Sun. **Credit** AmEx, MC, V. **Map 6/2B**
This friendly birreria-cum-winebar in a delightful square in Trastevere provides light meals at any time, as well as wines by the glass, a wide selection of beers, and an even wider range of whiskies.

Monti & Esquilino

Cavour 313
Via Cavour, 313 (06 678 5496). Metro Cavour/bus to Via Cavour. **Open** Oct-15 June 12.30-2.30pm, 7.30pm-12.30am, Mon-Sat; 7.30pm-12.30am Sun. *16 June-Sept* 12.30-2.30pm, 7.30pm-12.30am, daily. Closed Aug. **Credit** AmEx, DC, EC, MC, V. **Map 8/1C**
A friendly atmosphere (despite gloomy mahogany décor), a serious cellar and good snacks explain the eternal popularity of this wine bar at the Forum end of Via Cavour. Prices are reasonable, and there's a big selection of hot and cold snacks; in winter, they're especially strong on soups. With over 500 bottles on the wine list, choice is the only problem.

The Druid's Den
Via San Martino ai Monti, 28 (06 488 0258). Bus to Piazza Santa Maria Maggiore. **Open** 5pm-1am daily **No credit cards. Map 8/1C**

Like its rival the **Fiddler's Elbow**, this is a pub that was already well established before the current craze for all things Irish. A decent pint of Liffey water, plus football beamed in from the British Isles.

The Fiddler's Elbow
Via dell'Olmata, 43 (06 487 2110). Bus to Piazza Santa Maria Maggiore. **Open** 4.30pm-12.45am daily. **No credit cards. Map 8/1B**
One of the oldest, best known pubs in Rome, unchanged for years. Its narrow, basic wood-and-bench interior is smokey as ever, with the alternative feel that has long made it popular with students.

Trimani Wine Bar
Via Cernaia, 37b (06 446 9630). Bus to Via XX Settembre, Piazza Indipendenza. **Open** 11.30am-3pm, 5.30pm-12.30am, Mon-Sat. Closed Aug. **Credit** AmEx, DC, EC, MC, V. **Map 5/1A**
This wine bar offshoot of Rome's leading *enoteca* (*see p184*) has become a fixture in the few years since it opened; it offers an excellent choice of Italian regional wines, and high-quality pasta dishes, quiches, soups and crostini. Desserts are fabulous – especially *mousse al cioccolato*. It's advisable to book.

Aventino, Celio & Testaccio

L'Oasi della Birra
Piazza Testaccio, 41 (06 574 6122). Bus to Via Marmorata. **Open** 7.30pm-1am daily. Closed Sun in July & all Aug. **Credit** MC, V. **Map 7/2A**
If you take your beer seriously, this is a must. In the basement of a modest *enoteca* on Testaccio's market square, the Oasis of Beer has over 500 on offer, from Belgian Trappist brews to Jamaican Red Stripe (plus a decent wine list). It's one of few places where you can track down the products of Italian microbreweries such as the award-winning *Menabrea*. The accompanying food ranges from snacks (rolls, a well-stocked cheeseboard) to full-scale meals, with an Austro-Hungarian slant (goulash and strudel).

Prati

Il Simposio di Piero Costantini
Piazza Cavour, 16 (06 321 3210). Bus to Piazza Cavour. **Open** *enoteca* 4.30-8pm Mon; 9am-1pm, 4.30-8pm, Tue-Sat. *wine bar* 11.30am-3pm, 6.30pm-1am, Mon-Fri, Sun; 6.30pm-1am Sat. Closed Aug. **Credit** AmEx, DC, EC, MC, V. **Map 3/1B**
The well-stocked *enoteca* in the basement deserves a visit of its own, but the street-level wine bar has to be seen to be believed. Everything – the door, windows, the staircase – is covered with a wrought-iron vine and grapes motif; behind velvet drapes lies the restaurant, with hot dishes, salads, an encyclopaedic cheese board and delicious desserts. Prices are top-range – around L50,000 a head for a full meal – but so is quality. The wine list includes 2,000 Italian wines by the bottle, and a daily selection of around 20 by the glass – although mark-ups are on the high side for a place that still calls itself an *enoteca*.

Cafés & Bars

Rome's bars cater for extended people-watching and the short sharp espresso shot.

Caffè *for the comrades in* **Da Vezio**'s *temple to Communism (see page 159).*

Authentic Roman bars (or *caffè* – the terms are interchangeable) in salt-of-the-earth suburbs have zinc counters, lurid liqueurs, a steaming coffee machine, sad sandwiches, limp *cornetti* (Roman croissants), photos of football teams and floors strewn with sawdust and cigarette ends. The majority of their counterparts in the city centre have undergone post-modernisation treatment, trading the zinc counter for highly-polished wood; the other elements remain largely unchanged.

Whatever the décor, the fascinating cross-section of humanity frequenting them means that a visit to a Roman bar is rarely dull. There are still a few survivors from more splendid eras, while others offer such fantastic vantage points over the city that the interior decoration is immaterial.

All bars sell hot beverages, soft drinks and alcohol, together with sweets and chewing-gum. Some serve as late-night drinks stores or tobacconists. Then come the variations on the bar theme: *bar/ latteria* (selling dairy products); *bar/drogheria* (corner store incorporated); or *bar/tabacchi* (selling cigarettes, stamps etc). Other classifications tacked on after bar include *gelateria* (ice creams), *pasticceria* (fancy cakes) and *torrefazione* (coffee roasting). There are no licensing hours: have no qualms about ordering a grappa for breakfast.

Centro storico

Antica Pasticceria Bella Napoli
Corso Vittorio Emanuele, 246 (06 687 7048). Bus to Corso Vittorio Emanuele. **Open** 7.30am-9pm Mon-Fri, Sun. Closed two weeks Aug. **Map 3/2B**
Best known for its Neapolitan *dolci* such as *sfogliatelle ricce* (pastry with ricotta filling), and rum *babà*, to take away or eat on the spot with a *caffè*. Have your *sfogliatella* heated for a real treat.

Bar della Pace
Via della Pace, 3/7 (06 686 1216). Bus to Corso del Rinascimento. **Open** 9am-2am daily. **Map 3/2B**
Rome's eternally trendy Antico Caffè della Pace (but never known as such) continues to be a great (though expensive) place from which to survey passing fashion victims from wicker tables beneath the ivy. The same owner's equally modish pizzeria (*see* chapter **Restaurants**) is alongside.

Caffè Farnese

Via dei Baullari, 106 (06 6880 2125). Bus to Corso Vittorio Emanuele. **Open** 7am-2am daily. **Map 6/1B**
This *gelateria/pasticceria* is a popular meeting-place, offering a fine people-watching vista from Piazza Farnese to Campo de' Fiori from its outside tables. Coffee, cornetti and *pizza romana* are excellent.

Da Vezio

Via dei Delfini, 23 (06 678 6036). Bus to Largo Argentina. **Open** 7am-8.30pm Mon-Sat. **Map 6/1A**
Vezio Bagazzini is a legendary figure in the Ghetto area, on account of his extraordinary *bar/latteria* behind the former Communist Party HQ. Every square centimetre is filled with Communist icons and trophies – Italian, Soviet and Cuban. A place of pilgrimage for many *compagni*.

Dolce Vita

Piazza Navona, 70a (06 6880 6221). Bus to Corso del Rinascimento or Corso Vittorio Emanuele. **Open** 7.30am-2am daily. **Map 3/2A**
Tiny inside, but with plenty of tables on the square, Dolce Vita is a pleasant alternative to other more touristy bars on the piazza.

Latteria del Gallo

Vicolo del Gallo, 4 (06 686 5091). Bus to Corso Vittorio Emanuele. **Open** 8.30am-2pm, 5pm-midnight, Mon, Tue, Thur-Sun. Closed two weeks Aug. **Map 6/1B**
With its marble slab tables, this café in a side road between Campo de' Fiori and Piazza Farnese has remained impervious to passing fashions. Something of a *centro storico* institution, it's still popular with Rome's hippies and foreign residents.

Pascucci

Via di Torre Argentina, 20 (06 686 4816). Bus to Largo Argentina. **Open** 6.30am-midnight Mon-Sat. Closed three weeks Aug. **Map 6/1A**
This very modest bar in the centre of town has earned itself a reputation as milkshake heaven. Milk, though, isn't obligatory: no combination of fresh fruit froth (*frullato*) is too exotic here.

Sant'Eustachio

Piazza Sant'Eustachio, 82 (06 686 1309). Bus to Corso del Rinascimento. **Open** 8.30am-1am Tue-Sun. **Map 3/2A**
The most famous coffee bar in the city, with walls plastered with celebrity testimonials. The coffee is quite extraordinary – if very expensive. The espresso comes frothed up: the *schiuma* (froth) can be slurped out afterwards with spoon or fingers. Unless you specify *caffè amaro*, it comes heavily sugared. Asking for a cappuccino here is the equivalent of having 'tourist' tattooed across your forehead.

La Tazza d'Oro

Via degli Orfani, 84 (06 678 9792). Bus to Largo Argentina or Via del Corso. **Open** 7am-8.30pm Mon-Sat. Closed one week Aug. **Map 3/2A**
The powerful aroma wafting from this ancient *torrefazione* overlooking the Pantheon is a siren call to coffee lovers. It's packed with coffee sacks, tourists

and regulars who flock for *la monichella, granita di caffè* (coffee sorbet), and *cioccolata calda con panna* (hot chocolate with whipped cream) in winter.

Tucci

Piazza Navona, 94-100 (06 686 1547). Bus to Corso del Rinascimento. **Open** 9am-midnight Tue-Sun. **Map 3/2B**
A classic *bar/gelateria/ristorante*, with an outstanding view: seated outside in Piazza Navona, you can admire Bernini's fountains (though the mark-up on your bill can mar the pleasure), and from the back of the bar you can watch Italy's senators arriving for a day's politicking. Open daily in summer.

Tridente

Antico Caffè Greco

Via Condotti, 86 (06 678 5474). Metro Spagna/bus to Piazza San Silvestro. **Open** 8am-9pm daily. **Map 5/1C**
Founded in 1760, this venerable café was the one-time hangout of Casanova, Goethe, Wagner, Stendhal, Baudelaire, Shelley and Byron (*see p58*). Opposition to the French Occupation of 1849-70 was planned here. Today – under the ownership of a southern Italian consortium – it has its sofas packed with tourists, while locals cram the foyer.

Babington

Piazza di Spagna, 23 (06 678 6027). Metro Spagna/bus to Piazza San Silvestro. **Open** 9am-8.30pm, daily. **Map 5/1C**
Britons may not consider visiting tea-rooms abroad a priority, but will often be directed here by well-meaning Romans, convinced that they cannot survive without an overpriced pot of tea and plate of cakes. Founded by two British spinsters, Babington has occupied this prime location at the foot of the Spanish Steps for over a century.

La Buvette

Via Vittoria, 44 (06 679 0383). Metro Spagna/bus to Piazza San Silvestro. **Open** 7am-midnight Mon-Sat. Closed one week Aug. **Map 2/2A**
All polished wood and mirrors, the Buvette serves excellent coffee and great cakes in a plush, cosy atmosphere. A couple of pasta dishes and a wide range of salads are also served, for lunch only, June-Sept, and for lunch and dinner the rest of the year.

Café Notegen

Via del Babuino, 159 (06 320 0855). Metro Spagna/bus to Piazza del Popolo or Piazza San Silvestro. **Open** 7.30am-1am daily. **Map 2/2A**
An historic gathering spot for theatre people, artists and intellectuals, this century-old café prides itself on being a 'café in the French sense', serving hot and cold dishes and great cakes at any hour to sophisticated customers,seated in velvet booths. Threatened with eviction, but still fighting bravely at time of writing.

Canova

Piazza del Popolo, 16 (06 361 2231). Metro Flaminio/bus to Piazzale Flaminio or Piazza del Popolo. **Open** 8am-1am daily. **Map 2/2A**

According to tradition, Canova's clientele has always been right-wing, and at dagger's drawn with the left-wing rabble at **Rosati** (*see below*), across the square. There is little evidence of this now, although these mirror-image bars are still rivals for first place in the piazza. Good for catching the late afternoon sun. On summer evenings, it stays open into the small hours, until the last night-owl heads for home.

Ciampini al Café du Jardin
Viale Trinità dei Monti (06 678 5678).
Metro Spagna/bus to Piazza Barberini.
Open *Mar-Apr, Oct* 8am-5pm, *May-Sept* 8am-1am, daily. Closed Nov-mid-Mar. **Map 5/1C**
An open-air café surrounded by creeper-curtained trellises, with a pond in the centre. There's a selection of tasty sandwiches, pastas, cocktails, ices, and snack lunches, and it also serves a good breakfast. Plus there's a stunning view, especially at sunset.

Dolci e Doni
Via delle Carrozze, 85B (06 678 2913). Metro Spagna/bus to Piazza San Silvestro. **Open** 9am-8pm daily. Closed two weeks Aug. **Map 3/1A**
A tiny, bijou tea-room, renowned for its cakes and chocolates, which also specialises in breakfasts, brunches and quick quiche-and-salad lunches. Cakes to take away, and catering arranged.

Gran Caffè La Caffettiera
Via Margutta, 61a (06 321 3344).
Metro Spagna/bus to Piazza San Silvestro.
Open 9.30am-11pm daily. **Map 2/2A**
This huge café occupies the seventeenth-century Teatro Alibert. A warren of rooms, with décor ranging from eighteenth century (including original frescoes on the cross-beamed ceilings) to art nouveau. No crush at the counter: just under-stated (if a trifle over-priced) waiter service. Set breakfast from L18,000; light lunch around L25,000.

Rosati
Piazza del Popolo, 5 (06 322 5859). Metro Flaminio/bus to Piazzale Flaminio or Via Ripetta **Open** 7.30am-11.30pm daily. **Map 2/2A**
In a stunning situation on Piazza del Popolo, Rosati is the traditional haunt of Rome's intellectual left – Calvino, Moravia and Pasolini were regulars. The art nouveau interior is unchanged since its opening in 1922. Head *barista* Marco Frapietro will make you a *Sogni Romani*: orange juice with four kinds of liqueur in red and yellow – the colours of the city.

Via Veneto & Quirinale

Bar del Palazzo delle Esposizioni
Via Milano, 9 (06 482 8001/06 482 8540).
Bus to Via Nazionale. **Open** 10am-9pm Mon, Wed-Sun. **Map 5/2B**
The excellent bar at this major arts centre (*see p69*) has made it a mecca for local office staff, who also flock to eat at the buffet restaurant upstairs (*see p154*). The bar entrance is on the left of the *palazzo*, halfway up the stairs. Knockout fresh cakes.

Café Doney
Via Vittorio Veneto, 145 (06 482 1788). Metro Barberini/bus to Via Vittorio Veneto. **Open** 8am-1am Mon, Tue, Thur-Sun. **Map 5/1B**
A wonderful place at any time of day, whether for stand-up coffee or to sit down and relax on Via Veneto, watching doormen entice clients into nightclubs. Doney's had its place in the sun in the '50s and '60s, when it was a key meeting point for the Cinecittà set (Ava Gardner, Marcello Mastroianni, Tyrone Power, Anita Ekberg) and the Roman intelligentsia.

Café de Paris
Via Vittorio Veneto, 90 (06 488 5284).
Metro Barberini/bus to Via Vittorio Veneto.
Open 8am-1.20am Mon-Tue, Thur, Sun; 8am-2am Fri-Sat. **Map 5/1B**
In Via Veneto's Dolce Vita heyday **Café Doney** (*see above*) was definitely for the nobs, and Café de Paris across the road was for those with street-cred. Here you could be served in your jeans (quite something in those days), and listen to the *paparazzi* badmouth their prey. These days it's a bit squalid inside, so it's best to find a seat outdoors.

Catching the rays at **Canova** *(left).*

Trastevere

Bar Gianicolo
Piazzale Aurelio, 5 (06 580 6275). Bus to Via Carini.
Open 6am-3am Tue-Sun. **Map 6/2C**
Up the hill from Trastevere, wooden panels and benches lend this tiny bar at the site of Garibaldi's doomed battle with the French an intimate, chatty feel unusual in Rome. Fresh carrots and apples juiced on the spot, a range of exotic sandwiches and light meals and outside tables overlooking the Porta di San Pancrazio city gate make it a good spot for a drink, a snack or lunch.

Bar San Calisto
Piazza San Calisto (no phone). Bus or tram to Viale Trastevere. **Open** 5.30am-2am Mon-Sat. **Map 6/2B**
Green tourists get their coffee or beer on Piazza Santa Maria in Trastevere; locals who know better go to this bar, known locally as Marcello's. Unassuming and inexpensive, it's the haunt of arty and fringe types (plus a few questionable characters after sundown) downing beers or spooning an affogato (ice cream swamped with a liqueur).

*Kilos of cakes at **Dolci e Doni** (see page 160).*

Cecere
Via San Francesco a Ripa, 152. Bus or tram to Viale Trastevere. **Open** 6am-2am daily. **Map 6/2B**
A great selection of fresh, hot *cornetti*, turned out non-stop. Tired late-nighters – including a colourful transvestite crowd – throng the place after midnight.

Della Scala
Via della Scala, 4 (06 580 3610). Bus or tram to Viale Trastevere. **Open** 4pm-2am daily. **Map 6/2B**
A dark, smoky dive with a selection of wines by the glass, beers, and cocktails. The crowds that spill out from the few tables on Via della Scala testify to its popularity with late-night frequenters of Trastevere.

Di Marzio
Piazza Santa Maria in Trastevere, 15 (06 581 6095). Bus or tram to Viale Trastevere.
Open 7am-3am Tue-Sun.**Map 6/2B**
Piazza Santa Maria is not the cheapest place in Rome to sit out and have a drink, but if you do want to admire this square with a drink in your hand, Di Marzio, facing the church, is recommended.

Sacchetti
Piazza San Cosimato, 61/2 (06 581 5374). Bus or tram to Viale Trastevere. **Open** 5.30am-midnight Tue-Sun. **Map 6/2B**
The Sacchetti family runs one of the least touristy bars in Trastevere, with tables outside all year round and a big tea-room upstairs. Everything is own-made; *cornetti* and ricotta-filled *sfogliatelle romane* are memorable. The ice creams, hidden behind the bar in old-fashioned closed barrels, are delicious too.

Sala da Tè Trastè
Via della Lungaretta, 76 (06 589 4430). Bus or tram to Viale Trastevere. **Open** 5pm-1.30am daily. Closed two weeks July. **Map 6/2B**
On the main walkway from Viale Trastevere to Piazza Santa Maria, Trastè is particularly known for its cakes and serenity. One of few places in the area with teas as a speciality.

Monti & Esquilino

Antico Caffè del Brasile
Via dei Serpenti, 23 (06 488 2319). Bus to Via Nazionale. **Open** 6.45am-8.30pm Mon-Sat. Closed one week Aug. **Map 8/1C**
Despite EU norms banning the use of its centrepiece – a massive coffee-toasting machine – in the bar, this *torrefazione* on the characterful main street of Monti still retains its traditional atmosphere. Among its distinguished clientele was the current Pope, while he was still humble Cardinal Wojtyla.

Bar Gran Caffè dell'Opera
Via Torino, 140 (06 481 4881). Bus to Termini or Via Nazionale. **Open** 7am-11.30pm Tue-Sun. **Map 5/2B**
It says 'kaffè' above the door, a throwback to the 1970s, when a K looked vaguely revolutionary. Founded in 1880, like the opera house opposite, this cafe is more like a theme park than a bar. The walls

are covered with over 300 signed photos of each and every opera star to have appeared there in the last 130 years. Ideal for between-act or after-theatre snacks, when you can catch a glimpse of the artistes relaxing after the show.

Petrucci

Via Ettore Battisti, 129 (06 678 3720).
Bus to Piazza Venezia.
Open *Oct-May* 6.30am-midnight Mon-Fri, Sun; *June-Sept* 6.30am-12.30am daily. **Map 6/1A**
Busy all day, thanks to its position just off Piazza Venezia and its *tabacchi* counters, Petrucci really comes alive after dark, when the street outside is crammed with cars parked four-deep and traffic streaming into Piazza Venezia gets severely snarled as night-owls head inside for cigarettes and a drink. The later it gets, the more louche the atmosphere becomes. *Carabinieri* officers from the police station next door rub shoulders with crooks, drug dealers and transvestites.

Testaccio

Bar del Mattatoio

Piazza Orazio Giustiniani, 3 (06 574 6017). Bus to Via Galvani or Via Marmorata. **Open** 6am-9pm Mon-Sat. Closed two weeks Aug. **Map 7/2B**
A brick doll's house bar, with Gothic recesses in the front. One of the earliest-opening bars in Rome, it once catered for the meatworkers from the municipal slaughterhouse opposite; nowadays it serves the dawn revellers from Testaccio clubland.

Café du Parc

Piazza di Porta San Paolo (06 574 3363). Metro Piramide/bus or tram to Piazza di Porta San Paolo. **Open** 4.30am-1am Mon-Sat. **Map 7/2A**
This kiosk bar is the best place from which to admire the Pyramid of Cestius. The *gelati* are excellent, especially the *cremolati* – a kind of creamy sorbet. If they have it, try the raspberry; coffee and *stracciatella* are great too. Table service isn't cheap.

La dolce vita

Pasticcerie – cake shops – are dotted all over Rome, many of the most famous being in residential areas, handily placed for furnishing fresh *pastarelle* for Sunday lunch. Romans do most of their cake-scoffing at home, so cake shops are not normally places for sitting down.

Cream-filled items account for much of the cake trade: the whipped cream (*panna*) generally has very little sugar. Choux pastry varies wildly in quality, but when it's good, it melts in your mouth. Try the Sunday classic *la granatina*, a choux-bomb filled with *zabaglione* and cream and dusted with sugar granules.

Once there was such a thing as the Roman *cornetto* (croissant): low in sugar and even lower in fat, yeasty and light, an ideal accompaniment to morning coffee. Sadly it's now nearly extinct, ousted by the mass-produced, frozen/ reheated *cornetti* that are almost universal in bars. Seeking out somewhere where the real thing is still produced is a worthwhile experience: if you find it, have it sliced open and filled with whipped cream.

Bernasconi

Piazza Cairoli, 16 (06 6880 6264).
Tram to Via Arenula. **Open** 7am-8.30pm daily. Closed Aug. **Map 6/1B**
Centro storico. Cramped and inconspicuous like so many of Rome's best cake shops, but it's well worth fighting your way inside for *lieviti* (breakfast yeast buns) and excellent *cappuccino*. Bernasconi's *cornetti* are unbeatable, the real vintage variety. There's a lot else besides, and seasonal treats like *mini-colombe* (dove-shaped tea-cake) at Easter-time and Lenten fruit buns (*quaresimali*). Later in the day, pop in for a cream cake – possibly the best in Rome. Bigger cakes such as Sicilian *cassata* are also scrumptious.

La Caffettiera

Piazza di Pietra, 65 (06 679 8147).
Bus to Via del Corso. **Open** *Nov-May* 7am-9pm Mon-Sat; *June-Oct* 7am-9pm daily. **Map 3/2A**
Tridente. A temple of Neapolitan food. Politicians and mandarins from the nearby parliament buildings lounge in the sumptuous tea room, while lesser mortals bolt down coffee at the bar. The rum baba reigns supreme, but many ricotta-lovers rave over the crunchy *sfogliatella*, delicately flavoured with cinnamon and orange peel, and the *pastiera*, a rich tart filled with ricotta, orange-flower water, citrus peel and whole grains of wheat.

Cinque Lune

Corso del Rinascimento, 89 (06 6880 1005).
Bus to Corso del Rinascimento. **Open** 8am-9.30pm Tue-Sun. Closed Aug. **Map 3/2A**
Centro storico. One of the smallest cake shops in Rome, but packed with goodies to take away with you (coffee is not served in the shop). Another front-runner for the title of the best cream cakes in the city, with unbeatable choux pastry; they also do a great line in traditional Easter and Christmas cakes, including *pangiallo*, a luscious slab of dried fruit.

Dagnino

Galleria Esedra, Via VE Orlando, 75 (06 481 8660). Metro Repubblica/bus to Piazza della Repubblica or Termini.
Open 7am-10pm daily. **Map 5/1B**

Other parts of town

Prati

Antonini

Via Sabotino, 21-9 (06 3751 7845). Bus to Piazza Mazzini. **Open** 7am-9pm daily. **Map 2/1C**

In winter you can't move for fur coats. This high-class *pasticceria* is the place to come to buy cakes to take to that important lunch or dinner party; alternatively, eat them *in situ:* one *montebianco* (meringue, *marron glacé* spaghetti and cream) is a meal in itself. They also do a nice line in *tartine* – canapés topped with pate, caviar and other goodies.

Faggiani

Via Giuseppe Ferrari, 23/5 (06 3973 9742). Metro Lepanto/bus to Piazza Risorgimento. **Open** 7.30am-9pm Mon, Tue, Wed-Sun. Closed Aug. **Map 2/1C**

As pleasant for breakfast as for an evening *aperitivo*, this classic family bar with excellent coffee has one of Rome's finest *pasticcerie* attached. Worth coming to Prati to sample their *cornetti* and *budino di riso* (rice desserts), probably the best in Rome.

Northern suburbs

Bar lo Zodiaco

Via del Parco Mellini, 90 (06 3549 6744/06 3549 6640). Bus to Piazzale Medaglie d'Oro. **Open** 9am-1am daily.

Perhaps the best panoramic view to be had over the city – although it's quite a hike to get up the Monte Mario hill. Choose a clear day without too much smog or haze; the best views are at night. There's also a piano bar in the evening, and a restaurant for lunch and dinner. On summer weekends, the bar remains open into the small hours.

Mondi

Via Flaminia, 468a (06 333 6466). Bus to Via Flaminia. **Open** 7am-midnight Tue-Sun.

Dagnino: *if it's Sicilian and you can eat it...*

Monti & Esquilino. Stunning fifties decor and a chronic oversupply of tables set the scene for this corner of Sicily in the heart of Rome. If you can eat it or drink it and it's Sicilian, it's here: ice-cream in special buns, almond drinks, life-like marzipan fruits. Regulars come for crisp *cannoli siciliani* filled with ricotta and, above all, the baroque splendor of shiny green-iced *cassata,* uniting all the flavours of the south: the perfume of citrus, almond paste and the freshness and saltiness of ricotta.

Dolceroma

Via del Portico D'Ottavia, 20B (06 689 2196). Bus to Lungotevere Cenci/tram to Via Arenula. **Open** 9am-1.30pm, 3.30-8pm, Tue-Sat; 10am-1pm Sun. Closed July, Aug. **Map 6/1A**

Centro storico. Though it specialises in Viennese cakes, this is also the place for American-style carrot cake and chocolate chip cookies – ideal as presents, or if you are feeling homesick/bingey. Don't get hooked: prices are on the high side.

Forno del Ghetto

Via Portico d'Ottavia, 1 (06 687 8637). Bus to Largo Argentina/tram to Via Arenula. **Open** 8am-8pm Mon-Fri, Sun. Closed two weeks Aug; Jewish holidays. **Map 6/1A**

Centro storico. This tiny shop (officially *Pasticceria Il Boccione,* though no one knows it as such) run by three unwelcoming women, has no sign over the door, but is immediately recognisable by the line of slavering regulars outside. Unmissable, unforgettable damson and ricotta pies (or the chocolate and ricotta alternative), and unique *pizze,* solid bricks of moist dough and dried fruit.

Handling the Roman bar

For most Romans, bars are merely crowded places in which you down coffee in short sharp shots before rushing off to do whatever it is you have to do. When there's a crush, non-regulars are expected to pay at the *cassa* (cash desk) before ordering. If this seems daunting, don't fret: most bars serve more or less the same fare, so it won't be long before you know the range and are handling it like a veteran. Slap your *scontrino* (receipt) down on the bar (many Romans add L50-200 to get the *barista's* attention), and place your order.

With the exception of the odd local *bar/latteria*, higher prices are charged for sitting down, both inside and *all'aperto*. The price difference must be displayed on the wall behind the *cassa*. In particularly picturesque areas you may pay dearly for the privilege of taking the weight off your feet.

By law, all bars must have a *bagno* (lavatory) which can be used by anyone, whether or not they buy anything in the bar. The *bagno* may be locked; ask the cashier for the key (*la chiave per il bagno*). Bars must also provide gasping passers-by with a glass of tap water (*acqua dal rubinetto*), again with no obligation to buy.

Coffee

All Roman bars serve beer, wines, spirits, soft drinks, tea, but coffee accounts for 80% of their sales. There are many ways of drinking coffee, the most basic being the *espresso* (called simply *un caffè*, although *baristi* may presume you're asking for something less concentrated if you sound foreign) and the *cappuccino*. Italians only drink *cappuccino* for breakfast and mid-morning, and find it hilarious and faintly revolting that foreigners drink it after meals. Romans have an odd habit of drinking their *cappuccino* tepid (they've got things to do, and don't like waiting for it to cool), so you may prefer to ask for it *molto caldo* (very hot) or even *bollente* (boiling).

Variations on the *espresso*

caffè americano with a lot more water, in a teacup.
caffè corretto with a dash of liqueur or spirits (indicate which).
caffè freddo iced espresso, sugared unless you ask for a **caffè freddo amaro**.
caffè Hag espresso decaf.
caffè lungo a bit more water than usual.
caffè macchiato with a dash of milk.
caffè monichella with whipped cream.
caffè ristretto tooth-enamel removing coffee essence lining the bottom of the cup.
caffè al vetro in a glass.

Variations on the *cappuccino*

caffè latte more hot milk and less coffee
cappuccino freddo iced cappuccino, sugared unless you ask specifically for a **cappuccino freddo amaro**.
cappuccino senza schiuma without froth.
latte macchiato hot milk with a dash of coffee.

Drinks

Birra Rome has no appreciable beer culture, and beer in bars is peculiarly expensive. It is either *alla spina* (on tap) or *in lattina/bottiglia* (canned/bottled). *Alla spina* is served as *una birra piccola/media/grande* (33cl, 50cl, 1l).
Vino You can buy wine by the glass in most bars, but the quality of *un bicchiere di vino rosso/bianco* is generally fairly abysmal. The selection of bottles to take away is also limited and twice the price of an *enoteca* or shop. *Un prosecco* (dry sparkling white) is often a better bet. For a better class of claret, head for one of the *enoteche* listed on *pages 183-4*, or the watering holes in *chapter* **Wine Bars**.

Residents of the Cassia-Flaminia area swear this is the best *bar/pasticceria* in town. Its cakes and luscious *semi-freddi* (frozen ice cream-based desserts) are true works of art.

Southern suburbs – San Lorenzo

Bar Sanniti

Piazza dei Sanniti, 38/40 (06 495 8260). Bus or tram to Piazzale del Verano. **Open** 24 hours daily.
A good observation point for the grandly-named *Sala Palazzo Accademia Biliardo* – a beautiful early twentieth-century building dedicated to workers' leisure pursuits. The bar is frequented by rather dodgy-looking characters, among them aspiring pool hoods attracted by the serviceable *buffet freddo* and *latteria*,

and artists from the loft community of San Lorenzo. Useful place for picking up bus tickets at all hours.

EUR

Palombini

Piazzale Adenauer, 12 (06 591 1700). Metro Magliana/bus to Piazza Guglielmo Marconi. **Open** 7am-midnight daily. Closed two weeks mid-Aug.
In the imposing shadow of the **Palazzo del Civiltà del Lavoro** (the Square Colosseum, *see p100*) stands this airy pavilion, surrounded by sweeping gardens. Its huge patio area covered by a steel and plastic tent is a favourite meeting point for young Romans – the nearest Rome gets to Beverly Hills, and a good imitation. As a *gelateria*, *pasticceria* and snack supplier, it's also first-rate.

Ice Cream

When your brain's bursting with Berninis, soothe it with the true gelato experience.

Many bars in Rome boast a well-stocked freezer cabinet with a sign promising *produzione artigianale* (home-made ice creams). Generally speaking, this is a con. The contents may have been whipped up on the premises, but the lurid colours and chemical flavours come straight out of a tin. And while this doesn't necessarily mean the ice cream will be bad – indeed, in some cases this not-so-genuine-article can be very good indeed – it's good to be selective if you're seeking a truly unique *gelato* experience.

Ices to take away are served in a *cono* (cone) or cardboard *coppetta* (tub) of varying sizes, usually costing from L2,000-6,000. As well as the two main kinds, *frutta* or *crema*, there's also *granita* (a rougher version of the *sorbetto*), and *semifreddo*, usually a chilled sponge-and-cream pudding, like *tiramisù*.

As a general rule, ice creams kept in aluminium tubs inside the freezer cabinet are a safer bet than those in plastic ones. It shows, at the very least, that some thought has gone into appearances; it is also usually a good pointer to ice cream concocted on the premises rather than bought in wholesale from a factory. Also – obviously – the more garish the colours of the product, the more non-natural ingredients it has. True *gelato* artistes don't have their products on show at all: they are hidden away in closed tubs behind the counter.

When you've exhausted *gelato*, sample a *grattachecca*, the time-honoured Roman version of water-ice, consisting of hand-grated ice poured into a cup with flavoured syrup or juice on top. Rome was once full of kiosks selling this treat, but now only a handful maintain their authentic character. They are almost always on street corners (hence *angolo* in the addresses below), and most are closed in winter, opening only when their proprietors feel the weather is warm enough to warrant taking up the shutters. Opening hours tend to be erratic.

Centro storico

Alberto Pica
Via della Seggiola, 12 (06 686 8405). Bus to Largo Argentina/tram to Via Arenula. **Open** 8am-2am Mon-Sat; 4pm-3am Sun. **Map 6/1B**

Hand-grated ice and a dash of sticky syrup: the refreshing Roman grattachecca.

San Crispino: the world's best gelato?

Next to the regular bar and *tavola calda* sections is a small but excellent selection of some 20 flavours, among which the rice specialities stand out – imagine eating frozen, partially-cooked rice pudding and you'll start to get the picture. *Riso alla cannella* (cinnamon rice) is particularly fine.

I Tre Scalini

Piazza Navona, 28-32 (06 6880 1996). Bus to Corso Rinascimento or Corso Vittorio Emanuele. **Open** 8am-1am Mon, Tue, Thur-Sun. Closed Jan. **Map 3/2 AB**
The most famous bar in Rome's most famous square is above all famous for its speciality ice cream, the *tartufo* – a calorie-bomb chocolate ice cream with big lumps of chocolate inside. There are some 50 tables from which to view the square, and a tea room designed for tired English matrons on the first floor. Otherwise, opt to take your ice away and enjoy it next to Bernini's fountain, or do as the Romans do and stand at the crowded bar.

Tridente

Cremeria Monforte

Via della Rotonda, 22 (06 686 7720). Bus or tram to Largo Argentina. **Open** (approx) 10am-10pm Tue-Sun. Closed two weeks Aug. **Map 3/2A**
This *gelateria* handily situated around the corner from the Pantheon is a cut above the many others in the area. The white and orange chocolate flavours have big lumps of chocolate in them, and the

cremolati – fruity slushes – are delicious. On summer evenings the shutters don't come down until the early hours of the morning. True ice cream fiends should sign up for Monforte's *gelato*-guzzling competition, held each year in late July or early August.

Giolitti

Via Uffici del Vicario, 40 (06 699 1243). Bus to Via del Corso or Largo Chigi. **Open** 9am-1am Tue-Sat. **Map 3/1 A**
Perhaps the best-known *gelateria* in Rome, although by no means the best. Still, their range of flavours is vast, and some of them– marron glacé, *frutti di bosco, gianduia* – are truly excellent. The main bar has been a compulsory stop-off point on an evening *passeggiata* for several generations.
Website: www.giolitti.it

Via Veneto & Quirinale

Il Gelato di San Crispino

Via della Panetteria, 42 (06 679 3924). Metro Barberini/bus to Via del Tritone. **Open** 10am-12.30am Mon, Wed, Sun; 10am-2am Fri-Sat. Closed two weeks Jan. **Map 5/2C**
Far and away the best ice-cream in Rome – some would say the world. The secret of brothers Giuseppe and Pasquale Alongi is an obsessive control over the whole process, from the selection of ingredients through to method of preparation. Flavours change according to what's around in the markets – in summer the *lampone* (raspberry) and *susine* (yellow plum) are fabulous. Don't even think of asking for a cone: only tubs are allowed, as they 'interfere less with the purity of the product'. True devotees – of which there are many, as the traffic tangles outside show – shun the tourist-trap Trevi fountain branch and head out into the southern suburbs, where the miracle of San Crispino first occurred. The product, though, is equally exceptional in both places, and the central branch has the advantage – over and above its location – of offering tables and chairs (at no extra cost for sitting down) at which to rest your weary feet as you savour the Alongi brothers' delights.
Branch Via Acaia, 56 (06 7045 0412).

Trastevere

See also **Bar San Calisto** *and* **Sacchetti** *in chapter* **Cafés & Bars**.

Sora Mirella

Lungotevere degli Anguillara, angolo Ponte Cestio (no phone). Bus to Viale Trastevere or Ponte Cestio. **Open** *Mar-Sept* 10am-3am daily. **Map 6/2A**
Mirella styles herself *la regina della grattacheccha* (the queen of water ices), and there seems no reason to disagree. Her sons still grate the ice by hand with an iron glove. Sit on the Tiber embankment wall as you tuck into the *speciale superfrutta* – fresh melon, kiwi fruit and strawberry (or whatever's in season) and syrups served in a special glass.

Monti & Esquilino

Il Palazzo del Freddo di Giovanni Fassi

*Via Principe Eugenio, 65/7 (06 446 4740). Metro
Vittorio/bus or tram to Piazza Vittorio Emanuele.*
Open noon-midnight Tue-Fri; noon-1am Sat; 10am-
midnight Sun. **Map 8/1A**

From the pompous name and breathtakingly kitsch
interior to its splendid ices, Fassi is typically
Roman. It was founded in 1880 by Giovanni Fassi,
and its walls are adorned with Edwardian adverts
and Fascist-era posters extolling the virtues of the
shop's wares. Escape the appalling 1980s restoration and laughably contemptuous and irascible
service, and head into the '30s courtyard and loggia.
The ices are sublime: best of all are *riso* – rice
pudding – and the Palazzo's own invention, *la cater-
inetta*, a mysterious concoction of whipped honey
and vanilla.

Aventino, Celio & Testaccio

See also **Café du Parc** *in* **Cafés & Bars**.

Chiosco Testaccio

*Via Giovanni Branca, angolo Via Beniamino
Franklin (no phone). Bus to Via Marmorata or
Via Zabaglia.* **Open** *May-mid-Sept* noon-1.30am
daily. **Map 7/2B**

Still going strong after over 80 years in this working
class neighbourhood, although the ice is now cut by
mechanical means. The kiosk is painted a different
colour each year: the shade chosen for 1999 was avo-
cado green. Tamarind and *limoncocco* (lemon and
coconut), also available in liquid form) are the kiosk's
prime specialities.

Da Cristina

*Via Marmorata, angolo Largo M Gelsomini,
Testaccio (no phone). Bus to Via Marmorata.*
Open *June-Sept* 6am-3am, *Oct-May* 6am-8pm, daily.
Map 7/2A

An obligatory stop-off point for Testaccio residents
en route to the striking Fascist-era post office next
door, Cristina's kiosk does great coffee as well as
classic *grattachecche*, topped with delicious Fabbri
brand syrups and juices, plus a few liqueurs. Try
the vodka or *amaretto di Saronno*.

Giolitti a Testaccio

*Via Amerigo Vespucci, 35 (06 574 6006).
Bus to Via Marmorata or Piazza dell'Emporio.*
Open 7am-1am, Mon,-Tue, Thur-Sun. Closed two
weeks Aug. **Map 7/1A**

An institution in Testaccio, Giolitti (no relation to its
more famous namesake in the *Tridente*) makes good,
traditional creamy and fruity-flavoured ice-creams,
and a wicked *granita di caffè*. All of which taste better when consumed at its few road-side tables (or,
even better, and to avoid a hefty mark-up, around
the corner in Testaccio's pretty park). If you can't
face a whole ice, order a *caffè* (or a *cappuccino*)
freddo: half a glass of *granita di caffè* topped up
with iced coffee (and milk).

Prati

Pellachia

*Via Cola di Rienzo, 103 (06 321 0807).
Bus to Via Cola di Rienzo.* **Open** 6.30am-1am Tue-
Sun. Closed one week Aug. **Map 2/2B**

This bar on Prati's busiest shopping street produces
some of the best ice creams north of the river. The
perfect place to refresh body and soul after a bout of
retail therapy: the chocolate is a delight.

Northern suburbs

Duse

*Via Eleonora Duse, 1E (06 807 9300).
Bus or tram to Piazza Ungheria.* **Open** 8am-
midnight Mon-Sat. Closed one week Aug.

In this otherwise entirely residential neighbourhood,
Duse attracts well-off young *pariolini* (for which read
Chelsea/Valley girls and boys) on their motorbikes
and in their 4WDs. Late at night, the scene outside
looks like a well-brushed street party. Inside, the big
metal drums of the 30-odd flavours are stacked three
deep behind the counter. To start, try out their
cioccolato fondente (dark chocolate) or *cioccolato
bianco* (white chocolate).

San Filippo

*Via di Villa San Filippo, 2/10 (06 807 9314).
Bus or tram to Piazza Ungheria.*
Open 7am-midnight Tue-Sun.

From the outside, this seems like just another modest local *bar/latteria*, but don't pass it by, as this is
the home of some wicked ice creams, despite the limited selection. Sample the *nocciola* (hazelnut) and the
cioccolato – always the *gelato* connoisseur's litmus-
test flavours – or one of the big range of seasonal
fruits: watermelon (*anguria*), peach (*pesca*) or maybe
melon (*melone*).

Il Gelato di San Pancrazio

*Piazza San Pancrazio, 18 (06 5831 0338). Bus to
Piazza Ottavilla.* **Open** 8am-9pm Mon, Tue; 8am-2am
Wed-Sun.

Handily placed by the side entrance to the Villa
Pamphili park, on the western side of the Gianicolo
(*see chapter* **Children**), this likeable neighbourhood
gelateria is run by a cheerful group of lads with
sharp haircuts who take a real pride in their very
acceptable product.

Southern suburbs

Petrini dal 1926

*Piazza dell'Alberone, 16A (06 786 307). Metro Furio
Camillo/bus to Via Appia Nuova.* **Open** 10.30am-2am
Tue-Sun.

As its name implies, this *gelateria* a fair hike out of
the city centre has been purveying ice cream for
decades, and many still consider its product one of
the best in Rome. All its creamy flavours are delicious, but the *zabaione* and *nocciola* are particularly
mouth-watering.

Shopping

Prosciutto and pecorino, hand-made shirts, antique prints and high-style lamps: they're all there for you to find, providing you take your time.

Rome's designer outlets may be at the cutting edge of international fashion, but you'll find shopping here in many ways a very old-world experience. There are one-off shops galore, from jewellers to delicatessens and furniture restorers, but department stores are few and far between, and if you're craving for a decent-sized supermarket be prepared to toil out into the 'burbs.

Perhaps because nothing about it is streamlined, shopping in Rome is a serious business. Forget one-stop convenience shopping in a local mall, and savour the joys of stalking your prey through shop after shop, comparing quality, styles and prices. Time-consuming it may be, but the satisfaction of finding the Perfect Thing is infinitely greater.

In many Rome shops you'll find assistants who like to pretend that customers don't exist: in others, they think their vocation in life is to intimidate. Don't be put off. Perfect the essential lines *mi può aiutare, per favore?* (can you help me please) and *volevo solo dare un'occhiata* (I just wanted to have a look around): you're ready for any eventuality.

When you've found what you want, don't try bargaining: prices are fixed (unless you are buying in bulk from a small-scale outlet, or from an acquaintance). If ever you are not offered a *scontrino* (receipt) in any shop, ask for it: shops are required by law to provide one, and they and you are liable for a fine in the (unlikely) event of your being caught without it.

If you are not an EU resident take special care to keep your *scontrino*, as you are entitled to a VAT (IVA in Italian) **tax rebate** on purchases of personal goods over L300,000, providing they are exported unused and bought from a shop with the Europe Tax Free sticker. The shop will give you a form to show to customs when leaving Italy.

Opening times

An increasing number of city-centre shops are open non-stop from 9am to around 7.30pm, Mon-Sat. Even among shops that still shut for lunch, the traditional 1-4.30pm closedown is growing rarer, and shops are more likely to close just for an hour or so, 1-2pm or thereabouts. Times given below are winter opening hours: in summer (approximately June-Oct), shops that still opt for long lunches tend to re-open later, at 5pm or 5.30pm, staying open until 8-8.30pm. Most food stores close on Thursday afternoons in winter, and on Saturday afternoons in summer. Many non-food shops will be closed on Monday mornings.

Note too that **many shops close for at least two weeks each summer** (generally in August), with no guarantee that any one shop will opt for the same weeks every year. Where no holiday closing is indicated below, the shop stays open all year; where dates are given, they should be taken as approximate only. If you plan to go out of your way to visit a shop in summer try ringing first, to avoid finding a *chiuso per ferie* (closed for holidays) sign.

One-stop shopping

A handful of department stores has existed in central Rome for decades, but malls and giant hypermarkets are a relative novelty and, for obvious space reasons, tend to be confined to the outskirts of the city.

Centro Commerciale Cinecittà Due

Viale Palmiro Togliatti, 2 (06 722 0910).
Metro Cinecittà. **Open** 1-8pm Mon; 9.30am-8pm Tue-Fri; 9.30am-8.30pm Sat; 10am-8pm Sun.
Rome's foremost shopping mall, a glass and steel structure in the eastern suburbs housing 100 shops and eateries, including branches of many of the smartest fashion stores.

COIN

Piazzale Appio, 7 (06 708 0020). Metro San Giovanni/bus to Piazzale Appio or Piazza San Giovanni. **Open** 3.30-8pm Mon; 9.30am-1.30pm, 3.30-8pm, Tue-Sat. **Credit** AmEx, DC, EC, MC, V.
Middle-of-the-road store a stone's throw from San Giovanni in Laterano with some bargains – especially at the make-up counter. Romans go there for sensible skirts, or sheets that last. Excellent houseware department, and sturdy kids' clothes. The Cola di Rienzo branch has a supermarket.
Branch Via Mantova, 1b (06 841 6279) **Map 4/2A;** Via Cola di Rienzo, 173 (06 324 3319) **Map 2/2C.**

Oviesse

Viale Trastevere, 62/64 (06 589 5342). Bus or tram to Viale Trastevere. **Open** 3.30-8pm Mon; 9am-8pm Tue-Sat. **Credit** AmEx, DC, EC, MC, V. **Map 7/1B**
Run-of-the-mill lower range department store clothes, with some cheap and cheerful children's wear among them. In Trastevere's main drag, the store also has a basement supermarket.

Get your Millennium here

There are two major centres of worship in Rome: **Saint Peter's**, and the Olympic football stadium. But while you'll find no Christ-clutter at the latter, the shops around the Vatican mix their medals and statues with strips from every *Serie A* team, plus a big range of national squads too. The density of stripy shirts is in inverse proportion to proximity to the Vatican, so if it's pure religious tack you're after, begin your search well down Borgo Pio (**Map 3/1C**).

There, however, you may find that much of the space once given to Christs and Maries has lately been usurped by images of a grumpy-looking Capuchin monk, whose fanatical devotees themselves bear more than a passing resemblance to football fans. This is the miracle-working Padre Pio of Pietrelcina, a heroic battler against devils who after a long life spent annoying the Vatican was beatified in 1999, more one suspects to

humour his supporters than because the Church really wanted him in its pantheon of saints.

Fave five Roman take-homes

3-D posters (post-card versions available) where Christ changes miraculously into the Virgin Mary as you move him about (the ever-popular coyly blinking Christ is a viable alternative).

Pale green fluorescent mega-rosaries guaranteed to glow through all-night prayer vigils.

Do-it-yourself papal blessings (just fill in your name on the dotted line).

Holy Year mini-hammers and mini-trowels for knocking down and sealing up holy doors (*see p106*); available in a tasteful polished wood case.

Ceramic Swiss Guards bearing more than a passing resemblance to garden gnomes, topped with silver plate helmets and carrying silver plate halberds (note: from exclusive jewellers' only).

La Rinascente

Largo Chigi, 20 (06 679 7691). Bus to Piazza San Silvestro. **Open** 9am- 9pm Mon-Sat; 10.30am-8pm Sun. **Credit** AmEx, DC, EC, MC, V. **Map 3/1A**
Leading large-scale stores, good for classy jewellery and accessories, designer and off-the-peg clothing, and an extensive selection of lingerie. The Piazza Fiume branch has an excellent basement household department, and English-language desks at both give advice on tax-free shopping and shipping home. **Branch** Piazza Fiume (06 884 1231). **Map 4/2A**

Standa

Viale Regina Margherita, 117 (06 855 7427). Bus or tram to Piazza Buenos Aires. **Open** 3.30-8pm Mon; 9am-8pm Tue-Sat. **Credit** AmEx, DC, EC, MC, V. **Map 4/1A**
Italy's equivalent of Woolworths. Underwear is cheap; clothes are generally cheerful, with a middle-aged tinge. There is a basement supermarket.

Termini Drugstore

Below Termini Station. Metro Termini. **Open** 24 hours daily. **Map 5/2A**

Handy for last-minute snacks before train journeys, this underground mall has had a facelift and tried to move upmarket. Sheltering crowds of transsexuals, backpackers and homeless should be impressed.

UPIM
Piazza di Santa Maria Maggiore (06 446 5579). Bus to Piazza Esquilino or Termini. **Open** 9am-8pm Tue-Sat; noon-8pm Mon. **Credit** AmEx, DC, EC, MC, V. **Map 5/2A**
Lower-end-of-the-line fashion, plus toiletries and household goods.
Branches Via del Tritone, 172 (06 678 3336) **Map 5/2C**; Via Nazionale, 211 (06 484 502) **Map 5/2B**.

Antiques

Good but pricey places to look for antiques include Via del Babuino, Via Giulia and around Via de' Coronari, where dealers organise antiques fairs in May and October (*see chapter* **Rome by Season**). The dealers-cum-restorers who – weather permitting – picturesquely clutter up Via del Pellegrino may be cheaper, but quality dips in proportion to prices. The occasional bargain can be picked up in the antiques-meet-jumble markets (*see page 180*).

De Pillis
Via di Monte Giordano, 41 (06 687 9826). Bus to Corso Vittorio Emanuele. **Open** 8am-1pm, 2.30-7pm, Mon-Fri. Closed Aug. **No credit cards. Map 3/2B**
Alfonso De Pillis is primarily a furniture restorer, as the half-varnished items strewn in front of his workshop make obvious. But, in a dark room across the street – looking as it might have 400 years ago – he also has a small selection of furniture, large and small, for sale, at very honest prices.

La Sinopia
Via dei Banchi Vecchi, 21c (06 687 2869). Bus to Corso Vittorio Emanuele. **Open** 10am-1pm, 4-7.30pm, Mon-Sat. Closed Aug. **No credit cards. Map 3/2B**
More than an antiques shop, offering expert advice, valuations and design hints, plus courses in restoration, gilding and so on. The exquisite *objets* on show are not cheap, but prices are entirely reliable.

Artists' supplies & stationery

Artistica Roma
Via del Babuino, 22-4 (06 3600 0963). Metro Spagna/bus to Via del Babuino. **Open** 3.30-7.30pm Mon; 9am-1pm, 3.30-7.30pm, Tue-Sat. **Credit** EC, MC, V. **Map 2/2A**
A stone's throw from Rome's traditional artists' haunt, Via Margutta, Artistica Roma has a comforting jumble of artists supplies of all types.

Officina della Carta
Via Benedetta, 26B (06 589 5557). Bus to Piazza Sonnino. **Open** 9.30am- 1pm, 3.30-7.30pm, Mon-Sat. Closed two weeks Aug. **Credit** DC, MC, V. **Map 6/2B**

Beautiful hand-made paper is incorporated into albums, gift boxes, note books and a host of other items by the ladies of this tiny shop in Trastevere.

Vertecchi
Via della Croce, 70 (06 679 0155). Metro Spagna/bus to Piazza Augusto Imperatore. **Open** 3.30-7.30pm Mon; 9.30am-7.30pm Tue-Sat. **Credit** AmEx, DC, EC, MC, V. **Map 2/2A**
Stationery, pens, paints and wrapping paper, plus a big line in paper plates and stuff for parties.

Bookshops

Amore e Psiche
Via Santa Caterina da Siena, 61 (06 678 3908). Bus or tram to Largo Arenula. **Open** 3-8pm Mon; 9am-2pm, 3-8pm, Tue-Fri; 10am-8pm Sat, Sun. **Credit** AmEx, MC, V. **Map 3/2A**
Centrally-located store with a good range on psychology, poetry and the arts, and some English and French classics. Beautifully renovated in 1995.

Bibli
Via dei Fienaroli, 28 (06 588 4097/info@bibli.it). Bus to Piazza Sonnino. **Open** 5.30pm-midnight Mon; 11am-midnight Tue-Sun. **Credit** AmEx, DC, EC, MC, V. **Map 6/2B**
A bookshop unique in Rome, also functioning as a cinema, music venue and tea room. Over 30,000 books (some in English), and computers for browsing: the café offers salads, sandwiches and desserts. *Website: www.bibli.it*

Feltrinelli
Largo Argentina, 5a (06 6880 3248). Bus to Largo Argentina. **Open** 9am-8pm Mon-Sat; 10am-1.30pm, 4-7.30pm, Sun. **Credit** AmEx, DC, EC, MC, V. **Map 6/1A**
Excellent bookshops with big selections of art, photography, history and comic books, and titles in English and other languages. Also magazines, maps, postcards, posters, arty T-shirts and creative toys.
Branches Via del Babuino, 39/41 (06 3600 1899) **Map 2/2A**; Via Emanuele Orlando, 78-81 (06 487 0171) **Map 5/1B**.

Libreria M.T. Cicerone
Largo Chigi (06 6994 1554). Bus to Via del Corso or Largo Chigi. **Open** 9.30am-8pm Mon-Sat; 11am-1pm, 4-8pm, Sun. **Credit** AmEx, DC, EC, MC, V. **Map 3/1A**
A subterranean complex selling cut-price prints, antique and rare books, and comics. If you're interested in the history of Italian media, look out for Fascist-era newspapers with articles by Mussolini.

Libreria del Viaggiatore
Via del Pellegrino, 78 (06 6880 1048). Bus to Corso Vittorio Emanuele. **Open** 4-8pm Mon; 9am-2pm, 4-8pm, Tue-Sat. Closed one week Aug. **Credit** AmEx, DC, EC, MC, V. **Map 6/1B**
Specialists in travel literature, with books on Italy by Stendhal, Twain, Dickens, Goethe, Strindberg and Ruskin. English and French books too.

The street to find....

THEN...

Medieval Roman traders and craftsmen didn't like to go out on a limb: to ensure no customer was under any illusions about where to find a given product or service, they clustered together in streets that became known after their inhabitants. The area around **Campo de' Fiori** (even today home to a small flower – *fiore* – market) abounds with tributes to this age of high-density artisans.

Via dei Cappellari was the place to go for hats (*cappelli*), while paper (*carta*) products were found in **Via dei Cartari**. Jackets (*giubbotti*) were best bought in **Via dei Giubbonari**, keys (*chiavi*) in **Via dei Chiavari**, and crossbows (*balestre*) in **Via dei Balestrari**. For trunks (*bauli*), **Via dei Baullari** was (and to some extent still is) the place; for tin basins (*catine*), **Via dei Catinari**; for chairs (*sedie*), **Via dei Sederari** and for wicker baskets (*canestre*), **Via dei Canestrari**. The carpenters (*falegnami*) of **Via dei Falegnami** were a convenient stroll (along **Via dei Barbieri**, where they could have a shave along the way) from their nail (*chiodo*) suppliers in **Via dei Chiodaroli**.

...AND NOW...

Streets for...

Antiques Via de' Coronari, Via dei Banchi Nuovi, Via del Panico, Via del Pellegrino
Carpenters Via dei Capocci, Piazza de' Renzi
Carpets (Persian) Via del Babuino, Via Margutta
Designer clothes Via Condotti, Via Frattina, Via Borgognona
High-street/mid-range fashion Via Nazionale,

For baskets, try Via del Teatro Valle

Via del Corso, Via dei Giubbonari
Paper Via Monterone, Via di Torre Argentina
Wickerwork Via Monterone, Via del Teatro Valle, Via dei Sediari

---

Rinascita

Via delle Botteghe Oscure, 1/2 (06 679 7637). Bus to Piazza Venezia.
Open 10am-8pm, Mon-Sat; 10am-2pm, 4-8pm, Sun.
Credit AmEx, DC, EC, MC, V. **Map 6/1 A**
Traditionally a temple of left-wing culture, Rinascita now offers a good selection of modern literature, art and comic books, with one floor devoted to videos, many in the original language.

English-Language Bookshops

Anglo American Book Co

Via della Vite, 102 (06 679 5222). Bus to Piazza San Silvestro. **Open** 3.30-7pm Mon; 9am-1pm, 3.30-7.30pm, Tue-Sat. Closed one week Aug.
Credit AmEx, DC, EC, MC, V. **Map 5/1C**

A good selection of books in English, and a vast range of scientific and technical texts aimed at university students. What they don't have, they'll order.

The Corner Bookshop

Via del Moro, 48 (06 583 6942). Bus to Viale Trastevere. **Open** 3.30-8pm Mon; 9.30am-1.30pm, 3.30-8pm, Tue-Sat; 11am-1.30pm, 3.30-8pm, Sun.
Credit AmEx, DC, EC, MC, V. **Map 6/2B**
A hole-in-the-wall store, covering fiction, non-fiction and general interest books – in all, 25,000 titles in an incredibly small space at non-rip-off prices.

Economy Book & Video Center

Via Torino, 136 (06 474 6877). Bus to Via Nazionale. **Open** 3-8pm Mon; 9am-8pm Tue-Sat. Closed one week Aug.
Credit AmEx, DC, EC, MC, V. **Map 5/2B**

Although anything but economical, this bookshop imports the latest from London and New York, and deals in second-hand books (check before buying anything new). There's also a good noticeboard for those seeking work, shelter or Italian lessons.
Website: www.agora.stm.it/kem.bookcenter

The English Bookshop
Via di Ripetta, 248 (06 320 3301).
Metro Flaminio/bus to Piazzale Flaminia. **Open** 10am-7.30pm Mon-Sat. Closed two weeks Aug. **Credit** AmEx, DC, EC, MC, V. **Map 6/2B**
A general bookshop with plenty of non-fiction and a good children's selection.

Feltrinelli International
Via Emanuele Orlando, 84 (06 482 7878).
Metro Repubblica/bus to Piazza della Repubblica. **Open** 9am-8pm Mon-Sat; 10am-1.30pm, 4-7.30pm, Sun. **Credit** AmEx, DC, EC, MC, V. **Map 5/1B**
Try here for your reading matter before subsidising other, over-priced English language bookshops. This attractive store offers fiction, poetry, drama, magazines, guide books and a good choice of kid's books.

The Lion Bookshop
Via dei Greci, 33 (06 3265 4007). Metro Spagna/bus to Piazza San Silvestro. **Open** 4.30-7.30pm Mon; 10am-7.30pm Tue-Sat. Closed Aug. **Credit** AmEx, DC, EC, MC, V. **Map 2/2A**
The Lion has long been a reference point for Rome ex-pats. Recently installed in a new location, it also offers a reading room where customers can browse over a tea or coffee.

Italica Books
Via dei Giubbonari, 30/9 (06 6880 5285/mmcdermott4@compuserve.com). Bus or tram to Via Arenula. **Open** 3-7pm Thur; otherwise by appointment. **No credit cards. Map 6/1B**
Not so much a bookshop as the home of charming Louise McDermott, who will help you find exactly the right rare, second-hand or antiquarian book in English about any Italian topic. Phone or e-mail for a catalogue and to place orders, which can be mailed.

Cosmetics & perfumes

Antica Erboristeria Romana
Via di Torre Argentina, 15 (06 687 9493). Bus to Largo Argentina. **Open** 8.30am-1pm, 2.30-7.30pm, Mon-Fri; 9am-1.30pm Sat.Closed two weeks Aug. **Credit** AmEx, DC, EC, MC, V. **Map 6/1A**
A curiosity shop founded in the eighteenth century, with banks of tiny wooden drawers, some marked with skulls and cross-bones. Herbal remedies, scented paper, liquorice and hellbane are all in stock.

Officina Profumo-Farmaceutico di Santa Maria Novella
Corso Rinascimento, 47 (06 687 9608).
Bus to Corso Rinascimento. **Open** 9.30am-7.30pm Mon-Sat; 10.40am-7.30pm Sun. **Credit** AmEx, EC, MC, V. **Map 3/2A**

Using recipes purportedly handed down from Dominican monks (not including, one suspects, their sun-screen range), the Florence-based Officina produces all sorts of all-natural beauty products.

Profumeria Materozzoli
Piazza San Lorenzo in Lucina, 5 (06 6889 2686).
Bus to Largo Chigi. **Open** 3.30-7.30pm Mon; 10am-1.30pm, 3.30-7.30pm, Tue-Sat. Closed two weeks Aug. **Credit** AmEx, EC, MC, V. **Map 3/1A**
Founded in 1870, this elegant *profumeria* stocks the sought-after Acqua di Parma line, and also has a vast range of bristle shaving brushes.

La Strega
Via dei Banchi Nuovi, 21b (06 6830 7567).
Bus to Corso Vittorio Emanuele. **Open** 3.30-7.30pm Mon; 9am-1pm, 3.30-7.30pm, Tue-Sat. Closed Aug. **Credit** AmEx, EC, MC, V. **Map 3/2B**
Natural cosmetics, plus a large range of vitamins imported from the US, and macrobiotic foodstuffs. *Website: www.lastrega.com*

Design & household

Azi
Via San Francesco a Ripa, 170 (06 588 3303).
Bus to Viale Trastevere. **Open** 9.30am-1.30pm, 4-8pm, Mon-Sat; 11am-1.30pm, 4-8pm, Sun. **Credit** AmEx, DC, EC, MC, V. **Map 6/2B**
Dust-collecter household objects at the cutting edge of Italian design, in a minute shop in Trastevere.

Ceramiche Musa
Via Campo Marzio, 39 (06 6871 242).
Bus to Largo Chigi. **Open** 3.45-7.30pm Mon: 9am-1pm, 3.45-7.30pm, Tue-Fri; 9am-1pm Sat. Closed Aug. **No credit cards. Map 3/1A**
Modern reproductions of traditional ceramic tiles with those gorgeous blues and greens that brighten bathrooms and kitchens all over Italy.

C.U.C.I.N.A.
Via del Babuino, 118a (06 679 1275).
Metro Spagna/bus to Piazza San Silvestro. **Open** 3.30-7.30pm Mon; 9am-7.30pm Tue-Sat. **Credit** AmEx, DC, EC, MC, V. **Map 2/2A**
A kasbah for cooks, this subterranean warehouse contains everything you might need to make and present Italian coffee, ice cream, pasta, pizza or roasts. Excellent too for fistfuls of well-priced espresso cups, or eccentric baking moulds.

Frette
Via del Corso, 381 (06 678 6862). Bus to Largo Chigi. **Open** 3.30-7.30pm Mon; 9.40am-7.30pm Sat. **Credit** AmEx, DC, EC, MC, V. **Map 3/1A**
The crispest (and costliest) of bed and table linens. **Branch** Via Nazionale, 84 (06 488 2641). Bus to Via Nazionale. **Map 5/2B**

Habitat
Via Cola di Rienzo, 197 (06 324 3233).
Bus to Via Cola di Rienzo. **Open** 3.30-7.30pm Mon; 10am-7.30pm Tue-Sat. **Credit** AmEx, EC, MC, V. **Map 2/2C**

As you might expect, the Italian version of Habitat tends to offer slicker goods at steeper prices; the range is also more limited than in its UK counterparts. Open occasional Sundays too.
Branches Viale Marconi, 259 (06 558 2701). Bus to Piazzale della Radio; Viale Regina Margherita, 18/20 (06 855 8641). Bus/tram to Viale Regina Margherita.

House and Kitchen
Via del Plebiscito, 103 (06 679 4208). Bus to Piazza Venezia. **Open** 10am-8pm Mon-Sat; 10.30am-7.30pm Sun. **Credit** AmEx, DC, EC, MC, V. **Map 6/1A**
An old-fashioned delight; selling all the prosaic essentials they don't sell anywhere else, plus, inexplicably, rain gear and wellies.

Leone Limentani
Via del Portico d'Ottavia, 47 (06 6880 6949) Bus to Largo Argentina/tram to Via Arenula. **Open** 4-8pm Mon; 9am-1pm, 4-8pm, Tue-Sat. Closed two weeks Aug. **Credit** AmEx, DC, EC, MC, V. **Map 6/1-2A**
If you can't match up your broken plate/cup/vase in this subterranean Aladdin's cave of high-piled crockery, chances are you won't find it anywhere.

Ornamentum
Via de' Coronari, 227 (06 687 6849). Bus to Corso Rinascimento. **Open** 4-7.30pm Mon; 9am-1pm, 4-7.30pm, Tue-Fri; 9am-1pm Sat. Closed Aug. **Credit** AmEx, DC, EC, MC, V. **Map 3/1B**
A temple to fabrics: silks, brocades and indescribably beautiful colours in furnishing fabrics. If you can't find what you want in Franco Inciocchi's vast selection, he'll look it out or have it made for you. He is a supplier to theatres and film studios.

Passamanerie Crocianelli
Via dei Prefetti, 37-40 (06 687 3592). Bus to Piazza Augusto Imperatore. **Open** 3.30-7.30pm Mon; 9.30am-1pm, 3.30-7.30pm, Tue-Sat. Closed Aug. **Credit** EC, MC, V. **Map 3/1A**
Sequins, silk borders and ropes in glorious, colourful abundance: if you ever need a thing to tie your curtains back with, here you'll be spoilt for choice.

Poignée
Via Capo le Case, 34 (06 679 0158). Bus to Piazza San Silvestro. **Open** 9.30am-1pm, 3.30-7pm, Mon-Fri; 9.30am-1pm Sat. Closed three weeks Aug. **Credit** AmEx, EC, MC, V. **Map 5/1C**
A treasure trove of knobs, knockers, and exotic curtain rails.

Ravasini
Via di Ripetta, 71 (06 322 7096). Bus to Piazza Augusto Imperatore. **Open** 10am-1pm, 4-7.15pm, Mon-Fri; 10am-1pm Sat. Closed three weeks Aug. **Credit** AmEx, DC, EC, MC, V. **Map 2/2A**
Glorious hand-painted ceramic tiles, sinks and door handles, from a regular range or made to order.

Spazio Sette
Via dei Barbieri, 7 (06 6880 4261). Bus to Largo Argentina. **Open** 3.30-7.30pm Mon; 9.30am-1pm, 3.30-7.30pm, Tue-Sat. Closed one week Aug. **Credit** AmEx, DC, EC, MC, V. **Map 6/1A-B**

Rome's slickest furniture and design store occupies all three floors of a Renaissance palazzo. Admire the latest in interior design beneath frescoed ceilings, with a lush garden courtyard outside the window.

Stock Market
Via dei Banchi Vecchi, 52 (06 686 4238). Bus to Corso Vittorio Emanuele. **Open** 3.30pm-8pm Mon; 10am-8pm Tue-Sat. Closed 10 days Aug. **Credit** AmEx, DC, EC, MC, V. **Map 3/2B**
This curious outlet shifts end-of-line kitchen goods, quirky light fittings and odd articles of furniture that no one else manages – or wants – to sell. Prices are often low. Film directors have been known to come slouching in on the look-out for props.

Tucano
Piazza dei Crociferi, 10 (06 679 7547). Bus to Largo Chigi. **Open** 2-7.30pm Mon; 9.30am-7.30pm Tue-Sun. **No credit cards. Map 5/2C**
Where bargain-conscious Romans go to pick up furniture, kitchenware, wooden toys and just about anything, depending on what happens to be in store at the time. Quality isn't high, but neither are prices.

Fashion
Bags, shoes, ties, leatherwear

Barrilà Boutique
Via del Babuino, 33a (06 3600 1726). Bus to Via del Babuino or Piazzale Flaminio. **Open** 2.30-8pm Mon; 9am-8pm Tue-Sat; 10.30am-7.30pm Sun. **Credit** AmEx, DC, EC, MC, V. **Map 2/2A**
Smart, high-fashion women's shoes at medium prices: big and beautiful colour ranges in many lines. **Branch** Via Condotti, 29 (06 679 3916). Bus to Piazza San Silvestro. Map **3/1A**

Borini
Via dei Pettinari, 86 (06 687 5670). Bus to Lungotevere dei Tebaldi or Corso Vittorio Emanuele/tram to Via Arenula. **Open** 3.30-7.30pm Mon; 9am-1pm, 3.30-7.30pm, Tue-Sat. Closed two weeks Aug. **Credit** AmEx, EC, MC, V. **Map 6/1B**
Borini's shoes – all made in the family workshop – are simple, elegant, created with an eye on current fashion trends and very, very durable. In view of which, the price tags are surprisingly restrained.

Carlotta Rio
Via Arco della Ciambella, 8 (06 687 2308). Bus to Largo Argentina. **Open** 4-8pm Mon; 9am-1.30pm, 4-8pm, Tue-Sat. Closed two weeks Aug. **Credit** AmEx, DC, EC, MC, V. **Map 6/1A**
Classic hand-made bags, shoes and sandals. Leather creations cost from L250,000, silk from L140,000. Ms Rio's showroom looks like an elegant living room.

DPM
Piazza Mastai, 7 (05 588 0771). Bus to Viale Trastevere. **Open** 2-7pm Mon; 10.30am-2.30pm, 3-7pm, Tue-Sat. **Credit** AmEx, DC, EC, MC, V. **Map 6/2B**
High-fashion no-name women's and men's shoes at affordable prices.

The designer drag

Once Rome's point of reference for culture-craving Grand Tourists, the tight grid of streets at the foot of the Spanish Steps is now the essential haunt of those hungering after the heights of Italian fashion. *Vie* Borgognona, Condotti and Frattina are peopled by the beautiful and the would-be beautiful, the wealthy and the would-be wealthy, and tourists in their thousands. Virtually all of Italy's best-known fashion names (and several foreign ones) set out their stalls in these three streets.

Shopping here has some particular rituals: many of the staff are drawn from that section of Roman shop assistants who seem to assume their vocation in life is intimidation, and their notions of the hierarchy of fashionable-ness and social standing can be as solidly set as the stones of the Vatican. Be prepared to face them down. For all of the following, take a bus to Piazza San Silvestro, or the Metro to Spagna. All, naturally, will accept any major credit card you have to offer. **Map 3/1A, 5/1C**

Designer labels

DKNY
Via Frattina, 44 (06 6992 3472). **Open** 1-8pm Mon; 10am-8pm Tue-Sat.
Dolce e Gabbana
Via Borgognona, 7d (06 678 2990).
Open 1-7.30pm Mon; 10am-7.30pm Tue-Sat.
Branch D&G, Piazza di Spagna, 82/3 (06 679 2294).
Fendi
Via Borgognona 4e, 4l, 36a-38b, 39-40 (06 679 7641/2/3/4). **Open** *Leather shop* 2-7.30pm Mon; 10am-7.30pm Tue-Sat; *furrier* 10am-8pm Mon-Sat.
Gianfranco Ferrè
Via Borgognona, 5b, 6, 6a (06 679 7445).
Open 2.30-7.30pm Mon; 10am-7pm Tue-Sat.
Gianni Versace
Via Borgognona, 25 (06 679 5037).
Open 3.30-7.30pm Mon; 10am-7.30pm Tue-Sat.
Branches **Versus**, Via Borgognona, 33/4 (67 83 977); Via Bocca di Leone, 26 (67 80 521).
Giorgio Armani
Via Condotti, 77 (06 699 1460).
Open 3-7pm Mon; 10am-7pm Tue-Sat.
Branches **Emporio Armani**
Via del Babuino, 140 (06 3600 2197); **Armani Jeans** Via del Babuino, 70a (06 3600 1848).
Max Mara
Via Condotti, 17-19a (06 6992 2104).
Open 3.30-7.30pm Mon; 10am-7.30pm Tue-Sat.
Branches **Max Mara** Via Frattina, 28 (06 679 3638); Via Nazionale, 28-31 (06 488 5870); Via Cola di Rienzo, 273 (06 321 5375). **Max&Co** Via Condotti, 46 (06 678 7946); Via Nazionale, 56 (06 481 7524); Via del Corso, 488 (06 322 7266).

Prada
Via Condotti, 92-5 (06 679 0897). **Open** 3-7pm Mon; 10am-7pm Tue-Sat; 1.30-7.30pm Sun.
Valentino
Via Bocca di Leone, 15 (06 679 5862).
Open 3-7.30pm Mon; 10am-7.30pm Tue-Sat.
Branch **Oliver** (younger range) Via del Babuino, 61 (06 3600 1906).

Davide Cenci

Via Campo Marzio, 1-7 (06 699 0681). Bus to Via del Corso. **Open** 3.30-7.30pm Mon; 9.30am-1.30pm, 3.30-7.30pm, Tue-Fri; 10am-7.30pm Sat.
Credit AmEx, DC, EC, MC, V. **Map 3/1A**

Out on a geographical limb (on the Tiber-side of Via del Corso, heading towards Piazza Navona), to show that it's a good cut above the rabble, is Davide Cenci, the place where Romans – male, female and their over-dressed offspring – come to fit themselves out in their classical best. Cenci has catered to Rome's wealthy since 1926, offering a 'made in Italy' treatment of classic suits, shirts, accessories and shoes.

Fausto Santini
Via Frattina, 120 (06 678 4114).
Metro Spagna/bus to Piazza San Silvestro.
Open 2-7.30pm Mon; 10am-7.30pm Tue-Sat.
Credit AmEx, DC, EC, MC, V. **Map 3/1A**
Santini is the city's most famous shoe designer, and
rightly so. His designs, for men and women, are
sleek, sophisticated, original, and yet surprisingly
durable. Alternatively, pick up a pair of last year's
models (in perfect condition) at the Santini-seconds
shop at Via Cavour, 106 (06 488 0934; **Map 8/1B**).
The price difference is astounding.

Furla
Via del Corso, 481 (06 3600 3619).
Bus to Piazza Augusto Imperatore. **Open** 3.30-
7.30pm Mon; 10am-7.30 Tue-Sat; 10.30am-7.30 Sun.
Credit AmEx, DC, EC, MC, V. **Map 2/2A**
Elegant, high-fashion handbags that are minimalist
in everything but their prices.
Branches Piazza di Spagna, 22 (06 6920 0363).
Metro Spagna/bus to Piazza San Silvestro **Map
5/1C**; Via Nazionale, 54-5 (06 487 0127) Bus to Via
Nazionale. **Map 5/2B.**

Gucci
Via Condotti, 8 (06 678 9340).
Metro Spagna/bus to Piazza Augusto Imperatore.
Open 3-7pm Mon; 10am-7pm Tue-Sat.
Credit AmEx, DC, EC, MC, V. **Map 5/1C**
The very finest designer luggage, shoes and hand-
bags, as well as watches, scarves and other acces-
sories. All items are displayed without price tags,
presumably to stop customers passing out.

Ramirez
*Via del Corso, 176 (06 679 5928). Bus to Largo
Chigi or Piazza San Silvestro.* **Open** 3.30-8pm Mon;
10am-8pm Tue-Sat; 11.30am-8pm Sun.
Credit AmEx, DC, EC, MC, V. **Map 3/1A**
Dependable chain of reasonably-priced high-street
fashion footwear for men and women.
Branches Via Frattina, 85 (06 679 2467); bus to Piazza
San Silvestro **Map 3/1A**. Via Cola di Rienzo, 151 (06
321 4357); bus to Via Cola di Rienzo **Map 2/2C.**

Settimio Mieli
*Via San Claudio, 70 (06 678 5979). Bus to Piazza
San Silvestro.* **Open** 1-7.30pm Mon; 10am-7.30pm
Tue-Sat. **Credit** AmEx, DC, EC, MC, V. **Map 3/1A**
Reasonably-priced leather gloves in all shapes and
colours, with a choice of linings.

Valentino Guido
Via Sistina, 16 (06 488 1619).
Metro Spagna or Barberini/bus to Piazza Barberini.
Open 10am-8pm Mon-Sat. Closed one week Aug.
Credit AmEx, EC, MC, V. **Map 5/1C**
Designer bags at warehouse prices.

Mid-range fashion

Bacillario
*Via Laurina, 41/3 (06 3600 1828). Metro Spagna/
bus to Piazza Augusto Imperatore.* **Open** 9.30am-
7.30pm Mon-Sat. **Credit** AmEx, V. **Map 2/2A**
Punks' paradise (if they haven't all passed away).
Leather jeans and jackets, see-through shirts, pre-
cipitous platforms and scrappy bikinis.

Big cheeses hang out at the **Volpetti** *deli (see page 183).*

Cisalfa

Via del Corso, 475 (06 3265 1519).
Bus to Piazza Augusto Imperatore. **Open** 3.30-
7.30pm Mon; 10am-7.30pm Tue-Sat; 11am-7.30pm
Sun. **Credit** AmEx, MC, V. **Map 2/2A**
City-centre offshoot of a chain selling top-quality
sports clothes and equipment at prices slightly lower
than those charged by smaller competitors.

Diesel

Via del Corso, 185 (06 678 3933).
Bus to Piazza San Silvestro. **Credit** AmEx, DC, EC, MC, V. **Map 3/1A**
Mon-Sat. **Credit** AmEx, DC, EC, MC, V. **Map 3/1A**
A retro-look for the masses in a slickly attractive setting, with whimsical window displays. Small
amounts of stock are tastefully spread out over the
two floors of this showpiece outlet.

Energie

*Via del Corso, 486 (06 322 7046). Bus to Largo
Chigi.* **Open** 9.30am-8pm Mon-Sat; 9.30am-1.30pm, 4-
8pm, Sun. **Credit** AmEx, DC, EC, MC, V. **Map 2/2A**
Trend-setter and follower, Energie is one of *the*
shops for Roman youth, particularly those from the
outskirts. Stocking the hippest labels, including its
own, it also charges higher-than-average prices.

Eventi

*Via della Fontanella, 8 (06 3600 2533). Bus to Via
del Corso or Piazza del Popolo.* **Open** 3.30-8pm Mon;
10am-1pm, 3.30-8pm, Tue-Sat. Closed two weeks
Aug. **Credit** AmEx, EC, MC, V. **Map 2/2A**
The '70s revisited, with '90s street-chic. One of few
places in Rome to have lurid synthetic tops that
clash superbly with tulip-embellished five-inch platforms. Also worth a visit for the décor: you change
in shower units, and try on shoes sitting on the loo.

One-off shops

Baco della Seta

Via Vittoria, 55 (06 679 3907).
Metro Spagna/bus to Piazza Augusto Imperatore.
Open 3.30-7.30pm Mon; 9.30am-1.30pm, 3.30-7.30pm,
Tue-Sat. Closed two weeks Aug.
Credit AmEx, DC, EC, MC, V. **Map 2/2A**
Beautiful, elegant women's day and evening wear,
all in pure silks of glorious hues. Prices, given the
fabrics, are not exorbitant.

Degli Effetti

Piazza Capranica, 93-4 (06 679 0202).
Bus to Largo Argentina/Via del Corso. **Open** 3.30-
7pm Mon; 10am-2pm, 3.30-8pm, Tue-Sat.
Credit AmEx, DC, EC, MC, V. **Map 2/2A**
Stunning – often OTT – clothes by Gigli,
Gaultier,Westwood et al. Horrendous prices.
Branch Piazza Capranica, 75-9 (06 679 1650).

Discount dell'Alta Moda

Via Gesù e Maria, 16A (06 361 3796).
Bus to Via di Ripetta. **Open** 3.30-7.30pm Mon;
9.30am-1pm, 3.30-7.30pm, Tue-Sat. Closed two weeks
Aug. **Credit** DC, EC, MC, V. **Map 2/2A**
Last season's men's and women's models from top
Italian designers, at 50% off the original price.

Mimmo Siviglia

Via della Vite, 63 (06 679 7474).
Bus to Piazza San Silvestro.
Open 9.30am-1pm, 3.30-7.30pm Mon-Sat. Closed
Aug. **Credit** AmEx, DC, EC, MC, V. **Map 5/1C**
A tiny store, so discreet that there's no name
showing outside, where cottons and silks wait to be
hand sewn into stylish shirts for fashion-conscious
executives.

O. Testa

*Via Frattina, 42 (06 679 1296). Metrp Spagna/
bus to Piazza San Silvestro.* **Open** 4-7.30pm Mon;
10am-1.20pm, 3.30-7.40pm ,Tue-Sat. Closed Aug.
Credit AmEx, DC, EC, MC, V. **Map 5/1C**
Classic men's knitwear and suits, off-the-peg (at
lower-than-big-name-designer prices), or entirely
made to order.
Branch Via Borgognona, 13 (06 679 6174). Metro
Spagna/bus to Piazza San Silvestro **Map 3/1A**.

Scala Quattordici

Via della Scala, 14 (06 588 3580).
Bus to Piazza Sonnino. **Open** 4-8pm Mon; 10am-
1.30pm, 4-8pm, Tue-Sat. Closed two weeks Aug.
Credit AmEx, MC, V. **Map 6/2B**
If you can't find a style, size or colour on the racks
here, Letterio and Maria Attanasio will invite you
to view a selection of multi-hued silks and other fine
fabrics in their studio, then create the made-to-
measure dress or suit of your dreams. Womenswear
only, and at a price.

Strada

*Via del Corso, 443 (06 687 8423). Bus to Piazza
Augusto Imperatore.* **Open** 2-7.30 Mon; 10.30am-8pm
Tue-Sat; 10.30am-1.30pm, 3.30-7.30pm, Sun.
Credit AmEx, DC, EC, MC, V. **Map 2/2A**
A long-term fixture by the church of San Carlo on
Via del Corso, Strada is an outlet for Italian and for-
eign designers. Men's and women's wear.

Xandrine

*Via della Croce, 88 (06 678 6201). Metro
Spagna/bus to Piazza Augusto Imperatore.*
Open 1.30-8pm Mon; 9.30am-8pm Tue-Sat. **Credit**
AmEx, DC, EC, MC, V. **Map 2/2A**
Acres of lace and sequins adorn extravagant party
and ball dresses, with shoes and bags to match; all
are made in-house.

Lingerie

Lingerie stores are found all over town, but
particularly in the area around Via Condotti. Most
markets have at least one *bancarella* selling
inexpensive underwear. The large **Rinascente**
department store (*see page 168*) is a good bet for
middle-range items.

Brighenti

*Via Frattina, 7 (06 679 1484). Metro Spagna/
bus to Piazza San Silvestro.* **Open** 3.30-7.30 Mon;
9.30am-1.30pm, 3.30-7.30pm, Tue-Thur; 9.30am-
7.30pm Fri, Sat. Closed two weeks Aug.
Credit AmEx, DC, EC, MC, V. **Map 5/1C**

Lingerie in glorious, silky shades by Dior, Nina Ricci, Ferrè and other major names in a beautiful, pastel-hued temple to luxury. Their own-name brand offers similarly opulent things at slightly lower (which has to be regarded as a relative concept here) prices. **Branch** Via Borgognona, 27 (06 678 3898). Metro Spagna/bus to Piazza San Silvestro. Open 3.30-7.30pm Mon; 10am-7.30pm Tue-Sat. **Map 5/1C**

Food & drink

With supermarkets a rarity in central Rome, food shopping is generally a marathon: **markets** (*see page 179*) are best for fruit and vegetables, while your corner *alimentari* (grocery store) will provide other basic necessities, from pasta and cheese to stock cubes and yoghurt. If you ever

Food markets

Fresh produce in abundance in Testaccio's covered market.

When peckishness strikes as you make your way along the tourist trail, steer clear of the rip-off fruit stalls lurking around every well-known monument. Head, instead, for a genuine food market.

Handiest for the *centro storico* sights is **Campo de' Fiori**, a bustling, colourful food and flower market in one of Rome's most picturesque squares. This is the most central, but definitely not the cheapest market in the city. If you're exploring **Monti** and **Esquilino**, plunge into the chaotic jumble around **Piazza Vittorio** (aka Piazza Vittorio Emanuele), where the usual Italian fresh produce, cheese and meats are supplemented by pulses, halal meat and sumptuous spices. In **Trastevere**, the market in **Piazza San Cosimato** retains some of its neighbourhood feel despite the tourist hordes. Even further from the beaten track is the covered market in **Piazza Testaccio**, where prices are considerably lower.

A handful of tiny central(-ish) street markets also just manage to keep their heads above water. They can be found in **Via dei Santi Quattro Coronati** a stone's throw from the Colosseum, **Via Milazzo** near Termini station, **Piazza Bernini** on the San Saba side of the Aventine hill, and in **Via G.B. Niccolini** in Monteverde Vecchio.

But for the real Roman salt-of-the-earth market experience, head for the suburbs. In **Monteverde Nuovo**, **Piazza San Giovanni di Dio** is inundated by a mass of humanity as the square is transformed into one of the cheapest places in the city to buy produce. Rivalling it for liveliness is the market in **Via Trionfale**, a short hike from the Vatican. Also near the Holy See is the **Piazza dell'Unità** covered market on Via Cola di Rienzo, one of few that open 7am to 8pm, Monday to Saturday.

Market hours

Food markets are open about 6am-2pm, Mon-Sat. Some stay open on Tuesday and Thursday afternoons, but how open they are depends on the whims of individual stall holders.

hanker for something more adventurous and/or exotic, head for stores like **Volpetti** or **Castroni**. For fresh (as opposed to long-life) milk or cream, your best bet is not a shop at all, but any bar labelled *latteria*.

Most deli products are sold by the *etto* (100g) rather than the kilo; when ordering ask for *un'etto*, *due etti*, and so on. (*see also* **Food vocabulary**, *in chapter* **Restaurants**). Many *enoteche* (wine shops) sell wine from large barrels by the litre (bring your own container); cheap this may be, but unless you're very lucky, the resemblance to paint-stripper may be more than a passing one.

See also **Select your wine** *in chapter* **Restaurants** *and* **La dolce vita**, *in chapter* **Cafés & Bars**.

Ai Monasteri
Corso Rinascimento, 72 (06 6880 2783).
Bus to Corso Rinascimento. **Open** 9am-1pm, 4.30-7.30pm Mon-Wed, Fri, Sat; 4.30-7.30pm Thur. Closed Aug. **No credit cards**. **Map 3/2A**
Founded in 1892, this dark, cavernous store sells wines, liqueurs, honey, herbs, preserves and other natural products, all grown or gathered at seven Italian monasteries.

Flea markets

Most Italians have little interest in second-hand clothes and bric-a-brac. Objects long considered design classics in the UK and US are regarded as rubbish here, and consequently there are good bargains to be had. In larger markets, like **Porta Portese** and **Via Sannio**, it's *de rigeur* to haggle. Starting prices for antiques are about double what most stallholders really expect. This doesn't necessarily require a great level of Italian. Broken English and/or gestures will suffice for most deals.

Atelier Ritz
Hotel Parco dei Principi, Via Frescobaldi, 5 (06 807 8189). Bus to Via Mercadante. **Open** *Sept-June* two Suns each month, 10am-7pm. **Admission** L3,000. **Map 4/1B**
Second-hand clothes, hats, shoes and other wearables, all, as befits this elegant end of town, by big-name designers.

Borghetto Flaminio
Piazza della Marina, 32 (06 588 0517). Tram to Piazza della Marina. **Open** *Sept-June* 10am-7pm Sun. **Admission** L3,000. **Map 2/1A**
A partly covered, partly open-air garage sale held in a well-heeled part of the city, although stallholders are required to keep prices relatively low. You can often find interesting trinkets and curios from the Fascist period.

Galleria delle Stimmate
Largo delle Stimmate, 1 (06 333 7884). Bus to Largo Argentina. **Open** *Sept-Apr* last Sun of each month, 10am-7.30pm Sun. **Map 3/2A**
At the upper end of what can be considered a flea-market, the 40 or so stalls near the Church of the Stigmata offer antique lace and amber, silver cutlery and jewellery galore.

Mercatino del Testaccio
Piazza Santa Maria Liberatrice (no phone). Bus to Via Marmorata. **Open** third Sun of each month, 9am-4pm. **Map 7/2A**
Small antiques, old clothes, records and knick-knacks from exotic climes, beneath the horse-chestnut trees of this pretty square in Testaccio.

Porta Portese
Viale Trastevere/Porta Portese (no phone). Bus or tram to Piazza Ippolito Nievo or Ponte Sublicio. **Open** 5am-2pm Sun. **Map 7/1-2B**
Although it feels long-established, the famous Sunday market in the streets between Porta Portese, Ponte Testaccio and Viale Trastevere has only been held since the 1940s. If you enter the market from Piazza Ippolito Nievo, you'll find dealers in antique furniture, Asian carpets, canework and mirrors; carry on southwards down Via Ettore Rolli to look at clothes, glass and ceramics, more antiques or African sculpture. **Via Porta Portese** is the market's main thoroughfare: at the Ponte Sublicio end, stalls sell mostly new items – CDs, tapes, kitchenware, jeans, fake Lacoste shirts and leather goods. Towards Ponte Testaccio you'll find second-hand clothes, as well as vendors of sunglasses, cigarette lighters and sad-eyed puppies. It's commonly said in Rome that if your camera or *motorino* is stolen, it's a good idea to look for it in Porta Portese. The trouble is, somebody may also try and pick your bag or pocket while you're there, so be extra careful.

Porta Portese 2
Corner of Via Palmiro Togliatti and Via Prenestina, Tor Sapienza (no phone). Bus to Via Prenestina. **Open** 6am-2pm Sun.
Suburban offspring of the original, selling virtually the same goods, but with less atmosphere.

Sotto i Portici
Piazza Augusto Imperatore (06 3600 5345). Bus to Piazza Augusto Imperatore **Open** *Sept-June* third Sun of each month, 10am-sunset. **Map 3/1A**
Drunks and tramps are ejected one Sunday a month from the Fascist-era porticos of this imposing square to make way for stalls selling just about everything in the antique and old-ish junk line.

Castroni

Via Cola di Rienzo, 196 (06 687 4383). Metro Ottaviano/bus to Piazza del Risorgimento. **Open** 8am-8pm Mon-Sat. **No credit cards**. **Map 2/2C**
A wonderful shop in Prati, near the Vatican, Castroni has Italian regional specialities, imported international foodstuffs: anything from Chinese noodles to Marmite and Vegemite.

La Corte

Via della Gatta, 1 (06 678 3842). Bus to Piazza Venezia or Via del Corso. **Open** 9.30am-1.30pm, 5-7.30pm Mon-Fri, 9.30am-1pm Sat. Closed Aug. **Credit** EC, MC, V. **Map 3/2A**

Englishman John Fort and his charming wife sell wonderful smoked fishy things in this tiny shop off Piazza del Collegio Romano. The place to go in Rome for smoked swordfish or (excellent) salmon.

Innocenzi

Piazza San Cosimato, 66 (06 581 2725). Bus to Viale Trastevere. **Open** 7am-1.30pm, 4.30-8pm Mon-Wed, Fri, Sat; 4.30-8pm Thur. Closed two weeks Aug. **No credit cards**. **Map 6/2B**
Pulses spill from great sacks stacked around this treasure trove of foodie specialities from all over the world. If the San Cosimato door is closed, try the side entrance, at Via Natale del Grande, 31.

From fake Lacoste to sad-eyed puppies, **Porta Portese** *flea market has it all.*

Underground

Via Francesco Crispi, 96 (06 3600 5345). Bus to Via del Tritone or Piazza San Silvestro. **Open** *Oct-June* first weekend of each month, 10am-8pm Sat, 10.30am-7.30pm Sun. **Admission** L3,000. **Map 5/1C**
For two days a month this vast underground car park near Via Veneto is cleared of vehicles and filled with antiques, junk, and collectors' items of all kinds – this is the place to off-load unwanted books, toys or any other clutter you may have. A useful multilingual Help Desk is also provided.

Via Sannio

Via Sannio (no phone). Metro San Giovanni/bus or tram to Piazzale Appio. **Open** 10am-1.30pm Mon-Fri; *May-Oct* 10am-2pm Sat; *Nov-Apr* 10am-6pm Sat. **Map 9/1A**

Less frenetic than Porta Portese, and a better place for good second-hand clothes. The main section consists of three covered corridors, a bit like an Arab bazaar, offering new clothing at reasonable prices; behind them are used and retro clothing sections. Many dealers have a one-price policy, as low as L2,000 on some stalls. At others, you haggle. Dig deep amid the junk: real bargains can be found.

Via Trionfale

Via Trionfale, 45 (no phone). Bus to Via Giuliana or Via Andrea Doria. **Open** 10am-1pm Tue.
Not a flea market at all but Rome's wholesale flower market, a little to the north-west of the Vatican and open to the trade only. Except, that is, on Tuesday morning, when the uninitiated can plunge into this leafy, sweet-smelling haven to buy plants or cut flowers.

Pasta all'Uovo

*Via della Croce, 8 (06 679 3102). Metro Spagna/
bus to Piazza San Silvestro.* **Open** 8am-1.30pm, 3.30-
7.30pm Mon-Wed, Fri, Sat; 8am-1.30pm Thur.
No credit cards. **Map 2/2A**
Fresh pasta, and multi-coloured packets of the dry
kind as well. Amaze and delight your dinner guests
back home with *favette* (penis pasta) or harlequin
tagliatelle, in fetching postmodern shades of
turquoise and lilac.

Volpetti

*Via Marmorata, 47 (06 574 2352).
Bus to Via Marmorata.* **Open** 8am-2pm, 5-8pm Mon,
Wed-Sat; 8am-2pm Tue.
Credit AmEx, DC, EC, MC, V. **Map 7/2A**
A Testaccio institution, Volpetti is one of the best
delis in Rome, with exceptional hand-made pasta
(try their pumpkin-filled tortelloni). Once in, it's hard
to get away without one of the jolly assistants load-
ing you up with samples of their wares – and persuading you to buy twice as much as you want. If
you can't get to Testaccio, check their website: they
will despatch all over the world.
Website: www.fooditaly.com; www.volpetti.com

Chocolates & similar delights

*See also **La dolce vita**, in chapter* **Cafés & Bars**.

La Bottega del Cioccolato

*Via Leonina, 82 (06 482 1473). Metro Cavour/
bus to Via Cavour.* **Open** 9.30am-7.30pm, Mon-Sat.
Closed one week July-Aug.
Credit AmEx, DC, EC, MC, V. **Map 8/1B**
An offshoot of **Moriondo**, this confectioner a stone's
throw from the Colosseum produces similarly delicious chocolates, all made on the premises.

Confetteria Moriondo e Gariglio

*Via del Pie' di Marmo, 21/2 (06 699 0856). Bus to
Via del Corso or Largo Argentina/tram to Largo
Argentina.* **Open** 9.30am-1pm, 3.30-7.30pm, Mon-Sat.
Closed Aug. **No credit cards**. **Map 3/2A**
A family-run chocolatiers that moulds and sells
dark, liqueur-filled confections, all on the premises.
At Easter and before Valentine's Day Romans queue
to have their special gifts sealed inside beautifully-
packaged chocolate eggs and hearts. Home
deliveries are made anywhere within Italy. Stays
open through lunchtime in the weeks prior to Easter
and Christmas.

Valzani

*Via del Moro, 37b (06 580 3792). Bus to Piazza
Sonnino.* **Open** 9am-8.30pm Wed-Sun. Closed June,
July, Aug. **No credit cards**. **Map 6/2B**
A Trastevere institution, having survived numerous eviction orders and the vissicitudes of sweet-
eating fashion. *Sachertorte* and spicy, nutty
pangiallo are specialities, but form just the tip of an
iceberg of cakey, chocolatey delights. The shop
opens daily prior to Christmas and Easter, when it's
full of out-of-this-world chocolate eggs. Amazing
decorated cakes made to order.

Ethnic foods

The area around **Piazza Vittorio**, now home to
a large slice of Rome's recent-immigrant population, is the best place to go in search of Indian,
Korean, Chinese or African foodstuffs. The Piazza
Vittorio market itself has stall selling halal and
kosher meat, and many other products. Kosher
products can also be found in shops in the **Ghetto**
(*see chapter* **Centro Storico**).

Korean Market

*Via Cavour, 84 (06 488 5060). Bus to Via Cavour or
Piazza Esquilino.* **Open** 9am-1pm, 4-8pm, Mon-Sat;
3.30-6.30pm Sun. **Credit** MC, V. **Map 8/1B**
An up-market emporium selling everything you'll
need for your Korean culinary creations, together
with exotic snacks and sweets.

Pacific Trading Co

*Viale Principe Eugenio, 17-21 (06 446 7934). Metro
Vittorio/bus to Piazza Vittorio.* **Open** 9.30am-1.30pm,
3.30-8pm, Mon-Sat. **No credit cards**. **Map 8/1A**
A huge range of foodstuffs from the Far East.

Health Foods

Il Canestro

*Via Luca della Robbia, 12 (06 574 6287).
Bus to Via Marmorata.* **Open** 8am-8pm Mon; 9am-
8pm Tue-Sat. **No credit cards**. **Map 7/2A**
Il Canestro offers a full range of natural health
foods, cosmetics and medicines, mostly from within
Italy, including some organic versions of regional
specialities. The Trastevere branch (*below*) also has
courses on nutrition-related themes and fields, and
alternative medicine.
Branch Via San Francesco a Ripa, 106 (06 581 2621).
Map 7/1B.

Drink

See also chapter **Restaurants**.

Buccone

*Via di Ripetta, 19/20 (06 361 2154).
Bus to Piazza Augusto Imperatore.*
Open 9am-8.30pm, Mon, Tue; 9am-midnight Wed-
Sat; 10am-7.30pm Sun. Closed three weeks Aug.
Credit AmEx, DC, EC, MC, V. **Map 2/2A**
In a seventeenth-century palazzo, this *enoteca* is
filled from floor to arched ceiling with wines and
spirits, all sub-divided by region – from cheap
Valpolicella to Brunello Riserva at over a million
lire.

Costantini

*Piazza Cavour, 16 (06 321 3210).
Bus to Piazza Cavour.* **Open** 4.30-8pm Mon; 9am-
1pm, 4.30-8pm, Tue-Sat. Closed Aug.
Credit AmEx, DC, EC, MC, V. **Map 3/1B**
A vast, cavernous cellar containing just about any
Italian wine you want, divided by region. Not the
cheapest place to buy wine in Rome, but certainly
one of the city's most extensive selections.

Enoteca Carso

Viale Carso, 37/39 (06 372 5866). Bus to Piazza Mazzini. **Open** 9am-10pm Mon-Sat. Closed three weeks Aug. **No credit cards.**

A unique pleasure: shelves buckle under the weight of wines and liqueurs, while film and TV people drown their sorrows in jugs of *verdicchio* at tables outside. Just north of Piazza Mazzini **Map 2/1C.**

Enoteca Vinicolo Angelini

Via Viminale, 62 (06 488 1028). Metro Termini/bus to Termini. **Open** 9am-2pm, 4-9pm, daily. Closed two weeks Aug. **Credit** AmEx, EC, MC, V. **Map 5/2B**

Wines and spirits from all over Italy and the world. A 1964 Barolo or Chianti Classico runs from L50,000 up, and there's also real Frascati (not the bleached stuff they put in bottles) from the barrel.

Trimani

Via Goito, 20 (06 446 9661). Bus to Piazza Indipendenza or Via XX Settembre. **Open** 8.30am-1.30pm, 3.30-8pm, Mon-Sat; 10am-1pm, 4-7.30pm, Sun. **Credit** AmEx, DC, EC, MC, V. **Map 5/1A**

The oldest, best wine shop in Rome, founded in 1821 by Francesco Trimani, whose descendent Marco still presides. Delivers anywhere in the world.

Gifts

La Bottega del Marmoraro

Via Margutta, 53b (06 320 7660). Metro Spagna or Flaminia/bus to Via del Babuino. **Open** 9am-1pm, 3.30-7.30pm Mon-Sat. **No credit cards. Map 2/2A**

A treasure-trove of things marble, from small pseudo-Roman inscriptions (can be made to order) to full-sized headless statues both modern and ancient.

La Chiave

Largo delle Stimmate, 28 (06 6830 8848). Bus to Largo Argentina. **Open** 10am-7pm Mon-Sat. **Credit** AmEx, DC, EC, MC, V. **Map 3/2A**

Silver jewellery from India and South America, children's toys and knicknacks, and wooden furniture.

Fratelli Alinari

Via Alibert, 16a (06 679 2923). Metro Spagna or Flaminio/bus to Piazzale Flaminio. **Open** 3.30-7.30pm Mon; 9am-1pm, 3.30-7.30pm Tue-Sat. Closed Aug. **Credit** AmEx, MC, V. **Map 2/2A**

Early photographs of Rome and elsewhere taken or collected by the pioneering Alinari brothers.

Palazzo delle Esposizioni

Via Milano, 9a (06 482 8540). Bus to Via Nazionale. **Open** 10am-9pm Wed-Mon. **Credit** AmEx, DC, EC, MC, V. **Map 5/2B**

A showcase for contemporary design. As well as a good bookshop it has a display of cookware, stationery, watches, games, lamps and other objects by top-name designers.

Studio Massoni

Via Canova, 23 (06 322 7207). Bus to Via Ripetta or Piazza Augusto Imperatore. **Open** 9am-1pm, 3-7pm Mon-Fri. **No credit cards. Map 2/2A**

Made-to-order plaster casts of just about any well-known statue or *objet* you care to have copied. A lot lighter to carry home than the real thing.

Jewellery & watches

Swatch Store

Via Condotti, 33a (06 679 1253). Metro Spagna/bus to Piazza San Silvestro. **Open** 9.30am-7.30pm Mon-Sat; 10.30am-1.30pm, 3.30-7.30pm, Sun. **Credit** AmEx, DC, EC, MC, V. **Map 3/1A**

Italians have turned limited edition Swatches into a cult. This is the place to come if you want to join.

Bulgari

Via Condotti, 10 (06 679 3876). Metro Spagna/bus to Piazza San Silvestro. **Open** 3-7pm Mon; 10am-1.30pm, 3-7pm, Tue-Sat. **Credit** AmEx, DC, EC, MC, V. **Map 5/1C**

Sweep past the unfriendly security to drool over the fantastically expensive creations in Rome's most traditional citadel of extravagant jewellery. The glittering watches are arranged in splendid isolation; browsing clients admire them from straight-backed antique chairs.

Hedy Martinelli

Via Mario de' Fiori, 59b (06 679 7733). Metro Spagna/bus to Piazza San Silvestro. **Open** 3.30-7pm Mon; 10am-7pm Tue-Sat. Closed Aug. **Credit** AmEx, DC, EC, MC, V. **Map 5/1C**

Stunning modern designs by Ms Martinelli. Consult your bank manager before considering a purchase.

Manasse

Via di Campo Marzio, 44 (06 687 1007). Bus to Via del Corso. **Open** 3.30- 7.30pm Mon; 10am-7.30pm Tue-Sat. **Credit** AmEx, DC, EC, MC, V. **Map 3/1A**

An exquisite, museum-like shop, justly famous for its collection of Russian antique jewellery and icons.

Massimo Maria Melis

Via dell'Orso, 57 (06 686 9188). Bus to Corso Rinascimento. **Open** 3.30-7.30pm Mon; 9am-1pm, 3.30-7.30pm, Tue-Sat. Closed two weeks Aug. **Credit** AmEx, DC, EC, MC, V. **Map 3/1A**

Faithful recreations in 21 carat gold of the jewels of the ancient world.

Tiny artefacts at **Siragusa**.

*Indie and underground, plus the best notice board in town at **Disfunzioni Musicali***.

Siragusa

Via delle Carrozze, 64 (06 679 7085).
Metro Spagna/bus to Piazza San Silvestro.
Open 10am-1pm, 3.30-7.30pm, Mon-Fri. Closed Aug.
Credit AmEx, MC, V. **Map 3/1 A**
Original Greek, Roman and Etruscan coins, stones and tiny artefacts, in modern gold and oxidised silver settings based on models from antiquity.

Records & music

Cassettes, records and CDs are more expensive in Italy than in the UK and especially the US Some world music and indie releases are difficult to track down, and even the range of classical music on offer is relatively limited.

Disfunzioni Musicali

Via degli Etruschi, 4-14 (06 446 1984).
Bus to Via Tiburtina. **Open** 10.30am-7.30pm Mon-Sat. **Credit** AmEx, DC, EC, MC, V.
Just a few steps from the university, this is one of the best places in Rome to buy underground and rare records, new and second-hand, including recent US and British indie releases.

Goody Music

Via Cesare Beccaria, 2 (06 361 0959). Metro Flaminio/bus to Piazzale Flaminio. **Open** 9.30am-2pm, 3.30-8pm, Mon-Sat. Closed two weeks Aug.
Credit AmEx, DC, EC, MC, V. **Map 2/1 A**
Tons and tons of dance, house, underground and rap vinyl mixes, plus equipment. DJs from all over Italy come here to find the latest tracks.

Ricordi

Via Cesare Battisti, 120 (06 679 8022). Bus to Piazza Venezia. **Open** 9am-7.30pm Mon-Sat; 3.30-8pm Sun. **Credit** AmEx, DC, EC, MC, V. **Map 6/1 A**
Rome's best-known music store, with two adjacent shops, for classical and pop. Ricordi also stocks videos, books and scores and instruments and sound equipment, for sale or hire. Concert tickets.

Rinascita

Via delle Botteghe Oscure, 5-6 (06 6992 2436).
Bus to Piazza Venezia.
Open 10am-8pm Mon-Sat; 10am-2pm, 2-8pm, Sun.
Credit AmEx, DC, EC, MC, V. **Map 6/1 A**
Conveniently central store with all the basics, plus a good collection of CD singles and the latest trends. Next door is the also-excellent bookshop (*see p171*).

Services

***Get a hair cut, your laundry done or your snaps printed.
Or get a ticket out of town.***

On arriving in Rome, throw away all your
preconceptions about how things should work.
Here, everyday services function according to their
own special rhythm, and the more Taoist your
attitude, the better off you're likely to be.

For additional services, the best places to look
are the city's English-language press, or the twice-
weekly *Porta Portese* (*see chapter* **Media**).

Dry cleaning & laundries

The city is bristling with *tintorie (*dry cleaners)
monoprezzo – which don't, despite the name,
charge the same (usually L3,500-L4,000) for all
items: tariffs rise stiffly if there's a pleat to be
ironed in. Most laundries do your washing for you,
charged by the kilo. The following are self-service:

Onda Blu
Via Lamarmora, 12 (06 446 4172).
Metro Vittorio/bus to Piazza Vittorio Emanuele.
Open 8am-10pm daily. **Map 8/1A**
Six kilos of clothes can be washed for L6,000, plus
the same again to dry them. Bright and friendly.

Wash and Dry
*Via della Pelliccia, 35 (055 580 480). Bus to Piazza
Sonnino.* **Open** 8am-9pm daily. **Map 6/2B**
Spanking-clean self-service laundrette in Trastevere.
L6,000 for an 8kg wash, L6,000 to tumble dry.
Branch Via della Chiesa Nuova, 15. Bus to Corso
Vittorio Emanuele. **Map 3/2B**

Hairdressers & beauticians

Most Rome hairdressers are closed on Mondays.
Appointments are not usually necessary, but you
must be ready to wait if you don't book. See also
parrucchieri and *estetiste* in the Yellow Pages.

Capelli Verdi
Via della Cisterna, 15 (06 581 8691).
Bus to Viale Trastevere. **Open** 10am-7pm Tue-Sat.
No credit cards. **Map 6/2B**
This salon, tucked away in a Trastevere backstreet,
uses only natural products. A cut and blowdry costs
L60,000, or L68,000 if you want henna treatment
thrown in. Men's haircuts cost L30,000.

Franco
Via Alessandro Volta, 18 (06 574 7817).
Bus to Via Marmorata. **Open** 8am-6.30pm Tue-Sat.
No credit cards. **Map 7/2A**

Franco spent years in the US, picking up basic
English without losing his Italian knack for effort-
less cuts. Wash, cut and blow-dry: L45,000. Massage,
Solarium and other beauty treatments also available.

Metamorfosi
*Via Giovanni Branca, 94 (06 574 7576). Bus to Via
Marmorata.* **Open** 9am-8pm Mon-Fri. Closed three
weeks Aug. **No credit cards**. **Map 7/2B**
This friendly no-frills neighbourhood beautician will
do you one of Rome's cheapest leg-waxes, plus mas-
sages, make-up and pampering of all sorts.

Locksmiths

Avoid the 24-hour emergency locksmiths under *fab-
bro* in the local Yellow Pages: their charges are little
short of robbery. Instead, go to a local hardware
shop (*ferramenta*) and ask if they can suggest anybody. If you're locked out of a house or flat at night,
call the fire brigade; to get into a locked car, call the
ACI (*see chapter* **Directory: Getting around**).

Opticians

Replacement lenses can usually be fitted
overnight; missing screws are dealt with on the
spot, often gracelessly but nearly always for free.
See also *ottica* in the Yellow Pages.

Capaldo Ottica
*Via delle Coppelle, 24 (06 687 7364). Bus to Corso
Vittorio Emanuele or Corso del Rinascimento.*
Open 4-8pm Mon; 9.30am-8pm Tue-Fri; 9.30am-1pm,
4-8pm, Sat. Closed two weeks Aug. **Credit** AmEx,
DC, EC, MC, V. **Map 3/1A**
Eye tests, designer specs and contact lenses.

Ottica Scientifica Tonel
*Via delle Convertite, 19/20 (06 679 2579). Bus to
Via del Corso or Piazza San Silvestro.* **Open** 3.30-
7.30pm Mon; 9.30am-1pm, 3.30-7.30pm, Tue-Sat.
Credit AmEx, DC, EC, MC, V. **Map 3/1A**
Eye tests, repairs, lenses, a big choice of glasses.

Photocopying

As well as specialised shops some *tabacchi* and sta-
tioners (*cartolerie*) will have photocopiers; as a rule,
however, give them a miss if you need crisp, clear
copies. In the streets around the university many
copy centres offer discounts to students.

D'Antimi

Viale Aventino, 73 (06 574 2084).
Bus to Viale Aventino. **Open** 8.30am- 1pm, 3.30-7pm,
Mon-Fri; 8.30am-1pm Sat.
Credit AmEx, DC, EC, MC, V. **Map 9/1C**
Reliable, high-standard photocopying of all shapes,
sizes and colours.

Xeromania

Viale Trastevere, 119 (06 581 4433). Bus to Viale
Trastevere. **Open** 9am-2pm, 3-7.30pm, Mon-Fri; 9am-
2pm Sat. **No credit cards. Map 7/1B**
An excellent general copy shop in Trastevere, which
also has a reliable fax sending and receiving service.

Photo developers

Film can be bought in specialist camera shops or
opticians'. See also *fotografia – sviluppo e stampa*
in the Yellow Pages.

Cocacolor

Via del Mascherino, 4-10 (06 687 9498).
Bus to Piazza Città Leonina or Piazza Risorgimento.
Open 8am-8pm Mon-Sat; 9am-6.30pm Sun.
Credit AmEx, DC, EC, MC, V. **Map 4/1B**
Two minutes' walk from Saint Peter's, Cocacolor
prepares large, glossy prints in an hour or two. More
expensive than most same-day services, but better
at the same time.

Fotocolor Lab

Piazza Buenos Aires, 20 (06 884 0670).
Bus to Via Po or Viale Regina Margherita.
Open 8.30am-1pm, 3.30-7pm, Mon-Fri. Closed two
weeks Aug. **Credit** MC, V. **Map 4/1A**
One of Rome's most respected professional
developers, Fotocolor Lab specialises in slides but
will do a good job on your colour prints as well.

Foto Express

Via delle Quattro Fontane, 7 (06 474 4278). Bus to
Piazza Barberini. **Open** 8am-7.30 daily. **Credit**
AmEx, DC, EC, MC, V. **Map 5/1B**
This one-hour service just off Piazza Barberini will
print up a 36-pic film for L24,000. Used and highly
regarded by many professional photographers.

Repairers

F Pratesi (Clinica della Borsa)

Piazza Firenze, 22 (06 6880 3720).
Bus to Via del Corso or Piazza San Silvestro. **Open**
9.30am-1pm, 3.30-7.30pm, Mon-Fri; 9.30am-1pm Sat.
Closed Aug. **No credit cards. Map 3/1A**
Specialises in repairing bags slit open by thieves.
Repairs take up to three days, and cost from L10,000.

Vecchia Sartoria

Via dei Banchi Vecchi, 19 (06 6830 7180).
Bus to Corso Vittorio Emanuele. **Open** 8am-1pm, 3-
7pm, Mon-Fri; 8am-1pm Sat. Closed three weeks Aug.
No credit cards. Map 3/2B
Run by a skilled traditional tailor and a seamstress,
who do clothing repairs quickly at reasonable prices.

Ticket agencies

Expect to pay *diritti di prevendita* (pre-sales
supplement) on tickets bought anywhere but at the
venue on the night. Branches of **Ricordi** (*see page
185*) sell concert tickets.

Orbis

Piazza Esquilino, 37 (06 482 7403). Bus to Via
Cavour or Piazza Esquilino. **Open** 9.30am-1pm, 4-
7.30pm, Mon-Fri. **No credit cards. Map 5/2A**
Tickets for most concerts, theatre and sporting events.

Travel agencies

See also *agenzie viaggi* in the Yellow Pages.

Centro Turistico Studentesco (CTS Student Travel Centre)

Via Genova, 16 (06 462 0431). Bus to Via
Nazionale. **Open** 9.30am-1pm, 2.30-7pm, Mon-Fri;
9.30am-1pm Sat. **Credit** MC, V. **Map 5/2B**
Student travel agency with discounts on air, rail and
coach tickets for all those in full-time education. CTS
services can also be used by non-students.
Branches: Corso Vittorio Emanuele, 297 (06 687
2672/3/4); Via degli Ausoni, 5 (06 445 0141).

Eurojet

Piazza della Repubblica, 54 (06 474 3980).
Metro Repubblica/bus to Piazza della Repubblica.
Open 9am-1pm, 2.30-6.30pm, Mon-Fri; 9am-12.30pm
Sat. **No credit cards. Map 5/2B**
Tickets for coach travel to most European cities.

Transalpino

Piazza Esquilino, 102 (06 487 0870). Bus to Piazza
Esquilino. **Open** 9am-6.30pm Mon-Fri; 9am-1pm Sat.
Credit AmEx, EC, MC. **Map 5/2A**
Discount rail tickets throughout Europe, and some
air tickets.
Branch: Termini station (06 488 0536).

Viaggi e vacanze

Via Laurina, 23 (06 321 9541). Metro Spagna/bus
to Via del Babuino. **Open** 9am-1pm, 2-6pm, Mon-Fri;
9am-1pm Sat. **Credit** AmEx, MC, V. **Map 2/2A**
Also known as American-Italian Lloyd, this agency
accepts credit card for rail as well as air tickets.
website: www.ginalmi.it

Video rental

The **Economy Book & Video Center** (*see page
171*) has over 2,000 English-language titles for
rent. Membership costs L50,000 a year. See also
noleggio videocassette in the Yellow Pages.

Videoteca Navona

Corso del Rinascimento, 13/15 (06 686 9823). Bus
to Corso del Rinascimento. **Open** 9am-8.30pm Mon-
Sat. **Credit** AmEx, MC, V. **Map 3/2A**
A huge selection of Italian and English-language
films. Lifetime membership costs L50,000 (or leave
a L50,000 deposit); L5,000 for a two-day rental.

Arts & Entertainment

Children

Its museums may be hands-off, but Rome's one big playground for inquisitive kids.

Paradox number one: Italy has the world's lowest birth rate – but you can't get away from kids, dressed up to the nines, running around restaurants, helping Daddy drive his Vespa. Paradox number two: Italy lets you take kids just about anywhere – and yet lays on very few facilities for them.

A visit to Rome with offspring in tow will bring you right up against these contradictions. Nobody will mind if you take your five-year-old to the opera, but you won't be able to barter good behaviour against a trip to a children's farm, because there aren't any. As for museums, Rome's are mostly of the hands-off variety.

For all that, there is no reason why your children should not have the time of their life in Rome. The key to their enjoyment is careful preparation; a children's guidebook to Ancient Rome, or to the myths and legends it generated can be the key to a successful family holiday (*see page 193* **Books**). And if all else fails, there are beautiful parks, and some of the world's most glorious ice cream (*see chapter* **Ice Cream**).

For further information, look in *Time Out Roma* under *Bambini*, *Roma C'e* under *Children's Corner*, or the *Trovaroma* supplement with Thursday's *La Repubblica* under *Città dei Ragazzi*. All in Italian, but quite easy to follow. *See also chapter* **Media**.

Telefono Azzurro

(19 696). **Open** 24 hours daily.
A freephone helpline for children and young people with child abuse problems (normally Italian-speaking only).

Transport

Most of the city centre is walkable with kids, which is just as well, as other transport options can be tricky. Buses are often crowded, so moving kids and/or a pushchair can be a major hassle. The 30b tram route, which runs from Piramide to the Villa Borghese, can be made into quite an adventure if trams are a novelty, and ends up conveniently close to the zoo. The stuffy Metro is limited in scope, and best avoided during rush hours.

On all city transport the **metre rule** applies: kids up to a metre tall go free. Above that, you need to get a full-price ticket for them.

Sightseeing with kids

Unire l'utile con il dilettevole (mix business with pleasure), Italians will tell you, and in Rome this advice goes a long way. With museums making few concessions to kids, and the majority of churches sure to bore the pants off your offspring, take ten minutes out to plan your visit. With a little swotting up on Roman history, you should be able to find (or failing that, invent) a fascinating fact or two to interest kids at each landmark. And when boredom sets in, it's good to know which park or *gelateria* is nearby.

If you're craving an hour or two of Renaissance art at the **Palazzo Barberini** (*see page 68*) or *Galleria Borghese* (*see page 66*), you should meet with little resistance: both are well-situated for a picnic in **Villa Borghese**, where you can while away the non-cultural part of your day by hiring bikes or a rowing boat on the artificial lake.

Due to open half a kilometre from the Villa Borghese sometime in 2000 is Rome's long-awaited Children's Museum (**Museo dei Bambini** *Via Flaminia, 80 (06 3600 5488). Bus to Via Flaminia. Website: www.mdbr.it*), where kids up to age 12 will be able to explore all the workings of a realistic play-city, from plumbing and car maintenance to commerce and communications. Also nearby is the **Immacolata Concezione** church (*see page 65*), where the bones of some 4,000 late lamented Capuchin monks have been tastefully arranged on the walls of five chapels.

Other churches might also appeal to your kids' sense of the macabre and wierd. Frescoes in **Santo Stefano Rotondo** (*see page 89*) depict martyrs being boiled in oil, devoured by dogs and other occupational hazards of the early Church. Just down the road, you can admire the frescoes and mosaics in **San Clemente** (*see page 86*) while junior travellers revel in the mystery of the place. Dark stairs descend through several layers of civilization, until you get a glimpse of the **Cloaca Maxima**, Rome's first sewer system, where the water still rushes noisily down to the Tiber.

San Clemente is a short walk from the Colosseum (*see page 40*) where even the most culture-weary of youngsters will love tales of gladiatorial gore (*see page 11*). To make the visit memorable, there are always self-styled centurions wandering about in full regalia who are happy to pose with kids for a couple of thousand lire.

The inevitable next stop is the **Roman Forum** (*see page 41*), where there's a high risk of kids' refusing point blank to waste time looking at what seem to be just heaps of stone. Don't make matters worse recounting that the Basilica Aemilia was built by censors Marcus Aemilius Lepidus and Marcus Fulvius Nobilior in 179 BC: they'll be chasing pigeons before the end of the sentence. Instead, point out the marks left by the coins that melted in the great fire which destroyed the building in AD 410, and you might grab their attention.

If this sounds like too much homework, invest in one of the tacky 'then and now' guidebooks on sale from the many souvenir stalls around the area. Finish your visit with a picnic on the **Palatine** (*see page 43*) and maybe a game of hide and seek among the remains of walls and aqueducts.

The **Vatican** (*see pages 103-110*) will be high on the list of adult priorities. Spice things up for children with a trip up the dome of **Saint Peter's**, from where you can peer down into the basilica or take in the sweeping views over the city outside. Note that carrying a toddler up into the dome is only recommended for the very fit. In the **Vatican Museums**, children may prefer the huge painted sixteenth-century maps and globes to the overwhelming crowds in the Sistine Chapel. The less crowded **Egyptian Museum** is full of grisly mummies and lush sarcophagi.

A surprise in each itinerary goes down well: the giant marble hands and feet in the courtyard of the **Capitoline Museums** (*see page 36-7*); the single huge marble foot at the beginning of Via Santo Stefano di Cacco, just off Piazza del Collegio Romano; the obelisk-bearing elephant in **Piazza della Minerva** (*see page 56*); and the charming **Fontana delle Tartarughe** (*see page 38*) in the Ghetto. And there's always coin-throwing at the **Fontana di Trevi** (*see page 55*).

Though most of Rome's museums take a dim view of kids' tactile explorations, there are a few that have enticing bits for junior. **Castel Sant'Angelo** (*see page 96*) is a historic pope-bunker full of passageways, turrets and dungeons, and the **Museo del Folklore** (*see page 75*) has fun waxwork tableaux and other exhibits depicting ordinary life in Rome in the last century. The **Centrale Montemartini** (*see **Capitoline Museums**, page 36*) holds Sunday morning drawing workshops for kids among its gleaming machinery and classical statues. When real antiquities bore your children, show them plaster versions of how it looked before the rot set in: the **Museo della Civiltà Romana** (*see page 101*) in EUR contains huge scale models of ancient Rome. It's also conveniently close to **Luna Park** and the **Piscina delle Rose** swimming pool (*see below*).

Martially-inclined kids will enjoy playing at ancient Roman soldiers along the stretch of Aurelian wall accessed from the **Museo delle Mura** (*see page 93*). And if air traffic controllers ever turn your homewards trip into a nightmare, try taking a ten-minute walk from Fiumicino airport to the nearby **Museo delle Navi Romane** (*Via Guidoni, 36, Fiumicino (06 652 9192); closed*

Swings & roundabouts

As you flounder with your peevish offspring through the urban labyrinth of historic Rome, you may be disinclined to believe that the city has a higher percentage of green areas than any other European capital. It does, though, and if you know where to look, a shady tree and/or swing is usually at hand.

If you're anywhere in the *Centro storico* or *Tridente* and it's grass and trees you're after, **Villa Borghese** (*see pages 66-7*) is your best bet: there are bikes to hire, boats to row, and swings and a climbing frame at the Via delle Belle Arti entrance. A couple of laps of the **Circus Maximus** (*see page 40*) will also sort out excess energy problems. In **Trastevere** the **Orto Botanico** (*see page 75*) is a quiet, lush bolthole, but offers nothing in the way of play equipment. For this, head up to the **Gianicolo** (*see page 75*), where there are pony rides and bumper cars. Beyond the Gianicolo to the west are the **Villa Pamphili**, with 184 hectares of parklands, and the charming **Villa Sciarra (Map 7/1C)**, with a well-equipped playground and a mini-roller coaster among rose beds.

Monti & Esquilino are off-puttingly built-up at first glance, but the **Villa Aldobrandini** (*see page 83*), on a terrace at the south-western end of Via Nazionale, the tiny haven in **Via Piacenza (Map 5/2B)** and the gardens hidden at the centre of **Piazza Vittorio Emanuele (Map 8/1A)** offer some respite. The **Aventine, Celio & Testaccio** abound with green. **Villa Celimontana** (*see page 95*) has swings and climbing frames galore, and there's a roller-skating track in the **Parco della Rimembranza (Map 7/2A)** near Porta San Paolo. High on the Aventine, you can survey the city skyline as your kids romp in the delightful **Giardino degli Aranci (Map 7/1A)**.

On Sunday, the **Via dei Fori Imperiali (Map 8/1-2C)** and the **Via Appia Antica** (*see page 102*) become car-free zones. Along the former, you'll find stiltwalkers, small theatre ensembles, one-person shows, dance performances, musical groups and clowns, and it's all free, though the hat gets passed after every show. The Via Appia offers the closest thing to a quiet country lane you'll find near central Rome.

Mon), where kids can see (in model form) what Roman ships were really like.

Out of town

The best child-oriented sights within reasonable distance of Rome are the bizarre Renaissance **Sacro Bosco** or *Parco dei Mostri* – Monster Park – at **Bomarzo**, huge scary sculptures that kids can climb in and on, and the fountains and cascades of Tivoli's **Villa D'Este** and nearby Hadrian's Villa for picnics. In **Bracciano**, the **Castello Orsini-Odescalchi** makes an interesting trip, with its many suits of armour and sixteenth-century loos. **Lago di Bracciano** and its smaller neighbour **Lago di Martignano** both have decent beaches and fairly clean water. The water on the coast near Rome is not the cleanest, but is, they say, improving each year; there are many beach clubs at **Ostia** or **Fregene**, and miles of sand at **Castelporziano**. For all places mentioned, *see chapter* **Trips out of Town**).

Walking tours

If you're in a group, or are willing to pay for a personalised tour, there are many cultural associations in Rome that offer in-depth information about a given area or museum, often complete with historical anecdotes that make dry facts more palat-

able for children. English-speaking guides can be found through **Gente e Paesi** *(06 8530 1755)* or **La Serliana** *(06 3972 0252)*, which specialises in children's tours.

Entertainment

For the **Bioparco** zoo and the **Museo di Zoologia**, *see page 67*.

Biblioteca Centrale per i Ragazzi (Central Children's Library)
Via San Paolo alla Regola, 16 (06 686 5116).
Bus or tram to Largo Argentina or via Arenula.
Open *Nov-mid-June* 9am-7pm Tue-Fri, 9am-1pm Sat; *mid-June-Sept* 9.30am-5pm Tue-Thur. Closed three weeks Aug. **Map 6/1B**
The library has a selection of English, French, German and Spanish books for tinies, and plans to offer an international range for older kids too. Non-residents can use the library, but not borrow books. From mid-June, and for most of the summer, the library moves to a park: call for information.

Luna Park (LUNEUR)
Via delle Tre Fontane (06 592 5933).
Metro Magliana/bus to Via delle Tre Fontane.
Open *Oct-Apr* 3-8pm Mon, Wed-Fri; 3pm-1am Sat; 10am-1pm, 3pm-10pm, Sun; *May-Sept* 5pm-1am Mon-Fri; 5pm-2am Sat; 10am- 1am Sun. **Admission** free; rides L1,000-5,000 each.

Rome's funfair is 30 years old, and it shows, but it's saved by the sheer theatricality of the rides and exhibits. There's a very respectable roller coaster, two haunted houses, a hall of mirrors, and boat, car and pony rides for smaller children.

Acquapiper

Via Maremmana Inferiore, km 29, Guidonia (0774 326 538). Metro to Ponte Mammolo, then COTRAL bus to Palombara/by car SS5 (Tivoli road) then SS5ter to Guidonia. **Open** *mid May-mid Sept* 9am-6pm Mon-Fri; 9am-7pm Sat, Sun.
Admission L15,000 adults entering before 2pm Mon-Fri; L20,000 adults entering after 2pm Mon-Fri; L20,000 adults entering before 2pm Sat, Sun; L17,500 adults entering after 2pm Sat, Sun; L15,000 4-10s; free under-4s. **Credit** AmEx, DC, MC, V.

This water park is off the road from Rome to Tivoli, and so can be combined with a trip to Villa Adriana or the Villa D'Este. It boasts a small children's pool with a tortoise waterslide, plus kamikaze slides and a wave machine for older ones. There are picnic areas, a restaurant and banks of video games too.

Piscina delle Rose

*Viale America 20 (06 592 6717).
Metro EUR Palasport/bus to Viale Europa.* **Open** *mid June-end Sept* 9am-7pm daily. **Admission** L18,000; L13,000 9am-2pm or 2-7pm only; L7,000 1-4pm only; free children under 1 metre tall.

A child-friendly pool and so apt to get a bit crowded, especially in the afternoon.

Gearing up for driving Daddy's truck.

Puppeteers and theatre

Italy's long and glorious puppet tradition centres on Sicily and Naples, but Rome also offers decent shows. Theatres open and close all the time, but two stalwarts remain that claim to be the only real *burattinai* (puppeteers) left. One is on the Gianicolo, run by Mr. Piantadosi and identifiable by the sign *Non Tirate Sassi!* (Don't throw Stones!). The other is in Largo K. Ataturk, EUR, near a Giolitti ice cream emporium. Both serve up Pulcinella, just as violent and mysogynistic as his English descendant Mr Punch, and deliver it in a Neapolitan accent so thick that most local kids understand it no better than foreigners do: it's the whacks on the head that count anyway.

Teatro Verde

*Circonvallazione Gianicolense, 10 (06 588 2034).
Bus or tram to Stazione Trastevere.* **Open** mid-Oct-end Apr. **Shows** 5pm Sat, Sun.
The best-known children's theatre in Rome, Teatro Verde offers puppets and acted plays in Italian. Visit the costume and prop workshop half an hour before the curtain goes up. Booking advisable.

Books

The English-language *Ancient Rome for Kids*, on sale in Feltrinelli bookshops (*see page 170*), gives succinct explanations of major sites, illustrated with drawings of Roman kids doing what kids did in ancient Rome. Or before you set out, pick up any of the following: Usborne's *Who Were the Romans?* for kids of six and up; The Usborne *Pocket Guide to Ancient Rome* for slightly older children; and, if your child fancies practising her language skills, The *Usborne Guide to Italian* is a phrase book for eight to 11 year-olds.

Babysitters/childcare

Higher-range hotels have their own babysitting services, and all but the most basic hotels will arrange a babysitter for you.

Angels

Vicolo del Babuino, 7 (06 3600 1724/0338 667 9718). **Rates** L10,000-L12,000 per hour.
Tried and tested English-speaking babysitters are provided by Brit Rebecca, who will also find nannies and domestic staff for longer-term visitors.

United Babies

Piazza Nicoloso da Recco, 9 (06 589 9481/06 575 9543). Bus or tram to Viale Aventino.
Rates vary depending on attendance.
American Lucy Gardner runs this bilingual playgroup for kids aged from about one to three years. Short-term stays can be arranged. Activities run from 8am-2.30pm, after which there is an optional babysitting service at L10,000 an hour until 6pm. Hot lunches provided. Closes in August.

Contemporary Art

Nice galleries: but if it's art you're after, try Milan or Turin.

If you're planning to use a trip to Rome to catch up on latest developments in the Italian art scene, prepare to be disappointed. Evidence of burgeoning creativity is more likely to be found in Milan, Turin and, lately, Naples or Venice. That said, many of Rome's 200-plus contemporary art galleries are hidden away in beautiful historic buildings and streets that are attractions in their own right.Also, the opening in 1999 of a huge and decidedly adventurous public exhibition space – the **Galleria Comunale d'Arte Moderna e Contemporanea ex-Birreria Peroni** in Nomentana (*see page 97*) – may help inject a bit of life into Rome's languid contemporary art scene.

Admission to the galleries below is free unless otherwise stated. If you use a wheelchair, it pays to ring before setting out: many of the private galleries listed are on upper floors with no lifts.

Art Gallery Banchi Nuovi

*Via Margutta, 29 (06 3265 0316).
Metro Spagna, Flaminio/ bus to Piazza del Popolo.* **Open** 4-8pm Mon; 10am-1pm, 4-8pm, Tue-Sat.
Closed July-Aug. **Map 2/2A**
This gallery consistently shows new artists, although its often hectic programme reveals a predilection for metaphysically inspired magic realism that is not to everybody's taste.

Associazione Culturale L'Attico

*Via del Paradiso, 41 (06 686 9846).
Bus to Corso Vittorio Emanuele.* **Open** 5-8pm Mon-Sat. Closed Aug. **Map 6/1B**
One of the most innovative galleries in Rome, a starting-point for new artists and a place for known names to introduce new directions in their work.

Associazione Culturale Sala 1

*Piazza di Porta San Giovanni, 10 (06 700 8691).
Metro San Giovanni/bus to Piazza San Giovanni in Laterano.* **Open** 5-8pm Tue-Sat.
Closed July, Aug. **Map 8/2A**
Sala 1 opened in 1970, and specialises in the international avant-garde. In 1998 it presented a show of Joyce-inspired Irish artists.

Associazione Culturale
Valentina Moncada

Via Margutta, 54 (06 320 7956). Metro Spagna/bus to Piazza del Popolo. **Open** 4-8pm Mon-Fri. Closed two weeks July, Aug, one week Sept. **Map 2/2A**
This picturesque garden conceals a series of purpose-built nineteenth-century artists' studios. Wagner, Liszt and Fortuny visited. It now specialises in the work of radical young artists.

Galleria Emanuela Oddi Baglioni

Via Gregoriana, 34 (06 679 7906). Metro Spagna/ bus to Via del Tritone. **Open** 10am-1pm, 4-7.30pm, Mon-Fri; *by appointment* 10am-1pm Sat .
Closed Aug. **Map 5/1C**
Mainly non-figurative Italian sculpture since 1960; the owners act as agents for young sculptors.

Galleria Gian Enzo Sperone

Via di Pallacorda, 15 (06 689 3525). Bus to Piazza San Silvestro. **Open** 4-8pm Mon; 10am-1pm, 4-8pm, Tue-Sat. Closed Aug, & Sat in June-Sept. **Map 3/1A**
Sperone is one of Rome's most prestigious art promoters, with a gallery in New York. He now frequently holds unusual, experimental shows.

Galleria Giulia

Via Giulia, 148 (06 6880 2061). Bus to Lungotevere dei Tebaldi. **Open** 4-8pm Mon; 10am-1pm, 4-8pm, Tue-Sat. Closed July-mid-Sept. **Map 3/2B**
Has carved a niche for itself with shows by New Pop artists, German Expressionists and Italian contemporary artists. Strong in graphic arts and sculpture.

Galleria Ugo Ferranti

Via dei Soldati, 25a(06 6880 2146). Bus to Corso Vittorio Emanuele or Corso del Rinascimento. **Open** *Nov-Mar* 11am-1pm, 5-8pm, Tue-Sat; *Apr-Oct* 10am-1pm, 4-8pm, Mon-Fri. Closed Aug. **Map 3/1B**
American and European conceptual art: owner Ferranti is constantly on the look-out for new artists.

Opera Paese Ex-Lanificio Luciani

Via di Pietralata, 157 (06 450 3797). Metro Pietralata, then bus to Piazza Sempione. **Open** 10.30am-1pm, 4-6.30pm, Mon-Fri. Closed two weeks July; Aug. **Admission** L3,000 (annual membership).
This converted industrial space in Rome's eastern outskirts is well worth a visit. It offers a cultural programme that includes concerts and seminars.

Stefania Miscetti

Via delle Mantellate, 14 (06 6880 5880). Bus to Lungotevere della Farnesina. **Open** *Oct-Apr* 4-8pm Tue-Sat; *May, June* 4-8pm Mon-Fri. Closed usually July-Sept, but ring to check. **Map 6/1C**
In a warehouse in Trastevere, this gallery holds unusual shows of sculpture and installations.

Studio d'Arte Contemporanea
Pino Casagrande

Via degli Ausoni, 7a (06 446 3480). Bus or tram to Via dei Reti or Piazza del Verano. **Open** 5-8pm Mon-Fri. Closed July 15–Sept 15.
In the hip area of San Lorenzo, Casagrande's loft-like exhibition space hosts some of Rome's most challenging exhibitions.

Film

Despite Benigni-fever, Rome's better at showing films than making them.

It's curious that a city so steeped in old media – marble, fresco, bronze, paint – should lend itself quite so readily to celluloid. But the Roman taste for theatre, from the chariot race to the baroque funeral, has been carried over intact into the dream factory. Only hardline historical purists manage to keep films like *La Dolce Vita*, *Ben Hur* or *Roman Holiday* from clouding their experience of the city. And the dirty realism of De Sica (*Bicycle Thieves*) or early Pasolini (*Accattone*) do nothing to dispel the myth: they simply add the run-down outer suburbs to our cinematic *caput mundi*.

These days, though, Rome is better at showing films than making them.

HOLLYWOOD ON THE TIBER

In 1999, for the first time ever, an Italian film picked up three Oscars. It would be wrong, though, to take the success of Roberto Benigni's Holocaust tearjerker comedy *La vita è bella* (*Life is Beautiful*) as a sign that Italian cinema is about to return to the glory days of the 1950s and '60s. The Academy plaudits arguably had as much to do with the energetic promotion of the film by US distributor Miramax as they did with Benigni's directorial finesse. Few would claim that *La vita è bella* is in the same league as earlier Italian Oscar winners such as Vittorio De Sica's *Ladri di biciclette* or Federico Fellini's *La strada*.

Nowadays, the famed Cinecittà studios in Rome's south-eastern suburbs work as much for television as on feature films. Domestic production averages out at around 100 films a year – a good third of which are so low-budget (and so dire) that they never make it onto a cinema screen. Crowd-pleaser sentimental comedies by actor-directors like Benigni or his fellow Tuscan Leonardo Pieraccioni take the lion's share of audiences, while serious dramatic fare tends to be restricted to a small but loyal arthouse following.

The nineties have also seen the death of those Italian genre films – whether Spaghetti Westerns or B-movie horror flicks – that tided cinema professionals over until the next 'serious' project. It is worth remembering that the most successful Italian film of all time was not a classic like *La Dolce Vita* or *Mamma Roma*, but the Spaghetti Western *They Call Me Trinity* by EB Clucher – pseudonym of director Enzo Barboni – which was seen in 220 countries.

MOVIEGOING IN ROME

Although the Cinecittà studios are no longer the home of a thriving, internationally respected local film industry, Italians are increasingly enthusiastic moviegoers. Rome especially has seen a picture palace renaissance in recent years: between 1993 and 1998 the number of screens in the city more than doubled, and audiences have kept pace.

This has been due partly to the conversion of older cinemas into two- or three-screen miniplexes, but also thanks to the creation of new, modern cinemas, especially in the outer suburbs. At the beginning of 1999 the city's first true multiplex opened – the 18-screen **Warner Village** in Parco de' Medici. Despite its location – almost halfway to Fiumicino airport – this US-style entertainment temple, complete with pizzeria, bar and shopping mall, is always packed with young Romans.

The Warner Village has driven yet another wedge into Italy's traditional cinema ownership duopoly. The Cecchi Gori Group and Silvio Berlusconi's Fininvest empire no longer have a stranglehold over the market; alongside international parvenus like the Warner group, more arthouse-oriented independents have also sprung up in recent years. The *Circuito Cinema* chain now controls six first-run outlets around the city, all of which offer a relief from Hollywood blockbusters and/or domestic comedies: the **Greenwich**, the **Intrastevere**, the **Nuovo Olimpia** and the **Quattro Fontane** (*all listed below*), two others, the Archimede and Mignon, plus the **Pasquino** English-language cinema and **Labirinto** cineclub. And there's always the **Nuovo Sacher** in Trastevere – owned by cult director Nanni Moretti, this first-run independent wears its cineaste credentials on its sleeve .

The downside is in the dubbing. Italian dubbers are widely recognised to be the best in the world, but that's no consolation for anyone who likes to hear films in the original language (*versione originale* – abbreviated as *V.O.* in publicity and newspaper listings). Anything that moves is dubbed, and subtitles are virtually unheard-of. There are now two permanent English-language cinemas – the recently spruced-up Pasquino and the Cecchi Gori-owned **Quirinetta**. At time of writing, though, only two other cinemas – the Alcazar and Nuovo Sacher – have a regular policy of showing their current films in *lingua originale* – both on

Monday. In addition, the Nuovo Olimpia often shows cinema classics in the original language, depending on the availability of a print.

Most of the *prima visione* (first-run) cinemas concentrate on fairly mainstream material; more varied and adventurous programmes can be found at the *cinema d'essai* (roughly, art cinemas) and cine clubs. For a standard 90-minute film, the four daily screenings will invariably be at 4.30, 6.30, 8.30 and 10.30pm; the box-office generally opens half an hour before the first showing. Credit card payment is still a rarity.

Summer is the time when all Rome closes, and cinemas have traditionally been no exception. Nowadays, most mainstream cinemas stay open all year, but many cinemas and most cine clubs still close completely in July and August. Compensation is found in the open-air cinemas and festivals around the city (*see page 199*).

The best source for information on what's on at any of the cinemas in Rome, including summer venues, is the local section of the daily newspapers *La Repubblica* and *Il Messaggero*.

First-run cinemas

All first-run cinemas offer lower prices for the first two screenings on Monday, Tuesday, Thursday and Friday – generally at 4.30 and 6.30 – and all day Wednesday. In 1999 this was pegged at L8,000 (L10,000 for some screens, like the Warner Village).

Alcazar
Via Cardinal Merry del Val, 14 (06 588 0099). Bus or tram to Viale Trastevere. **Tickets** L13,000; *reductions* L8,000. 210 seats. **Map 6/2B**
A red plush jewel, and one of the first major Rome cinemas to screen its current film in the original language (generally English) on Mondays. For the last two showings it's wise to book ahead (tickets must be picked up 30 minutes beforehand).
Air-conditioning. Disabled: wheelchair access.

Dei Piccoli
Viale della Pineta, 15, Villa Borghese (06 855 3485).Metro Spagna/bus to Porta Pinciana. **Tickets** L7,000 afternoon showings Mon-Fri; L8,000 evenings, afternoon showings Sat, Sun. 63 seats. **Map 4/2B**
Built in 1934 as a children's theatre in the Villa Borghese park, the tiny, beautifully restored Dei Piccoli now presents a selection of children's films (in Italian only) each afternoon. In the evening it shows independent first-run films; it also stages occasional themed seasons with offerings from the Italian Film Archives.
Air-conditioning. Disabled: wheelchair access.

Greenwich
Via Giovanni Battista Bodoni, 59 (06 574 5825). Metro Piramide/bus to Via Marmorata or Via Zabaglia. **Tickets** L13,000; *reductions* L8,000. Sala 1: 220 seats; Sala 2: 150 seats; Sala 3: 60 seats. **Map 7/2B**

A three-screen house in an anonymous residential street in trendy Testaccio, the 'Green-witch', as locals call it, is extremely popular with younger Romans. It's strong on Italian and international art-house films. There is also a small bar.
Air-conditioning. Disabled: wheelchair access, toilets.

Intrastevere
Vicolo Moroni, 3a (06 588 4230). Bus to Ponte Sisto. **Tickets** L13,000; *reductions* L8,000. Sala 1: 210 seats; Sala 2: 120 seats; Sala 3: 35 seats. **Map 6/2B**
In a seventeenth-century palazzo in a Trastevere backstreet, this three-screen arthouse outlet specialises in European and American independents. It occasionally screens its ongoing films in *lingua originale* on Mondays – but ring to check.
Air-conditioning. Disabled: wheelchair access, toilets.

Nuovo Olimpia
Via in Lucina, 16g (06 686 1086).
Bus to Via del Corso or Piazza San Silvestro.
Tickets L12,000; *reductions/cinema classics* L8,000.
Sala 1: 260 seats; Sala 2: 93 seats. **Map 3/1A**
The Nuovo Olimpia is in a lane just off Via del Corso. It alternates Italian and foreign independents in its Sala 1 with restored cinema classics in Sala 2. The latter change every week, are often shown in *lingua originale*, and are offered at a lower price of L8,000.
Air-conditioning. Disabled: wheelchair access, toilets.

Nuovo Sacher
Largo Ascianghi, 1 (06 581 8116).
Bus or tram to Viale Trastevere. **Tickets** L13,000;
reductions L8,000. 360 seats. **Map 7/1B**
The Nuovo Sacher is owned and run by film director Nanni Moretti, who bought it out of irritation at the poor state of film distribution in Rome. It has become a meeting place for local cinematic talent, and makes an effort to support independent Italian filmmakers – with initiatives such as a short-film festival in July, in the open-air arena alongside the cinema – as well as presenting strong art-house titles from abroad on long runs (Ken Loach, Iranian director Abbas Kiarostami and, of course, Moretti's own films are firm favourites). Films are usually shown in VO on Mondays and Tuesdays.
Air-conditioning. Disabled: wheelchair access, toilets.

Pasquino
Piazza Sant'Egidio, 10 (06 580 3622).
Bus or tram to Viale Trastevere. **Tickets** *Sala 1* L12,000; *Sala 2 & 3* (Pasquino Club) L8,000 Mon-Fri; L10,000 Sat, Sun, with L2,000 membership card (valid two months). Screen 1: 165 seats; Screen 2 (Pasquino Club): 80 seats; Screen 3: (Pasquino Club): 50 seats. **Map 6/2B**
Rome's historic English language-cinema used to be a fleapit with dodgy sound, but a 1998 refurbishment has turned it into a modern cinema with dodgy sound. It has a rare talent for choosing just the film you don't want to see – but the opening of two new video-projection screens (the so-called 'Pasquino Club') means that the occasional gem does appear. Programmes change each Friday.
Air-conditioning. Disabled: wheelchair access .

On location in Campo de' Fiori.

Quattro Fontane

Via Quattro Fontane, 23 (06 474 1515).
Bus to Via Nazionale. **Tickets** L13,000; *reductions*
L8,000. Sala 1: 350 seats; Sala 2: 200 seats;
Sala 3: 140 seats; Sala 4: 70 seats. **Map 5/2B**
The showcase miniplex of new indie distribution
cartel *Circuito Cinema*, the Quattro Fontane is a
designer cinema with state-of-the-art sound system
and a small bar in the foyer. Small domestic indies
often get their only Italian run in Sala 4.
Air-conditioning. Disabled: wheelchair access, toilets.

Quirinetta

Via M. Minghetti, 4 (06 679 0012). Bus to Via del
Corso or Piazza San Silvestro. **Tickets** L13,000;
reductions L8,000. 366 seats. **Map 5/2C**
A large, old-fashioned movie house that the Cecchi
Gori group has offered up as an English-language
cinema, in competition with the historic **Pasquino**.
The schedule depends on what American titles
Cecchi Gori happen to be distributing at the time.
Air conditioning.

Warner Village

Viale del Parco dei Medici, 135 (info & phone
bookings 06 6585 5111). Train (Tiburtina-Ostiense-
Trastevere to Fiumicino line) to Muratella, then 10
min. walk. **Tickets** L14,000; *reductions* L10,000. 18
screens, varying from 140 to 386 seats.
When this temple to the American Way of
Moviegoing opened in early 1999, Rome leapfrogged
from having not a single multiplex worth the name
to having one of the largest in Europe. The 18
screens mean that you can turn up just about any
time between 1pm and 10.30pm (earlier and later at

weekends) and choose from among the films
starting in the next half hour; there's also a bar, a
restaurant, shops, and plenty of Warner Bros
merchandising. But the location – on the airport side
of Rome's southern sprawl – and poor public transport links make your own wheels a near necessity.
Air conditioning. Car park. Disabled: wheelchair
access, toilets.

Cinema d'Essai & Cineclubs

Cinema d'essai are generally small and cheap, and
feature mainly classics or prestige contemporary
cinema, often in *versione originale*. It is in these cinemas and the still smaller cine clubs that the full
range of international cinema and the best of the
Italian cinema heritage can be seen. All are private
ventures, except the **Palazzo delle Esposizioni**,
the municipal arts centre. Some clubs also re-
screen films that suffered from truncated first
releases. Some *centri sociali* (*see chapter* **Music:**
Rock, Roots & Jazz) also offer screenings of
alternative or difficult-to-see films. A membership
card (*tessera*) is required by many clubs, but they
can be bought at the door for a minimal charge.

L'Arsenale

Via Giano della Bella, 45 (06 4470 0084).
Metro Bologna/bus to Piazza delle Province. **Tickets**
L5,000, with annual membership card (L7,000). 70
seats. Closed June-Sept.
A student-run film club near the University,
L'Arsenale organises regular original-language
screenings: ring for information.

On location

'Vieni, Marcello, vieni!'. Anyone trying to do an impromptu remake of the most famous scene from *La dolce vita*, in which Anita Ekberg and Marcello Mastroianni get wet in the Trevi Fountain, is almost certain to be arrested by the resident policeman. Nevertheless, Rome is still full of classic locations for film pilgrims. You could walk the following list, but for the full Roman effect, do it by Vespa (for hire companies, *see chapter* **Directory**).

Within the Walls

Stazione Termini

Most hours of the day and night Termini station is a scene of barely-controlled chaos, enclosed within an architectural frame of rationalist purity. This feeling is nowhere better encapsulated than in the long dolly shot at the end of Fellini's *Ginger and Fred* (1986).

Via Veneto

These days, the street made famous by Fellini's *La dolce vita* (1960) is full of big hotels, offices and sad nightclubs frequented by men with toupées. Of the cafés, the **Doney**, inside at least, still has something of the old glamour; the **Café de Paris** (once the paparazzi's favourite hangout) has lost it (for both, *see p160*). Fellini never filmed here

anyway; the whole thing was reconstructed at Cinecittà.

Via Margutta

This pretty lane between Piazza di Spagna and Piazza del Popolo is now full of art galleries, antique shops and high-rent flats, but in the 1950s its denizens and prices still verged on the bohemian. It was here, at number 51, that Gregory Peck had his bachelor flat, the compact size of which so charmed princess-on-the-lam Audrey Hepburn in William Wyler's *Roman Holiday* (1953). 'Is this the elevator?' she asked; 'This is my room', he replied.

Trevi Fountain

It was a night in the middle of March, 1959, and it was freezing. Anita really did wade into the fountain in her evening gown, as a huddle of bemused locals and theatre returnees looked on. Fellini liked to film with an audience: he turned his megaphone on them and said, 'Where would you find another woman like this? I've made her do things a circus horse wouldn't do. And now I'm going to throw her into the water.'

Piazza Venezia

Possibly the ugliest building of all time, the **Vittoriale** monument that dominates the piazza, was used by Peter Greenaway in *The Belly of an*

Azzurro Scipioni

Via degli Scipioni, 8 (06 3973 7161) Metro Lepanto/bus to Via Marcantonio Colonna. **Tickets** *Sala Chaplin* L10,000, *Sala Lumière* L10,000, for monthly *tessera*. Sala Chaplin: 130 seats; Sala Lumière: 60 seats. **Map 2/2C**

Best-known of the *d'essai* cinemas, with two screens: the Sala Chaplin, showing more recent art-house successes, and Sala Lumière, with a video projector, devoted to cinema classics and themed seasons. Run by director Silvio Agosti. By a house rule, streetsweepers get in free.

Detour

Via Urbana, 47a (06 487 2368). Metro Cavour/bus to Santa Maria Maggiore. **Tickets** L6,000 with membership card (L2,000). **Map 5/2B**

A small but committed cineclub near Santa Maria Maggiore, with an eclectic programme alternating cinema classics, world cinema, shorts, and more. *Disabled: wheelchair access.*

Grauco

Via Perugia, 34, Prenestino (78 24 167). Bus or tram to Piazzale Prenestino. **Membership** L10,000 per year (includes one ticket). **Tickets** L5,000-L8,000. 35 seats.

The tiny Grauco concentrates on powerful independent cinema from around the world, often in *versione originale*, with a particular day of the week often devoted to one country. On Saturday and Sunday afternoons kids' classics are screened (in Italian). Films are usually shown at 7pm and 9pm.

Labirinto

Via Pompeo Magno, 27 (32 16 283). Metro Lepanto/bus to Via Giulio Cesare. **Open** box office 6pm, last show 10.30pm, daily. Closed Aug. **Membership** L3,000 per year (Sept-Sept). **Tickets** L9,000. Sala A: 100 seats; Sala B: 60 seats; Sala C: 45 seats. **Map 2/2B**

A three-screen complex, old but comfortable, which usually shows re-runs of the best of the previous season's releases. Films are rarely in VO. *Air-conditioning.*

Palazzo delle Esposizioni

Via Nazionale, 194 (06 488 5465). Metro Repubblica/bus to Via Nazionale. **Open** 10am-9pm Mon, Wed-Sun. **Admission** (per day, to whole arts centre) L15,000, students and OAPs L8,000. 200 seats. **Map 5/2B**

Mainly a venue for large-scale art exhibitions (*see p69*), the Palazzo is also a popular meeting-place for

Architect (1987) as an allegorical 'machine for viewing Rome'. (The *Belly* by the Pantheon, *above*). Next door in the Piazza del Campidoglio is the place where the alienated academic of Tarkovsky's *Nostalgia* (1983) sets fire to himself, a reaction some of those who have seen the film may feel a certain sympathy with.

Further afield

Via Montecuccoli

It's now an anonymous and not especially down-at-heel residential street between Piazzale Prenestina and the railway tracks. But in the 1940s this was frontierland, the working-class edge of town; it was here (at number 17) that the Anna Magnani character lived in Rossellini's stirring *Roma città aperta* (1945), and here that she was gunned down by the German soldiers who were taking her son away – one of the Italian cinema's most memorable images.

Via Tuscolana

Another Anna Magnani location. Pasolini's *Mamma Roma* (1962) – which features the actress as yet another proletarian Mother Courage – was set in this tough area of tenements. The contrast between the hand-to-mouth existence of the families who lived here just after the war and the illusions turned out in the nearby dream factory of Cinecittà was exploited to good effect in Luchino Visconti's 1951 satire of the movie business, *Bellissima*.

Garbatella

Due south of the Aventine, this smiling proletarian garden suburb was built during the 1910s and early 1920s. Its charming twisting lanes, red ochre houses and bursts of bougainvillea provided one of the key locations for Roman director Nanni Moretti's cinematic love letter to his home town in the opening sequence of *Caro Diario* (1993, *below*).

filmgoers. Film cycles are presented in the cinema, the Sala Rossellini, almost every week: it could be a Fellini retrospective, a season of modern Dutch films, or a special on Woody Allen. Watch out for the uncomfortable and occasionally broken seats. *Air-conditioning.*

Festivals & summer programmes

Around the beginning of July, as cinemas are closing and box-office figures take a nose-dive, Rome becomes a great place to take in a movie. A plethora of second-run or arthouse open-air cinesplurges spring up under the **Estate Romana** (Roman Summer) umbrella (*see page 7*), many in breathtaking settings. In addition, there are several *arene* (fixed open-air screens) that provide a chance to catch up with that blockbuster you missed, or take in obscure underground classics.

There are also two regular mini-festivals, *Cannes a Roma* and *Venezia a Roma*, which show original-language films from these major European festivals about two weeks after they close (in May and September respectively). Venues

change annually: check local papers for details. Festivals and *arene* come and go, but the following are regular summer fixtures:

Cineporto

Parco della Farnesina, Farnesina.
Bus to Foro Italico. **Information** *(06 3600 5556).*
Dates July, Aug. **Tickets** L10,000.
The venue for one of the most successful and popular summer festivals is in the park by the Olympic Stadium. Two separate screens, each showing two dubbed films a night, often recent releases. Live concerts are presented between shows on many nights.

Massenzio

Information *(06 4423 8002).* **Open** 9am-6pm Mon-Fri. **Dates** July, Aug. **Tickets** L10,000.
The biggest and most politically correct of Rome's open-air film festivals, featuring about 200 films each year. The venue changes every year: in 1999 it came to rest in Via Appia Antica, 42. The imaginative programmes are organised around directors, actors, countries, genres or themes; there is usually one large viewing area with more commercial programming, and a smaller arthouse space. Films are usually dubbed.

Gay & Lesbian

Rome's gays go global with World Pride 2000.

Despite the odd bout of finger-wagging from the Vatican, Italy has long been notably free of anti-gay legislation. In the first half of this century, life was cheap, attitudes were relaxed, and boys were both. Today, the spread of affluence has broken the traditional link between poverty and sexual availability, although off-duty national servicemen have sometimes been known to turn wrist-engineers for a small fee.

Politically, the election as mayor of leading Green Francesco Rutelli in 1994 looked like good news for Rome's gays. Now into his second term, Rutelli left a bitter taste in many mouths with his earlier, much-publicised courtship of Rome's gay community. Apart from his appointment of a token gay councillor and a brief presence on one Pride march, he has been more concerned with currying Vatican favour than meeting gay needs. There has been suppression of the traditional outdoor scene, and the slash-and-burn deforestation

*The fences are up at **Monte Caprino**.*

of cruising spots continues. Even Rome's nudist beach (*see page 201*) is under attack, with the council fencing off the offending strip of dunes along the coast. The only consolation is that there's no fence that can long resist determined queers with wire-cutters.

Outdoors, indoors

Older Romans talk about the hedonistic delights once available along the banks of the Tiber, at the Circus Maximus (before bushes were uprooted) or inside the Colosseum (before railings were put up). In recent years, popular outdoor sites have included the Monte Caprino side of the Capitoline, Piazzale Gramsci, opposite the British Academy, the *galoppatoio* (yes, horse-riding) section of the Villa Borghese and the park behind the Palazzo della Civiltà del Lavoro in EUR. Even in these hallowed places, however, lighting has been improved, pissoirs demolished and concealing shrubs severely pruned.

This won't be a problem for those who are less at ease with street cruising. Gay life is moving indoors: albeit with characteristic Roman caution, a whole gamut of venues is emerging. Self-styled 'sex clubs' and dark rooms are springing up, and the city now boasts a Rome Leather Club. There are still few places, though, where gay men can meet during the day: gay terrace cafés have yet to hit the Eternal City.

Personal safety

Discretion is the keyword. Although Romans pride themselves on their worldly acceptance of human variety, public effusions are best avoided. The police are as likely to protect you as they are to harass.

AIDS

Contrary to the situation in many countries, most Italians with AIDS are victims of infected needles rather than unsafe sex, although the high percentage of addicts involved in prostitution has led to a spill-over.

Transvestites & transsexuals

When gay pioneer Mario Mieli published *Homosexuality and Liberation* in 1977 (English edition published by Gay Men's Press, 1980), trans-vestites were seen as the cutting edge of gay politics. These days in Rome the vast army of South American *viados*, and some home-grown transvestites, do little more than satisfy the needs of the sex industry.

The *Buco*

Perhaps one of the best-established and most attractive bastions of Roman gay life, *Il Buco* (the hole) is a short stretch of beach nestling unexpectedly between the family-fun resorts of **Ostia** and **Torvaianica** (*see pages 236-7*). Gay men and women of all ages flock to the *Buco* from June to September, to enjoy sun and sand (the far-from-crystal-clear nature of the water means that 'sea' can't really be added to the list of enjoyments).

Nudism was once the order of the day; bathing suits are now tolerated. The atmosphere is generally laid-back: the lapping of waves is interrupted only by the beach's own disco – appropriately called the Cow Goes to the Sea – organised by the *Mucca Assassina* crew at weekends (ring **Circolo Mario Mieli** for details).

Getting there *by car* take Via Cristoforo Colombo to Ostia, turn left at the coast and drive for about 8km/5 miles (an '8km' milestone marks the spot); *by train and bus* take from Roma-Ostia Lido station (Metro Piramide) to Lido di Ostia-Cristoforo Colombo. Then 07/ bus (summer months only), from outside the station to the last stop; from here it's a 10-15 min walk.

The **Circolo Mario Mieli** has given increasing space to transsexual issues, and its cultural programmer and ringmaster/mistress Vladimir Luxuria is a constant presence on TV, not always to the liking of more traditional gay campaigners.

Terminology

Even quality newspapers use euphemisms such as *ambiguo* (ambiguous) and *diverso* (different). The most widely-used term is *gay*; alternatives like *frocio* (homosexual) and *finocchio* (fennel – don't ask) change their politics according to who's using them.

Bars & clubs

Rome's gay venues open and close at an alarming rate, so a phone call to check the bar still exists is a good idea before you slip into something sexy. Some bars charge no entrance fee but oblige you to buy a drink. A growing number of venues ask you to show an **Arcigay** annual membership card, which costs L20,000, can be bought in any venue that requires you to have it, and gives you admission to many clubs throughout Italy. Some bars, though, still have their own membership cards, valid only in the individual venue and usually costing L3,000. In most bars you are given a printed slip on which the barman ticks off what

you consume; you pay the total amount on leaving. Be careful not to lose your slip, as you're liable for a stiff penalty if you do.

Alcatraz

Via Aureliana, 39 (06 4201 3286).
Metro Repubblica/bus to Via XX Settembre.
Open 10pm-2am Thur-Sun. **Admission** with Arcigay card. **Map 5/1B**
New disco-cum-sex bar, situated next to the Europa sauna for those who like to go from sweat and steam to, erm, sweat and steam in one easy move. Neat prison theme and a youngish crowd.

L'Alibi

Via di Monte Testaccio, 40-47 (06 574 3448).
Bus to Via Marmorata, Via Galvani or Lungotevere Testaccio. **Open** 11pm-4.30am Wed-Sun.
Admission free Wed-Fri, Sun; L20,000 Sat (includes first drink). **Map 7/2B**
The Alibi paved the way for Testaccio's boom as a quarter with an alternative feel (*see chapter* **Nightlife**) and is still one of Rome's few full-time gay discos. Just as well it's good. Two floors in winter, three in summer; the roof garden is its best feature. There's a good sound system, floor-shows and a noticeably competitive atmosphere.

L'Apeiron

Via dei Quattro Cantoni, 5 (06 482 8820). Metro Cavour/bus to Via Cavour. **Open** 10.30pm-3.30am Mon-Sat. **Admission** free with annual membership card (L5,000). Compulsory first drink. **Map 8/1B**
The bar and lounge area are dominated by a fuzzy screen offering MTV; downstairs a dank ante-room shows porn videos to get punters in the mood before entering the darkroom. A mixture of timid suburbanites and hardened darkroom devotees.

Hangar

Via in Selci, 69 (06 488 1397).
Metro Cavour/bus to Via Cavour. **Open** 10.30pm-2am Wed-Mon. Closed three weeks Aug.
Admission with Arcigay card. **Map 8/1B**
Rome's oldest gay bar, opened in 1983 by American John Moss. Hangar maintains its friendly but sexy atmosphere whether it's half full (occasionally midweek) or packed (weekends and Mondays). Two bars are linked by a long, dark passage; the pissoir is reputed to be livelier. There are porn video shows on Monday nights.

K Men's Club

Via Amato Amati, 6-8 (0347 622 0462).
Bus to Via Casilina. **Open** 11pm-3am Mon-Thur; 11pm-4am Fri; 11pm-5am Sat; 4pm-4am Sun.
Admission with free membership card: L10,000 Mon-Thur (includes first drink); L15,000 Fri; L18,000 Sat; L13,000 Sun (includes first drink).
One of gay Rome's hardest and furthest-flung recent additions, K Men's Club is the city's first SM/leather venue. Its main attraction, however, is its variety of well-equipped dark areas and its occasional midweek 'total naked' parties. Definitely not for the faint-hearted.

K 2 Day
Via A Dulceri, 30 (0347 622 0462). Bus to Via Casilina. **Open** 4-10pm Wed-Sun. Closed June-Sept. **Admission** with free membership card.
Rome's only daytime gay sex club. Just the place if you fancy an early evening stroll with like-minded folk through the various darkrooms of a cellar bar.

Knast
Via A. Jandolo, 9 (06 6994 2419). Tram to Viale Trastevere/bus to Lungotevere Ripa. **Open** 10.30pm-2.30am Wed-Mon. **Admission** with free membership card (compulsory first drink). **Map 6/2A**
One of a growing number of beer'n'sex cellars, Knast has several areas, although most of the mixed clientele heads for the porn-film parlour. The butch German name and glint of chains suggest heavy goings-on, but candles and dark drapes owe as much to Queen Victoria as her consort. Friendly staff.

Max's Bar
Via A. Grandi, 3a (06 7030 1599). Metro Manzoni/bus to Piazza di Porta Maggiore. **Open** 10.30pm-2.30am daily. **Admission** L10,000 Mon-Thur, Sun; L15,000 Fri; L20,000 Sat (prices include first drink).
A stone's throw from one of the city's liveliest transvestite prostitution areas east of Piazza Vittorio Emanuele (**Map 8/1A**). Its dance floor and bar are rumoured to be popular with bus drivers, which may explain its bluff, chummy charm, and why it attracts a fair share of Rome's over-fifties.

Shelter
Via dei Vascellari, 35 (no phone). Tram to Viale Trastevere/bus to Lungotevere Ripa. **Open** 9pm-3am daily. **Admission** with free membership card. **Map 6/2A**

One of the more relaxed gay venues in the city. The atmosphere tends towards coffee and chat rather than cruise and choose. Shelter is one of the few places where gay men and women get together and enjoy company, cocktails and desserts.

Skyline
Via degli Aurunci, 26/28 (06 444 0817). Bus to Via Tiburtina. **Open** 10.30pm-2am Tue-Fri, Sun; 10.30pm-3am Sat. **Admission** with Arcigay card.
A compact club in San Lorenzo. The décor is a strange hybrid – between military fatigues and stainless steel slick. The crowd is relaxed and mixed, with constant toing and froing between the bar and the cruisy balcony and dark areas. Hosts the Leather Club Roma on Wednesday evenings, and organises the occasional leather, biker or bear event.

Residencies/one-nighters
Mucca Assassina (Killer Cow), the DJ crew based at the **Mario Mieli** gay centre, run the largest and best one-nighters around Rome. On Fridays from October to June they're at **Alpheus** (*see chapter* **Nightlife**), after which they often transfer to the Buco (*see page 201*), although it's worth calling the Mario Mieli centre to check on summer locations and programmes.

The crew mixes a standard disco diet with novelty theme evenings (uniform night is popular). The success of the *Mucca* with Roman youth of all sexual orientations has inspired a series of otherwise straight clubs (from trendy **Goa** to the terminally tedious **Gilda** (*see chapter* **Nightlife**) to indulge in midweek 'gay' one-nighters. Check local listings for latest band-wagon jumpers.

Pride 2000: the Other Jubilee

Not all the 30-odd million visitors expected in Rome for 2000 Holy Year (*see page 106*) will be seeking plenary indulgences. The international gay community will mark the beginning of the new millennium with the first ever **World Pride** event. That celebration will take place in the Eternal City.

There's a certain poetic justice to this: history shows that holy years and homosexuality go hand in hand. One of Pope Boniface VIII's motives for calling the first ever Holy Year in 1300 was to divert attention from rumours of papal sodomy. His efforts were scuppered by no less a person than Dante, who ensured posterity never forgot Boniface's proclivities by having him make a guest appearance in his Seventh Circle – that corner of hell reserved for lovers of the unspeakable vice.

The all-too-predictable objections to holding the event in the Capital of Catholicism were not slow in coming, from outside and inside the gay community. Many activists were less than happy about what they saw as a confrontational response to the Vatican's own jamboree.

But with disagreements put to one side, a 15-acre village is to be erected near Tiburtina station in preparation for the 1-9 July 2000 bash. Apart from the usual worthy stands and conference facilities, there will be bars and restaurants, not to mention discos, a pool and a sports centre where you can tone up the odd muscle in time for the 8 July march through the city. A gay marathon is also planned. Book early, and you might even get to pitch your tent in the nearby purpose-built camp site. Absolutely no comment. *Website: www.worldpride2000.com*

'Cultural programmer' Vladimir Luxuria all dressed up at **Mucca Assassina**. *See page 202.*

Europa Multiclub

Via Aureliana, 40 (06 482 3650). Metro Repubblica/bus to Via XX Settembre. **Open** 3pm-midnight Mon-Thur; 2pm-6am Fri, Sat; 2pm-midnight Sun. **Admission** L25,000 with Arcigay card; discounts after 11pm Fri, Sat. **Map 5/1B**

Rome's largest and smartest sauna, with a friendly staff and mixed clientele. Leave your togs in the multi-coloured lockers and cruise on down to the steam, sweat and romantically star-lit booths. The only place in Rome to do all night weekend sessions.

Mediterraneo Sauna

Via Villari, 3 (06 7720 5934). Metro Manzoni/bus to Via Merulana. **Open** 2-11pm daily. **Admission** L20,000 with Arcigay card. **Map 8/2A**

Tasteful décor and an emphasis on hygiene distinguish this sauna from many others. The steam room and jacuzzi provide repose prior to the exertions of the 'relax rooms' on the upper and lower levels.

Information/organisations

There are about 30 gay activist organisations in Italy, mostly in the north. Foremost is the Bologna-based **Arcigay** network.

Arcigay Caravaggio

Via Lariana, 8 (06 855 5522). Bus to Via Salaria. **Open** 4-8pm Mon-Fri; 5-8pm Sun.

Rome branch of the Bologna-based group. Responsible for political, social and welfare activities; also runs a helpline and a Sunday meet.

National HQ: Piazza di Porta Saragozza, 2, 40123 Bologna (051 580 563)

Circolo Mario Mieli di Cultura Omosessuale

Via Corinto, 5, or on the corner of Via Efeso/Via Ostiense (06 541 3985/fax 06 541 3971). Metro San Paolo/bus to Via Ostiense. **Open** 10am-6pm Mon-Fri.

The most important gay, lesbian and trans-gender group in Rome, a base for debates and events .Their one-nighters, run by *Mucca Assassina*, are highly popular. The centre also offers a counselling service and AIDS/HIV testing and care facilities. *Website: www.mariomieli.it*

Publications

Aut

Via Corinto, 5 (06 54 13 985).

A monthly magazine published by the **Circolo Mario Mieli**. Interesting articles and an up-to-date listings page; available free at many gay venues.

Marco

Edizioni Moderne, Casella Postale (PO Box) 17182, 20170 Milano (02 2951 7490).

Contact mag with ads and amateurish photographs, sometimes sexy, occasionally depressing and often hilarious.

Outlets & publishers

Babele

Via dei Banchi Vecchi, 116 (06 687 6628). Bus to Corso Vittorio Emanuele. **Open** 9.30am-7.30pm Mon-Sat. **Map 3/2B**

The only exclusively gay and lesbian bookshop in Rome. The small space contains a big selection of books (with a well-stocked English section), videos, guides, and magazines. Useful noticeboards.

Babilonia

Babilonia Edizioni, Casella Postale (PO Box) 11224, 20110 Milano (02 569 6468).
Italy's principal gay publishing house, responsible for a fairly lively monthly magazine, *Babilonia* (L10,000, at selected newsstands) and the annual Italian/English *Guida Gay* (L20,000), which gives comprehensive information on gay life in Italy.

Cobra Videofilms

Via Giolitti, 307/313 (06 4470 0636).
Metro Vittorio/bus to Piazza Vittorio Emanuele.
Open 9am-7.45pm Mon-Sat. **Map 5/2A**
A well-stocked (for Rome) small chain of gay/hetero video shops, with monthly arrivals from abroad. Specialises in 'trans' material. Over-18s only.
Branch: Via Barletta, 23 (06 3751 7350). **Map 2/2C**

Europa 92

Via Vitelleschi, 38/40 (06 687 1210).
Bus to Piazza del Risorgimento. **Open** 3-7.45pm Mon; 9.15am-1.30pm, 3-7.45 pm, Tue-Sat. **Map 3/1C**
Hard by the Vatican, this predominantly gay video shop also sells magazines and a variety of gadgets.

Newsstands

Edicole (open-air news-stands) are often good for gay books, videos and other material. Around Termini there are several with a fair amount of material on display by day, and masses by night.
Edicola Antrilli *corner of Via Giolitti/Via Gioberti.*
Edicola Di Fabrizio *corner of Piazza dei Cinquecento/Via Gaeta.*
Edicola Lazzari *corner of Piazza dei Cinquecento/Via Volturno.* **All Map 5/1-2A**
Edicola Camponeschi *corner of Piazza Colonna/Largo Chigi.* **Map 3/1A**

Lesbian Rome

There are two distinct factions in *Roma lesbica*. The older lesbian groups have their roots in the feminist movement of the Seventies, and continue to claim separate identity from men, gay or straight. They meet at the **Buon Pastore** centre. Younger lesbians meet at **Circolo Mario Mieli** or are part of the **Arci-Lesbica** association. Joint ventures like *Mucca Assassina* get good turn-outs from both gay men and lesbians, and the **Shelter** café (*see above*) is also popular with women.

Although Rome has yet to host a permanent lesbian club or disco, there are one-nighters and events for an occasional good night out. Check the notice board at the **Babele** bookshop (*see above*), stop by the Buon Pastore, or ring Arci-Lesbica or Circolo Mario Mieli for the latest happenings.

See also **Shelter**, *page 202*.

Jolie Cœur

Via Sirte, 5 (06 8621 5827). Bus to Viale Eritrea.
Open 10pm-5am Sat. **Admission** L12,000.
Saturday is women's night at this club in the northern suburbs, which now has a karaoke room and billiard table. On the dance floor, it's strictly techno. A friendly atmosphere, and no men allowed.

La Stanza dei Frutti Rubini

Via Corinto, 5 (06 54 13 985).
Metro San Paolo/bus to Via Ostiense.
Open 8.30-11pm Wed. **Admission** free.
Laid-back women-only event at **Circolo Mario Mieli**.

Information

Libreria delle Donne: Al Tempo Ritrovato

Via dei Fienaroli, 31d (06 581 7724). Tram to Viale Trastevere. **Open** 3-8pm Mon; 10am-8pm Tue-Sat.
No credit cards. **Map 6/2B**
Bookshop with a well-stocked lesbian section (including some titles in English) and a helpful, information-packed noticeboard.

Organisations & events

Arci-Lesbica Roma

Via dei Monti di Pietralata, 16 (06 418 0369).
Metro Tiburtina. **Open** 9-10.30pm Thur.
A spin-off from Arcigay, Arci-Lesbica offers a helpline and organises get-togethers twice a week, plus special events through the year. Occasional residencies at local nightspots: phone for information.
Website: www.women.it/~arciles/roma

Collegamento fra le lesbiche italiane

Buon Pastore, Via della Lungara, 19 (06 686 4201).
Bus to Lungotevere della Farnesina.
Open 7-9pm Tue. **Map 6/1C**
Formed in 1981, this separatist group meets in the Buon Pastore women's centre in Trastevere once a week to discuss politics. It's strictly women-only, but you don't need to be a member to take part. Organises conferences, literary evenings, concerts, dances, holidays and an annual Masqued Ball.

Coordinamento Lesbiche Romane

Buon Pastore, Via della Lungara, 19 (06 686 4201).
Bus to Lungotevere della Farnesina.
Open phone for details. **Map 6/1C**
The little sister of the lesbian associations, the CLR was set up in 1995 to facilitate contacts among lesbians throughout Italy. Separatist at heart.

Zipper Travel Association

Via Castelfidardo, 18 (06 48 82 730). Metro Castro Pretorio/bus to Piazza Indipendenza. **Open** 10am-6pm Mon-Fri. **Credit** AmEx, MC, V. **Map 5/1A**
The only travel agency in Italy offering customised travel for gay women.

Media

Frustrating papers, compulsively awful TV, good news programmes.

Newspapers

Italian newspapers can be a frustrating read. Stories tend to be long and indigestible, so you have to wade through reams of copy to find out what the point is. Often there isn't one.

Italian journalists are so terrified of missing anything that they hang out together in packs. As a result, their stories often look suspiciously alike. Similarly, editors rarely take their cue from anything other than the previous evening's TV news, and readers commonly complain that dailies look like photocopies of each other.

On the plus side, Italian papers are delightfully unsnobbish, and happily blend serious news with crime and human-interest stories. If politics bore you, turn to the *cronaca* (i.e., anything that isn't politics, economics or sport) pages where, even with a rudimentary reading knowledge of Italian, you will be happily transfixed by blow-by-blow reconstructions of the bloodiest murders, and in-depth pop-psychoanalytical deconstructions of wife-bashing cases. Or just make straight for the serious stuff: football.

Although several papers have country-wide distribution, by tradition the Italian press is local. Rome's major dailies are *La Repubblica*, *Il Messaggero* and the right-wing *Il Tempo*. Milan's *Corriere della Sera* has a Rome section. News dailies, whether local or national, are short on sensationalist scandal-mongering: if you're hankering after tabloid-style dirt, try magazines. Sports coverage in the dailies is extensive, but if you're not sated there are the top-selling sports rags *Corriere dello Sport*, *La Gazzetta dello Sport* and *Tuttosport*.

National dailies

Corriere della Sera

To the centre of centre-left, the solid, serious, best-selling *Corriere* is good on crime and foreign news.
Website: www.rcs.it

Il Manifesto

A reminder that, though the Berlin Wall is a distant memory, there is still some corner of central Rome where hearts beat Red. And where some decent journalism – especially of a cultural bent – is turned out.
Website: www.ilmanifesto.it

Il Messaggero

A fixture on top of the ice cream cabinet of every Roman bar, *Il Messaggero* is the Roman daily par

excellence. Particularly useful for classified ads – with many flat rents – on Thursdays and Sundays.
Website: www.messaggero.it

L'Osservatore Romano

The Vatican's official newspaper was an organ for liberal Catholic thought during the 1960s and '70s, but now, under the guiding hand of Opus Dei, it reflects the conservative orthodoxies issuing from the top. Weekly editions in English

La Repubblica

The centre-ish, left-ish *La Repubblica* is good on the Mafia and the Vatican, and comes up with the occasional major scoop on its business pages. It has a tendency to pad out news with pseudo-intellectual waffle, and to slip in scandal-mongering under a very thin veneer of serious reporting.
Website: www.repubblica.it

La Stampa

Part of the massive empire of Turin's Agnelli family (Fiat is another), *La Stampa* has good (though, inevitably, pro-Agnelli) business reporting. Rather dull, and often frustratingly incomplete.
Website: www.lastampa.it

L'Unità

A beacon of Italian journalism in the mid-'90s, when edited by Walter Veltroni, who was whisked off to the government and the *Democratici di sinistra* party; the dull, disorientated paper has yet to recover.
Website: www.unita.it

Foreign press

The *Financial Times, Wall Street Journal* and *International Herald Tribune* (this last with an *Italy Daily* supplement) can be found on most newsstands in the city centre. Other British dailies arrive on the afternoon of the the the same day, but you may have to wait until Monday for Sunday papers (shorn of colour supplements). US papers are likely to be slightly more out of date.

Magazines

With the naked female form blazoned across their covers most weeks, Italy's serious news magazines are not always distinguishable from the soft porn among which they are often lodged on newsstands. But *Panorama* and *L'Espresso* provide a generally high-standard round-up of the week's news

For tabloid-style scandal, try *Gente* and *Oggi*, with their weird mix of sex, glamour and religion, or the execrable *Eva 3000, Novella 2000* and *Cronaca Vera*, which specialise in hacks' bizarre and imaginary renditions of intimate conversations between blurry personalities snapped from the top of tall trees with arm-length lenses.

Internazionale (www.internazionale.it) is an excellent digest of bits and pieces gleaned from the world's press. *Diario della Settimana (www.diario.it)* is informed, urbane and has some good investigative journalism. The biggest seller of them all, though, is *Famiglia Cristiana* – available in any Catholic church – which alternates Vatican line-toeing and Vatican-baiting, depending on the state of relations at any given time between the Holy See and the idiosyncratic Paoline monks who produce it.

Listings & small ads magazines

Porta Portese

Essential reading for anyone looking for a place to live in Rome; published twice a week, on Tuesday and Sunday. Place ads free on 06 70199; sections include household goods and cars, as well as houses and flats to rent or buy.

Roma C'è

A weekly guide with comprehensive listings for theatre, music venues, dance, film and nightlife. On newsstands on Thursday. English-language section.

Solocase

Houses for sale and to rent. On newsstands every Saturday.

Time Out Roma

Same format as the London version, but in Italian. Features on events and unusual facets of Roman life.

Wanted in Rome

A good source of essential information and upmarket housing ads for ex-pats.

Television

Italy has six major networks (three owned by the state broadcaster **RAI**, three belonging to Silvio Berlusconi) plus the two channels operated across most of the country by second-ranking **Telemontecarlo**. When these have bored you – and unless you're in the mood for soaps, interminable games shows or political chat shows ending in a shouting free-for-all, they soon will – there are any number of local stations to provide hours of channel-zapping fun. Most of the fare on offer is compulsory awful, although if you're in the market for revolutionary cellulite treatments, exotic vegetable choppers or tacky paste jewelry, you're in the right place. Reports of late-night stripping housewives are exaggerated, but not without some basis in truth.

The standard of TV news and current affairs programmes varies from channel to channel and show to show; all, however, offer a breadth of international coverage that's genuinely impressive. For local news, catch the *TG Regionale*, after the 7pm and 10.30pm news programmes on **RAI 3**.

Radio

The three state-owned stations (**RAI 1**, 89.7 MHz FM, 1332 KHz AM; **RAI 2**, 91.7 MHz FM, 846 KHz AM; **RAI 3**, 93.7 MHz FM) play classical and light music, and have endless chat shows and excellent regular news bulletins.

Other stations

For UK and US chart hits, mixed with home-grown offerings, try some of the following –
Radio Capital 95.8 Mhz FM.
Radio 105 96.1 Mhz FM.
Radio Centro Suono 101.3 MHz FM.
Radio Città Futura 97.7 MHz FM. Italy's most PC 24-hour station. *Radiofax*, at 10am daily, lists the day's events in Rome.
Radio Kiss Kiss Network 97.250 MHz FM.
Vatican Radio 93.3 MHz FM; 1530 KHz AM. The world news, as seen through the distorting lenses of the Catholic Church, can be heard in English at 8.30am, 12.30pm and 6.15 pm. A considerably more upbeat news features programme in English is broadcast at 7am and 9.50pm.

Rome on-line

Innumerable websites provide information on Rome as padding for more-or-less overt advertising. For some less commercial data, try *www.comune.roma.it* (Italian only), the Rome city council's site, or *www.beniculturali.it* (English pending), the site of the cultural heritage ministry. *Time Out* has its own site at *www.timeout.com/rome*, and the **Enjoy Rome** agency (*see chapter* **Directory**) provides information at *www.enjoyrome.com*.

Sport & Fitness

Romans get passionate over Roma vs Lazio, but few are spurred into getting out their kit and working up a sweat themselves.

Romans are passionate about sport, and above all football (*calcio*), but a great deal more passion is put into spectating and/or pontificating about any game than ever is into participating in one. Which is perhaps just as well, because the city provides far more and far better facilities for professionals than it does for amateurs.

The 1960 Olympic Games and the 1990 football World Cup left Rome with a substantial legacy of high-class professional facilities, despite the fact that much of the money allocated to the World Cup was frittered away on meaningless prestige projects. Most of the sports centres that do exist in the city, especially the ones located in accessible central areas, are private, and require a hefty annual membership fee for any use of their facilities. If, on the other hand, you want to experience sport the traditional Roman way (sitting down), you could do worse than catching a soccer game at the Stadio Olimpico.

Football

Rome has two first-rank clubs, **AS Roma** (more information on *www.asromacalcio.it*) and **SS Lazio** (check out *www.sslazio.it*), both of which share the **Stadio Olimpico**, on the north bank of the Tiber in the Foro Itálico complex. City derbies are hotly contested affairs, but the fans' rivalry rarely ever leads to violence.

Between them Roma and Lazio have won three titles in *Serie A*, Italian football's first division. In the last few years Lazio have become one of Italy's richest soccer clubs, thanks to massive investment from owner Sergio Cragnotti and a stock market flotation. Lazio has bought in raft-loads of star players and regularly pushed for the title in recent seasons, and in 1999 the club won the last-ever European Cup-Winners' Cup and qualified for the 1999-2000 Champions' League. Roma, meanwhile, in spite of its followers' belief in themselves as the city's more 'authentic' club, have been in the doldrums for years, after a spell of glory and a *Serie A* title in the early '80s.

As with almost everything else in Italy, Roman soccer is politicised: Roma's supporters traditionally hail from the left - be it working-class or intellectual - while Lazio is seen as the team of the right, drawing support from the wealthy Parioli district and the countryside around the city.

Most fan attention is focused on the *Serie A* Championship and European competitions; the Italian Cup (*Coppa d'Italia*) is a second-rate affair. League games are traditionally played on Sunday, but, beginning with the 1999-2000 season, one match will also be played and broadcast live on Saturday evening. Cup and European games are played during the week, usually on Tuesdays and Wednesdays.

Tickets can be bought directly from the Stadio Olimpico box office, from the club merchandising outlets listed below, and from **Orbis** (*see page 187*). Once inside the stadium, Lazio fans opt for the *Curva Nord*, while the Roma faithful occupy the *Curva Sud* (north stand and south stand – where tickets are cheapest). For better (and more expensive) seats, ask for the *Tribuna Tevere* or *Tribuna Monte Mario*.

Stadio Olimpico

Viale dello Stadio Olimpico (ticket office 06 323 7333). Bus to Piazza Mancini or Lungotevere Maresciallo Cadorna/tram to Piazza Mancini.
If you get off your bus or tram in Piazza Mancini, follow the crowds over the Ponte Duca d'Aosta bridge across the Tiber to reach the stadium. Tickets cost around L30,000-L120,000; even the cheap seats have a reasonable view.

Essential accessories

These shops stock full ranges of official strips and club merchandise:

Lazio Point

Via Farini, 34 (06 482 6768). Metro Vittorio Emanuele/bus to Piazza Vittorio Emanuele or Via Principe Amedeo. **Open** 9am-7pm Mon-Sat. **Credit** AmEx, MC, V. **Map 5/2A**

Punto Roma

Via Paolina, 8 (06 482 1664). Metro Cavour/bus to Piazza Esquilino or Via Merulana. **Open** 9am-1pm, 4-7.30pm, Mon-Sat. **Credit** AmEx, MC, V. **Map 8/1B** **Branch** Via Angelo Emo, 59 (06 3972 1567). Metro Ottaviano.

Golf

Golf is an exclusive game in Italy. In most clubs, including those listed below, you have to produce a membership card of your home club, together with proof of your handicap, before you're allowed to play. It is not normally necessary, though, to be introduced by a member. Green fees, including those quoted below, are normally charged per day rather than per round.

Circolo del Golf di Roma

Via Appia Nuova, 716a (06 780 3407).
Metro Colli Albani, then taxi. **Open** 8am-sunset Tue-Sun. **Rates** L80,000 Tue-Fri; L110,000 Sat, Sun; *club hire* L35,000; *driving range* L18,000 Tue-Fri; L35,000 Sat, Sun (use of range included in green fees).
Non-members can take part in competitions on Sundays.

Country Club Castelgandolfo

Via Santo Spirito, 13, Località Pavona Laghetto. (06 931 2301). Metro Anagnina, then taxi. **Open** 8am-8pm daily. **Rates** L70,000 Tue-Fri; L90,000 Sat, Sun. *Electric cart hire* L60,000 Mon-Fri; L70,000 Sat, Sun. *Trolley hire* L10,000. *Club hire* L35,000. *Driving range* L10,000 (use of range included in green fees).
This course near the papal summer residence outside Rome was designed by leading American golf architect Robert Trent Jones inside a volcanic crater, and is overlooked by its distinguished sixteenth-century club house.

Gyms

Many of Rome's gyms are as snooty as they are expensive, and unless you're wearing all the latest varieties of lycra and have a perfect figure it's easy to feel a mite self-conscious inside them. Public gyms do exist, but they are few and far between and hard to find. Some of the more luxurious hotels also have their own fitness centres.

The facilities listed below are all private clubs.

New Body Image

Via Enrico Fermi, 142 (06 557 3356).
Bus to Viale Marconi. **Open** 9.30am-9pm. Closed Aug. **Membership** L80,000 per month.
This women-only centre in EUR offers all kinds of health and beauty treatment, and no inital sign-up fee is required. Fitness facilities include a weight room, aerobics classes and a sauna.

Roman Sports Center

Villa Borghese, Viale del Galoppatoio, 33 (06 320 1667/06 321 8096/06 322 3665).
Bus to Via Veneto. **Open** 9am-10pm Mon-Sat; Sun 11am-5pm. **Membership** L2,100,000 for 15 months; L50,000 per day. **Map 4/2C**
Strictly speaking you need to be introduced by a member to use the facilities here, but the rules are often bent, and day membership is available. Rome's largest health centre, it includes three aerobic rooms, sun beds, saunas, hydromassage pools, two gyms, squash courts and two Olympic-size swimming pools. There is a second centre on Largo Somalia, north-west of the Villa Ada park (take the bus to the end of Viale Libia).
Branch Largo Somalia, 60 (06 8621 2411/06 8621 2481).

Jogging

Crowds of people and omnipresent cars make a jog through central Rome a memorably unpleasant experience. That aside, the best bet is to make for one of the parks. The leafy avenues of **Villa Borghese** are popular with locals at weekends, when you can hire rollerblades and bikes if and when your feet get tired.

Many joggers opt for **Villa Doria Pamphili**, on the western side of the Gianicolo and Trastevere (bus to Porta di San Pancrazio), which has work-out stations along the trail. Other options are **Villa Ada**, with paths running between ponds and lakes (bus to Via Salaria), and **Parco di Monte Mario**, north of Prati (bus to Via Trionfale) for a stiff, uphill workout. For a feel of ancient Rome try working out in the **Circo Massimo**, but go early or late, as it gets hot, dusty and crowded with tourists during the day. Serious runners congregate just south of the *Circo* on the stretch of lawn running along **Via delle Terme di Caracalla**, opposite the ancient Roman baths of the same name.

The **Rome City Marathon**, held each spring, is slowly making a name for itself in international running circles, although it remains an essentially Roman event. A city-to-sea race is also held during the spring (*see page 5*).

Swimming

Despite Rome's torrid summer temperatures, pools are not numerous in the city and, apart from a few far-flung exceptions, those that do exist are privately run. The beaches near Rome are not particularly inviting; you're better off making a day of it and exploring parts of the coast a little further afield (*see chapter* **Trips out of Town**).

Alternatively, make your way to one of the following private pools:

Oasi della Pace

Via degli Eugenii, 2 (06 718 4550).
Metro Arco di Travertino then bus 765.
Open *June-Sept* 9.30am-6pm daily.
Admission L15,000 Mon-Fri; L18,000 Sat, Sun.
A pleasant open-air pool off the ancient **Via Appia Antica** (*see p102*), surrounded by tall hedges and cypresses. Facilities are fairly simple.

La Piscina delle Rose

Viale America, 20 (06 592 6717). Bus to Palasport.
Open *June-Sept* 9am-7pm daily.
Admission L18,000 full day, L13,000 half day (9am-2pm; 2pm-7pm), L7,000 1pm-4pm; free for children under 1m tall. *Ten-day ticket* L120,000.
Rome's largest public pool, an open-air pool in the heart of Mussolini's EUR exhibition district south of the city (*see p100*). It has good facilities for small children, and often gets crowded. *See also chapter* **Children**.

Football action (Lazio in blue, Roma red and yellow) ...

...football devotion....

...and football passion.

Hotel Pools

Due to the cramped spaces of central Rome there are no hotels in the heart of the city that also offer swimming pools. In leafier areas around the outskirts of town, though, there are several hotels, most of them part of international chains, which have pools that can also be used by non-residents. *See also chapter* **Accommodation**.

Cavalieri Hilton

Via Cadlolo, 101 (06 3509 2950).
Bus to Piazzale Medaglie D'Oro.
Open *May-Sept* 9am-7pm daily. **Admission** L60,000 per day, L30,000 under-12s, Mon-Fri; L90,000 per day, L45,000 under-12s, Sat, Sun.
Luxurious hotel pool on the north side of the city with fabulous views down the Monte Mario hill across Rome. Prices include a towel and use of showers; there is one Olympic-size swimming pool, and a smaller pool for children, with hydromassage.

Holiday Inn

Via Aurelia Antica, 415 (06 6642).
Bus from Via di Porta Cavalleggeri to Aurelia Antica/infrequent Holiday Inn shuttle bus service from Piazza Santa Maria Maggiore.
Open *June-Sept* 9am-7pm daily. **Admission** L40,000 per day Mon-Fri; L50,000 Sat, Sun.
Another upper-range hotel with a fine pool on the outskirts of the city, located along one of ancient Rome's consular roads, just west of the Villa Pamphili park.

Parco dei Principi

Via Frescobaldi, 5. (06 854 421). Bus to Via Paesiello or Via Mercadante/tram to Viale Rossini.
Open *May-Sept* 9.30am-6pm daily. **Admission** L45,000 Mon-Fri; L60,000 Sat, Sun. **Map 4/1B**
A more centrally-located outdoor pool, set in its own gardens on the edge of the Villa Borghese, and much favoured by local swimmers (especially at weekends). There is a 20% discount for children.

Romans in the ruck

They might prefer a pizza to a pint, but Italy's rugby players are for real. Twenty four clubs from the north and centre of the peninsula play in a highly competitive league, and Italy's national XV has recorded victories over France, Ireland and Scotland. In 2000, moreover, Italy finally makes its debut as a regular among Europe's major rugby countries in the all-new-look *Six* Nations Championship. Home matches will be played at the **Stadio Flaminio**, directly north of the Piazza del Popolo along the Via Flaminia (information 06 3685 7832; bus or tram along Via Flaminia to Viale Tiziano).

Rome also boasts a first-class club rugby side in **RDS Roma**, who play their league matches at the **Stadio Tre Fontane**, amid the wide-open spaces of EUR south of the city (Metro Magliana/bus to Viale delle Tre Fontane). For information on forthcoming games and tickets, call 06 592 1840.

Tennis

Every May Rome hosts the Italian Open tennis tournament, one of the most important European clay court tournaments outside the Grand Slam, for men and women (*see page 6*). It's worth a visit just to take a stroll through the venue: the Mussolini-built **Foro Italico**, a vast sports complex set in the shadow of the **Stadio Olimpico** and filled with giant (and camp) marble statues of Roman athletes. The tennis isn't bad either, with most of the world's top players taking part.

Foro Italico
Viale dei Gladiatori, 31 (06 3685 8218). Bus to Piazza Mancini or Lungotevere Maresciallo Cadorna/tram to Piazza Mancini.

Circolo della Stampa
Piazza Mancini, 19 (06 323 2452). Bus/tram to Piazza Mancini. **Open** 9am-11pm Mon-Fri; 9am-8pm Sat, Sun. **Court hire** *singles/50 minutes* L16,000; *doubles/50 minutes* L22,000; *floodlights* L20,000 (singles), L26,000 (doubles)
Owned by the Italian journalists' association, but friendly and open to non-members, the Circolo offers both clay and synthetic grass courts. There's no dress code, but studded trainers are not allowed.

Riding

Italy's annual show-jumping Grand Prix arguably boasts horse-riding's most beautiful arena: the Piazza di Siena, in the leafy surroundings of Villa Borghese (*see page 6*). The **Concorso Salto Ostacoli Internazionale** (CSIO – international show-jumping competition) takes place in May (for information, 06 3685 8326).

Il Galoppatoio
Via del Galoppatoio, 25 (06 322 6797). Metro Spagna/bus to Via Veneto. **Open** 8.30am-6pm Tue-Sat; 8.30am-2pm Sun. Closed Aug. **Rates: adults** *initial sign-up fee* L400,000 per year; *lessons* L300,000 (minimum 10 lessons, plus L35,000 insurance); **under-18s** *initial sign-up fee* L100,000 per year; *lessons* L200,000 per month. **Map 4/2C**
Rome's most exclusive riding club, deep in the Villa Borghese, has a predictably snooty atmosphere and prices to go with it. Lessons last one hour, and can be booked between 8-10am or 3-6pm.

Hotel dei due Laghi
Localita' Le Cerque (06 9960 7059). Train to Anguillara from Ostiense or Trastevere/Cotral bus from Lepanto to Anguillara; then a long walk.
Best reached by car, this hotel and riding school is lodged in a spectacular position between Lakes Bracciano and Martignano, north of Rome. Round off your riding day with some excellent food in the hotel restaurant; riding lessons cost L35,000 per hour, and are for guests only. Non-residents can take part in monthly drag-hunting meets.
Website: www.venere.it/lazio/due-laghi

Tennis at the **Foro Italico.**

Theatre & Dance

Spectacular settings and high-class festivals set Roman theatre-going apart.

Rome has some unparalleled venues for theatre and dance, but you have to search very hard to find anything outstanding or cutting-edge about the fare on offer during the regular season. To compensate, the **RomaEuropa festival** and the **Festival D'Autunno** bring a flurry of international activity in a daunting array of excellent theatre and dance productions (*see page 213*).

For the rest of the year, Rome can seem a sleepy backwater. However, a night at the theatre here has rewards all of its own.

First, there is the pleasure of watching theatre-going Romans: theatres are the city's see-and-be-seen venues *par excellence*. Then there are Rome's 80-plus theatres themselves: the **Teatro dell'Opera** with its frescoes, red and gold seats and boxes and enormous central chandelier; the **Teatro Argentina** with its perfect proportions; the **Teatro Valle,** resembling a miniature opera house; and the stunning new **Teatro India,** fashioned out of an old soap factory.

The main theatre season runs from October to May, when theatres stick doggedly to their own specialities. Costly productions by star directors such as Luca Ronconi and Gabriele Lavia are to be found at the publicly-funded **Teatro Argentina,** which occasionally hosts dance as well. The **Sala Milloss** stages the Opera House's lower-profile dance productions and the odd concert, as does the rather moldy **Teatro Brancaccio. Teatro Valle**'s programme usually includes reworked Greek classical theatre, and works by modern British and American playwrights in Italian; the fashionable **Teatro Sistina** is the place to go for musicals and light Italian musical comedies; while the **Teatro Flaiano,** with its plush blue velvet interiors, has lately transformed itself into an opera theatre.

For anglophones and hankerers after the completely different Anglo-Saxon approach to theatre culture, Rome's most interesting venue is the **Teatro dell'Orologio,** home to the young and upbeat Off Night Repertory Theater, Rome's only permanent English-speaking drama com-pany. For fringe theatre, head for the **Vascello.**

Foreign academies occasionally organise arts festivals in Rome, tending to favour the **Palazzo delle Esposizioni** as the venue for what are often excellent avant-garde productions. The **Teatro Agorà** holds a season that includes international theatre productions in English.

Dance

The **Teatro Olimpico** has Rome's best dance stage, and always has a few dance events in its very varied, high-class annual music season. The **Teatro dell'Opera** always includes a classical ballet or two in its programme, but administrative problems have resulted in haphazard artistic management. The *corps de ballet* is in a sorry state, even though international *étoiles* often lend their glittering presence for the first few nights of major productions.

Programme information

Rome-based dailies such as *La Repubblica* and *Il Messaggero* carry theatre and dance listings, as do the weekly *Time Out Roma* and *Roma C'è* magazines. Tickets can be bought at theatres themselves, or at agencies (*see p187*).

Main public theatres

Palazzo delle Esposizioni
Via Nazionale, 194 (06 474 5903).
Bus to Via Nazionale. **Open** 10am-9pm Mon, Wed-Sun. Closed Tue. **Map 5/2B**
Rome's only multi-cultural arts centre has a cinema, lecture hall and a dance space. *See also p69.*

Teatro Nazionale – Sala Milloss
Via del Viminale, 51 (06 4782 5140). Metro Termini/bus to Via Nazionale. **Box office** 10am-7pm daily. **Shows** *Sept-May* 4.30pm Mon; 9pm Tue, Thur, Fri; 4.30pm, 9pm Sat; 5.30pm Sun. **Map 5/2A**
Venue for the Teatro dell'Opera's not-so-prestigious productions.

Teatro dell'Opera
Via Firenze, 72 (06 4816 0255/06 481 7003).
Bus to Via Nazionale. **Box office** 10.45am-5pm Tue-Sun. **Shows** varies. **Map 5/2B**

Out of season

Rome's theatre and dance offerings can appear tame during the official winter season. Out of season, however, the city abounds with high-class productions in settings that no city in the world can beat. The **Teatro dell'Opera** is responsible for a stunning annual under-the-stars season of dance and opera – which, though, has a nasty habit of running into bureaucratic obstacles, and has been forced to change venues several times in recent years. In 1999 the **Olimpico** football stadium hosted popular (and cheap) opera productions.

Many of the best out-of-season shows are international productions brought to Rome by the **RomaEuropa Festival**, which has ballooned from being a small but classy summer happening organised by the French Academy into a major date in the international calendar. It was once a summer-only affair, but many of the festival's best events are now held back until autumn. Which brings it into direct competition with the **Festival d'Autunno**: his event is the result of a concerted effort to bring productions from festivals such as the Edinburgh Fringe and Avignon to Rome.

For **RomaEuropa**, *see pages 7 and 219.*

Festival d'Autunno

Associazione Cadmo, Via Flaminia 61 (06 320 2102). Metro Flaminio/bus to Via Flaminia. **Box office** at individual venues, **Map 2/1 A** *Website: www.enteteatrale.it/Festival.htm*

Summer venues

Anfiteatro della Quercia del Tasso

Passeggiata del Gianicolo (06 575 0827). Bus to Piazza Sonnino or Lungotevere Sanzio. **Box office** from 7pm each evening at the Anfiteatro; 9am-2pm Mon-Sat at Teatro Anfitrione, Via San

*Small gladiators at **Ostia Antica**.*

Saba, 24. **Shows** 9.15pm Mon-Sat, July-Sept; occasional afternoon matinees. **Map 6/1C** An ancient amphitheatre on the Gianicolo, specialising in classic Greek and Latin theatre and eighteenth-century Venetian comedy. Matinée performances for children.

Giardino degli Aranci

Via di Santa Sabina (06 3973 9700). *Metro Circo Massimo/bus to Via di Santa Sabina.* **Box office** from 8.30pm Tue-Sun. **Shows** 9pm Tue-Sun. **Map 7/1 A** This beautiful park on the Aventine is transformed into a theatre for the summer. One play per season, often classic comedies and tragedies.

Teatro Romano di Ostia Antica

(06 687 5445). Train to Ostia Antica from Stazione Roma-Ostia Lido. **Box office** from 6pm daily; also at Teatro Argentina *(see below).* **Shows** 8.30pm daily, July. This wonderfully-preserved Roman theatre, set amid the ruins of ancient Rome's main port *(see pp236-7),* hosts prestigious productions of Roman and Greek classics. The seats are stone: you are advised to take your own cushion.

Rome's official venue for opera and dance is a beautiful theatre with excellent acoustics and unruly unions. *See also page 216.*

Teatro di Roma – Argentina

Largo Argentina, 52 (06 6880 4601). *Bus or tram to Largo Argentina.* **Box office** 10am-2pm, 3-7pm, Mon-Sat. **Shows** *Oct-June* 9pm Mon-Wed, Fri, Sat; 5pm Thur, Sun. **Map 6/1 A** Beautiful headquarters of the Teatro di Roma., with a range of exchange programmes and productions in conjunction with other state-subsidised theatres.

Teatro di Roma – India

Lungotevere Papareschi (06 6840 0008). *Bus to Piazzale della Radio.* **Box office** details not available at time of writing.

Opened late in 1999, the India is Rome's newest and most modern space for performances of all kinds. Situated in a former soap factory in a semi-abandoned industrial area south of the centre; its brief, according to Teatro di Roma's indefatigable artistic director Mario Martone, is to make high-profile international experimental theatre and dance a regular feature in this otherwise tradition-orientated city. It will have spaces for seminars, lectures and anything else that fails to slot comfortably into staider venues.

Teatro Valle

Via del Teatro Valle, 23a (06 6880 3794). Bus to Corso Vittorio Emanuele or Largo Argentina. **Box office** 10am-7pm Tue-Sat; 10am-1pm Sun. **Shows** 9pm Tue, Fri, Sat; 5pm Wed, Thur, Sun. **Map 3/2A**

A beautiful little theatre, with one of the city's highest-quality repertoires, including very good reworkings of classics.

Commercial/smaller venues

Salone Margherita Bagaglino
*Via Due Macelli, 75 (06 679 1439/06 679 8269).
Metro Spagna/bus to Piazza San Silvestro or Via del
Tritone.* **Box office** 9.30am-10pm Tue-Sun.
Shows 9.30pm Tue- Sat, 6pm Sat, Sun **Map 5/1C**
Rome's nearest equivalent to a Parisian dinner-theatre, frequented by the city's upper crust.

Teatro degli Artisti
*Via San Francesco di Sales, 14 (06 6880 8438). Bus
to Lungotevere Farnesina.* **Box office** 7.30pm until
beginning of show. **Map 6/1C**
Mainly a contemporary dance stage, it also provides
a space for young experimental theatre groups.

Teatro Belli
*Piazza Sant'Apollonia, 11A (06 589 4875). Bus to
Lungotevere Sanzio or Piazza Sonnino.* **Box office**
11am-1pm, 5-9pm, Tue-Sat; 3.30-5.30pm Sun. **Shows**
Sept-May 9pm Tue-Sat; 5.30pm Sun. **Map 6/2B**
Small, private theatre with an emphasis on Italian
plays and dialect theatre.

Teatro Colosseo
*Via Capo d'Africa, 5 (06 700 4932). Metro
Colosseo/bus to Piazza del Colosseo.*
Box office 8-10pm Tue-Sat. **Shows** *Sala Grande*
8.30, 10.30pm Tue-Sat; 5.30, 7.30pm Sun; *Ridotto Sala
A* 8.30pm Tue-Sat, 5.30pm Sun; *Ridotto Sala B*
10.30pm Tue-Sat, 7pm Sun. **Map 8/2B**
The Colosseo provides a showcase for young Italian
directors and actors.

Teatro della Cometa
*Via del Teatro di Marcello, 4 (06 678 4380). Bus to
Piazza Venezia or Via del Teatro di Marcello.* **Box
office** 10am-1pm, 4-9pm, Tue-Sat; 10am-1pm, 4-5pm
Sun. **Shows** 9.15pm Tue-Sat; 5pm Sun. **Map 6/1A**
Fringe theatre hosting farces or socially-aware drama.

Teatro Eliseo
*Via Nazionale, 183 (06 488 2114).
Bus to Via Nazionale.* **Box office** 10am-1pm, 4-7pm,
Tue-Sun. **Shows** 8.45pm Tue, Thur-Sat; 5pm Wed,
Sat, Sun. **Map 8/1C**
A huge, rather dreary theatre, which nevertheless is
an important venue for mainstream productions.

Teatro Flaiano
*Via Santo Stefano del Cacco, 15. Bus or tram to
Largo Argentina. (06 679 5696/06 678 7424).* **Box
office** 10am-1pm, 4-7pm, Tue-Sun. **Map 3/2A**
A pretty theatre decorated in blue velvet, the Flaiano
also hosts literary presentations and lectures.

Teatro Ghione
*Via delle Fornaci, 37 (06 637 2294).
Bus to Piazza di Porta Cavalleggeri.* **Box office**
10.30am-1pm, 4-8pm, Tue-Sun. **Shows** 9pm Tue,
Wed, Fri, Sat; 5pm Thur, Sun.

This velvet-swathed Victorian theatre stages a prestigious music season from September to May.

Teatro Greco
*Via Ruggero Leoncavallo, 16 (06 860 7513).
Bus to Largo Somalia.* **Box office** before shows.
Shows 9pm daily.
A new dance venue in north-east Rome, connected
to one of the city's most prestigious dance schools.

Teatro Olimpico
*Piazza Gentile da Fabriano, 17 (06 326 5991). Bus
to Piazza Mancini.* **Box office** 11am-7pm daily.
Shows 9pm daily, Oct-May.
A vast, recently renovated theatre with excellent
acoustics, and an interesting programme of music,
dance and theatre.

Teatro dell'Orologio
*Via de' Filippini, 17a (06 6830 8735/06 6830
8330). Bus to Corso Vittorio Emanuele.*
Box office *Sept-June* 4-8pm Tue-Sat; 4-6pm Sun.
Shows *Sala Grande* 9pm Tue-Sat; 5.30pm Sun; *Sala
Caffèteatro* 9pm Tue-Sat; 6pm Sun; *Sala Arnaud*
9pm Tue-Sat; 5pm Sun. **Map 3/2B**
Fringe theatre, home to the English language theatre season produced by the Off Night Repertory.

Teatro Quirino
*Via Marco Minghetti, 1 (06 679 4585). Bus to Via
del Corso.* **Box office** 10am-1pm, 3-7pm, Tue-Sat;
10am-1pm, 3.30-5pm, Sun. **Shows** 9pm Tue, Fri, Sat;
5pm Wed, Thur, Sun. **Map 5/2C**
Productions of serious classics and tragedies by big
name directors and major Italian casts.

Teatro Rossini
*Piazza Santa Chiara, 14 (06 6880 2770). Bus to
Largo Argentina.* **Box office** 10.30am-1pm, 4-9pm,
Tue-Sun. **Shows** 9pm Tue, Thur-Sat; 5pm Wed, Sat,
Sun. **Map 3/2A**
A cosy old theatre with a programme dedicated to
original dramas and Roman dialect reworkings.

Teatro Sistina
*Via Sistina, 129 (06 420 0711).
Bus to Piazza Barberini/ metro Barberini.*
Box office 10am-1pm, 3.30-7pm, daily.
Shows 9pm Tue-Sat; 5pm Sun. **Map 5/1C**
Glitzy Italian musicals and even glitzier international variety hits.

Teatro Vascello
*Via Giacinto Carini, 72 (06 588 1021). Bus to Via
Carini.* **Box office** 5.30-8.30pm Tue-Sat; 3-5pm Sun.
Shows 9pm Tue-Sat; 5pm Sun. **Map 7/1C**
Independent theatre that presents some fairly decent
experimental theatre and dance productions, plus
conferences and workshops.

Teatro Vittoria
*Piazza Santa Maria Liberatrice, 8 (06 574 0170/06
574 0598). Bus to Via Marmorata.* **Box office**
10am-1pm, 4-7pm, Mon; 10am-7pm Tue-Sat; 10am-
1pm Sun. **Shows** 9pm Tue-Sat; 5pm Sun.
Cavernous venue in Testaccio, specialising in
translated texts and international variety.

Music: Classical & Opera

Rome's music scene is buzzing as the Auditorium nears completion.

After decades of stagnation, Rome's classical music scene is buzzing. Renzo Piano's state-of-the-art **auditorium** (*see page 218*) is slowly rising from its foundations, and the city's musical establishment is jockeying for a place in the new order. In the process, some august musical institutions are sure to come in for a shake-up.

Italy's prodigal son, Giuseppe Sinopoli, now artistic director of Rome Opera, has ambitions of Wagnerian dimensions. With city councillors fawning at his feet, Sinopoli seems set for a central role as the city's musical life prepares to move into the three-hall auditorium complex. One thing is certain: he will either make or break classical music in the city. His champions would do well to remember that Sinopoli's divorce from London's Philharmonia followed some of the nastiest, most critical reviews in living memory.

ENSEMBLES & SEASONS

The top job in Rome's musical scene remains the directorship of the **Accademia Nazionale di Santa Cecilia**, Italy's most prestigious academy, founded by Palestrina himself in the sixteenth century. The current chairman, Bruno Cagli, appointed Myung-Whung Chung as principal conductor for a much-needed overhaul of the orchestra. Gone are the days of jobs for boys: Chung has set international standards for recruitment. He has also signed recording contracts with Deutsche Grammophon, Philips and Decca, but more drilling is needed to get the orchestra up to world standard. Rome, though, continues to attract some of the world's greatest conductors: Valery Gergiev, Wolfgang Sawallisch, Andrew Davis and Yuri Temirkanov, among others. Programming reflects the Accademia's rather conservative audience, for whom composers like Janacek seem daringly modern, but Cagli has begun to change things with autumn festivals dedicated to single composers, and a pioneering commitment to classical/popular cross-overs. Artists such as Keith Jarret, Madredeus and Michael Nyman have featured recently on the Santa Cecilia programme.

Undoubtedly world-class, the chamber music season hosts just about anyone who is anyone in the music world. The Santa Cecilia summer season at the remarkable outdoor venue in **Villa Giulia** is always interesting (*see page 67*), as is the children's season.

The **Accademia Filarmonica Romana**, founded 1821, is a newcomer compared with Santa Cecilia, but can boast composers like Rossini, Donizetti, Paganini and Verdi among its founders. Traditionally it combines the activities of a choir school (with a repertoire reflecting the dubious taste of its director, Father Pablo Colino) with a varied season of chamber music, early music, ballet and chamber opera. Under its new artistic director, composer Matteo D'Amico, multimedia productions by stage directors such as Bob Wilson and Peter Stein have added to the rich range of offerings, and more space has been made for contemporary music. The concert season runs from September to May in the Accademia's own venue, the **Teatro Olimpico**.

Newest and smallest of the major concert-providers, the **Istituzione Universitaria dei Concerti** (IUC), was founded after World War II to help bring a bit of life to Rome's culturally-dead campus. Today the IUC offers a varied season around a core programme of often outstanding international and Italian recitals and chamber music at the campus's main auditorium, the **Aula Magna**. There's a refreshing emphasis on early music, non-classical musicians and unusual sound textures. The IUC serves a mixed audience, with elderly subscribers drawn by the afternoon concerts, and students and university staff on cut-rate subscriptions dominating the evening series. It's also a forum for Rome débuts of young international competition winners and composers.

Last but certainly not least is Rome's **Teatro dell'Opera**. Never one of Italy's truly great opera houses, it has been teetering on the brink of total collapse for decades. With its staff of thousands and scandalously limited number of productions and performances each year, it is remarkably inefficient even by Rome standards. During the early 1990s the place was run by Giampaolo Cresci, a self-proclaimed musical ignoramus, under whose guidance it notched up its only major achievement of recent years: the biggest deficit of any opera house ever – a staggering 60 billion lire. Since then a long succession of *sovrintendenti* (administrators) have all thrown in the towel, defeated by the political favours system and the paralysis of the hyper-unionised orchestra and stagehands.

The recent appointment of super-bureaucrat Francesco Ernani as *sovrintendente* is hailed as the last chance for the opera. He has promised to balance the books and tame the unions. After an acrimonious battle, Sinopoli has been given artistic and musical direction, which will mean much more Wagner than anyone in Rome really wants. It remains to be seen whether this heavyweight duo can put an end to Rome's tradition of first-night walk-outs by musicians, and guarantee a reasonable number of European-level performances. In the fraught 1999 season things weren't looking too hopeful. Traditionally, top-name singers rarely stay around much after the opening night. Keep a close eye on the cast list for second-rate substitutes, and check the reviews. Seats are expensive.

Tickets

Getting hold of tickets used to involve all-night queueing, but now computer pre-sales are the order of the day. Don't get too excited: phone booking is still light years away. Most good inexpensive seats for big-name concerts are taken by subscribers, so keep an eye out for concerts that are *fuori abbonamento* (non-subscription). Seats for chamber and early music performances are usually in good supply. Almost all venues now pre-sell single tickets for concerts immediately after subs close, which means that tourists often miss out, but you can try an agency (*see p187*); these charge a booking fee. If you have time, a trip to the box office is still the best way. Go at least a week in advance, with cash (plastic can be touch and go).

Tickets for high-demand opera performances are sometimes sold only at the last minute: ring for details. Prices for decent seats at main auditoria, and cheap seats at the opera, start at around L30,000, plus a 10% booking fee.

Auditoria

Auditorio Pio

Via della Conciliazione, 4 (06 6880 1044).
Bus to Lungotevere Vaticano.
Concerts Oct-June. **Box office** 10.30am-1.30pm, 3-6pm, Mon, Tue, Thur-Sun; until interval on concert days. **Map 3/1C**
Since it was first rented from the Vatican in 1958, this has been the 'temporary' home of the **Accademia Nazionale di Santa Cecilia** concert series. Bearing more resemblance to an oversized school hall than a concert hall, it has acoustics that have been greatly improved over the years, but few will be sorry to leave it when the new auditorium (*see page 218*) is ready. It's worth spending more for good seats: tickets for single concerts are sold in two phases: from mid-October (Oct-Jan concerts) and from February (Feb-Jun concerts).

Aula Magna dell'Università la Sapienza

Piazzale Aldo Moro. Metro Policlinico/bus or tram to Viale Regina Elena. **Concerts** Oct-June.
Box office *Lungotevere Flaminio, 50 (06 361 0051/fax 06 3600 1511/*
segretaria.ius@concentrüuc.it). Bus/tram to Piazza Mancini. **Open** 10am-1pm, 2-6pm, Mon-Fri.
With its kitsch Fascist décor, but reasonable acoustics, the Aula Magna is the principal auditorium for the IUC season. Tickets can be bought ahead from the IUC headquarters at Lungotevere Flaminio, or at the Aula Magna immediately before concerts. *Website: www.cercertiiuc.it*

Sala Casella

Via Flaminia, 118 (06 320 1752).
Bus to Piazza Mancini/bus or tram to Via Flaminia.
Box office at **Teatro Olimpico** (*see below*).
The in-house concert hall of the **Accademia Filarmonica**, restored and equipped to the highest level in terms of acoustics, comfort and safety. Seats an intimate 180, and its atmospheric interior is ideal for offbeat programmes.

Teatro Olimpico

Piazza Gentile da Fabriano (06 326 5991).
Bus or tram to Piazza Mancini.
Box office 11am-7pm daily; from 8pm on concert days. **Concerts** Sept-May.
A very successful cinema conversion has created one of the most attractive venues in Rome for all types of performances: comfortable, with good acoustics, even in cheaper seats. Owned by the **Accademia Filarmonica**, it's used for their Thursday concerts. *See also chapter* **Theatre & Dance**.

Teatro dell'Opera di Roma

Via Firenze, 72 (06 481 601/06 4816 0255).
Bus to Via Nazionale. **Box office** 9am-5pm Mon-Sat; 9am-1.30pm Sun; also until 15 minutes after the beginning of performances. **Map 5/2B**
The lavish late nineteenth-century *teatro all'italiana* interior comes as quite a surprise after Mussolini's angular façade and tacky potted palms. There are towering rows of boxes, loads of stucco, frescoes and gold paint everywhere. Acoustics vary greatly – the higher (and cheaper) seats are unsatisfactory. Splash out on a box – it's part of the experience.

Churches

There is nothing in Rome to compare with the church music tradition of cities like Vienna and London. Of the great city basilicas, only **San Giovanni in Laterano** and **Santa Maria Maggiore** still bother to maintain a choir and do a weekly sung mass. **Saint Peter's** has a football stadium acoustic and lousy choirs to match, and among the city's monasteries and convents, only **Sant'Anselmo** manages some decent plainchant. Kitsch amplification in places like San Giovanni completely destroys the effect of what singing

*Against all odds, productions still make it on stage at the **Teatro dell'Opera**: Aida, in 1999.*

there is. The only really outstanding church choir is that of the *Russicum*, the Eastern Rite church opposite Santa Maria Maggiore.

To make matters worse, the church hierarchy does not allow paying concerts. There are some free concerts by visiting choirs, so it's worth keeping an eye on posters at church entrances. Sadly, the preferred venue, **Sant'Ignazio**, is a massive barn with acoustics wholly unsuited to music-making. Get there early and grab a seat in the very front row – anywhere else is a waste of time.

Organ buffs should make a bee-line for the splendidly restored 1670s instrument in **San Giovanni de' Fiorentini** in Via Giulia (played for mass at noon on Sunday; **Map 3/2B**) and the Luca Blasi organ in San Giovanni in Laterano (played after 10am mass). There are organ concerts at **San Marcello al Corso** in Piazza San Marcello, 5 (**Map 5/2C**), and **San Carlo ai Catinari** in Piazza Cairoli, 117 (**Map 6/1A**).

Musical associations

In the '80s and early '90s, while the city's major cultural institutions were languishing in mediocrity, these smaller associations took up much of the slack. Concert programmes and musical workshops usually run from November (when associations often seek new members) to May.

Associazione Il Tempietto

Via Appia Nuova, 154 (06 7720 9128/fax 06 7720 0905/tempietto@alt.it) .
An energetic organisation that gives young and relatively inexperienced performers a public forum.

Concerts are held at Sala Baldini in Piazza Campitelli and the Basilica of San Nicola in Carcere in winter (both **Map 6/1A**), and the Teatro di Marcello in summer (nightly). *See also p219.*
Website:
http://members.it.tripod.de/tempietto/index.html

Associazione Musicale Romana

Via dei Banchi Vecchi, 61 (06 686 84 41; amr.it@agora.stm.it).
Concerts Mar, June-July, Sept. **Box office** at individual venues before concerts.
The AMR presents an interesting summer season for a select few in the Botanic Gardens (Largo Cristina di Svezia, 23b; **Map 6/1B**). Programmes includes Gershwin and Piazzola as well as mainstream chamber music. Don't miss the short but sweet annual organ festival in September, when the superb instrument in San Giovanni de' Fiorentini is played by big names, or the harpsichord festival, in the spectacular French academy in Villa Medici at the top of the Spanish Steps, in March. Tickets can be bought through **Easy Ticket** (*www.tkts.it*; 24-hour phone booking, 166 22 166).
Website: www.agora.stm.it/amr/

Associazione Nuova Consonanza

Via S. di Saint Bon, 61 (06 37 00 323; fax 06 37 20 0 26;nuovaconsonanza@iol.it;).
Concerts May, June, Oct-Dec. **Box office** at individual venues before concerts.
The Associazione organises the prestigious autumn **Festivale di Nuova Consonanza**, presenting the best in contemporary music. There is also a short spring season, and lectures and seminars. Two other contemporary music groups specialise in electronic music: **CRM**, which runs a spring festival (06 446

4161), and **Musica Verticale**, which organises an autumn festival (0765 36 386).
Website: http://users.iol.it/nuovaconsonanza/

Club Orpheus

Viale Ruggero Bacone, 8 (06 4781 8485/ fax 06 4781 8444). **Concerts** Oct-May. **Venue** Teatro Ghione, Via delle Fornaci, 37 (06 637 2294). **Box office** at Teatro Ghione, 30 minutes before concerts.
Singing and singers are the emphasis of this group, which organises operatic and lieder recitals of outstanding quality. The voices range from great names to rising young stars (Nicolai Ghiaurov and Raina Kabaivanska, to Sylvia McNair, Anna Tomowa-Sintow, Rockwell Blake and Simon Keenlyside). Also presents piano recitals and the odd chamber music performance. A must for opera fans.

Il Gonfalone

Oratorio del Gonfalone, Via del Gonfalone. Bus to Lungotevere Sangallo. **Concerts** Oct-June.
Information & Box office Vicolo della Scimmia, 1b (06 687 5952). *Bus to Lungotevere Sangallo.* **Open** 9am-1pm Mon-Fri; 9.30am-5pm Sat. **Map 3/2B**

The Gonfalone has its own orchestra, choir and venue: the **Oratorio del Gonfalone** (although at time of writing this was under restoration, and concerts were being held at the **Oratorio Caravita** in Via del Caravita, 7; **Map 3/2A**). Phone ahead to check the current venue. It specialises in chamber music, and hosts performances by excellent visiting groups from around Italy.

Choirs

One of the healthiest areas of Rome's musical life is the amateur choral scene, which ranges from big singalong choirs like C.I.M.A to church choirs and earnest early music groups. In autumn many choirs place advertisements for new members.

Agimus

Via dei Greci, 18 (06 36 00 18 24). **Map 2/2A**
The **Associazione Giovanile Musicale** is the principal choral organisation in Rome. In addition to performances, it organises concerts in venues like the church of San Teodoro al Palatino (**Map 8/2C**).

The nameless auditorium

Rome has had to do without a proper purpose-built concert venue since 1933, when Mussolini, always keen for a photo opportunity, personally dealt the first blow in the demolition of the city's concert hall, the *Augusteo*. The venerable old building happened to stand above the remains of the **Mausoleum of Augustus** (*see page 57*), and *Il Duce* wanted the mausoleum as the centrepiece in a celebration of his Imperial hero.

Vows to provide the city with a new concert venue were forgotten as World War II loomed. Since then, an interminable string of projects has been presented, then left on shelves to gather dust. In 2000, however, Rome's concert-goers will finally get what they've been waiting for. If, that is, all goes to plan.

The new auditorium – its very name is a matter of controversy, with several options still being argued over at time of writing – has been designed by Renzo Piano (of Centre Pompidou fame), and is taking shape on a former wasteland site in the northern suburb of Flaminia, not far from the Stadio Flaminio. Work on the three-hall complex was initially held up by the inevitable ancient finds. Foundation-digging ground to a halt as archaeologists unearthed a small farmhouse discovered on the site; a statue of a river god had to be closely scrutinised before Piano could incorporate it into his overall scheme. Contractual squabbles, too, halted work on occasion. It was not long before the original,

pre-Millennium inauguration date of November 1999 had to be scrapped.

Undaunted, the city council presented Plan B: a grand opening in October 2000, just in time to dominate the tail end of Holy Year celebrations (*see page 106*). And just to make it clear there's no ignominy attached to this all-too-familiar failure to meet deadlines, it was decided to interrupt building work in December 1999 for a one-off inaugural concert among the cement mixers.

Whenever the auditorium opens for business, there can be no doubt that Piano's complex will raise Rome's status on the international music scene, providing the infrastructure needed to host world-class events. As Piano's three computer-mouse-shaped concert halls (*see photo, page 30*) rose out of the ground, only one question has remained: can the Eternal City really afford this state-of-the-art luxury?

The city council, with an eye to financial viability, insisted on bumping up seating capacity in the 500-seat hall to 750, making it double as a theatre. It also appointed private-sector managers to run things. If the Auditorium is to mark a real departure in Roman culture, however, city hall must now find a solution to the biggest threat of all: the bureaucrat-vs-union battles that have turned so many Opera seasons into an excruciating farce.
Auditorio
Via P. de Coubertin. Bus to Piazza Euclide.

Coro Romani Cantores

Corso Trieste, 165 (06 44 24 05 61).
Specialises in early music, usually accompanied by
period instruments.

New Chamber Singers

*Chiesa di San Paolo entro le Mura, Via Napoli, 58
(06 5091 7241/06 488 3339).* **Map 5/2B**
This rather exclusive amateur choir, long directed
by Keith Griggs, organist of the Episcopalian
church, is now conducted by Wijnand van de Pol
from the rival Anglican church.

Coro della Scuola Popolare di Musica di Testaccio

*Via Monte Testaccio, 91 (06 575 9308/fax 06 575
7940/spmt@flashnet.it).* **Map 7/2A**
Gutsy music-making is the order of the day at this
remarkable music school. The SPMT runs courses
on just about every aspect of music, and hosts a
staggering range of jam sessions and happenings.
Website: www.itaca.com/spmt/

Open-air festivals

Teatro dell'Opera

Via Firenze, 72 (06 481 601). Bus to Via Nazionale.
Box office 9am-5pm Mon-Sat; 9am-1.30pm Sun.
Since 1997 the Opera's outdoor season has been
installed at the **Stadio Olimpico** *(see p207)*, while
its old home, the spectacular **Baths of Caracalla**,
have been declared off-limits for opera performances, but continue to be used for concerts. Check
July newspapers for performance details and the latest developments in the running battle between the
opera and the archaeologists.

Accademia of Santa Cecilia at Villa Giulia

*Piazzale di Villa Giulia, 9 (06 6786428/ 06 678
0742/06 683 3242/credit card sales 06 6880 1044/
06 3938 7297). Bus or tram to Via Flaminia or
Viale delle Belle Arti.*
Concerts end June-end July. **Map 2/1A**
Probably the most beautiful setting for outdoor
music in Rome, the exquisite Renaissance courtyard
of the Etruscan museum also boasts the city's best
outdoor acoustics. Staged through July, the series
used to include international orchestras, but belt-
tightening has led to greater dependence on local
artists. Symphony concerts, plus something out of
the way, with classical/popular cross-overs, gypsy
bands or even gospel choirs.

RomaEuropa Festival

*Via XX Settembre, 3 (06 4201 3467/ toll-free 800
795 525/fax 06 48 90 40 30/romaeuropa@srd.it).*
Box office at individual venues.
Organised in collaboration with the French
Academy (Villa Medici), the German Academy (Villa
Massimo) and other Rome international cultural centres, this wide-ranging festival highlights contemporary European culture in the breathtaking
gardens of the academies themselves. The indoor
autumn season (Oct-Nov) is mostly ballet, but

always includes some concerts. *See also p7, and
chapter* **Theatre & Dance**).
Website: www.romaeuropafestival.com

Concerti del Tempietto

Temporary venue *Cortile di San Teodoro, Via di
San Teodoro.* **Map 8/2C**
From 2000 *Teatro di Marcello, Via del Teatro di
Marcello, 44 (06 7720 9128/ fax 06 7720
0906/tempietto@alt.it). Bus to Via del Teatro di
Marcello.* **Box office** from venue two hours before
concerts. **Map 6/2A**
From November to July Associazione Il Tempietto
organises concerts in Sala Baldini and in the nearby Basilica of San Nicola in Carcere *(see p46)*, but
during the summer months they move *al fresco* for
their nightly 8.30pm concerts. Rather low-level musi-
cally, but both the temporary home and the Teatro
di Marcello are beautiful outdoor venues.

Rome Festival

*Cortile Auditorium Virgilio, Via Giulia, 38.
(06 3979 9868). Bus to Lungotevere dei Tebaldi or
Piazza della Chiesa Nuova.* **Box office** before
concerts. **Map 6/1B**
A low-budget summer festival of opera, operetta and
popular classics directed by *maestro* Fritz Maraffi.
The cool outdoor venue is a major draw.

Out of town festivals

Festival dei Due Mondi, Spoleto

*Piazza Duomo, 8, 06049 Spoleto (0743 44 700/
toll-free 800 565 600/spoletofestival@krenet.it).*
Dates June-July.
Perhaps Italy's most famous performing arts
festival and certainly its most international, Spoleto
is recovering some of the dynamism of its early
years. Founded over 40 years ago by Gian Carlo
Menotti, and now under the direction of his son
Francis, it has always showcased modern opera, theatre, film and music, but includes almost everything
from gypsy horse shows to grand opera, visual art
and even science. Romans flock in early summer to
the cooler climes of Umbria. More off-beat performances may be under-booked, but are often the best.
Check the highly informative and efficient website
for programmes and booking.
Website: www.spoletofestival.net

Festival Pontino

*Castello Caetani Sermoneta/Abbazia di Fossanova,
Priverno (0773 605 551/fax 0773 605 548).*
Dates June-July.
Composer Goffredo Petrassi always draws excellent
musicians from all over Europe to his small-scale
festival of orchestral and chamber music in two out-
standingly beautiful venues: the medieval Castello
Caetani in the pretty hill town of Sermoneta (near
Ninfa, *see page 245*), and the abbey of **Fossanova**,
one of Italy's few 'real' Gothic churches *(see page
244)*. A contemporary music festival also takes
place in June. Ticket sales are at the door only.
Website: www.panservice.it/festivalpontino

Music: Rock, Roots and Jazz

No musical caput mundi, but dig deep and Rome has something for everyone.

For the kind of person who'd consider travelling to London, Paris or even the States to take advantage of an exciting live music scene, Rome isn't going to be high up on any list of 'happening' cities. To be fair, though, its back-water reputation is not entirely merited. Sure, international stars often limit the Italian leg of their world tours to a quick hop over the border to play Milan, but not all of them do. And in any case, it's the local scene that's worth coming for: armed with a bit of inside information, you'll find that the Eternally-surprising City has something for everyone.

WHAT TO EXPECT

Until the recent appearance of the **Palacisalfa** in EUR, Rome had always lacked a good large-scale music venue. The **Palaeur** and **Foro Italico** sports venues have often hosted concerts, but both are far from ideal. Now, the city finally has a decent space for larger concerts, in the shape of a sports stadium that actually lends itself to music, with bearable acoustics. All that remains to be done is to overcome the damaging lack of professionalism in organizing concerts… And to rescind strict decibel-level rules and absurd curfews.

Smaller bands have fewer troubles. The *centri sociali* – semi-legal squats – and the organisations that revolve around them do a great job of providing cheap, alternative facilities.

Winter months in Rome are dominated by local rock and Latin bands, with the occasional visit from foreign stars and big-name Italian favourites such as Pino Daniele, or homegrown rapper Lorenzo Cherubini, alias Jovanotti. Other local names that you may not know, but might find interesting, include **Almamagretta**, an Adrian Sherwood/African Headcharge-inspired dub band; **Casino Royale**, for hip hop Italian-style; and popular rap group **Sud Sound System**. There's also a string of Italian World Beat bands such as **Novalia** and **Agricantus** that are well worth checking out: for more synthetic sounds look out for **Matt 101**, **MSB**, and **Surya Lab**.

As for local jazz, piano and accordion player **Antonello Salis** is always good, as is **Roberto**

Home-grown rapper Jovanotti.

Gatto, who plays almost every week: just head for **Big Mama**. For R&B and soul fans, Rome has long been home to American ex-pat **Herbie Goins**, who was one of the singers to pass through Alexis Korner's many bands in the 1960s (Mick Jagger was another).

In the summer months, clubs close and outdoor venues move to the fore. This is the time when international acts are most likely to make an appearance in Rome. Whatever's on offer, the joy of sitting under the stars, often in beautiful, historic surroundings, can turn any night into something special.

GIG-GOING

Concert listings can be found in the weekly *Time Out Roma* magazine, in papers like *Il Manifesto* and *La Repubblica* (especially in its Thursday

Trovaroma supplement), and in the weekly magazine *Rome C'è*, which has an English section. **Radio Città Futura** (97.7 FM) lists the day's events (Italian only) on Take Five at 6.30pm daily (*see chapter* **Media**). Whatever your source of information, bear in mind that times should be read as vague suggestions rather than definite data: a phone call can save you a wasted trip.

One peculiarity of Roman clubs is the *tessera* (membership card), which you will have to buy at the door. You're not being ripped off: this is the law. *Tessere* are usually valid for the season, and will often entitle you to free entry on subsequent visits. Sometimes there is an entrance fee on top of the price of the *tessera*, which may or may not entitle you to a free drink. Many clubs double up as live music and DJ venues at different times; for more on their dance club side, *see also chapters* **Gay & Lesbian** *and* **Nightlife**.

Venues

Akab
Via di Monte Testaccio, 69 (06 574 4485).
Bus to Via Marmorata or Via Galvani.
Open 10pm-4am Wed-Sat. **Admission** L15,000-25,000. **No credit cards. Map 7/2A**
Situated near the Mattatoio (*see p85*), Akab presents a mix of musical styles, as well as some cabaret and theatre nights. DJ after the gigs.

Alpheus
Via del Commercio, 36 (06 574 7826).
Bus to Via Ostiense. **Open** 10pm-4.30am Tue-Sun. **Admission** L10,000 Tue, Wed, Thur, Sun; L20,000 Fri including drink; L15,000 Sat; *July-Aug* 10pm-4.30am Fri, Sat. **Credit** AmEx.
A former cheese factory, near a huge gasworks, with three big halls featuring live rock, Latin, world music and jazz, followed by a disco. There's a pizzeria and an ice-cream parlour in the garden. Admission fees may rise for special concert events. Plenty of street parking – but be sure to pay the self styled 'parking attendant', or you might return to find a vital piece of your car missing. Friday night hosts the *Mucca Assassina* crew (*see page 202*).

Brancaleone
Via Levanna, 11 (06 8200 0959).
Bus to Piazza Sempione. **Open** 10.30pm-5.00am Thur-Sun. **Admission** donation of L5,000 expected; concerts may cost more. **No credit cards.**
One of Rome's *centri sociali* – semi-legal social centres – which hosts regular concerts, local and international. The stage is large and the amplification decent. Recommended.

Circolo degli Artisti
Via Casilina Vecchia, 42 (06 7030 5684).
Bus to Via Casilina or Piazza D. Pigneto.
Open 9pm-3am Tue-Sun. **Admission** varies depending on the event; L7,000 three-month membership card. **No credit cards.**

A long-running, vibrantly eclectic alternative venue that has recently upped sticks to a new locale. The Circolo's new home, south-east of Termini, isn't quite as concert-friendly as the old one by Piazza Vittorio, but they still organise an un-pin-downable range of local concerts several days a week. *Wheelchair access.*

Fonclea
Via Crescenzio, 82A (06 689 6302).
Bus to Piazza Cavour or Piazza Risorgimento. **Open** *end Sept-June* 8.30pm-2am daily. **Admission** L10,000 for special events. **Credit** MC, V. **Map 3/1C**
Restaurant, pub and cellar featuring soul, Latin, and funk. Local acts are more likely to take the stage than international ones.

Frontiera
Via Aurelia, 1,051 (06 6618 0110). Drive west along Via Aurelia, beyond Grande Raccordo.
Open 9pm-late Thur-Sun: closing times vary. **Admission** depends on event. **No credit cards.**
One of the bigger venues in Rome, and the one where you're most likely to find a name band. The tricky part is getting to Rome's western outskirts; you'll need a car. Situated in the middle of a motorway roundabout, it's easy to miss it. DJs often appear when the concert is finished. *Wheelchair access.*

Horus Club
Corso Sempione, 21 (06 8689 9181).
Bus to Piazza Sempione. **Open** 9pm-3am Wed-Sat. **Admission** L20,000 or more, depending on the event. **Credit** AmEx, DC, EC, MC,V.
One of few music venues in the north of the city, and a good place to avoid other tourists, the Horus is a former cinema with billiard tables, seats and a bar. It has presented visiting acts of the calibre of Fun Loving Criminals, Courtney Pine and Steve Earle; programming policy is eclectic. DJs appear after gigs. *Wheelchair access.*

Jive
Via Giuseppe Libetta, 7 (06 574 5989).
Bus to Via Ostiense/ metro Garbatella. **Open** *July-May* 9.30pm-3.30am daily; *June* 9.30pm-3.30am Thur-Sat **Admission** membership L10,000; remainder depends on event. **No credit cards.**
Once known as the Classico, this stylish club features local African, Latin and funk groups and special DJ nights. There are regular outdoor gigs in summer, which come highly recommended. *Wheelchair access.*

Il Locale
Vicolo del Fico, 3 (06 687 9075). Bus to Corso Vittorio Emanuele or Corso Rinascimento. **Open** 10pm-3am; closing day varies. Closed June-Sept 15. **Admission** L10,000. **No credit cards. Map 3/2B**
A long-standing, popular hangout for local musicians and theatre people, Il Locale features mostly Italian bands playing their own compositions, with occasional theatre, cabaret and films. *Wheelchair access.*

Music moves outdoors

When clubs close down for the summer, outdoor festivals abound. The official **Estate Romana** (Roman Summer) is the mother of all festivals, running from mid-June through August (*see page 7*), and attracting many foreign acts to the stunning venues that are set aside for the occasion. There are also plenty of other, only relatively smaller-scale events through the summer.

Smaller festivals occur during the rest of the year too. By far the most impressive non-summer event is the annual free outdoor May Day **(Primo Maggio)** concert in Piazza San Giovanni. Organised by the major trade unions (*see page 6*), this traditional fixture in Rome's music calendar usually attracts an international star or two and a slew of home-grown ones, plus crowds that invariably number hundreds of thousands.

Along Came Jazz

Various venues in Tivoli (0774 313755). Bus from Ponte Mammolo. **Dates** last week of June, first week July. **Admission** free.
This jazz festival runs for two or three days at the beginning of July in **Tivoli**, 30km east of Rome (*see pages 237-9*), and features mainly Italian musicians, such as Antonello Salis, Pino Minafra or Mauro Orselli, together with a few international guests such as Evan Parker.
Website: www.alongcamejazz.org

Fiesta Capannelle

Via Appia Nuova, 1,245 (06 7129 9855/ 06 7834 6587/06 718 2139). Bus along Via Appia Nuova to Ippodromo Capannelle. **Dates** mid-June-Aug. **Admission** L12,000.
Top international names in Latin American music – including Cuban and Caribbean stars – and reggae perform here at Rome's largest racecourse – in the far south-east of the city down the Via Appia Nuova. Latin American food, rhythms and atmosphere take over the track from June through to August.

Jazz and Image Festival

Villa Celimontana (06 7049 5005/06 589 7807). Bus to Piazza della Navicella or Colosseum. **Dates** June-Aug. **Admission** L10,000. **Map 9/1B**
Organised by the **Alexanderplatz** jazz club (*see page 224*), this is the best outside venue in which to hear jazz in summer. In the glorious, leafy Villa Celimontana park on the Celio hill, a formal garden dotted with ancient remains and trickling fountains, international and local bands play under spreading branches. There are also film and video projections.

RomaEuropa Festival

Various venues in Rome (06 474 2286/toll-free 800 795525). **Dates** mid-July-July, Oct-mid Nov. **Box office** at individual venues. **Admission** depends on event.
This eclectic performing-arts festival now ranks as one of the top international events of its kind (*see also p7 and chapters* **Music: Classical & Opera** *and* **Theatre & Dance**). It's the classical offerings that predominate, but RomaEuropa has hosted the likes of Manu Dibango, Cesaria Evora and gypsy groups from Andalusia and Pakistan.

Roma Incontra il Mondo

Villa Ada, Via di Ponte Salaria ([06 418 0369). Bus to Via Salaria. **Dates** end June-Sept. **Admission** L5,000-L10,000.
One of the most beautiful sites in Rome: the banks of a small lake in the forested grounds of the Villa Ada, north-east of Villa Borghese. 'Rome Meets the World' is a festival of world music, jazz and roots groups. There's a range of stalls offering international food, a bar and a small market selling ethnic goods and books.

Roma Live Festival

Viale Olimpiadi, Largo de Bosis (06 4423 3226). Bus to Lungotevere Maresciallo Cadorna. **Dates** mid-June-end July. **Admission** depends on event.
The sports facilities around the **Stadio Olimpico** football stadium (*see p207*) provide a huge festival site during the summer months, with outdoor concerts, cinema, discos, kiddies' play areas, restaurants and bars. It's one of the few venues that manages to get the big international names to play in Rome in summer, although sloppy organization has meant that in the past concerts have been cancelled at the last minute, or gone ahead with only a handful of spectators. You have been warned.

Testaccio Village

Viale del Campo Boario (06 5728 7661). Bus to Piazza dell'Emporio or Via Galvani. **Dates** June-Sept. **Admission** L10,000. **Map 7/2B**
Many of Testaccio's clubs (*see chapter* **Nightlife**) move outside for the summer season, to this quiet area behind Rome's former slaughterhouse. Concerts, which begin at 10pm, include international and Italian rock, jazz, Latin and funk. But come earlier, for food, markets, stalls and bars, and then stay on for the DJs.

Crowds of hundreds of thousands turn up for the annual May Day concert in Piazza San Giovanni in Laterano.

Palacisalfa

*Viale dell'Oceano Atlantico, 271. (information 06
474 7668) Bus to Viale dell'Oceano Atlantico.*
Open depends on event. **Admission** depends on
event. **No credit cards.**
This large new venue on the very southern edge of
EUR (*see p100*) is actually an indoor sports hall. It
has better acoustics than **Palaeur**, its older rival as
a sports-cum-concerts venue, and is slightly less cavernous. Now a major venue for big-name acts.
Wheelchair access.

Palaeur

*Piazzale Dello Sport (information 06 3976 0420).
Metro EUR Palasport/bus to Palazzo dello Sport.*
Until recently, Nervi and Piacentini's saucer-shaped
Palaeur (built for the 1960 Olympics, and also
known as the Palazzo dello Sport) was the only
megastar-sized venue in town – which never
stopped (and still doesn't stop) smaller acts playing
it, often with disastrous results. The acoustics are
appalling, and it's somewhat less atmospheric than
an empty aircraft hangar. The arrival of
Palacisalfa has brought blessed relief.
Wheelchair access.

Villaggio Globale

*Lungotevere Testaccio (06 5730 0329). Bus to
Lungotevere Testaccio or Piazza dell'Emporio.* **Open**
daily; concert times vary. **Admission** L5,000-L15,000
depending on event. **No credit cards. Map 7/2B**
An ex-slaughterhouse that's probably Rome's largest
alternative venue. The huge central courtyard is used
for open-air concerts in summer. The fact it's a *centro sociale* keeps prices low, and the fact that it's the
only *centro sociale* anywhere near the centre of town
makes it very popular amongst Roman youth.
Wheelchair access.

Jazz

Alexanderplatz

*Via Ostia, 9 (06 3974 2171). Metro Ottaviano/
bus to Piazza Risorgimento.* **Open** Oct-June 9pm-
1.30am Mon-Sat. **Admission** membership L12,000
for two months; tourists free with passport.
Credit AmEx, DC, EC, MC, V.
Creole and Roman dishes are served up with live
jazz, which is usually played by visiting American
names. Dinner reservations are taken. One of Italy's
most famous jazz venues, it moves to Villa
Celimontana every summer to organize the open-air
Jazz and Image Festival (*see p222*).

Big Mama

*Vicolo San Francesco a Ripa, 18 (06 581 2551).
Bus/tram to Viale Trastevere.* **Open** Oct-June
9.30pm-1.30am daily. **Admission** membership
L20,000 per year; L10,000 monthly; extra charge for
star acts. **No credit cards. Map 7/1B**
Deep in the heart of Trastevere, this is the home of
blues in Rome, but Big Mama also presents visiting
and local jazz, American singer-songwriters, and
local and out-of-town blues.

Latin American

Rome's thriving Latin American and Caribbean
community and its resident musicians, added to a
constant stream of visiting bands, has created a
healthy Latin music scene. One of the longest-
established local groups is **Yemaya Orchestra**,
formed in 1975 by the Flores brothers Cairo and
Henry. Others include **Caribe**, **Sabor Cubano**,
Trio Berimbau, **Connexion Sonora** and
Diapson. Look out for **Besito de Coco**, one of
Rome's most famous salsa and merengue DJs, and
one of very few women spinning records in Roma.

As for visitors, Tito Puente, Oscar D'Leon, Celia
Cruz and Los Van Van make frequent appearances
in Rome. Many summer festivals feature Latin
events, but the focal point is the **Fiesta
Capannelle** (*see page 222*).

Berimbau

*Via dei Fienaroli, 30B (06 581 3249). Bus to Piazza
Sonnino or Viale Trastevere/ tram to Viale
Trastevere.* **Open** Sept-June 10.30pm-3am Wed-Sun.
Admission L10,000 Wed, Sun; L15,000 Thur, Fri;
L20,000 Sat. **No credit cards. Map 6/2B**
Colours and sounds of Brazil, in this cocktail bar fea-
turing live music, a disco, and Rome's most cos-
mopolitan clientele.

Bossa Nova

*Via degli Orti di Trastevere, 43 (06 581 6121). Bus
or tram to Viale Trastevere.* **Open** 10pm-3am Tue-
Sun. Closed Aug. **Admission** free, but you must buy
a drink (L12,000). **No credit cards. Map 6/1C**
A friendly club with Brazilian music every night.
Great for uninhibited dancing while you watch
videos of Rio, but very pricey for drinking.

Caruso

*Via di Monte Testaccio, 36 (06 574 5019).
Bus to Via Marmorata or Via Galvani.* **Open** Sept-
May 10pm-3am Tue-Sun; June 10pm-3am Thu-Sat.
Admission membership L15,000 per month.
No credit cards. Map 7/2A
A Testaccio club specialising in live Latin sounds
from Rome-based Caribbean and Brazilian
musicians. Also mounts rock gigs and hip hop
events.Always packed, too, for the Sunday disco
night, which features rock, hip hop, rap and salsa.

African

Stazione Ouagadougou

*Via della Lungaretta, 75 (06 659 0030).
Bus or tram to Viale Trastevere.* **Open** 8.30pm-2am
Tue-Sun. Closed July, Aug. **Admission** free.
No credit cards. Map 6/2A-B
The only place in Rome that features live African
music. This small bar has superb African décor, an
art gallery where paintings and photography are
displayed, and African food and beer. Plus
wonderfully friendly staff.
Wheelchair access.

Nightlife

Dance by the abbatoir or party in an underground 'cathedral': it's the venues that make Rome's nightlife unique.

The ancient Romans, who debauched and partied their Empire into the ground, would have had little time for their sedate descendants. For most modern Romans, a good night out is a long lazy dinner and a stroll through the city centre with an ice cream. That said, the city also has a few good clubs, loads of flashy '70s-style discos, interesting late-night bars, and the weird and wonderful world of *centri sociali*. Ibiza it is not, but then Ibiza doesn't offer the stunning beauty of night-time Rome.

Party night is Saturday, when party animals hop into poppa's car and head for the clubs of Rimini and Riccione on the Adriatic – or even across the border into Slovenia, where there are no regulations to check rave extremes. The effect of this migration on drink-related road deaths is dramatic. The less adventurous/foolhardy remain in town. If you're a fan of commercial hip hop or Eurodisco, Rome may be your idea of paradise. If not, one week's clubbing in the Eternal City and you might just decide to concentrate on sightseeing instead, which would be a shame: there are some gems.

What is known locally as 'black music' – watered-down R'n'B chart fodder – is what most clubs are playing: think Fugees, think Puff Daddy, and now please think of something else. Failing this, the music tends to be garage or house. For something out of the ordinary, seek out alternative scenes: the *centri sociali* play host to most of Rome's independent and experimental music, not to mention after-hours bars, parties and raves.

Places

Discobars – places that look and feel like bars, but have people dancing – are very popular in Rome. **Testaccio** is one of the city's liveliest quarters after dark. The area around **Via della Pace** in the *centro* has long been Rome's most fashionable hang-out for the seriously trendy. **Trastevere** and **San Lorenzo** also offer happy hunting grounds for bar-hopping, as does well-heeled **Parioli** to the north– but consider your finances if you intend to become a regular there.

Prices

Romans love not having to pay for things, and will exploit even the most tenuous connection with the owner/bouncer/DJ to avoid coughing up. In some places simply being female is enough to get past the man at the door. Entry prices are generally higher than in the UK or US – owners need to subsidise the freeloaders, and compensate for Italians' very low

alcohol consumption. Your ticket often includes a 'free' first drink; free or low-price entry sometimes-means you are *obliged* to buy at least one drink once you get inside. In order to fall into a different tax category some clubs and discobars define themselves as private clubs; you then have to fill out a membership card, which generally costs nothing.

Discobars & clubs

Akab

Via di Monte Testaccio, 69 (06 578 2390). Bus to Via Marmorata or Via Galvani. **Open** 10pm-4am Wed-Sat. **Admission** L15,000-25,000 depending on event (incl one free drink. **No credit cards. Map 7/2A**
This '80s-style designer-vibe venue in Testaccio hosts live acts followed by soul, dance, R&R, house and R&B, depending on the band or the evening. Down in the cellar is the area they call the **Cave** (*see below*). Make friends with the bouncers and you might avoid the queue. *See also chapter* **Music: Rock, Roots & Jazz**.

L'Alibi

Via di Monte Testaccio, 40/47 (06 574 3448). Bus to Via Marmorata or Via Galvani. **Open** 11pm-4am Wed-Sun. **Admission** free Wed, Thu; L20,000 Fri, Sat; L15,000 Sun. **No credit cards. Map 7/2B**
This gay club becomes more hetero-tolerant during summer months, when the glorious roof terrace is opened up. There's live music upstairs, and generally a more mixed crowd: the basement has a great sound system, thumping out house hits and '70s and '80s classics. *See also chapter* **Gay & Lesbian**.

Alien

Via Velletri, 13-19 (06 841 2212). Bus to Piazza Fiume. **Open** *Sept-May* 11pm-4am Tue-Sat; *June-July* 11pm-4am Fri, Sat. **Admission** L20,000-30,000. **Credit** AmEx, DC, EC, MC, V. **Map 4/2A**
This big, flashy disco comes with all the trimmings: strobes, scantily-clad dancers on the bar, two rooms with different DJs ... but music tends to be uninspired house, trance and garage. There are sometimes experimental evenings, when musicians play along with the DJ. The crowd are mainly under-25s; there's also a cringeworthy 'VIP room', a serious turn-off.

Alpheus

Via del Commercio, 36 (06 574 7826). Metro Piramide/bus to Via Ostiense. **Open** *Sept-June* 10pm-4.30am Tue-Sun; *July, Aug* 10pm-4.30am Fri, Sat. **Admission** L10,000 Tue, Wed, Thur, Sun; L20,000

(incl one drink) Fri; L15.000 Sat. **Credit** AmEx.
Right in front of a disused gasworks, this spacious multi-room venue caters for a variety of live bands, theatre and cabaret, plus DJs every night. The central pink bar, with its kitsch fountain and sculpture, unfortunately matches the rest of the club's decor – cheesy to say the least. Students get in free on Wednesdays. Also home to the *Mucca Assassina* gay nights (*see chapter* **Gay & Lesbian**) on Fridays. *See also chapter* **Music: Rock, Roots & Jazz.**

Anima
Via Santa Maria dell'Anima, 57 (06 686 4021).
Bus to Corso Vittorio Emanuele or Corso del Rinascimento. **Open** *Sept-June* 10.30pm-4am Tue-Sun. **Admission** L10,000 Wed, Thur; L15,000 Fri, Sat; free Sun. **No credit cards. Map 3/2B**
Wacky décor and a central location by Piazza Navona make Anima worth a pitstop. It's more bar than disco, but the music can be good, varying from hip hop to house, drum'n'bass and jungle.

B-Side
Via degli Stradivari (06 588 3842).
Bus to Piazza Ponte Testaccio or Via Ettore Rolli.
Open 11pm-3am Thur-Sat. **Admission** L20,000.
No credit cards. Map 7/2B
A new location for this once-trendy club. The music remains the same, however: 'black', house and funky.

Black Out
Via Saturnia, 18 (06 7049 6791).
Metro Re di Roma/bus to Piazza Tuscolo.
Open *Sept-June* 10pm-4am Thur-Sat; **Admission** L15,000-20,000. **No credit cards. Map 9/2A**
Brit pop, rock, grunge and Indie music are the speciality, with the odd goth track thrown in for good measure, in this long-running stawart of the Rome club scene.
Wheelchair access.

Brancaleone
Via Levanna, 11 (06 8200 0959).
Bus to Piazza Sempione. **Open** 10.30pm-5.00am Thur-Sun. **Admission** donation expected (L5,000).
No credit cards.
One of the best run *centri sociali*, boasting a cinema, recording studio and library, but, best of all, a decent bar, a quality stage for concerts and some of the best amplification to be found amongst *centri*. Friday nights are the most popular; techno, drum'n'bass and big beat are what you'll hear during the session, known simply as **Agatha**. Live acts and guest DJ sets on a regular basis. *See also chapter* **Music: Rock, Roots & Jazz.**

Cave
Via di Monte Testaccio, 68 (06 578 2390).
Bus to Via Marmorata or Via Galvani. **Open** *Oct-June* 10pm-3am Mon-Sat. *July-Sept* 10pm-3am Wed-Sat **Admission** L15,000 Mon-Wed, Fri, Sat; L10,000 Thur. **No credit cards Map 7/2A**
Beneath **Akab** (*see above*), this offers a cool cave downstairs, a big bar upstairs and interesting music

ranging from hip hop to ethno-jazz. A venue that's worth a visit.

Circolo degli Artisti
Via Casilina Vecchia, 42 (06 7030 5684).
Bus to Via Casilina or Piazza D. Pigneto. **Open** 9pm-3am Tue-Sun. **Admission** varies; L7,000 three-month membership card. **No credit cards.**
Big new venue for a long-established *centro sociale* (the old club was knocked down to make way for an indoor market) which mixes live acts with DJs. Fridays are 'black' and rock; Saturdays tend towards disco from the 70's to the 90's. *See also chapter* **Music: Rock, Roots & Jazz.**
Wheelchair access.

DDT
Via dei Sabelli, 2 (06 495 8338)
Bus or tram to Piazzale Verano. **Open** 10.30pm-3am Tue-Sat. **Admission** varies; L5,000 three-month membership card. **No credit cards.**
One of the few late-night venues in San Lorenzo. A long underground bar and disco, playing anything from Big Beat to Latin, with a side-order of rock.
Wheelchair access.

Dome Rock Cafè
Via D. Fontana, 18 (06 7045 2436). Bus or tram to Piazza San Giovanni. **Open** *Sept-June* 10pm-3am daily. **Admission** free. **No credit cards. Map 8/2A**
In the shadow of San Giovanni in Laterano, this new and trendy discobar has built a good reputation in a short time. Live acts every week: music ranges from hip hop to indie via acid jazz – pot luck, really, but a good selection of beer and a lively atmosphere.

Dub Club
Via dei Funari, 21A (06 6880 5024).
Bus to Piazza Venezia or Via del Teatro di Marcello.
Open 11.30pm-4am. **Admission** L10,000-L20,000.
No credit cards. Map 6/1A
Formerly occupied by B-Side (*see above*) and formerly very trendy, this small, smoky, sweaty discobar plays mainly funk, 'black', R&B, house and of course, dub. The air conditioning helps in summer.
Wheelchair access.

Ex-Magazzini
Via Magazzini Generali, 8 bis. (06 575 8040).
Bus to Via Ostiense. **Open** 9pm-4.30am daily.
Admission L10,000-L15,000. **No credit cards.**
Trendy discobar with DJs playing rock, electro, big beat and/or jungle. There's a small stage downstairs for live acts, and the upstairs bar has a glass panel in the floor, so you can watch the throng dancing below you (and they watch you watching them…).

Forte Prenestino
Via Delpino. (06 2180 7855).
Bus/tram to Via Prenestina.
Open virtually always; call first. **Admission** donation expected (L5,000). **No credit cards.**
If you're looking for something different then this *centro sociale* in a nineteenth-century fortress simply has to be seen. From the dry moat and the maze of tunnels to the underground 'cathedral', it's a part of Rome

Ex-Magazzini *(left): trendy discobar.*

rarely seen by tourists. Try Friday and Saturday for dancing, when you'll probably hear reggae, dub and/or drum'n'bass. Concerts are often held in the two courtyards in summer. There's an international arts festival in spring, and a *Festa del Non-Lavoro* (Non-Labour Day) celebration each 1 May.

Gender

Via Faleria, 9 (06 702 5829).
Metro San Giovanni/bus to Via Appia Nuova.
Open 11pm-4am Tue-Sun. Closed one week Aug
Admission L60,000 Tue; L20,000 Wed-Sun.
Caligula might have enjoyed himself here. Gender is the only real fetish club in Rome – a rubber-clad dungeon with all mod cons, including private cabins for you and your choice of companion. Almost too seedy for words and not for the faint-hearted; also, note the prices (*see also p229*).

Gilda

Via Mario de' Fiori, 97 (06 678 4838). Metro
Spagna/bus to Piazza San Silvestro. **Open** *Sept-June*
11pm-4am Tue-Sun. **Admission** L40,000 (incl one drink). **Credit** AmEx, DC, EC, MC, V. **Map 5/1C**
Don't even think about it unless you are (1) an ageing film star, (2) a politician of the deeply slimy variety or (3) very rich/drunk/stupid. All silicone and no soul, Gilda is a dame no one should touch even with a pair of sterilized tongs.

Goa

Via Libetta, 13 (06 574 8277). Metro Garbatella/bus to
Via Ostiense. **Open** 11pm-4am Tue-Sat. **Admission**
L15,000-L30,000. **Credit** AmEx, DC, EC, MC, V
Ethnically-inspired club – incense, exotic artefacts, slide projections and those things you plug yourself

into to chill out. Currently among Rome's trendiest. Music is hip hop via tribal to house, courtesy of Rome's DJ star Giancarlino.
Wheelchair access.

Hang-out

Via Ostiense, 131 (06 578 3146). Metro
Garbatella/bus to Via Ostiense. **Open** 9pm-2am Tue-Sun. **Admission** L10,000-L15,000. **No credit cards.**
Discobar serving food in the evening; it gets funky later with DJs playing 'black', R'n'B and house.
Wheelchair access.

Piper

Via Tagliamento, 9 (06 841 4459). Bus to Via
Tagliamento or Corso Trieste. **Open** 11pm-4am
Thur-Sat; 4-8pm Sun. **Admission** L20,000 Thur, Fri; L16,000 Sat before 8pm, Sun; L30,000 Sat after 8pm.
Credit AmEx, DC, EC, MC, V. **Map 4/1A**
A classic among Roman discos, this huge subterranean Saturday Night Fever-style venue launched many Italian pop stars of the '60s, many of whom are still about and have an alarming tendency to return to their roots (now heavily dyed) at the Piper. Saturday and Sunday afternoon it hosts Fever sessions for teenagers. Saturday nights on the other hand are (at least for the moment) gay, and popular.

Qube

Via di Portonaccio, 212 (06 438 1005).
Metro Tiburtina/bus to Via Tiburtina or Via di
Portonaccio. **Open** 11pm-4am Thur-Sun.
Admission L10,000-L20,000. **No credit cards.**
Hugely successful club with classic disco lights and three bars, plus second-floor chill-out room with sofas and pool tables. Thursday is student night.

Radio Londra

Via di Monte Testaccio, 65b (06 575 0044). Bus to Via
Marmorata or Via Galvani. **Open** 9pm-3am Wed-Mon.
Admission L10,000. **No credit cards Map 2/7A**.
Listen to rock, blues and dance while you eat your chips and sandwiches. Live acts too.
Wheelchair access.

Villaggio Globale

Lungotevere Testaccio (06 5730 0329).
Bus to Lungotevere Testaccio or Piazza dell'Emporio.
Open daily, times vary. **Admission** L5,000-L15,000 depending on event. **No credit cards**.
This collection of buildings and yards once used to be the municipal slaughterhouse (*see chapter* **Aventino, Celio & Testaccio**), but now large sections of the bits that haven't fallen down are occupied by one of Rome's most active *centri sociali*. The central courtyard is used for concerts in summer. Around the edge are multi-lingual, multi-cultural activities of all descriptions. Fears that the *Villaggio Globale* would be evicted to make room for an artsy-crafty centre providing a front for a shopping mall have not been wholly quelled by city hall, which has, however, promised that the 'Global Village' will be given some room inside the huge complex to continue its activities. *See also chapter* **Music: Rock, Roots & Jazz**.

ROME

rocking the world for over 25 years

restaurant • bar • boutique

Via Vittorio Veneto 62A
00187 Roma

Tel.064203051
Fax.0642030552

A walk on the wild side

Your first impression of Rome's nightlife might not be one of pure joy. So-called 'black' music may not be up your street, and you may not want to hear Cher just one more time. On first impressions, you might be forgiven for feeling something's definitely missing.

Don't despair, Rome does have a thriving alternative scene. *Centri sociali* (such as **Brancaleone** *(page 226)*, **Forte Prenestino** *(page 226)* and **Villaggio Globale** *(page 227))* are a good place to start. For information, pick up fliers in clothes and record shops all over the centre of Rome. If a DJ is called Stigmata, Coresect or Spleen, make sure you wear black.

If that isn't off the beaten path enough, then perhaps **Gender** *(see page 227)* is what you're after. Don't let its quiet residential surroundings fool you. The music doesn't count for much, but then, that's not why the club is popular. It will probably be the crucifix you'll notice first: someone is likely to be chained to it. The vaulting horse isn't there just for show either. This little bit of Roman decadence thrives virtually unnoticed just five minutes' walk from San Giovanni in Laterano. There's a selection of whips, should you feel that way inclined, and, if you like your privacy, there are private cubicles available. If you prefer company, try the dark room. The bar is best described as industrial. Sure, it's not for everyone, but it can be a relief to discover that there's more to Rome than flashy clubs and trendy bars.

Late bars & eating-places

Eating late can be a problem in Rome. Turn up at most restaurants at midnight and you're likely to be told *la cucina è chiusa* – the kitchen's closed, the cook's gone home. Pubs *(see chapter* **Wine bars & birrerie***)* can be a good bet for late snacks, and some wine bars serve cold cuts and salads into the wee hours. Bars in the centre, especially around Via della Pace, tend to stay open well into the morning.

Bar della Pace
Via della Pace, 4 ,5, 7 (06 686 1216). Bus to Corso del Rinascimento or Corso Vittorio Emanuele. **Open** 9am-2am Tue -Sun; 3pm-2am Mon. **Map 3/2B**
Rome's prime posing spot for pseudo-intellectuals. The ivy-clad location is as beautiful as prices are horrific. A must for first-time visitors to the Eternal City looking for old-style Roman glamour.

Bar del Fico
Piazza del Fico, 26-28 (06 686 5205). Bus to Corso del Rinascimento or Corso Vittorio Emanuele. **Open** 9am-2am Mon-Sat; noon-2am Sun. **Map 3/2B**
Round the corner from Bar della Pace, the Fico has come into its own recently, hiking prices accordingly and attracting a very cool crowd. Nice fig tree.

La Base
Via Cavour, 274 (06 474 0659). Metro Cavour/bus to Via Cavour. **Open** 8pm-5am daily. **Map 8/1B**
Combined bar and pizzeria that stays open all night, frequented into the small hours by hungry clubbers and transvestites.

Hemingway
Piazza delle Coppelle, 10 (06 686 4490). Bus to Via del Corso or Corso del Rinascimento. **Open** 8.30pm-2am daily. **Map 3/1A**
Classy, decadent hole, with comfy sofas. Work off day-after doldrums with Sunday brunch (11am-4pm). A great winter bar.

Jonathan's Angels
Via della Fossa, 16 (06 689 3426). Bus to Corso del Rinascimento or Corso Vittorio Emanuele. **Open** 8pm-2am Mon; 5.30pm-2am Tue–Sat; 2pm-2am Sun. **Map 3/2B**
Spectacular in summer, with its abundant candles. The interior is decked out with religious-style paintings of Jonathan and his Harley. Great *fragolino* wine, and far and away the best loo in Rome.

Selarum
Via dei Fienaroli, 12 (06 581 9130). Bus to Piazza Sonnino. **Open** *June-Sept* 9pm-2am daily **Map 6/2B**.
Bamboo seats and blue lighting create a laid-back atmosphere in Selarum's leafy courtyard. Serves cocktails and food (lunch 11am-3pm daily) and often has live music. Prices on the high side.

Stazione Ouagadougou
Via della Lungaretta, 75 (06 581 2510). Bus to Piazza Sonnino. **Open** 10pm-2am Tue-Sun.**Map 6/2A**
Gorgeous African bar, awash with African art. It hosts exhibitions and live music, and serves African food every weekend. Overwhelmingly friendly. *See also chapter* **Music: Rock, Roots & Jazz**.

La Vineria
Piazza Campo de' Fiori, 15 (06 6880 3268). Bus to Corso Vittorio Emanuele or Via Arenula. **Open** 9.30am-3pm, 5pm-1.30am Mon-Sat; *mid June-mid-Oct* 5pm-1.30am Sun. **Map 6/1B**
Known to the cognoscenti as Giorgio's, the Vineria now runs a close second to the Colosseum as Rome's trademark monument. On summer evenings, the crowd spills out to take over the Campo; in winter it becomes more demure and cosy, so you can take

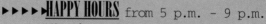

Five outside...

As the thermometre rises and indoor venues get seriously sweaty, head for the great outdoors, where Rome's nightlife continues unabated. **Selarum** (*page 229*) is a little oasis in the heart of Trastevere; relax in your cane garden chair, sip your long cool drink, and soak in low-key music – some of it live – after a hard day's sightseeing.

Further afield, you can chill out Fridays at **Agatha at Brancaleone** (*see page 226*). The dancefloor's closed, but the garden definitely isn't. The music is drum'n'bass, techno-electro and big beat, and the 1,000+ crowd party to the mixing skills of Riccardo Petitti and Paul Toohill. There are guest DJs from all over Europe almost every week, and live bands frequently take the stage.

Slightly nearer the centre, the green and luscious Villa Ada throbs to ethnic beats in the **Roma Incontro Il Mondo** festival (*see page 222*). You might not necessarily have expected to spend your Roman Holiday enjoying Iranian music while munching on Egyptian food, but the setting is pure Roman, and it's a great way to spend an evening.

South of the centre, the new **Circolo Degli Artisti** (*see page 226*) moves its activities into its huge outdoor space for the hot season. Still further out, the Capanelle racetrack on Via Appia Nuova hosts the **Fiesta Capanelle** (*see page 222*), the annual under-the-stars feast of Latin American rhythms, sounds and food. Reggae too. Very popular, and very, very crowded.

Brancaleone: *1,000+ crowds sweat it out at 'Agatha' on Fridays.*

your time browsing the wine selection, or just get your lips around a Vecchia Romagna. *See p156.*

Late kitchens

The following restaurants and *pizzerie*, listed in *chapter* **Restaurants**, usually keep their kitchens open until midnight, but it's always best to phone ahead and check: **Antico Arco, Antico Bottaro, Arancia Blu, ATM, 'Gusto, Maccheroni, Margutta Vegetariano, Osteria dell'Ingegno, Pachì, Panattoni, Papà Baccus, Tuttifrutti, Taverna Angelica,** and **Trattoria Pizzeria della Pace.**

Newspapers

Late-night news-stands are a great Roman tradition. Many vendors swap their day-time displays for more off-the-wall stock (and large quantities of porn) after dark. Here are some options for party animals (*see also chapter* **Gay & Lesbian**):

Via del Corso across from Piazza Colonna
Via Veneto two stands in different places
Piazza Sonnino in Trastevere
Piazza del Cinquecento in front of Termini

Trips Out of Town

Trips Out of Town

Beyond Rome's streets and piazze lie ancient villas, beaches, lakes, quiet country towns and cool mountain air.

All roads may lead to Rome, but look at it another way and they all lead out of the city as well. The green belt known as the *campagna romana*, praised and criticised alternately by generations of travellers of the Grand Tour, and more prey to hypermarkets and sprawling dormitory towns. But, though the journey no longer takes you through an unbroken landscape of ruins, grazing sheep, wild flowers and the occasional rustic hut, there are plenty of destinations very worth a day trip or a longer stay.

The Etruscan sites of **Cerveteri** and **Tarquinia** north of Rome, the historic town of **Viterbo**, the villas and gardens of **Tivoli** and the **Castelli Romani** to the east, plus a slew of fascinating churches, monasteries and hot springs, provide respite from the urban crush. There are natural gems too: **Lake Martignano**, the **Treia**

valley and the **Lucretili** mountains are all under an hour away. A little more perseverance is required to get to the more attractive beaches north and south of the city, or the serious mountains of the **Parco Nazionale di Abruzzo**, but, especially in summer, the effort is worth it.

Getting there

By bus

The Lazio transport authority COTRAL (*see* chapter **Directory**) has bus services to nearly all destinations within the region. Buses leave from several termini within Rome, each serving a different direction and following roads that roughly correspond to the ancient Roman *vie consolari*, but ae now one- or two-lane highways (*strade*

Like an out-sized sandcastle, the Castello Orsini *in* **Santa Severa**. *See page 243.*

statali or SS). Places outside Lazio which have poor or no train connections (such as L'Aquila) are served by private or regional bus lines. Many operators have offices in or near Piazza dei Cinquecento or Piazza della Repubblica. For schedules and fares, visit the *capolinea* (terminus) you need; you can phone for information, but staff are usually Italian-speaking only, and getting through can be near-impossible.

COTRAL Information

Information *freephone 800 431 784.*
Open 9am-1pm, 2-5pm, Mon-Fri.
Head office *Via Volturno, 65 (06 575 31). Bus to Piazza dei Cinquecento.* **Open** 8am-1.40pm, 2.10-4.40pm, Mon-Fri; 8am-1.40pm Sat. **Map 5/1A**

COTRAL bus stations

North-west: Lepanto
Information *Via Cassia destinations 06 321 4827; Via Aurelia destinations 06 324 4724.*
Metro Lepanto/bus to Viale Giulio Cesare.
For the coastal route north (Cerveteri, Civitavecchia, Tarquinia), and Lake Bracciano area (Via Aurelia/ Cassia). **Map 2/2B**
North: Saxa Rubra
Information *06 332 8333.*
Train from Piazzale Flaminio.
For Viterbo and the north (Via Cassia/Flaminia/Tiberina).
North-east: Stazione Tiburtina
Information *06 4424 2419. Metro Tiburtina.*
For Farfa and Rieti (Via Salaria/Nomentana)
East: Ponte Mammolo
Information *06 418 1338. Metro Ponte Mammolo.*
For Tivoli, Subiaco, Prenestina and the east (Via Tiburtina/Prenestina).
South-east: Anagnina
Information *06 722 2153. Metro Anagnina.*
For Ciampino airport, Palestrina (also frequent services from Ponte Mammolo Metro station), Castelli Romani, Frosinone and area (Via Appia/Anagnina/ Tuscolana/Casalina/Fiuggina).
South-west: EUR Fermi
Information *06 592 0402.*
Metro EUR Fermi/bus to Viale America.
For the coastal route south: Latina, Anzio, Terracina (Via Pontina).

By road

Rome is surrounded by a ring road, the *Grande Raccordo Anulare* (GRA), which links up with the network of motorways (*autostrade*) and *strade statali* (SS). A third lane on the GRA – the long drawn-out construction of which has led to spectacular hold-ups – was nearing completion as this guide went to press. Even so, traffic can be intense, especially in rush hours and on Friday and Sunday evenings. From Rome, *autostrada* A1 (the *autostrada del sole*) leads north to Florence and Milan, and south to Naples. The A24 heads east to L'Aquila and the Adriatic, the A12 up the coast to Civitavecchia. Motorways are quick, but tolls are high. You can save on time (but not costs) at toll

stations by using an *autostrada* card (*Viacard*), which is available from all *tabacchi* shops (*see* chapter **Directory**).

The *strade statali* that fan out from Rome are commonly known by their ancient consular names – Aurelia, Salaria, Tiburtina etc – as well as numbers, even on road signs. They can be quite slow. Signposting can be very efficient, non-existent, or an infuriating mixture of both.

Before longer journeys, it's advisable to check whether there may be delays due to road works. Ring the ACI automobile club's 24-hour information number, 06 44 77 (English-speaking staff), or listen to the 103.3 FM Isoradio channel (occasional English-language bulletins in summer). For details of the ACI and more on driving in Italy and car hire, *see chapter* **Directory**.

By train

Train tickets can be bought at stations or travel agents with an FS (*Ferrovie dello Stato* – State Railways) sign. At Termini and other main stations there are automatic ticket machines with instructions in several languages. There is a 20 per cent discount on ordinary tickets (not supplements) for those aged under 26 with the *Carta Verde* card (which costs L40,000 for one year). For information on taking wheelchairs on trains, *see* chapter **Directory: Disabled travellers.**

At stations, check that you are waiting at the right ticket window: some handle ordinary tickets, *Eurostar* tickets and high-speed supplements (*supplementi rapidi*); some also take advance bookings (*prenotazioni*), and some are for bookings only. International trains have their own window.

The FS has promised a radical reorganisation of fare structures, but until this happens ticket prices are directly related to kilometres travelled. Slower trains (the *diretti, espressi, regionali* and *interregionali*) are very cheap, but a system of supplements means that faster services – *InterCity* (IC), *EuroCity* (EC), *Eurostar Italia* (ES) – are closer to the European norm. The first two cost about 50 per cent more than slower trains, *Eurostar* (not to be confused with channel tunnel trains) overdouble.

The second-class fare between Rome and Naples, for example, is L37,500 by *Eurostar* (105 min), L28,500 by *InterCity* (105-120 min) and L18,000 by *diretto, espresso* or *interregionale* (125-160 min). Advance reservation (for no extra charge) is obligatory on ES trains on Fridays and Sundays, and all week and on other trains at certain peak times of year. An R inside a square on train timetables indicates this; it is a good idea to check when purchasing your ticket. Booking a seat on IC and internal EC routes costs L5,000 extra, and is well worth it even when not obligatory to avoid standing in a packed corridor, especially on Friday and Sunday evenings. If your ES, IC or EC train arrives more than 30 minutes late and you have a seat booking, you can get the supplement reembursed at the booth marked *rimborsi*.

Rome's larger stations, including Termini, Tiburtina and Ostiense, accept all major credit cards in theory, but in practice the machines are frequently out of order. To make sure of getting on your train, take cash as well. Most travel agents persist in accepting cash only for train tickets.

You must stamp your ticket – and any supplements you have – in the yellow machines by each platform **before boarding the train**: failure to do so can lead to a hefty fine. Being foreign and looking forlorn can get you off the hook.

All Italian stations now have the same information number: 147 888 088: operates daily, 7am-9pm; Italian-speaking only. A private company offers a 24-hour service, seven day a week on 166 105 050; calls cost L2,500 plus tax. For Eurostar information call 06 474 2155.

Near Rome

Ostia Antica

If it weren't for the lack of a backdrop like Vesuvius, Ostia Antica would be as famous as Pompeii: it certainly conveys just as uncannily what everyday life was like in a working Roman town. Ostia was Rome's main port for over 600 years, until its decline in the fourth century AD.

Thereafter, river mud and sand gradually buried the town, which had the effect of preserving most buildings from the second storey down. Visit on a sunny weekday, and bring a picnic to eat under the pines or on the steps of the amphitheatre, as it's a place that needs to be taken at a leisurely pace.

The main street, the **Decumanus Maximus**, runs from the **Porta Romana**, the gate facing Rome, for almost a kilometre, past the **amphitheatre** and **forum**, before forking left to reach what used to be the seashore (which is now about 3km away at **Lido di Ostia**, *see page 237*). The right fork, the **Via delle Foce**, leads to the Tiber. On either side of these main arteries is a network of intersecting lanes, and it's here that the most interesting discoveries can be made, scrambling over truncated walls and half-hidden mosaics.

Behind the amphitheatre is the **Forum of Corporations**, ringed by offices and shops with mosaics referring to the trades practised by the ancient guilds. Don't miss the **Thermopilium**, an ancient Roman bar, complete with marble counter, a fresco advertising the house fare and a garden with fountain out the back; the elegant fourth century **House of Cupid and Psyche**; and the fine mosaics in the **House of the Dioscuri**. The **museum** has a good collection of artefacts from the site, including bas-reliefs of scenes of ordinary life, and two rooms on the eastern and Mithraic cults (*see page 95*) especially prominent in Ostia.

The medieval fortified village of Ostia, five minutes walk from the entrance to the excavations, has a brick castle, built in 1483-6 for the future Pope

River mud preserved ancient Rome's main port, **Ostia Antica**.

The sea may be murky but at least it's wet. A make-shift shower at **Capocotta**.

Julius II, and some picturesque cottages that were once set aside for workers in the nearby salt pans.

Information & transport
Information *06 5635 8099*.
Open *Excavations* Apr-Oct 9am-7pm (last entrance 6pm) Tue-Sun; *Nov-Mar* 9am-5pm (last entrance 4pm) daily; *museum* (currently closed for restoration) 9am-2pm Tue-Sun. **Admission** L8,000.
Getting there *by train* from Ferrovia Roma-Lido station (next to Piramide Metro); Ostia Antica is the sixth station along, and the excavations are a ten-minute walk from the station.

Rome's seaside

In a word (or two): forget it. The local riviera for Romans is the Lido in **Ostia**, with dark sandy beaches lined by private, pay-on-entry beach clubs that fill to bursting every summer, and a murky sea. Those desperate for a swim are advised to head towards **Torvaianica**, 11km (7 miles) further south, where the water is at least a bit cleaner. The Capocotta nudist beach – about 9km (6 miles) south of Ostia (look for the milestone) – is also acceptable, and free, with a sprinkling of beach-hut bars (*see also chapter* **Gay & Lesbian Rome**). If you're looking for discos, grilled fish and *racchettone* (beach tennis), the resorts north of Ostia – such as **Fregene**, **Ladíspoli** and **Santa Marinella** – will not disappoint. Romans flock

here every summer, by day and for night-time discos, but for secluded beaches and clean sea you must travel further afield (*see pages 243-6*).

Transport
Getting there: **Ostia** *by train* from Ferrovia Roma-Lido station next to Piramide Metro; for full-on beach umbrellas, get out at Lido Centro; for **Capocotta** and **Torvaianica** go to the end of the line (Cristoforo Colombo) and take bus 071 or 061.
Fregene *by bus* COTRAL from Lepanto;
Ladíspoli and **Santa Marinella** *by train* FS Roma-Civitavecchia line.

Tivoli & Palestrina

The town of Tivoli, founded by an Italic tribe, was conquered by the Romans in 338 BC. The surrounding area became a popular location for country villas, and Tivoli itself was littered with temples. A favourite destination for day trips from Rome, its greatest attractions are the largest of the Roman Imperial villas, the **Villa Adriana**, and the Renaissance **Villa d'Este**.

Also worth looking at are the **Villa Gregoriana**, a wild park in a rocky gorge, next to two waterfalls; the cathedral of **San Lorenzo**, which contains a famous thirteenth-century wood-carving of the *Descent from the Cross*; and a very well preserved circular Roman **Temple of Sybil**. Up at the top of the town is a fifteenth-century castle built by Pope Pius II, the **Rocca Pia**. Nearby is **Palestrina**, a medieval town built on the remains of a temple to an ancient oracle. A few kilometres east of Tivoli is the small town of **Castelmadama**, where a Palio (traditional horse race) is held every July (*see page 7*). Also, if you have any children to entertain with you, take note that not far from the road between Tivoli and Rome is the **AcquaPiper** water park (*see chapter* **Children**).

Villa Adriana (Hadrian's Villa)

(0774 530 203). **Open** *Apr-Sept* 9am-6.30pm, *Oct-Mar* 9am-4pm, daily. **Admission** L8,000.

Hadrian started work on this huge and grandiose country retreat in the mountains near Tibur (ancient Tivoli) in AD 118. It was completed in 134, and later used by several other emperors. In the centuries following the fall of the Empire it became a luxury quarry for later builders, but it was never destroyed completely; the restored remains, lying between olive groves and cypresses, are still impressive (you can look at a model in the pavilion to get an idea of its original size). Hadrian was a great traveller, and in his old age built himself replicas of some of his favourite buildings. After dinner he could stroll in the shade of the arcaded *Stoa Poikile* (painted porch), with its huge pool, and feel he was back in Athens conversing with the

Water gushes at the **Villa d'Este**.

Stoics (who got their name from their favourite meeting place); or he could recline around the pool in the *Canopus* (a replica of the sanctuary of Serapis near Alexandria), surrounded by Egyptian statues – a reminder of the emperor's favourite, a Greek boy called Antinous, who had drowned in Egypt. If he was feeling particularly miserable, he could take a trip through his reconstruction of Hades, the underworld – a series of underground passages to the east of the *Odeion* or Greek theatre. And for moments of private reflection there was the *Teatro Marittimo* (naval theatre), a charming circular study in the middle of an artificial pool. The complex also included extensive guest and staff apartments, dining rooms, assembly halls and libraries, baths and a stadium.

The whole villa complex was connected by underground passages (*cryptoportici*), a private subway that gave welcome relief from the beating sun.

Villa d'Este

(0774 312 070). **Open** *May-Sept* 9am-6.30pm, *Oct-Apr* 9am-one hour before sunset, Tue-Sun. **Admission** L8,000.

This lavish villa was built over a Benedictine monastery in 1550 for Cardinal Ippolito d'Este, son of Lucrezia Borgia, purely as a pleasure palace. Inside the villa – by Mannerist architect Pirro Ligorio – there are frescoes and paintings by Correggio, da Volterra and Perrin del Vaga. The main attraction, though, is the garden, beautifully cool and refreshing, with huge, elaborate and ingenious fountains. The *Fontana dell'Organo Idraulico* used water pressure to compress air and play tunes like an organ; another, the Owl Fountain, imitated an owl's song. The villa has become frayed at the edges over the centuries, and restoration is a struggle: the musical fountains have not made a sound for years, but others have regained their original splendour. Note too the *Rometta* – a miniature model of the Tiber Island in Rome, with the Capitoline Wolf and several other buildings in the background.

Museo Archeologico Prenestino, Palestrina

Piazza della Cortina, Palestrina (06 953 8100). **Open** *Mar* 9am-5pm, *Apr* 9am-6pm, *May* 9am-6.30pm, *June-Aug* 9am-7.30pm, *Sept* 9am-5.30pm, *Oct* 9am-5pm, *Nov-Feb* 9am-4pm, daily. **Admission** L4,000 including excavations.

The attractive town of Palestrina, south-east of Tivoli, was built over a huge temple, parts of which date back to the sixth century BC, dedicated to the oracle Fortuna Primegenia. The ancient Etruscan town here, *Praeneste*, fought many wars with the Romans before it was defeated in 87 BC. The temple was rebuilt on a grander scale, and *Praeneste* became a favourite holiday resort – Pliny the Younger had a villa here. After the oracle shut up shop in the fourth century AD, the medieval town was built on top. Bombing during World War II exposed the huge extent of the remains.

A round temple with a statue of the goddess Palestrina originally stood where the seventeenth-century **Palazzo Colonna-Barberini** is now. Today it houses the museum. Its star exhibit is the second century BC Nile mosaic – a work admired by Pliny, which came from the most sacred part of the temple, where the cathedral now stands. It is an intricately detailed, brightly-coloured representation of the Nile in flood from Ethiopia to Alexandria, showing warriors hunting exotic animals, people dining, goddesses preaching and birds galore. Palestrina's other claim to fame is as the birthplace of Giovanni da Palestrina, the sixteenth-century composer.

Information & transport

Tivoli tourist office *Largo Garibaldi (0774 311 249)*. **Open** 9am-2.30pm Mon, Sat; 9am-2.30pm, 3-6pm, Tue-Fri.
Villa Gregoriana: **Open** *Sept-May* 9.30am-one hour before sunset, *June-Aug* 10am-7.30pm, Tue-Sun. **Admission** L2,500.
Getting there: **Tivoli** *by bus* COTRAL from Ponte Mammolo; *by car* 32km/20 miles, by A24 or Via Tiburtina (SS5); *by train* from Termini or Tiburtina to Avezzano, stops at Tivoli (very slow).
Palestrina *by bus* COTRAL from Ponte Mammolo; *by car* 39km/24 miles, by Via Prenestina (SS155).
Where to eat On the approach road to Villa Adriana is the **Adriano** *Via di Villa Adriana 194 (0774 382 235)*, a surprisingly untouristy restaurant that's great for *al fresco* eating in summer. In Tivoli itself, next to the church of Sant'Antonio, is the **Antica Hostaria dei Carrettieri** *Via Domenico Giuliani 55 (0774 330 159; closed Wed)*, which has built up a solid reputation in recent years; run by two Sardinian sisters, it does great pasta dishes and meat or fish *secondi*. Palestrina is not well-supplied with good places to eat; grab a roll or take a picnic.

The Castelli Romani

The tame volcanoes that make up the Alban Hills have long provided refuge for Romans on Sunday outings or *scampagnate*, with plenty of *trattorie* and local wine to soothe away urban angst. The 16 small towns dotted around the hills that make up the Castelli Romani are not all equally worth a visit, but there is plenty of good eating and walking, and wonderful sights such as Frascati's **Villa Aldobrandini**, the **Abbazia di San Nilo** at Grottaferrata and beautiful **Lake Nemi**.

Most of the modern-day Castelli are creations of the struggle for power and influence between Rome's noble families (the Savelli, Colonna, della Rovere), who took turns to put their scions on the papal throne through the Middle Ages and Renaissance (*see chapter* **History**). In pre-Classical times this area was the centre of the Latin League, whose capital, *Alba Longa*, above **Lake Albano**, has now made way for **Castel Gandolfo**, summer residence of the Pope. Subjugated by Rome, the Castelli became a favourite summer haunt of Roman patricians – no fewer than 43 villas are

Nemi, *home to a Diana cult. See page 242.*

known to have existed on the hills around now-deserted Tuscolo, where there are the remains of a Roman amphitheatre. Their Renaissance successors also built a string of villas.

Frascati is the closest of the Castelli to the city, and offers perhaps the most satisfying balance of food, wine and culture. Pick up a map of the town at the tourist office. Of the numerous Renaissance villas sprinkled over the hillside behind the town, only the garden of the seventeenth-century **Villa Aldobrandini** is visitable. The villa was built in 1598-1603 by Giacomo della Porta for Cardinal Pietro Aldobrandini, whose uncle had just become Pope Clement VIII. In nearby **Villa Torlonia** – now a public park – Carlo Maderno's sixteenth-century *Teatro delle Acque* fountain is still impressive, although now rather decrepit. There is also an elegant smaller fountain by Bernini.

The name 'Frascati' is synonymous with uninspiring Italian table wine, but you'd do well to give it another try. Local topers claim that it has to be drunk *sul posto* – on site – and, quaffing it fresh from the barrel in a cool cellar, you may well agree. There are a number of wine shops around town: cavernous rooms in which jugs of wine and hearty snacks are served. Particularly characteristic is the den run by **Carlo Taglienti** at Via Sepolcro di Lucullo, 8 (on the left of Corso d'Italia, just before the turn for the Villa Aldobrandini).

Etruscan Lazio

Over the centuries, people have projected their obsessions onto the Etruscans. Herodotus was so impressed by their art that he decided they must have come from Greece. For DH Lawrence, they were creative souls trampled underfoot by the jackboots of the Roman Empire. He particularly admired the apparent sexual equality of Etruscan society, suggested by countless scenes, in wall-paintings and on sarcophagi, in which couples recline in attitudes of intimate enjoyment.

However, comparatively little is really known about the Etruscans, and their language has not been deciphered. It is known that they were more sophisticated than the early Romans, and passed on to them many of their engineering techniques. Their houses were built of wood, so the only parts of Etruscan towns that have survived are tombs, dug down into volcanic rock.

The territory occupied by the Etruscan League covered a wide area, but for practical purposes Etruscan Lazio can be considered as the wide strip stretching from just north of Rome to the Tuscan border, with most of the important towns (**Cerveteri**, **Tarquinia** and **Vulci**) set on hills a few kilometres from the coast. If you have a car and a decent map, it's also worth considering a trip to **Norchia**, a spectacular cliff-face necropolis between Tarquinia and Viterbo.

For an overview of the Etruscans' talents, have a look at the Etruscan Museum at **Villa Giulia** in Rome (*see page 67*) before setting out for the sites. The contents of many tombs have ended up here or in the Vatican's **Museo Gregoriano** (*see page 108*). The only on-site museum with exhibits of the same quality is at Tarquinia.

Cerveteri

Cerveteri has atmosphere. Beneath the pines, this town of the dead – with streets, *piazze* and tidy little houses – is one of the most touching archaeological sites in Italy. There's a good-humoured feel about the place, despite the fact that, like most Etruscan sites, it consists almost solely of tombs.

In the drab modern town, the sixteenth-century Orsini castle is home to the small **Museo Nazionale di Cerveteri**, with secondary finds from Cerveteri and the nearby port of **Pyrgi** (*see page 243*). Much more interesting is the **Banditaccia Necropolis** 1km from the piazza.

Etruscan *Kysry*, romanised as *Caere*, was a vast, prosperous town with three ports, one of the great trading centres of the Mediterranean between the seventh and fifth centuries BC. It was situated further along the same volcanic spur that is occupied by the modern town, but covered an area 20 times greater. Similarly, the visitable area of the necropolis represents only a small part of its total extent.

The earliest tombs date from the seventh century BC; the latest are from the third, by which time there had been a progressive impoverishment of tomb size and decoration. Don't miss the well-preserved sixth-century BC **Tomba dei Capitelli**, the fourth-century BC **Tomba dei Rilievi**, with bas-reliefs of weapons and domestic utensils, and the three parallel streets of fifth- and sixth-century BC cube-shaped tombs between the **Via degli Inferni** and **Via delle Serpi**. Ask an attendant to accompany you to the **Tomba degli Scudi e delle Sedie** outside the main gate, with its chairs carved out of tufa rock and bas reliefs of shields adorning the walls (bring a torch).

Information

Museo Nazionale di Cerveteri *(06 994 1354).*
Open *Apr-Oct* 9am-7pm, *Nov-Mar* 9am-4pm, Tue-Sun. **Admission** free.
Banditaccia Necropolis:
Open *Oct-Apr* 9am-4pm, *May-Sept* 9am-7pm, Tue-Sun. **Admission** L8,000.
Getting there: *by bus* COTRAL from Lepanto; *by car* 44km (27 miles) by A12 or Via Aurelia (SS1); *by train* from Termini, Tuscolana, Ostiense or Trastevere to Cerveteri-Ladispoli station (6km out of town), then local bus.

Tarquinia

Tarquinia's tombs are hidden beneath a grassy hill, peppered with modern entrances like a crazy fallout shelter. But they have the art that Cerveteri lacks: over 100 vividly-coloured painted tombs giving an insight into Etruscan life. Tarquinia provokes our curiosity, with scenes of work and social life, athletic contests, mysterious rituals and erotic encounters.

In order to limit atmospheric pollution, only ten tombs are open. Start off in the **Museo Nazionale** in Piazza Cavour, which has one of the best Etruscan collections outside Rome. Its chief exhibit is a pair of fourth-century terracotta winged horses from a temple, proof that the Etruscans could model with as much finesse as the Greeks. There are also fine sarcophagi, imported Greek vases, and some tomb paintings moved here to ensure their preservation.

To see the best paintings in situ, head for the **necropolis**, about 2km (1.25 miles) out of town.

Fun-loving Etruscans romp in tomb paintings from **Tarquinia**.

The sixth-century **Tomba della Caccia e della Pesca** (generally open on weekends in summer) has delightful fishing and hunting scenes; in the **Tomba dei Leopardi** couples recline in a banqueting scene (note the man passing his partner an egg – a recurrent symbol, though experts disagree as to what of). There is a similar scene with dancers in the elegant **Tomba delle Leonesse**. Finally, the **Tomba dei Tori**, one of the oldest, has a scene of Achilles waiting to ambush Troilus, and another containing *un po' di pornografico*, as Lawrence gleefully (but ungrammatically) described it. The modern town bristles with medieval defensive towers, and its twelfth-century church of **Santa Maria di Castello** dominates the plain below.

Information & transport
Museo Nazionale di Tarquinia & Necropolis *(0766 856 036)*. **Open** 9am-7pm Tue-Sun. **Admission** L8,000.
Getting there: *by bus* COTRAL from Lepanto, change at Civitavecchia; *by car* 91km/56.5 miles, by A12 and Via Aurelia (SS1); *by train* (irregular) from Termini or Ostiense to Tarquinia.
Where to eat: **Le Due Orfanelle** *Via Vicolo Breve, 4 (0766 856 307; closed Tue)*. Follow signs to the church of San Francesco to find this excellent, reasonably-priced *trattoria*.

Tuscania

In Tuscania it's the post-Etruscan bits that stand out – even though the town itself was dealt a devastating blow by a major earthquake in 1971. The town boasts two Romanesque-Lombard churches, **San Pietro** and **Santa Maria Maggiore**.

The Colle San Pietro, on which they stand, was the site of an Etruscan and then Roman settlement; fragments of the pre-Christian acropolis are incorporated into the apse of San Pietro. Founded in the eighth century, the church was reworked from the eleventh to the thirteenth, when the adjacent bishop's palace and towers were added. The façade is startling: three-faced trifons, snakes and dancers owe more to pagan culture than Christian iconography. The interior has a Cosmatesque pavement and twelfth-century frescoes. Santa Maria Maggiore was built at the same time, with tamer beasts on its marble façade, and a more harmonious interior.

The main Etruscan find in the town is in the small **archaeological museum**, in the cloisters of **Santa Maria del Riposo** convent. Inside, four generations of the same Etrusco-Roman family gaze from the lids of their sarcophagi.

Information & transport
Tuscania archaeological museum *(0761 436 209)*. **Open** 9am-7pm Tue-Sun. **Admission** free.
Getting there: *by bus* COTRAL from Saxa Rubra (summer only; in winter bus to Viterbo, then change); *by car* 85km/53 miles, Via Cassia (SS2) to Vetralla, then local road.
Where to eat: Tuscania has one of northern Lazio's best restaurants, **Al Gallo** *Via del Gallo 22 (0761 443 388, closed Mon)*. Gourmet dishes and an extensive wine list raise it above the usual *trattoria di campagna*; there are also twelve bedrooms, if you can't face the journey back.

*Bucolic cherubs at the Villa Falconieri in palazzo-packed **Frascati**. See page 239.*

Grottaferrata is a small, lively town whose main street leads down to the tenth-century **Abbazia di San Nilo**, a mainly Romanesque monastery fortified in the fifteenth century by Michelangelo's patron Pope Julius II. The abbey church of **Santa Maria** has a fine twelfth-century campanile, and an even finer carved marble portal. Inside, the Cappella di San Nilo contains frescoes by Domenichino. The **museum** contains pieces of Classical sculpture and frescoes originally from the nave of the church.

Of all the Castelli, **Nemi** is definitely the most picturesque – so try to avoid visiting on a Sunday, when it fills up with Roman strollers. Perched on the edge of Lake Nemi's tree-covered crater is a site once used for worship by the cult of Diana. For Romans, the medieval village nearby, beneath the Ruspoli family castle, is synonymous with strawberries. They're grown in greenhouses by the lake, and heavily promoted, particularly in the village's Strawberry Festival in June. On the other side of the lake is **Genzano**, which holds an annual Corpus Christi Flower Festival (early June), when the town's main streets are beautifully decorated with elaborate carpets of flowers.

Information & transport

Frascati tourist office *Piazzale Marconi 1 (06 942 0331).* **Open** *Apr-Oct* 8am-2pm Mon, Sat; 8am-2pm, 4-7pm, Tue-Fri. *Nov-Mar* 8am-2pm Mon, Sat; 8am-2pm, 3.30-6.30pm, Tue-Fri.
Villa Aldobrandini: Open *Mar-Oct* 9am-1pm, 3pm-6pm, *Oct-Mar* 9am-1pm, 3pm-5pm, Mon-Fri only. **Admission** free, but permit must be obtained from tourist office.

Abbazia di San Nilo *abbey* **Open** 5.30am-7.30pm daily. **Admission** donation expected; *museum* **Open** 8.30am-noon, 4.30-6pm, Tue-Sun. **Admission** free.
Getting there: *by bus* COTRAL from Anagnina; *by car* A2 or Via Tuscolana (SS5) to Grottaferrata (18km/11 miles), Frascati (20km/12.5 miles); Via Appia (SS7) to Genzano (29km/18 miles), Nemi (33km/20.5 miles); *by train* from Termini-Laziale station, lines run to Frascati and Castel Gandolfo/Albano. The latter is very picturesque.
Where to eat In **Frascati** you're spoilt for choice. Among the crowd, **Cacciani** *Via Armando Diaz, 13 (06 942 0378; closed Mon & mid-Aug)*, stands out as one of the best restaurants in the Castelli (with prices to match). For something simpler, try **Zarazà** *Viale Regina Margherita 2 (closed Mon & Aug)*. In **Grottaferrata** don't miss **Al Fico Nuovo** *Via Anagnina, 134 (06 945 9276; closed Wed & second half Aug)*. It's well worth the 15-minute uphill trek out of town (on the Rocca Priora road) for the home-made *fettuccine*, cool garden terrace and delicious house wine. The best place to eat in **Nemi** is **Lo Specchio di Diana** *Corso Vittorio Emanuele, 13 (06 936 8016)*. There's a terrace overlooking the lake, and pizzas so huge they arrive on two plates.

Lake Bracciano & its region

This large, sparklingly clean lake about 40km (24 miles) north of Rome is surrounded by picturesque villages and sailing, windsurfing and canoeing clubs. Swimming is possible all around the lake, but the best spots are just north of Bracciano town on the western shore, and on the east side south of Trevignano. **Anguillara**, the nearest lakeside town to Rome, may take its name from the lake's eels (*anguille*), or a Roman villa built on this corner (*angolo*) of the lake shore. In ancient times this was already a site for holiday homes. The medieval town is perched on a rocky crag, and especially beautiful at sunset. There are great views from the belvedere overlooking the lake.

Bracciano is the main town on the lake, dominated by the **Orsini-Odescalchi Castle**, built in 1470, with fine apartments decorated by Antoniazzo Romano and the Zuccari brothers. Close by is **Lago di Martignano**, a quieter, smaller, offshoot of the Bracciano crater. There's a small beach, and you can rent sailing boats, pedalos and canoes. You need a car to get there: turn sharp right at the little chapel before Anguillara, follow the road past a drinking trough and go left on a track (signposted *lago*) for 3km. Parking at the top of the path down to the lake will cost you L5,000.

Trevignano, to the north, is a medieval town with a pleasant *lungolago* (lakeside promenade), with bars and restaurants. It's best reached on the Via Cassia, which leads past the ruins of **Veio**, Rome's great Etruscan rival in the fifth century BC. If you turn right instead of left at the Trevignano junction on the Cassia you will come to **Calcata**, isolated on a volcanic spur above the verdant **Valle del Treia**. This picturesque village is a mecca for ageing hippies, and there's no shortage of wholefood snackbars and ethnic jewellery shops. It's also the hub for several spectacular walks, some of which are marked (the non-marked ones tend to disappear under nettles each summer). The one-and-a-half-hour trek along the valley to **Mazzano**, via the Etruscan necropolis of **Narce**, is recommended.

Information & transport
Castello Orsini-Odescalchi, Bracciano *(06 9980 4348)*. **Open** 10am-noon, 3-6.30pm, Tue-Sun. **Admission** L11,000.
Getting there *by bus* COTRAL from Lepanto; *by car* Via Braccianense (SS493) to Anguillara (32km/20 miles), Bracciano (40km/25 miles); Via Cassia (SS2) to Trevignano (43km/26.5 miles), Calcata (45km/28 miles); *by train* from Termini, Tiburtina, Ostiense to Anguillara or Bracciano.
Where to eat: In **Bracciano**, **Vino e Camino** *Via delle Cantine 11 (06 9980 3433, dinner only, closed Mon)* is an excellent wine bar with tables outside just around the corner from the Castello Orsini, offering snacks and more substantial meals.

Further afield

The coast north of Rome

In **Santa Severa**, 54km (33.5 miles) north-west of Rome, the four-square **Castello Orsini** squats like an outsized sandcastle on the beach. Inside it

there is a proper little village, with its church, a chapel with fourteenth-century frescoes, and a fountain. The castle is now owned by the town council, which organises concerts there in summer, and lets out some of the tiny seventeenth-century cottages as holiday homes. Next to the castle are the remains of the once-busy Etruscan port of **Pyrgi**, the main sea outlet of Cerveteri (*see page 240*) and the site of an important sanctuary to the Etruscan goddess *Uni* (Roman *Juno*). There's a small museum of finds from the excavations, the **Antiquarium**. The beach to the right of the castle is fine for a swim, so long as you don't look too closely at the colour of the water.

Continuing northward, the power stations, Sardinian ferries and industrial waste of **Civitavecchia** scupper the theory that the further you travel from Rome, the cleaner it gets. It's not until you reach the border with Tuscany that things start to improve again. The first village across the boundary, **Chiarone**, consists of a dainty railway station, a shop, a couple of bars and a few houses – but it has the first clean sea and sandy beach this side of Rome, and a gently shelving shoreline makes it ideal for kids. Behind the dunes is a good campsite, the **Chiarone** (0564 890 101; open May-Sept).

You can walk along the beach from here all the way (12km/7.5 miles) to the hill at **Ansedonia**. This is the site of the Etruscan town of Cosa, and now bristles with upmarket holiday villas. Halfway along, just beyond **Lago di Burano**, an important protected bird sanctuary, is the **Marina di Capalbio**, marked by the incongruous bulk of the **Casale di Macchiatonda**, a former hunting lodge. For many years this has been the beach resort for Rome's monied Left, although according to recent reports they are currently forsaking villas in the hills behind the shore for houses in the beautiful walled village of **Capalbio** itself (7km/4 miles inland). Without a car the only way to get here directly from Rome is to take a train to Capalbio station, and walk or hitch the 3km (2 miles) to the beach.

Beyond Ansedonia the mountainous promontory of **Monte Argentario** rises out of the sea. It's joined to the mainland by three narrow isthmuses. On the central one the historic town of **Orbetello** bulges out like a swollen knuckle, while the southernmost, the **Tombolo della Feniglia**, is a nature reserve with a healthy colony of deer and many species of aquatic birds, visible from the shore facing the lagoon. A path (walkers and cyclists only) under shady umbrella pines runs the whole length of the Tombolo (to get there, take the Porto Ercole bus from Orbetello Scalo station and ask to be put off at *il bivio per la Feniglia*). From the tombolo path, you can cut across to a beach that – because it's inaccessible by car – is among the emptiest in mainland Italy (although in high season 'empty' may be a relative concept). One piece of advice: the mosquitoes that frequent the lagoons are monsters. Come prepared.

Information

Pyrgi Antiquarium *(0766 570 194)*.
Open 9am-1pm Tue, Thur, Sat. **Admission** L8,000.
Getting there: Santa Severa
by bus COTRAL from Lepanto; *by car* 54km/33.5 miles, by A12 or Via Aurelia (SS1); *by train* (infrequent) from Termini, Ostiense or Trastevere to Santa Severa, then 1km walk to beach.
Chiarone, Capalbio, Monte Argentario *by car* A12 or Via Aurelia (SS1) to Chiarone (124km/77 miles); *by train* from Termini, Ostiense or Trastevere to Chiarone and Capalbio (infrequent: 4/5 per day in summer; you may need to change at Civitavecchia) and Orbetello Scalo (around 10 per day in summer).
Where to eat: In **Santa Severa** there's a good beach trattoria right next to the castle, **L'Isola del Pescatore** *(0766 740 145)*, open daily from Easter to late September. On the beach in **Chiarone** is the bar/trattoria **L'Ultima Spiaggia** *(0564 890 295, open 1 June-20 Sept)*. The **Bar della Stazione** in **Capalbio** is a front for an excellent cheap *trattoria (0564 898 424, closed Tue in low season)*. You can also eat on Capalbio beach at the pricey but atmospheric **Carmen Bay** *(0564 893 196; open Sat, Sun Easter-end May, Oct; daily June-Sept)*.

The coast south of Rome

The ports of **Anzio** and **Nettuno** were the site of massive Allied landings in 1944, and are now surrounded by giant war cemeteries. Neither town has much to recommend it except fish restaurants. Anzio is also the jumping-off point for ferries to the **Pontine Islands**, of which the two largest, **Ponza** and **Ventotene**, are popular summer venues that have retained most of their Mediterranean charm. A mixture of pastel-painted architecture, rocky coves and curious Roman remains makes them well worth a stopover. They can also be reached from Formia, Terracina and, in summer, the Roman port of Fiumicino.

The first cleanish sea south of Rome is at ~~Sabaudia, the Fascist answer to Bournemouth.~~ It stands in the **Parco Nazionale del Circeo**, next to a large artificial lake. The beaches (1km from town) are clean and sandy, and the sea is fairly acceptable. Looming to the left is **Monte Circeo**, said to be where Odysseus was waylaid by the enchantress Circe while his men were changed into pigs. On the other side of the rock a road leads up to **San Felice Circeo**, a pretty little town that becomes a poseurs' paradise each summer.

About 20km (12.5 miles) inland from **Sabaudia**, below the town of Priverno, is the Cistercian **Abbazia di Fossanova**. Recent restoration has exposed the elegance of its early Gothic architecture, with a gorgeous rose window and Cosmati mosaics on the unfinished façade. Saint Thomas Aquinas died here, and his room can be visited.

Terracina is a port-town with two centres. The pleasant modern part is down by the sea, and along the Via Flacca. The medieval town above lies on top of the forum of the Roman port of *Anxur*. Its cathedral was built out of the main hall of a Roman temple to Augustus; above the portico is a twelfth-century mosaic frieze, while below it is a big basin that was reputedly used for boiling Christians. The paving slabs in the piazza are those of the old forum, and just beyond is a gate and stretch of the ancient Via Appia. Bombing during World War II uncovered these ancient remains and made space for the modern town hall and **archaeological museum**. The museum was closed for restoration at time of writing, but due to open during 2000. Up above the town, and spectacularly lit at night, is the first century BC **Temple of Jupiter** (follow the signs to the hospital and carry on up), which offers views along the coast from Circeo to Gaeta.

Between Terracina and Sperlonga the beaches are almost all sown up by private beach facilities. **Sperlonga** itself is a very pretty seaside resort with some of the cleanest sea in central Italy. The whitewashed medieval town on the spur overlooking the two beaches, its narrow lanes lined with potted geraniums, boutiques, bars and restaurants, fills up with well-heeled Romans in summer months. The **archaeological museum**, at the end of the fine sandy beach to the south of the town, contains some important second century BC sculptures depicting scenes from the story of Odysseus. The visit includes a tour of **Tiberius' Villa and Grotto**.

There are some pretty sandy coves between Sperlonga and Gaeta, but you will often have to pay to park on the road (L3,000-5,000) and to use the steps down to beaches, even if they themselves are *spiaggie libere* (free-access beaches).

If you get tired of the beach, consider hopping inland to **Fondi**. This thriving little town contains two fine medieval churches, a chunk of megalithic wall, a splendidly intact castle and one of the biggest open-air markets in the region, good for second-hand clothes and delicious local produce (every Sunday morning).

The last resort along this stretch of coast is **Gaeta**, a town of great strategic and historical importance. It was the last stronghold of Francis II of Naples against Garibaldi's Piedmontese troops, falling on 13 February 1861 to end 130 years of Bourbon rule in southern Italy. The modern lower town clusters around the harbour; the old medieval walled town has more tackily-adorned Madonnas in wall-niches than Naples, and an impressive twelfth-century castle. **Serapo** beach, to the north, is long, wide and very crowded in summer.

The ghost gardens of Ninfa

Ninfa, local legend says, was named after a nymph so upset at the loss of her lover that she cried copiously enough to form a stream. That same stream, they say, is the one that today still flows cold and crystal clear though what surely count as some of Italy's most beautiful gardens, which ramble romantically through the ruins of a mysterious, abandoned medieval town just north of the Via Appia, south-east of Rome.

The origins of the town of Ninfa are obscure. That it existed in the eighth century is certain, and by the tenth century it was an important bulwark of the papal states against the marauding Normans. In the twelfth century it made the mistake of supporting a rival to the then pope, and was sacked by the pontiff's defender, Holy Roman Emperor Frederick Barbarossa. It rallied, though, and by the early 1380s it had seven churches and 150 large *palazzi*. Shortly afterwards, however, Ninfa came definitively to grief in one of the inter-clan wars that were then devastating the area.

What warfare did not destroy, malaria finished off, and Ninfa was gradually left as a deserted ruin. The Caetani family, who acquired it in the fourteenth century, showed little interest in their ghost estate for centuries. It was not until the 1920s, in fact, when Don Gelasio Caetani decided to plant his vast collection of exotic species there, that Ninfa got its second lease of life. The result of Don Gelasio's botanical dabbling is a place of pure magic, where climbing roses cascade over crumbling masonry, flowering trees shed blossoms on manicured lawns, and the air is rich with perfumes emanating from countless bursts of colour.

Donna Lelia Caetani, last of the family line, died in 1977, leaving Ninfa in the hands of the Caetani Foundation. The area around the ruined village is now a bird sanctuary, thronged with herons and egrets, managed by the Foundation, the WWF, and LIPU, Italy's society for the protection of birds.

Information & transport

Ninfa Gardens: Open *Apr-Oct* 9am-noon, 3-6.30pm, first Sat, Sun of each month.
Admission L12,000.
Only a limited number of visitors are allowed, so tickets are best purchased in advance in Rome from:
WWF *Viale Giulio Cesare, 128 (06 372 3646).*
Metro Lepanto/bus to Viale Giulio Cesare.
Open 10am-7pm Mon-Fri.
Fondazione Caetani *Via delle Botteghe Oscure, 32 (06 6880 3231).*
Bus or tram to Largo Argentina. **Open** 8am-7pm Mon-Fri; 8am-noon Sat.
Getting there: Not easy without a car. *By car* Via Appia (SS7) to Tor Tre Ponti, then follow signs to Latina Scalo, Norma and Ninfa (65km/40 miles). *by train* from Termini to Latina Scalo, then haggle with waiting taxi-drivers for the 9km/5.5 mile ride to the Gardens.

*A weeping nymph cried a river in the botanical gardens of **Ninfa**.*

Information & transport

Abbazia di Fossanova *(0773 93 061)*. **Open** *Oct-Mar* 8am-noon, 3.30-5.30pm, *Apr-Sept* 8am-noon, 4-7.30pm, daily. **Admission** donation expected.
Terracina archaeological museum *(0773 702 220)*. **Open** *May-Sept* 9am-1pm, 5-7pm, Tue-Sat, 8am-1pm Sun; *Oct-Apr* 9am-2pm Mon-Sat. **Admission** free
Sperlonga archaeological museum & Tiberius' Villa *(0771 54 028)*. **Open** 9am-one hour before sunset daily. **Admission** L4,000.
Getting there: *by bus* COTRAL from EUR Fermi; *by car* Via Appia (SS7) or Via Pontina (SS148) to Sabaudia (93km/58 miles), Terracina (105km/65 miles), or Sperlonga (123km/76 miles); *by train* from Termini for Anzio and Nettuno; from Termini, Tiburtina or Ostiense to Priverno (for buses to Sabaudia and buses/trains to Terracina), Fondi (for buses to Sperlonga), and Formia (for buses to Gaeta).
Where to eat, drink & dance:
In **Anzio**, **Da Alceste al Buon Gusto** *Piazzale Sant'Antonio 6, (06 984 6744, closed Tue)* is one of the best of the town's many seafood resturants.
Terracina offers plenty of options; good value is **Bottega Sarra 1932** *Via Villafranca 34 (0773 702 045, closed Mon)*, not far from the cathedral. It's also worth making a gastronomic detour inland to **Fondi**, where the unpronounceable **Vicolo di 'Mblo** *Corso Italia 126 (0771 502 385, closed Tue)* offers the best of the region's cooking (homemade pasta, baked fish with olives, good desserts).
In **Sperlonga** head for the family-run **La Bisaccia** *Via Romita 25 (0771 545 76; open Wed-Mon)*, in the modern lower town, for great fish; in the old quarter of **Gaeta** **Antico Vico** *Vico II del Cavallo 2 (0771 465 116, closed Wed)*. is another reliable place for a well-priced seafood meal Not to be missed in this area are the *mozzarella di bufala* and little black olives from Gaeta, sold in stalls along the road.
All along the coast there are plenty of **beach discos**, an Italian summer institution. Evergreen party palaces on Lungomare Circe in **San Felice Circeo** are **La Stiva** (no phone) and **Valentino Notte** *(0773 784 310)*, a romantic disco/piano bar that could be a Barry Manilow fan's idea of heaven.
Enea's Landing *(0771 741 713)* on Via Flacca in **Gaeta** is a popular club with a funky atmosphere.

Viterbo

Originally an important Etruscan town and then an insignificant Roman one, Viterbo was fortified in the eighth century by the Lombard King Desiderius as a launching pad for sacking Rome. As well as enduring many bloody internal battles, Viterbo also managed to get caught up in the medieval quarrels between the Holy Roman Empire and the Church. Depending on which way the wind blew, the town played host to popes and anti-popes, several of whom relocated here when things in Rome got too hot to handle. Gregory X was elected pope in Viterbo and lasted a month; Hadrian V died on arriving in town; and John XXI was killed a year after his election when his bedroom floor in the Papal Palace collapsed.

Viterbo was badly bombed in World War II, but has been meticulously restored, and the town still retains its historic appearance. Wandering around the narrow streets you will stumble across medieval laundries, ancient porticos, imposing towers and crenellated buildings. You will also notice that there are lions (the symbol of Viterbo) and fountains everywhere.

The medieval quarter of **San Pellegrino** lies at the southern edge of the city, flanked by Piazza della Morte. Across the bridge is the elegant twelfth-century – but much altered and restored – **cathedral of San Lorenzo**. Next door to it is the **Palazzo Papale**, built for the popes in the thirteenth century and restored in the nineteenth. From the Loggia outside, newly elected popes would bless the people of Viterbo. Nearby, off Via San Lorenzo, is the pretty church of **Santa Maria Nuova**, from the twelfth century, with an ancient head of Jupiter on the façade, and a pulpit from where Saint Thomas Aquinas preached. Behind the church are the remains of a small Lombard cloister (always open).

Piazza del Plebiscito is dominated by the **Palazzo Comunale** town hall (1500). Its arched doorway opens onto a lovely courtyard with a seventeenth-century fountain and a view across the Faul valley below; a staircase leads to the Senate rooms, which are usually open to the public in the morning. At the top of the stairs is the Chapel of the Commune, sealed off by glass, displaying, as if in a shop window, two huge canvasses by Sebastiano del Piombo and a *Visitation* by Bartolomeo Cavarozzi. From the piazza, Via Roma leads past the **Fontana dei Leoni** into Corso d'Italia, where at number 11 there is the **Caffè Schenardi**, a fifteenth-century hotel that has been a café since 1818. Mussolini had breakfast here in 1938, at the third table on the right.

Taking Via Cavour out of Piazza del Plebiscito, past the impressive thirteenth-century **Fontana Grande**, Via Garibaldi leads up to the **Porta Romana**. Just inside the gate on the left is the fine church of **San Sisto**, parts of which date back to the ninth century. It has a unique chancel raised a full fifteen steps above the nave, and two curious twisting columns.

Outside the walls, opposite Porta della Verità, is the twelfth century **Santa Maria della Verità**, with some of the most Tuscan frescoes outside of Tuscany in the Gothic **Cappella Mazzatosta**, painted by local boy Lorenzo di Viterbo in 1469. The charming *Marriage of the Virgin* panel was badly damaged in the war, and reconstructed from 16,000 pieces. The chapel pavement has remains of maiolica decoration; other fragments are in the V&A in London. In the old convent next door is the renovated **Museo Civico**, with Etruscan finds and works of art from local churches, and two canvases by Sebastiano del Piombo.

Wallowing in sulphurous mud in the Bagnaccio *hot springs near* **Viterbo**.

Within a 7km (4.5 miles) radius of the city, but accessible only by car, there are several bubbling pools of sulphurous water. Local residents like to sit around in them on Sundays, smeared in greeny-white clay, listening to the football on the radio or chatting. The best place to wallow is the **Bagnaccio**, where four basins of varying degrees of heat are scooped out of the glaring white clay. To get there, leave Viterbo by the Porta Fiorentina on the Montefiascone road, and after 5km (3 miles) turn left onto the road to Marta. After another kilometre you'll see a Roman ruin on your left with a tree growing out of it. Just before this, an unpaved road branches off to the Bagnaccio.

If you're in Viterbo on 3 September, you can attend the *festa* of Santa Rosa. At 9pm the citizens parade a 30m (98ft)-high illuminated tower (*la macchina*) around the town. A new one is built every five years – on one occasion it was so high that it swayed out of control, and in the panic 21 people were trampled to death. In the **Museo della Macchina di Santa Rosa** models and photos document the festival's history. The body of Santa Rosa herself lies shrivelled in a glass tomb in the church of her name.

Information & transport

Viterbo tourist office: APT *Piazza San Carluccio, in courtyard of Zaffera restaurant (0761 304 795)*. **Open** 9am-1pm, 1.30-3.30pm, Mon-Fri; 9am-1pm Sat. **Museo Civico** *(0761 348 275)*. **Open** *Apr-Oct* 9am-7pm, *Nov-Mar* 9am-6pm, Tue-Sun. **Admission** L6,000.

Museo della Macchina di Santa Rosa *Via San Pellegrino 60 (0761 345 157)*. **Open** *Apr-Oct* 10am-1pm, 4-8pm, Wed-Sun; *Nov-Mar* 10am-1pm, 4-7pm, Fri-Sun. **Admission** free)

Getting there: *by bus* COTRAL from Saxa Rubra; *by car* A1 or Via Cassia (SS2) to Viterbo (85km/53 miles); *by train* FS from Ostiense or Trastevere to Viterbo. Also slow, infrequent services from the COTRAL Roma-Nord station in Piazzale Flaminio.

Where to eat: A reasonably-priced restaurant serving good food in a friendly, family atmosphere is the **Porta Romana** *Via della Bontà, 12 (0761 301 118; closed Sun)*, near the church of San Sisto. More upmarket but equally good value is **Enoteca La Torre** *Via della Torre 5 (0761 226 467, closed Sun)*, with creative versions of local pasta, meat and fish dishes; alongside the extensive wine list, there is even an olive oil and a mineral water list.

Around Viterbo

Villas & parks

The villas in northern Lazio, like those in Tivoli and the Castelli Romani, were commissioned by families whom the lottery of ecclesiastical power had briefly raised to preeminence. They were not just country retreats, but personal and political statements. **Villa Farnese**, **Villa Lante** and the mysterious **Sacro Bosco** at Bomarzo were all commissioned in the sixteenth century by patrons related to one other. They also used the same architects, artists and craftsmen – chiefly those busy Mannerists Sangallo and Vignola.

Sacro Bosco, Bomarzo

(0761 924 029). **Open** *May-Sept* 8am-7pm, *Oct-Apr*
8am-sunset, daily. **Admission** L15,000 adults;
L13,000 3-8 year olds; L13,000 groups.

An important town in the Roman Empire, Bomarzo
was largely owned from the beginning of the fourteenth century by the powerful Orsini family. The
park of *Il Sacro Bosco*, also known as the *Parco
dei Mostri* or 'Monster Park', is situated just
below the town, and was built by Duke Vicino
Orsini (1523-84) shortly after his wife died. This,
though, is more a bizarre Renaissance theme park
than a dignified retreat for a bereaved husband.
Taking advantage of the volcanic peperino stone
that dotted his estate, Orsini spent years filling the
park with surreal, sometimes grotesque sculptures,
which were completely at odds with the
conventional tastes of his day. Lurking in the
undergrowth are a skewed, leaning house and
enormous, absurd beasts, which children (and
adults) are free to clamber on; a huge elephant
mauls a Roman soldier, and giants brawl. The park
was much appreciated by Salvador Dali, who
played a part in publicising it and making it one of
Lazio's most popular tourist attractions. Its present
owners have done all they can to destroy the
overgrown mystery of Vicino's original park, but
some of the old magic still filters through.

Villa Farnese, Caprarola

(0761 646 052). **Open** *Nov-Feb* 9am-4pm,
Mar-mid-Apr, mid Sept-Oct 9am-4.30pm, *mid Apr-
mid Sept* 9am-6.30pm, Tue-Sun. **Tours** *of villa &
park* 10am, 11am, noon, 3pm, 5pm Tue-Sat; 10am,
noon, 3pm Sun. **Admission** L4,000.

The little town of Caprarola is dwarfed by the
imposing Villa Farnese, one of Italy's great
Mannerist villas. It began as a castle, designed by
Sangallo the Younger and Peruzzi, but was taken
over by Vignola in the 1560s. As you approach the
villa it appears to be only two storeys high, but climb
the semi-circular ramps and the ground floor
appears. Vignola raised and extended the approach
road, burying the lower storeys of the existing houses to provide an optimum view of the villa. Inside, a
wide spiral staircase, which the villa's owner,
Cardinal Alessandro Farnese, used to climb on
horseback, leads up to the *Piano Nobile*, the only part
open to the public. In the *Salone dei Fasti Farnese*
are frescoes depicting the heroic deeds of the Farnese
family: note the Farnese Pope Paul III in the act of
excommunicating Henry VIII of England. The *Sala
dei Sogni* – the cardinal's winter bedroom – has
bizarre allegorical scenes intended to induce sweet
dreams. There is also a room with frescoed maps of
the world from 1500, and another in which whispers
rebound from wall to wall. Behind the villa are two
formal gardens (included in the ordinary tour) and
the *barchino*, a steep, wooded park that leads up to
the fountains of the *Giardino Grande* and the
Palazzina del Piacere summer house. This part of the
grounds can only be visited with one of the guided
tours of the whole villa and park.

Villa Lante, Bagnaia

(0761 288 008). **Open** *gardens only* guided visits
every half-hour, 9.30am-half an hour before sunset
Tue-Sun. **Admission** L4,000.

The town of Bagnaia lies beneath the gardens and
park of Villa Lante. The villa was built in the 1570s
for Cardinal Gambara (perhaps to a design by
Vignola), and is a superb example of Renaissance
landscape gardening. The two identical palaces are
surrounded by a geometrically perfect formal Italian
garden, punctuated with fountains and pools. Fed
by a spring at the top of the garden, water cascades
down over five terraces, performing spectacular
water-games to impress and surprise guests. Not all
are still working, but the ropework cascade and
stone dining table with central wine-cooling rivulet
can still be admired. Inside the *palazzini* (closed at
time of writing, but supposedly due to reopen for
summer 2000) are frescoes by the Zuccari brothers,
and a series of paintings of the Lazian villas.

Transport

Getting there: Bomarzo *by bus* COTRAL from
Saxa Rubra, change at Viterbo; *by car* A1 to
Attigliano exit, then SS204 (90km/56 miles); *by train*
from Termini or Tiburtina to Attigliano-Bomarzo on
Orte line (5km from park). **Caprarola** *by bus*
COTRAL from Lepanto; *by car* Via Cassia (SS2), then
road to Ronciglione/Caprarola (60km/37 miles).
Bagnaia *by bus* COTRAL from Saxa Rubra, change
at Viterbo; *by car* A1 to Attigliano or Orte exit, then
SS204 (90km/56 miles); *by train* from Roma-Nord/
Piazzale Flaminio to Bagnaia, change at Viterbo.

The Vico & Bolsena lakes

A group of Lazian shepherds once asked Hercules
to demonstrate his powers. Ever ready to show off,
Hercules picked up his club, thrust it deep into the
ground and challenged the shepherds to extract it.
Sure enough, they were too weak and Hercules had
his moment of glory, whereupon fresh water
gushed forth, filled the hole and created **Lago di
Vico**, a beautiful lake surrounded by forests and
wetlands, and now part of a nature reserve with
good marked paths.

The much larger **Lago di Bolsena**, in the heart
of Etruscan Lazio, is great for sailing, windsurfing
and swimming. There are good beaches all around
it, but especially on the road from **Gradoli** to
Capodimonte. In mid-lake there are two pri-
vately-owned islands. **Isola Bisentina** was a
papal summer residence, and has a Via Crucis with
seven Renaissance churches and chapels by
Antonio da Sangallo. **Isola Martana** was where
the daughter of Ostrogoth king Theodoric (*see
chapter* **History**) was imprisoned and killed by
her husband Teodato in the fifth century. Boats to
Bisentina leave from Capodimonte (Navigazione
La Bussola, 0761 870 760) and Bolsena
(Navigazione Alta Lazio, 0761 798 033) in summer.

On the eastern shore of the lake is **Bolsena**, a
charming medieval town with a castle housing an

archaeological museum. There's also a fifteenth-century church, **Santa Caterina**, and, at **Poggio Moscioni** (1km along the Orvieto road) the remains of Roman **Volsinium**, with an amphitheatre, walls and houses. Heading south is Capodimonte, with a little harbour and a Farnese castle built by Sangallo the Younger. **Marta** is a pretty medieval and Renaissance town on the river Marta, where it joins the lake.

To the south-east is **Montefiascone**, a hilltop town dominated by the huge dome of **Santa Margherita** – the third largest dome in Italy. At the bottom of the town is **San Flaviano**, a twelfth-century church containing the tomb of Bishop Fugger, the German prelate who named the local wine; it is built on top of an earlier church that faced the opposite way. On his travels, the monk was accompanied by an assistant who went ahead marking places where the local wine was good with an *'Est!'* (here). At Montefiascone it merited an *'Est! Est!! Est!!!'* Uncharitable souls have suggested that without the story this ordinary little wine would have sunk without trace, but nowadays a local producer, Poggio dei Gelsi, has set about salvaging its reputation, with some success.

Information & transport

Bolsena archaeological museum
(0761 798 630). **Open** *Apr-Sept* 9.30am-1.30pm, 4-8pm, Tue-Sun; *Oct-Mar* 10am-1pm Tue-Fri, 10am-1pm, 4-8pm, Sat, Sun. **Admission** L5,000.
Volsinium: Open 9am-1.30pm Tue-Sun. **Admission** free.
Getting there *by bus* COTRAL from Saxa Rubra (in winter change at Viterbo); *by car* Via Cassia (SS2) to Montefiascone (100km/62 miles), Capodimonte (108km/67 miles), Bolsena (116km/72 miles).
Where to eat
A number of restaurants in **Marta** serve fish from sea and lake. Try **Gino al Miralago** *Lungolago Guglielmo Marconi, 58 (0761 870 910; closed Tue except in Aug).*

Into the mountains

When the city gets too hot and the sea too crowded, smart Romans head for the hills. There are some serious mountains (2,000m/6,500ft-plus) within an hour and a half of the capital, but you don't need to go that far to find clean air, good walks and some unspoilt villages.

The nearest range is the **Monti Lucretili**, only 40km (25 miles) north-east of Rome (you can see them on a clear day from the Gianicolo). Nevertheless, this Regional Park has remained relatively untouched by the metropolis. A good base is the pretty hill town of **Licenza**, with the remains of Horace's country retreat, the Sabine Farm, close by. From **Civitella di Licenza**, a tiny hamlet just outside the town, it's possible to climb **Monte Pellecchia** (1,368m/4,490ft), the highest peak in the Lucretili, in about two and a half hours.

Another good walk is the hour trek to the upland plain of **Il Pratone**, from the end of the Monte Morra road above the village of **Marcellina**.

On the other side of the A24 *autostrada*, beyond the tree-covered slopes of the **Monti Ruffi**, the long, bare crest of the **Monti Simbruini** stretches away to the south-east, marking the border between Lazio and Abruzzo. Since 1982 the whole of the Lazio side has been a Regional Park, which at least means that further development of dire ski resorts like those at Monte Livata and Campo Staffi has been curbed. The big tourist draw of the area is the town of **Subiaco**, in the eastern foothills, with its twin monasteries of **Santa Scolastica** and **San Benedetto**. From here you can go by car or ski-lift to Monte Livata and the plain of Campo dell'Osso, starting-point for the easy ascent of **Monte Autore** (1,855m/6,100ft; one hour), at the top of which you will find a magnificent view. Other launching-pads for long, solitary hikes are the hamlets of **Camerata Nuova** and **Vallepietra**, both served by infrequent buses from Rome's Ponte Mammolo terminus.

Across the regional boundary and some distance south-east is one of Italy's oldest national parks, the **Parco Nazionale di Abruzzo**. It contains breathtaking mountain scenery, and a range of fauna that includes the rare Apennine brown bear (the park's symbol), chamois, wolves and golden eagles. The park's administrative centre and only town of any size is **Pescasseroli**, which fills up with second-homers in summer. Information on hostels, refuges and campsites and detailed maps can also be obtained from information offices in the more attractive villages of **Opi** or **Civitella Alfadena** further up the valley.

From the latter, one of the best of the many walks in the park (all clearly marked and colour-coded – this one is itinerary I1) leads up through the beech woods of Val di Rosa to the **Passo Cavuto**. From here you can traverse (chamois sightings possible) to the refuge of **Forca Resuni** (1,952m/6,400ft). You begin your descent here (itinerary I4), via the Valle Jannanghera, back to the starting-point. In all, the trek should take about six hours. For something less strenuous, wander up the beautiful valley of the **Camosciara** (itinerary G6) or alongside the torrent of **Valle Fondillo** (F2 – the best route for would-be bear-spotters).

Transport

Getting there: *by bus* COTRAL from Ponte Mammolo to all destinations in Lazio: Abruzzo National Park, ARPA (06 4423 3928) runs a service to Pescassèroli (buses depart from Tiburtina); *by car* A24 or Via Tiburtina (SS5) to Licenza (54km/33.5 miles) or Subiaco (72km/44.5 miles); A24 then A25 to Abbruzzo National Park; *by train* very slow, very infrequent services from Termini or Tiburtina to Avezzano will take you to some (not all) mountain destinations in Lazio and Abruzzo.

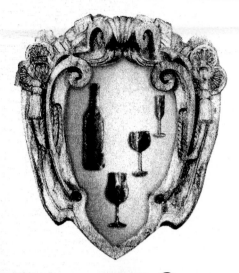

Directory

Directory

Getting Around

Arriving in Rome

By air

Through Fiumicino Airport

Fiumicino Airport Information (06 65 951). **Open** 24 hours daily. Rome's main airport, also known as Leonardo da Vinci, is about 30 km (18 miles) from the city, and handles all scheduled flights.

There is an **express rail service** between Termini station and the airport, which takes about 30 min and runs hourly approx 7am-10pm, daily Tickets in either direction cost L15,000. The regular service from Fiumicino takes 25-40 min, and also stops at Trastevere, Ostiense, Tuscolana and Tiburtina stations. Trains leave about every 15 min (less often on Sundays), 6.25am-11.27pm (5am-10.30pm to Fiumicino). Tickets are L8,000.

You can buy tickets for both these services from automatic machines in the main airport lobby and rail stations, from the Alitalia office in front of the central platforms, from the ticket office (open 7am-9pm), and the airport *tabacchi*. Some carriages have access for wheelchair users (*see p272*).

Ostiense is close to Piramide metro station, for trains to the city centre, but depending on your final destination in Rome you may find it more convenient to get off at one of the other stations, particularly when the metro is closed. Stamp your ticket in the machines on the station platform before boarding.

During the night, a bus service (*information 06 6595 4552*) runs between Fiumicino (from outside the arrivals hall) and Tiburtina in Rome. Tickets cost L7,000 from automatic machines. Buses leave Tiburtina at 12.30am, 1.15am, 2.30am and 3.45am, stopping at Termini 10 minutes later. Departures from Fiumicino are at 1.15am, 2.15am, 3.30am and 5am. Neither Termini or Tiburtina station are attractive places at night, and it's advisable to get a taxi directly from there to your final destination.. Metro line B, which passes through Tiburtina, closes at midnight, and buses are scarce.

A **taxi** into Rome from Fiumicino will cost at least L80,000, including a surcharge (L11,500 from Fiumicino, L14,000 from Rome) for the airport trip. Use only yellow or white officially licensed cabs lined up at ranks (ignore all touts). *See also p258*.

Through Ciampino Airport

Ciampino Airport Information (06 794 941). **Open** 24 hours daily. Ciampino, about 15 km (9 miles) south-east of the city, is mainly a military air-base, but is also used by charter flights to Rome. Getting to and from there can be a hassle. The best way into town is by **COTRAL bus** to Anagnina metro station on Line A, which links with Termini. Buses for Anagnina leave from the front of the arrivals hall every 30-60 min, 6.50am-11.40 pm daily (6.10am-11pm, Anagnina to Ciampino), and the fare is L2,000. Tickets can be bought from an automatic machine in the arrivals hall and the newsstand in the departures hall. A **taxi** to the centre will set you back about L70,000.

Airlines

Major airlines can be reached on the following numbers:
Alitalia *Main office: Via Leonida Bissolati, 11 (domestic flights 06 65 641; international flights 06 65 642). Metro Barberini/bus to Via Bissolati.* **Open** 9am-6pm Mon-Fri. **Credit** AmEx, DC, EC, MC, V. **Map 5/1B** *Termini station branch;* **Open** 6.30am-9pm. *Fiumicino Airport (06 65 641);* **Open** 24 hours daily.

Before you go

Customs

EU citizens do not have to declare goods imported into or exported from Italy for their personal use, as long as they arrive from another EU country.
For non-EU citizens, the following limits apply:
• 400 cigarettes or 200 small cigars or 100 cigars or 500 grams (17.64oz) of tobacco.
• One litre of spirits (over 22 per cent alcohol) or 2 litres of fortified wine (under 22 per cent alcohol); 50 grams (1.76oz) of perfume.
There are no restrictions on the import of cameras, watches or electrical goods. Visitors are also allowed to carry up to L20 million in cash.

Insurance

EU nationals are entitled to reciprocal medical care in Italy, provided they have an E111 form, available in the UK from Health Centres, post offices and Social Security offices. This will cover you for emergencies, but using an E111 naturally involves having to deal with the intricacies of the Italian state health system,

and for short-term visitors it's better to take out health cover under private travel insurance. Non-EU citizens should take out private medical insurance for all eventualities before setting out from home.

Visitors should also take out adequate property insurance before setting off for Italy. If you rent a vehicle, motorcycle or moped, make sure you pay the extra charge for full insurance cover, and sign the collision damage waiver when hiring a car.

Visas

EU nationals and citizens of the USA, Canada, Australia and New Zealand do not need visas for stays of up to three months. For EU citizens, a passport or national identity card valid for travel abroad is sufficient, but all non-EU citizens must have full passports. In theory, all visitors have to declare their presence to the local police within eight days of arrival. If you're staying in a hotel, this will be done for you. If not, contact the **Questura Centrale**, the main police station, for advice (*see also p270*).

British Airways *Via Leonida Bissolati, 54 (147 812 266 8am-8pm Mon-Fri; 9am-5pm Sat). Metro Barberini/bus to Via Bissolati.* **Open** 9am-5pm Mon-Fri. **Credit** AmEx, DC, EC, MC, V. **Map 5/1B**
Fiumicino Airport (06 6501 1513). **Open** 7am-6.30pm daily.
Qantas *Via Leonida Bissolati, 54 (06 5248 2725). Metro Barberini/bus to Via Bissolati.* **Open** 9am-5pm Mon-Fri. **Credit** AmEx, DC, MC, V. **Map 5/1B**.
Fiumicino Airport (06 6501 0468). **Open** 9am-5pm Tue-Sat.
TWA *Via Barberini, 67 (06 47 211 reservations/06 47 241). Metro Barberini/bus to Piazza Barberini.* **Open** 9am-5pm Mon-Fri. **Credit** AmEx, DC, EC, MC, V. **Map 5/1B**
Fiumicino Airport (06 6595 4921). **Open** 7.30am-1pm, 2.30-4pm daily.

By bus

There is no central long-distance bus station in Rome. Most international and national coach services terminate outside the following metro stations: Lepanto, Ponte Mammolo and Tiburtina (routes north); Anagnina and EUR Fermi (routes south). For more information, *see page 235.*

By train

Most long-distance trains arrive at **Termini** station, which is also the centre of the metro and city bus networks. The station is a pickpocket's haven, so watch your wallets and luggage. Trains arriving by night stop at **Tiburtina** or **Ostiense**, both some way from the centre of Rome. The metro, bus routes 649 and 492, or night bus 42N (to become 40N in 2000), run from Tiburtina into the city. If you arrive at Ostiense after midnight, it's advisable to take a taxi to your final destination.

Some trains also bypass Termini during the day. The Napoli Express to and from Paris, for example, only stops at Ostiense. Many trains also stop at more than one station in Rome, and it may be more convenient to get off at one of the smaller stations rather than go into Termini.

For information on buying train tickets, *see pages 235-6.* When travelling on any Italian train **remember that you must stamp your ticket – and any supplement – in the yellow machines at the head of each platform before boarding the train.** Failure to do this can result in a L50,000 fine, plus the price of the ticket from the point where you are nabbed to the train's final destination. Looking contrite and sounding foreign, though, can persuade all but the nastiest ticket inspectors to let you off. If you forget to stamp your ticket, seek out an inspector as soon as possible after boarding the train and have it clipped.

The principal stations in Rome, and some of the suburban ones, are:

Ostiense
Piazzale dei Partigiani (06 575 0732). Metro Piramide/bus to Piazzale Porta San Paolo. **Map 7/2A**

Stazione di Piazzale Flaminio (Roma Nord)
Piazzale Flaminio (06 361 0441). Metro Flaminio/bus to Piazzale Flaminio.

Stazione Termini
Piazza dei Cinquecento (06 484 972/06 485 938/fax 06 4730 6916). Metro Termini/bus to Termini. **Map 5/2A**

Stazione Tiburtina
Circonvallazione Nomentana(06 4424 5104). Metro Tiburtina/bus to Piazza Stazione Tiburtina.

Stazione Trastevere
Piazzale Biondo, Trastevere (06 589 5615). Bus or tram to Circonvallazione Gianicolense.

Public transport

The Rome transport system is made up of three companies. The city transport authority, **ATAC**, runs the orange buses and trams (some of which, to fool you, are green) that operate within the city. The regional transport body **COTRAL** (formerly ACOTRAL, and signs often show the old name)

is responsible for the blue buses (some of which, to really confuse you, are orange) operating within the Lazio region, and for Rome's two metro lines. COTRAL also operates three suburban railway lines in the Rome area from Termini, Porta San Paolo and Roma Nord stations. Local lines of the FS, the state railway, are also integrated into the city transport network.

Travelling on public transport is pretty safe, even at night, but be wary of pickpockets and gropers on crowded buses, and especially the 64 route between Termini and the Vatican.

Buses & trams

ATAC buses and trams are the mainstay of Rome's transport network. There are nine tram routes, mainly serving suburban areas, and an express tram service that links Largo Argentina to Trastevere and the western suburbs. Trams and buses share the same tickets and pricing system. Owing to continual changes in the network, however, routes and numbers are subject to change: if you plan to use public transport, it's a good idea to pick up a copy of the latest city bus map, available free from the ATAC kiosk outside Termini, or for L8,000 from most news-stands.

Buy tickets before getting on a bus or tram – they are not sold on board (*see page 255* **Tickets**).

ATAC
Information Via Volturno, 65 (06 4696 4444). Metro Termini/bus to Termini station. **Open** 7.30am-7pm daily. **Map 5/2B**
The main ATAC information desk has English-speaking staff, although its phone line (8am-8pm Mon-Sat) is Italian-speaking only. ATAC offers tickets for all the transport network. Automatic ticket machines are scattered throughout the city centre.

COTRAL Information
Via Volturno, 65 (06 57 531/ toll-free 800 431 784). **Open** 8am-1.40pm, 2.10-4.40pm, Mon-Fri; 8am-1.40pm Sat.

Daytime services

All ATAC routes, except the special night services, run between about 5.30am and midnight daily, with a frequency of from 10 to 45 minutes, depending on the route. You are expected to board buses and trams by the rear or front doors, and get off by the middle doors. When buses are crowded, it can be impossible to work your way through to the central doors, so it's acceptable to use the nearest exit you can find – although the driver may not open the door you're next to if no one's getting on: perfect the art of yelling '*può aprire dietro, per favore?*' ('can you open the back doors please?').

Each bus stop (*fermata*) lists stops on each route in the direction to be followed. Because of the many one-way systems, buses do not necessarily follow the same route on return journeys. If you're not sure where to get off, say the name of your destination to other passengers, who will usually be happy to help.

Useful Routes

Useful daytime buses include:
Colosseum, Roman Forum: 75, 85, 87, 115, 117, 175, 186, 13B (tram), metro B (Colosseo).
Largo Argentina
(for Campo de' Fiori, Pantheon, Ghetto): 46, 56, 60, 62, 64, 70, 81, 87, 115, 186, 492, 628, 8 (tram).
Piazza Navona:
70, 81, 87, 115, 116, 186, 492, 628.
Piazza San Silvestro/Via del Tritone (for *Tridente*):
52, 53, 56, 58, 58B, 60, 61, 62, 71, 85, 95, 115, 116, 160, 175, 850.
Piazza Venezia:
46, 56, 60, 62, 64, 70, 75, 81, 87, 95, 160, 170, 186, 68, 716.
Stations: Termini 16, 36, 36B, 37, 38, 38B, 64, 75, 105, 115, 157, 170, 175, 217, 310, 317, 319, 360, 492, 649, 714, 910, H, metro A, metro B (Termini); **Tiburtina** 11, 168, 111, 211, 409, 490, 492, 495, 649, metro B (Tiburtina); **Ostiense** 95, 280, metro B (Piramide). **Trastevere**: 23, 56, 280, 8 (tram). **Vatican**, St. Peter's: 23, 34, 64, 81, 80, 492, 982, metro A (Ottaviano). **Villa Borghese**:
2, 53, 95, 116, 490, 495, 910.

A small fleet of **electric mini-buses** also plies the centre. The 115, 116, 116T, 117 and 119 connect places such as the Pantheon, Piazza di Spagna, Campo dei Fiori, and Piazza Venezia with Via Veneto and Termini. It's a bit like trundling around on a milk float, but they're handy when it's too hot to walk, and views are good.

Tour buses

The **110** is a city tour bus run buy ATAC. It leaves Termini at 10.30am, 2pm, 3pm, 5pm and 6pm, and makes a tour of the city taking in sights such as the Colosseum (where you get off for 15 min), Circo Massimo, Piazza Venezia (15 min), St. Peter's (20 min), Piazza del Popolo and Via Veneto before returning to Termini. The two and a half hour tour costs L15,000.

ATAC also offers a **three-hour tour** of Rome's major basilicas, costing L15,000. It leaves Termini at 10am and 2.30pm, stopping at St. Peter's (20 min), San Paolo fuori le Mura (15 min), and San Giovanni in Laterano (15 min).

Tickets for both tours can be bought at Piazza Cinquecento, in front of Termini. For bookings or information, phone 06 4695 2256 (open 9am-7pm daily).

Night Buses

There are currently 27 night routes, which run from about 12.10am to 5.30am daily. They run every 30 minutes to an hour, and the schedule for each route (identified by an N after the number) is written on bus stops. The following routes are particularly useful:
42N or **40N**, from Tiburtina station to Termini;
78N between the Vatican and Termini.

Metro

Rome has only two metro lines, which form a rough cross on the map, with the hub at Stazione Termini. **Line A** runs from the south-east to the north-west, **line B** from EUR in the south to the north-eastern suburbs. Both lines are open from 5.30am to around midnight, daily.

On Sundays it is possible to travel with bicycles on metro line B and on the connecting railway line to **Ostia** (*see page 236-7*) from Porta San Paolo; just stamp an extra ticket at the barrier before the start of your journey, and use the front carriage of the train only.

Tickets

The same tickets are valid on all city buses, trams and metro lines. They must be bought before boarding, and are available from the ATAC automatic ticket machines (scattered throughout the city), information centres, some bars and newstands and all *tabacchi* shops (*see page 267*).

When you board a bus or tram, you must stamp tickets in the machines by the rear and/or front doors. If travelling without paying looks an easy option, bear in mind that there *are* ticket inspectors around, and that if you are caught you will be fined L100,000 on the spot.

Timed Ticket (Biglietto Integrato a Tempo – BIT)

Valid for 75 minutes, during which you can use an unlimited number of ATAC buses, plus one trip on the metro; this ticket costs L1,500.

Integrated Ticket (Biglietto Integrato Giornaliero – BIG)

This ticket costs L6,000, is valid for one day and covers all the systems (except Fiumicino airport) in the urban network, whether ATAC, COTRAL or the FS suburban trains.

Weekly Ticket (Carta Integrata Settimanale – CIS)

Costs L24,000 and covers all the bus routes and the metro system, including the lines out to Ostia.

Monthly Ticket (Abbonamento Mensile)

Monthly tickets cost L50,000 for unlimited travel on the entire metropolitan transport system. Note that monthly tickets are valid for a calendar month, not for one month from the day you buy them, so may not be useful if you arrive mid-month.

Regional Ticket (Biglietto Integrato Regionale Giornaliero – BIRG)

This is a one-day ticket covering rail travel within the Lazio region. The price varies according to the zone of your destination. For example, a ticket to Frascati and back costs L8,500, while for Sperlonga the price is L17,000. The BIRG is valid on the metro, buses and the FS (second class only) but not on routes to and from Fiumicino airport.

The Language

Any attempt at spoken Italian – no matter how incompetent – will be appreciated.

Italian is spelt as it is pronounced, and vice versa. Traditional grammars will always tell you that the stress usually falls on the penultimate syllable, but this is a very dodgy rule: accents must be learnt by trial and error.

There are two forms of address in the second person singular: *Lei*, which is formal and should be used with strangers and older people; and *tu*, which is informal. The personal pronoun is usually omitted.

PRONUNCIATION

Vowels

a – as in **a**sk.
e – like a in **a**ge (closed e) or e in s**e**ll (open e).
i – like ea in **ea**st.
o – as in h**o**tel (closed o) or in h**o**t (open o).
u – as in b**oo**t.

Consonants

Romans have a lot of trouble with their consonants, and take much stick for it from Italians from other regions. **C** often comes out nearer **g**; **n**, if in close proximity to an **r**, disappears.

Remember that **c** and **g** both go soft in front of **e** and **i** (becoming like the initial sounds of check and giraffe respectively).

An **h** after any consonant makes it hard. Before a vowel, it is silent.

c before **a**, **i** and **u**: as in **c**at.
g before **a**, **i** and **u**: as in **g**et.
gl: like lli in mi**lli**on.
gn: like ny in can**y**on.
qu: as in **qu**ick.
r: always **r**olled.
s: has two sounds, as in **s**oap or ro**s**e.
sc: like the sh in **sh**ame.
sch: like the sc in **sc**out.
z: can be sounded ts or dz.

USEFUL PHRASES

hello and goodbye (informal) – ciao, salve.
good morning – buon giorno.
good evening – buona sera.
good night – buona notte.
please – per favore, per piacere.
thank you – grazie.
you're welcome – prego.
excuse me, sorry – mi scusi (formal), scusa (informal).
I'm sorry, but… – mi dispiace…
I don't speak Italian (very well) – non parlo (molto bene) l'italiano.
I don't/didn't understand (anything at all) – non capisco/ho capito (niente).
how much is (it)? – quanto costa? or quanto viene?
open – aperto.
closed – chiuso.
entrance – entrata.
exit – uscita.

TIMES & TIMETABLES

could you tell me the time? – mi sa dire l'ora?
it's – o'clock – sono le (number).
it's half past – sono le (number) e mezza.
when does it (re-)open? – a che ora (ri)apre?
does it close for lunch? – chiude per pranzo?

DIRECTIONS

(turn) left – (giri a) sinistra.
(it's on the) right – (è a/sulla destra.
straight on – sempre diritto
where is…? – dov'è…?
could you show me the way to the Pantheon? – mi potrebbe indicare la strada per il Pantheon? (Note: ask several people, and take the most-frequently-proffered directions. Romans would rather make something up than disappoint the visitor by saying they don't know.)
is it near/far? – è vicino/lontano?
would it be better to take the bus or can I walk? – sarebbe meglio prendere l'autobus, o posso andare a piedi? (Bear in mind that Romans consider walking uncool, and will tell you it's miles away if it's more than a couple of hundred metres.)

TRANSPORT

car – macchina.
bus – autobus.
coach – pullman.
taxi – tassì, taxi.
train – treno.
tram – tram.
plane – aereo.
ferry – traghetto.
bus stop – fermata (d'autobus).
station – stazione.
platform – binario.
ticket/s – biglietto/biglietti.
one way – solo andata.
return – andata e ritorno.
(I'd like) a ticket for – (vorrei) un biglietto per…
where can I buy tickets? – dove si comprono i biglietti?
fine – multa.
are you getting off at the next stop? (i.e. get out of my way if you're not) – che, scende alla prossima?
I'm sorry, I didn't know I had to stamp it (the lament of foreigners alarmed at the threat of a heavy fine for not having stamped their tickets before getting on the train or bus) – mi dispiace, non sapevo che lo dovevo timbrare.

COMMUNICATING

phone – telefono.
fax – fax.
stamp – francobollo.
how much is a stamp for England/Australia/the United States? – quanto viene un francobollo per l'Inghilterra/l'Australia/ gli Stati Uniti?
how much does it cost per minute/page? – quanto viene al minuto/alla pagina?

can I send a fax? – posso mandare un fax?
can I make a phone call? – posso
telefonare/posso fare un colpo di telefono?
can I borrow the telephone directory?
– mi può prestare l'elenco telefonico?
letter – lettera.
postcard – cartolina.
e-mail – posta elettronica, e-mail.
net-surfer – navigatore.
courier – corriere, pony.

SHOPPING

I'd like to try the blue sandals/black
shoes/brown boots
– vorrei provare i sandali blu/le scarpe nere/gli
stivali marroni.
do you have it/them in other colours?
– ce l'ha in altri colori?
I take (shoe) size … – porto il numero …
I take (dress) size… – porto la taglia …
it's too loose/too tight/just right
– mi sta largo/stretto/bene.
100 grams of … – un etto di …
300 grams of … – tre etti di …
can you give me a little more/less?
– mi dia un po' di più/meno?
one kilo of … – un kilo (chilo) di …
five kilos of ... – cinque chili di …
a litre/two litres of … – un litro/due litri di …

ACCOMMODATION

a reservation – una prenotazione.
I'd like to book a single/twin/double room –
vorrei prenotare una camera singola/doppia/
matrimoniale.
you must have a room for me; I booked weeks
ago – è impossibile che non ci sia una camera per
me; ho prenotato settimane fa.
I'd prefer a room with a
bath/shower/window over the courtyard –
preferirei una camera con vasca da
bagno/doccia/finestra sul cortile.
can you bring me breakfast in bed?
– mi porti la colazione al letto?

EATING & DRINKING

I'd like to book a table for four at eight
– vorrei prenotare una tavola per quattro alle otto.
this is lukewarm; can you heat it up?
– è tiepido; me lo può riscaldare?
this wine is corked; can you bring me
another bottle, please?
– questo vino sa di tappo; mi può portare un'altra
bottiglia per favore?
that was poor/good/(really) delicious
– era mediocre/buono/(davvero) ottimo.
if it's not a family secret,
could you give me the recipe?
– se non è un secreto della famiglia, mi potrebbe
dare la ricetta?
the bill – il conto.
is service included? – è incluso il servizio?
I think there's a mistake in this bill
– credo che il conto sia sbagliato.

there's a fly in my soup
– c'è una mosca nella mia zuppa.
See also **Translating the Menu** *in chapter
Restaurants.*

FEMALE SELF-DEFENCE

no thank you, I can find my way by myself
– no grazie, non ho bisogna di una guida.
I'm not interested – non mi interessa.
can you leave me alone?
– i vuole (or vuoi – informal – if you want to
make it clear you feel very superior)
lasciare in pace?
if you don't leave me alone, I'll call the police –
se non mi lascia (or lasci – informal)
in pace, chiamerò la polizia.
fuck off – vaffanculo.

OR ALTERNATIVELY …

thank you, I'd been hoping someone like you
would come along
– grazie, speravo di trovare qualcuno come Lei.
I'd love to go for a spin on your Vespa
– mi piacerebbe tanto fare un giro con
Lei in Vespa.
I'd love to see your etchings
– mi piacerebbe molto vedere le sue incisioni.
you are the man/woman of my dreams
– Lei è l'uomo/la donna dei miei sogni.

DAYS & NIGHTS

Monday – lunedi.
Tuesday – martedi.
Wednesday – mercoledi.
Thursday – giovedi.
Friday – venerdi.
Saturday – sabatò.
Sunday – domenica.
yesterday – ieri.
today – oggi.
tomorrow – domani.
morning – mattina.
afternoon – pomeriggio.
evening – sera.
night – notte.
weekend – fine settimana or, more usually,
weekend.
have a good weekend! – buona domenica!
see you tomorrow/on Monday! – a domani!/
a lunedi!

NUMBERS

0 zero; 1 uno; 2 due; 3 tre; 4 quattro; 5 cinque;
6 sei; 7 sette; 8 otto; 9 nove; 10 dieci; 11 undici;
12 dodici; 13 tredici; 14 quattordici; 15
quindici; 16 sedici; 17 diciasette; 18 diciotto;
19 dicianove; 20 venti;
30 trenta; 40 quaranta; 50 cinquanta; 60
sessanta; 70 settanta; 80 ottanta; 90 novanta;
100 cento;
200 duecento; 1,000 mille; 2,000 duemila;
1,000,000 un milione.

Taxis

Licensed taxis are painted white or yellow, and have a meter. If anyone comes up to you at Termini or any of the other major tourist magnets, muttering 'Taxi?' always refuse, as they are likely to charge you up to 400 per cent more than the normal rate.

Taxi fares & surcharges

When you pick up a taxi at a rank or hail one in the street, the meter should read zero. As you set off, it will begin to indicate the minimum fare, currently L4,500 for the first 200m, after which the charge goes up rapidly according to time and distance. There are surcharges on Sundays, public holidays and for trips to and from the airport, plus L2,000 for each item of luggage placed in the boot. L5,000 is also added to the basic fare between 10pm and 7am. For taxis to Fiumicino the supplement is L14,000; to Ciampino, L10,000.

Most of Rome's taxi drivers are honest; if, however, you suspect you're being ripped off, make a note of the driver's name and number from the metal plaque inside the car's rear door. The more ostentatiously you do this, the more likely you are to find the fare returning to its proper level. Report complaints to the drivers' co-operative (the phone number of which is shown on the outside of each car) or, in serious cases, the police.

Taxi ranks

Ranks are indicated by a blue sign with *Taxi* written in white, but are often identifiable by the number of people in the queue rather than the presence of taxis. In the central area there are ranks at Largo Argentina, the Pantheon, Piazza Venezia, Piazza San Silvestro, Piazza Sonnino (Trastevere), Piazza di Spagna and Termini station.

Phone Cabs

You can phone for a taxi from any of the following companies. When your call is answered, name the street and number, or the name and location of a bar, club or restaurant where you wish to be picked up. You will then be given the taxi code-name (always a location followed by a number) and a time, as in *'Bahama 69, in tre minuti'* (Bahamas 69, in three minutes). A radio taxi will start the meter from the moment your call is answered.

Cooperativa Samarcanda (*06 55 51*). Credit card facilities.
Cosmos Radio Taxi
(*06 88 177/06 88 22*).
Società Cooperativa Autoradio Taxi Roma (*06 35 70*).
Società la Capitale Radio Taxi (*06 49 94*).

Driving

Having a car in Rome can be great fun, or a huge liability. At first glance, Roman driving resembles the chariot race in Ben Hur, until you realise that it's like a high-speed conversation, with its own language of glances, light flashing and ostentatious acceleration, all carried out with panache.

If you do use a car in the city, some tips to be borne in mind are listed below. Short-term visitors should have no trouble driving with their home licences, although if they are written in different scripts or less common languages an international licence can be useful. EU citizens are obliged to take out an Italian driving license after being resident for one year. Remember:

• In spite of the common practise among Italians, you are required by law to wear a seat belt at all times, and to carry a warning triangle in your car.
• Keep your driving licence, Green Card, vehicle registration and personal ID documents on you at all times.
• Do not leave anything of value (including a car radio) in your car. Take all your luggage into your hotel when you park.
• Flashing your lights in Italy means that you will NOT slow down (contrary to British practice).
• If traffic lights flash amber, you should STOP and give way to the right.
• Watch out for death-defying mopeds and pedestrians. By local convention, pedestrians usually assume they have the right of way in the older, quieter streets without clearly-designated pavements.

Restricted areas

Large sections of the city centre are closed to non-resident traffic during business hours, and sometimes in the evening. The municipal police stand guard over these areas, and they may fine you if you are caught trying to get in, or wheel-clamp your vehicle if you do manage to slip through the net and park, in which case you'll have to pay a fine and a charge to have the clamp removed. If you are in a hired car or have foreign plates and are stopped, you can sometimes get through by unscrupulous means. Just mention the name of a hotel in the area you want to enter, and you will often be waved on.

Breakdown services

It is advisable to join a national motoring organisation, like the AA or RAC in Britain or the AAA in the US, before taking a car to Italy. They have reciprocal arrangements with the **Automobile Club d'Italia** (**ACI**), which offers assistance in the case of a breakdown, and can provide useful general information. Even for non-members, the ACI is the best number to call if you have any kind of breakdown.

If you require extensive repairs and do not know a mechanic, pay a bit more and go to a manufacturer's official dealer, as the reliability of any garage depends on long years of building up a good client-mechanic relationship. Dealers are listed in the Yellow Pages under *auto*, along with specialist repairers such as *gommista* (tyre repairs), *marmitte* (exhaust repairs)and *carrozzerie* (bodywork and windscreen repairs). The English Yellow Pages, available from most English bookshops (*see page 171*) has a list of garages where English is spoken.

Automobile Club d'Italia (ACI)

(*06 49 981/24-hour emergency phone line 116/24-hour information phone line 06 44 77*).
The ACI has English-speaking staff and provides a range of services for all foreign drivers, free or at low prices. Members of associated organisations are entitled to basic repairs free, and to other services at preferential rates. Non-members will be charged, but prices are generally reasonable. Phone 06 44 77 for information on ACI services, driving regulations and customs formalities in Italy, and traffic and weather information. It is not necessary to have membership to use the phone lines.

Parking

A system in which residents park free and visitors pay has recently been introduced to many areas of the city, and is efficiently policed: watch out for tell-tale blue lines. Parking fees are paid at pay-and-display ticket dispensers, at the rate of L2,000 per hour. In some areas you can park free after a certain time at night (usually after 11pm), or at weekends, so check the instructions on the machine before feeding it with coins. For longer stays, a L50,000 parking card, available from *tabacchi*, allows you to deduct parking fees gradually, and saves having to search your pockets for small change.

Elsewhere, anything resembling a parking place is up for grabs, with some exceptions: watch out for signs by entrances saying *Passo carrabile* (access at all times), *Sosta vietata* (no parking), and disabled parking spaces marked by yellow stripes on the road. The sign *Zona rimozione* (tow-away area) means no parking, and is valid for the length of the street, or until the next tow-away sign, with a red line through it denoting the end of the restricted area. If a street or square has no cars parked in it, you can safely assume it's a seriously-enforced no-parking zone.

Although your car is fairly safe in most central areas, you may prefer to pay the hefty rates charged by underground car parks to ensure the vehicle is not tampered with. The two listed here are centrally located.

Central car parks
Villa Borghese
Open 24 hours daily. **Rates** L1,800 per hour for up to 4 hours; L1,500 per hour for 4-24 hours; L23,000 for 24 hours. **Map** 4/2C
Valentino *Via Sistina, 75e (06 678 2597).* **Open** 7am-1am Mon-Sat; 7am-12.30am, 6pm-1am, Sun. **Rates** L40,000 for 24 hours. **Map** 5/1C

Car pounds
If you do not find your car where you left it, it has probably been towed away. Phone the municipal police (*Vigili Urbani*) on 06 67691 and quote your number plate to find out which of the various car pounds it has been taken to.

Petrol
Most petrol stations sell unleaded petrol (*senza piombo* or *verde*) and regular (*super*). Diesel fuel is *gasolio*. Liquid propane gas is *GPL*. All petrol stations have full service during weekdays. Pump attendants do not expect tips. At night and on Sundays many stations have automatic self-service pumps that accept L10,000 or L50,000 notes, in good condition. Unofficial 'assistants' will do the job for you for a small tip (L500-L1,000).

Car hire
To hire a car you must be over 21 – in some cases 23 – and have held a licence for at least a year. You will be required to leave a credit card number or a substantial cash deposit. It's advisable to take out collision damage waiver (CDW) and personal accident insurance (PAI) on top of basic third party insurance. Companies that do not offer CDW are best avoided.

Avis
Via Sardegna, 38a (06 4282 4728). Metro Spagna/bus to Via Vittorio Veneto. **Open** 8am-8pm Mon-Fri; 8am-1pm, Sat; 8am-1pm Sun. **Credit** AmEx, DC, EC, MC, V. **Map** 4/2B
Branches:
Fiumicino Airport (06 6501 1531). **Open** 7am-midnight daily. *Ciampino Airport (06 7934 0195).* **Open** 8.45am-12.30pm, 2.15-8pm, Mon-Fri; 10am-3.30pm Sat; noon-8pm Sun. *Termini station (06 481 4373).* **Open** 7am-8pm Mon-Fri; 8am-6pm Sat; 8am-1pm Sun. **Map** 5/2A

Maggiore Budget
Fiumicino Airport (06 6501 0678/toll-free 1478 67067). **Open** 7am-midnight daily. **Credit** AmEx, DC, MC, V.
Branches:
Termini station (06 488 0049). **Open** 7am-8pm Mon-Fri; 8am- 6pm Sat; 8am-noon Sun. *Ciampino Airport (06 7934 0368).* **Open** 7.30am-8.30pm Mon-Fri; 8.30am-2pm, 4.30pm-8.30pm, Sat, Sun.

Moped, scooter & cycle hire
To hire a scooter or moped (*motorino*) you need a credit card, an identity document and/or a cash deposit for the hire company. Helmets are required on motorbikes, bikes of over 50cc, and on all *motorini* for anyone under the age of 18. For bicycles, it is normally sufficient to leave an identity document rather than pay a deposit. For mopeds up to 50cc you need to be over 14; a driver's licence is required for anything over 125cc.

Apart from the companies listed below, there are useful pay-and-ride bike hire stands with similar rates outside Spagna metro, in Piazza del Popolo (near Rosati), by the carpark under Villa Borghese, and at the tiny bar in Piazza di Ponte Milvio, at the start of the pleasant cycle path that takes you out of central Rome along the banks of the Tiber .

Happy Rent
Via Farini, 3 (06 481 8185). Bus to Via Cavour. **Open** 9am-7pm Mon-Sun. **Credit** AmEx, EC, MC, V. **Map** 5/2A Friendly outlet with special offers and tourist advice. Daily rates: bikes L15,000; mopeds L44,000; scooters L60,000; 600cc bikes L120,000.

Romarent
Vicolo dei Bovari, 7A (phone/fax 06 689 6555). Bus to Corso Vittorio Emanuele. **Open** 8.30am-7pm daily. **Credit** AmEx, DC, MC. **Map** 3/2A As well as bike, moped and motorbike hire, Romarent also offers guided bike and scooter tours in English, French and Spanish. Bike rental for one day costs L15,000-L20,000; for seven days L75,000-L100,000. Mopeds range from L35,000-L140,000 for one day, L190,000-L350,000 for seven days. A 650cc motorbike costs L180,000 for one day and L840,000 for seven.

Scoot a Long
Via Cavour, 302 (06 678 0206). Metro Cavour/bus to Via Cavour. **Open** 9am-8pm daily. **Credit** AmEx, MC, V. **Map** 8/1C Based near the Colosseum, this company offers special student discounts. Daily and weekend rates for mopeds are from L50,000 and L80,000 (scooters L80,000 and

L140,000). For a week you can pay anything between L250,000 and L350,000. Motorbikes are also available. A deposit of L200,000, plus a passport is required.

Scooters for Rent
Via della Purificazione, 84 (06 488 5485). Metro Barberini/bus to Piazza Barberini. **Open** 9am-7pm daily. **Credit** AmEx, EC, MC, V. **Map 5/1C**

Daily rentals of *motorini* cost L50,000, smaller Vespas L60,000 and scooters L80,000. For a week's rental, you pay five days' cost instead of seven. L300,000 deposit is required.

Treno e Scooter Rent
Stazione Termini (06 4890 5823/ fax 06 4891 9539). **Open** 9am-7am daily. **Credit** AmEx, EC, MC. **Map 5/2A**

Located on Termini forecourt near the taxi rank, Treno e Scooter Rent is a joint venture between the railway and Piaggio, suppliers of bikes and *motorini* to around half of Italy. A moped can be rented for L55,000-L100,000 a day, or L230,000-L400,000 for a full week. They also have bicycles for hire, for charges of from L10,000-L18,000 a day, L35,000-L54,000 per week.

Essential Information A-Z

Business

If you're doing business in Rome, a stopover at your embassy's commercial section (*see page 261*) is always a good first move. There you will find trade publications, reports, databases of fairs, buyers, sellers and distributors, and helpful initial advice.

As ever in Italy, any personal recommendations will smooth your way immensely. Use them shamelessly and mercilessly.

Business services

Auditors & Accountants
Arthur Andersen & Co
Via Campania, 47 (06 482 971/fax 06 482 3684).
Coopers & Lybrand *Via delle Quattro Fontane, 15 (06 46 62 00 71/fax 06 488 5318).*
Deloitte Touche
Via Flaminia Vecchia, 495 (06 332 2841/fax 06 3322 8282).
KPMG Peat Marwick Consultants *Via Petrolini, 2 (06 809 711/06 8069 0002/fax 06 8077 518).*

Banks
Consult the white pages of the phone book under *banca* for listings of Italian and international bank headquarters (*sede*) and branches.

Business Centres
Finding temporary office space and services can be difficult in Rome. The following provide basic facilities, including conference and secretarial services.
Centro Uffici Parioli
Via Lima, 41 (06 8530 1350/fax 06 8449 8332).
Dollaro Express
Via S. de Saint Bon, 61 (06 370 1107/fax 06 3735 3335).
Pick Center *Via Attilio Regolo, 14 (06 328 031/06 3280 3227).*

Conference organisers
Rome offers superb facilities for conferences in magnificent palazzi and castles. Most of the major hotels can cater for events of all sizes (*see chapter* **Accommodation**). If you don't wish to handle the details yourself, a number of agencies will smooth the way for you.
Rome At Your Service
Via E. Orlando, 75 (06 484 583/06 482 5589/fax 06 484 429).
Studio Ega *Viale Tiziano, 19 (06 328 121/fax 06 324 0143).*
Tecnoconference *Via Udine, 30 (06 440 4271/fax 06 440 4272/ roma@tecnoconference.it).*
Triumph Congressi
Via Proba Petronia, 3 (06 3972 7707/fax 06 3973 5195).

Interpreters
Berlitz *Via Cesare Beccaria, 84 (06 320 1160/fax 06 320 1159/berlitz.info@berlitz.it.*
CRIC *Via dei Fienili, 65 (06 67 87 950/fax 67 91 208).*

Law firms
These companies specialise in international corporate and finance law.
John Greaves & Co *Via Cavour, 278 (06 482 1610/fax 06 4890 4188).* English solicitors and international lawyers.
Studio Legale Guerreri *Via 4 Fontane, 15 (06 488 3979/fax 06 482 9686).*
Tonon & Associates
Via Arenula, 21 (06 6880 3000/ fax 06 6813 4047).
Offices in Milan, New York and Los Angeles.

Couriers (international)
DHL
(06 790 821/Toll free 800 345 345). Website:www.dhl.it

Federal Express
(Toll Free 800 833 040).

TNT
(national 06 232 908/ fax 06 2326 7979/international 06 232909/fax 06 2326 7930.

UPS
– United Parcel Service
(Toll-free 800 877 877).

Couriers (local)
Boy Express
(06 4890 0109).

Presto
(06 3974 1111).

Speedy Boys
(06 39 888).

Drugs

If you are caught in possession of drugs of any type, you will be taken before a magistrate. If you can convince him or her that the tiny quantity you were carrying was for purely personal use, then you will be let off with a fine or ordered to leave the country.

Habitual offenders will be offered rehab. Anything more than a tiny amount will push you into the criminal category: couriering or dealing can land you in prison for up to 20 years. It is an offence to buy or sell drugs, or even to give them away. Sniffer dogs are a fixture at most ports of entry into Italy; customs police take a dim view of visitors entering with even the smallest quantities of narcotics, and they are nearly always refused entry.

Electricity

Most wiring systems work on 220v, which is compatible with British-bought appliances. With US 110v equipment you will need a current transformer. A few systems in old buildings are 127v. Buy two-pin adaptor plugs before leaving for Italy, as they will almost certainly cost more here. Otherwise, they can be bought at any electrical shop (look for *Casalinghi* or *Elettricità*).

Embassies & consulates

Listed below are embassies of the main English-speaking countries. A full list is found under *Ambasciate* in the telephone directory. Except where indicated, consular offices, which provide most services of use to tourists and the general public, share the same address as embassies.

American Embassy
Via Vittorio Veneto, 119 (06 46 741). Metro Barberini/bus to Piazza Barberini or Via Veneto. Emergency duty officer 24 hours daily. **Map 5/1B**

Australian Embassy
Via Alessandria, 215 (06 852 721). Bus to Via Nomentana. **Map 4/2A**

British Embassy
Via XX Settembre, 80a(06 482 5551/06 482 5441/fax 06 4890 3073). Bus to Piazzale Porta Pia. **Map 5/1A**

Canadian Embassy
Embassy *Via G B de Rossi, 27(06 445 981).* **Consulate**: *Via Zara, 30(06 445 981). Bus to Viale Regina Margherita.*

Irish Embassy
Piazza Campitelli, 3(06 697 9121). Bus to Piazza Venezia. **Map 6/1A**

New Zealand Embassy
Via Zara, 28 (06 441 7171). Bus to Viale Regina Margherita.

South African Embassy
Via Tanaro, 14 (06 852 541). Bus to Piazza Buenos Aires or Via Tagliamento. **Map 4/1A**

Health

Emergency health care is available for all travellers through the Italian national health system and, by law, hospital casualty departments

must treat all emergency cases free. However, if you're only visiting for a short time, it's worth taking out private health insurance (*see page 252*).

Hospitals

If you need urgent medical care (but not an ambulance) it is best to go to the *Pronto soccorso* (casualty department) of the nearest hospital. The hospitals listed below are open 24 hours a day. If you have a child needing emergency treatment, head only for the excellent casualty department at the **Ospedale Bambino Gesù**.

Ospedale Fatenbenefratelli
Isola Tiberina (06 683 7299). Bus to Piazza di Monte Savello or Lungotevere degli Anguillara or Piazza Sonnino. **Map 6/2A**

Ospedale Pediatrico Bambino Gesù
Piazza Sant'Onofrio, 4 (06 68 591). Bus to Via del Gianicolo or Via Giacinto Carini. **Map 3/2C** Website: www.obg-irrcs.it.

Ospedale San Giacomo
Via Canova, 29 (06 36 261). Metro Spagna/bus to Via del Corso. **Map 2/2A**

Ospedale San Giovanni
Via Amba Aradam, 8 (06 77 051). Metro San Giovanni/bus to Piazza San Giovanni. **Map 9/1A**

Policlinico Umberto I
Viale Policlinico, 155 (06 49 971). Metro Policlinico/bus or tram to Viale Regina Elena.

Pharmacies

Pharmacies (*farmacia*, identified by a large red or green cross) will give informal medical advice for straightforward ailments, as well as making up prescriptions from a doctor. Over-the-counter drugs such as aspirins are considerably more expensive in Italy than in the UK or US. Most pharmacies also sell homeopathic and veterinary medicines, and all will check your height/weight/ blood pressure on request.

Anyone who requires regular medication should bring adequate supplies of their drugs with them. Also, take care to know the chemical (generic) rather than brand name of medicines you need. They may only be available in Italy under different names.

Normal opening hours are from 8.30am to 1pm, 4pm to 8pm, Monday to Saturday. The best-stocked pharmacy in the city is the one in the Vatican, which always has a range of medicines not found on Italian territory.

Outside of normal hours, a duty rota system operates. A list by the door of any pharmacy indicates the nearest ones that will be open at any time. The daily rota is also published in local papers. At duty pharmacies there is a surcharge of L5,000 per client (but not per item) when the main shop is shut and only the special duty counter is open. The following pharmacies always follow unusual hours:

Farmacia del Senato
Corso Rinascimento, 50 (06 6880 3985). Bus to Corso Rinascimento. **Open** 24 hours Mon-Fri; Sat, Sun shifts vary. Closed three weeks Aug. **Map 3/2A**

Farmacia della Stazione
Piazza dei Cinquecento (corner of Via Cavour; 06 488 0019). Metro Termini/bus to Termini. **Open** 24 hours daily. **Credit** Amex, DC, EC, MC, V. **Map 5/2A**

Farmacia del Vaticano
Porta Sant'Anna entrance, Città del Vaticano (06 6988 3422). Metro Ottaviano/bus to Piazza del Risorgimento. **Open** 8.30am-6pm Mon-Fri; 7.30am-1pm Sat. **No credit cards. Map 3/1C**

Internazionale
Piazza Barberini, 49 (06 487 1195/fax 06 871 195). Metro Barberini/bus to Piazza Barberini. **Open** 24 hours Mon-Fri; shifts vary Sat, Sun. **Credit** EC, MC, V. **Map 5/1B**

Piram
Via Nazionale, 228 (06 48 80 754). Metro Repubblica/bus to Via Nazionale. **Open** 24 hours daily. **Credit** MC,V. **Map 5/2B**

Contraception

Condoms are on sale near check-outs in supermarkets, or over the counter in pharmacies. They are relatively expensive. *See also page 217*

Help lines & agencies

See also chapter **Gay & Lesbian** *and p271.*

Alcoholics Anonymous

An active English-speaking support group holds meetings at the church of San Paolo, Via Napoli, 56, on Monday, Wednesday and Friday at 8pm,and on Saturday and Sunday at 7pm, and at Saint Andrew's Presbyterian Church (Via XX Settembre, 7) on Tuesday and Thursday at 7pm.

Drogatel

(Toll free 800 016600)
A freephone government-run drug helpline, open from 9am-9pm.

Narcotics Anonymous

(06 86 04 788)
Meetings are held (usually in Italian) at venues across the city. A recorded message gives the current timetable and addresses.

Samaritans

(06 70 45 44 44/06 70 45 44 45).
Staffed by native English speakers, this confidential help and counselling line was set up for the diplomatic and expatriate community.

Dentists

For serious dental emergencies, make for the hospital casualty departments listed above.

Charles Kennedy

Via Fonte di Fauno, 29 (06 5783 3639). Metro Piramide/bus or tram to Viale Aventino.

George Eastman Clinic

Viale Regina Elena, 287 (24-hour emergency number 06 844 831). Metro Policlinico. **Open** *7.30am-1.30pm Mon-Sat.*

Internet & e-mail

You can caper in cyberspace or check e-mail at ever-more internet points around the city.

Bibli

Via dei Fienaroli, 28 (06 588 4097/info@bibli.it). Bus to Piazza Sonnino. **Open** *5.30pm-midnight Mon; 11am-midnight Tue-Sun.* **Rates** *L12,000 per hour.***Map 6/2B**

Bookshop, cultural centre, excellent restaurant and internet point in a quiet Trastevere backstreet (*see also p171*).

Internet Café

Via dei Marrucini, 12 (06 445 4953). Bus to Via Tiburtina or Viale Pretoriano.
Open *9am-2am Mon-Fri; 5pm-2am Sat, Sun. Closed one week Aug.* **Rates** *before 9pm L8,000 per hour, L5,000 per half hour; after 9pm L10,000 per hour, L6,000 per half hour.*
On the San Lorenzo side of Termini, this friendly café does drinks and snacks as well as providing 22 computers (including two Macs) for surfing. They'll also print, scan, and supply you with floppies.

The Netgate

Piazza Firenze, 25 (06 689 3445). Bus to Via del Corso.
Open *10.30am-10.30pm, Mon-Sat. Closed one week Aug.* **Rates** *L10,000 per hour; L5,000 for 20-min mail check; L100,000 for 11 hours.*
Map 3/1A
This clinical but very functional internet point in the heart of the *Tridente* has 35 work stations, and offers laser printing, fax, scanning and digital photo services.
Website: www.thenetgate.it

Left luggage

The left luggage office by platform two of Termini station is open 5.20am to 12.20am daily, and Fiumicino airport has left-luggage offices in its international (24 hours daily) and domestic (7.15am-11.15pm daily) terminals. If you're staying in a hotel, staff are generally willing to look after your luggage for you during the day, even after you have checked out.

Lost property

Anything mislaid on public transport, or stolen and subsequently discarded, may turn up at one of the lost propery offices (*ufficio oggetti rinvenuti*) listed below.

ATAC

Via Volturno, 65 (06 581 6040/toll free 800 431 784). Metro/bus to Stazione Termini. **Open** *8.30am-1pm Mon, Fri; 8.30am-1pm, 2.30-6pm, Tue-Thur.* **Map 5/1A**

Anything found on the city bus and tram network may turn up here.
Website:www.atac.roma.it

COTRAL

For property lost on the metro, phone *06 487 4309*; if you have lost anything on COTRAL buses, phone *06 57 531* or *06 591 5551*.

FS/Stazione Termini

Via Giovanni Giolitti, 24 (06 4730 6682). Metro Termini/bus or tram to Termini. **Open** *7am-11pm daily.***Map 5/2A**
Articles found on the state railway anywhere in the Rome area are sent here – the office is near platform 1.

Mail & postal services

In ancient times a letter from Rome to Bari took three days. Today the same journey can frequently take a great deal longer. The Italian postal system is notoriously unpredictable. Letters can and sometimes do arrive in reasonable time, but this is never something that you can rely on. Private couriers (*see page 260*) are quicker, but substantially more expensive.

To ensure speedy delivery abroad, use the **Vatican Post Office**, which is run in association with the Swiss postal service .

There are local post offices (*ufficio postale*) in each district, which are open from 8.25am to 6pm, Monday to Friday (8.25am-2pm in August), and from 8.25am to 1.30pm on Saturday and any day preceding a public holiday. They close two hours earlier than normal on the last day of each month. Main post offices in the centre of town have longer opening hours and a range of additional services, including fax facilities. For postal information of any kind, phone the central information office on 160.

Centro Pacchi (Parcels Office)

Via Monterone, 1c (Information 160). Bus to Largo Argentina or Corso del Rinascimento.
Open *9am-6pm Mon-Fri; 9am-2pm Sat.* **Map 3/2A**

Parcels can be sent from any post office, but this is the only branch where they can be sent insured. Given the general unreliability of the postal system, it is advisable to send any package worth more than L100,000 from this office.

Posta Centrale (Central Post Office)

Piazza San Silvestro, 18/20 (06 679 3064/information 160). Bus to Piazza San Silvestro. **Open** 9am-6pm Mon-Fri; 9am-2pm Sat (closes at noon last Sat of month). **Map 5/2C**
This is the hub of Rome's postal system, although the other main post offices have many of the same services. Letters sent Poste Restante/General Delivery (*Fermo Posta*) to Rome should be addressed to *Roma Centro Corrispondenza, Posta Centrale, Piazza San Silvestro, 00186 Roma.* You will need your passport to collect letters, and you have to pay a small charge. At the San Silvestro office, the fax service remains open until midnight.

Other Main Offices

Piazza Bologna, 39 (06 4424 4406). Metro Bologna/bus to Piazza Bologna.
Via Marmorata, 4 (06 574 3809). Metro Piramide/bus to Via Marmorata. **Map 7/2A**
Viale Mazzini, 101 (06 3751 7611). Bus to Viale Mazzini. **Map 2/1B**
Via Taranto (06 7004350). Metro San Giovanni.
Via Terme di Diocleziano, 30. (06 4745602). Bus to Termini station. **Map 5/2A**

Poste Vaticane (Vatican Post Office)

Piazza San Pietro; Vatican Museums complex (06 6988 3406). Bus to Piazza del Risorgimento.
Open 8.30am-7pm Mon-Fri; 8.30am-6pm Sat. **Map 3/1C**
There are branches of the Vatican post office on either side of St. Peter's square, and another within the Vatican Museums complex. Charges are a little higher than the Italian system (L900 for letters within the EU and L1,300 for a letter to the US). You must use Vatican stamps, and mail must be posted in the special Vatican post boxes.

Stamps & charges

Stamps can be bought at *tabacchi* (*see page 267*) or from post offices. A letter of up to 20 grams costs L800 to any destination within the EU, L1,300 to the USA or Canada, and L1,400 to Australia or New Zealand.

Most post boxes are red and have two slots, *Per la Città* (for Rome) and *Tutte le Altre Destinazioni* (for everywhere else). There are also blue post boxes decorated with the EU star symbol: these are for international mail only. All going well, a letter will take about five days to the UK and eight to the US.

To speed things up, mail can be sent *Raccomandata* (registered; L4,000 extra) or *Espresso* (express; L3,600 extra). If it is essential that letters reach their destination quickly, use the *CAI-Posta Celere* service (available only in main post offices), which promises 24-hour delivery in Italy and two-to-three day delivery abroad.

Telegrams & telexes

These can be sent from main post offices. The telegraph office at the Posta Centrale on Piazza San Silvestro (entrance 18) is open 24 hours a day. Alternatively, you can dictate telegrams over the phone. Dial 186 from a private phone and a message in Italian will tell you to dial the number of the phone you're phoning from. You will then be passed to a telephonist who will take your message.

Money

The Italian currency is the *lira* (plural *lire*). Coins for L50 and L100 each come in three different sizes; there are also coins for L200 and L500. Each of the six denominations of bank notes carries a picture of a famous Italian; between Maria Montessori on the L1,000, and the L100,000 note with its portrait of Caravaggio come notes for L2,000, L5,000, L10,000 and L50,000. A L500,000 also exists.

In many shops and businesses, assistants will throw up their hands in horror if asked to change L50,000 or

L100,000 notes when you're buying something inexpensive. When changing money, ask for it to be changed into smaller-denomination notes.

Prices are rounded up to the nearest L50. By law, you must be given a full receipt (*scontrino fiscale*) for any transaction. Some places may try to avoid giving you a receipt for tax reasons, in which case it is your right (and according to the *guardia di finanza* police, your duty) to ask for one. In the unlikely event of your being accosted by a police officer as you exit a shop, you, as well as the shopkeeper, are liable for a fine if you do not have proof of payment for goods you have purchased.

Italy is a part of the European single currency zone, meaning that – at least in theory – business transactions should be carried out in Euros, and prices will increasingly be quoted both in *lire* and Euros. Euro notes and coins will come into circulation and replace the *lira* in 2002.

Banks & foreign exchange

Most banks are open from 8.30am to 1.45pm and 2.45pm to 4.30pm, Monday to Friday. Some central branches have extended hours, opening until 6pm on Thursdays and 8.30am to 12.30pm on Saturdays. All banks are closed on public holidays, and staff work reduced hours the day before a holiday, usually closing around 11am.

Banks usually have better exchange rates than private bureaux de change (*cambio*). It's a good idea to take a passport or other identity document whenever you're dealing with money, particularly to change travellers' cheques or withdraw money on a credit card. Commission rates vary considerably: you can pay from nothing to L10,000 for each transaction. Watch out for 'No Commission' signs, as the rate of exchange will almost certainly be terrible.

Many bank cash machines (*Bancomat*) can be used with major credit cards or banking cards that carry the Eurocard/Maestro/Cirrus symbols (up to L500,000 per day). Most banks will also give cash advances against a credit card, but this varies according to the bank, and many refuse to do so if you do not have a PIN number.

Many city centre branches have automatic cash exchange machines, which accept notes in most currencies. Notes need to be in good condition.

If you need to have money sent from home, the best method is via American Express, Thomas Cook or Western Union (*see below*).

Main post offices also have exchange bureaux. Commission is L1,000 for all cash transactions, L2,000 for travellers' cheques up to the value of L100,000, and L5,000 for larger amounts. Only American Express travellers' cheques are accepted. *See page 263* **Mail & postal services**.

American Express
Piazza di Spagna, 38 (06 67 641). Metro Spagna/bus to Piazza San Silvestro. **Open** *travel agency and credit card transactions* 9am-5.30pm Mon-Fri; *financial services* 9am-7pm Mon-Fri, 9am-2pm Sat. **Map 5/1C**
All the standard AmEx services, such as travellers' cheque refund service, card replacement, Poste Restante, and a cash machine that can be used with AmEx cards. Money can be transferred from any American Express office in the world within 24 hours.

Thomas Cook
Piazza Barberini, 21 (06 482 8182/fax 06 482 8085). Metro Barberini/bus to Piazza Barberini. **Open** 8.30am-7.30pm Mon-Sat; 9am-1.30pm Sun. **Map 5/1B**
The three branches of Thomas Cook are among the very few exchange offices open on Sunday. A 2.5%

commission is charged on all transactions apart from Thomas Cook, MasterCard and Swiss Bankers' travellers' cheques, which are cashed free of charge. MasterCard holders can also withdraw money here. Money can be transferred to the Rome branches from any Thomas Cook branch in the UK.
Branches *Via della Conciliazione, 23/25 (06 6830 0435).* **Open** 8.30am-7.30pm Mon-Sat; 9am-5.30pm Sun. *Via del Corso, 23 (06 320 4723).* **Open** 9am-8pm Mon-Sat; 9.30am-1.30pm Sun.

Western Union Money Transfer
Agenzia Tartaglia, Piazza di Spagna, 12 (Toll free 800 464 464). Metro Spagna/bus to Piazza San Silvestro. **Open** 9am-6pm Mon-Fri. **Map 1/1C**
The quickest, though certainly not the cheapest, way to send money, which should arrive within the hour. The commission is paid by the sender, on a sliding scale.

Credit cards

Italians have an enduring fondness for cash, but persuading them to take plastic has become considerably easier in the last few years. Nearly all hotels of two stars and above now accept at least some of the major credit cards, and Eurocheques are also accepted – albeit grudgingly – with the necessary guarantee card.

If you lose a credit or charge card, phone one of the emergency numbers listed below. All lines are freephone numbers, have English-speaking staff and are open 24 hours a day.
American Express *(800 864 046).*
Diner's Club *(800 864 064).*
Eurocard/Carta Si (including **Mastercard** and **Visa**) *(800 018 548).*
MasterCard *(800 870 866).*
Visa *(800 877 232).*

Public holidays

On public holidays (*giorni festivi*) virtually all shops, banks and businesses are closed, although (with the exception of May Day, August 15 and Christmas Day) bars and restaurants generally tend to stay open.

The public holidays are as follows: **New Year's Day** (*Capo d'anno*), 1 January; **Epiphany** (*La Befana*), 6 January; **Easter Monday** (*Pasquetta*); **Liberation Day**, 25 April; **May Day**, 1 May; **Patron Saints' Day** (*San Pietro e San Paolo*), 29 June; **Feast of the Assumption** (*Ferragosto*), 15 August; **All Saints'** (*Tutti santi*), 1 November; **Immaculate Conception** (*Festa dell'Immacolata*), 8 December; **Christmas Day** (*Natale*); **Boxing Day** (*Santo Stefano*).

Limited public transport runs on 1 May and Christmas afternoon. Holidays falling on a Saturday or Sunday are not celebrated the following Monday; however, if a holiday falls on a Thursday or a Tuesday, many people will take the Friday and Monday off as well. *See also pages 5-8.*

Public toilets

If you need a toilet, the easiest thing is usually to go to a bar (which won't necessarily be clean or provide toilet paper). There are modern lavatories at or near most of the major tourist sites (few of which are disabled-friendly, *see pages 272-3*); the majority of these have attendants, and you must pay a nominal fee to use them. Fast food joints and department stores also come in handy.

Queuing

Lining up one behind the other doesn't come easy to Romans, but, despite the apparent chaos, queue-jumpers are usually given short shrift. Hanging back deferentially, on the other hand, is taken as a clear sign of stupidity, and if you're not careful the tide will sweep contemptuously past you. In busy shops and bars, be aware of who is in front of and behind you and, when it's your turn, assert your rights emphatically.

Emergencies

Thefts or losses should be reported immediately at the nearest police station (of the *Polizia di stato* or the *Carabinieri, see page 266*). There you will be helped to make a written statement (*denuncia*) essential for reclaiming your lost belongings if they are found, and for making insurance claims. You should also report the loss of your passport to your consulate or embassy (*see page 261*). Report the loss of a credit card or travellers' cheques immediately to your credit card company (*see page 265*)

National emergency numbers
Police *Carabinieri* (English speaking helpline) 112; *Polizia di stato* 113
Fire service *Vigili del Fuoco* 115
Ambulance *Ambulanza* 118
Car breakdown *Automobile Club d'Italia, ACI* 116

Domestic emergencies
If you need to report a malfunction in any of the main services, the following emergency lines are open 24 hours a day. Which of the two Rome electricity companies (ACEA or ENEL) you should call will be indicated on your electricity meter.
Electricity ACEA *(06 57 991; emergency number toll-free 800 22 88 33)*; ENEL *(answering machine 16 441; operator 06 321 2200)*.
Gas Italgas *(06 57 391/toll-free 800 803 020)*.
Telephone Telecom Italia *(188)*.
Water ACEA *(06 575 171; toll-free 800 229 988)*.

Religion

There are over 400 Catholic churches throughout the city: several hold mass in English. The main British Catholic church is **San Silvestro** at Piazza San Silvestro, 17A (06 679 7775). **San Patrizio**, which is at Via Boncompagni, 31 (06 488 5716), is the principal Irish church in Rome, and the American Catholic church is **Santa Susanna**, at Via XX Settembre, 14 (06 482 7510).

For information on papal audiences *see chapter* **The Vatican City**. Some of the non-Catholic denominations and religions represented in Rome are listed below, with the times of their main services or prayer times.

American Episcopal Church
Saint Paul's-within-the Walls, V ia Napoli, 58 (06 488 3339). Metro Repubblica/bus to Via Nazionale. **Services** 8.30am, 10.30am Sun. **Map 5/2B**

This socially active church also has services in Spanish for its large Filipino congregation. The crypt is used for, among other things, English meetings of Alcoholics Anonymous.

Anglican
All Saints, Via del Babuino, 153B (06 3600 1881). Metro Spagna/bus to Via del Corso. **Services** 6pm Tue-Thur; 10.30am Sun. **Map 2/2A**
The church was opened in 1887, but the Rome chaplaincy dates from 1816, when services were held in the chaplain's rooms in Piazza di Spagna. Today it hosts an active programme of cultural events, including regular, high-quality concerts. Times are liable to change, so ring ahead.

Jewish
Comunita Israelitica di Roma Lungotevere Cenci (06 684 0061). Bus to Piazza di Monte Savello. **Map 6/2A**
There are services every day but the times vary throughout the year. Guided tours of the synagogue are offered from the museum, the **Museo di Arte Ebraica** (*see p51*).

Methodist
Ponte Sant'Angelo Church, Via del Banco di Santo Spirito (06 686 8341).Bus to Corso Vittorio Emanuele. **Services** 10.30am Sun. **Map 3/1B**

Muslim
La Moschea di Roma, Viale della Moschea (06 808 2167). Train to Campi Sportivi.
Paolo Portoghesi's masterpiece is always open to Muslims for prayer. It can also be visited by non-Muslims from 9-11.30am on Wednesday and Saturday.

Presbyterian (Church of Scotland)
Saint Andrew's, Via XX Settembre, 7 (06 482 7627). Bus to Via XX Settembre. **Services** 11am Sun. **Map 5/1B**
The church is also used by Korean Presbyterians.

Safety & police

Muggings are fairly rare in Rome, but pickpockets and bag snatchers (including children operating singly or in gangs) are particularly active in the main tourist areas. You will find that a few basic precautions greatly reduce a street thief's chances:

Points to remember
• Don't carry wallets in back pockets, particularly on buses. If you have a bag or camera with a long strap, wear it across the chest and not dangling from one shoulder.
• Keep bags closed, with your hand on them. If you stop at a pavement café or restaurant, **do not** leave bags or coats on the ground or the back of a chair where you cannot keep an eye on them.
• Avoid attracting unwanted attention by pulling out large wads of notes to pay for things at street stalls or in busy bars.
• When walking down a street, hold cameras and bags on the side of you towards the wall, so you're less likely to become the prey of a motorcycle thief or *scippatore*.
• If you see groups of ragged children brandishing pieces of cardboard, avoid them or walk by as quickly as possible, keeping tight hold on your valuables. They'll wave the cardboard to confuse you while accomplices pick pockets or bags.

If you are the victim of crime call the police helpline (*see left* **Emergencies**) or go immediately to the nearest police station and say you want to report a *furto*. A *denuncia* (written statement) of the incident will be made by or for you. It is unlikely that your things will be found, but you will need the *denuncia* for making your insurance claim.

The principal *Polizia di Stato* station, the **Questura Centrale**, is at Via Genova, 2 (06 46 861; **Map 5/2B**). The addresses of others, and of the *Carabinieri*'s *Commissariati*, are listed in the phone book under *Carabinieri* and *Polizia*. Incidents can be reported to either force.

Smoking

Smoking is not permitted in public offices (including post offices, police stations, etc) or on public transport. For where to buy cigarettes, see *Tabacchi*.

Tabacchi

Tabacchi or *tabaccherie* (identified by signs with a white T on a black or blue background) are the only places where you can legally buy tobacco products of any kind. They also sell stamps, telephone cards, tickets for public transport, lottery tickets and the stationery required when dealing with Italian bureaucracy.

Most *tabacchi* proper keep shop hours; many, however, are attached to bars and, through that supplementary outlet, can satisfy your nicotine cravings well into the night.

Telephones

Although pressures of competition have led to some price cuts, the Italian telephone company (*Telecom Italia*) still operates one of the most expensive systems in Europe, particularly for international calls. The minimum charge for local call from a private phone is about L150 (L200 from public one); normal rate for a minute to the UK is L1,070; to the rest of northern Europe L1,245; to the US L1,237; and to Australia and New Zealand

L2,421. In all cases it costs more if you use a public phone.

One way to keep costs down is to phone off-peak (10pm to 8am Monday to Saturday, and all day Sunday). Another is to avoid using phones in hotels, which may carry extortionate surcharges. Phoning from a phone centre (*see below*) costs the same as from a phone box, but is more convenient for long-distance calls since you avoid the need for large amounts of change or several phone cards. Additional services are listed in the local phone book, the *elenco telefonico*.

Phone numbers

All normal Rome numbers begin with the area code 06, and this must be used whether you call from within or outside the city. All numbers beginning with 800 are freephone lines (until recently, these began 176: you will still find old-style numbers listed, in which case replace the prefix with 800). For numbers beginning 147 you will be charged one unit only, regardless of where you're calling from or how long the call lasts.

Phone numbers within Rome generally have eight digits, although some of the older numbers may have seven or less. If you try a number and cannot get through, it may have been changed to an eight digit number. If you have difficulties, check the directory or ring enquiries (12) to check.

Public phones

Rome has no shortage of public phone boxes (although they tend to be clustered in areas where the traffic makes it impossible to hear) and many bars have payphones. Most public phones only accept phone cards (*schede telefoniche*); a few also accept major credit cards. Telephone cards cost L1,000, L5,000, L10,000, L15,000, and L25,000 and are

available from *tabacchi* (*see left*), some newspaper stands and some bars. Beware: phone cards have expiry dates (usually 31 December or 30 June) after which you won't be able to use them. Irritatingly, the Vatican City has its own special phone cards, obtainable from the Vatican post offices (for the same prices) and usable only within the City State. To use public coin phones you will need L100, L200 and L500 coins. The minimum charge for a local call is L200.

International calls

To make an international call from Rome, dial 00, then the appropriate country code: Australia **61**; Canada **1**; Irish Republic **353**; New Zealand **64**; United Kingdom **44**; United States **1**. Then dial the area code (for calls to the UK, omit the initial zero of the area code) and the number.

To phone Rome from abroad, dial the international code (00 in the UK), then 39 for Italy and 06 for Rome, followed by the individual number. To make a reverse charge (collect) call, dial 170 for the international operator in Italy. Alternatively, to be connected to the operator in the country you want to call, dial 172 followed by a four-digit code for the country and telephone company you want to use (for the UK and Ireland this is the same as the country code above; for other countries see the phone book). If you are placing a collect call from a phone box, you will need to insert a L200 coin, which will be refunded after your call.

Phone centres

Phone centres pop up all over Rome and disappear just as fast. They handle international calls and are generally cheaper than public phones: you give the attendant the number you want to ring and you're allotted a booth. Phone centres can be found in the main hall at Termini station, on Via Marsala outside Termini, and at Piazza Risorgimento.

Faxes

These can be sent from most large post offices (*see page 264*), which will charge you for the units used, plus a surcharge per sheet. They can also be sent from some photocopying outlets. In all cases, the surcharge will be hefty. Some do-it-yourself fax/phones can be found in main stations and at Fiumicino airport.

Operator services

All these services are open 24 hours daily.
Operator and Italian Directory Enquiries (12).
International Operator (170).
International Directory Enquiries (176).
Communication problems on national calls (182).
Communication problems on international calls (176).
Wake-up calls (114); an automatic message will ask you to dial in the time you want your call, with four figures on a 24-hour clock, followed by your phone number.
Tourist information (110/06 488 991).

Mobile phones

Owners of GSM phones can use them in Italy, but reception can be patchy in some of central Rome's narrower streets.

Time & weather

Italy is one hour ahead of British time, six hours ahead of US EST. Rome can sizzle at over 40°C in July and August, when humidity levels can also be high. Spring and autumn are usually warm and pleasant, although there may be occasional heavy showers, particularly in March, April and September. Between November and February you cannot rely on good weather, and might either come across a week of rain, or crisp, bright

(sometimes even warm) sunshine. The compensation is the comparative scarcity of fellow tourists.

Tipping

Foreigners are expected to tip more than Italians, but the 10 per cent customary in many countries would be considered generous even for the richest-looking tourist. Most locals leave L100 or L200 on the counter when buying drinks at the bar and, depending on the standard of the restaurant, L2,000 to L10,000 for the waiter after a meal. Many of the larger restaurants now include a 10 or 15 percent service charge. Tips are not expected in family-run restaurants, although even here a couple of thousand is always appreciated. Taxi drivers will be happy if you round the fare up to the nearest whole L1,000.

Tourist information

The offices of Rome's tourist board, **APT**, and the state tourist board, **ENIT**, have English-speaking staff, but a surprisingly limited amount of information, and what they tell you can be unreliable or out of date.

An extra effort, however, is being made in preparation for the 2000 Holy Year. The Rome city council now has well-stocked green-painted tourist information kiosks in:
Castel Sant'Angelo
(Piazza Pia, 06 6880 9707).
Map 3/2B
Largo Goldoni (06 6813 6061).
Map 3/1A
Piazza delle Cinque Lune (by Piazza San Agostino, 06 6880 9240).
Map 3/1A
Piazza San Giovanni in Laterano (06 7720 3535).
Map 8/2A
Santa Maria Maggiore (Via del Olmata, 06 4688 0294). **Map 8/1B**
Stazione Termini (Piazza del Cinquecento; 06 4782 5194).
Map 5/2A
Via dei Fori Imperiali (Piazza del Tempio della Pace, 06 6992 4307).
Map 8/1C

Via Nazionale (by the Palazzo delle Esposizioni; 06 4782 4525).
Map 5/2B
Piazza Sonnino (06 5833 3457).
Map 6/2B
These are the best places for checking up on changes to opening hours. For the 2000 Jubilee (*see pages 25, 106*), the city council's **Agenzia per il Giubileo** (*Website: www.giubileo.it*) has set up multi-media points providing historical and other data on Holy Years through the ages, plus tourist information, in the **Museo del Risorgimento** beneath the **Vittoriale** monument on the Forum side of Piazza Venezia (**Map 6/1A**), in the **Auditorio Pio** near the Vatican (Via della Conciliazione, 4, **Map 3/1C**), and on the Via Giolitti side of Termini station (**Map 5/2A**).

For more personal service, the private agency **Enjoy Rome** can be recommended: their English-speaking staff are friendly and well-informed. The local press is another useful source of information (*see chapter* **Media**).

Azienda Provinciale per il Turismo di Roma (APT)

Head office: *Via Parigi, 11 (06 488 991). Metro Repubblica/bus or tram to Piazza della Repubblica.* **Open** 8.15am-7.15pm Mon-Fri; 8.15am-1.45pm Sat. **Information** *from: Via Parigi, 5 (06 4889 9253/06 4889 9255).* **Open** 8.15am-7.15pm Mon-Fri; 8.15am-1.45pm Sat. **Map 5/1B** The APT provides free brochures on various attractions and events in Rome and Lazio, and a rather basic map. No hotel booking service. **Offices** *Stazione Termini (06 487 1270/06 482 4078). Metro Termini/bus or tram to Termini.* **Map 5/2A Open** 8.15am-7.15pm daily. *Fiumicino Airport (06 6595 6074/06 6595 4471).* **Open** 8.15am-7.15pm daily.

Enjoy Rome

Via Varese, 39 (06 445 1843/ fax 06 445 0734/info@enjoyrome.com). Metro Termini/bus to Termini. **Open** 8.30am-1pm, 3.30-7pm, Mon-Fri; 8.30am-2pm Sat.
This friendly English-speaking company is a very handy place for information and advice. The office is just east of Termini railway station, and provides an accommodation-

booking service and left luggage facilities, both for free. They also arrange walking tours (three-hour tours in Rome: L25,000 under-26, L30,000 over-26) and Pompeii (L70,000).
Website: www.enjoyrome.com

Ufficio Informazioni Pellegrini e Turisti
Piazza San Pietro (06 6988 4466). Bus to Piazza Risorgimento. **Open** 8.30am-7pm Mon-Sat. **Map 3/1C**
The Vatican's own tourist office. Its English-speaking staff will give you all the information you need on the Holy See, plus a free pamphlet.

Maps
A basic street map is available free from APT offices, information kiosks and McDonald's branches, but better ones can be bought at newspaper stands and in bookshops. The official metro and bus map, available from ATAC information centres (*see page 268*) has detailed street plans, with the transport systems clearly marked.

Veterinary care
For the nearest public veterinary clinic, consult *Azienda Unità Sanitaria Locale – servizio veterinario* in the phone book.

Students

The three state universities, **La Sapienza**, **Tor Vergata** and **Roma Tre**, and the private **LUISS** (*Libera Università Internazionale degli Studi Sociali*) offer exchanges with other European universities through the EU's *Erasmus* programme. Several American universities also have campuses in Rome, which students attend on exchange programmes.

There are also private Catholic universities, which run some of Italy's most highly respected faculties of medicine. The student scene, however, is dominated by La Sapienza. Specialist bookshops are mostly found in neighbouring San Lorenzo and Viale Ippocrate.

Bureaucracy/services
Foreigners studying on any type of course in Italy must obtain a student's permit from the police (*see page 270*). Apart from student offices in the universities themselves, there are private agencies that deal with the paperwork of enrolments.

Centro Turistico Studentesco (CTS)
Via Genova, 16 (06 462 0431). Bus to Via Nazionale. **Open** 9am-1pm, 3-7pm, Mon-Fri; 9am-1pm Sat. **Map 5/2B**
The CTS student travel centre issues student cards giving discount travel tickets, hostels or language courses.

Nuovo Centro Servizi Universitari
Viale Ippocrate, 160 (06 445 5741/06 445 7768). Metro Policlinico. **Open** 8.30am-7pm Mon-Fri.

This private agency takes charge of enrolment, registration for exams and all other time-consuming details. Along with the L10,000 membership fee, there are travel offers and discounts to concerts and cinemas.

Libraries
If you expect to use Rome's libraries for research, be ready for red tape, restricted hours and patchy organisation. Many libraries do not have computer catalogues, so finding a book can be a frustrating experience.

All libraries listed below are open to the public. Other specialist libraries can be found under *Biblioteche* in the phone book. It is always useful to take an identity document with you; plus, in some cases, a letter from your college or tutor stating the purpose of your research will be required. *See also pages 170-2* **Bookshops**).

Archivio Centrale dello Stato (State archives)
Piazzale Archivi (06 592 6204). Metro EUR Fermi. **Open** *Sept-mid July* 8.30am-7pm Mon-Fri; 8.30am-1.30pm Sat; *mid July-Sept* 8.30am-1.30pm Mon-Sat.
This efficiently-run archive has original documents, historical correspondance and many other items. Get there before midday to order the ones you want, which must be consulted in situ. Most can be photocopied.

Biblioteca Alessandrina
Piazzale Aldo Moro, 5 (06 447 4021). Metro Policlinico/bus to Viale dell'Università. **Open** 8.30am-7.30 pm Mon-Fri; 8.30am-1pm Sat.
La Sapienza's main library is grossly inefficient for the needs of a huge university.

Biblioteca Nazionale
Viale Castro Pretorio, 105 (06 49 891). Metro Castro Pretorio/bus to Viale Castro Pretorio. **Open** *Sept-mid July* 8.30am-7pm Mon-Fri; 8.30am-1.30pm Sat; *mid July-Sept* 8.30am-1.30pm Mon-Sat. Closed two weeks mid-Aug.
The Biblioteca Nazionale holds 80% of everything that is in print in Italy, as well as books in other languages. The system is not computerised, however, so finding what you need is challenging, to say the least.

Biblioteca dell'Università Gregoriana
Piazza della Pilotta, 4 (06 322 2155). Bus to Piazza Venezia. **Open** 8am-6.30pm Mon-Fri; 8am-12pm Sat. **Map 5/2C**
Much better organised than La Sapienza's library, but books are not allowed off the premises.

Biblioteca Vaticana
Via di Porta Angelica (06 6987 9411). Metro Ottaviano/bus to Piazza Risorgimento. **Open** 9am-5.30pm Mon-Fri. Closed mid-July to mid-Sept. **Map 3/1C**
To consult the Vatican tomes, students need a letter signed by a professor stating the purpose of their research.

British Council Library
Via delle Quattro Fontane, 20 (06 478 141). Metro Barberini/bus to Piazza Barberini. **Map 5/2B**
Good English teaching resource centre.assport

The British School at Rome
Via Gramsci, 61 (06 321 3454/06 326 4931). Bus or tram to Viale delle Belle Arti. **Open** 9.30am-1pm, 2-7.30pm, Mon-Fri. **Map 4/1C**
The reading room of the British School contains English and Italian books on every aspect of Rome, especially archaeology, art history and topography. To be admitted, students need two photos and a letter from a museum or university. No lending facilities.

Directory *(vertical side tab)*

Living & working in Rome

Rome has over 200,000 registered foreign residents, who are here (temporarily or permanently) for a wide variety of reasons: work, study, political asylum, religion or love.

To help newcomers get started, **Welcome Neighbor** (06 3036 6936) is a group of English-speaking ex-pats who organise talks on various aspects of living in Rome.

Anyone staying here is obliged by the Italian state to pick up a whole series of forms and permits. The basic set is described below. EU citizens should have no difficulty getting their documentation once they are in Italy, but non-EU citizens are advised to enquire at an Italian embassy or consulate in their own country before travelling. There are agencies that specialise in obtaining documents for you if you can't face the procedures yourself – for a price (see *Pratiche e certificati – agenzie* in the Yellow Pages).

Carta d'Identita (Identity card)

Foreigners resident in Rome should have an ID card. You'll need three passport photographs, a *permesso di soggiorno*, and a special form that will be given you at your *circoscrizione* – the local branch of the central records office, which will eventually issue the card. To find the office for your area, look in the phone book under *Comune di Roma: Circoscrizioni*.

Codice Fiscale (Tax code)

Anyone working in Italy needs one of these plastic cards. It is essential for opening a bank account or setting up utilities contracts. Take your passport and *permesso di soggiorno* to the tax office, *Ufficio Imposte Dirette*, in Via della Conciliazione, 5 (06 688 241; open 8.30am-noon Mon-Sat), fill in a form and return a few days later to pick up the card. It can be posted on request.

Partita IVA (VAT number)

The self-employed or anyone doing business in Italy may also need this. It costs L250,000, and most people pay an accountant to handle the formalities. Make sure you cancel it when you no longer need it: failure to do so may result in a visit from tax inspectors years later.

Permesso di Soggiorno (Permit to stay)

EU citizens need one of these if they're staying in Italy for over three months; non-EU citizens should (but usually don't) apply for one within eight days of their arrival in Italy. Take three passport photographs, your passport, and proof you have some means of supporting yourself/reason to be in Italy (preferably a letter from an employer or certificate of registration at a school or university) to the nearest *Commissariato* (police station; see the phone book under *Polizia di Stato*), or the **Questura Centrale** (main police station), Via Genova, 2 (06 46 861) between 9am and 12.30pm (people start queuing at 7am) . For information call 06 4686 2928 (8am-noon, 5-7pm, Mon-Fri).

Permesso di Lavoro (Work permit)

In theory, all non-Italian citizens employed in Italy need a work permit. Application forms can be obtained from the **Ispettorato del Lavoro**, Via Cesare de Lollis, 6 (06 444 931; open 9am-12.30pm, 2.45-4.30pm, Mon-Thur; 9am-noon Fri, Sat). The form must be signed by your employer; you then need to take it with your *permesso di soggiorno* and a photocopy back to the *Ispettorato*. Don't rush: often the requirement is waived, or employers arrange it for you.

Residenza (Residency)

This is your registered address in Italy, and you'll need it to buy a car, get customs clearance on goods brought from abroad, and many other transactions. Take your *permesso di soggiorno* (which must be valid for at least another year) and your passport to your local *circoscrizione* office (*see* **carta d'identità**). They will check that rubbish collection tax (*nettezza urbana*) for your address has been paid (ask your landlord about this) before issuing the certificate.

Opening a bank account

In general Italian banks are less customer-friendly than those in other parts of the world. Be prepared to provide the bank of your choice (choose one that's easy to get to; it makes life a lot easier if you do all transactions at your own branch) with a valid *permesso di soggiorno* or *certificato di residenza*, your *codice fiscale*, proof of regular income from an employer (or a fairly substantial sum to deposit) and, of course, your passport. Charges are higher than in most other European countries.

Work

Casual employment can be hard to come by, so try to sort out work before you arrive. English-language schools and translation agencies are mobbed with applicants, so qualifications and experience count. The UN Food and Agriculture Organisation is a large but picky employer.

The classified ads paper *Porta Portese* has a daunting number of job advertisements. Other good places to look are *Wanted in Rome* and noticeboards in English-language bookshops (*see pages 120-2 and chapter* **Media**). You can also place an ad yourself in any of the media above. For serious jobs look in *Il Messaggero*, the *Herald Tribune* and *La Repubblica*.

Accommodation

Best places to look for accommodation are again *Porta Portese, Wanted in Rome*, and English-language bookshops. Look out for *affittasi* (for rent) notices on buildings, and check classifieds in *Il Messaggero* on Thursday and Sunday.

When you move into an apartment, it's normal to pay a month's rent in advance plus two months' deposit, which should be refunded when you move out, although some landlords create problems over this. You'll probably get a year's contract (lease), normally renewable. If you rent through an agency, expect to pay the equivalent of two months' rent in commission.

Women's Rome

As you're walking down the street being whistled and hissed at, pursued by squadrons of Vespa-riders and generally hassled, take comfort in the fact that Italian men are often all mouth and no trousers. Compared with many others in Europe, Rome is actually quite a safe city for women, and as long as you stick to central areas it is still one of the few cities where you can still walk alone late at night without wishing you'd brought your mace.

For women on their own, common sense will usually be enough to keep potential harassers at bay. If you're not interested, ignore them and they'll probably go away. Alternatively, duck into the nearest bar: they'll give you up as a lost cause and look for a new victim.

Young Roman blades head for Piazza Navona, Piazza di Spagna and Fontana di Trevi to pick up foreign talent. If you prefer to enjoy Rome's nocturnal charm in peace, you're better off in the areas around Campo dei Fiori, Testaccio and Trastevere. The area around Termini station gets seriously seedy after sundown.

Accommodation

The vast majority of Rome's hotels and *pensioni* are perfectly suitable for women travellers, but if you're uneasy about walking around at night, avoid those near Termini station and around Via Nazionale, a major shopping artery that becomes pretty deserted once the shops are shut. Stick to the more populated areas in the *centro storico* where you can still get good prices and enjoy the night-life without too much fret. Otherwise, some convents offer

a bulwark against the city's perceived threats, as well as a bed. If you don't feel like getting to a nunnery, Rome also has women-only hostels (*see also page 127*).

Casa Tra Noi

Via Monte del Gallo, 113 (06 3938 7355/fax 06 3938 7446). Bus to Via Monte del Gallo. **Rates** *single* L95,000; *double* L164,000; mini-apartments for 4 L312,000. **Credit** AmEx, DC, EC, MC,V. The management of this hostel is religious but fairly low-profile. Inside a safe though somewhat anonymous complex, the rooms are comfortable and clean, and breakfast is included. Situated close to the Vatican, on the west side of the Gianicolo.

Suore Pie Operaie

Via di Torre Argentina, 76 (06 686 1254). Bus to Largo di Torre Argentina. **Rates** L25,000 per person. **No credit cards.** **Map 3/2A**
Right in the centre, this hostel has ten rooms with two or three beds in each. Women only; 10.30pm curfew. Book ahead: cheap rates make it exceptionally popular.

Health

Tampons (*assorbenti interni*) and sanitary towels (*assorbenti esterni*) are cheaper in supermarkets, but you can also get them in pharmacies and *tabacchi*.

Consultori familiari (Health & family planning centres)

Each district has a *Consultorio familiare*, run by the local health authority, and EU citizens with an E111 form are entitled to use them, paying the same low charges for services and prescription drugs as locals. They also give advice and help on contraception, abortion and gynaecological problems. The pill is freely available on prescription; abortions are legal when performed in state-run hospitals. For gynaecological emergencies, head for the *Pronto soccorso* at your nearest hospital (*see p261*). The most centrally-located *consultori* are: *Via Arco del Monte, 99a (06 6880 3545). Bus or tram to Largo Argentina/ tram to Via Arenula.* **Open** 11.30am-5pm Mon; 9-11am Tue; 9am-6pm Wed; 9am-2pm Thur, Fri. **Map 6/1B**

Via San Martino della Battaglia, 16 (06 773 0555). Bus to Termini. **Open** 8.30am-12.30pm Mon-Sat. **Map 5/1A**

AIED

Via Toscana, 30/31 (06 4282 5314). Metro Barberini. **Open** 9am-7pm Mon-Fri; 9am-1pm Sat. **Map 4/2B**
Viale Gorizia, 14 (06 855 7731). Bus to Corso Trieste. **Open** 9am-1pm, 2-7pm, Mon-Fri; 9am-1pm Sat. These private family-planning clinics offer check-ups, contraceptive advice, menopause counselling and smear tests. Once you buy a membership card (*tessera*) for L10,000, check-ups cost L65,000. Smear tests cost L25,000; follow-up visits are free.

Artemide

Via Sannio, 61 (06 7047 6220). Metro San Giovanni. **Open** 10am-7pm Mon-Fri. **Map 9/1A**
This private clinic offers gynaecological check-ups (L90,000) and smear tests (L30,000), together with a wide range of other tests and services. Appointments can be made at 24 hours' notice, and emergencies are invariably taken immediately.

Helplines & crisis centres

Dial 112 or 113 in case of emergency. For more specific help or counselling, try one or more of the following:

Centro Provinciale d'Accoglienza per Le Donne Che Non Vogliono Subire Violenze

Viale di Villa Pamphili, 100 (06 581 0926/06 581 1473). Bus to Viale di Villa Pamphili. **Open** 24 hours daily. A short-stay hostel for female victims of domestic violence, and their children, plus a 24-hour emergency line.

Centro Anti-Violenza

Via delle Tre Canelle, 15 (06 678 0537/06 678 0563). **Open** 24 hours daily. A helpline for victims of sexual violence. The women-only volunteers at the *Centro Anti-Violenza* offer legal assistance and psychological support, and some are English-speaking.

Telefono Rosa

06 683 2690/06 683 2820/06 683 2675. **Open** 10am-1pm, 4-7pm, daily. Provides sympathetic counselling and sound legal advice to women who have been victims of either sexual abuse or sexual harassment.

Disabled travellers

There's no denying that Rome is a difficult city for disabled people, especially for anybody in a wheelchair. You'll almost certainly have to depend on other people more than you would at home. But if you're prepared to accept its shortfalls and considerable obstacles, a stay in Rome can prove a rewarding challenge.

It won't take long to understand why you don't see many people in wheelchairs in central Rome, and why those you do see are nearly always accompanied. Narrow streets make life difficult for those who can't flatten themselves against a wall to let passing vehicles by, while the cobblestones turn even wheelchairs with excellent suspension into bone-rattlers. Getting onto pavements – and off again at the other end – is made well-nigh impossible by bumper-to-bumper parked cars. Once off the streets, you're faced with the problems of old buildings with narrow corridors, lifts that, if they're there at all, are too small, and toilets at the top or bottom of impossibly steep staircases.

Blind and partially sighted people, meanwhile, often find that there's no curb at all between the road proper and that bit of street that pedestrians are entitled to walk along (the one exception is a smooth brick walkway laid into the cobblestones leading from the Trevi Fountain to Piazza Navona, along which braille notes on bronze plaques give historical explanations of landmarks en route).

There have been improvements. Lifts, ramps and special toilets are being installed in museums, stations and public offices, and although willingness has not always been matched by careful thinking (you may be expected to levitate up a couple of steps to reach that brand-new toilet or lift), these days you're more likely to be treated like a human being.

The **Enjoy Rome** agency and, if you're lucky, the official **APT** tourist office (*see page 268*), have a selection of information for disabled people.

Information

CO.IN

Via Enrico Giglioli, 54a (tel/fax 06 2326 7504/coin@inroma.roma.it). **Open** 9am-5pm Mon-Fri.
CO.IN (short for Consorzio Cooperative Integrate) publish a multilingual guide, *Roma Accessibile*, which should be available (but often is not) at the APT (*see p268*) and lists disabled facilities at museums, restaurants, stores, theatres, stations, hotels and so on, and has a map of Rome showing disabled parking places. It has been fully revised for 2000. To be sure of obtaining a copy, contact CO.IN directly and have it sent to you; the guide is free but you will be asked to pay postage. The *consorzio* will also organise guided tours in Rome and all over Italy, and transport for disabled people.

COINtel

(06 2326 7695). **Open** 24 hours daily.
A phone information line run by CO.IN and Rome city council. Staff speak Italian and English and answer questions on accessibility in hotels, buildings and monuments. CO.IN also has an information service in Italian and English for the whole country. The toll-free number (800 271027) can only be dialed from within Italy. *Website: http://andi.casaccia.enea.it/hometur.htm*

Transport

Rome is in the process of making the whole of its **bus** network accessible to wheelchairs. The specially-adapted red and silver buses are already a common sight.

They have extra-large central doors and an access ramp; inside, there is a space where a wheelchair can be secured. Rome's disabled have been slow to take advantage of this boost to their mobility, so be prepared for some surprise from other bus users if you actually use the facilities. At time of writing, the routes served by these buses were as follows. Note that not all buses on these routes are wheelchair-friendly; disabled passengers should resign themselves to letting a couple of old-style buses go by before an appropriate one arrives.
H Piazza dei Cinquecento (Termini station)-Via Nazionale-Piazza Venezia-Viale Trastevere-Casaletto.
23 Piazzale Clodio-Piazza Risorgimento (Vatican Museums, Saint Peter's)-Lungotevere-Via Marmorata-Piramide (metro B)-Via Ostiense-San Paolo fuori le mura.
31 Piazzale Clodio-Villa Pamphili-Piazza Isaac Newton.
44 Piazza Venezia-Piazza Bocca della Verità-Via Dandolo (Villa Sciarra)-Piazza Ottavilla (Villa Pamphili)-Piazza San Giovanni da Dio-Monteverde Nuovo.
64 Termini-Via Nazionale-Piazza Venezia-Corso Vittorio Emanuele-Vatican.
75 Piazza Indipendenza-Via Cavour-Colosseum (metro B)-Viale Aventino-Piramide (metro B)-Via Marmorata-Via Dandolo-Monteverde Vecchio.
157 Eastern suburbs-Porta Maggiore-Termini.
170 Termini-Via Nazionale-Piazza Bocca della Verità-Testaccio-Trastevere station-Viale Marconi EUR.
280 Piazza Mancini (Stadio Olimpico)-Piazza Mazzini-Lepanto (metro A)-Piazza Cavour-Lungotevere-Via Marmorata-Piramide (metro B)-Ostiense station.
590 follows the route of metro A between Prati and Cinecittà.
913 Piazza Augusto Imperatore-Piazza Cavour-Lepanto (metro A)-Via Andrea Doria-Via Trionfale.
116, 117, 118, 119 The electric buses that serve the *Centro Storico.*
Tram 8 Largo Argentina-Viale Trastevere-Casaletto.

On the **metro**, line A is something of a no-go area, although to compensate there is the 590 service (*see above*). All stations on line B have lifts, disabled WCs and special parking spaces, with the exception of Circo Massimo, Colosseo and Cavour (southbound).

Most **taxi** drivers will carry wheelchairs (they have to be folded); if possible, phone and book a cab rather than hail one in the street (*see page 258*).

The state **railway** (FS) is introducing some special easy-access carriages. To ascertain which trains have wheelchair facilities, call (or go to) the *Ufficio disabili* ('office for the disabled') at the station from which you plan to depart (Termini, beside platform 1, 06 488 1726; Ostiense 06 4730 5066; Tiburtina 06 4730 7184), or consult the official timetable, which shows a wheelchair symbol next to accessible trains. Twenty-four hours prior to departure, the disabled traveller or someone representing him/her must go to the *Ufficio disabili* in the appropriate station to fill in a form requesting assistance. Reserve a place, also, when buying a ticket, and make sure you arrive three quarters of an hour before departure time.

This procedure also applies to all train services to and from Fiumicino **airport**. When coming to Rome, you should, in theory, call Fiumicino Airport station (06 4730 5300) to arrange for help the day before your arrival; in practise, you'll be helped onto the train anyway.

Both Rome's airports have facilities such as adapted toilets. Inform your airline of your needs: they will contact the office at Fiumicino or Ciampino, where you will be able to use special facilities and waiting rooms on arrival and departure.

Sightseeing

Well-designed ramps, lifts and toilets are being installed in many museums. Among sites with full facilities are the **Vatican Museums** and **Castel Sant'Angelo**, **Galleria Doria Pamphili**, **Palazzo delle Esposizioni** and **Palazzo Venezia**, the **Galleria Nazionale d'Arte Moderna** and **Galleria Borghese** in Villa Borghese, and the **Bioparco** zoo. COINtel (*see above*) provides up-to-date information on disabled facilities, and can arrange for specialised guides.

Museum

06 321 4218. **Closed** Aug.
A volunteer group, Museum offers tours of some galleries and catacombs for people with mobility or especially visual problems (individuals or groups). A small fee to cover costs is charged. Museum guides – some of whom speak English, and when they can't an interpreter can be arranged – have braille notes, copies of some of the main paintings in relief, and permission to touch sculptures and other artefacts in the museums. Guides also seek to make works of art comprehensible to the non-seeing with music cassettes and recorded text. Braille guidebooks are available for further reading.

For general information in English call the number above; to arrange tours of individual sites, call: **Capitoline Museums** 06 503 4253; **Galleria Comunale di Arte Moderna** 06 5730 0551; **Museo Barracco** 06 513 9855 or 06 7981 1080; **Museo della Civiltà Romana** 06 592 3951 or 06 508 9318; **Vatican Museums & Saint Peter's** 06 331 4839. Museum also organises tours of the **Catacombs of Santa Domitila**, and of the **Pretestato** catacombs, normally closed to the public. More venues will be added during 2000.

Places to stay & eat

Financial incentives from the 2000 Holy Year committee mean the number of accessible **hotels** is increasing: CO.IN (*see above*) have the latest details. Cheaper hotels and *pensioni*, often on upper floors of old *palazzi*, can be a problem. If you

have special needs, make them known when you book.

The following hotels listed in *chapter* **Accommodation** have adapted rooms: **Atlante Star**; **Crowne Plaza Minerva**; **Plaza**; **Scalinata di Spagna**; **Celio**; **Fontanella Borghese**; **Hotel Locarno**; **Margutta**; **Nerva**; **Rinascimento**; **Ostello della Gioventú Foro Italico** (youth hostel).

Local by-laws now require **restaurants** to have disabled access and toilets; in practise, few have made the necessary alterations. However, if you phone ahead and ask for an appropriate table, most will do their best to help. In summer, the range of outdoor restaurants makes things easier. Getting to toilets, though, can be difficult or impossible.

Most bars open onto the street at ground level, and/or have tables outside in summer. Again, though, most bar toilets are tiny dark holes down long flights of steps.

Toilets

Public toilets accessible to wheelchair users are very scarce. The most central are near the boating pond in **Villa Borghese**, by **Colosseum** metro station, and in Via Ripetta in the *Tridente* (*see pages 53-61*). They can also be found in Termini, Tiburtina and Ostiense stations. Bear in mind too that most McDonald's have wheelchair-friendly loos.

Wheelchair hire

Ortopedia Colosseo

Via San Giovanni in Laterano, 16 (06 700 5709/06 700 1727/fax l'ufficio ortopedico 06 709 6331). Bus to Piazza del Colosseo. **Open** 8.30am-1pm, 2.30pm-7pm, Mon-Fri; 8.30am-1pm Sat.
Ortopedia Colosseo rents wheelchairs of all kinds – including antiques – starting at L45,000 per day. No delivery, but the shop does have special arrangements with some of Rome's larger hotels.

Directory

Further Reading

Ancient Rome

Catullus *The Poems*
Catullus' poems are well worth a read: sometimes malicious, sometimes pornographic, and occasionally exquisite.
Dudley, Donald *Roman Society*
A concise account of the history of Rome from the ninth century BC until the fourth century AD: recommended if you want a broad overview which includes culture, politics and economics.
Gibbon, Edward *The Decline and Fall of the Roman Empire*
The definitive account; to be dipped into.
Grant, Michael *History of Rome*
This, like all Grant's books on the ancient world, is highly readable and full of useful factual information.
Graves, Robert *I, Claudius; Claudius the God*
Damning portraits of the imperial family – especially the women – which help flesh out the historical facts.
Juvenal *Satires*
A contemporary view of ancient Rome's seedy underbelly.
Lawrence, DH *Etruscan Places*
Lawrence frolics empathetically through countryside formerly inhabited by sensual Etruscans.
Lefkovitch, Mary and Fant, Maureen *Women's Life in Greece and Rome*
A riveting collection of extracts, covering everything from ancient gynaecology to how to select a wet-nurse.
Massie, Allen *Augustus; Tiberius; Caesar*
Popular rewrites of history, in biographical or autobiographical form. Strong on ancient history, while bringing emperors and their families to life.
Ovid *The Erotic Poems*
Includes raunchy, ironic love poems, a manual on cosmetics, and the *Ars Amores*, a handbook for cynical lovers, which got the poet banished from Rome. Ted Hughes' 1997 translation of *Metamorphoses*, called *After Ovid*, is compelling.
Pomeroy, Sarah *Goddesses, Whores, Slaves and Wives*
A readable, meticulously researched account of the lives of women in ancient Rome and Greece.
Sear, Frank *Roman Architecture*
An accessible overview of ancient Roman architecture and building techniques, with plenty of illustrations.
Shakespeare, William *Julius Caesar*
Get into the mood for a visit to the Forum with a re-reading of this classic.
Suetonius, Gaius *The Twelve Caesars*
Salacious, scandal-packed biographies of Roman rulers from Julius Caesar to Domitian. A great read.
Virgil *The Aeneid*
The founding myth of Rome, written as propaganda for Augustus. A great yarn.

History, Art, Religion & Culture

Cellini, Benvenuto *Autobiography*
Bitchy, slanderous and egotistical tales of the Renaissance goldsmith's street brawls, sexual conquests and art.
Ginsborg, Paul *A History of Contemporary Italy*
Excellent introduction to the ups and downs of post-war Italy.
Hebblethwaite, Peter *In the Vatican*
Opinionated insights into the inner workings of the Vatican.
Hibbard, Howard *Bernini*
An accessible interpretation of Bernini's work, with pictures.

Hibbert, Christopher *Biography of a City*
An engaging, effortlessly readable account of Rome's history, from the Etruscans to Mussolini. Great illustrations too.
Levey, Michael *The High Renaissance*
A readable, well-illustrated guide to the era of Raphael, Michelangelo *et al*.
Masson, Georgina *Courtesans of the Italian Renaissance*
A revealing, entertaining study of the most famous courtesans of the fifteenth and sixteenth centuries. Like all books by this indomitable American traveller, contains fascinating anecdotal insights into Roman life.
Morton, HV *A Traveller in Rome*
Classic Roman guide book. Written in the 1950s and still highly readable.
Ranke-Heinemann, Uta *Eunuchs for the Kingdom of Heaven*
An engagingly witty critique of the Catholic church's attitude to sex, from Saint Jerome to JPII.
Stille, Alexander *Excellent Cadavers*
The story of the rise, successes, failure and ultimate assassinations of anti-Mafia prosecutors Giovanni Falcone and Paolo Borsellino.
Vasari, Giorgio *Lives of the Artists*
This sixteenth century biography of great masters was the first art history book but is purely Florentine in outlook: chiefly responsible for consigning the artists and craftsmen of Rome to the dustbin of history.
Warner, Marina *Alone of all her Sex*
An impressive, stimulating and beautifully written account of the cult of the Virgin Mary.
Wittkower, Rudolf *Art and Architecture in Italy 1600-1750*
Everything you ever wanted to know about the Baroque. Loads of illustrations and photos.
Yallop, David *In God's Name*
A sensational but fun tale of Vatican intrigue and the death of Pope John Paul I.

Fiction

Davis, Lindsay *Venus in Copper (etc)*
Series of lightweight comic crime thrillers set in ancient Rome.
Dibdin, Michael *Vendetta (etc)*
Thriller set in deftly-evoked contemporary Rome, where cop-hero Aurelio Zen hangs out in the *Vineria* on Campo de' Fiori. Other Zen adventures continue the theme.
Hawthorne, Nathaniel *The Marble Faun*
A quaint, moralising novel about two female artists in Rome. Stilted characters, but a page-turner nonetheless.
James, Henry *The Portrait of a Lady (etc)*
James' adoration of Rome is legendary, and some of his greatest works are set here. Try *Portrait, Daisy Miller*, and a couple of gushing essays in *Italian Hours*.
Morante, Elsa *History*
A brilliant evocation of everday life for a Roman woman during and after World War II.
Moravia, Alberto *Roman Tales; Two Women (etc)*
Grandfather of post-war Italian literature, Moravia was a keen observer of Roman life, though his literary clout sometimes outstripped the quality of his work.
Wharton, Edith *Roman Fever*
Stinging short story from 1911 about two old American ladies in Rome reminiscing about the past.
Yourcenar, Marguerite *The Memoirs of Hadrian*
A sombre novel, told by Hadrian as he approaches death.

Index

Advertisers' Index

Please refer to the relevant sections for
addresses/telephone numbers

Maps

Worldwide Calling Made Easy.

172-1022

It's EASY to call back to the U.S. or from one country to another from Italy:

1. Dial 172-1022 – the WorldPhone® toll-free access number for Italy.

2. Follow the instructions or hold for an MCI WorldCom operator.

The MCI WorldCom Card® gives you...

- Operators who speak your language.
- Customer Service 24 hours a day.
- Great MCI WorldCom rates in the U.S. and abroad.

Villa Ada

Viale Regina Margherita

4-5

2-3

Via Flaminia

Villa Borghese

■ Stazione
Roma-Viterbo

PRATI

VIA VENETO

Via Nomentana

Castel
Sant'Angelo

Via
Condotti

Piazza di
Spagna

CITTÀ DEL
VATICANO

TRIDENTE

Stazione
Roma-Termini

QUIRINALE

CENTRO
STORICO

MONTI

GIANICOLO

Teatro di
Marcello

Colosseo

ESQUILINO

Foro
Romano

Viale di Trastevere

TRASTEVERE

Fiume Tevere

Circo
Massimo

CELIO

AVENTINO

Terme di
Caracalla

6-7

TESTACCIO

Stazione
Roma-Ostia

8-9

Via Ostiense

Stazione
Ostiense

Via Gianicolense

OSTIENSE

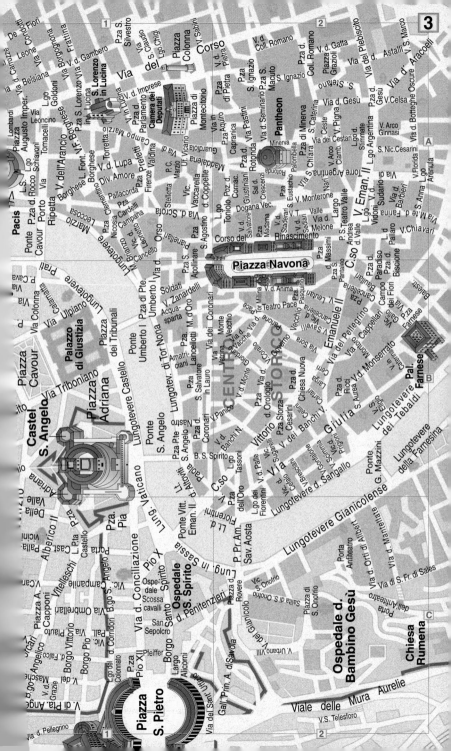

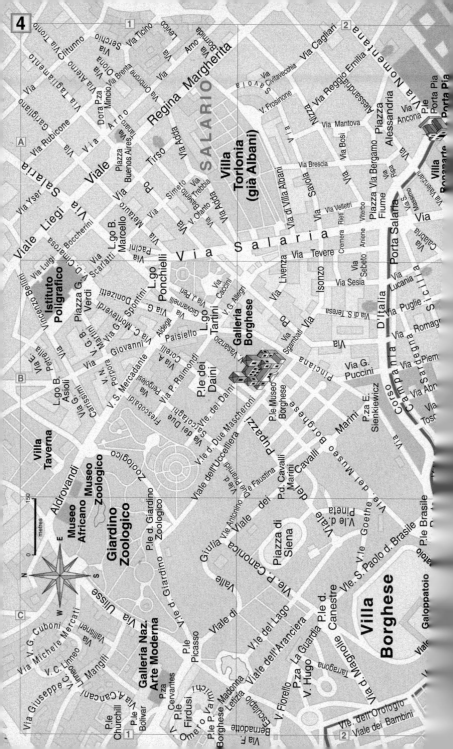

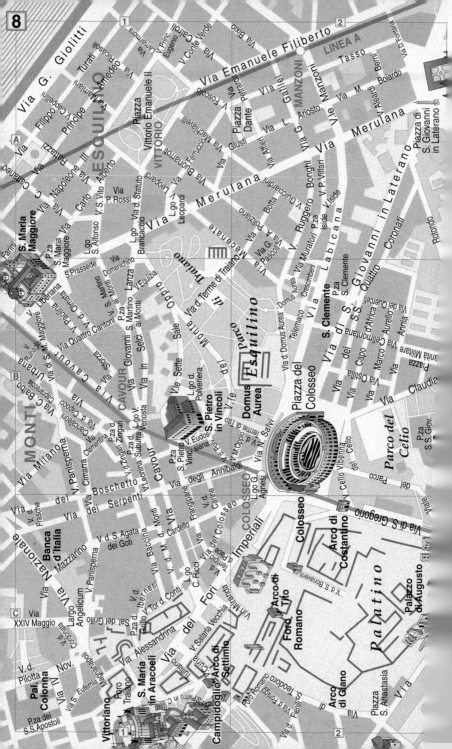

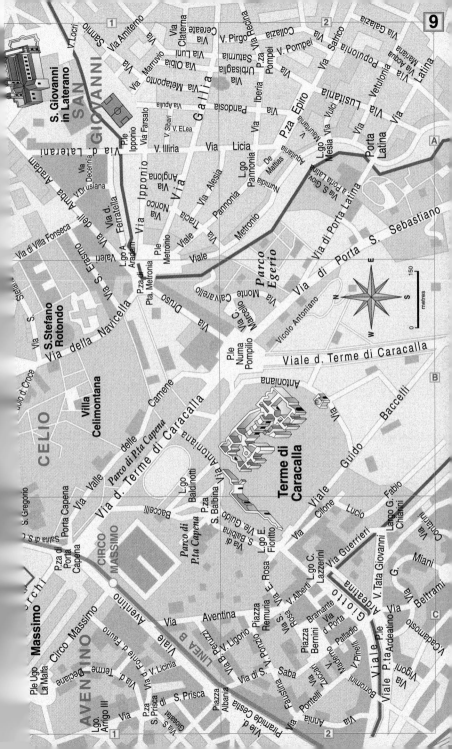

Street Index

Monserrato via 3 B2
Monte Aureo rampa di 6 B2
Monte Calvarello via 9 B2
Monte della Farina via,3 A2
Monte Giordano via 3 B2
Monte Oppio via 8 B2
Monte Oppio viale del 8 B1
Monte Tarpeo via 6 A2
Monte Testaccio via di 7 A2
Monte Vecchio via 3 B2
Montebello via 5 A1
Montecavallo salita 5 C2
Montecitorio pza di 3 A1
Monterone via 3 A2
Monteverdi via 4 B1
Montoro via 3 B2
Moro via del 6 B2
Moroni vicolo 6 B2
Mura Gianicolensi
viale delle 7 C1
Mura Portuensi
viale delle 7 B1
Muratori via 8 A2
Muratte via 5 C2
Muro Torto viale del 2 A1
Museo Borghese pzale 4 B2
Museo Borghese
viale del 4 B2
Napoleone III via 8 A1
Napoleone pzale 2 A2
Napoli via 5 B2
Nari via 3 A2
Nastro via 3 B1
Natale del Grande via 6 B2
Navi lungtvre delle 2 B1
Navicella via della 9 B1
Navona pza 3 B2
Nazareno via 5 C2
Nazionale via 5 B2
Nenni ponte 2 B1
Nerva via 5 B1
Nicosia pza 3 A1
Nievo pza 7 B2
Nievo via 7 B2
Nizza via 4 A2
Nomentana via 4 A2
Numa Pompilio pzale 9 B2
Novembre via 9 B2
Obelisco viale dell' 2 A2
Oca via dell' 2 A2
Olmata via 8 B1
Olmetto via 6 B2
Ombrellari via 3 C1
Ombrone via 4 A1
Orlando via 5 B1
Oro pza dell' 3 C2
Orologio pza dell' 3 B2
Orologio viale dell' 2 A2
Orsini via 2 B2
Orso via dell' 3A1
Orti di Alibert via 3 C2
Orti di Trastevere
via degli 7 B1
Ostiense pzale 7 A2
Ostiense via 7 A2
Ostilia via 8 B2
Ottaviano via 2 C2
Ovidio via 2 C2
Pace via della 3 B2
Paganica via 3 A2
Pagano via 5 B1
Paglia via della 6 B2
Paisiello via 4 B1
Palatino ponte 6 A2
Palermo via 5 B2
Palestro via 5 A1
Pallacorda via 3 A1
Pallaro largo 3 A2
Pallavicini via 3 C1
Palle via 3 A2
Palline vicolo 3 C1
Palombella via 3 A2
Panetteria via 5 C2
Panieri via dei 6 B2
Panisperna via 8 B1
Pannonia largo 9 B2
Pannonia via 9 B2
Paola via 3 B1
Paolina via 8 B1
Paradiso pza del 3 B2
Parco del Celio viale del 8 B2
Parco di Villa Corsini
via dei 6 C2
Parigi via 5 B1
Parione via 3 B2
Parlamento pza 3 A1
Parma via 5 B2
Pascarella via 7 C2
Pascoli via 8 A2
Pasquino pza 6 B1
Pastini via 3 A2
Pastrengo via 5 B1
Pellegrino via 3 B2
Pellegrino via dei 6 B2
Pellicia via della 6 B2
Penitenza via della 6 B2
Penitenzieri via dei 3 C1
Penna via 2 A2
Peretti via 6 A2
Petrarca via dei 6 B1
Piacenza via 5 B2
Pianellari via 3 A1

Piave via 5 A1
Picasso pzale 4 C1
Pie di Marmo via 3 A2
Piemonte via 4 B2
Pierleoni lungtvre di 6 A2
Pietra pza 3 A2
Pietra via 3 A2
Pigna via 3 A2
Pilotta pza 5 C2
Pilotta via 5 C2
Pinciana via 4 B2
Pincio salita del 2 A2
Pineta viale della 4 C2
Pio borgo 3 C1
Pio X via 3 C1
Pio XII pza 3 C1
Piombo vicolo del 6 A1
Piramide Cestia viale 7 A2
Pirgo via 9 A2
Pisanelli via 2 B1
Piscinula pza in 6 A2
Plauto via 3 C1
Plava via 2 C1
Plebiscito via del 3 A2
Po via 4 A1
Poerio via 7 C1
Poli pza 5 C2
Policlinico viale del 5 A1
Poliziano via 8 A2
Polveriera largo 8 B1
Polveriera via della 8 B1
Pompei pza 9 A2
Pompei via 9 A2
Pompeo Magno via 2 B2
Ponte Rotto via del 6 A2
Ponte S Angelo pza 3 B1
Ponte Testaccio pzale di 7 A2
Ponte Umberto I 3 B1
Ponte Umberto I pza 3 B1
Pontefici via 2 A2
Ponziani pza 6 A2
Popolo pza del 2 A2
Porcari via 3 C1
Porta Anfiteatro 3 C2
Porta Angelica via di 3 C1
Porta Ardeatina viale di 9 C2
Porta Capena 9 C1
Porta Capena pza di 9 C1
Porta Castello largo 3 C1
Porta Castello via 3 C1
Porta Latina 9 A2
Porta Latina via di 9 A2
Porta Metronia pza di 9 B1
Porta Pia 4 A2
Porta Pia pzale 4 A2
Porta Pinciana 4 C2
Porta Pinciana via di 5 C1
Porta Portese 7 B1
Porta S Pancrazio largo 6 C2
Porta S Paolo 7 A2
Porta S Paolo pza di 7 A2
Porta S Sebastiano via 9 B2
Porta Salaria 4 A2
Porta Settimiana 7 B1
Portico d'Ottavia via del 6 A1
Porto Ripetta pza di 3 A1
Portuense lungtvre 7 B1
Portuense pzale 7 B1
Portuense via 7 B1
Pozzo delle Cornacchie
via 3 A2
Prati lungtvre 3 B1
Prefetti via 3 A1
Prigioni vicolo delle 3 B2
Principe Amedeo via 5 A2
Principe di Savoia galleria
3 C2
Principe Eugenio via 8 A1
Principe Savoia Aosta
ponte 3 C2
Propaganda via 5 C1
Publicii clivo dei 7 A1
Puglie via 4 B2
Pupazzi viale dei 4 B2
Purificazione via 5 C1
Quattro Cantoni via 8 B1
Quattro Fontane via delle 5 B2
Querceti via del 8 B2
Querini via 7 A1
Quirinale via del 5 B2
Quirino via 2 B2
Quirinale pza del 5 C2
Rasella via 5 C2
Rattazzi via 8 A1
Reggio Emilia via 4 A2
Regina Margherita ponte 2 B2
Regina Margherita viale 4 A1
Renella via della 6 B2
Renzi pza del 6 B2
Repubblica pza della 5 B2
Riari via dei 6 C1
Ricasoli via 8 A1
Ricci largo 8 C1
Ricci pza 3 B2
Rinascimento corso 3 A2
Ripa Grande porto di 7 A1
Ripa via 4 A2
Ripetta passeggiata di 2 A2
Risorgimento pza 2 C2
Robbia via 7 A2

Rolli via 7 B2
Roma Libera via 6 B2
Romagna via 4 B2
Romita via 5 B1
Rosmini via 5 A2
Rosolino Pilo pza 7 C1
Rossi via 8 A1
Rotonda pza 3 A2
Rotonda via 3 A2
Rovere pza 3 C2
Ruinaglia via 5 B2
S Agata dei Goti via 8 C1
S Agostino pza 3 A1
S Alberto Magno via 7 A1
S Alessio pza 7 A1
S Alessio via 7 A1
S Alfonso largo 8 A1
S Ambrogio via 6 A1
S Anastasia pza 8 C2
S Andrea della Valle pza 3 A2
S Andrea delle Fratte via 5 C1
S Angelo borgo 3 C1
S Angelo ponte 3 B1
S Anna via 3 A2
S Anselmo pza 7 A1
S Anselmo via 7 A1
S Apollinare pza 3 B1
S Aurea via 3 B2
S Balbina pza 9 C1
S Balbina via 9 C2
S Bartolomeo all' Isola
pza 6 A2
S Basilio via 5 B1
S Bernardo pza 5 B1
S Bonaventura via 8 C2
S Calisto pza 6 B2
S Calisto via 6 B2
S Caterina via 3 A2
S Cecilia pza 6 A2
S Cecilia via 6 A2
S Chiara via 3 A2
S Claudio via 3 A1
S Clemente pza 8 B2
S Cosimato pza di 6 B2
S Cosimato via 6 B2
S Crisogono via 6 B2
S Domenico via di 7 A1
S Dorotea via 6 B2
S Egidio pza 6 B2
S Eligio via 3 B2
S Erasmo via 9 B1
S Eufemia via 8 C1
S Eugenio via 2 A1
S Eustachio pza 3 A2
S Felice via 3 A2
S Francesco a Ripa via 6 B2
S Francesco d'Assisi pza 7 B1
S Francesco di Sales via 3 C2
S Gallicano via 6 B2
S Giacomo via 2 A2
S Giovanni Decollato via 6 A2
S Giovanni della Malva p.6 B2
S Giovanni in Laterano
p. di 8 A2
S Giovanni in Laterano
via di 8 A2
S Gregorio pza 8 C1
S Gregorio salita di 8 C2
S Gregorio via 8 C2
S Ignazio pza 3 A2
S Ignazio via 3 A2
S Isidoro pza 5 C1
S Isidoro via 5 C1
S Lorenzo in Lucina pza 3 A1
S Macuto pza 3 A2
S Marcello via 5 C2
S Marco pza 6 A1
S Marco via 3 A2
S Maria del Pianto via 6 A1
S Maria in Cappella 6 A2
S Maria in Cosmedin 6 A2
S Maria in Trastevere pza 6
B2
S Maria in Via via 5 C2
S Maria Liberatrice pza 7 A2
S Maria Maggiore pza 8 A1
S Maria Maggiore via 8 B1
S Martino ai Monti via 8 B1
S Martino ai Monti via 8 B1
S Martino della Battaglia
via 5 A1
S Massimo via 4 B2
S Michele via 7 B1
S Nicola Cesarini via 3 A2
S Nicola da Tolentino
salita 5 B1
S Nicola da Tolentino via 5 B1
S Nicola da Tolentino
vicolo 5 B1
S Onofrio pza 3 C2
S Onofrio salita di 3 C2
S Onofrio vicolo 3 C2
S Pantaleo pza 3 B2
S Paolo a Regola via 6 B2
S Paolo della croce via 9 B1
S Pietro in Montorio pza 6 C2
S Pietro in Vincoli pza 8 B1
S Pietro pza 3 C1
S Prassede via 8 B1
S Prisca pza 9 C1

S Prisca via 9 C1
S Rocco largo 3 A1
S Saba via 9 C2
S Sabina via 7 A1
S Salvatore in Lauro pza 3 B1
S Sebastianello rampa 5 C1
S Sebastianello via 5 C1
S Silvestro pza 3 A1
S Stefano Rotondo via 8 A2
S Stefano via 3 A2
S Susanna largo di 5 B1
S Susanna via 5 B1
S Teodoro via 8 C2
S Teresa via 4 B2
S Tullio via 5 A1
S Vincenzo via 5 C2
S Vitale via 5 B2
S Vito via 8 A1
SS Apostoli pza 5 C2
SS Apostoli via 5 C2
SS Giovanni e Paolo pza 8 B2
SS Quattro Coronati
via dei 8 B2
Sabini via 3 A1
Sabino via 2 C1
Salandra via 5 B1
Salaria Vecchia via 8 C1
Salaria via 4 A1
Sallustiana via 5 B1
Sallustio pza 5 B1
Salumi via dei 6 A2
Salvatore via del 3 A2
Salvi via 8 B2
San Sepolcro via 3 C1
Sangallo lungtvre 3 B2
Sanità Militare pza 8 B2
Sannio via 8 A1
Sant' Uffizio via del 3 C1
Santa Maria dell' Anima via 3
B2
Santa Melania via 7 A1
Santi via 3 A2
Santo Spirito borgo 3 B1
Sanzio lungtvre 6 B2
Sapri via 5 A1
Sardegna via 4 B2
Sassia lungtvre 3 C1
Saturnia via 9 A2
Savella clivo di 7 A1
Savelli via 3 B2
Savelli vicolo 6 B1
Savoia F. via 2 A2
Savoia L. via 2 A2
Savoia via 4 A2
Scala via della 6 B2
Scanderbeg pza 5 C2
Scauro clivo di 8 B2
Scavolino via 5 C2
Schiavoni largo 3 A1
Scimmia via 3 B2
Scipioni via degli 2 C2
Scrofa via della 3 A1
Scuderie via 5 C2
Sediari via dei 3 A2
Seggiola via 6 B1
Selci via in 8 B1
Sella via 5 B1
Seminario via 3 A2
Serpenti via dei 8 B1
Servili pza 7 A2
Sette Sale viale 8 B1
Sforza Cesarini pza 3 B2
Sforza via 8 B1
Shawky pza 2 A1
Sicilia via 4 B2
Siena pza 4 C2
Sienkiewicz pza 4 B2
Simeto via 4 A1
Sistina via 5 C1
Sisto ponte 6 B1
Soldati via 3 B1
Solferino via 5 A1
Somma Campagna via 5 A1
Sonnino pza 6 B2
Sora via 3 B2
Spagna pza di 5 C1
Spaventa via 5 B1
Specchi via degli 6 B1
Sprovieri via 7 C1
Stamperia via 5 C2
Statuto via 8 A1
Stelletta via 3 A1
Stimmate largo 3 A2
Sublicio ponte 7 A1
Suburra pza 8 B1
Sudario via del 3 A2
Sugarelli vicolo 3 B2
Tabacchi vicolo 6 B2
Tacito via 3 B1
Tagliamento via 4 A1
Tasso via 8 A2
Tassoni largo 3 B2
Teatro di Marcello via dei 6 A1
Teatro Pace via dei 3 B2
Teatro Valle largo 3 A2
Teatro Valle via 3 A2
Tebaldi lungtvre dei 3 B2
Telemaco via 8 B2
Tempio della Pace
via dei 8 C1
Tempio di Diana pza 7 A1
Tempio di Diana via 7 A1

Tempio del 6 A2
Terme Deciane via delle 9 C1
Terme di Caracalla
viale delle 9 B1
Terme di Diocleziano
via d. 5 A2
Terme di Tito via delle 8 B2
Terme di Traiano via 8 B1
Testaccio lungtvre 7 A1
Testaccio pza 7 A2
Testaccio ponte 7 B2
Thorwaldsen pza 2 A1
Tiburzi via 8 B2
Ticino via 4 A1
Tirso via 4 A1
Tittoni via 8 B2
Tomacelli via 3 A1
Toniolo largo 3 A1
Tor de' Conti via 8 C1
Tor Millina via 3 B2
Tor Nona lungtvre di 3 B1
Torino via 5 B2
Torre Argentina via di 3 A2
Torretta via 3 A1
Toscana via 4 B2
Traforo via dei 5 C2
Trastevere viale 6 B2
Traversari via 7 C2
Trevi pza di 5 C2
Triboniano via 3 B1
Tribunali pza dei 3 B1
Trilussa pza 6 B2
Trinità dei Monti pza 5 C1
Trinità dei Monti
viale 5 C1
Tritone largo 5 C2
Tritone via del 5 C1
Tulliano via 8 C1
Turati via 8 A1
Uccelliera viale dell' 4 B1
Uffici del Vicario via 3 A1
Ulpiano via 3 B1
Umberto I traforo 5 C2
Umbria via 5 B1
Umiltà via dell' 5 C2
Unità pza dell' 2 C2
Urbana via 5 B2
Urbano VIII via 3 C2
Vaccarella vicolo 3 A1
Vacche via delle 3 B2
Valadier via 2 B2
Valadier viale 2 A1
Valdina vicolo 3 A1
Vallati lungtvre dei 6 B2
Valle delle Camene via 9 B1
Valle Giulia viale di 4 B1
Vantaggio via del 2 A2
Vascellari via 6 A2
Vascello via 6 C2
Vaticano lungtvre 3 C1
Veneto via 5 B1
Venezia pza 6 A1
Venezia via 5 B2
Venezian via 6 B2
Venosta largo 8 B1
Verdi pza 4 B1
Vergini via delle 5 C2
Versilia via 5 B1
Vespucci via 7 A1
Vetrina via 3 B2
Vicenza via 5 A1
Villa Albani via di 4 A2
Villa Fonseca via 9 A1
Villa Medici viale di 2 A2
Villa Peretti largo di 5 A2
Villari via 8 A2
Viminale pza del 5 B2
Viminale via 5 A2
Virgilio via 3 B1
Vite via della 5 C1
Viterbo via 4 A2
Vittoria via 2 A2
Vittorio borgo 3 C1
Vittorio Emanuele II
corso 3 B2
Vittorio Emanuele II pza 8 A1
Vittorio Emanuele II
ponte 3 C1
Volta via 7 A2
Vulci via 9 A2
XX Settembre via 5 B1
Zanardelli via 3 B1
Zingari pza degli 8 B1
Zingari via 8 B1
Zoccolette via delle 6 B2
Zucchelli via 5 B1

Worldwide Calling Just Got Easier

The MCI WorldCom Card is designed specifically to keep you in touch with the people that matter the most to you. We make international calling easy.

Use your MCI WorldCom Card with the WorldPhone Toll-Free Access Numbers for an easy way to call when traveling worldwide.

REFERENCE GUIDE FOR MCI WORLDCOM CARD CALLING IN THE U.S. AND WORLDWIDE

Calls within the U.S.*
Dial 1-800-888-8000, then enter your Card number + PIN and the area code and phone number.

International Calls from the U.S.
Dial the 1-800-888-8000 plus your Card number + PIN as well as 011 + Country Code and City Code + phone number.

Calls from outside the U.S. back to the U.S. or to another country
Dial the WorldPhone toll-free access number of the country you're calling from. Follow the voice instructions or hold for a WorldPhone operator to complete a call.

COUNTRY	WORLDPHONE TOLL-FREE ACCESS #
Austria (CC) ◆	0800-200-235
Belarus (CC)	
From Brest, Vitebsk, Grodno, Minsk	8-800-103
From Gomel and Mogilev regions	8-10-800-103
Belgium (CC) ◆	0800-10012
Bulgaria	00800-0001
Canada (CC)	1-800-888-8000
Croatia (CC) ★	0800-22-0112
Cyprus ◆	080-90000
Czech Republic (CC) ◆	00-42-000112
Denmark (CC) ◆	8001-0022
Egypt ◆ (Outside of Cairo, dial 02 first)	355-5770
Finland (CC) ◆	08001-102-80
France (CC) ◆	0800-99-0019
Germany (CC)	0800-888-8000
Greece (CC) ◆	00-800-1211
Hungary (CC) ◆	00▼800-01411
Ireland (CC)	1-800-55-1001
Israel (CC)	1-800-940-2727
Italy (CC) ◆	172-1022
Japan (CC) ◆ To call using KDD ■	00539-121▶
To call using IDC ■	0066-55-121
To call using JT ■	0044-11-121
Liechtenstein (CC) ◆	809-8000
Luxembourg (CC)	0800-0112
Macedonia (CC) ◆	99800-4266
Malta	0800-89-0120
Monaco (CC) ◆	800-90-019
Morocco	00-211-0012
Netherlands (CC) ◆	0800-022-9122
Norway (CC) ◆	800-19912
Poland (CC) ÷	00-800-111-21-22
Portugal (CC) ÷	800-800-123
Romania (CC) ÷	01-800-1800

COUNTRY	WORLDPHONE TOLL-FREE ACCESS #
Russia (CC) ◆ ÷	
To call using ROSTELCOM	747-3322
(For Russian speaking operator)	747-3320
To call using SOVINTEL	960-2222
San Marino (CC) ◆	172-1022
Saudi Arabia (CC)	1-800-11
Slovak Republic (CC)	00421-00112
Slovenia	080-8808
Spain (CC)	900-99-0014
Sweden (CC) ◆	020-795-922
Switzerland (CC) ◆	0800-89-0222
Turkey (CC) ◆	00-8001-1177
Ukraine (CC) ÷	8▼10-013
United Kingdom	
(CC) To call using BT ■	0800-89-0222
To call using CWC ■	0500-89-0222
United States (CC)	1-800-888-8000
Vatican City (CC)	172-1022

(CC) Country to-country calling available to/from most international locations.
÷ Limited availability.
▼ Wait for second dial tone.
▲ When calling from public phones, use phones marked LADATEL.
■ International communications carrier.
★ Not available from public pay phones.
● Public phones may require deposit of coin or phone card for dial tone.
● Local service fee in U.S. currency required to complete call.
▶ Regulation does not permit Intra-Japan calls.
◆ Available from most major cities.

*Includes calls from/within Canada, Puerto Rico, and the U.S. Virgin Islands.

To apply for a card call MCI WorldCom's local office at: 800-014340

or ask your local operator to place a collect call (reverse charge) to MCI WorldCom in the U.S. at: 1-712-943-6839

For more information visit
http://www.mci.com/worldphone

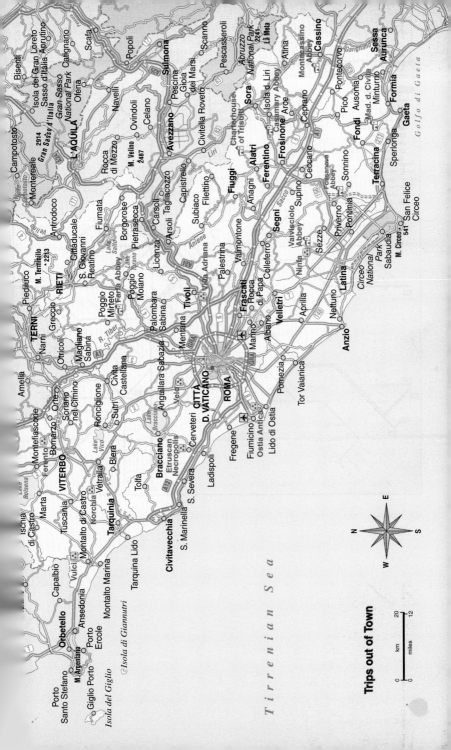

metro e ferrovie metropolitane

ATAC/COTRAL